MCSE WINDOWS NT 4.0 CERTIFICATION TRACK

CANDIDATES MUST PASS FOUR REQUIRED AND TWO ELECTIVE EXAMS

W9-CUH-548

Global Knowledge Network™ Certification Press provides the best information available to help you get certified!

SELECT FOUR REQUIRED EXAMS

REQUIRED
EXAM #:
70-67

Implementing
Microsoft Windows NT
Server 4.0
MCSE Windows NT Server 4.0 Study Guide
(Exam 70-67)
ISBN: 0-07-882491-5

REQUIRED
EXAM #:
70-58

Networking Essentials
MCSE Networking
Essentials Study Guide (Exam 70-58)
ISBN: 0-07-882493-1

REQUIRED
EXAM #:
70-73

Implementing and Supporting
Microsoft Windows NT
Workstation 4.0
MCSE Windows NT Workstation 4.0 Study
Guide (Exam 70-73)
ISBN: 0-07-882492-3

REQUIRED
CHOOSE
EXAM# 70-73
OR
EXAM# 70-98

EXAM #:
70-98

Implementing and Supporting
Microsoft Windows 98
MCSE Windows 98 Study Guide
(Exam 70-98)
ISBN: 0-07-882532-6

REQUIRED
EXAM #:
70-68

Implementing and Supporting
Microsoft Windows NT Server
4.0 in the Enterprise
MCSE Windows NT Server 4.0 in the Enterprise
Study Guide (Exam 70-68)
ISBN: 0-07-882490-7

PLUS

TWO ELECTIVE EXAMS

EXAM #:
70-59

Internetworking with Microsoft
TCP/IP on Windows NT 4.0
MCSE Microsoft TCP/IP on Windows NT 4.0
Study Guide (Exam 70-59)
ISBN: 0-07-882489-3

EXAM #:
70-87

Implementing and Supporting
Microsoft Internet Information
Server 4.0
MCSE+Internet Internet Information Server
4.0 Study Guide (Exams 70-87, 70-79, 70-88)
ISBN: 0-07-882560-1

EXAM #:
70-81

Implementing and Supporting
Microsoft Exchange Server 5.5
MCSE Exchange Server 5.5 Study Guide
(Exam 70-81)
ISBN: 0-07-882488-5

EXAM #:
70-88

Implementing and Supporting
Microsoft Proxy Server 2.0
MCSE+Internet Internet Information Server
4.0 Study Guide (Exams 70-87, 70-79, 70-88)
ISBN: 0-07-882560-1

EXAM #:
70-18

Supporting Microsoft System Management
Server 1.2

EXAM #:
70-28

System Administration for Microsoft SQL
Server 7.0

EXAM #:
70-85

Implementing and Supporting Microsoft SNA
Server 4.0

EXAM #:
70-29

Implementing a Database Design on SQL
Server 7.0

FOR COMPLETE DETAILS, VISIT MICROSOFT'S TRAINING AND CERTIFICATION WEB SITE AT **http://www.microsoft.com/train_cert/**

MICROSOFT CERTIFIED SYSTEMS ENGINEER

MCSE NT Workstation 4.0

Study Guide

(Exam 70-73)

Syngress Media, Inc.

Osborne McGraw-Hill

Berkeley New York St. Louis San Francisco Auckland Bogotá Hamburg London Madrid Mexico City Milan Montreal New Delhi Panama City Paris São Paulo Singapore Sydney Tokyo Toronto

Osborne McGraw-Hill
2600 Tenth Street
Berkeley, California 94710
U.S.A.

For information on translations or book distributors outside the U.S.A.,
or to arrange bulk purchase discounts for sales promotions, premiums, or
fund-raisers, please contact Osborne/**McGraw-Hill** at the above address.

MCSE NT Workstation 4.0 Study Guide

1234567890 DOC DOC 901987654321098

ISBN 0-07-882492-3

Publisher	**Copy Editor**	**Illustrator**
Brandon A. Nordin	Kathleen Faughnan	Lance Ravella
Editor-in-Chief	**Indexer**	**Series Design**
Scott Rogers	David Heiret	Roberta Steele
Acquisitions Editor	**Proofreaders**	**Cover Design**
Gareth Hancock	Pat Mannion	Regan Honda
Project Editor	Stefany Otis	**Editorial Management**
Cynthia Douglas	Carroll Proffitt	Syngress Media, Inc.
Technical Editor	**Computer Designer**	
Shaun Taylor	Jani Beckwith	
	Mickey Galicia	
	Roberta Steele	

From Global Knowledge Network

At Global Knowledge Network we strive to support the multiplicity of learning styles required by our students to achieve success as technical professionals. In this series of books, it is our intention to offer the reader a valuable tool for successful completion of the MCSE Certification Exam.

As the world's largest IT training company, Global Knowledge Network is uniquely positioned to offer these books. The expertise gained each year from providing instructor-led training to hundreds of thousands of students worldwide has been captured in book form to enhance your learning experience. We hope that the quality of these books demonstrates our commitment to your lifelong learning success. Whether you choose to learn through the written word, computer-based training, Web delivery, or instructor-led training, Global Knowledge Network is committed to providing you the very best in each of those categories. For those of you who know Global Knowledge Network, or those of you who have just found us for the first time, our goal is to be your lifelong competency partner.

Thank you for the opportunity to serve you. We look forward to serving your needs again in the future.

Warmest regards,

Duncan Anderson
Chief Operating Officer, Global Knowledge Network

January 12, 1998

Dear Osborne/McGraw-Hill Customer:

Microsoft is pleased to inform you that Osborne/McGraw-Hill is a participant in the Microsoft® Independent Courseware Vendor (ICV) program. Microsoft ICVs design, develop, and market self-paced courseware, books, and other products that support Microsoft software and the Microsoft Certified Professional (MCP) program.

To be accepted into the Microsoft ICV program, an ICV must meet set criteria. In addition, Microsoft reviews and approves each ICV training product before permission is granted to use the Microsoft Certified Professional Approved Study Guide logo on that product. This logo assures the consumer that the product has passed the following Microsoft standards:

- The course contains accurate product information.
- The course includes labs and activities during which the student can apply knowledge and skills learned from the course.
- The course teaches skills that help prepare the student to take corresponding MCP exams.

Microsoft ICVs continually develop and release new MCP Approved Study Guides. To prepare for a particular Microsoft certification exam, a student may choose one or more single, self-paced training courses or a series of training courses.

You will be pleased with the quality and effectiveness of the MCP Approved Study Guides available from Osborne/McGraw-Hill.

Sincerely,

Becky Kirsininkas
ICV Program Manager
Microsoft Training & Certification

The Global Knowledge Network Advantage

Global Knowledge Network has a global delivery system for its products and services. The company has 28 subsidiaries, and offers its programs through a total of 60+ locations. No other vendor can provide consistent services across a geographic area this large. Global Knowledge Network is the largest independent information technology education company, offering programs on a variety of platforms. This enables our multi-platform and multi-national customers to obtain all of their programs from a single vendor. The company has developed the unique Competence Key™ software tool and methodology, which can quickly reconfigure courseware to the proficiency level of a student on an interactive basis. Combined with self-paced and on-line programs, this technology can reduce the time required for training by prescribing content in only the deficient skills areas. The company has fully automated every aspect of the education process, from registration and follow-up, to "just-in-time" production of courseware. Global Knowledge Network, through its Competus consultancy, can customize programs and products to suit the needs of an individual customer.

Global Knowledge Network Classroom Education Programs

The backbone of our delivery options is classroom-based education. Our modern, well-equipped facilities, staffed with the finest instructors, offer programs in a wide variety of information technology topics, many of which lead to professional certifications.

Custom Learning Solutions

This delivery option has been created for companies and governments that value customized learning solutions. For them, our consultancy-based approach of developing targeted education solutions is most effective at helping them meet specific objectives.

Self-Paced and Multimedia Products

This delivery option offers self-paced program titles in interactive CD-ROM, videotape and audio tape programs. In addition, we offer custom development of interactive multimedia courseware to customers and partners. Call us at 1-888-427-4228.

Electronic Delivery of Training

Our network-based training service delivers efficient competency-based, interactive training via the World Wide Web and organizational intranets. This leading-edge delivery option provides a custom learning path and "just-in-time" training for maximum convenience to students.

ARG

American Research Group (ARG), a wholly-owned subsidiary of Global Knowledge Network, one of the largest worldwide training partners of Cisco Systems, offers a wide range of internetworking, LAN/WAN, Bay Networks, FORE Systems, IBM, and UNIX courses. ARG offers hands on network training in both instructor-led classes and self-paced PC-based training.

Global Knowledge Network Courses Available

Networking Foundation
- Understanding Computer Networks
- Emerging Networking Technologies
- Telecommunications Fundamentals
- Computer Telephony Integration
- Understanding Networking Fundamentals
- Essentials of Wide Area Networking
- Implementing T1/T3 Services
- Introduction to LAN/WAN Protocols
- Internetworking with Bridges, Routers and Switches
- Cabling Voice and Data Networks
- Upgrading and Repairing PCs
- Introduction to Web Development Fundamentals
- Building a Web Site
- Web Security
- Building Electronic Storefronts
- Project Management for IT Professionals
- Advanced Project Management
- Communication Skills for IT Professionals

Internetworking
- Emerging Networking Technologies
- Understanding Network Fundamentals
- Essentials of Wide Area Networking
- Frame Relay Internetworking
- Introduction to LAN/WAN Protocols
- Internetworking with Bridges, Routers and Switches
- Migrating to High Performance Ethernet
- Network Troubleshooting
- Multi Layer Switching and Wire-Speed Routing
- Cabling Voice and Data Networks
- Internetworking with TCP/IP
- Troubleshooting TCP/IP Networks
- Network Management
- ATM Essentials
- ATM Internetworking
- Cisco Router Security and Performance Tuning
- OSPF Design and Configuration
- Border Gateway Protocol (BGP) Configuration
- Managing Switched Internetworks

Authorized vendor training
Cisco Systems
- Introduction to Cisco Router Configuration
- Advanced Cisco Router Configuration
- Installation and Maintenance of Cisco Routers
- Cisco Internetwork Troubleshooting
- Cisco Internetwork Design
- Catalyst 5000 Series Configuration
- Cisco LAN Switch Configuration
- Configuring, Monitoring and Troubleshooting Dial-Up Services
- Cisco AS5200 Installation and Configuration
- Cisco Campus ATM Solutions

Bay Networks
- Bay Networks Router Installation and Basic Configuration
- Bay Networks Router Configuration and Management
- Bay Networks Accelerated Router Configuration
- Bay Networks Advanced IP Routing
- Bay Networks Hub Connectivity
- Bay Networks Centillion Switching

FORE Systems
- Introduction to ATM
- ATM Enterprise Core Products
- ATM Enterprise Edge Products

IBM
- Authorized IBM NETeam Education

Operating systems & programming
Microsoft
- Windows NT 4.0 Workstation
- Windows NT 4.0 Server
- Windows NT Networking with TCP/IP
- Windows NT 4.0 Security
- Enterprise Internetworking with Windows NT 4.0

- Essentials of UNIX and NT Integration

UNIX
- UNIX Level I
- UNIX Level II
- Mastering UNIX Security
- Essentials UNIX & NT Integration

Programming
- Practical JavaScript for Web Development
- Java Programming
- PERL Programming
- Advanced PERL with CGI for the Web
- C++ Programming Featuring Microsoft's Visual C++

TCP/IP & network security
- Internetworking with TCP/IP
- Troubleshooting TCP/IP Networks
- Network Management
- Network Security Administration
- Mastering UNIX Security
- Cisco Router Security and Performance Tuning
- Windows NT Networking with TCP/IP
- Windows NT 4.0 Security

High speed networking
- Essentials of Wide Area Networking
- Implementing T1/T3 Services
- Frame Relay Internetworking
- Integrating ISDN
- Fiber Optic Network Design
- Fiber Optic Network Installation
- Migrating to High Performance Ethernet
- ATM Essentials
- ATM Internetworking

DIGITAL UNIX
- UNIX Utilities and Commands
- DIGITAL UNIX v4.0 System Administration
- DIGITAL UNIX v4.0 (TCP/ip) Network Management
- AdvFS, LSM, and RAID Configuration and Management
- DIGITAL UNIX TruCluster Software Configuration and Management
- UNIX Shell Programming Featuring Kornshell
- DIGITAL UNIX v4.0 Security Management
- DIGITAL UNIX v4.0 Performance Management
- DIGITAL UNIX v4.0 Intervals Overview

DIGITAL OpenVMS
- OpenVMS Skills for Users
- OpenVMS System and Network Node Management I
- OpenVMS System and Network Node Management II
- OpenVMS System and Network Node Management III
- OpenVMS System and Network Node Operations
- OpenVMS for Programmers
- OpenVMS System Troubleshooting for Systems Managers
- Configuring and Managing Complex VMScluster Systems
- Utilizing OpenVMS Features from C
- OpenVMS Performance Management
- Managing DEC TCP/IP Services for OpenVMS
- Programming in C

Hardware Courses
- AlphaServer 1000/1000A Installation, Configuration and Maintenance
- AlphaServer 2100 Server Maintenance
- AlphaServer 4100, Troubleshooting Techniques and Problem Solving

Alta Vista
- Installing and Configuring AltaVista Firewall 97 on Windows NT
- Installing and Configuring AltaVista Tunnel 97 on Windows NT
- Installing and Configuring AltaVista Firewall 97 on Digital UNIX
- Installing and Configuring AltaVista Tunnel 97 on Digital UNIX

Networking
- Digital MultiSwitch 900 Configuration and Installation
- Digital GIGAswitch/Ethernet Installation and Configuration
- Digital Gigaswitch/FDDI Installation and Management
- Digital ATM Solutions Installation and Configuration

ABOUT THE CONTRIBUTORS

Syngress Media creates books and software for Information Technology professionals seeking skill enhancement and career advancement. Its products are designed to comply with vendor and industry standard course curricula and are optimized for certification exam preparation. Contact them at www.syngress.com.

Cameron Brandon (MCSE, CNE, CNA, MCPS:Internet Systems, A+) is a Network Engineer/Administrator with Computer Systems, and lives in the greater Portland, Oregon, area. His specialty is Windows NT with BackOffice Integration.

Cameron participated in the Intel migration to Windows NT in Oregon, the largest migration of its kind in history. He completed his MCSE, CNE, CNA, MCPS:Internet Systems, and A+ certifications in five months' time, which shows what you can do if you set your mind to it.

Stace Cunningham is a Systems Engineer with SDC Consulting located in Biloxi, Mississippi. SDC Consulting specializes in the design, engineering, and installation of networks. Stace received his MCSE in October, 1996 and is also certified as an IBM Certified LAN Server Engineer, IBM Certified OS/2 Engineer, IBM Certified LAN Server Administrator, Microsoft Certified Product Specialist, IBM Certified LAN Server Instructor, and IBM Certified OS/2 Instructor.

Stace has participated as a Technical Contributor for the IIS 3.0 exam, SMS 1.2 exam, Proxy Server 1.0 exam, Exchange Server 5.0 and 5.5 exams, Proxy Server 2.0 exam, and the revised Windows 95 exam.

His wife Martha and daughter Marissa are very supportive of the time he spends on the computers located throughout his house. Without their love and support he would not be able to accomplish the goals he has set for himself.

Mike Swisher (MCSE) is a 1st Lieutenant in the United States Air Force. He is a communications officer serving at Keesler Air Force Base in Mississippi. His current duties have him designing a networking infrastructure with NT as the primary network operating system for the entire base (more than 10,000 users). He has received numerous awards in his three years in the military. Two years in a row he was selected as the 81st Training Support Squadron Company Grade Officer of the Year. He also distinguished himself by graduating top in his class at the Air Force's Basic Communications Officer Course. He enjoys water skiing and—of course—computers. His hometown is Rock Hill, South Carolina.

Michael D. Kendzierski (MCT, MCSE) works as a Systems Engineer for New Technology Partners, the 1997 Microsoft Solution Provider Partner of the Year. He received his Bachelor's degree from Providence College and has recently completed graduate work at Boston University. He is currently dividing his time between the Midwest and New England, providing consulting, development, and project management for Fortune 100 companies. When he's not fooling around with Visual Basic, he can be found roaming the country searching for a local Starbucks. He welcomes e-mail and can be reached at Mkendzierski@worldnet.att.net.

Harry Flowers (MCPS) has been a Systems Administrator for more than 15 years. He has a B.S. degree in Mathematics/Computer Science from Rhodes College, and currently works as one of a small group of systems administrators responsible for central computing systems at the University of Memphis in Memphis, Tennessee. He supports several Windows NT servers for both academic and administrative systems as well as other Microsoft BackOffice products, such as Exchange and Systems Management Server. Harry is also a Windows NT consultant and trainer for Open Road Technologies.

Tony Hinkle (MCSE, CNE) is from southern Indiana, is farm-raised, and holds a Bachelor's degree in Business Accounting from Oakland City University. His accounting career was quickly terminated by destiny, and he moved into the field of computer services. Although he started as a hardware technician, he knew that operating systems and networking would be his fields of excellence. With the assistance of his employer, Advanced Microelectronics, Inc., Tony completed the requirements to become a CNE, an A+ Certified Technician, and an MCSE.

Tony enjoys reading, Frisbee, Scrabble, computing, and participating in most non-contact sports. His claims to fame include being able to chirp like a cricket, knowing the alphabet backward, not owning a television, and knowing how many bytes are in an ATM packet. Tony thanks all of those who have helped to instill in him the knowledge, experience, and self-confidence necessary to excel in his field.

Todd Kiker is a consulting MCSE and CNE in the Southern California area, specializing in large-scale Windows NT implementations and support staff training. He is actively involved in advanced client/server technological development spanning multiple disciplines, including internetworking, network operating systems, and security.

Ed Wilson is a Senior Networking Specialist with Full Service Networking, a Microsoft Solution Partner, in Cincinnati, Ohio. A former Naval officer, Ed has been working with computers for nearly 15 years in a variety of industrial and corporate settings. He teaches adult education computer classes on an assortment of Windows-related topics including Powerpoint, Access, and Internet Explorer at Maysville Community College. He is a graduate of the University of Mississippi and Maysville Community College, and a Microsoft Certified Systems Engineer.

Technical Review by:
Shaun Taylor, a Network Consultant, Technical Editor, and full-time trainer in Ottawa, Ontario, Canada. Shaun is a Microsoft Certified System Engineer holding nine Microsoft certifications. He is also a Certified NetWare Administrator.

From the Classroom sidebars by:
Shane Clawson is a principal in Virtual Engineering, a consulting and engineering firm specializing in network consulting and technology process re-engineering. Shane has more than 20 years' experience as an instructor and in the in networking field. He is a Microsoft Certified System Engineer and a Microsoft Certified Trainer who has been working with NT since its inception and teaches for Global Knowledge Network. He specializes in Microsoft networking and BackOffice products. Shane may be reached at ShaneCSE@msn.com.

ACKNOWLEDGMENTS

We would like to thank the following people:

- Rich Kristof of Global Knowledge Network for championing the series and providing us access to some great people and information. And to Patrick Von Schlag, Rhonda Harmon, Marian Turk, and Kevin Murray for all their cooperation.

- To all the incredibly hard-working folks at Osborne/McGraw-Hill: Brandon Nordin, Scott Rogers, and Gareth Hancock for their help in launching a great series and being solid team players. In addition, Cynthia Douglas, Steve Emry, Anne Ellingsen, and Bernadette Jurich for their help in fine-tuning the book.

- Bruce Moran of BeachFront Quizzer, Mary Anne Dane of Self-Test Software, John Rose of Transcender Corporation, Parmol Soni of Microhard Technologies, and Michael Herrick of VFX Technologies.

- Gene Landy of the MIT Enterprise Forum for his support and encouragement, not to mention his incredible legal expertise. And to Tom Warren for handling all our IS needs with a smile.

- And to Holly Heath at Microsoft, Corp. for being patient and diligent in answering all our questions.

CONTENTS

The Global Knowledge Network Advantage

Linking the Classroom to the Real World

Global Knowledge Network is the largest independent IT training company in the world, training more than 150,000 people every year in state-of-the-art network training centers or on location with major corporate customers. In addition, it is a Cisco Systems Training Partner, a Bay Networks Authorized Education Center, a FORE Systems Training Partner, and an Authorized IBM NETEAM Education provider. Now, for the first time, all of Global Knowledge Network's classroom expertise and real-world networking experience is available in the form of this Microsoft Certified Professional Approved Study Guide.

This book's primary objective is to help you prepare for and pass the required MCSE exam so you can begin to reap the career benefits of certification. We believe that the only way to do this is to help you increase your knowledge and build your skills. After completing this book, you should feel confident that you have thoroughly reviewed all of the objectives that Microsoft has established for the exam.

In This Book

This book is organized around the actual structure of the Microsoft exam administered at Sylvan Testing Centers. Most of the MCSE exams have six parts to them: Planning, Installation and Configuration, Managing Resources, Connectivity, Monitoring and Optimization, and Troubleshooting. Microsoft has let us know all the topics we need to cover for the exam. We've followed their list carefully, so you can be assured you're not missing anything.

In Every Chapter

We've created a set of chapter components that call your attention to important items, reinforce important points, and provide helpful exam-taking hints. Take a look at what you'll find in every chapter:

- Every chapter begins with the **Certification Objectives**—what you need to know in order to pass the section on the exam dealing with the chapter topic. The icon shown at left identifies the objectives within the chapter, so you'll always know an objective when you see it!

exam
Watch

- **Exam Watch** notes call attention to information about, and potential pitfalls in, the exam. These helpful hints are written by MCSEs who have taken the exams and received their certification—who better to tell you what to worry about? They know what you're about to go through!

EXERCISE

- **Certification Exercises** are interspersed throughout the chapters. These are step-by-step exercises that mirror vendor-recommended labs. They help you master skills that are likely to be an area of focus on the exam. Don't just read through the exercises; they are hands-on practice that you should be comfortable completing. Learning by doing is an effective way to increase your competency with a product.

- **From the Classroom** sidebars describe the issues that come up most often in the training classroom setting. These sidebars give you a valuable perspective into certification- and product-related topics. They point out common mistakes and address questions that have arisen from classroom discussions.

- **Q & A** sections lay out problems and solutions in a quick-read format:

QUESTIONS AND ANSWERS

I am installing NT and I have HPFS...	Convert it before you upgrade. NT 4 does not like HPFS.

- The **Certification Summary** is a succinct review of the chapter and a re-statement of salient points regarding the exam.

- The **Two-Minute Drill** at the end of every chapter is a checklist of the main points of the chapter. It can be used for last-minute review.

- The **Self Test** offers questions similar to those found on the certification exams, including multiple choice, true/false questions, and fill-in-the-blank. The answers to these questions, as well as explanations of the answers, can be found in Appendix A. By taking the Self Test after completing each chapter, you'll reinforce what you've learned from that chapter, while becoming familiar with the structure of the exam questions.

Some Pointers

Once you've finished reading this book, set aside some time to do a thorough review. You might want to return to the book several times and make use of all the methods it offers for reviewing the material:

1. *Re-read all the Two-Minute Drills*, or have someone quiz you. You also can use the drills as a way to do a quick cram before the exam.

2. *Re-read all the Exam Watch notes.* Remember that these are written by MCSEs who have taken the exam and passed. They know what you should expect—and what you should be careful about.

3. *Review all the Q & A scenarios* for quick problem solving.

4. *Re-take the Self Tests.* Taking the tests right after you've read the chapter is a good idea, because it helps reinforce what you've just learned. However, it's an even better idea to go back later and do all the questions in the book in one sitting. Pretend you're taking the exam. (For this reason, you should mark your answers on a separate piece of paper when you go through the questions the first time.)

5. *Take the on-line tests.* Boot up the CD-ROM and take a look. We have more third-party tests on our CD than any other book out there, so you'll get quite a bit of practice.

6. *Complete the exercises.* Did you do the exercises when you read through each chapter? If not, do them! These exercises are designed to cover exam topics, and there's no better way to get to know this material than by practicing.

7. *Check out the web site.* Global Knowledge Network invites you to become an active member of the Access Global web site. This site is an online mall and an information repository that you'll find invaluable. You can access many types of products to assist you in your preparation for the exams, and you'll be able to participate in forums, on-line discussions, and threaded discussions. No other book brings you unlimited access to such a resource. You'll find more information about this site in Appendix C.

MCSE Certification

Although you've obviously picked up this book to study for a specific exam, we'd like to spend some time covering what you need to complete in order to attain MCSE status. Because this information can be found on the Microsoft web site, www.microsoft.com/train_cert, we've repeated only some of the more important information. You should review the train_cert site and check out Microsoft's information, along with their list of reasons to become an MCSE, including job advancement.

As you probably know, to attain MCSE status, you must pass a total of six exams —four requirements and two electives. One required exam is on networking basics, one on NT Server, one on NT Server in the Enterprise, and one on a client (either Windows NT Workstation or Windows 95 or 98). There are several electives from which to choose. The most popular electives now are on TCP/IP and Exchange Server 5. The following table lists the exam names, their corresponding course numbers, and whether they are required or elective. We're showing you the NT 4.0 track and not the NT 3.51 track (which is still offered).

Exam Number	Exam Name	Required or Elective
70-58	Networking Essentials	Required
70-63	Implementing and Supporting Microsoft Windows 95 or 98	Required (either 70-63/ 70-98 or 70-73)
70-67	Implementing and Supporting Microsoft Windows NT Server 4.0	Required

Exam Number	Exam Name	Required or Elective
70-68	Implementing and Supporting Microsoft Windows NT Server 4.0 in the Enterprise	Required
70-73	Implementing and Supporting Microsoft Windows NT Workstation 4.0	Required (either 70-73 or 70-63)
70-14	Supporting Microsoft System Management Server 1.2	Elective
70-59	Internetworking with Microsoft TCP/IP on Windows NT 4.0	Elective
70-81	Implementing and Supporting Microsoft Exchange Server 5.5	Elective
70-85	Implementing and Supporting Microsoft SNA Server 4.0	Elective
70-87	Implementing and Supporting Microsoft Internet Information Server 4.0	Elective
70-88	Implementing and Supporting Microsoft Proxy Server 2.0	Elective
TBA	System Administration for Microsoft SQL Server X	Elective
TBA	Implementing a Database Design on SQL Server X	Elective

The CD-ROM Resource

This book comes with a CD-ROM full of supplementary material you can use while preparing for the MCSE exams. We think you'll find our book/CD package one of the most useful on the market. It provides all the sample tests available from testing companies such as Transcender, Microhard, Self Test Software, BeachFront Quizzer, and VFX Technologies. In addition to all these third-party products, you'll find an electronic version of the book, where you can look up items easily and search on specific terms. The special self-study module contains another 300 sample questions, with links to the electronic book for further review. There's more about this resource in Appendix B.

How to Take a Microsoft Certification Examination

by John C. Phillips, Vice President of Test Development, Self Test Software
(Self Test's PEP is the official Microsoft practice test.)

Good News and Bad News

If you are new to Microsoft certification, we have some good news and some bad news. The good news, of course, is that Microsoft certification is one of the most valuable credentials you can earn. It sets you apart from the crowd, and marks you as a valuable asset to your employer. You will gain the respect of your peers, and Microsoft certification can have a wonderful effect on your income.

The bad news is that Microsoft certification tests are not easy. You may think you will read through some study material, memorize a few facts, and pass the Microsoft examinations. After all, these certification exams are just computer-based, multiple-choice tests, so they must be easy. If you believe this, you are wrong. Unlike many "multiple guess" tests you have been exposed to in school, the questions on Microsoft certification examinations go beyond simple factual knowledge.

The purpose of this introduction is to teach you how to take a Microsoft certification examination. To be successful, you need to know something about the purpose and structure of these tests. We will also look at the latest innovations in Microsoft testing. Using *simulations* and *adaptive testing,* Microsoft is enhancing both the validity and security of the certification process. These factors have some important effects on how you should prepare for an exam, as well as your approach to each question during the test.

We will begin by looking at the purpose, focus, and structure of Microsoft certification tests, and examine the effect these factors have on the kinds of questions you will face on your certification exams. We will define the structure of examination questions and investigate some common formats. Next, we will present a strategy for answering these questions. Finally, we will give some specific guidelines on what you should do on the day of your test.

Why Vendor Certification?

The Microsoft Certified Professional program, like the certification programs from Lotus, Novell, Oracle, and other software vendors, is maintained for the ultimate purpose of increasing the corporation's profits. A successful vendor certification program accomplishes this goal by helping to create a pool of experts in a company's software, and by "branding" these experts so that companies using the software can identify them.

We know that vendor certification has become increasingly popular in the last few years because it helps employers find qualified workers, and because it helps software vendors like Microsoft sell their products. But why vendor certification rather than a more traditional approach like a college degree in computer science? A college education is a broadening and enriching experience, but a degree in computer science does not prepare students for most jobs in the IT industry.

A common truism in our business states, "If you are out of the IT industry for three years and want to return, you have to start over." The problem, of course, is *timeliness*; if a first-year student learns about a specific computer program, it probably will no longer be in wide use when he or she graduates. Although some colleges are trying to integrate Microsoft certification into their curriculum, the problem is not really a flaw in higher education, but a characteristic of the IT industry. Computer software is changing so rapidly that a four-year college just can't keep up.

A marked characteristic of the Microsoft certification program is an emphasis on performing specific job tasks rather than merely gathering knowledge. It may come as a shock, but most potential employers do not care how much you know about the theory of operating systems, networking, or database design. As one IT manager put it, "I don't really care what my employees know about the theory of our network. We don't need someone to sit at a desk and think about it. We need people who can actually do something to make it work better."

You should not think that this attitude is some kind of anti-intellectual revolt against "book learning." Knowledge is a necessary prerequisite, but it is not enough. More than one company has hired a computer science graduate as a network administrator, only to learn that the new employee has no idea how to add users, assign permissions, or perform the other day-to-day tasks necessary to maintain a network. This brings us to the second major characteristic of Microsoft certification that affects the questions you must be prepared to answer. In addition to timeliness, Microsoft certification is also job task oriented.

The timeliness of Microsoft's certification program is obvious, and is inherent in the fact that you will be tested on current versions of software in wide use today. The job task orientation of Microsoft certification is almost as obvious, but testing real-world job skills using a computer-based test is not easy.

Computerized Testing

Considering the popularity of Microsoft certification, and the fact that certification candidates are spread around the world, the only practical way to administer tests for the certification program is through Sylvan Prometric testing centers. Sylvan Prometric provides proctored testing services for Microsoft, Oracle, Novell, Lotus, and the A+ computer technician certification. Although the IT industry accounts for much of Sylvan's revenue, the company provides services for a number of other businesses and organizations, such as FAA pre-flight pilot tests. In fact, most companies that need secure test delivery over a wide geographic area use the services of Sylvan Prometric. In addition to delivery, Sylvan Prometric also scores the tests and provides statistical feedback on the performance of each test question to the companies and organizations that use their services.

Typically, several hundred questions are developed for a new Microsoft certification examination. The questions are first reviewed by a number of subject matter experts for technical accuracy, and then are presented in a beta test. The beta test may last for several hours, due to the large number of questions. After a few weeks, Microsoft Certification uses the statistical feedback from Sylvan to check the performance of the beta questions.

Questions are discarded if most test takers get them right (too easy) or wrong (too difficult), and a number of other statistical measures are taken of each question. Although the scope of our discussion precludes a rigorous treatment of question analysis, you should be aware that Microsoft and other vendors spend a great deal of time and effort making sure their examination questions are valid. In addition to the obvious desire for quality, the fairness of a vendor's certification program must be legally defensible.

The questions that survive statistical analysis form the pool of questions for the final certification examination.

Test Structure

The kind of test we are most familiar with is known as a *form* test. For Microsoft certification, a form usually consists of 50–70 questions and takes 60–90 minutes to complete. If there are 240 questions in the final pool for an examination, then four forms can be created. Thus, candidates who retake the test probably will not see the same questions.

Other variations are possible. From the same pool of 240 questions, *five* forms can be created, each containing 40 unique questions (200 questions) and 20 questions selected at random from the remaining 40.

The questions in a Microsoft form test are equally weighted. This means they all count the same when the test is scored. An interesting and useful characteristic of a form test is that you can mark a question you have doubts about as you take the test. Assuming you have time left when you finish all the questions, you can return and spend more time on the questions you have marked as doubtful.

Microsoft may soon implement *adaptive* testing. To use this interactive technique, a form test is first created and administered to several thousand certification candidates. The statistics generated are used to assign a weight, or difficulty level, for each question. For example, the questions in a form might be divided into levels one through five, with level one questions being the easiest and level five the hardest.

When an adaptive test begins, the candidate is first given a level three question. If it is answered correctly, a question from the next higher level is presented, and an incorrect response results in a question from the next lower level. When 15–20 questions have been answered in this manner, the scoring algorithm is able to predict, with a high degree of statistical certainty, whether the candidate would pass or fail if all the questions in the form were answered.

When the required degree of certainty is attained, the test ends and the candidate receives a pass/fail grade.

Adaptive testing has some definite advantages for everyone involved in the certification process. Adaptive tests allow Sylvan Prometric to deliver more tests with the same resources, as certification candidates often are in and out in 30 minutes or less. For Microsoft, adaptive testing means that fewer test questions are exposed to each candidate, and this can enhance the security, and therefore the validity, of certification tests.

One possible problem you may have with adaptive testing is that you are not allowed to mark and revisit questions. Since the adaptive algorithm is interactive, and all questions but the first are selected on the basis of your response to the previous question, it is not possible to skip a particular question or change an answer.

Question Types

Computerized test questions can be presented in a number of ways. Some of the possible formats are used on Microsoft certification examinations, and some are not.

True/False

We are all familiar with True/False questions, but because of the inherent 50 percent chance of guessing the correct answer, you will not see questions of this type on Microsoft certification exams.

Multiple Choice

The majority of Microsoft certification questions are in the multiple-choice format, with either a single correct answer or multiple correct answers. One interesting variation on multiple-choice questions with multiple correct answers is whether or not the candidate is told how many answers are correct.

EXAMPLE:

Which two files can be altered to configure the MS-DOS environment? (Choose two.)

Or

Which files can be altered to configure the MS-DOS environment? (Choose all that apply.)

You may see both variations on Microsoft certification examinations, but the trend seems to be toward the first type, where candidates are told explicitly how many answers are correct. Questions of the "choose all that apply" variety are more difficult, and can be merely confusing.

Graphical Questions

One or more graphical elements are sometimes used as exhibits to help present or clarify an exam question. These elements may take the form of a network diagram, pictures of networking components, or screen shots from the software on which you are being tested. It is often easier to present the concepts required for a complex performance-based scenario with a graphic than with words.

Test questions known as *hotspots* actually incorporate graphics as part of the answer. These questions ask the certification candidate to click on a location or graphical element to answer the question. As an example, you might be shown the diagram of a network and asked to click on an appropriate location for a router. The answer is correct if the candidate clicks within the *hotspot* that defines the correct location.

Free Response Questions

Another kind of question you sometimes see on Microsoft certification examinations requires a *free response* or type-in answer. An example of this type of question might present a TCP/IP network scenario and ask the candidate to calculate and enter the correct subnet mask in dotted decimal notation.

Knowledge-Based and Performance-Based Questions

Microsoft Certification develops a blueprint for each Microsoft certification examination with input from subject matter experts. This blueprint defines the content areas and objectives for each test, and each test question is created to test a specific objective. The basic information from the examination blueprint can be found on Microsoft's web site in the Exam Prep Guide for each test.

Psychometricians (psychologists who specialize in designing and analyzing tests) categorize test questions as knowledge-based or performance-based. As the names imply, knowledge-based questions are designed to test knowledge, while performance-based questions are designed to test performance.

Some objectives demand a knowledge-based question. For example, objectives that use verbs like *list* and *identify* tend to test only what you know, not what you can do.

EXAMPLE:
Objective: Identify the MS-DOS configuration files.
Which two files can be altered to configure the MS-DOS environment? (Choose two.)

    A. COMMAND.COM

    B. AUTOEXEC.BAT

    C. IO.SYS

    D. CONFIG.SYS
    Correct answers: B,D

Other objectives use action verbs like *install, configure*, and *troubleshoot* to define job tasks. These objectives can often be tested with either a knowledge-based question or a performance-based question.

EXAMPLE:
Objective: Configure an MS-DOS installation appropriately using the PATH statement in AUTOEXEX.BAT.
Knowledge-based question:
What is the correct syntax to set a path to the D:\APP directory in AUTOEXEC.BAT?

    A. SET PATH EQUAL TO D:\APP

    B. PATH D:\APP

    C. SETPATH D:\APP

    D. D:\APP EQUALS PATH
    Correct answer: B

Performance-based question:

Your company uses several DOS accounting applications that access a group of common utility programs. What is the best strategy for configuring the computers in the accounting department so that the accounting applications will always be able to access the utility programs?

    A. Store all the utilities on a single floppy disk, and make a copy of the disk for each computer in the accounting department.

    B. Copy all the utilities to a directory on the C: drive of each computer in the accounting department, and add a PATH statement pointing to this directory in the AUTOEXEC.BAT files.

    C. Copy all the utilities to all application directories on each computer in the accounting department.

    D. Place all the utilities in the C:\DOS directory on each computer, because the C:\DOS directory is automatically included in the PATH statement when AUTOEXEC.BAT is executed.

Correct answer: B

Even in this simple example, the superiority of the performance-based question is obvious. Whereas the knowledge-based question asks for a single fact, the performance-based question presents a real-life situation and requires that you make a decision based on this scenario. Thus, performance-based questions give more bang (validity) for the test author's buck (individual question).

Testing Job Performance

We have said that Microsoft certification focuses on timeliness and the ability to perform job tasks. We have also introduced the concept of performance-based questions, but even performance-based multiple-choice questions do not really measure performance. Another strategy is needed to test job skills.

Given unlimited resources, it is not difficult to test job skills. In an ideal world, Microsoft would fly MCP candidates to Redmond, place them in a controlled environment with a team of experts, and ask them to plan, install, maintain, and troubleshoot a Windows network. In a few days at most, the experts could reach a valid decision as to whether each candidate should or should not be granted MCSE status. Needless to say, this is not likely to happen.

Closer to reality, another way to test performance is by using the actual software, and creating a testing program to present tasks and automatically grade a candidate's performance when the tasks are completed. This *cooperative* approach would be practical in some testing situations, but the same test that is presented to MCP candidates in Boston must also be available in Bahrain and Botswana. Many Sylvan Prometric testing locations around the world cannot run 32-bit applications, much less provide the complex networked solutions required by cooperative testing applications.

The most workable solution for measuring performance in today's testing environment is a *simulation* program. When the program is launched during a test, the candidate sees a simulation of the actual software that looks, and behaves, just like the real thing. When the testing software presents a task, the simulation program is launched and the candidate performs the required task. The testing software then grades the candidate's performance on the required task and moves to the next question. In this way, a 16-bit simulation program can mimic the look and feel of 32-bit operating systems, a complicated network, or even the entire Internet.

Microsoft has introduced simulation questions on the certification examination for Internet Information Server 4.0. Simulation questions provide many advantages over other testing methodologies, and simulations are expected to become increasingly important in the Microsoft certification program. For example, studies have shown that there is a very high correlation between the ability to perform simulated tasks on a computer-based test and the ability to perform the actual job tasks. Thus, simulations enhance the validity of the certification process.

Another truly wonderful benefit of simulations is in the area of test security. It is just not possible to cheat on a simulation question. In fact, you will be told exactly what tasks you are expected to perform on the test. How can a certification candidate cheat? By learning to perform the tasks? What a concept!

Study Strategies

There are appropriate ways to study for the different types of questions you will see on a Microsoft certification examination.

Knowledge-Based Questions

Knowledge-based questions require that you memorize facts. There are hundreds of facts inherent in every content area of every Microsoft certification examination. There are several keys to memorizing facts:

■ **Repetition** The more times your brain is exposed to a fact, the more likely you are to remember it.

■ **Association** Connecting facts within a logical framework makes them easier to remember.

■ **Motor Association** It is often easier to remember something if you write it down or perform some other physical act, like clicking on a practice test answer.

We have said that the emphasis of Microsoft certification is job performance, and that there are very few knowledge-based questions on Microsoft certification exams. Why should you waste a lot of time learning file names, IP address formulas, and other minutiae? Read on.

Performance-Based Questions

Most of the questions you will face on a Microsoft certification exam are performance-based scenario questions. We have discussed the superiority of these questions over simple knowledge-based questions, but you should remember that the job task orientation of Microsoft certification extends the knowledge you need to pass the exams; it does not replace this knowledge. Therefore, the first step in preparing for scenario questions is to absorb as many facts relating to the exam content areas as you can. In other words, go back to the previous section and follow the steps to prepare for an exam composed of knowledge-based questions.

The second step is to familiarize yourself with the format of the questions you are likely to see on the exam. You can do this by answering the questions in this study guide, by using Microsoft assessment tests, or by using practice tests. The day of your test is not the time to be surprised by the convoluted construction of Microsoft exam questions.

For example, one of Microsoft Certification's favorite formats of late takes the following form:

Scenario: You have a network with…
Primary Objective: You want to…
Secondary Objective: You also want to…
Proposed Solution: Do this…
What does the proposed solution accomplish?

  A. satisfies the primary and the secondary objective

  B. satisfies the primary but not the secondary objective

  C. satisfies the secondary but not the primary objective

  D. satisfies neither the primary nor the secondary objective

This kind of question, with some variation, is seen on many Microsoft Certification examinations.

At best, these performance-based scenario questions really do test certification candidates at a higher cognitive level than knowledge-based questions. At worst, these questions can test your reading comprehension and test-taking ability rather than your ability to use Microsoft products. Be sure to get in the habit of reading the question carefully to determine what is being asked.

The third step in preparing for Microsoft scenario questions is to adopt the following attitude: Multiple-choice questions aren't really performance-based. It is all a cruel lie. These scenario questions are just knowledge-based questions with a little story wrapped around them.

To answer a scenario question, you have to sift through the story to the underlying facts of the situation, and apply your knowledge to determine the correct answer. This may sound silly at first, but the process we go through in solving real-life problems is quite similar. The key concept is that every scenario question (and every real-life problem) has a fact at its center, and if we can identify that fact, we can answer the question.

Simulations

Simulation questions really do measure your ability to perform job tasks. You must be able to perform the specified tasks. There are two ways to prepare for simulation questions:

  1. Get experience with the actual software. If you have the resources, this is a great way to prepare for simulation questions.

2. Use official Microsoft practice tests. Practice tests are available that provide practice with the same simulation engine used on Microsoft certification exams. This approach has the added advantage of grading your efforts.

Signing Up

Signing up to take a Microsoft certification examination is easy. Sylvan operators in each country can schedule tests at any testing center. There are, however, a few things you should know:

1. If you call Sylvan during a busy time period, get a cup of coffee first, because you may be in for a long wait. Sylvan does an excellent job, but everyone in the world seems to want to sign up for a test on Monday morning.

2. You will need your social security number or some other unique identifier to sign up for a Sylvan test, so have it at hand.

3. Pay for your test by credit card if at all possible. This makes things easier, and you can even schedule tests for the same day you call, if space is available at your local testing center.

4. Know the number and title of the test you want to take before you call. This is not essential, and the Sylvan operators will help you if they can. Having this information in advance, however, speeds up the registration process.

Taking the Test

Teachers have always told you not to try to cram for examinations, because it does no good. Sometimes they lied. If you are faced with a knowledge-based test requiring only that you regurgitate facts, cramming can mean the difference between passing and failing. This is not the case, however, with Microsoft certification exams. If you don't know it the night before, don't bother to stay up and cram.

Instead, create a schedule and stick to it. Plan your study time carefully, and do not schedule your test until you think you are ready to succeed. Follow these guidelines on the day of your exam:

1. Get a good night's sleep. The scenario questions you will face on a Microsoft certification examination require a clear head.

2. Remember to take two forms of identification—at least one with a picture. A driver's license with your picture, and social security or credit cards are acceptable.

3. Leave home in time to arrive at your testing center a few minutes early. It is not a good idea to feel rushed as you begin your exam.

4. Do not spend too much time on any one question. If you are taking a form test, take your best guess and mark the question so you can come back to it if you have time. You cannot mark and revisit questions on an adaptive test, so you must do your best on each question as you go.

5. If you do not know the answer to a question, try to eliminate the obviously wrong answers and guess from the rest. If you can eliminate two out of four options, you have a 50 percent chance of guessing the correct answer.

6. For scenario questions, follow the steps we outlined earlier. Read the question carefully and try to identify the facts at the center of the story.

Finally, I would advise anyone attempting to earn Microsoft MCSE certification to adopt a philosophical attitude. Even if you are the kind of person who never fails a test, you are likely to fail at least one Microsoft certification test somewhere along the way. Do not get discouraged. If Microsoft certification were easy to obtain, more people would have it, and it would not be so respected and so valuable to your future in the IT industry.

1

Overview of Windows NT Workstation 4.0

Windows NT was created by Microsoft to fill a need for a 32-bit, stable, reliable, secure operating system. Some older operating systems were not able to ensure reliable performance, while others had no means of securing access to the computer, or even of restricting access to certain files or folders. Reliability and security are just two of the features that make Windows NT the premier operating system on the market today, not only for desktop computers but for high-powered, mission-critical enterprise servers. Throughout this chapter, you will learn just how advanced NT 4.0 is as we explore its many features, such as 32-bit preemptive multitasking, support for multiple processors, the ability to run on different architectures, and C2-compliant security. The Windows NT architecture has been optimized to ensure stability and performance through the use of modular components that work together, including protected subsystems for running applications. Since NT is designed to be a network operating system, it includes all of the features that you need to communicate and coexist with many different types of network architectures. You can cluster your computers in smaller workgroups, or take advantage of the Windows NT domain for large-scale central management of users and computers.

CERTIFICATION OBJECTIVE 1.01

Development of Windows NT

Microsoft Windows NT began life in 1988 as a project intended to develop a new, more advanced operating system than any that Microsoft had ever created. This new operating system was envisioned to be able to run on different hardware architectures, offer extensive security, provide multiprocessing support, and maintain compatibility. The project was five years in the works, and the results were finally released as Windows NT 3.1 and Windows NT Advanced Server 3.1 in 1993. The 3.1 designation referred to the similarities with the Windows 3.x operating system that was also available. Windows NT could run Windows 3.x applications and DOS applications, even though NT was not a DOS-based operating system like Windows 3.x.

The market was not swift to adopt Windows NT until after the release of the second version of the new operating system, entitled Windows NT 3.5. Release 3.5 still showed the familiar Windows 3.x user interface, but contained significant changes from the first release of NT, including a couple of new names: Windows NT Workstation and Windows NT Server. These names defined the role of the operating system more clearly than the first release. The next release of NT, entitled 3.51, was also significant. Many portions of the operating system were rewritten, and many new features were added. Some of these features included long filename support, WINS, DHCP, compression, and performance improvements. While there still was plenty of work to do before NT could command a major share of the market dominated by Novell NetWare, release 3.51 began to legitimately challenge NetWare in the network operating system area. But the best was yet to come.

With the release of Windows 95, the graphical interface, complete with the Start menu, Explorer, Task bar, and shortcuts, became a big hit. The latest version of NT, entitled Windows NT 4.0, includes this familiar interface. Because many users were already familiar with the interface, there was no learning curve to impede the acceptance of this new release, and now NT stands poised to dominate the market. After all, the point of an operating system is to make it easier to use a computer. Administrators who were responsible for Windows 95 already have a very good understanding of how to navigate and use the various features of the NT interface, such as the Explorer, the Control Panel, and the Registry. Administrators who were responsible for supporting an earlier version of NT, such as NT 3.51, are probably even more familiar with the underlying features of NT Workstation.

The overwhelming acceptance of Windows NT in the computing world creates a great demand for qualified professionals to support new NT networks. This is where *you* come in—the future Microsoft Certified System Engineer and highly trained technical mercenary.

Microsoft's Goal for Windows NT

The primary goal for Windows NT has always been to provide high-performance computing for users whose needs are not currently being met by Microsoft's other mainstream operating systems. Microsoft understands that NT is not for everybody, and provides the other desktop operating systems to fulfill other users' needs. Windows 95 was not as widely adopted as Microsoft anticipated, so many business environments are still using decaying operating systems such as Windows 3.*x*, and now are ready to upgrade, most likely by making the jump to Windows NT. Later in the chapter we will discuss the differences between the various operating systems to help you determine which one to implement in a given situation. NT Workstation should typically find itself in a business environment alongside NT Server, providing a total client/server solution for any sized business. Although these two operating systems can be separated, they were created to complement each other. They have similarities, but NT Server has been optimized for resource sharing and includes some utilities that are not provided with Workstation, including domain management tools, and greater support for the entire BackOffice suite.

Networking is obviously the wave of the future, and Microsoft is aiming to build networks with NT Workstation on every desktop and NT Server as the back end, combined with several of the Microsoft BackOffice products. The company has already dominated the desktop operating system market, and hopes to increase its presence in the networking arena to provide a total networking solution.

Microsoft has positioned NT to take part in the Internet and, especially, corporate intranets. Products such as Internet Information Server work with NT to provide access to the Internet, or the ability to browse an intranet. Peer Web Services for NT Workstation give you the ability to publish web pages on your company's intranet, or test content for the Internet Information Server without having to run NT Server. With Peer Web Services you can create your own web site, complete with FTP and Gopher support, from your NT Workstation.

CERTIFICATION OBJECTIVE 1.02

Features of Windows NT Workstation

With every new version of Windows NT, the available features become more impressive. Not only is the operating system becoming more stable, it also has improved networking capabilities, security, and compatibility. At first glance, the majority of NT's features revolve around the graphical interface or cosmetic adjustments to services found in the previous release. While few new substantial features are added with each release of NT, what already exists in the product is very substantial compared to the offerings of other operating systems. In the next few sections of this chapter we review the major features native to Windows NT and learn what they add to the overall robustness of this operating system.

Portability

A business network operating system must be able to support not only small businesses, but also complex corporate networks of the most powerful machines available. Many companies require the absolutely fastest systems available for processing power. While Intel remains the processor of choice for home and business, enterprise networks demand greater performance. With this in mind, Microsoft planned from the beginning on making Windows NT support a number of processor architectures. No other Microsoft operating system has been able to be run on so many different architectures. This flexibility allows you to customize each installation of NT to the architecture you feel best supports the function of your system. For example, if you have several file servers running Windows NT that do not experience heavy workloads, they could perform just fine with an Intel processor. However, if you have an application server that experiences tremendous workloads, it could benefit from having a faster processor to meet the demand. Before we go any farther, let's discuss these concepts in greater depth.

Portability is the capability of Windows NT to be "ported" to other architectures, such as DEC Alpha, MIPS, and Motorola's PowerPC. Different CPU architectures often work quite differently. The most notable examples of these differences can be found in Intel processors and Reduced Instruction Set Computing (RISC) processors. DEC Alpha, MIPS, and PowerPC processors are all based on the RISC design, which allows for fast, efficient processing of smaller numbers of instructions. (A small number of instructions can be executed very fast.) Intel processors are based on the Complex Instruction Set

Computing (CISC) design, and are often referred to as "*x*86" processors. You may not feel the need to run your NT Workstation on anything but an Intel processor unless your computer experiences heavy workloads. Windows NT Server, however, benefits greatly from NT's capability to be ported to other architectures.

Source codes for the various processor architectures differ, and that is why you see separate folders on the Windows NT Workstation CD-ROM for each processor type. If NT could not be ported to the more powerful RISC-based processors, it would not be popular in enterprises that demand more processing power. Processor speed for the RISC-based chips is around 500MHz, while Intel just released 300MHz processors.

While the NT operating system interface is the same for whatever processor architecture it runs on, portions of NT had to be rewritten for the new architectures. NT can be ported to other architectures because it is written in the C programming language, a platform-independent language. Other Microsoft operating systems, such as MS-DOS and Windows 95, were not written in C and therefore could only be ported to a non-Intel-based architecture with difficulty. Hardware-specific portions of the NT operating system that cannot be ported without modification were written in assembly language, thus allowing those portions simply to be recompiled on new platforms. You will learn later about the Hardware Abstraction Layer and its importance in making this portability possible.

POSIX

The Portable Operating System Interface (POSIX) is a standard developed by the Institute of Electrical and Electronic Engineers (IEEE) for file naming and identification. Windows NT supports POSIX as an environment subsystem, just as it supports the OS/2 and Win32 subsystems. The POSIX subsystem makes it possible for UNIX applications to run on NT, bringing NT one step closer to being the operating system of choice for companies that must support existing business applications. Microsoft has high hopes that NT can compete for the market share currently held by Novell and UNIX, and POSIX compatibility is important for making Windows NT a contender. POSIX compliance includes conforming to conventions such as case-sensitive naming, hard links, and additional time stamps.

Networking

The computer networking industry exploded in the last decade, and although Windows NT got a late start, it is picking up speed and challenging other competitors in this area. As mentioned earlier, the current networking arena is dominated by Novell NetWare. There are many other formidable foes that NT will have to challenge, however, such as UNIX, Banyan Vines, and legacy systems like the IBM AS/400. Microsoft is aware of this competition and, perhaps surprisingly, has designed NT to coexist and communicate with several operating environments, including:

- Novell NetWare
- Banyan Vines
- DEC Pathworks
- UNIX networks
- AppleTalk networks
- IBM LAN Server
- IBM SNA networks
- Windows 95 networks
- Windows for Workgroups networks
- Microsoft LAN Manager

As you can see from the preceding list, Windows NT can coexist with most of the popular networks available today. The most popular of the network environments is Novell NetWare, which NT supports heavily. Both Novell and Microsoft realize the importance of providing communication between these two giant network operating systems.

exam
ⓦatch

Novell integration is heavily tested on almost every MCSE exam.

Windows NT supports the following protocols for communicating in the various operating environments:

- TCP/IP
- NetBEUI
- NWLink (Microsoft's own 32-bit IPX/SPX protocol for NetWare support)
- AppleTalk
- DLC

Transmission Control Protocol/Internet Protocol (TCP/IP) is the choice for most networks these days. TCP/IP is the protocol of the Internet and of many company networks. I would not venture to say that TCP/IP is the protocol for most company networks because of the large installed base of Novell NetWare, which uses the IPX/SPX protocol. TCP/IP is the default protocol used during installation of Windows NT. TCP/IP lets you communicate with UNIX machines, mainframe computers, Apple networks (that use TCP/IP, not AppleTalk), and even NetWare networks (that use TCP/IP, not IPX/SPX). Although TCP/IP is extremely popular, it is a bit more difficult to implement. Each workstation and server requires a unique IP address before it can communicate on the TCP/IP network. You must manually assign these addresses, unless you use the Dynamic Host Configuration Protocol (DHCP) to ease the burden. You learn more about DHCP and TCP/IP in later chapters.

NetBIOS Extended User Interface (NetBEUI) is a small, efficient protocol that evolved over ten years ago when computer networks were much smaller than today, and did not require routers to connect to different networks. Although NetBEUI is the fastest protocol supported by NT, it is not routable, and therefore support for this protocol is dwindling except on smaller networks that do not use routers.

NWLink is Microsoft's interpretation of the patented IPX/SPX protocol owned by Novell. This protocol allows NT systems to communicate with NetWare systems that use IPX/SPX. Although designed for communication with NetWare networks, NWLink can be a very good choice as a primary protocol if TCP/IP is not implemented. This protocol is much easier to configure and support than TCP/IP, but is not nearly as widely accepted outside of the Novell world.

AppleTalk is the protocol designed for communicating with Macintosh computers. This protocol is not as commonly used because communication with Macintosh computers can be achieved through use of the TCP/IP protocol. AppleTalk is required for Services for Macintosh.

Data Link Control (DLC) is commonly used for accessing mainframes or stand-alone printers that have network cards installed. This protocol is different from the other protocols mentioned in that it is not used for communications between computers. You can free up a valuable IP address for printers with network cards by implementing DLC.

exam
Watch

The test will have you choose an appropriate protocol for use in a given situation. Nothing tricky here, just make sure you know what each protocol is used for.

It is worth mentioning that most of the software applications for communicating with these operating environments are built into Windows NT Workstation. They can be installed on your workstation computer as needed. You can even have multiple protocols installed on your system to communicate with the different environments on your network. These protocols would all communicate through the same network card, transparent to the user. The more protocols being used at once, however, the slower the system performance, so you should use only the protocols you need.

Interoperability is the key to survival if you intend to vie for market share in the networking area. Windows NT not only integrates with other network operating systems, it also provides tools to facilitate a smooth migration from those systems to NT Workstation. This feature makes it possible for you to roll out such a migration in phases while you continue to provide support for applications that require the original environment. There is also a tool built into NT Server that enables a quick and easy migration from NetWare networks to NT.

Multitasking

Handwritten note: Multitasking => uses only one processor

Multitasking is the ability to run several applications at once using one processor. The rapid execution of the different applications makes them appear as if they are all running at once. Multitasking is not the same as *multiprocessing*, which uses more than one processor. The multitasking model must be upgraded to the multiprocessing model if more than one processor is present in the system.

There are two types of multitasking: preemptive and cooperative.

Preemptive

Handwritten note: Preemptive => take over w/o consent

Preemptive multitasking gives the operating system the ability to take control of the processor without the consent of the application. This is the most common type of multitasking in Windows NT.

There are two ways the operating system can take control of the processor from the application:

- When the time slice (or *time quantum*) for the task runs out.

- When a task with a higher priority is ready to be executed. The lower priority task must yield control to the higher priority task.

Cooperative

Cooperative multitasking, or *non-preemptive multitasking*, requires an application to check the queue for other waiting applications and relinquish control to those applications. Earlier Windows operating systems, such as Windows 3.*x*, used cooperative multitasking to run 16-bit applications. Under those systems, if a cooperatively tasked application did not relinquish control of the CPU, it could prevent other applications from running properly; oftentimes the system would lock up or become unresponsive. The system was at the mercy of poorly written applications. This is one reason why older operating systems were not as stable as NT.

Multithreading

Windows NT uses a method known as *multithreading*, which makes different tasks performed within the same application appear as if they are running simultaneously. Every running application is considered a *process*, and every process can spawn one or more *threads*. Threads are the smallest units of execution in a process. Each thread is assigned a priority, which can be higher or lower than the priority of the process in which the thread is contained. A process or thread with a lower priority must yield control to one with a higher priority.

On a single-processor system, threads from multiple processes appear to run at the same time, even though only one thread is executed at a time. On a system with multiple processors, however, the threads can actually execute simultaneously.

Multithreaded applications must be written carefully to avoid conflicts between threads. For example, when one process creates another, the processes can share information by using a shared address space. Any thread spawned by either process also has access to that address space. Execution must be carefully synchronized to avoid having one thread alter or destroy information that another thread needs.

Multiprocessing

Scalability allows Windows NT to easily increase performance by adding more processors in the system to take advantage of *multiprocessing*. Windows NT Workstation provides support for two processors. NT Server can support more processors, including OEM versions that can provide support for up to 32 processors. Your workstation will probably not need more than one processor, but if you require extreme processing power for multimedia or CAD work, then it is nice to know NT Workstation will allow at least one more processor to be added to the system. Multiprocessing allows threads, which are small components of applications, to run on any processor.

Multiprocessing can be broken into two discreet categories:

- ■ Asymmetric Multiprocessing (ASMP)
- ■ Symmetric Multiprocessing (SMP) A processor would not be idle

Asymmetric Multiprocessing uses one processor for the operating system functions, and any other processors are used for user threads. Since the operating system uses the same processor for its processing, it is fairly easy to add more processors to application processing to suit your needs. The disadvantage with ASMP is that one processor can be nearly idle while the other processor is being heavily used. The processor that is idle will not be able to assist the other processor because it is reserved for one of two functions: the operating system or the applications. However, this is resolved with Symmetric Multiprocessing (SMP).

Symmetric multiprocessing is the ability of threads to be processed simultaneously by any processor in the system. Not only do user threads run on any processor in the system, but the operating system itself can also use all available processors. This is a significant increase in performance because the operating system can be very demanding and tax the system resources. If the operating system is performing many executions while the user threads remain idle, the operating system can take advantage of the processors where it could not in ASMP. This is the multiprocessing method of choice.

File Systems

Windows NT can utilize different file systems depending on the capabilities you require. Windows NT has introduced the New Technology File System (NTFS) for greater flexibility, security, and performance provided by the operating system. Windows NT also has maintained compatibility with its predecessors by providing support for the File Allocation Table (FAT) file system, which was introduced with the very first version of MS-DOS and has been used in Windows 3.x and Windows 95, as well as OS/2. The Compact Disc File System (CDFS) also is supported as a file system for CD-ROM media.

FAT

The FAT file system has been the most supported file system for Microsoft operating systems for many years. It has been sufficient for these previous operating systems, but NT requires greater functionality that is not provided with FAT. The FAT file system has limitations with respect to security, reliability, and hard drive capacity. However, that doesn't mean you shouldn't use FAT with NT. Microsoft even recommends using a FAT partition as your primary partition, so that you can perform diagnostics on the partition in an emergency. This would allow you to boot the computer from the floppy and run surface scanning and data recovery tools on the FAT partition. The sensitive information could still be inaccessible on an NTFS partition contained on the same system. Of course, you can format all your partitions with NTFS and your system will work just fine. In the event that your system partition has problems, you can use an NT boot disk to gain access to your system, or you can use the Emergency Repair Disk that you created. If you make your system completely NTFS, you are taking full advantage of the built-in security features of NTFS for local directory and file security. When we are talking about partitions not being accessible to FAT, we need to clarify that this is on the local computer. If you dual-boot between operating systems with both FAT and NTFS partitions, the NTFS partition is not visible in the operating system that does not support NTFS. A file that is stored on a partition formatted with the NTFS file system still can be shared over the network, regardless of whether the client that is accessing the file supports the NTFS file system.

With the Windows 95 operating system, enhancements were made to FAT, and the new version was called Virtual File Allocation Table (VFAT). VFAT enables the use of long filenames, while maintaining the 8.3 naming convention for older applications viewing the same file. It does this by writing two files on the disk: the actual long filename, and a FAT-compatible 8.3 version. VFAT gives users with FAT partitions the enhancement of long filename support without the complete transition to NTFS. You do not receive any of the benefits of the NTFS file system, such as security and compression. Windows NT just refers to VFAT as FAT.

NTFS

NTFS is the file system of choice for the Windows NT operating system, because it can support the new features of Windows NT. Among these features is the capability to assign attributes to files for security reasons. You can limit use of a file or folder to a certain user or group by assigning the appropriate permissions directly to the file or folder. NTFS allows these extended attributes to be stored with the file or folder itself, listing all users or groups that have access to the object. A compression attribute can be set for files and folders, as well. This attribute enables you to compress the contents of a file or folder, without compressing the entire volume. Another reason to choose

NTFS allows compression [handwritten margin note]

NTFS is the larger capacity hard disk support. FAT has too much overhead when it comes to large-capacity hard disks. It is common today to see drives over 6GB, which would not be used effectively if they were formatted as a FAT volume.

NTFS support larger capacity hard disks

NTFS security is implemented at the local level and works with the network shares to produce the most restrictive permissions across the network.

Security

In order for an operating system to be accepted in a business environment, it must be capable of fulfilling security needs—allowing some to view or modify the data, and restricting access by others. This type of security is another strong feature provided with Windows NT. NT can restrict access right down to the file level for greater security. This may be necessary when a folder is shared by a group of users, but access to a certain file in that folder is restricted to fewer users. Even if a directory is shared with full control, the presence of file-level security overrides this directory permission.

file-level security overrides directory share

NT is also C2-compliant, which makes it a National Security Agency trusted product. This enables NT to be used in high security areas such as government installations, banking institutions, or any other company requiring secure handling of sensitive data. This is a major breakthrough for the operating system. NT is one of the first mainstream operating systems to be awarded this compliance. With this C2 compliance, companies and agencies can benefit from NT's ease of use without compromising security. Here is a general breakdown of the requirements for becoming a C2-compliant operating system:

- ■ **Secure logon**   Users must have the proper credentials in order to access any of the resources located on the system.

- ■ **Access control**   Resource owners can determine who can access resources, and the nature of that access.

- ■ **Auditing**   The system can audit successful and failed attempts to access system resources.

- ■ **Memory protection**   A process cannot read another process's data without permission.

[handwritten margin notes:]
User Manager
set what y want
to audit

Event View
sees what has
been audited

NT has the capability not only to audit access to resources, but also to audit security changes, process tracking, logons, and system restarts. This capability lets you track down attempts at malicious activity on your network. The Event Viewer reports these successful or failed attempts based on what activity you have decided to audit in User Manager. There are many different events, and if you were to audit all of these events, you would have a security log a mile long. It is best to determine which events you feel are critical to your organization, and begin testing the auditing of events on the accompanying log files.

Multiple Clients

A *client* is most commonly defined as the workstation accessing the resources in a Client/Server model. A Windows NT network uses an NT server, and can support multiple client workstations of different operating system types.

- MS-DOS
- Windows 3.*x*
- Windows 95
- Windows NT Workstation
- Macintosh
- OS/2

A Windows NT network can contain any or all of these client workstations. Each operating system is subject to its own limitations or benefits. For example, Windows NT Workstation is used in conjunction with NT servers to take full advantage of its increased security, stability, and reliability. But using multiple clients of different operating systems on your network is also beneficial, for a number of reasons.

- These clients can be migrated to Windows NT Workstation in phases.
- Some applications are not yet supported in Windows NT and must be used on these platforms.
- Some machines on the network are not capable of running NT, and no plans are in order for these systems to be upgraded.

■ Other operating systems may provide benefits that are not available with NT.

A migration to Windows NT can be complicated, and can take a long time to implement. If the migration is done gradually, you can make adjustments to the migration process along the way for the systems yet to be migrated. You also can continue to make these resources available for a certain period of time after the migration, to verify that they are working correctly in the new environment. I was involved in an NT migration at Intel that started with NT 3.51. By the time we were finished, NT 4 had been in release for months.

Businesses come to depend on certain applications. If those applications are not supported by NT, a migration could be very disruptive. Even if an application can be upgraded to support NT, it might not be cost effective for the company to do so. The previous operating system can function just as it did before, while still participating on the NT network and providing users with the resources they have been accustomed to. This is the reason why legacy applications are still in existence in some business environments. Administrators face tough decisions when planning for a migration, because if just one required application cannot function correctly, the whole migration process is hampered. Windows NT Workstation is a very demanding operating system. All hardware requirements must be met and must be compatible before the system can run NT. This is expensive for a business that already has a lot of systems in production. You would have to convince management that the system upgrade and migration to NT Workstation would increase efficiency. If you could not, you would have to run older systems with another operating system on the NT network alongside the newer NT Workstations. Windows NT domains can support these other operating systems and enable them to access resources, but a standard for desktop computers is now broken. You now have more than one operating system that must be taken into consideration from now on.

On systems such as laptops, NT Workstation does not provide benefits, such as power management, that other operating systems such as Windows 95 provide. NT Workstation may also be too demanding in terms of resources for these systems.

A client also can be the software that enables communications for various network services. You can have multiple clients installed to take advantage of differing network services provided on your network. For example, you might install multiple clients to support the Client Services for Microsoft Networks, and the Client Services for NetWare Networks. Once you configure the network clients, the communication is transparent to the user. This transparency is achieved through the use of the *redirector.* Just like it sounds, the redirector redirects data from the local machine to a remote machine.

Compatibility

Maintaining compatibility is important in any release of an operating system, and Windows NT is no different. Some companies have found out why not maintaining backward compatibility is referred to as "corporate suicide." Even though a new product can be a significant advancement, if it is not compatible with the sizeable investments of software that a company wishes to maintain, the gain may not be worth the trouble. NT was originally planned not to support any older applications, but those plans were soon changed to support business applications. NT has remained compatible with previous Windows operating systems by support for the FAT file system, a 16-bit application subsystem as implemented by the Virtual MS-DOS Machine (VDM), and network and protocol support for previous Windows clients.

We discussed compatibility with the file systems in the earlier sections. Application compatibility is maintained through the various subsystems, most notably the virtual MS-DOS machine which runs both MS-DOS and Windows 3.*x* applications. MS-DOS applications are run in the VDM, which is the DOS emulator. Windows 3.*x* applications, which were created to run in MS-DOS, are also run in this VDM, but they require yet another emulator called Win16 on Win32 (WOW). These emulators can fool an application into believing it has full access to the system resources, just as it did when it was run on its native operating environment. Even more amazing is that Windows NT does not have any DOS code in the operating system at all. This is in contrast to the previous operating systems that required DOS to run correctly. This is why the NT Virtual DOS Machine is so important to NT. It is provided not only to support the DOS applications you may be using, but also to support the Windows applications that require DOS in order to operate.

An important feature of the WOW emulator is how calls are made between the WOW and Win32 subsystems. NT uses a process called *thunking* to translate the calls from one subsystem to another. Different rules for each format must be applied.

Not only can NT support these older applications through use of the subsystems, it can improve performance in most cases. For example, a DOS application is not multitasking in its original DOS environment. However, when it is run in the Windows NT 32-bit VDM, it can be multitasked with other DOS VDMs that are running, or with other applications running on the system. Each DOS application that is run will create a new VDM that is fully independent of other VDMs. This provides for greater stability for the system if the DOS application is misbehaving, because the application only crashes itself.

Next time you feel as if your NT Workstation system is locked up just like it used to get in Windows 95, press CTRL-ALT-DEL and see how fast your system responds. The window almost always comes up, no matter what the condition of the operating system at that moment. Closing down the faulty application can be tricky sometimes. When closing down an ill-behaved application, you typically see a dialog box prompting you to wait a few seconds longer, or to kill the unresponsive application. Sometimes you have to enter the Windows NT Task Manager and manually end the processes that you know are being unresponsive. This is unfortunate, but needs to be done sometimes.

16-bit Windows applications have the option of being run in one memory space, just as they were in their native environment, or being run in a separate memory space. If the applications are run in one memory space, the chance that one faulty 16-bit application will bring down every application sharing that space is increased. (However, if they are run in the same NTVDM, and an application stops responding, you can end the application as a process, and the other applications continue to work.) When the applications are run in their own separate memory space, if one application crashes, applications running outside the memory space are not affected. This is a welcome feature for users of many older 16-bit applications who were having trouble with misbehaving applications in the past. For example, if you are running four applications and one is not behaving appropriately, you can isolate this one application and run it in its own memory space, where it will no longer affect the other applications. You do have the option of running all of the 16-bit applications in their own memory space, but the memory space requires extra overhead. If you have the necessary resources to run each application in its own space, you should do so for extra protection. Be aware that some applications expect to share space with other applications. When they are run in their own memory space, they may not be able to function correctly.

exam
ⓦatch

The exam will present a scenario with a mix of applications, such as DOS and Windows applications, and ask you what would be the result if application x were to crash. How would the other applications currently running be affected? Study how the subsystems react to each other, and how the applications run within the subsystem.

Storage

An operating system must be able to anticipate future growth of hardware and components. One area that has been continually improving is storage. Hard disk and RAM capacities are increasing at an alarming pace. Luckily, Windows NT supports a large amount of RAM (4GB) and an even larger capacity of hard disk space (16 exabytes). Windows NT also can support removable media such as SyQuest, Bernoulli, and other magneto-optical devices. These drives are often used as offline devices for data archiving to tapes or compact discs, but also can be used for online storage in addition to the hard disks. The removable media are not quite as fast as hard disks, but they can be removed and placed in other devices, or stored offline for later use.

With your hard disk drives you can enable the use of striping, which spreads the data among several (a minimum of two) hard disks in the system, which can be read by the hard disk controllers at once. This greatly increases disk I/O performance. It is not a fault tolerant method, and a failure of one of the stripe set members results in a loss of the entire stripe set. You also can configure the hard disks in your system to use a volume set. A volume set takes areas of free space on any drive of a partition and creates one logical drive. This is useful when you have areas of the disk that are too small to be worthwhile. Once again, this is not a fault tolerant feature. Both of these methods will be discussed in later chapters.

Architecture of Windows NT

The Windows NT architecture can be daunting, but an understanding of how and why NT works is critical. Refer to Figure 1-1 as you study this topic. It is interesting to see how many components are involved. Windows NT Workstation is designed as components that are responsible for their own functions. These modular components comprise the NT architecture. The major components of the architecture are the Hardware Abstraction Layer (HAL), the Kernel, the Executive (System Services), and the Environment

FIGURE I-I

The Windows NT architecture, and the modes by which it is accessed

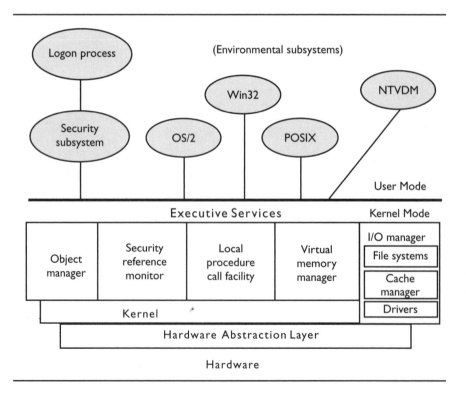

subsystems. How a process accesses the hardware is determined by what mode the process is running in: User Mode or Kernel Mode.

User Mode

Most NT code is stored and most applications run in User Mode. This is also the mode in which the environment subsystems that we discussed earlier are executed. User Mode is designed to prevent applications from bringing down the operating system. If a process is running in User Mode, it cannot access the hardware directly. It must call upon the operating system to access the hardware. This provides stability for the operating system by providing a protective barrier against a misbehaving application. User Mode is also called Nonprivileged Processor Mode.

Kernel Mode

Kernel Mode, also called Privileged Mode, has direct access to hardware and software resources in the system. Calls for hardware functions from applications running in User Mode must be translated into Kernel Mode instructions before the hardware can be accessed. The data must then be retranslated into User Mode when it is returned to the application. An important note about the release of NT 4 is that some components of NT that used to run as User Mode components now run as Kernel Mode components. These are the Window Manager, GDI, and graphics device drivers.

The Hardware Abstraction Layer separates the Kernel from the hardware to provide an intermediary layer, so that the Windows NT Kernel does not have to perform communication with the hardware. You should understand that the User Mode applications never call the hardware directly. These calls are handled only by the Windows NT Executive. Because of this, HAL is the most common reason why DOS and Windows applications are incompatible with NT. These applications expect to communicate directly with the hardware, and will not run if they are not given this privilege. Not only do you need another HAL for each hardware platform, you need two for each processor architecture. One is for supporting a single processor, and the other is for supporting multiple processors.

The Windows NT Kernel is the most important portion of the NT architecture, and is designed to be small and efficient to handle operating system events. This is the core of the operating system. The Kernel is small because the other components of NT provide their own functions and leave the Kernel to perform its duties. Additional components can be added without affecting or disrupting the Kernel itself. This is important when porting Windows NT to other processor architectures. One of the most important duties of the Kernel is to manage the use of threads, which can be defined as units of execution. Not only does the Kernel manage the threads, it is responsible for creating and scheduling them. These threads are assigned a priority from 0 - 31. (A higher number means a higher priority.) The Kernel must send threads to be processed based on this priority, or preempt a thread that has used up the time slice given to it.

The Executive (System Services) provides the operating system services that the Kernel is too busy to perform. The Kernel is actually part of the NT Executive, and together they are responsible for the entire system. The NT Executive is responsible for numerous major components.

- Object Manager is responsible for managing objects used to represent resources in the system.

- Process Manager monitors the status and usage of processes and threads.

- Virtual Memory Manager (VMM) manages the system's virtual memory pool, in which the hard disk is used to simulate RAM.

- Local Procedure Call Facility (LPC) is responsible for processes that share information on the local machine.

- Security Reference Monitor (SRM) is responsible for enforcing the security policies by verifying credentials of users and groups.

- I/O Manager is responsible for all input and output for the file system, I/O devices, and redirectors.

- Window Manager (USER) creates the screen interface.

■ Graphics Device Interface (GDI) is the graphics engine that interprets graphic requests and displays them.

The Environment subsystems provide support for the various application types that can be run, such as POSIX, Win32, and OS/2. Such applications require a particular environment, which is mimicked by the Environment subsystem. Environment subsystems are considered *sub*systems, because they can perform independently of other subsystems. They are described as *protected*, because other subsystems do not have the right to access another application's subsystem. Each of the major subsystems is described below:

Win32
The primary subsystem for Windows NT, Win32 is used for all user input and output, and is called upon by the other subsystems for services. An interesting note is that the OS/2 subsystem originally was going to be the primary subsystem for Windows NT, until the surprising success of Windows 3.*x*.

MS-DOS and Win16
MS-DOS and Win16 were included within Windows NT to provide backward compatibility with older DOS and Windows applications. Most applications being used in their native operating environments now can be used in NT. The use of the NTVDM enables these applications to run properly. This is described in detail earlier in the chapter.

POSIX
The POSIX subsystem was included to support open standards, mostly for application support for UNIX platforms. The POSIX subsystem is discussed in greater detail in later chapters on file systems.

OS/2
The OS/2 subsystem was originally planned to be much more significant in NT, but dwindling support has decreased the need for OS/2 compatibility.

The OS/2 subsystem is protected and can be preemptively multitasked, and also can translate the Win32 calls. However, the OS/2 subsystem does not support graphical applications. It can support only Character Mode applications, which are scarce. Therefore, the OS/2 support is very limited.

Memory Architecture

Windows NT has made significant improvements in its memory architecture. The most important features that comprise the NT memory architecture are as follows:

- Virtual Memory
- Demand Paging
- 32-bit, flat address space

Virtual Memory allows your NT Workstation to use the hard disk to simulate RAM as needed. NT uses a system called *paging* to move an unused portion of memory to the hard disk, and to retrieve the data when it is needed. This also can be called *demand paging*. NT accomplishes this through use of the Virtual Memory Manager, and the paging file. It is VMM's job to determine which data has been paged to the disk, and to keep track of the physical memory addresses used by this data. The paging file is the actual file on the hard disk where this information is paged to and from. You will learn more about the paging process and configuring the paging file for use with NT in later chapters.

The 32-bit flat address space is used in Windows NT instead of the segmented memory architecture used in MS-DOS and Windows 3.*x*. Segmented memory architecture used a 16-bit addressing model to access memory locations using a segment/offset method. (This method is akin to a map grid. You find the location of F7, for example, by moving over to column F, and down to row 7. The segment and the offset are comparable to columns and rows.) It took valuable system resources to map these memory references. The 32-bit flat address space means that applications can access up to 2GB of RAM, rather than the 64K segments that were previously used. This is what other non-Intel processors use as their address scheme, therefore NT is more compatible with these processor architectures.

Comparing Workstation with Other Operating Systems

Windows NT represents the pinnacle of desktop operating systems to date. Its power, compatibility, security, and ease of use make NT Workstation, quite possibly, the best workstation operating system. It's more stable than Windows 3.x or Windows 95. It's easier to use than the SPARCstation. And it's more compatible than OS/2. Since Microsoft dominates the market as far as desktop operating systems go, you will most likely be choosing among various Microsoft operating systems in your organization. You must understand the features of each operating system in order to make a wise decision. There is nothing wrong with using a combination of desktop operating systems in your organization. This can be an effective way to cater to the capability and purpose of the computer. There are ramifications to implementing a mixed network, mostly involving compatibility. If your organization uses certain applications throughout the company, each platform has to be able to support those applications. (For example, if you use Microsoft Office for Windows 95 or NT in your company, how could the 16-bit operating systems, such as Windows 3.x, share documents and worksheets created in these versions? Workstations using an older version of the Office suite couldn't read the formats created using the Windows 95 or NT versions. The newer version of Office could read the formats of older versions, but it doesn't work the other way.) These considerations must be weighed when making operating system decisions. You should plan an extensive period for testing in a lab environment. Install the new operating system, and all the applications you plan on using. Determine if there are any incompatibilities before the upgrade. If there are, will you upgrade to a newer version? Discontinue the use of the application? Find another, equal application from another vendor that does support your new operating system? Or just not upgrade to the new operating system?

Workstation vs. Server

The choice between NT Workstation and NT Server depends on the use of the machine. If you use the machine as a source for applications, files, or print services, it would be wise to choose NT Server over Workstation, because NT

Server is optimized for these types of services. That is not to say that you cannot share files or print devices with NT Workstation. You can share these services just as you would with NT Server, but you might decide between the two based on how many of these services a given machine shares at one time. If other users often log on locally to the system, you might elect to use NT Workstation. (Logging on directly into NT Servers should be reserved for administrators qualified to support NT Server.) If you need services available for sharing at all times, however, choose NT Server. Any processing required for a user sitting directly at the system detracts from the capability to share resources such as applications and files. However, you can administer the domain from a workstation without the need to log on locally at the server. Table 1-1 shows a detailed breakdown of the various differences between the two operating systems.

| TABLE 1-1 | Workstation vs. Server |

Feature	Windows NT Workstation	Windows NT Server
Processor support	2	4 (out of the box), 32 maximum
RAID Fault Tolerance	No	RAID 5 Striping with parity, and disk mirroring
Domain Logon validation for clients	No	Yes
Directory replication	Import	Import and Export
Services for Macintosh	No	Yes
RAS Connections	1	256
Inbound Client sessions	10	Unlimited
Configurable Server service	No	Configurable for application server, file/print, or balanced throughput
Minimum RAM	12MB	16MB
Minimum Disk space	120MB	130MB
Caching	Better throughput for local access	Better network throughput
BackOffice support	Limited	Yes

Other than the features just listed, the two operating systems are very much alike. One of the most important differences mentioned in Table 1-1 is the number of inbound client sessions available. The limit of 10 client sessions to your NT Workstation is a drawback if you are using your workstation to share files or applications. If you are constantly reaching this limit, transfer these services over to an NT Server so all users can access the resources in a timely manner. After all, that is the purpose of resource sharing: to give users access to files, printer, and applications. The other important difference is that NT Server is optimized for network throughput and NT Workstation is optimized for better local access.

The hardware requirements of the two operating systems are quite similar. This is, of course, the bare minimum. It would be wise to increase the amount of RAM on the NT Server to 32MB or more, to increase response time. Even more than 32MB of RAM is recommended if your NT Server is also running any of the BackOffice products.

The limitations of NT Workstation when it comes to fault tolerance are also important. Although you can stripe the data on NT Workstation to increase the disk I/O, there is not an option for disk striping with parity. This is a feature supported in NT Server that enables you to re-create the data in the stripe set if one of the members of the stripe set fails. NT Server uses the parity information to re-create the data. Another fault tolerant feature that NT Workstation does not support is the capability to mirror drives. NT Server can mirror the information from one drive to another to eliminate the possibility of data loss if one of the drives fails. Although these features would be useful for some users in NT Workstation, their absence does not pose a big concern. If you participate on an NT network, you should save all of your important information to the server, where the data will be backed up during the regularly scheduled backup routine for the servers. If your workstation hardware fails, you need only replace the failed devices, in this case a hard disk, reinstall NT and your applications, and you are back up and running.

Workstation vs. Windows 95

Your choice between Windows NT Workstation and Windows 95 for a client workstation depends on your working environment. For the average home user, Windows 95 is the logical choice. This might not be the case in special situations, so I'll discuss the differences between the two operating systems in this section. Table 1-2 shows the differences between Windows 95 and Windows NT.

There are many applications and programs available for the Windows 95 operating system. Most of these will run on NT Workstation. When run in Windows NT, they might receive a performance increase. We have learned earlier that NT runs DOS applications in their own subsystem, and preemptively multitasks the VDM. This results in a performance increase. Windows applications benefit in terms of greater stability, because they can be

TABLE 1-2   Workstation vs. Windows 95

Feature	Windows NT Workstation	Windows 95
Hardware	Minimum 486DX/33, 12MB RAM	Minimum 386/20, 4MB RAM
Devices supported	Not as many as Windows 95	More than Windows NT
Power Management	No	Yes
Plug and Play	No, but can detect some devices	Yes
Security	Maximum security	Can participate in an authenticated domain environment
Stability	Much greater than Windows 95	Improved over predecessors,, but still prone to errant applications
File system	NTFS or FAT	FAT
Compatibility	Good, but some applications still have problems	Very compatible with existing applications
Multiprocessor support	Yes	No
Capability to run on different architecture	Yes	No
Preemptive multitasking	Yes	Yes
Protocol support	TCP/IP, NetBEUI, DLC, NWLink, AppleTalk	TCP/IP, NetBEUI, DLC, NWLink, AppleTalk
Remote Access	Yes	Yes

run in their own separate memory space. This prevents an errant application from bringing down other applications sharing the same space, as often happened in their native operating environments. If you are using your home system for games, you will find a few that refuse to run in NT. NT is not the preferred game machine, due to the fact that some of these games expect to have access to the hardware. This can be remedied by dual-booting between Windows 95 and NT. On my own computer, I have to dual-boot between the two operating systems because of a scanner that is not supported under Windows NT.

Windows 95 would also be used on systems that do not meet the hardware requirements of NT, or devices in the system that do not adhere to the strict Hardware Compatibility List provided for NT. Windows 95 runs on a 386/20 with 4MB of RAM, although very poorly. Windows NT requires at least a 486DX/33 with 12MB of RAM. If you require plug and play functionality, you have to choose Windows 95 for now, because NT is not plug and play-compatible as of yet. Our company uses Windows 95 on the laptops, because so many users complained about sluggish performance by NT, and the lack of power management.

Home users also don't have much use for the added security features that NT provides. Its capability to restrict file and folder access for users or groups probably would never be used. Neither would its capability to audit successful and failed attempts to access system resources.

The new NTFS file system offers home users and business users considerable advantages over the FAT file system of Windows 95.

- NTFS supports larger capacity hard disks than FAT.

- Compression for individual files and folders comes in handy when you need extra space, or for files or folders that will not be accessed for a period of time.

- NTFS has less file system overhead than the FAT file system, and therefore maximizes valuable hard disk space.

- Hot fixing, commonly known as sector sparing, automatically moves the contents of a sector that is found to be bad, and marks that sector as unusable. This is transparent to the user, but only available if you are using SCSI devices.

As we mentioned earlier, the added security with the NTFS file system might not mean much to home users, but in a business setting this is a very valuable feature.

Windows 95, unlike NT, doesn't support the creation of stripe and volume sets—features that any user would find beneficial.

Another distinction between the two operating systems is the cost. Windows NT Workstation costs more than Windows 95. If you feel you have the computer to support NT and are aware of the factors involved with your decision, the higher cost for NT might be a worthwhile investment in terms of performance and features.

CERTIFICATION OBJECTIVE 1.04

When to Use a Domain vs. a Workgroup

Windows NT supports the use of a workgroup or domain for the managing and sharing of resources for users. In any network of computers, resources are shared, and clients access the shared resources. Each of the models, workgroup and domain, supports the sharing of resources, but they do so in different ways. The choice of workgroup or domain is based on the network environment and several other factors. Important factors to consider in deciding between the two are the number of users who will share the resources, and their technical knowledge.

Workgroup Model

The workgroup model, illustrated in Figure 1-2, is most often used in a small group of users, due to the way resources are managed and shared. Each computer in the workgroup must maintain the account information for each user in the workgroup. This is because there is no central means of providing authentication for users. If you were to change your account information, you would have to change your account information on every computer that you access in the workgroup before you can access resources. This gets more complicated as more users are added to the workgroup. If your workgroup

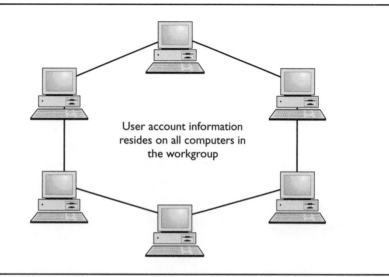

FIGURE 1-2

The Workgroup Model for managing and sharing resources on a network

User account information resides on all computers in the workgroup

consists of fewer than ten users, the workgroup model provides an effective way of sharing information, provided all the users who participate in the workgroup have the technical ability to share system resources and manage account information. This is the most complicated facet of the workgroup environment, but the workgroup model is much easier than the domain group model in terms of user account management and access to resources.

Pros

- Easier to install than a domain.
- Does not require NT Server or another server for authentication.
- No central point of failure.

Cons

- Requires users to have knowledge about sharing resources and account management.

■ Not for groups of more than ten computers.

■ Account information must be kept on every computer that participates in the workgroup.

Domain Model

Under the domain model, a Windows NT Server acts as a domain controller. The domain controller authenticates users into the domain before they can access resources that are a part of the domain. See Figure 1-3 for an illustration. These resources can be located on the NT Server, or any computer on the network. The domain model is strongly recommended for networks of ten computers or more. The domain model is also recommended, regardless of the number of participating computers, if you require central control of user management or resource access. For this reason the domain model is by far the model of choice for businesses. It enables an administrator to centrally manage the accounts in the domain, including account policies that regulate password restrictions such as length of password, password age, and account lockout. The administrator also can add users to groups, give the user special permissions, and disable or delete accounts from the Windows NT tools including User Manager available in NT Workstation, or User Manager for Domains in NT Server.

As we indicated earlier, in the workgroup model user account information is kept on each computer that participates in the workgroup. In the domain model, the user account information database can be shared by users or groups, and also is shared by the servers in the domain. These servers require access to this database if they are to perform logon validation for users. They are, most likely, the Primary Domain Controller or a Backup Domain Controller. You will learn more about these types of servers in later sections of the book.

The domain model has a few variations when you are using more than one domain, as in the case of large enterprise networks with separate divisions or departments. Domains can be organized as physical or logical divisions within a company. For example, a domain model based on physical locations would include domain names such as Buffalo and Seattle. An example of a domain model based on logical groupings of computers would be domain names such as

Accounting and Sales. Either way, the domain should be named to illustrate its purpose. You will learn more about domains and the various domain models as you continue towards your MCSE with the Windows NT Server exam, and especially the Windows NT Server in the Enterprise exam. For now, we are just clarifying the differences between the workgroup and domain models.

Figure 1-3 can be a little misleading. We have stated that a domain controller is needed to authenticate users upon logging on to the domain. Why are there two NT Servers in the illustration? One of the servers is the Primary Domain Controller (PDC), which is at the top of the NT domain hierarchy. The PDC is responsible for the changes to the directory database. Any adjustments by the administrator are recorded in this database on the PDC. There would be one PDC for each domain. The other computer in the illustration is a Backup Domain Controller (BDC). The BDC maintains a copy of the directory database that has been replicated from the PDC. The BDC can authenticate user logons with this database. Therefore, any of the domain controllers can be used for authenticating the client workstations.

FIGURE 1-3

The Domain Model is for large networks, and provides central control over user management and resource access

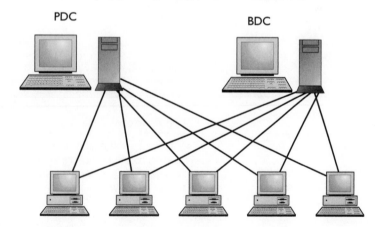

User account information is stored on a domain
controller to authenticate users for the domain

PDC

BDC

Pros

- Provides a central source for user account management and resource management.
- Can support a large number of users.
- Can coexist with other domains in the organization.

Cons

- Central point of failure if backup domain controllers are not used.
- More difficult to install and configure.

Now that you have seen the two models, here are possible scenario questions relating to the topic:

QUESTIONS AND ANSWERS

I want central control...	Use the domain model. It gives you central control over user accounts.
I have a large number of users...	Use the domain model. The workgroup model is unwieldy for more than ten users.
We have inexperienced users...	Use the domain model. The workgroup model requires that users know how to share and manage accounts for other users on their own systems.
We do not have a server...	Use the workgroup model. This is one advantage of the workgroup. You do not need to dedicate a machine to authenticating user accounts.

CERTIFICATION OBJECTIVE 1.05

Hardware Qualifier Disk Tool

There is a tool provided with Windows NT Workstation that can identify installed hardware and settings for you to examine before your upgrade to Windows NT. It is the Windows NT Hardware Qualifier Disk (NTHQ). You can use this tool to verify that your system and components are going to be supported under the new operating system. I strongly recommend using this tool to verify the compatibility of your system before you upgrade. You should use it on all systems you upgrade, unless they are of the same model, or contain the very same components. Using this tool is much more efficient than trying the upgrade and finding your system is not compatible. NTHQ also can be used for troubleshooting Windows NT after it has been installed. In the next exercise we will create the Windows NT Qualifier Disk.

For these exercises, you need a floppy disk and access to the Windows NT Workstation CD-ROM.

EXERCISE 1-1

Creating the Windows NT Hardware Qualifier (NTHQ) Disk

1. Insert the Windows NT Workstation CD-ROM

2. If Autoplay is enabled, the Windows NT Workstation screen appears. If Autoplay is not enabled you have to bring up Explorer to search the CD-ROM.

3. Click the Support folder.

4. Click the Hqtool folder.

5. Insert a 3.5" 1.44MB floppy disk.

6. Click the MAKEDISK.BAT file.

   The program then copies a disk image file to the floppy for the program.

7. Label the disk NT Qualifier Disk.

In the next exercise we will use the disk you just made to check our system for compatibility with Windows NT. The disk is bootable, so we don't have to make it a system disk.

EXERCISE 1-2

Using the Windows NT Hardware Qualifier Disk

1. Reboot the computer you wish to check with the floppy disk in the drive.

2. You see a prompt that the system is preparing NTHQ.

3. After some activity, you see the Main Graphical Menu, which tells you what the program does. It prompts you to indicate whether you want to continue with device detection. Click Yes to continue.

4. Click Yes if you receive another prompt for detection. The detection process takes approximately 3-5 minutes.

5. After the detection, you are at the screen with general system information. You can click various components in the system, such as the motherboard, video, and storage, and view their properties. The Help file button gives you an extensive overview of the process and how to analyze the results. This file also says that the program is not for Windows 95 or Windows NT. Do not be concerned if you are running one of these operating systems, because we are booting up to the floppy, not the operating systems. The warning refers to the act of clicking the icon from within the Windows 95 or NT operating system to access the program.

6. Click the compatibility button to see which devices conform to the NT Hardware Compatibility list.

   I have three devices listed here, two of which match the NT Hardware Compatibility List, and a third, which is a video accelerator card that does not match the list.

7. Click Exit once you have finished viewing the system information, and restart the system without the floppy in the drive.

NTHQ allows you to forecast potential incompatibilities before they happen. With this information you can replace the device, or just not install Windows NT on a particular machine.

CERTIFICATION SUMMARY

Windows NT Workstation is an advanced operating system, with features that make it a great choice for businesses and individuals requiring a robust operating system. The architecture of Windows NT is comprised of modular components. The memory architecture of Windows NT has been enhanced by the addition of Virtual Memory, which allows your NT Workstation to use the hard disk to simulate RAM as needed. With the 32-bit flat address space, your system can access up to 4GB of virtual memory.

The file system created for the Windows NT operating system is NTFS. NTFS takes advantage of the new features available with NT, such as security, compression, and large hard disk support. NT has remained compatible with previous Windows operating systems by support for the FAT file system, a 16-bit application subsystem, the virtual MS-DOS machine (VDM), and network and protocol support for previous Windows clients. The Windows NT Hardware Qualifier Disk is a tool for verifying that your system and components are going to be supported under the new operating system.

Security in NT has been increased to include file and folder permissions, user and group permissions, and auditing of attempts to access system resources. NT requires a user logon before any resources are available to the user.

Windows NT can support multiple client workstations of different operating system types. For network support, NT Workstation can manage and share resources according to the workgroup model or the domain model.

 # TWO-MINUTE DRILL

- ❏ Windows NT's most important advancements are in the areas of portability, POSIX, networking, multitasking, multithreading, multiprocessing, and security.

- ❏ *Portability* is the capability of Windows NT to be "ported" to other architectures, such as the DEC Alpha, MIPS, and Motorola's PowerPC.

- ❏ *POSIX* is a standard developed by the Institute of Electrical and Electronic Engineers (IEEE) for file naming and identification.

- ❏ *Multitasking* is the ability to run several applications at once using one processor. This can be either preemptive or cooperative.

❑ *Multithreading* uses processes that spawn multiple *threads*, which have priorities assigned to them. These threads are executed based on their priority, or until their time slice is up.

❑ *Multiprocessing* is the capability of the system to increase processing power by adding more processors. There are two categories of multiprocessing: Asymmetric and Symmetric.

❑ How a process accesses the hardware is determined by what mode the process is running in: User Mode or Kernel Mode.

❑ The major components of the NT architecture are the Hardware Abstraction Layer (HAL), the Kernel, the Executive (System Services), and the Environment subsystems.

❑ The *Hardware Abstraction Layer* (HAL) separates the Kernel from the hardware to provide an intermediary layer, so that the Windows NT Kernel does not have to perform communication with the hardware.

❑ The *Kernel* is responsible for creating, managing, and scheduling threads.

❑ The *Executive* (System Services) component provides services that the Kernel does not perform.

❑ The *Environment subsystems* provide support for the various application types that can be run, such as POSIX, Win32, and OS/2. They mimic the original environment the application expects to see.

❑ The most important features of the NT memory architecture are Virtual Memory, Demand Paging, and 32-bit, flat address space.

❑ *Virtual Memory* allows your NT Workstation to use the hard disk to simulate RAM as needed.

❑ *Demand paging* is the term used to describe the process of moving pages of memory to and from the disk as needed.

❑ The 32-bit flat address space allows your system to access up to 4GB of virtual memory.

❑ The most important factors to consider when deciding between workgroup or domain model are the number of users that will take part in the sharing of resources, and their technical knowledge.

❑ The Windows NT Hardware Qualifier Disk (NTHQ) is a tool provided with Windows NT Workstation that identifies installed hardware and settings for you to examine before your upgrade to Windows NT.

SELF TEST

The following questions will help you measure your understanding of the material presented in this chapter. Read all the choices carefully, as there may be more than one correct answer. Choose all correct answers for each question.

1. What does RISC stand for?

    A. Reduced Information Source Code

    B. Reduced Instruction Source Code

    C. Reduced Instruction Set Computing

    D. Reduced Information Set Computing

2. Windows NT is written in the _____ language.

3. _____ applications use conventions such as case-sensitive naming and hard links.

4. What does TCP/IP stand for?

    A. Transport Control Protocol/Internet Protocol

    B. Transmission Controlled Protocol/Internet Protocol

    C. Transport Compatible Protocol/Internet Protocol

    D. Transmission Control Protocol/Internet Protocol

5. (True/False) DLC is the protocol used for communicating with DEC Pathworks networks.

6. What is the fastest network protocol supported by NT?

    A. DLC

    B. NetBEUI

    C. TCP/IP

    D. NWLink

7. I have one DOS application running, and a suite of five 16-bit applications running. One of the 16-bit applications continually crashes when I use the DOS application. What is the best way to keep this from happening?

    A. Run the DOS application in its own VDM.

    B. Run all of the 16-bit applications in a separate memory space.

    C. Run the faulty application with a higher priority than the other 16-bit applications.

    D. Run the faulty application in a separate memory space.

8. Windows NT Workstation provides support for up to _____ processors.

9. (True/False) If you share a file that is on a FAT partition over the network, the file cannot be seen by non-NTFS-compatible operating systems.

10. NT uses a process called _____ to translate the calls from one subsystem to another.

11. Which is not a component of the Windows NT Executive?

A. Process Manager

B. Security Reference Monitor

C. Process Scheduler

D. Object Manager

12. (True/False) Environment subsystems are run in User Mode.

13. Kernel Mode is also commonly referred to as _____.

14. _____ is the term used to describe the process of moving paging files to and from the disk as needed.

15. How many inbound client connections does NT Workstation support?

A. 1

B. 5

C. 10

D. Unlimited

16. How many RAS connections does NT Workstation support? How many does NT Server support?

17. I have a network of 4 computers with very inexperienced users. Which model (workgroup or domain) would be the better choice for my network, and why?

A. Workgroup model, because you have fewer than ten users.

B. Workgroup model, because you do not have a server to act as domain controller.

C. Domain model, because you have very inexperienced users.

D. Domain model, because you can expand to include more computers in the future.

18. What is the lowest level of the Windows NT operating system architecture?

2

Installing Windows NT 4.0 Workstation

T he planning phase for Windows NT 4.0 Workstation is the most important part of an installation. If you take time to think out your hardware requirements, you can reduce the amount of downtime caused by incompatible hardware and installation problems. There are so many options to consider when doing a Windows NT Workstation installation that you want to make sure that you do not overlook any important details.

Part of the planning phase is deciding how to partition your hard disk. You can split your hard disk into many partitions or you can use just one. Determining how big your partitions should be can help you decide what type of file system to use: FAT or NTFS. For the exam, you must know the advantages and disadvantages of each file system.

Once you have planned your Windows NT 4.0 Workstation installation, you can decide what type of installation to perform. You have many different options: You can install Windows NT from a CD-ROM, over the network, or perform an upgrade from a previous version of Windows. An important part of the exam deals with how you decide what version of the Windows NT setup utility to use, so make sure that you understand which setup utility can be used when.

Part of knowing how to install Windows NT Workstation involves knowing how to remove Windows NT Workstation from your computer. There are a couple of different methods and you must know them both. You have to know how to remove Windows NT system files, the NT boot loader, and NTFS partitions.

To become certified, you'll be quizzed to make sure that you understand every detail of the planning and installation process for Windows NT 4.0 Workstation. For example, Microsoft wants to make sure that you understand the importance of the Hardware Compatibility List and its role during installation. They want to make sure that you understand the advantages of using the NTFS file system or why you might be required to use a FAT partition. Microsoft wants you to know which version of the NT setup utility you will use and why.

The information covered in this chapter fully describes the basics of planning and performing a Windows NT 4.0 Workstation installation. It also gives you a grounding for more complicated topics covered in later chapters, like differences in file systems, protocol suites, and network connectivity.

CERTIFICATION OBJECTIVE 2.01

Hardware Requirements

In today's world, computers are more powerful than ever before. Just a few years ago it was not even thinkable that a computer could do the work that Windows NT can do today. This expansion in technology comes at a price, namely the high hardware requirements of networking operating systems such as Windows NT 4.0 Workstation. Microsoft Windows NT 4.0 Workstation demands a lot of resources to run effectively.

Minimum Hardware Requirements

The *minimum* requirements for Windows NT Workstation x86 are:

- Intel processor 486/33 or higher (Pentium, Pentium-Pro, Pentium II)
- 12MB of RAM for x86 (Intel) (16 – 32MB of memory is recommended)
- 120MB of free hard disk space
- CD-ROM drive (or have access to a network share or CD-ROM)
- VGA or higher resolution graphics card
- Microsoft mouse or compatible pointing device

If you follow the minimum hardware requirements for Microsoft NT 4.0 Workstation you might be able to run a few applications, but you will not see a great boost in performance. The minimum hardware requirements are shallow at best and are not recommended if you are running many resource-intensive operations at once. If you try and run Windows NT 4.0 with the minimum requirements you are going to lose a lot of functionality and performance. The type of user you are and the software you have installed determine the hardware that works the best for you. For example, a power user needs a lot of memory to do heavy multitasking, whereas a developer might need a fast processor in order to compile code.

You need to know the hardware requirements for Windows NT 4.0 Workstation: 12MB RAM for an Intel processor or 16MB RAM for a RISC processor, a 120MB hard disk, and a 486/33MHz processor. Also remember that you cannot upgrade or install Windows NT 4.0 on a 386 no matter how much memory the computer has.

Recommended Hardware

The following hardware is *recommended* for users who want to get the most out of Windows NT 4.0 Workstation:

- Intel Pentium, Pentium-Pro, Pentium II Processor
- 32 – 48MB of RAM for x86 (Intel)
- 2GB of free hard disk space—this amount allows enough space for large pagefile and software applications
- Bootable CD-ROM drive
- SVGA or higher resolution, 3D graphics card
- Microsoft mouse or compatible pointing device
- 33.6 modem or ISDN adapter to connect to the Internet
- 10/100MB network interface card with a PCI bus for greater throughput

Hardware Compatibility List

Windows NT offers many options to help configure your machine to your personal needs. For example, you can install backup devices, modems, ISDN adapters, network interface cards, and scanners. If you want a machine with more than the minimum requirements, you should look for one that has a lot of memory (RAM) and an excellent processor. These two key features will have the greatest effect on how your computer runs once all of the applications are installed.

Before selecting any hardware, the first thing you should do is check the Hardware Compatibility List (HCL) provided by Microsoft as a detailed inventory of all supported and tested hardware for Windows NT 4.0. In order for a vendor's hardware device to appear on the HCL, the device must pass a series of tests given directly by Microsoft. These tests help ensure that no hardware problems will occur when you install Windows NT 4.0. Microsoft examines and tests the various hardware devices so that you do not have to.

Importance of the HCL

If you encounter a hardware problem during installation because you're running unsupported hardware, you are going to encounter problems with support. Microsoft cannot support hardware they have not tested. They will do their best to help you out, but they cannot guarantee anything. Simply said, Microsoft does not support hardware that does not appear on the HCL, so please check the HCL before beginning an installation.

To find the most current version of the HCL, check out Microsoft's web site, Windows NT newsgroups, or the latest version of Microsoft TechNet. Microsoft updates the HCL periodically, as new and updated hardware passes compatibility testing.

If for some reason your hardware does not appear on the HCL, it does not necessarily mean that your hardware will not work with NT 4.0. It takes time before new hardware appears on the list. You can always check for the latest drivers on the vendor's web site or use the hardware drivers that were distributed from the hardware vendor.

Hardware Device Drivers

Just as you want to make sure that your hardware devices are Windows NT compatible, it is also smart to have the required device drivers handy in case the Windows NT setup program does not detect your hardware. During installation, Windows NT queries your computer and tries to recognize all your hardware devices, including the processor and the hard disk, and to determine the amount of memory. During the graphical mode of setup, Windows NT also tries to detect the rest of your hardware devices, such as the network card and the video adapter. Just in case Windows NT makes a mistake during the installation process, you can add the correct drivers on your own.

In an effort to make hardware detection easier, Microsoft includes the tool NTHQ (NT Hardware Query) on the Windows NT 4.0 Workstation CD-ROM in the \Support\Hqtool directory. This MS-DOS-based program can help you solve any problems you have installing Windows NT. You can start NTHQ from the floppy disk and use it to detect your hardware and settings for troubleshooting. You can also use it to determine whether your hardware meets the HCL standards.

To run NTHQ:

1. Run Windows NT and insert a blank 3.5-inch floppy disk into the floppy drive.

2. Run MAKEDISK.BAT from the \Support\Hqtool directory on the Windows NT Workstation CD-ROM.

3. Leave the floppy disk in the drive and restart your computer. Your computer restarts, with NTHQ running.

CERTIFICATION OBJECTIVE 2.02

Configuring a Disk

Before you begin installing Windows NT 4.0, you need to understand some basic information about your hard disk. In particular, you need to be familiar with creating and deleting partitions on different types of disks, as described in the following sections. You'll get to know which tools to use when configuring a disk and what their advantages are by configuring a disk with a single or multiple partitions.

Partitioning the Hard Disk

It is common to partition the hard disk before you install Windows NT 4.0 to make installation easier. If you have a large hard disk, you can set up as many partitions as necessary. If you have a smaller hard disk, you might create only one partition or only a couple of small ones. Partitioning the disk ahead of time is a more flexible approach than using Window NT 4.0 Disk Administrator after the system is running.

A *partition* is a logical division of a physical disk. After partitioning the hard disk, you need to decide which partition will be the system partition and which will be the active partition. The *active partition* is the partition that the operating system will boot from; it is often called the *boot partition.* If you decide to install Windows NT 4.0 somewhere other than the boot partition, that other partition is the *system partition.* If you install Windows NT on your boot partition, it becomes both your boot partition and your system partition.

Once you finish partitioning the hard disk, you can format your drives. This is the final step before you begin the installation procedure.

It is a good idea to make your disk partitions as large as possible, so that you have enough room to install all of your applications and still leave enough room for your pagefile. Depending on the size of your hard disk, you can leave it all one size or keep the system files on a smaller partition of 200MB.

Remember that Windows NT 4.0 does not support the High-Performance File System (HPFS) or the OS/2 file system. Unlike previous versions of NT, you cannot install Windows NT on an HPFS partition. You have the option of converting an existing HPFS partition to NTFS, or you can delete the old partition using the FDISK.EXE utility and create a File Allocation Table (FAT) partition instead.

FAT Partitions

The File Allocation Table (FAT) file system is used predominantly for MS-DOS and Microsoft Windows systems, such as Windows 3.*x* and Windows 95. To allow for backward compatibility, Windows NT fully supports the FAT file system. This support is also supplied because of FAT's universal acceptance and accessibility by other operating systems. If you are going to use a RISC computer, such as an Alpha or MIPS machine, you must have a 2MB FAT partition for your system files.

The FAT file system has the following characteristics:

- Good for smaller hard disks of 200 – 400MB because of overhead.
- Does not offer any file or directory security.
- Does not protect files through the security features of Windows NT.
- Good if your system needs to be accessible through DOS or OS/2, but can be easily fragmented.
- Can accept partitions up to 2GB.
- Handles hard disks under 511MB.
- Universally accepted as a file system.
- Necessary if you wish to dual-boot between NT and DOS or OS/2.
- Cannot take advantage of fault tolerance.
- Needed for dual-boot capability with MS-DOS and Windows 95.
- Uses the 8.3 naming scheme.

The newest version of the FAT file system is called FAT-32. FAT-32 allows for large hard disk support. With FAT-32, your partitions can surpass the 2GB limit. However, Windows NT 4.0 does not support FAT-32, and you cannot install on any partition formatted with FAT-32. (Windows NT 5.0 is expected to recognize the FAT-32 file system.)

NTFS Partitions

The New Technology File System (NTFS) is the file system of choice for Windows NT. By installing Windows NT on an NTFS partition, you can take advantage of many of the NTFS features that are inherent in Windows NT, most notably security. NTFS provides granular security to both files and directories on the local workstation. This level of security is not available on a FAT partition.

Another reason to use an NTFS partition with NT is fault tolerance. NTFS supports many fault tolerant options that are part of the Windows NT operating system, including logging all changes to the file system.

Note that once a partition is formatted as an NTFS partition, you cannot convert it back to a FAT partition.

NTFS is characterized by:

- Better support for hard disks over 500MB.

- File and directory security that allows you to specify access levels.

- Complete Windows NT security model support, so you can specify who is allowed what kind of access to files or directories on the network and the local machine.

- Recognition only by Windows NT. When a computer is running another operating system (such as MS-DOS or OS/2), that operating system cannot access files on an NTFS partition on the same computer.

- Capability for expanding partitions beyond 2GB.

- Allowing up to 255 characters per filename.

- Fast access, recoverable and secure.

- Support for partitions as large as 16 exabytes.

Creating and Deleting Partitions

You can create or delete partitions in either Windows NT or MS-DOS. When you begin a new installation it is a good idea to start by removing any existing partitions on the hard disk and creating new ones. This allows you to customize your partitions for your exact needs.

If you are using MS-DOS, you create or delete partitions using the fixed-disk setup program FDISK.EXE. Depending on what version of FDISK.EXE you use, you can eliminate non-DOS partitions and create new ones. If you are running Windows NT, you can create both NTFS and FAT partitions using the Disk Administrator tool found in the Administrative Tools common group. You can also convert existing FAT and HPFS partitions to

NTFS using Disk Administrator, but you cannot later convert an NTFS partition back to a FAT partition.

Besides FDISK.EXE, there are other options for removing partitions. These include DELDISK.EXE, a third-party utility such as Partition Magic, or Delpart from the Windows NT 3.1 Resource Kit. Whenever you use these utilities, make sure you are certain before removing the partitions—once you delete them they are gone for good.

| EXERCISE 2-1 |

Partitioning a Hard Disk Using FDISK.EXE

If you want to partition your hard disk, you have to first delete all other partitions before starting over. Using FDISK.EXE, you can partition the disk according to your needs.

Before you begin, it is important to remember that there is a specific order in which each partition can be deleted from the hard disk. You must delete any non-DOS partitions first, logical partitions second, the extended partition third, and the primary partition last. When removing an NTFS partition, make sure that the partition is not an extended partition. If it is, FDISK.EXE will remove the NTFS partition, but ruin the hard disk.

The reverse order applies when you create partitions. You must first create a primary partition, then an extended partition, then logical partitions, and finally you can convert to NTFS if you are using Windows NT.

If you currently have an HPFS partition, you have two options with Windows NT. You can either delete the partition and create a FAT partition in its place, or convert the HPFS partition to NTFS. Unlike previous versions of Windows NT, Windows NT 4.0 Workstation does not support installations that use existing HPFS partitions.

DELETING PARTITIONS   To delete existing partitions:

1. Boot your computer to MS-DOS.

2. At the command prompt, type

   ```
   FDISK.EXE
   ```

   You are now running the fixed-disk setup program.

3. To display your partition information, press 4.

4. Press ESC to continue.

5. Select **3** to indicate that you want to delete partitions.

6. Decide which partition to delete and press the number associated with it.

7. Type the volume label of the partition to verify the deletion.

8. Type **Y** to confirm.

9. Press ESC to continue.

CREATING PARTITIONS To create new partitions:

1. Create the primary DOS partition.

   Do not use all of the free space unless you have a very small partition.

2. Create the extended DOS partition.

3. Create a logical partition or individual partitions on the extended partition.

4. Convert your FAT partition either by using the CONVERT utility during Windows NT setup or by using Disk Administrator from Windows NT \ Administrative Tools (Common Group).

5. Select option **2** to make one of your partitions active (usually this is your boot partition).

6. Type the number of your partition to mark it as active.

7. Press ESC to continue.

8. Press ESC again to continue and exit FDISK.EXE.

9. Reboot your computer to make the changes take effect.

10. Format your active partition by typing:

```
A:\format C: /S
```

    This formats your C: partition with the necessary system files so that you can boot your machine.

EXERCISE 2-2

Converting an Existing FAT Partition to NTFS

To take advantage of the NTFS file system's capabilities after you have installed Windows NT on a FAT partition, you can convert your FAT partition to NTFS.

To convert a FAT partition to NTFS:

1. Log on to your computer as Administrator.

2. Click Start Menu | Programs | Command Prompt.

3. At the command prompt, start the CONVERT.EXE conversion utility by typing:

   ```
   C:\CONVERT D: /FS:NTFS
   ```

   This converts the D: partition to NTFS.

4. Reboot the computer to create the file system.

   You must reboot because you do not have exclusive rights to the file system (NT cannot access the hardware directly). During the boot up process, the file system begins converting the FAT partition to NTFS.

EXERCISE 2-3

Re-Creating Windows NT Boot Floppies

If you ever misplace or lose the three setup floppies included with Windows NT 4.0, you can make a new set using the NT setup utilities WINNT.EXE or WINNT32.EXE. If you are running Windows NT, you can use WINNT32.EXE with the /OX switch. If you are running any other version of Windows, use WINNT.EXE with the /OX switch.

exam
ⓦatch

This question often appears on the NT 4.0 Workstation exam, so be prepared.

You'll need three blank, formatted floppy disks and the NT 4.0 Workstation source files to complete this exercise.

To re-create the Windows NT boot floppies:

1. Log on to your computer as Administrator.

2. Insert the Windows NT 4.0 CD-ROM into the CD-ROM drive.

3. Click Start Menu | Programs | Command Prompt.

4. At the command prompt, specify your CD-ROM drive.

5. Make sure that you are in the Windows NT /I386 directory where the Windows NT setup utility is located.

6. If you are running a version of Windows NT, type

   ```
   D:\WINNT32.EXE /OX
   ```

7. If you are running an operating system other than Windows NT (such as DOS or Windows 95), type

```
D:\WINNT32.EXE /OX
```

The dialog box shown in Figure 2-1 appears and prompts you for the location of the Windows NT 4.0 source files. From here on, the WINNT32.EXE utility guides you through the process of creating the boot floppies.

Bootable CD-ROM Drives

Some of today's computers allow you to boot your system directly from the CD-ROM drive. While this is helpful in some environments, it can cause considerable problems when setting up Windows NT. I never recommend using this functionality with Windows NT 4.0; always use a command prompt or simple batch file. A related problem occurs if the Windows NT 4.0 CD-ROM is left in the CD-ROM drive. This oversight can sometimes cause the computer to hang indefinitely during the initial setup phase. Rather than continuing with NT setup, the computer tries to boot from the CD-ROM. This is a known problem with Windows NT setup, and one you should take care to avoid.

FIGURE 2-1

The Installation/Upgrade dialog box is the first one presented by WINNT32.EXE /OX

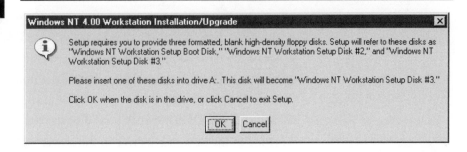

Windows NT 4.00 Workstation Installation/Upgrade

Setup requires you to provide three formatted, blank high-density floppy disks. Setup will refer to these disks as "Windows NT Workstation Setup Boot Disk," "Windows NT Workstation Setup Disk #2," and "Windows NT Workstation Setup Disk #3."

Please insert one of these disks into drive A:. This disk will become "Windows NT Workstation Setup Disk #3."

Click OK when the disk is in the drive, or click Cancel to exit Setup.

OK   Cancel

CERTIFICATION OBJECTIVE 2.03

Installation Options

Microsoft has included many different options for installing Windows NT 4.0 Workstation. You can install from the network, the local hard disk, or the CD-ROM drive. There are also options for upgrading, running fresh installations, and running multiple installations. Because every user does not require the same type of installation, many different command line switches are available, to allow for floppy-less or unattended installations, for example, or one to create the three setup floppies.

EXERCISE 2-4

Creating a Network Share of the Windows NT Workstation 4.0 Installation Files

If you are going to be doing multiple installations of Windows NT 4.0, you can keep the source files in a network share to allow multiple installations to run at once. This speeds up the installation time since the installation files are copied directly to the hard disk and not run off the CD-ROM. Also, anyone who has network access can begin a Windows NT installation.

To create a network share for NT Workstation 4.0 installation files:

1. Log on as Administrator.

2. Create a directory on an NTFS partition on the server. Name this directory I386.

3. From the Windows NT Workstation CD-ROM, copy all of the files in the /I386 directory to the new folder named I386.

4. Share the directory named I386.

5. Set directory permissions on the folder for those who should have access to the source files.

6. Use your MS-DOS network boot disk to start the network services.

7. Once connected, map a drive to the server and the share point of the installation files.

8. Navigate to the /I386 directory. This is where the Windows NT setup utility will be.

9. At the DOS prompt type

   `F:\I386\WINNT.EXE /B`

   The /B switch in this command begins a floppy-less Windows NT installation.

Unattended Installations

Out in the real world the unattended installation feature can prove a useful tool for setting up Windows NT. This utility allows you to install large numbers of NT workstations very quickly and with minimum effort. This tool is great to use in situations such as rollouts or upgrades to multiple installations. It can save a lot of time over having to go around and perform manual installations. The UNATTEND.TXT file can provide information in response to any question that comes up during the installation, such as type of network drivers, values of TCP/IP parameters, values for the display configuration, types of file systems, or correct time zone. Here is the switch syntax for running this file during setup:

`WINNT.EXE /B /U:UNATTEND.TXT /S:d:\I386`

The /B switch after WINNT.EXE sets up NT without creating the three standard boot floppies. The /U switch signifies an unattended installation and specifies the name of the file (usually UNATTEND.TXT). The /S switch tells NT where to look for the UNATTEND.TXT file during installation. The setup program runs uninterrupted until it finishes, then prompts the user to log on.

OK, I can hear your first questions: What if there are different configurations? And how do you change things like IP addresses, computer names, or hardware settings? This is where the *Unique Database File* or UDF comes in. The UDF is divided into sections with UniqueIDs that describe any changes to the UNATTEND.TXT file, and that override the information in that file. All that you must specify during setup is which UniqueID should be parsed. When you run the setup procedure (probably just a simple batch file to connect to the server), enter the switches needed to tell the computer where to find the UDF, as follows:

```
WINNT.EXE /B /U:UNATTEND.TXT /S:d:\I386 /T:c:
/UDF:test_ID,D:\UDF_File
```

As we learned earlier, we need to run the UNATTEND.TXT file as part of the installation procedure. The /T switch signifies a temporary directory to dump into and the /UDF switch is the name of the UDF that will be parsed. Here, test_ID is the UniqueID that is going to be looked at and changed according to the parameters listed in the UDF. The last part of the command gives the path to the UDF, in this case on the D: drive under the name UDF_File. Again, this UDF information overrides any section specified in the UNATTEND.TXT file.

EXERCISE 2-5

Using the SYSDIFF Utility to Customize an Installation

The SYSDIFF.EXE utility is used to pre-install applications during Windows NT setup. It takes before-and-after snapshots of your installation and creates a OEM directory that can be used as part of the installation. The snapshots capture the Registry and files that are located on the computer, or any other drives. This is why it is important to have a fresh installation—you don't want the snapshot to pick up any other files from other software applications.

SYSDIFF.EXE can be found on the Windows NT 4.0 Workstation CD-ROM in the \Ntwks40a\Support\Deptools\I386\ directory, or on the NT 4.0 Workstation Resource Kit CD-ROM in the \Ntrk_40\I386\ Setup directory. This utility works well and is documented in Microsoft's *Guide to Automating Windows NT 4.0 Setup* Word document.

As prerequisites to performing this exercise, you need to have SYSDIFF.EXE, SYSDIFF.INF, a fresh Installation of Windows NT 4.0 Workstation, and a software application that you want to install.

To customize an installation using SYSDIFF.EXE:

1. Begin with a newly installed version of NT 4.0 Workstation.

    This is the basis for the rest of the installations, so it should be as generic as possible.

2. Copy SYSDIFF.EXE and SYSDIFF.INF to the hard disk of the local workstation. SYSDIFF.INF must be installed in the same directory as

SYSDIFF.EXE. SYSDIFF.INF is used to exclude changes to certain settings in the Registry or the pagefile, or to exclude any drives or partitions that would otherwise be taken during the initial snapshot.

3. Using SYSDIFF.EXE, take a snapshot of the fresh installation by typing:

```
C:\SYSDIFF.EXE /SNAP C:\SNAP.IMG
```

The /SNAP switch causes SYSDIFF.EXE to take a snapshot of your fresh installation and create a file named SNAP.IMG as output. (You can name the snapshot output file whatever you like.)

4. Load your software application according to its instructions.

5. After you finish installing the software application, take another snapshot of the finished package or of the difference between the two. Type

```
C:\SYSDIFF.EXE /DIFF C:\SNAP.IMG C:\DIFF.IMG
```

The /DIFF switch causes SYSDIFF.EXE to take a snapshot of the installation after the software application is loaded. The C:\SNAP.IMG file is compared to the C:\DIFF.IMG file, which contains the changes since the software application has been installed. These changes include any additions to the Registry or new files. The DIFF.IMG file becomes the basis for automatically installing applications. (As with the snapshot file, you can name the difference file anything you want.)

6. Add the /INF switch to the SYSDIFF.EXE command.

This switch builds a OEM directory beneath the /I386 directory to store the needed changes, and calls an .INF file that automatically sets up the pre-installed application.

```
C:\SYSDIFF.EXE /INF /U /m C:\DIFF.IMG F:\I386
```

The /INF switch creates an .INF file that sets up the pre-installed applications that were loaded as part of Windows NT setup. The /U switch generates a Unicode text file. (The default is ANSI codepage, but that does not affect the end results.) The /m switch causes the profile to be mapped to the default user so that everyone who logs onto the workstation has access to the installed applications. C:\DIFF.IMG is the location of the difference file. F:\I386 is the location of the Windows NT source files, where the OEM directory is built. Also in the OEM directory are the CMDLINES.TXT file and the .INF file that contain the instructions for pre-installing the applications. CMDLINES.TXT is made up of commands that call specific sections of the .INF file that set up the applications. Here is an example:

```
[Commands]
"Rundll32 setupapi,InstallHinfSection DefaultInstall 128
.\ThisIsWhateverInfFIleThatYouCreate.INF"
```

The name of this file is whatever you named your difference file, but with the .INF extension. This file contains the Registry changes needed to install the applications. The command in CMDLINES.TXT makes a direct call to a specific section in the .INF file. All that is left to do is reinstall NT 4.0 Workstation on the target computers. When these changes are through, NT 4.0 Workstation will install on as many workstations as necessary, with the applications already installed.

exam
ⓦatch

One of the trickiest parts of this exam involves the questions on Unattended Installations. Remember that the three files necessary to complete an unattended installation are:

- ■ *SYSDIFF.EXE* *This executable file pre-installs software applications.*

- ■ *UNATTEND.TXT* *This script file outlines the setup for Windows NT Workstation.*

- ■ *Unique Database File (UDF)* *This file allows you to set up unique parameters for the installation, such as computer names or TCP/IP addresses.*

Network Installations vs. CD-ROM Installations

There are many different ways to install Windows NT 4.0 Workstation. What you need to know is what type of installation will work best for you. Do you want to walk around from machine to machine and install Windows NT from a CD-ROM? Or do you want to keep the source files in a central location and use the network to perform installations? Each choice carries various advantages and disadvantages. Performing a CD-ROM installation can be considerably faster if you only have to install one machine. If multiple machines need to be installed then a network install might be your best option. However, performing multiple installations from the network can take a long time if all installations are done at once and the server is slow. Once you decide your basic approach, you can begin the procedures for installation.

CD-ROM Installations

If you are installing Windows NT 4.0 Workstation from the CD-ROM, you need the three NT setup disks to begin installation unless you are going to use the /B switch and do a floppy-less installation. The three setup disks install a mini version of Windows NT on your computer that aids in the setup process.

EXERCISE 2-6

Beginning a Windows NT Workstation 4.0 Installation from CD-ROM (Intel-Based Computers, Floppy-Less Installation)

If you want to save time, you can perform a floppy-less installation with the Windows NT setup utility. Rather than waiting to be prompted for each of the three boot floppies, with this approach you copy the files from the CD-ROM directly to the hard disk. If you are using an earlier version of Windows NT, you can use the WINNT32.EXE setup utility; if you are using any version of MS-DOS or Windows, you can use WINNT.EXE.

Make sure you have the Windows NT 4.0 Workstation CD-ROM before beginning this exercise.

To install NT 4.0 from CD-ROM on an Intel-based computer:

1. Place the CD-ROM into the CD-ROM drive.

2. Go to a Command Prompt to navigate to the CD-ROM drive.

3. Specify the drive that contains the CD-ROM.

4. Make sure you are at the root of the /I386 directory to get to the setup utility.

5. If you are running an early version of Windows NT, type **WINNT32.EXE /B** at the command prompt. For all other versions, type **WINNT.EXE /B**.

   ```
   D:\I386\WINNT.EXE /B
   ```

   The /B switch designates a floppy-less install. Most installations are run this way.

EXERCISE 2-7

Beginning a Windows NT Workstation 4.0 Installation from the Network for DOS Computers (Floppy-Less Install)

For this exercise, you need the MS-DOS network boot floppy and a network share point that contains the source files or /I386 directory for Windows NT 4.0 Workstation or for the Network CD-ROM.

To install NT 4.0 from CD-ROM on a DOS-based computer:

1. Using your MS-DOS boot disk, establish a connection to the share point containing the setup files. (By default this is the /I386 directory.)

2. From the network share, make sure that you are in the root of the /I386 directory. This is where you will find the setup utility, WINNT.EXE.

3. Since this exercise assumes you are not currently running an earlier version of Windows NT, you need to type **WINNT.EXE /B** at the command prompt.

   This begins the installation process for Windows NT 4.0. Since you are performing a floppy-less installation, you have to use the /B switch. The installation parameters should look like this.

   ```
   F:\I386\WINNT.EXE /B
   ```

EXERCISE 2-8

Beginning a Windows NT Workstation 4.0 Installation from the Network for Windows 95 Computers (Floppy-Less Install)

Since you cannot upgrade Windows 95 to a Windows NT workstation, you need to begin a fresh installation. Because it is more convenient, this exercise performs a floppy-less installation from Windows 95.

For this exercise you need a Windows 95 computer and a network share point that contains the Windows NT 4.0 Workstation source files.

To perform an NT 4.0 installation from the network for a Windows 95 machine:

1. In Windows 95, open up Command Prompt and connect a network drive to the share point that contains the Windows NT 4.0 source files or /I386 directory.

2. Verify that you are in the network share point that contains the Windows NT 4.0 Workstation source files.

3. Run the 16-bit version of the setup utility, WINNT.EXE, by typing:

```
F:\I386\WINNT.EXE /B /w
```

It should be noted that this is not a recommended feature in Windows NT and is not officially supported by Microsoft. It bypasses some safety features during installation, so use this method at your own risk.

EXERCISE 2-9

Beginning a Windows NT Workstation 4.0 Installation from the Network for Windows NT Version 3.51 and Earlier Computers (Floppy-Less Install)

For this exercise, you need to be running an earlier version of Windows NT, so that you can run the WINNT32.EXE setup utility. This version takes advantage of Windows NT's processing power and 32-bit capability. WINNT32.EXE runs much faster than WINNT.EXE because it is a 32-bit multithreaded application. Windows NT can take advantage of its speed during installation.

For this exercise, you need a network share point that contains the Windows NT 4.0 Workstation source files.

To install NT 4.0 Workstation from the network for earlier versions of Windows:

1. Log on as Administrator.

2. Go to the MAIN program group.

3. Click the MS-DOS icon.

4. Map to a network drive that contains the NT 4.0 Workstation source files. (For example, type **Net use Z: \\Server_Name\I386**.)

5. Make sure that you are in the /I386 directory. (This directory contains the WINNT32.EXE setup utility.)

6. At the command prompt, type

```
Z:\I386\WINNT32.EXE /B
```

Floppy Installations

When you install Windows NT Workstation, you always have the option of installing from the three setup floppies included with the product.

EXERCISE 2-10

Beginning a Windows NT Workstation 4.0 Installation from the Installation Boot Floppies

For this exercise, you need the three NT setup boot floppies and the Windows NT 4.0 Workstation CD-ROM.

To install NT 4.0 Workstation from the original boot floppies:

1. Turn on your computer and insert the boot disk labeled Windows NT Setup Disk 1.

2. When the operating system prompts you, insert Windows NT Setup Disk 2.

3. When prompted, insert the Windows NT 4.0 Workstation CD-ROM and follow the instructions that appear.

4. Insert the third NT setup disk to add drivers if the system requests them.

The Setup Utility

To set up Windows NT 4.0 Workstation you need to use either the WINNT.EXE or WINNT32.EXE setup utilities to begin installation. The operating system you are currently using determines which version of the Windows NT setup utility you use:

- WINNT.EXE is a 16-bit version, used to begin installation from a CD-ROM, from the network, or from any type of MS-DOS-based installation. This utility cannot be used with Windows NT.

- WINNT32.EXE is a 32-bit version, used to begin any installation or upgrade under any version of Windows NT. WINNT32.EXE is much faster than WINNT.EXE. Also, when you run WINNT32.EXE and files are being copied from the server's share into the WIN_NT.~LS directory on the local hard drive, Windows NT is still running.

The setup utility can be run at the command prompt, through Windows Explorer, delivered via SMS, or as a batch file. Other options can be selected, such as the switch that controls floppy-less installations (/B) and unattended installations (/U).

Using the Windows NT Setup Program

You are about to install Windows NT and you must decide which version of the Windows NT setup utility you are going to use. You can use the 16-bit version, WINNT.EXE, if you are going to install Windows NT from a network installation or any non-NT version of Windows. If you are using any version of Windows NT, you have only one choice—the 32-bit version, WINNT32.EXE. Although both versions do exactly the same thing WINNT32.EXE is quicker since it takes advantage of NT's processing power.

For this exercise, you need the Windows NT 4.0 Workstation source files (either CD-ROM or network share point).

To run the Windows NT setup utility:

1. Insert the Windows NT Workstation 4.0 CD-ROM into the CD-ROM drive.

   ■ If you are running a previous version of Windows NT, run WINNT32.EXE by typing:

   ```
   F:\I386\WINNT32.EXE
   ```

   ■ If you are performing an installation from the network, from CD-ROM, or from MS-DOS, run WINNT.EXE by typing:

   ```
   F:\I386\WINNT.EXE
   ```

2. Insert Setup Disk 1 to begin installation.

3. Insert Setup Disk 2 when prompted.

4. If needed, enter Setup Disk 3.

5. Continue installing Windows NT 4.0 Workstation as usual.

The syntax you use to run either WINNT.EXE or WINNT32.EXE is the same:

```
WINNT.EXE [/S:sourcepath] [/I:inf_file]
[/T:drive_letter] [/X] [/B] [/O[X]] [/U:answer_file]
[/UDF:id, [UDF_file]]
WINNT32.EXE [/S:sourcepath] [/I:inf_file]
[/T:drive_letter] [/X] [/B] [/O[X]] [/U:answer_file]
[/UDF:id, [UDF_file]]
```

Refer to Table 2-1 for an explanation of the various switches and options.

TABLE 2-1 WINNT.EXE and WINNT32.EXE Switches and Options	/S:sourcepath	Specifies the location of the Windows NT files.
	/T:drive_letter	Forces the setup utility to place temporary files on the specified drive. Use this option if you are going to install Windows NT on a different partition.
	/B	Causes the boot files to be loaded on the system's hard drive rather than on floppy disks, so that floppy disks do not need to be loaded or removed by the user.
	/OX	Specifies that the setup utility create boot floppies for a CD-ROM or floppy-based installation.
	/I:inf_file	Specifies the location of an answer file that provides answers for the user.
	/X	Prevents the setup utility from creating the boot floppies. Use this switch when you already have setup boot floppies.
	/O	Specifies that the setup utility create only boot floppies.
	/U:answer_file	Specifies the location of an unattended answer file that provides answers the user would otherwise be prompted for during installation.

Upgrading from Windows 95

Upgrading from Windows 95 to Windows NT 4.0 Workstation is not an officially supported option in this release of NT. However, an undocumented /W switch is available. You must use it with caution; if you have problems do not call Microsoft because they will not be able to help you.

Upgrading Other Operating Systems

It *is* possible to upgrade your existing MS-DOS, Windows 3.*x*, or Windows NT operating system to Windows NT 4.0. For Windows 3.*x* and Windows NT 3.*x*, you can save your existing configuration settings and have them apply in your Windows NT 4.0 Workstation environment. The operating system you are currently using determines what version of the Windows NT setup utility you can use for an upgrade. If you're running an earlier version of Windows NT, use WINNT32.EXE. For all other upgrades and non-Windows NT versions, run WINNT.EXE.

Upgrading from MS-DOS

The MS-DOS operating system can be easily upgraded or dual-booted with Windows NT 4.0. Using the WINNT.EXE setup utility, you can perform any type of installation available. When upgrading an MS-DOS-based system, the Windows NT setup program installs the Windows NT boot loader to let the user choose which operating system to use each time the system is started.

Upgrading from Windows 3.x for MS-DOS

It is possible to install Windows NT in the same directory as an existing version of Windows 3.*x.* Windows NT places its system files in a \<windows root>\SYSTEM32 directory. The Windows NT setup program also places some files that can be used with any version of Windows, such as .BMP files, in the \<windows root> directory.

If you choose not to install Windows NT into the same directory as Windows 3.*x,* Windows 3.*x* Program Manager groups will not be available under Windows NT. If Windows NT is installed in the same directory as Windows 3.*x,* the setup process imports the Windows 3.*x* program groups into Windows NT.

When you install Windows NT on top of Windows 3.*x,* all of your .INI file data, .GRP file data, and REG.DAT data is migrated into the new Windows NT environment.

FROM THE CLASSROOM

How to Keep a 30-Minute NT Installation from Ruining your Whole Weekend

An NT installation could take 30 minutes or three days. The need for a three-day effort is often the result of insufficient planning. There are three areas where problems commonly occur during installation. Forethought can go a long way toward preventing frustrations down the road.

The first problem area is hardware. NT is quite particular about compatible hardware. Check the Hardware Compatibility List (HCL)

FROM THE CLASSROOM

before you buy or install hardware. If a make or model is not listed, beware. It might be compatible, but you should do some checking. We got a call from a client who wanted us to come and complete his NT installation, which was giving him trouble. When we got to the site, he handed us an SCSI adapter and the instruction booklet. Now, picture the size of a dollar bill folded in half. This was the size of the hardware manual. On its pages were installation instructions in four languages, none of which I recognized (and I speak six). I didn't have to check the HCL to know that this adapter was not going to be listed, but the client was still enthused about the adapter because he had paid $19.95 for it! You can imagine the conversation we had with the vendor: "Hello, we have one of your adapters and were wondering if you supported Windows NT?" Response: "I'm sure we do. Huh, by the way, what is Windows NT?"

You encounter the second problem area early in the installation process, when you must choose which partition will hold the NT system files and what size it will be. We recommend installing the system files on a separate partition. You don't want to make the partition too big (wasting space that could be used for data) and you don't want to make it too small. We had a client using a partition size of 250MB, which

seemed reasonable to him, as it was twice the minimum size recommended. The *gotcha* came when he tried to add more services and found that there wasn't enough room. In a situation like this, absent a third-party utility, you'd have no choice but to tear down the partition and reinstall NT.

The third problem area is the network card. You should identify the NIC parameters before you start the installation. NT might auto-detect the NIC, and it might not. While NT recognizes many network cards, it might not recognize the IRQ, I/O, or DMA settings of the NIC you have installed. In the classroom, we try to use the same NIC (and settings) in all machines, and we give the students this information for their installations. Still, in a class of ten students, two will get the settings wrong, and another will accept the defaults that NT presents, which is also incorrect. They can't finish the installation until they go back and correct the settings. The catch is that, while most NICs have a program that tests the NIC and tells you what the settings are, you cannot access this program while you are doing the installation. And if you are doing an over-the-network installation and pick the wrong NIC, you can't connect to the server to install the proper NIC later.

—By Shane Clawson, MCT, MCSE

Performing a New Installation

OK, you are now ready to perform a new installation. Here is a simple checklist of information and preliminary actions that will help you avoid any problems along the way:

- Check the HCL to make sure that your hardware is going to be compatible.

- Make sure you have the NT 4.0 Workstation CD-ROM available.

- Partition your hard disk according to your needs.

- Make sure you have all relevant network information (TCP/IP, computer name, domain, permissions to add the computer to a domain, and so on).

- If you are upgrading your system, be sure to back up all of the important files currently on your computer to either a network share or a tape storage device.

- Gather all the driver diskettes and configuration settings for third-party hardware like tape drives or mass storage devices.

- Make sure you have a blank floppy disk for the Emergency Repair Disk (ERD). Use a 3.5-inch 1.44MB disk for the ERD. Although the ERD is optional for running Windows NT, it is always good practice to be safe rather than sorry with your computer. It only takes seconds to make an ERD and that can save you hours upon hours later. Make sure that you create an ERD during installation and update it every time you make changes to your configuration, such as restructuring partitions, adding new disk controllers and other software, or installing new applications.

- If you are doing a network installation, make sure you have network access to the Windows NT Workstation files.

Installing NT for Dual-Boot Purposes

Windows NT has no problem dual-booting between operating systems. You can install multiple versions of Windows NT on an NTFS or FAT partition, or another operating system on a FAT partition, such as MS-DOS or Windows 95. When you first install Windows NT Workstation on the boot partition, Windows NT takes control of your boot menu and creates an entry for itself and for MS-DOS if installed on a FAT or an NTFS partition. If you are dual-booting between Windows 95 and NT and they are on the same partition, make sure that you do not convert the file system from FAT to NTFS because Windows 95 or MS-DOS cannot recognize NTFS partitions. Operating systems that are currently supported include MS-DOS, Windows 95, and OS/2 versions 1.1 and 1.3. OS/2 version 2.*x* might work, but it is not supported.

If you are installing another version of NT for dual-boot purposes, make sure that you install each version of Windows NT in a separate directory. If you install them in the same directory, it will upgrade your NT build. The NT boot loader is smart enough to recognize another version of Windows NT and will update the BOOT.INI file.

Third-Party Options

There are third-party utilities like Boot Commander available that take control of your computer and create separate partitions so that all of your operating systems coexist happily. You can install Novell, Linux, Windows NT, OS/2, or any other operating system and they will all work together in separate hard disk spaces. Instead of Windows NT's Boot Loader taking control of the operating system, Boot Commander does it for you.

Setting Up Windows NT Workstation 4.0

After using the setup utility to begin the installation, the setup files are copied to the local hard disk to speed the installation. This is much faster than accessing them from a network share point or CD-ROM since the files are stored locally. Once all of the files are copied to the local hard disk, text mode setup begins. This part of setup tries to identify your hardware and begins asking you questions about how you would like to set up Windows NT 4.0 Workstation according to your specifications. You also have the chance to add any drivers in case Windows NT does not identify all of your hardware.

Once your computer finishes rebooting after text mode setup, the graphical portion of setup begins. In this section you're prompted for information such as network settings, monitor settings, and specific user information. After the graphical portion of setup finishes, the computer saves your configuration, reboots, and you can begin using Windows NT 4.0 Workstation.

Hardware Identification

After the Windows NT setup utility copies the installation files to the local hard disk, Windows NT tries to identify what type of hardware is in your computer. Among other things, NT looks for the processor type (x86, MIPS®, ALPHA, or PPC), motherboard type (PCI, VESA, MCA, EISA, or ISA), hard disk controllers, file systems (FAT or NTFS), the amount of free space on your hard disk, and the amount of memory in your system. If your hardware is not detected correctly during this phase, you can almost be guaranteed that setup will fail during the graphical mode phase.

Again, this points out the importance of the Hardware Compatibility List. Setup should run smoothly if your hardware is listed on the HCL. If the setup process cannot find all of your hardware devices, or if you have additional devices such as mass storage devices or non-supported hardware, add the necessary drivers when setup asks you.

Partition Selection

During the partition selection stage of setup, you can select the partition on which the operating system will be installed. It is a good idea to have all of your partitions set up before you begin so that you do not have the hassle of trying to set them up while installing the operating system. You can use the MS-DOS FDISK.EXE utility to create new partitions or delete existing partitions.

Once you decide which partition you want to install Windows NT 4.0 Workstation on, you can either leave the current file system as is or you can convert the file system to NTFS. It is a good idea to convert your file system to NTFS if you are not going to be dual-booting with MS-DOS or Windows

95 to take advantage of some of the features NTFS provides for Windows NT, like security, performance, and fault tolerance.

Hard Drive Examination

Before beginning a Windows NT installation, you want to be certain that there are no problems with your hard disk, such as bad clusters, physical flaws, or a corrupted boot sector that might prohibit Windows NT from successfully installing. Windows NT gives you two options for examining your hard disk automatically during setup: You can perform an exhaustive examination or a simple one. Because the time difference involved between the two approaches is negligible, you should usually perform an exhaustive examination.

Graphical Portion of Setup

The Windows NT graphical setup wizard guides you through the final stages of the setup process. During this phase, you must provide the setup program with information such as your computer's name, what additional components you want to install, and what networking you want to set up. The NT networking phase asks you for the network card type, the protocol, and the monitor settings. Once NT has all of this information, it processes the settings, finalizes setup, and saves your configuration. This is the last phase before the setup process reboots your system and lets you log on.

EXERCISE 2-12

Proceeding with the Graphical Portion of the Windows NT Workstation 4.0 Installation Process

1. Select Typical at the Configuration Options page, and click Next.

2. Enter your name and your organization in the Name and Organization field, and click Next.

3. Enter the default Administrator account password, and confirm it when the system prompts you. (Make sure that you do not forget this password!) Click Next to continue.

4. Select Yes to create an Emergency Repair Disk. (The ERD is not actually created until the graphical part of the setup process ends.)

5. Select Install Most Common Components (if you want to, you can install additional components later), and click Next to continue.

6. Click Wired to Network, and click Next.

7. Select Search for Network Adapter. Windows NT should find your adapter instantly if your adapter is on the HCL. If Windows NT does not find your adapter, choose Select from List and add the correct adapter.

8. Select TCP/IP.

9. Select Use DHCP. Only select DHCP if you have a DHCP server; otherwise, the system prompts you for TCP/IP information.

10. Click Next to install the components.

11. Click Next to start the network.

12. Select either Workgroup or Domain, and enter your Workgroup or Domain information. If you are joining a domain, make sure that you have a username and password with privileges to Add Workstations to the Domain, or that the computer account has already been created on the master account database by your network administrator.

13. Click Next to continue.

14. Click Finish.

15. Enter the correct time zone and date/time properties. Verify that these settings work (typically, you can click Test to review them).

16. Click OK to continue.

17. Insert a blank disk to create the ERD.

18. When the system finishes creating the ERD, remove the disk, label it, and save it. The system saves the configuration and reboots.

19. Log on to Windows NT Workstation.

Configuration Options

You can choose from the following options when configuring Windows NT Workstation:

■ **Typical**   Installs the default settings and most commonly used optional components. This is the recommended option.

■ **Portable**   Takes advantage of setup options for portable or laptop computers.

■ **Compact**   To save disk space, does not install any optional components. This option is useful for installing on old computers where disk space is at a premium.

■ **Custom**   Lets you pick and choose what options you want to install depending on your system configuration. This option gives you the most flexibility for installing Windows NT.

Supplying User Information and a Computer Name

The setup process prompts you for user information and a computer name to be used for licensing agreements and product registration.

User Information

The user information you supply is used for registration and licensing purposes. The setup process asks you who owns the license for the software you are installing. Enter your name and the name of the organization that sent you the software.

Computer Name

The computer name you supply identifies your computer on the network. The name must be a NetBIOS-compatible name of 15 characters or less. It must be unique on the network. If you are using WINS in your network, your computer name will be registered dynamically when the computer boots or a user logs onto the network.

Creating an Emergency Repair Disk

During setup, you are asked if you want to create an Emergency Repair Disk (ERD). This step is optional, but it is highly recommended. If you ever have to repair a damaged version of Windows NT, if your computer ever crashes because of a bad installation, a corrupted registry, a bad boot sector, or if it is unable to start NT Workstation, you'll be glad that you made an ERD. The vital information it contains may help you repair the workstation.

If you decide not to create an ERD during installation, you can create one later by running RDISK.EXE after Windows NT finishes booting. (Just type **RDISK.EXE** at the command prompt.) The information stored in the WINNT\REPAIR folder on your local workstation is copied to the ERD.

Although you cannot repair all Windows NT problems using an ERD, this disk gives you a fighting chance. Remember that the ERD you create on one computer is for that computer *only*, and should never be used on another computer. (While it is possible to use an ERD on another computer with similar hardware, it is not recommended and not supported by Microsoft.)

Emergency Repair Disk Contents

An ERD contains the following system information that is necessary to rebuild a broken machine. The following files are copied from the Winnt\System32\Repair directory to the Emergency Repair Disk in compressed form:

- **AUTOEXEC.NT**   Used for MS-DOS applications running the _DEFAULT.PIF

- **CONFIG.NT**   Used for MS-DOS applications running the _DEFAULT.PIF

- **DEFAULT**   Registry key HKEY_USERS\DEFAULT

- **NTUSER.DA**   Copy of user profiles

- **SAM**   Registry key HKEY_LOCAL_MACHINE\SAM

- **SECURITY**   Registry key HKEY_LOCAL_MACHINE\SECURITY

- **SYSTEM**   Registry key HKEY_LOCAL_MACHINE\SYSTEM

- **SOFTWARE**   Registry key HKEY_LOCAL_MACHINE\ SOFTWARE

Creating an Emergency Repair Disk

The purpose of an Emergency Repair Disk is to create a backup of your system files in case of an operating system failure.

For this exercise, all you need is one blank floppy disk.

To create an ERD:

1. Insert a blank disk into the floppy disk drive.

2. At the command prompt, type

   ```
   C:\RDISK.EXE /S
   ```

   The /S switch instructs the system to update the information in the WINNT\REPAIR directory on your local workstation.

3. When the system asks if you want to create an ERD, choose Yes.

4. After you create the ERD, make sure you label the disk clearly with the name of the system and the date, and store it in a safe place so that you don't overwrite it or misplace it unintentionally

Initiating a Recovery with Your Emergency Repair Disk

Once you have created an ERD, it is helpful to know what to do with it in case you ever have to repair your system.

For this exercise, you need an ERD, the Windows NT setup boot floppies, and the Windows NT 4.0 operating system source files.

To initiate a recovery from an ERD:

1. Boot your computer from the Windows NT setup floppies, stopping after you insert NT Setup Disk 2.

2. When the system asks whether you want to perform a recovery, answer Yes.

3. Insert the ERD.

4. Choose Recovery.

Remaining Installation Steps

The remaining steps needed to complete the installation of Windows NT Workstation include supplying information about network adapters, protocols, workgroups or domains, and display settings. It is a good idea to gather this information beforehand, and verify that all of the hardware is listed on the HCL.

Network Settings

Windows NT 4.0 Workstation is a network operating system, and offers features specific to participating in a networking environment. You can hook up directly to a LAN, or you can be connected to a network remotely if you have enough bandwidth to dial up. In order to start the network, you must make sure that you enter the correct settings during installation. Make sure that you have the correct driver disks for your network adapter in case Windows NT does not detect your card. Also make sure that you enter the correct information about the protocols to use. If you enter the wrong TCP/IP address or specify the wrong frame type during installation, serious network problems could result once your computer finishes setup.

Network Access

There are three options available under Network Settings that allow you to access a network in the following ways:

■ **Across a wire** This is the most common type of connection. Depending on your network adapter, you can connect via Ethernet or Token-Ring. Both of these connection types have distinct advantages and disadvantages depending on your environment. The most obvious difference between the two is speed. An Ethernet Category 5-type connection can reach speeds of 100MB per second, while a Token-Ring connection can reach speeds of only 16MB per second. Although these are the top speeds for each connection type, the actual performance speed depends on network traffic on your LAN or WAN, and will probably be lower.

■ **Across a cable** If you do not have a hub or Local Area Network to connect to, you can connect two computers with a special type of cable called a Null-Modem cable. This cable takes the place of a hub and allows two computers to talk directly to one another instead of sending data to a hub first.

■ **Via dial-up access** This type of connection is much slower than being connected directly to the network. The speed of your modem or ISDN line limits the speed of your connection. Windows NT has special features that help with slow connections, but you probably do not want to run any applications over a dial-up connection unless you have a lot of time or a really fast connection.

Configuring the Adapter Card

Your network card should be auto-detected during setup, but if it is not, you must enter the IRQ, the I/O address, and the base memory address. If these settings are not correct, the network fails to start when you log on, and you receive a message while booting up that a service or driver failed to load. Usually the hardware vendor for your card provides you with a network configuration diskette that tells you exactly what the settings should be. Verify these settings before you begin the setup process to save time. As you configure your card, you'll be asked whether you are wired to the network or connecting via the Remote Access Service (RAS).

WIRED TO THE NETWORK This is the most common configuration. If you select this option, you will be directly connected to the network through your network adapter via a cable that connects you to an RJ-45 jack or a BNC connector.

REMOTE ACCESS If you choose to set up remote dial-in capabilities, the Remote Access Service installs itself and you must enter the setting for your modem. You can also select the Dial-Up option from your logon menu during startup.

Network Adapter Configuration

Depending on your network card, you can let Windows NT try to auto-detect it, you can select it manually from a list, or you can add drivers to help Windows NT identify it.

Selecting an Adapter Card

To make sure that you have supported hardware in your machine, check the Hardware Compatibility List before choosing a network card. Remember: Microsoft does not support hardware that does not appear on the HCL.

You can choose one of the following options for determining how your network card is selected:

- **Select from list**   If your network card is not auto-detected and you know what network card is presently in your computer, you should select this option. A list appears and you can select your card from those choices. If you do not see your network card in the list provided by Windows NT setup, you can select Have Disk and provide the network drivers yourself from the disk provided by the hardware manufacturer.

- **NT finds/selects**   If your network card can be auto-detected you will save yourself a great amount of trouble. Windows NT setup tries to set up your card automatically depending on what your hardware resources are. Located in the "Guide to Automating Windows NT 4.0 Setup" is a list that Microsoft provides of detectable network cards. This is a very helpful option to choose.

Without Adapter Card

If you do not have a network adapter card installed in your computer, select MS Loopback Adapter. Once you do, the following procedure allows you to detect a problem with the network adapter or the network adapter driver and work around the network adapter installation problems during Windows NT Setup:

1. In the Network Settings dialog box, remove all network adapters from the Installed Adapter Cards list.

2. Choose Add Adapter and select the MS Loopback Adapter and click Continue.

3. The only configuration information required for the MS Loopback driver is Frame Type. Valid frame types are:

- 802.3 (Ethernet)

■ 802.5 (Token-Ring)

■ FDDI

Choice of frame type is not critical, so selecting 802.3 should be sufficient. If you've experienced a problem caused by a network adapter hardware conflict or driver problem, the setup program should now continue. The MS Loopback Adapter also can be used to isolate configuration problems from hardware problems on existing Windows NT installations.

You need to know what to do if you want to install your network protocols but you do not have a network card. You can install the MS Loopback Adapter to take the place of the card, and then install the network card once the setup procedure is complete.

Select Protocols

Windows NT uses protocols to communicate with other computers. As long as the computers are using the same protocol, they will be able to communicate. Some protocols are used to communicate with different computers. The protocol suite TCP/IP is used on the Internet for communication, IPX/SPX is used to connect to Novell networks and DCL is used to connect computers to Hewlett-Packard printers or mainframes. Depending on who you need to communicate with will depend on what protocols you will install during Windows NT setup.

Three Default Protocols

Windows NT 4.0 communicates to other workstations and computers on the network using different types of protocols. The protocols installed on your Windows NT Workstation determine what type of computers your NT Server can communicate with. To allow for the widest range of communication, Windows NT Workstation offers many different types of protocols that can be installed, including TCP/IP, IPX/SPX, and NetBEUI. Each of these protocols has advantages and disadvantages. Some protocols, like NetBEUI, are not routable or cannot talk to other networks on the other side of a router. Examples of two routable protocols are TCP/IP and IPX/SPX. TCP/IP is used regularly on the Internet, and IPX/SPX is used primarily to communicate with Novell networks.

Depending on the specific needs of your networks, you will need to install some of these protocols. It is important to note that having more protocols installed on your Windows NT Workstation causes more traffic than if you just install only one. For example, if you have an NT Server that has the protocols NetBEUI, IPX/SPX, and TCP/IP installed, you might create a network traffic overload. When you try to communicate with another computer on the network, your workstation tries to talk to the destination computer with each and every protocol! Even if you are using only TCP/IP, your server will first try to communicate using NetBEUI, then IPX/SPX, and finally TCP/IP. This can cause a lot of unwanted network traffic. For maximum performance, you should remove the unused protocols from your server.

TCP/IP   TCP/IP stands for Transmission Control Protocol/Internet Protocol and is an industry-standard suite of protocols designed for local and wide-area networking. TCP/IP was developed in 1969 as the result of a Defense Advanced Research Projects Agency (DARPA) research project on network interconnection.

This protocol has gained most of its popularity through its wide use for Internet communication, connecting computers together throughout the world. TCP/IP is known for being both reliable and routable, and for being able to talk to foreign networks.

Windows NT TCP/IP allows users to connect to both the Internet and to any machine running TCP/IP and providing TCP/IP services, including some applications that require TCP/IP to function.

Advantages of the TCP/IP protocol include:

- Provides connectivity across operating systems and hardware platforms. This protocol is the backbone of the Internet. If you need to connect to the Internet, you need this protocol.

- It's routable, meaning that you can talk to other networks through routers.

- Very popular. (Think of all of the computers on the Internet.)

- Some applications need TCP/IP to run.

- Provides connectivity across operating systems and hardware platforms. Windows NT can FTP to a UNIX workstation.

- Offers Simple Network Management Protocol (SNMP) support. (Used to troubleshoot problems on the network.)

- Offers Dynamic Host Configuration Protocol (DHCP) support. (Used for Dynamic IP addressing.)

- Offers Windows Internet Name Service (WINS) support. Resolves Windows NetBIOS names on the network.

NWLINK IPX/SPX-COMPATIBLE TRANSPORT   The most common use of the IPX/SPX protocol is connecting to Novell networks. You should also select this protocol if you use any applications that need IPX/SPX. Make sure that when selecting IPX/SPX, you pick the correct frame type.

NWLink is simply a protocol by itself and it does not allow a Windows NT workstation to access files or printers on a NetWare server. To access files or printers on a NetWare server, you have to make sure that you have Microsoft's Client Service for NetWare (CSNW) installed or Novell's NetWare Client for Windows NT. You can also use IPX/SPX to gain access to an NT Server that has Gateway Services for NetWare installed or a SQL Server that is using the NWLink protocol to communicate.

You should remember the following information about IPX/SPX:

- Ability to connect to Novell networks.

- You might need this protocol to connect to an application server running IPX/SPX.

- You need Client Services for NetWare to gain access to files and printers that reside on a NetWare server.

exam
ⓦatch   *It is important that you pick the correct frame type when selecting the IPX/SPX protocol. A question about it will probably appear on the exam.*

NETBEUI   Because of its speed, the NetBEUI protocol is best suited for Local Area Networks that do not connect to the Internet. The main limitation of this protocol is that it is not routable. Remember the following characteristics of NetBEUI:

- Very fast.
- Only used for Local Area Networks (LANs).
- Additional protocols may be added if necessary.

DLC   The DLC protocol is used to connect to printers using the Hewlett-Packard network attachment cards (internal or external) and mainframes.

exam
ⓦatch

The protocol required to connect to a Hewlett-Packard printer is often a test question.

The DLC protocol is used primarily for:

- Accessing IBM mainframes (usually with 3270 applications).
- Printing to HP printers connected directly to the network.

APPLETALK   The AppleTalk protocol is used to communicate with Macintosh networks. Generally, an NT Server with Services for Macintosh will use this protocol to communicate with the Macintosh clients.

POINT-TO-POINT TUNNELING PROTOCOL   Point-to-Point Tunneling Protocol allows users to create secure, virtual private intranets over public networks like the Internet. This technology simply allows the Remote Access Service (RAS) to create secure private networks and allows for secure communication over public data lines.

Enter Settings for Workgroups and Domains

In this section of setup, you have to decide whether to make your computer a member of a workgroup or a domain. For workstations participating in a small network of computers not requiring central administration, the workgroup environment should work best. For workstations in a larger environment that need security, central administration, and access to data across the network, you should join an existing domain.

A *workgroup* or *peer-to-peer network* is generally used in environments using 10 workstations or fewer that do not require central administration. A workgroup is also usually used for a small group of workstations that need access to resources on other computers in the workgroup. In a workgroup, every workstation that participates in the workgroup is its own local administrator. Workgroup computers manage their own local resources through their local account database. All user accounts are stored locally on the workstation instead of on a domain controller. Workgroup computers do not share security with other computers in the workgroup or rely on other computers to provide security for their local resources.

If you choose a workgroup, NT prompts you for the local machine account username and password that allows you to log on to the local workstation. Make sure that you keep this information in a safe place. If you lose or forget the password for the local machine account, you have to reinstall Windows NT Workstation to recover your workstation.

The Domain Environment

A domain environment is used for large numbers of computers that require central administration, centralized security, and access to resources on other computers. In a domain, all user accounts are stored in a common account database that resides on a primary domain controller and is replicated to all of the backup domain controllers. Like a workstation, a domain has a unique name that identifies it. Users who have domain accounts are subject to the security and policies of the domain. A domain provides logon validation to enforce security throughout the domain.

If you select a domain to join, you need to make sure that you have sufficient privileges for joining the domain. Normally, you have to have Account operator privilege, or be given this specific privilege in User Manager for Domains. Once this information is entered and validated, your computer becomes a member of the domain. You can also add the workstation to the domain prior to installation so you are not prompted during Windows NT setup. After the necessary domain information has been entered, you are prompted for the password for the system's local administrator account. Like a workgroup configuration, this administrator account provides access to the local machine.

Miscellaneous Settings

You are almost finished with your Windows NT 4.0 Workstation installation. If you have gotten this far, you just have to fill in some trivial information like date, time and time zone. Once these settings are complete, you are almost ready to save your configuration, reboot the computer, and log on to your brand new Windows NT 4.0 Workstation.

Date and Time

You should select your date and time depending on your geographic location. Just enter the time, date, and time zone. Windows NT stamps files with Greenwich Mean Time plus the number of hours to the specified time zone. This is helpful in situations where the absolute time of file creation may be required. If a file created on the West Coast is modified on a computer on the East Coast, the file timestamp maintains correct information.

Display Properties

The Display Properties screen allows you to configure your video adapter and monitor settings. Standard VGA with 16 colors is the default.

■ **Video Adapter**   In case Windows NT cannot find your video adapter card during setup, you can choose your adapter from a list or provide the setup program with drivers supplied by you from your hardware vendor. If you cannot set up the video adapter, you can choose VGA resolution and then set up your adapter once installation finishes. If for any reason Windows NT fails to come up because of video resolution problems, you can choose VGA mode during the boot process and then fix your display settings.

■ **Monitor Settings**   How powerful your video adapter is has a direct
effect on what type of monitor settings you can use. What type of
monitor you have also has an effect on what type of monitor settings
you can use. Check whether your monitor is on the Hardware
Compatibility List. If it appears there, you should not have a problem
with installation. If you do have a problem, you can choose VGA
settings and change the video and monitor settings once Windows NT
setup is finished and you log on to your workstation.

■ **Default**   If you choose the default settings, you get whatever settings
Windows NT detects during setup. You can always change the default
settings once you log on to your workstation.

CERTIFICATION OBJECTIVE 2.04

Removing Windows NT 4.0 Workstation

If you are not happy with your Windows NT installation or operating system,
you always have the option of removing Windows NT. There are a couple of
ways to do this, depending on how your system is configured and what type of
file system you are using with Windows NT Workstation. Whatever method
you choose to remove Windows NT, you need to perform a few steps using
either FDISK.EXE or a third-party tool such as Partition Magic.

Remove the NTFS Volume, If Necessary

Although an NTFS partition is difficult to remove, it can be done with a
variety of partition utilities. Some of these tools include FDISK.EXE, Partition
Magic, DELDISK.EXE, or Delpart. If you use FDISK.EXE to remove an
NTFS partition, you have to follow a clearly defined set of steps. Other
partition tools work equally well, but require more care.

Deleting an NTFS Partition

If you are trying to remove an NTFS partition from your hard disk, you have to use an executable called FDISK.EXE. FDISK.EXE removes the NTFS or non-DOS partition from your hard disk as long as your NTFS partition is not on an extended partition. You will lose any data on the NTFS partition, so back up the data prior to starting.

To delete an NTFS partition:

1. Start Windows NT installation from floppy disks or a CD-ROM.

2. When you are prompted, type **D** to remove the partition.

Located on the Windows NT 3.51 resource kit is the NTFS partition removal utility, Delpart. Delpart can remove an NTFS partition quickly and easily. All you have to do is tell which NTFS partition you need removed and Delpart takes care of the rest. If you use this utility, make sure that you save your changes once you decide which partition to remove.

Change the Boot Operating System

To completely remove Windows NT from your hard disk, you have to change the boot operating system. To change the boot operating system, you can use a command-line executable (SYS) to change the system files from Windows NT to MS-DOS. After the computer finishes rebooting after you "SYS" the hard disk, you can boot straight to MS-DOS.

Changing the Boot Loader to MS-DOS in an Existing FAT Partition

If you need to remove NT from a FAT partition, you have to issue the SYS command on the boot drive that Windows NT is located on. The SYS command replaces the NT boot sector with the MS-DOS boot sector and allows your computer to boot from MS-DOS. If your system files reside on the C: drive, then you need to SYS the C: drive. If your system files reside on the D: drive, then you use the SYS command on the D: drive, and so on. After you replace the boot sector on your hard drive, you still have to remove the Windows NT system files. These can be removed with the DELETE command. To change the boot loader to MS-DOS in an existing FAT partition:

1. Insert your MS-DOS boot disk into your floppy drive.

2. Turn your computer on and let it begin booting from the floppy drive.

3. At the MS-DOS prompt on the A: drive type

   ```
   A:\sys c:
   ```

4. Now that you have regained the boot sector from Windows NT, remove the NT system files by typing:

   ```
   A:\Del C:\Pagefile.sys
   A:\Del C:\Boot.ini
   A:\Del C:\Ntldr
   A:\Del C:\Ntdetect.com
   A:\Del C:\Bootsect.DOS
   ```

   or by typing:

   ```
   A:\Del C:\Ntbootdd.sys
   ```

   If you have a SCSI adapter on your computer, you also have to delete the file NTBOOTDD.SYS. This file resides only on computers using SCSI drives or adapters. To make sure that you have gotten rid of all your Windows NT files, type **DEL *.***.

EXERCISE 2-17

Creating an MS-DOS Boot Partition

To create an MS-DOS partition, you need to use the MS-DOS utility, FDISK.EXE. This utility allows you to create a partition and make it active. To create an MS-DOS partition:

1. Insert the MS-DOS boot disk that contains the FDISK.EXE and FORMAT.COM programs.

2. At the command prompt, type

   ```
   A:\FDISK.EXE
   ```

3. Using the FDISK.EXE program, make sure that there are no existing partitions on your hard disk.

4. To create an MS-DOS partition, select option 1.

5. Tell the computer how big you want the primary partition to be (for example, 500MB).

6. Press ESC.

7. To make the partition active, select option 2. Tell the computer which partition you want to make active.

8. Reboot the computer and keep the floppy in the drive.

9. When the computer finishes booting from the floppy, type the following command at the command prompt:

```
A:\Format C: /S
```

This command formats the C: drive with the MS-DOS system files. You can now boot off of the C: partition.

If You Currently Have a FAT Partition

If you currently have a FAT partition and you want to make the partition bootable, all you have to do is format the drive with the /S switch. This places the MS-DOS system files onto the drive.

```
A:\Format C: /S
```

You will be prompted to verify the format before any action can take place. Once this is done the drive will be formatted.

If You Currently Do Not Have a FAT Partition

If you are using an HPFS partition, you have to convert the file system to NTFS in order to install Windows NT 4.0. NT 4.0 does not support HPFS. If you are using an NTFS partition, the only way to install Windows NT is through an existing version of NT.

If you have an NTFS partition you must first remove the partition by using FDISK.EXE.

Remove Windows NT from a FAT Partition

Removing Windows NT from a FAT partition is much easier than removing Windows NT from an NTFS partition. To remove Windows NT from a FAT partition, you basically just delete the NT files and directories from the hard disk. Once this is completed, you can remove the NT loader by using the SYS command.

Removing NT from a FAT Partition

If you want to remove Windows NT from a FAT partition you use the MS-DOS command DELTREE.EXE to remove directories, and the DEL command to remove files. This eliminates any existing sections of the Windows NT installation.

To remove NT from a FAT partition:

1. Insert the MS-DOS boot disk that contains the DELTREE.EXE command.

2. Turn on your computer and boot off of the MS-DOS boot disk.

3. Delete the Winnt or %Systemroot% directory by typing the following command at the MS-DOS command prompt:

   ```
   A:\Deltree C:\Winnt
   ```

4. Remove the Windows NT system files by typing:

   ```
   A:\Del C:\PAGEFILE.SYS
   A:\Del C:\BOOT.INI
   A:\Del C:\NTLDR
   A:\Del C:\NTDETECT.COM
   A:\Del C:\BOOTSECT.DOS
   ```

You should now have all of the Windows NT system files and directories removed from your computer.

CERTIFICATION SUMMARY

The information in this chapter relates directly to what you will be tested on in the Windows NT 4.0 Workstation exam. Through the detailed explanations and exercises provided, you should feel better prepared to pass this exam. Let's review what was covered. The following examples are taken directly from the exam preparation page on Microsoft's web site, which explains exactly what will be covered on the exam. You should make sure you understand these key points before taking the exam.

In this chapter you have learned how to create unattended installation files, and used an UNATTEND.TXT file to create a script to automate Windows

NT Workstation installations. This technique allows you to roll out multiple Windows NT Workstations at once.

The exam will ask you to choose the appropriate file system to use in a given situation. Your choices include the NTFS, FAT, and HPFS file systems. The NTFS file system is made especially for Windows NT. By using NTFS on your partitions you can take advantage of its security features, fault tolerance, and performance. We also looked at the FAT file system. The FAT file system gives you more flexibility with other operating systems, but you will not be able to make use of some of Windows NT's security features. Lastly we looked at the HPFS file system. HPFS is no longer supported with Windows NT 4.0, so you must either delete the HPFS partition or convert the partition to NTFS during setup. We looked at security on the workstation and NTFS provides that for us. If you want security for your workstation you need to use NTFS security for an NTFS partition. NTFS gives you both file and directory security with Windows NT. Remember that you cannot set file permissions or use auditing on a FAT partition.

An important part of the exam covers dual-boot systems. If you decide to dual-boot between Windows 95, MS-DOS, and Windows NT, you need a FAT partition. Windows 95 and MS-DOS are unable to recognize any NTFS partition. If you are using NTFS, however, you can install multiple versions of Windows NT without any problem.

For installation exercises, we installed Windows NT Workstation on an Intel platform in a given situation. The first step in installing Windows NT 4.0 is verifying the hardware requirements. If your hardware meets the specifications, you can decide what type of installation to use. Along with the CD-ROM and network installation options, you can use the /B switch for a floppy-less installation. You need to remember that for any previous version of Windows NT you have to use the 32-bit setup utility, WINNT32.EXE. For all other versions of MS-DOS or Windows, you need the 16-bit version, WINNT.EXE. We also set up a dual-boot system in a given situation. Dual-booting between Windows NT and either MS-DOS or Windows 95 is possible. You can dual-boot with MS-DOS or Windows 95 if you have a FAT partition. If you dual-boot with Windows NT you can have either an NTFS partition or FAT. If you are setting up the machine from scratch, you should install Windows 95 first and then Windows NT.

In case something goes wrong with a Windows NT Workstation or its installation, you can remove Windows NT Workstation by either deleting the partition using the fixed-disk setup program, FDISK.EXE, or by using the SYS command to replace the Windows NT boot sector with the MS-DOS boot sector.

Besides installing Windows NT 4.0 workstation, you also can upgrade to Windows NT Workstation 4.0. Remember that you can only upgrade from MS-DOS, Windows 3.*x*, and previous versions of Windows NT. Upgrading from Windows 95 is not an option. For multiple installations, you can configure a server-based installation for wide-scale deployment. To configure a server-based installation, you must use all the tools provided as part of the installation process, including SYSDIFF.EXE (which pre-installs applications as part of setup), an UNATTEND.TXT file (which serves as a script for answering setup questions), and Unique Database Files (UDFs) (which replace content-specific information such as computer names and TCP/IP information).

TWO-MINUTE DRILL

- ❏ To witness the power of NT 4.0 Workstation, you should adhere to the recommended hardware requirements.

- ❏ The first thing you want to do is check the Hardware Compatibility List (HCL).

- ❏ Microsoft provides the Hardware Compatibility List as a detailed inventory of all supported and tested hardware for Windows NT 4.0.

- ❏ In order for Windows NT to be installed successfully, you must have an active partition (a "primary boot partition") of at least 120MB that is formatted as either FAT or NTFS.

- ❏ Windows NT installations are accessible from the network, local hard disk, or CD-ROM.

- ❏ There are also the options for upgrading, running fresh installations, and performing multiple installations.

❑ There are many different command-line switches available that allow you to perform floppy-less or unattended installations, or to create the three setup floppies.

❑ Remember that the files necessary to complete an unattended installation are SYSDIFF.EXE, UNATTEND.TXT, and Unique Database Files (UDFs).

❑ It is highly recommended that you create an Emergency Repair Disk (ERD). The ERD is a tool used to repair a damaged version of Windows NT.

❑ For a large number of installations, administrators may choose to install Windows NT over the network.

❑ To install network protocols without a network card, install the MS Loopback Adapter, and then install the network card once installation is finished.

❑ DLC is the protocol used to connect to printers using the Hewlett-Packard network attachment cards (internal or external) and mainframes.

❑ Whichever method you choose to remove Windows NT, there are a couple of steps that require using FDISK.EXE or a third-party tool such as Partition Magic.

❑ To remove Windows NT from a FAT partition, you basically just delete the NT files and directories from the hard disk. Once this is completed, you can remove the NT loader using the SYS command.

SELF TEST

The following questions will help you measure your understanding of the material presented in this chapter. Read all the choices carefully, as there may be more than one correct answer. Choose all correct answers for each question.

1. Holden wants to upgrade his workstation to Windows NT 4.0 Workstation. What choices does he have?

   A. Windows 3.1

   B. Windows 95

   C. Windows NT 3.51

   D. OS/2

2. Phoebe's boss wants her to install Windows NT 4.0 Workstation onto some legacy hardware. What choices does she have?

   A. 386/20, 48MB of RAM, 2.3GB hard disk

   B. 486/33, 16MB of RAM, 1.0GB hard disk

   C. 200 Pentium Pro, 64MB of RAM, 4.5GB hard disk

   D. 486 /100, 8MB of RAM, 3.0GB hard disk

3. Nuala Anne wants to verify that all of the hardware that she is going to use for Windows NT workstation is compatible. How should she verify the hardware?

   A. Call the hardware vendor.

   B. Check the Hardware Compatibility List.

   C. Ask her Network Administrator.

   D. Doesn't matter, Windows NT is compatible with everything.

4. To partition your hard disk you use the _____.EXE utility.

5. Ken accidentally lost his three setup floppies for installing Windows NT 4.0 Workstation. What command-line utility can he use to re-create them?

   A. WINNT.EXE /NO

   B. WINNT.EXE /B

   C. WINNT.EXE /U

   D. WINNT.EXE /OX

6. Dermot is doing top-secret work and wants to take advantage of Windows NT's security model. He is using a Pentium II 266, 4.3GB hard disk with 64MB of RAM. What file system should he use?

   A. HPFS

   B. NFS

   C. NTFS

   D. FAT

7. Danielle needs to install Windows NT 4.0 from the network from an MS-DOS workstation client and does not need to

create floppies. What setup utility should she use?

A. WINNT32.EXE /B

B. WINNT32.EXE /OX

C. WINNT.EXE /B

D. WINNT.EXE /U

8. Michael was instructed to come up with a plan to implement unattended installations throughout his company's enterprise-wide network. He also needs to pre-install applications and set up machine-specific parameters such as computer names and IP addresses. What files does Michael need to use?

A. Windiff.exe

B. SYSDIFF.EXE

C. UNATTEND.TXT

D. Unique Database Files

9. Your company has just purchased four new Hewlett-Packard printers for your network. TCP/IP is already installed on your network yet you cannot connect to the printers. What protocol must be installed to talk to the HP printers?

A. IPX/SPX

B. AppleTalk

C. DLC

D. Point-to-Point Tunneling Protocol

10. You accidentally edited the Registry of your computer. After you restart your computer, Windows NT will not load. What will help you restore your system?

A. Emergency Repair Disk

B. RESTORE.EXE

C. SYSDIFF.EXE

D. Windows NT 4.0 Server CD-ROM

11. While installing Windows NT 4.0 Workstation, you encounter errors during installation of your network card. You still want to install a network device to continue the installation. What option should you pick?

A. 3COM EtherLink III

B. 56K modem

C. MS Loopback Adapter

D. Arcnet adapter

12. What command lets you change the boot loader on your hard disk from Windows NT to Microsoft DOS?

A. ROLLBACK.EXE

B. SYS.EXE

C. DELTREE.EXE

D. RESTORE.EXE

13. Holly is upgrading a previous installation of Windows NT Workstation 3.51 to Windows NT Workstation 4.0. She already has the three Windows NT setup floppies.

What version of the Windows NT setup utility can she use?

A. WINNT.EXE /B

B. WINNT32.EXE /OX

C. WINNT32.EXE

D. WINNT.EXE /U

14. What are the benefits for using NTFS partitions on your Windows NT 4.0 Workstation?

A. Adapts to Windows NT security model.

B. Compatible with UNIX workstations.

C. Fault tolerant.

D. Best for hard disks over 500MB.

MICROSOFT CERTIFIED SYSTEMS ENGINEER

3

Configuring Windows NT Workstation 4.0

CERTIFICATION OBJECTIVES

3.01   Windows NT Control Panel

3.02   System Settings vs. User Settings

3.03   Windows NT Registry

After the initial installation of Windows NT Workstation, the majority of the configuration of software and hardware is done in the Control Panel. We will explore the options in the Control Panel for configuring system settings, which are available to all users on the system, and user settings, which are customized on an individual basis. We also will learn how to configure various hardware devices such as network cards, SCSI and IDE adapters, and CD-ROM drives for use with Windows NT. The chapter concludes with an overview of the Registry, which is the central repository for hardware and software settings configured via the applets in the Control Panel, or by accessing the Registry itself.

CERTIFICATION OBJECTIVE 3.01

Windows NT Control Panel

The Windows NT Control Panel is where the majority of your NT Workstation configuring is done. If you need to adjust a setting in Windows NT, chances are you will do it here. The Control Panel is basically a front end to the Registry, the central repository for configuration information (discussed later in the chapter). The icons in the Control Panel represent applets where specific changes can be made to the hardware or software through a graphical interface. See Figure 3-1 for an illustration of the Windows NT Control Panel.

If you have been using Windows 95 you are used to the Control Panel already. Some of the icons are unchanged, but a few icons were not in Windows 95, such as Devices, SCSI Adapters, Server, and Services. These require extra attention, whereas the features in the other icons remain the same as they did in Windows 95. Some of the icons that were in Windows 95 are not available in Windows NT, the most notable being the Add New Hardware icon. This was used in Windows 95 to detect new hardware, and since NT is not plug and play at this time, the icon has no use in NT. One of the most commonly used areas of the Control Panel in Windows 95 was the Device Manager, with which you could view and configure all the devices in your system in one area. The exclusion of Device Manager in NT was disappointing to many.

It is very common to see other icons in the Control Panel other than those provided by Windows NT. Third-party programs and utilities can add an icon in the Control Panel to centralize the configuring of hardware and software. A computer purchased from a leading manufacturer with software preinstalled most likely has a few vendor-specific icons. As you continue on towards your MCSE, you will find Windows NT Server will have more Control Panel icons for server-related configurations that NT Workstation does not provide. Some of these include icons for configuring Novell NetWare related services. And finally, some Control Panel icons are not present until certain hardware or software is installed in your system. For example, the Open Database Connectivity (ODBC) icon will not become available until you install a database application, such as Access or SQL.

As an NT administrator you must not be afraid of the Control Panel. You should be familiar with everything that the Control Panel is capable of. Even if you are not familiar with some of the less popular areas of the Control Panel such as UPS, Telephony, Tape devices, and Ports, you will use these as a support professional. The more time you spend with the various applets now, the less time you will have to spend when you are in the field as an MCSE.

FIGURE 3-1

Windows NT Control Panel, showing the icons through which changes can be made to hardware or software

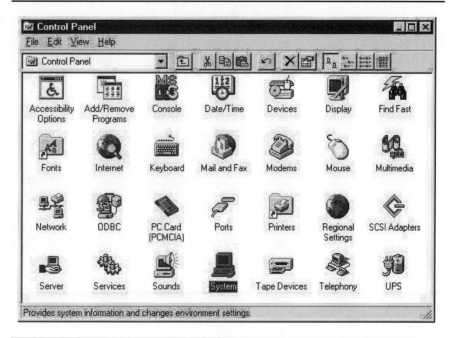

The exam will ask you which Control Panel icon you would select to configure a certain device. They can be tricky!

Accessing the Control Panel

There are a number of ways to access the Control Panel, and chances are you will use most of them. Here are a few ways you can access the Control Panel:

- From the Start menu, under Settings (the most common way).
- Through the My Computer icon on the desktop.
- At the bottom of the left pane in the Windows NT Explorer.

Anyway you go, you get to the same place. However, there a number of ways to get to the various applets contained in the Control Panel:

- By right-clicking the desktop and selecting Properties, you are brought to the Display Control Panel applet.
- Right-clicking the Network Neighborhood icon on the desktop and selecting Network will lead you to the Network Control Panel applet.
- When you right-click the My Computer icon and select Properties, you will be brought to General tab of System Properties.
- Double-clicking the time in the taskbar will bring up the Date/Time properties.
- Double-clicking the PCMCIA icon on the taskbar will bring up the PC Card properties.

Not only can you access the Control Panel from the above methods, you can make a desktop shortcut to the entire Control Panel, or you can make shortcuts to the various applets that are contained within the Control Panel.

The Printers icon in the Control Panel is actually a shortcut. You can access the printer information from this shortcut, or you can use the icon that is provided in the My Computer icon. You also can access the Printers from the Start menu by selecting Settings and clicking the Printers icon. We will discuss printers and printing issues in later chapters, but it is important to know where to access this applet because you will use this in your job as an NT

Administrator often. One thing users cannot live without is the ability to print, and when they cannot print you hear about it in a hurry. You are expected to fix the problems, so be sure and spend plenty of time learning the configuration and troubleshooting of printers. This is one weapon you want to have in your MCSE arsenal.

Since I access the Control Panel so much, I found that using the keyboard can be a fast way to maneuver. For example, if I were going to access the Control Panel from the desktop, I would use CTRL-ALT to open the Start menu, press S for the Settings menu, press the right arrow to open the Control Panel, and press ENTER. If you practice, you can get there fast. The best part is that the keyboard shortcuts work on most NT Workstations and Servers. Once I reach the Control Panel, I press the letter that corresponds to the icon I want to access, such as N for Network, and then I press ENTER.

CERTIFICATION OBJECTIVE 3.02

System Settings vs. User Settings

You should be aware of the distinction between system settings and user settings, because some configuration settings in the Control Panel affect every user that uses the system, and others affect only a specific user. For example, as an Administrator I log on with administrative rights to the system that I use to configure a user's system. I need to know which settings are system settings and which are user settings. If I adjust system settings, I know they affect every user on the system. If the settings I adjust are user settings, I have to decide if those settings that have been changed are just for me, or available for every user's profile. When I install a program I need to remember to make a shortcut to the program to be accessible for all users. Usually, I do this by placing a shortcut in the Winnt\profiles\all users\desktop, or Winnt\profiles\all users\Start menu. If I don't remember to make those shortcuts, when the user logs in he doesn't see the application I just installed. For example, if I adjusted the paging file setting on a user's computer I know that I don't have to replicate those changes for the other users that access the system, because it is a system setting.

Since the configuring of system settings is critical, only Administrators should be given the rights. Too many things can go wrong if you give a user who is not as well trained as you the ability to configure these settings. You could either log on to the user's computer as the Administrator of the local machine, or log in as yourself (with administrative rights) if you are participating in an NT domain. You will learn more about rights and permissions, as well as NT domains in later chapters, but for now it is important to know that only administrators should be configuring system settings.

The icons that are highlighted in Figure 3-2 represent the settings that a user may change for her user profile. Changing mouse, keyboard, and display drivers affects other system users, and these changes cannot be performed without privileges.

Learning the differences between system and user settings is critical before you assign rights and permissions to other users. When you grant explicit

---

FIGURE 3-2

The icons selected are those that are commonly configured on a per-user basis

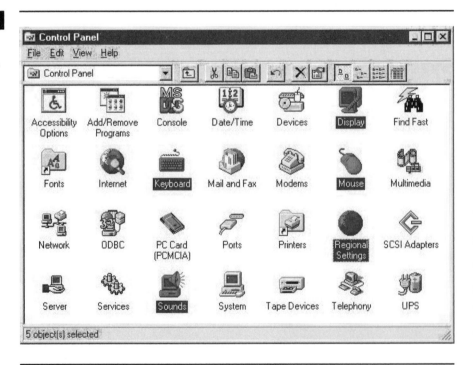

rights to users you want to know what they can and cannot do when it comes to system and user settings. It may not be your intention to give a user the right to configure system settings. In later chapters you learn about rights and permissions that allow you to assign rights to special users whom you would like to have configure system settings. Only a select few on the network should have the ability to change system settings, and they should be trained professionals like yourself.

I encourage you to create a user on your system that does not have administrative rights and see what this user can and cannot do. Sometimes it's tricky, because some icons, buttons, and tabs do not appear for a user without rights. Many options are grayed out, as well. I once tried to have a user adjust a setting that he said was not there. I insisted that it was there, and he should look harder. I was getting frustrated until I realized he did not have the rights to the setting. For him, it was not there. When we are the administrators of our local machines we take for granted all of the system and user settings we can modify. Change a setting as an administrator, then log in as the user, with fewer rights, and see if the changes affected the user's profile. This is good practice for when you have administrative rights on your own NT network.

System Properties

The system properties dialog box contains advanced settings that should not have to be reconfigured very often. There are some tabs that contain very important configuration information, as you will see later in the section. As mentioned before, you can also reach the System Properties by right-clicking the desktop as well as the icon in the Control Panel. Just because this applet is called System does not mean that it is the only place where you can configure system settings. Many of the applets in the Control Panel can be used to configure system settings that are reflected for all users logging in to the system.

General Tab

The general tab of the System applet, illustrated in Figure 3-3, gives you a quick reference for information such the operating system version you are

FIGURE 3-3

General tab

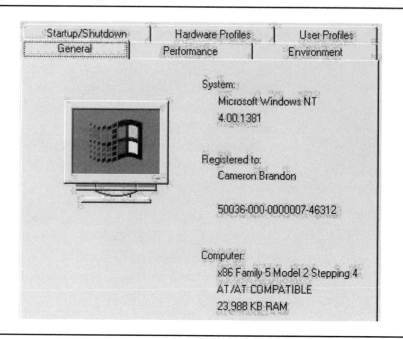

running, how much memory is installed, and who the product is registered to. I mostly use it to see the total amount of RAM in a user's system, or to see if a service pack is installed, and jump directly to the Performance tab to make paging file settings based on the size of the RAM I just received. One thing I noticed after installing Microsoft's Internet Explorer 4 is that it registered itself with this General tab, with the version and build number of the product. There is nothing on this tab for you to modify.

Performance Tab

The two settings that can be adjusted in the Performance tab, as you can see in Figure 3-4, are the Application Performance and Virtual Memory settings. You won't spend much of your time configuring these settings after your initial NT Workstation is configured. However, if you are serious about performance-tuning your system, you should be familiar with these settings.

FIGURE 3-4

Use the Performance tab
to adjust Application
Performance and Virtual
Memory settings

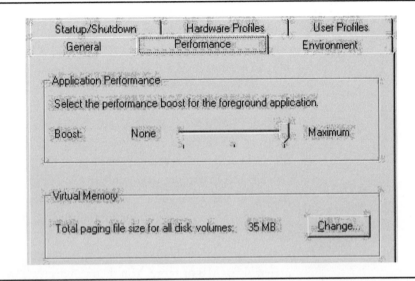

In order to understand the effect of the Application Performance setting, you must understand how a user interacts with the application. When you are using an application, it is in the foreground and most often the title bar is dark blue rather than gray. The computer boosts the program's priority to increase the response for the user. Priority is the number assigned to represent the importance of tasks in relation to one another. They are ranked on a scale of 1 to 31, with 31 being the most critical. When the user switches to another application, the program that was in the foreground now loses its boost in priority. For example, when you have an application in the foreground, by default it receives a priority of 9. When it becomes a background application, it loses two priority levels and drops down to a level of seven. The Application Boost setting will affect how the foreground application responds when multiple applications are running. If you feel the background applications are not getting enough processing time, you can reduce performance boost for the foreground application. However, if you feel the foreground application is not receiving enough processing time, you can increase the performance boost for the foreground application.

It is very important to have the Virtual Memory setting configured correctly. The rule is to set the initial paging file size to the size of your RAM plus 11 – 12MB. You can see that I have 24MB of RAM, so the initial paging file size is set to 35MB. I may be in need of some more RAM because I received an error message a few minutes ago, indicating that I was out of memory while I had a few applications open. Even with a maximum of 85MB I still ran out of memory. This is to show you that NT really does require plenty of RAM, and a correctly set paging file. If NT has to expand the paging file size, you'll notice, as this is not a good thing. You should allow a considerable maximum paging file size so NT doesn't have to expand the paging file size while you are working with several applications open.

There are two guidelines for configuring the paging file size. The first has been addressed in the previous paragraph. The rule for the initial paging file size can be flexible if you have a large amount of RAM in the system, preferably 64MB or more. You then can decrease the size of your paging file. The other guideline is that placing the paging file on separate drives can increase performance. Both disk drives are accessing information at the same time with increased throughput. The paging file does not have to be one file. If the recommended paging file size for your system is 35, you can have two 18MB paging files located on separate drives that function collectively as a paging file. There is one other small rule about the minimum paging file size. It is recommended that your paging file be at least 22MB. If the paging file size recommendation is 11 – 12MB plus the size of your RAM, that would mean that your installed RAM would equal 10MB. For Windows NT that is a scary thought.

Those are the basic rules that govern the use of the paging file. Remember, a paging file is no substitute for plenty of RAM in your system. Information is read from RAM much faster than from a hard disk. With the prices of RAM decreasing, it is a good investment to make, and your paging file will thank you.

exam
ⓦatch

You may get a question on the exam concerning the correct paging file size for a given situation. Remember the recommendations.

Virtual Memory

The term "virtual" refers to something that appears to be working although it is not. In the case of virtual memory, it means using the hard disk or paging file to simulate RAM when you have run out. NT uses *pages* that are swapped to the hard disk and brought in and out of memory as needed. Of course, the hard disk is much slower than RAM. If you receive the error message, "Your system is running low on virtual memory," you need to increase the size of your paging file. The paging file is actually a file called PAGEFILE.SYS, and is located in the root directory of the drive you specify in the Virtual Memory dialog box. Look at Figure 3-5 for an illustration of the Virtual Memory dialog box on my system. You can see in my E: root directory in Explorer a 35MB PAGEFILE.SYS. (Explorer first had to be configured to view hidden files, because the PAGEFILE.SYS is hidden.)

Windows NT makes better use of the paging file than any of the Windows predecessors, so don't let past experiences with adjusting and using the paging file worry you. (This file used to be called the *swap file*. You could create *permanent* swap files that used the same space each time, or *temporary* swap files that were created at each system startup. The temporary swap file could be scattered all over the disk. If you ran out of disk space, this scattering could be problematic. It took longer for the hard disk heads to read from a fragmented swap file.) The Windows NT paging file also can become fragmented and yield the same result: poor performance. Here is a quick exercise in what you could do to improve your system performance if your paging file is fragmented.

EXERCISE 3-1

Moving the Paging File to Another Drive

This exercise requires a second hard disk, or at least another partition to work effectively.

1. Open the Control Panel and select System.
2. Click the Performance tab.
3. Click the Change button.
4. Highlight the currently allocated paging file.

5. In the Initial Size box, enter the number 0.

6. Click the Set button.

7. Select the drive or partition on which you want to place the new paging file.

8. Enter the initial size for your paging file. This could be the recommended size of 12MB plus the size of your installed RAM.

9. Click the Set button.

10. You have to restart the computer for the changes to take effect.

What this exercise accomplished was to move the paging file from a possibly fragmented region of your disk or partition, into a new partition or onto a new disk where the paging file is covering contiguous space.

You can use NT's Performance Monitor to view paging file activity and determine the correct size for the paging file. (You will learn more about the

---

FIGURE 3-5

Control paging file size from the Virtual Memory dialog box

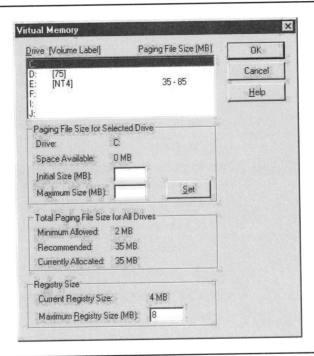

Performance Monitor in later chapters. For now we are configuring our paging file based on the recommendations provided by Microsoft, which will be sufficient for most users.) When your system experiences *paging*, NT is accessing the paging file in order to read, from the hard disk, required information that is not in RAM. The Performance Monitor also indicates whether excessive paging is decreasing system performance, requiring additional RAM. When paging gets really bad, the system begins *thrashing*. (That definitely sounds worse than paging!)

At the Virtual Memory window, shown in Figure 3-5, you can see how your currently allocated paging file size compares to the recommended paging file size. It is best to make the paging file size equal to or greater than this recommended size, unless you have a significant amount of memory, as described earlier.

The last setting in the dialog box is for the Maximum Registry Size. This is not a grave concern. You have two options: Limit the Registry to a certain size (not suggested), or just let it grow larger. I cannot think of a reason why you would want to limit the size. The Registry is growing for a reason. It is storing more hardware, software, and security settings.

Startup/Shutdown Tab

The Startup/Shutdown tab is used to adjust the settings for startup, but also allows you to adjust recovery settings. See Figure 3-6 for an illustration of this dialog box. The System Startup section is a graphical means of modifying the BOOT.INI, which is a read-only text file in the root directory of the system partition. Everything that you can do in the System Startup section you can do in the BOOT.INI. In fact, there are many more features that can be changed that are not shown in the System Startup section. The BOOT.INI is covered in later chapters, and should be thoroughly understood.

The operating system shown in the Startup window is selected as the default operating system—the one that is started once the allotted 30 seconds have passed. Be sure to select the operating system in which you spend most of your time. If you boot the system unattended, you want your main operating system to appear when you return after the timer has expired. You can change the default operating system by selecting another from the Startup pull down window. The 30 second timer is also adjustable. You could lower the timer to

FIGURE 3-6

At the Startup/Shutdown tab, adjust setting for startup and recovery

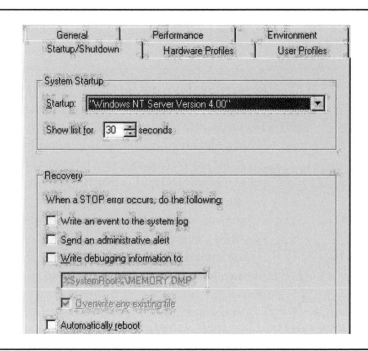

give yourself just enough time to select the proper operating system, but not too much time where NT takes too long to boot. If you have installed Windows NT Workstation on the same computer as Windows 95, you can see that it did an excellent job of creating the system startup menu with a selection for Windows 95. This was the smoothest operating system addition I have ever seen. But if you go the other way—installing NT Workstation first, and then going back and installing Windows 95—the process won't go as smoothly, because Windows 95 overwrote the nice system startup and Master Boot Record for NT. It's not that difficult to revert to the old NT system startup menu, which you can read about elsewhere in this book.

Recovery Options

The Recovery section of the Startup/Shutdown dialog box allows you to configure your system to act in the case of a critical STOP error. STOP errors do not happen often, but you should know the available recovery options.

■ The event can be written to the system log. In a business setting, you want to have the event on record to know when the STOP error occurred. A home user usually sees the error take place, and doesn't need to write the event to the system log.

■ An administrative alert can be sent. In a business setting, the administrator should be notified immediately if a computer has experienced a STOP error. In a home setting the user is the administrator, so sending this message is unnecessary.

■ Debugging information is something you probably are not trained to interpret. It is a detailed analysis of everything happening at the time of the Kernel STOP error. This dump could be sent for analysis to Microsoft Support personnel, to determine the cause of the STOP error. In later chapters on Troubleshooting, you learn which tools to use to view the memory in the dump.

You can configure your system to perform all of the above recovery options or none. A home user doesn't need most of them. However, if you are responsible for a corporate NT network, you should select most, if not all of the recovery options. System downtime is costly in the business world, and these options enable you to react promptly in an emergency.

Environment Tab

The environment tab allows you to modify system variables for the computer. See Figure 3-7 for an illustration of the Environment dialog box. Some variables seldom have to be modified. For example, why would you want to change the PROCESSOR_ARCHITECTURE from x86 to anything else? The PATH statement is the exception. With this statement, you dictate the path of directories that is followed to find information when the computer cannot find a file. The system searches the directories you specify in the order you specify, until it finds the desired file. If the file is not found, an error message is issued. The PATH statement was very popular for use with DOS and older Windows operating systems. It's still important, even if you don't see it so much anymore.

The PATH statement in the
Environment tab gives the
system another means to
find a required file

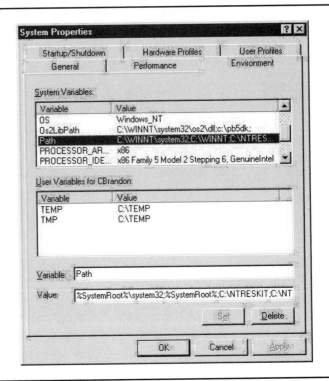

Here is one trick I have found useful with respect to the Path statement: If I
install a fresh copy of NT in another directory, I modify the PATH statement
to look in the existing Winnt\System32 directory for the files it needs to run
Windows applications. Before I came up with this idea, I used to reinstall the
applications so that the correct files could be placed in the new system
directory. I would run the application, and if a DLL file was indicated as
missing, I would find it in the old directory and copy it to the new system
directory. Then I would start the application again. If I got another error
message, I would move the DLL file again. This process would continue until
the application started properly. But what if the program did not indicate
which DLL is missing? Well, then I was out of luck. In any case, why add the
files again when I can just tell NT to look elsewhere for them? This trick of
modifying the PATH statement fixes everything. (If only I had been an MCSE

earlier!) In the next exercise we will adjust the PATH statement to add another directory to the search path. Let's use the Program Files directory to practice adding another directory.

Modifying the PATH Statement

1. Open the System tab in the Control Panel.
2. Click the Environment tab.
3. Scroll down until PATH is visible.
4. Highlight the PATH statement. At the bottom of the dialog box the current path is displayed in the Value edit box.
5. Move to the end of the path displayed in the Value edit box and add the following:

   ;C:\Program Files
6. Click the Set button.

Notice that the directories in the Value field are separated by a semicolon. The computer uses the %SystemRoot% statement to insert the drive on which your system root is located—in this exercise, the C drive.

The other common user variable that you can modify in the Environment tab is the TEMP directory setting. Most people leave the TEMP directory as the default. The purpose of the TEMP directory is to place files that are currently being used by the operating system. In most cases Windows automatically deletes them when it is finished. This is not always the case, though. If you look in your TEMP directory right now, chances are you have files left over for unknown reasons. You should not delete them unless you know what they are. They could be TEMP files for an application that is currently running. (I recently had to break this rule when I was called to help a user who had run out of disk space. His TEMP directory held about 50MB of stuff, and all of the leftover files began with the tilde symbol, so it did not appear that he was using it as anything other than a TEMP directory. I deleted all of the temp files while the system was running, because he only had a few kilobytes of disk space left. I bet you can't wait until you are an MCSE to encounter these situations!)

Hardware Profiles

A hardware profile is an alternate configuration you can select from a startup to specify various options. Laptop users employ one hardware profile for the docked configuration, and another for the undocked, or *travel* configuration. I have seen other users specify one profile for network connectivity, and another for the local system. This is reminiscent of the old days when we tried to conserve valuable conventional memory, when playing a computer game that demanded a lot of memory, by creating a different profile that loaded only the drivers required to play a game. I found hardware profiles to be especially helpful when troubleshooting a machine, or testing different configurations without destroying the original working configuration. For example, if I am installing a modem and its resources are conflicting with the mouse, I can make a hardware profile for the original configuration in which the mouse worked. This way, I can have something to fall back on should the modem installation make the situation worse, which it usually does. After I am done troubleshooting, I use one hardware profile most of the time. I delete the other to avoid the Hardware Profiles menu on bootup.

To make a new hardware profile, just copy the existing hardware profile, which is called Original Configuration (Current). You can rename the new hardware profile. If NT cannot decide which profile to use for startup, it asks you which profile you would like to boot to. You can configure NT to wait a specified period of time before it boots to the default hardware profile, or you can have NT wait indefinitely for you to make a choice.

User Profiles Tab

There is much more to the User Profiles tab than first appears. From this dialog box you can copy and delete profiles, or change the type of profile that is used. Before we continue, we need to understand user profiles and the different types available. (You learn more about user profiles in later chapters.)

A user profile stores user preferences such as screen savers, last documents used, and environmental settings such as program groups and network connections. When you log off, the changes are saved so that the next time you log in, the settings are just as you left them. The profile starts as the default user and then becomes saved in the user's logon name in the system root, which is usually C:\Winnt under Profiles.

You can see in Figure 3-8 where NT will store user preferences. This is good for administrators to know, whether they make applications and files available to everyone on the system, or just to a select few. All Users is the default that is used as a model for all users who log on to the system. Just select the user that you would like to have a program or shortcut, and copy it to the Desktop or Start menu, whichever you prefer. This is the kind of thing I do on a daily basis when installing software as an NT Administrator, so you may want to practice it.

You have the option of making a profile a *roaming profile,* which is a profile stored on another computer, most likely a server. The roaming profile enables you to keep your user preferences in one location so that any changes you make to the profile are used on any computer that you log into. If you did not have a roaming profile, you would have a profile for each computer you log into, and any changes you make to that profile are not accessible on other

FIGURE 3-8

Copy User Profiles to Desktop or Start Menu under All Users

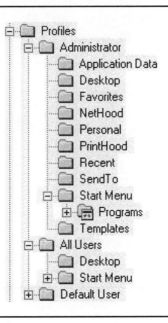

computers. I usually make my profile into a roaming profile so I can have shortcuts to commonly used areas available regardless of the user's machine. This way I don't have to browse the network to find everything I need while the user is watching impatiently. You enable a roaming user profile by specifying a path to the profile in User Manager.

Services

Clicking the Services icon in the Control Panel brings up the window shown in Figure 3-9. This feature is new to users of Windows 95. It shows you what services are running on the system. Not only can you stop, start, or pause services, you have the option of configuring them for system startup.

Services are important because they run even when a user is not logged on. This enables NT to perform tasks such as replication and scheduling in the background. Although it appears that NT is not doing anything when no user is logged in, many services are running. This is especially true of NT Server. The Services icon becomes much more valuable when you are using Windows NT Server, due to the number of services added when you install the various BackOffice products such as SQL Server, SMS, and Exchange. These products

FIGURE 3-9

From the Services applet, you can start, stop, pause, and configure services

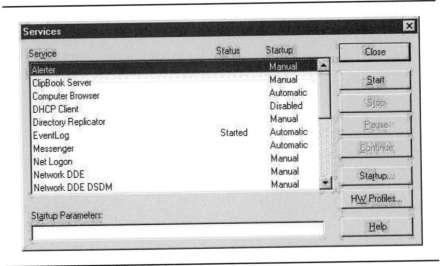

install services that have to be monitored as well as stopped and started for various reasons. You have to stop services when updating the software, or when installing applications requiring the use of that particular service. Many times you have to stop and start a service for a configuration change to take effect. Pausing the service allows the existing users to continue their work without allowing any new users to access the resources. This is an effective and considerate way to let users access the resources without abruptly stopping the service and causing potential data loss. You even can send the users a polite message notifying them the system will be taken down for maintenance, and give them opportunity to save the data they are working on.

Here is an example of how the skills you learn while becoming an MCSE help you to solve problems in the real world: I have been using the Services applet, trying to troubleshoot an application. Whenever I try to start the service I get an error message. I can't use that portion of the application if the service is not running. In this case the application is Microsoft's Exchange Server. The service will not start, because I have an Exchange database that is corrupt. I make adjustments on the database, and try to start the service. If the service starts correctly, I have fixed the problem. If it does not start, I still have work to do. You can see how useful the Services applet can be when troubleshooting problems.

Figure 3-10 is the dialog box showing the three startup configuration options for a service: automatic, manual, and disabled. Automatic starts the service without your intervention. Manual configures the service to not start until you choose to start it. Disabled means the service will not start at all until you change the setting to automatic or manual.

Earlier in the chapter you learned about hardware profiles. The H/W Profiles button in the Service startup allows you to configure the services for the various hardware profiles that you have enabled on the system. This means you can specify one hardware profile that is to have the service started, while another profile will not start that service. You can isolate hardware profiles while you adjust system settings so as not to affect the other hardware profiles.

I wanted to share another example of a situation in which you might use services. Recently, when I was renaming a file, I received the following message: "There has been a sharing violation. The source or destination file may be in use." At first I thought I had renamed the file to a name that was

FIGURE 3-10

The Startup dialog box for a service, showing the three configuration options

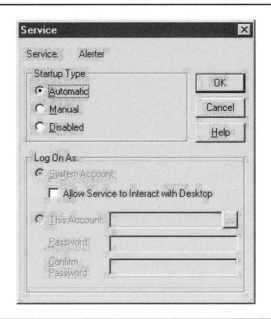

already being used. Not finding another file with that same name, I looked to see what applications might be open and using that same file. No other application was open. Finally, I remembered the services. Once I stopped the service, I could rename the file.

Here is another situation that could have taken a turn for the worse if not for my knowledge of services: I was restoring data from a tape backup. (No, I did not accidentally delete anything. I was testing the backup and restore process just in case I did accidentally delete something!) I was using one backup program that could not restore the data, so I quit that application and started another backup program. I received an error message upon opening the second program saying the tape device driver was loaded, but the backup device could not initialize. I made sure that the other program was not running, but still had no luck. Restarting the computer did not solve the problem, either. When I went to the Services icon in the Control Panel, I saw that the first program had services that were started automatically. Once I stopped these services, the other backup program started correctly.

An inexperienced NT user, unfamiliar with services, might not have solved the problem. If another person were to try to use the second backup program later and received the error message, he could have torn apart the entire system looking for the answer. With a grasp of services, you can quickly diagnose and solve such problems.

Date/Time Icon

This icon allows you to adjust the date and time of your system, as well as the time zone. This applet can also be reached by double-clicking the clock in the task bar. Adjusting the date and time is self-explanatory, so I will not spend a lot of time with configuration. However, you should note that you have the option of automatically adjusting for daylight savings, or manually making the adjustment. If you support hundreds of computers, you don't want to go around to each computer and manually adjust the time every six months. The date and time are important for updating file stamps such as last accessed, scheduled events, and e-mail messages. These don't sound that important, but what if an internal NT system procedure had to check the timestamps of files during synchronization, or replication? The computer may not get updated correctly, because the timestamp would show a date later than the other computers.

Sometimes I get called out to adjust the time setting on an NT Workstation, because the user did not have the appropriate rights. If you need administrative rights to change the setting, chances are it is a system setting that affects every user who logs into the system. I once had an e-mail correspondent ask me to send him a newspaper so he could place some bets. I had no idea what he was talking about until another person told me my e-mail messages were being time stamped with a date two months in the future! I had made an adjustment to find out what day of the week my birthday would fall on, and had forgotten to set it back.

Display Icon

From the Display icon, the user can customize desktops, icons, screen savers, and pointers. An NT Administrator often helps less experienced users with these settings. There is also an area in the Control Panel where graphics card manufacturers place several more tabs of configurations relating to the features of their cards. Don't be surprised if you see upwards of eight tabs of configuration settings for the adapter and display environment. With the installation of Microsoft Internet Explorer 4, a tab called Web was added to the Display icon. It allows you to view your desktop as a web page. This is the new feature of the Internet browser that makes your desktop active so you can view web pages directly on it.

Background Tab

The background tab lets you choose a pattern or wallpaper to be used for your background (what some refer to as the desktop). Once you choose an image, you can tile the image to cover the entire background, or leave it as one tile in the middle of the screen. If you use pattern for the background, the option to tile or center will be grayed, because a pattern is a small picture already tiled.

Screen Saver Tab

There is nothing complex about the screen saver tab. It allows you to choose a screen saver, and to password protect the screen saver. If you set the Password Protect option, a password dialog box is displayed when you interrupt the system while the screen saver is running. This may be a nuisance for home users, but in a corporation it is considered a security feature. Just imagine if you left your computer suddenly while logged in as Administrator, and someone came along and deleted every file on the computer. This is an important feature when you become an MCSE and you are the Administrator of your own network. Follow this next exercise to make sure you know how to select a new screen saver.

EXERCISE 3-3

Selecting a Screen Saver

1. Open the Display icon in the Control Panel.
2. Click the Screen Saver tab.
3. Use the Screen Saver pull-down menu to select the screen saver you wish to use. Click the preview button to see if you like it.

4. Check the Password Protect button.

5. Set the time to wait before the screen saver becomes active.

6. Click OK to exit.

I don't use screen savers that use too many system resources, especially on Windows NT Server. The CPU-intensive screen savers may look cool, but at the price of precious CPU cycles. I also don't use screen savers that often, because of too many instances when Windows 95 and some laptops didn't wake up when I tried to access the computer again. I know Windows NT is much better, but I hate rebooting just because the screen saver locked up the system.

Appearance Tab

The Appearance tab lets you change all of the default colors of the dialog boxes, icons, and borders. Someone could probably spend hours in here trying all the different settings. This area is also important for visually impaired users who require special settings. It allows the user to change the size, color, and brightness of dialog boxes and icons to improve legibility. Just like the Sounds icon in the Control Panel, the Appearance tab lets you load schemes, or create and save your own schemes.

Plus! Tab

The Plus! tab is left over from the Windows 95 Plus Pack enhancements to the display applet. It lets you change the default icons for desktop icons such as My Computer and the Recycle bin. Since the enhancements are self-explanatory, here are some of the available options:

- Smooth edge of screen fonts.
- Use large icons.
- Show window contents while dragging.
- Show icons using all possible colors.
- Stretch background wallpaper to fit the screen.

Settings Tab

Of all the sections available in the display applet, the Settings tab will be the most important to you. As your tastes change (or your eyes get worse) you can change the resolution of the desktop to suit your needs. I found that I usually require a large desktop to maintain multiple windows, so I have selected the resolution of 1024 by 768. The larger the resolution, the more can be displayed on the screen at once. Windows 95 (without third-party utilities) would require you to reboot the computer for the changes to take effect, but NT can adjust the resolution immediately. However, NT cannot adjust the color depth immediately, and will require a reboot for those changes to take effect. This is a nice feature if you frequently require resolution changes for the different applications you are using. The color depth is not changed as frequently as the screen resolution. A color depth of 65K or more should be sufficient to make images pleasant to look at. Remember, these settings are all conditional upon your graphics subsystem. The better your card, the larger the resolution and deeper the color depth you can use. A good graphics card could enable you to use a resolution of 1280 or greater with a color palette of 65K or more. Use the test feature to see what is the maximum your graphics card and monitor can handle and adjust accordingly. If you have not discovered for yourself already, the Settings tab of Display Properties (shown in Figure 3-11) appears when you right-click the desktop and select Properties.

The List All Modes button is useful for selecting a mode that is supported by the system. This area displays all of the modes available, including various color depths, resolution and refresh frequency. I use this as an alternative to adjusting each of the settings from the main Settings window. Sometimes you have the refresh rate and color depth you want, but when you select the screen resolution size it changes the values that you had previously adjusted.

The most important configuration you can make in this section is the adding and removing of display adapters. The display adapters are system settings present for every user on the system. Only Administrators can change the display adapter. In the next exercise you change the video adapter. Please note that there are many different types of adapters, offering many different options.

With the Settings tab,
change the desktop
resolution to suit your
needs

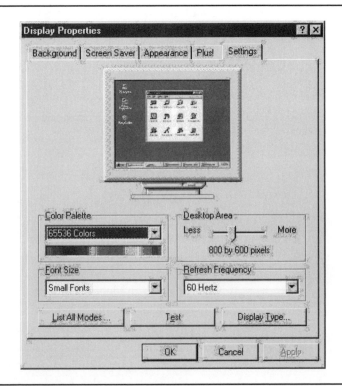

Changing Video Adapters

1. Access the Control Panel Display icon.

2. Click the Settings tab.

3. Choose Change Display Type.
   Information on your current adapter is shown. Note that you can
   change the monitor type from here also.

4. Choose Change.

5. In most cases, a dialog box with the compatible devices appears.
   If the driver you would like to use is not on this screen, select
   Show All Devices.

6. All of the available manufacturers and models of video adapters are displayed. Select the driver that matches the hardware you want to install. If you want to select a safe display driver that is compatible, select the Standard Display Adapter (VGA) from the Standard Display types at the top of the Manufacturers list. If the display adapter you would like to use is not shown on the list, select the Have Disk button and insert the vendor provided disk.

7. You now see the driver that you have just chosen in the Adapter type window.

8. Select the Close button.

9. You now are at the Settings window, and you may be able to select Change the Screen Resolution and Color Depth for the new adapter.

10. When you select the Close button, you may be prompted to restart the computer, depending on the changes you have made.

If you have made an incorrect choice when configuring your display driver and the system will not boot, Windows NT has the capability to boot in VGA mode. VGA mode can be selected from the Windows NT Startup menu, and will enable a universal VGA driver that lets you boot into Windows, where you can restore the original display adapter, or correct any action that caused the incompatibility. This makes it very easy to recover from a display mishap. I used this capability recently when a user received an error from the monitor during bootup concerning a scan rate. I thought the monitor had gone bad and was almost ready to replace it when I decided to boot into VGA mode. Once I accessed the Display properties while I was in VGA mode, I saw that the resolution size was set to 1152 and the refresh frequency was set to 72Hz. I made changes and rebooted the system and it worked fine. Another thing to be mindful of is the refresh frequency. If you set this too high, whenever NT reboots it may bring you back to the Display Property tab.

Modem Icon

The Modem icon in the Control Panel is where you configure the modem for use with the computer. This applet is one of the few areas where Windows NT detects your hardware. You are prompted for Windows NT to try to detect your modem if you have not configured one already. Since the installation of a modem is fairly straightforward, we need do only a brief overview of the procedure.

When you click the Modem icon in the Control Panel, either you are prompted for NT to try to detect a new modem, or you see the screen in Figure 3-12, with a modem already configured. If you do not have a modem configured and would like to install one, you have the option of letting NT try to detect your modem, or to select your modem from a list. If you are selecting your modem from a list and your device is not listed, click the Have Disk button to provide a disk supplied by the manufacturer for your modem. Once you have selected a modem, you are prompted for a COM port that you would like to install the modem on. After you have selected the port, NT either completes the installation or prompts you for Telephony settings, if this is the first time you have configured them.

FIGURE 3-12

The Modems Properties dialog box displays all modem configurations

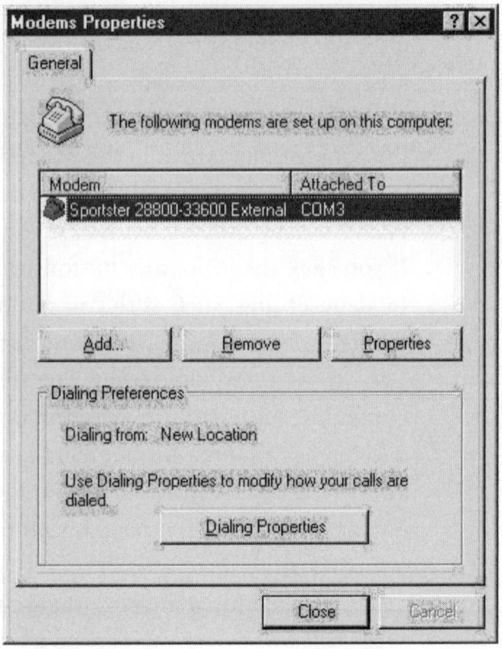

Telephony settings are used by TAPI-compliant devices and applications to store settings for such things as locations, calling cards, and area codes. Each of these devices can access the settings, which are stored in a *dialing location* that is comparable to a profile. You can define a dialing location for each place you dial from, and configure it with appropriate information so you do not have to adjust the setting each time you make a call. For example, you can include the number nine as a prefix for one dialing location to enable you to access an outside line. You could configure another dialing location to let you use your calling card. Dialing locations are also referred to as *Dialing Properties*. If you did not configure these locations when you installed the modem, you can always set them up later through the Telephony icon in the Control Panel. If you connect to various sources, such as an Internet provider, a remote work site, or several different bulletin board systems (BBSs), you can define each of them and then select the one you would like to use for a particular session. When I set a Dial-Up Networking property for my Internet provider, I pulled the settings for the provider onto the desktop in plain sight so my wife could find them easily. (She's not an MCSE like me!) You also can click the Dialing Properties button on the Modems Properties page to modify how your calls are dialed.

As Figure 3-12 illustrates, you can add and remove modems by clicking the appropriate button in the Modems Properties box. Each time you add a modem it's as if you never had a modem in the system. NT asks if you would like it to detect the modem, or if you would like to select one from the list. If you click the Properties button you can view and configure some of the modem settings, such as the maximum speed. A friend told me his 28.8 modem was so fast, he could connect to his Internet provider at 115200bps. I was going to explain to him that this is the speed at which your computer is communicating with the port and not the actual speed of the modem, but I decided not to burst his bubble. Don't worry if you didn't know either. I am guilty of the same thing. The computer must communicate with the port at a higher speed because it has to compress and uncompress the data before it is transmitted.

If you need to, you can configure the connection settings such as the data bits, parity, and stop bits for the modem under the Connection tab in the properties of a particular modem. You probably will not have to adjust any of these settings. There is even an Advanced tab with flow control and error control settings that you will also probably never have to configure. There is more concerning these settings and the serial port overview under the section on the Ports icon in the Control Panel.

An important feature of the Modems icon in the Control Panel is that once you have configured your modem(s), it will be accessible by all the applications that require a modem, such as your Dial-Up Networking (DUN) and Remote Access Service (RAS). These programs call upon the properly configured modem to communicate. Here is a good way to understand the relationships among all these devices and programs that we just learned:

- You click a hypertext link from a Word document. This link is a URL on the Internet.
- Word requires RAS or DUN, because the request is not local.
- RAS or DUN initializes the modem.
- The modem dials according to the telephony properties.

Tape Devices Icon

In order to use the Windows NT built-in backup utility, you need to have a compatible backup device installed. You install and configure the backup device by clicking the Tape Devices icon, which brings up the dialog box shown in Figure 3-13. NT actually detects the device and installs the appropriate driver. Installing the tape device is the easy part of backing up. The difficult part is configuring NT to back up, restore, and catalog. Or even worse, you could be using a third-party product that has too many features to keep straight.

Devices Tab

This tab in the Tape Devices windows shows you the tape devices currently in the system. You can select the Properties button to view the settings such as SCSI port, bus number, and target ID. The Detect button automatically detects and installs the appropriate driver. You can see that the status of the device driver also is displayed.

FIGURE 3-13

Click the Tape Devices icon to configure and install a backup device

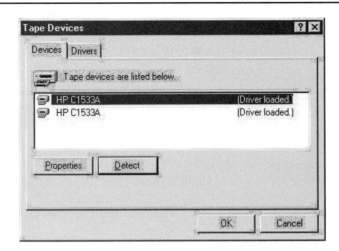

This next exercise demonstrates how to add a tape device and the appropriate device driver to Windows NT. For the purpose of the exercise, we'll assume that you do not already have a tape device on your system. (If you already had such a device installed, you could skip the step for installing the physical device.) We're not using the Detect feature of Windows NT in this exercise, because we're assuming there would be nothing for NT to detect.

EXERCISE 3-5

Adding a Tape Device and Driver to Windows NT

1. Begin by physically installing the tape device. Make any settings changes to jumpers if necessary. This would include setting the SCSI ID, or setting the Master/Slave settings for IDE devices.

2. Start the computer and boot to NT Workstation.

3. Access the Tape Devices icon in the Control Panel.

4. Select the Drivers tab.

5. Click Add.

6. Select your device from the list of manufacturers and models available. If the driver for your device is not present, click Have Disk and supply the disk with the driver provided by the manufacturer.

7. Click OK.

8. Provide the path to the NT Workstation CD-ROM if necessary.

9. Restart the computer for the changes to take effect.

If you do not have a tape device and you were installing a driver just for the exercise, you can use that driver for the next exercise, in which case we will *remove* a tape device driver.

Removing a Tape Driver and Device

1. Open the Control Panel and select the Tape Devices icon.

2. Select the Drivers tab.

3. Highlight the device you want to remove, and select the Remove button.

4. Confirm your intention to remove the device.

5. The driver for the tape device is now removed.

Drivers Tab

As you witnessed in the last two examples, the Drivers tab is where the installation and removal of device drivers takes place. Since a device driver can be thought of as controlling the device, adding or removing a driver essentially removes your ability to communicate with the device. The next step in removing the driver, if you were not going to use the device anymore, would be physically removing the device from the system.

When I was installing a third-party backup utility, I was prompted to remove the device and drivers from NT so that I could have sole ownership of them. I don't understand why this is necessary. I would have to go to a catalog and order tape that was backed up using Windows NT backup before the upgrade. This is the sort of thing to anticipate if you are going to be an NT Administrator, or any network administrator for that matter. You must stick with one solution, or else risk not having other devices or programs (or in this case, previous backup tapes) remain compatible with your new solution. Being aware of the ramifications of a decision will make you a great Administrator.

Network Icon

The Network icon in the Control Panel may be the most important applet available. If you do not participate in a network, it's of no use to you. But to other users, such as network administrators, this applet is essential to everyday survival. I am not exaggerating when I say that I visit the box illustrated in Figure 3-14 every few hours at my job. Here are a few examples of what you can configure in the Network applet:

- Install and configure a network adapter.

- Configure the TCP/IP protocol, and add support for other protocols such as IPX/SPX, and NetBEUI.

- Change the computer name and the domain in which it will participate.

- Bind and unbind protocols to adapters.

- Add support for the Remote Access Service (RAS) and Simple Network Management Protocol (SNMP).

Anything that has to do with network hardware and software for your workstation can be configured here. In the next exercise we install a network adapter, which gets the ball rolling for the other network options covered in

---

FIGURE 3-14

The Network Identification dialog box, where a network administrator spends a lot of time

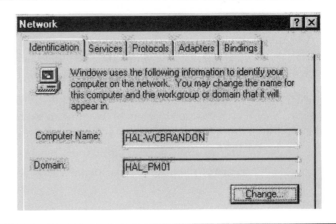

later chapters, such as adding protocol support. Refer to Figure 3-15 for an illustration of the Adapters tab box.

EXERCISE 3-7

Installing a Network Adapter

In order to complete this exercise, you must have a network adapter card to install and configure. If you don't have a network card, you can install the MS Loopback Adapter located with the other network drivers. With this adapter, you can add protocols and services just as you could with any other driver provided by Windows NT.

1. Open the Control Panel by selecting Start, and then Settings.

2. Click the Network icon to bring up the network configuration applet.

3. Click the Adapters tab.

4. Click Add.

FIGURE 3-15

Install a network adapter at the Adapters tab of the Network icon in the Control Panel

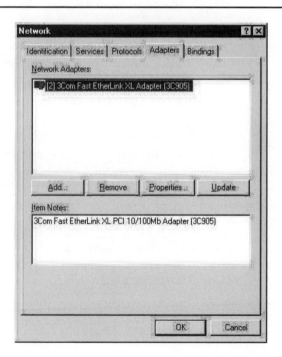

5. A list of network adapters appears. Select the correct adapter for the card you are installing. If your network card is not in the list of adapters, choose Have Disk. If you do not have a network card to install, choose the MS Loopback Adapter.

6. Depending on your card, you get a dialog box that will display additional configuration information that you have to provide. This can be the difficult portion of the install. Most likely, the dialog box will ask you for IRQ and Port Address for the card. These settings can be ascertained by using the configuration disk that shipped with the network card. It is very important not to lose network adapter card disks with the utilities for configuring the card. I usually turn off the system, install the new network adapter, and then boot with system disk (if the network utility disk is not bootable) and run the configuration utility. This allows you to assign an IRQ, port address, transceiver type, and duplex type, among other things. If you don't use this disk to configure your network adapter card, you have to guess at the network card's settings. If NT were plug and play, this installation would be much different.

7. If you chose the MS Loopback Adapter for your card, then you have to specify the frame type. It doesn't matter in this case, because we aren't using the card. Just accept the default.

8. The network card is now installed. In order for the settings to take effect, you have to reboot the computer.

An unfortunate incident happened to me once as a result of an improper network card setting. I had the misfortune of downing the entire network, and I don't mean a network of 3-5 computers. Our network has about 20 servers and over 200 workstations. When the phone began ringing and the users were looking out of their cubicles at me, I knew I was in trouble. Not knowing the cause of the problem, I called everyone I could think of for a solution. The main Ether switch had no more blinking lights indicating activity. We got out the switch documentation to find out what each light represents. We thought the switch itself might have gone bad, until we saw that the collision light had come on. After a few minutes, someone remembered I had just started installing NT Server on another computer. He proposed that the network card might be bad and could be chattering on the network. When he unplugged the network cable from the card, the Ether switch collision light turned off, and the blinking activity lights began appearing. When he plugged the cable back in to the card, the light for 100MB throughput on the card was on, rather than the 10MB light. He asked if I had configured the card to autodetect the network speed, and I remembered not even checking the speed while I configured the card. This situation could have had devastating results. I will always pay more attention when I am configuring devices. I hope you will too.

If you receive the error, "At least one service or driver failed during system startup. Use Event Viewer to examine the event log for details", just after configuring the card, the settings are not correct. Open Event Viewer in the Administrative Tools to verify this. You might not get the exact reason why the device failed, but at least you will know where to begin troubleshooting the problem.

The settings you choose in Windows NT must match the settings that the device is physically set to. This is very important for network cards, as well as modems and sound cards. Don't try guessing. Use the utilities provided with the card, and please do not throw the utilities away after you are finished. You will need them again if you have to adjust the card at a later date. You should write down the settings and attach them to the computer, so the next person who has to configure that device knows at a glance what device is installed and how it is configured.

EXERCISE 3-8

Removing a Network Adapter

Removing a network adapter is simple, but you should make a note of the settings such as DNS, WINS, and TCP/IP information before you remove the card. Knowing these will make configuring the next card much easier. You learn much more about these settings in later chapters. In this next exercise we remove an adapter from your system. This can be the adapter you installed in the previous exercise.

1. Open the Network icon in the Control Panel.

2. Click the Adapters tab.

3. Select the adapter you want to remove from the list.

4. Click the Remove button.

5. A message will ask you to confirm your actions. Click Yes to continue.

UPS Icon

The icon with the battery and the power cord is the icon for the Uninterruptible Power Supply, or UPS. Clicking this icon brings up the dialog box in Figure 3-16. The UPS is a device connected through the serial port that keeps power running to a system in the event of an emergency, such as a blackout. UPS can keep a computer running for several minutes while you shut it down correctly. The computer can also be configured to allow a safe shutdown without Administrator intervention, rather than remaining on until the UPS runs out of power. A power surge or spike can be fatal to a computer, so you should protect critical computers, such as servers, with UPS devices. You use this feature more when you are an Administrator of an NT network, because most of the important computers are protected by a UPS system.

FIGURE 3-16

UPS protects the system in the event of power failure

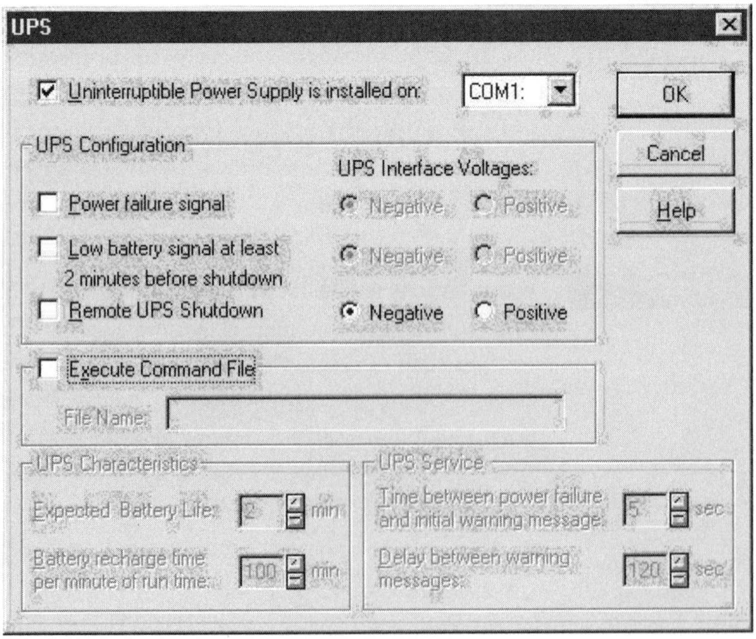

Adding Support for an Uninterruptible Power Supply

Since most of us do not have access to a UPS, we will configure the settings as if UPS is present in the system.

1. Click the UPS icon in the Control Panel.

2. Add support for the UPS by specifying which COM port the UPS is connected to. This allows more configuration options to become available.

3. You want the UPS to send a signal if the power supply fails, so check the box marked Power Failure Signal in the UPS Configuration area.

4. You also want to be notified when the UPS is running low on battery power, and how much time you have before the battery is depleted. Check the Low Battery Signal At Least 2 Minutes Before Shutdown box.

5. If you would like the option to remotely shut down the UPS, check the box marked Remote UPS Shutdown.

6. If you have a file or alert that you have made specially for this situation, enter the filename in the Execute Command box.

7. The UPS Characteristics portion of the dialog box depends on your UPS, because the amount of battery life varies by model. Consult the documentation provided with the UPS.

8. The UPS Service portion is used to configure the initial and subsequent attempts to send warning messages to the Administrator and the users.

In addition to the UPS icon in the Control Panel, the UPS vendor may provide another Control Panel icon for viewing the status of the UPS devices. Here you can find valuable information concerning self-tests, diagnostics and logging, as well as some of the features provided with the Control Panel UPS icon. (On the Control Panel for my company's server, which has the UPS device installed, there is not even an icon for the UPS anymore! The vendor must have removed the icon because it conflicts with device settings already present in their software. This might be a good idea to consolidate configuration utilities.)

Ports Icon

This icon yields a number of windows (shown in Figure 3-17) from which you can configure the *serial ports*. Not only can you add and remove serial ports, you can also adjust the baud rate, data bits, stop bits, parity, and flow control. The advanced option lets you manually adjust the resources for the port, including the IRQ and I/O port address. You won't want to override the default port values unless you are an experienced user. These settings can also be overridden in the Modem properties dialog box.

If you are not very familiar with serial ports, here is a quick summary. Serial ports, or *communication ports* (COM ports) are, of course, used to communicate. Note that a mouse is considered a communications port. Serial ports use asynchronous communications, which append stop and start bits to the data to signal the beginning and end of a byte. The receiving computer strips off the start and stop bits and reassembles the data. Synchronous communication requires that the two communicating devices share the same

FIGURE 3-17

The many configurable settings in the Ports icon

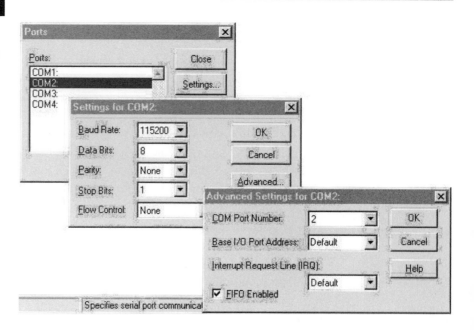

clock signal so they do not waste the overhead of appending start and stop bits to each byte of information. That is why synchronous communication is much faster. In the Ports icon you can configure the port for the amount of data bits, use of the stop bit, and parity for error detection if necessary. If you are not experienced with serial communications, you should leave these settings at the default. The other device would have to be set exactly like your device in order to communicate. (Just in case you were wondering, FIFO Enabled means First In, First Out buffer—the first data in the buffer will be the first out when the buffer becomes full.)

You can use the Ports icon to see the ports you have available before you install a communications device such as a modem. If the modem requires manual configuration such as jumpers, you can jumper the modem accordingly. If you can't use the default IRQ or I/O assignments for your ports because of conflicts with other devices, you can change them. This flexibility allows you to cater the NT port assignment settings to older legacy devices that were not very configurable. You must match the settings on both the device and in the ports icon for the device to work. That is the most difficult portion of the installation of these devices. It would be easier if you only had to configure the device one time. This is why you must keep your configuration disks after you configure your devices. You will need them later if the devices settings have to be changed. This is also why some companies have hardware inventory stickers on the sides of computers, showing the contents and configuration of the devices. When you see a computer that you are not familiar with, how are you going to know what brand network card it is, let alone what the card is configured for? You must be prepared for these situations. Learn where to go to find this information, and gather the correct information from the utility to be effective.

Add/Remove Programs Icon

The Add/Remove Programs icon is for the adding and removing of software, including the components that are part of the operating system, as well as third-party programs. Unfortunately, only 32-bit Windows applications that register themselves can be removed automatically by Windows, and not many applications do this. Microsoft is good about making most of their software capable of being removed from this uninstall window. And it is becoming more popular for software makers to have an item in their program group that uninstalls the application, rather than forcing the user to access the Add/Remove Programs icon. You should check all these areas to be sure the application can be removed safely, before you try to remove the program manually.

Using the Add/Remove Program Control Panel to Remove Software

For this exercise you must have an application that you are willing to remove from your system. You could use the program that you just installed in the preceding exercise. I will be using Microsoft's Office 97. I chose this because, rather than removing the entire Office suite, it brings up the setup program used when installing Microsoft Office. This lets me reinstall, add, or remove software, or remove all components from the system.

1. If you are not in the Control Panel Add/Remove programs, click the Start menu, select Settings, and then Control Panel. From there, select Add/Remove Programs.

2. On the Install/Uninstall tab, select the program that you want to remove.

3. Click the Add/Remove button

What you see next depends on the application. Some programs begin uninstalling themselves immediately, and others bring up the setup program you used when you first installed the program. When I chose Office 97 to remove, it brought up the setup program and I chose Add/Remove software. The next screen is the Options list of available components of the Office suite. I choose to uninstall Outlook, so I deselect it and select Continue. The setup program now begins removing Outlook. Mastering uninstalling and adding or removing components is important with Microsoft products, because they have so many. You may find that you don't need all the components you got when you installed the program, and want to remove them. This can easily be done in this utility.

Install/Uninstall Tab

The Install/Uninstall tab (shown in Figure 3-18) is one of the many ways you can install software. Just because you install software by this method does not mean that Windows automatically can remove it. This is reserved for 32-bit applications that were mentioned in the previous section. I usually don't use this method for installing applications. Opening My Computer and selecting the drive that contains the setup information is easier. But what is nice about installing applications via this Install/Uninstall tab is that it searches the floppy drive and CD-ROM drive for the setup program.

FIGURE 3-18

You can install software with the Install/Uninstall tab, but it's not always the best way

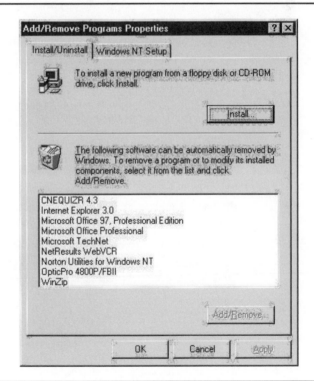

Using the Add/Remove Program Control Panel to Install Software

This exercise demonstrates the installation of an application via the Add/Remove Programs feature. This means you do not have to search through Explorer to find the correct executable, because NT will search for the setup program for you. Even if you don't install applications this way, it is always helpful to know all of the different methods of installing applications.

1. Open the Add/Remove Programs icon in the Control Panel.

2. Click the Install button.

3. Insert the floppy disk or CD-ROM containing the program you want to install.

4. NT will search the floppy and the CD-ROM for the executable to start the program.

5. If NT is unable to locate the setup program, it prompts you to enter the path to the file. You also can select the Browse button to find the file yourself.

6. Once NT finds the correct setup program, click Finish to begin the installation of the program.

With the advent of AutoPlay, it is becoming much easier to install software. All you have to do in some cases is insert the CD-ROM, and click one or two buttons, and the application is installed. Installing a program may not be the hard part, because most programs have good default choices that make installation easier. However, you should learn all of the options available with the software to make an intelligent decision on whether to deviate from those default options. A case in point is the installation of Windows NT Workstation. Should you use the typical or the custom setup? You should know the differences and try them both. There may come a time when you need to install NT Workstation with special features not available in the typical setup.

Windows NT Setup Tab

The Windows NT Setup tab (see Figure 3-19) allows you to go back and add or remove Windows components. This is an easy way to remove a component from Windows that is no longer needed. Or you might use this feature if you

Windows NT Setup tab offers an easy way to remove components that are no longer needed

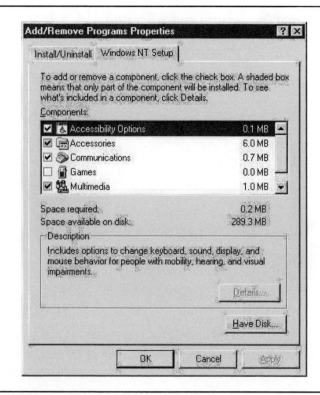

forgot to install the correct components when NT initially was installed. You have to provide the Windows NT CD-ROM to install applications not previously installed. It is a wise investment to have the source files on the hard disk, or out on a network share where you do not have to provide the CD-ROM every time something is added to NT. This is especially important in large companies.

Table 3-1 gives you a quick summary of the components that are available to add or remove.

SCSI Adapters Icon

The most important fact to remember about the SCSI Adapters icon in the Control Panel is that, in addition to SCSI adapter information, it contains

TABLE 3-1

Components
Check Boxes

Tab	Components
Accessibility Options	no additional components
Accessories	Calculator, Character Map, Clipboard Viewer, Clock, Desktop Wallpaper, Document Templates, Imaging, Mouse Pointers, Object Packages, Paint, Quick View, Screen Savers, WordPad
Communications	Chat, HyperTerminal, Phone Dialer
Games	FreeCell, Minesweeper, Pinball, Solitaire
Multimedia	CD Player, Jungle Sound Scheme, Media Player, Musica Sound Scheme, Robotz Sound Scheme, Sample Sounds, Sound Recorder, Utopia Sound Scheme, Volume Control
Windows Messaging	Internet Mail, Microsoft Mail, Windows Messaging

information about IDE devices. This sounds strange, but it's true. If you have IDE devices in your system you can view them through this dialog box, but you are limited in what you can configure. SCSI devices, on the other hand, enable you to do much more.

Most home users other than power users will not use SCSI devices, since they cost more and are more difficult to configure. However, SCSI devices are popular in the business environment for their performance and expandability. An MCSE often comes across SCSI devices and is responsible for supporting them, so you must learn to install and configure them. Here are a few of the concerns about SCSI installation and configuration that you should be aware of:

- SCSI devices needed to be terminated correctly. This includes both ends of the bus.

- SCSI devices need to have proper device ID numbers assigned. Since a SCSI adapter can support seven devices, it becomes more difficult to assign device ID numbers properly.

- There are more compatibility concerns with NT than with IDE devices. Find out if your SCSI device is on the hardware compatibility list before you install the device.

■ If your boot device is a SCSI device, it has to be configured before Windows NT can boot properly.

SCSI devices provide many advantages once they are properly configured. Here are a few of the advantages of SCSI:

■ Faster than IDE.

■ Can have up to seven devices per adapter. IDE can have four.

■ Has a controller onboard to do some of the processing.

■ Allows use of more external devices such as scanners, CD-ROMs, and optical drives.

Devices Tab

The Devices tab is where you see the SCSI and IDE devices in your system. Notice how the devices are arranged according to the device to which they are connected. You can see that the Dual-Channel PCI IDE Controller in Figure 3-20 has a Quantum Fireball and a Conner hard disk as master and slave on the primary IDE controller. There is also a Matshita CD-ROM as the master of the secondary IDE controller. SCSI devices are no different. They are shown just like the IDE devices, with the adapter and the devices that are connected to the adapter. This is a good graphical representation of how the devices are configured in your system. You can view the properties of each of the devices by highlighting the device and selecting the Properties button. The Devices window will show you the settings the device is using, such as target ID, SCSI port, and bus number. You can also view the resources for devices by selecting the Resource tab. This will show you resources such as Input/Output Range, and Interrupt Request. Actually, in my current setup nothing in the Devices tab of the SCSI Adapters utility is configurable. You may have different devices that can be configured. I have two IDE controllers, a SCSI controller, a SCSI hard disk, and an IDE CD-ROM drive.

Drivers Tab

The Drivers tab of the SCSI Adapters dialog box is where you add and remove device drivers. Choose this tab when you want to make upgrades, since you

FIGURE 3-20

SCSI Adapters dialog box
displaying IDE devices and
their interrelationships

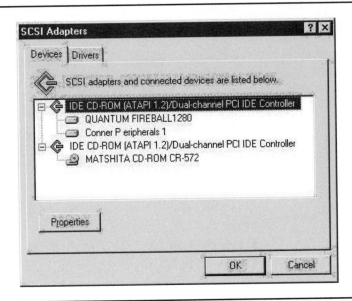

need to remove the old driver (in the sense that you remove its ability to communicate with a device) and add a new one. If you are removing an existing driver to add a new device, you must also physically remove the old device from your system. We use the Drivers tab to add and remove drivers in the exercises that follow.

If you are having difficulty configuring SCSI devices, Microsoft has provided a SCSI utility with Windows NT called the SCSI Investigator. It only supports the two major SCSI adapter manufacturers Adaptec and Buslogic, but these two manufacturers comprise the majority of the SCSI adapter market. SCSI Investigator lets you configure your devices properly to avoid conflicts and termination problems. The next exercise covers the creating of the SCSI tool disk. For the exercise, you must have a DOS-based computer to make the boot disk. If you do not have any SCSI adapters in your system, you can still make the SCSI tool disk, but it will be of no use to you.

Creating the SCSI Tool Disk

1. Boot to DOS. If your NT Workstation does not have DOS installed, use a computer that does.

2. Use the SYS C: A: command to transfer the system files from your C: drive to your A: drive to make the disk bootable.

3. Insert the Windows NT Workstation CD-ROM. (Please note that your CD-ROM drivers have to be loaded to access the CD-ROM.)

4. Insert a 1.44 floppy disk into the drive.

5. Change to the drive that your CD-ROM is located on.

6. Change to the SCSI tool directory by typing: **CD \SUPPORT\SCSITOOL**

7. Type **MAKEDISK** to begin.

For the next exercise we use the SCSI Investigator to verify the correct settings for our installed SCSI adapters. You are limited in what you can configure with the SCSI Investigator, but it still is a great tool to have around for viewing SCSI device settings.

EXERCISE 3-13

Using the SCSI Tool to View SCSI Device Settings

1. Reboot the computer that has the SCSI devices installed that you would like to verify or configure.

2. Select your choice from the following startup menu:

   A. Adaptec Controllers

   B. Buslogic controllers

   C. None of the above

   D. (Default) All above controllers

3. The SCSI Investigator begins loading drivers required for operation.

4. If prompted to continue, select Yes and wait as the SCSI investigator detects your SCSI devices.

5. It should find the SCSI adapters, and display the settings.

6. Click SCSI Devices to view all of the devices currently connected to the SCSI adapter.

7. Verify that the settings are correct and that all of your devices are detected.

8. You can print the settings for your records if you like, or you can view and print the SCSI.TXT file that was created.

Installing and configuring a SCSI adapter can be very challenging. With more experience, you become more comfortable with the procedures. If you learn how to use the SCSI Investigator, you can use it when you are configuring SCSI devices. Keep a copy of this disk with you, or add it to your computer toolkit for troubleshooting devices. You may feel you know the settings of your SCSI devices inside and out, but what happens when you try to troubleshoot someone else's? You need to be aware of what the current configuration is in order to resolve conflicts.

The next exercise will involve installing a SCSI adapter. If you do not have a SCSI adapter to install, try to visualize the steps as we go.

EXERCISE 3-14

Installing a SCSI Adapter

1. Manually configure the SCSI adapter if it is required. In order to find an available address and IRQ assignment, you could use NT diagnostics. You have to configure the termination for the device you are installing in relation to the other SCSI devices in your system.

2. Physically install the device.

3. While your computer boots up, access the software configuration program. This is usually done by a certain keystroke, such as CTRL-A.

4. Configure the device based on the available settings you gathered from NT diagnostics.

5. Reboot again, this time to Windows NT.

6. Select the SCSI Adapters icon from the Control Panel.

7. Select the Drivers tab.

8. Click Add.

9. Select the driver for the device you just installed. If a driver is not provided, click the Have Disk button and insert the vendor-provided disk with the device driver.

10. Enter the path for the Windows NT CD-ROM if prompted.

11. Restart your computer for the changes to take effect.

One thing to keep in mind is that most SCSI problems occur from improper termination. You have to terminate the last device correctly. Luckily, devices are becoming autoterminating, which removes the hassle of determining which device should be terminated. The best way to get used to configuring SCSI devices is just to get a few and try different combinations of settings and configurations. You don't want to be in the MCSE field without a grasp of SCSI devices, because configuring them requires experience and a thorough understanding.

For the next exercise, we will be removing a SCSI adapter. This could be the SCSI adapter that you just installed. Once again, if you don't have a SCSI adapter in your system, try to visualize these steps.

EXERCISE 3-15

Removing a SCSI Adapter

1. Click the SCSI Adapters icon in the Control Panel.
2. Click the Driver tab.
3. Select the driver that you wish to remove.
4. Click Remove.
5. If you are prompted to confirm your intentions, select Yes.
6. Click Close.
7. Shut down the system, remove the device, and restart your system for the changes to take effect.

Although NT does a great job of detecting your CD-ROM drive at installation, there comes a time when you have to replace your obsolete drive and add a new one. Unfortunately Windows NT is not plug and play as of yet, so you have to install and configure the CD-ROM yourself. This is not very difficult. You actually can go through the installation of the CD-ROM in the next exercise with us, or you can pretend that you have installed the drive already, and are now configuring the driver.

EXERCISE 3-16

Installing a CD-ROM Drive

1. Enter the SCSI Adapters applet in the Control Panel.
2. Click the tab for Drivers.
   I currently have an IDE CD-ROM ATAPI (1.2)/Dual-channel PCI IDE Controller that I am removing and reinstalling for this exercise.
3. Choose the Add button to add a driver.

4. Select your driver from the list. If it is not on the list, select the Have Disk button and provide a disk supplied by the manufacturer for your device.

I received a message informing me that the drivers are currently installed on the system, and asking if I would like to use them rather than copying them from disk. You probably do not receive this message and have to reboot the system for the changes to take effect.

This next exercise involves removing a CD-ROM drive—more specifically, a driver that controls the device. Use this option if you are upgrading your CD-ROM and removing the older drive from your system.

EXERCISE 3-17

Removing a CD-ROM Drive

1. Open the SCSI Adapters icon from the Control Panel.
2. Click the Drivers tab.
3. Highlight the driver you would like to remove.
4. Click the Remove button.

You have now removed the driver from your system. You now can shut off the system and physically remove the device, if you are actually preparing to upgrade the CD-ROM.

Server Icon

The Server icon in the Control Panel fooled me at first, because I thought it was only for Windows NT Server. This is not the case. If you are making shares accessible to other users, your computer is acting like a server. This applet gives you a summary of which shares are available to users, and which users are currently accessing shares. You have the resources that others are accessing. You would like to know who is accessing your system, how many files they have open, and how long they have been on. This applet is for just that purpose. The Usage Summary in the first dialog box, shown in Figure

3-21, has the following dynamic (updated continually based on usage) resource settings:

- **Sessions**   The number of remote users currently accessing the computer.

- **File Locks**   The number of file locks by users.

- **Open Files**   The number of open files by the users.

- **Open Named Pipes**   A named pipe allows one process to communicate with another remote or local process. You learn about Named Pipes in later chapters.

Clicking the Shares button displays the shares that you currently have available and number of users connected to each share. You can see how long a user has been using your shared resources. If there are users connected that you do not want, you can highlight and click the disconnect button, or you can disconnect all users. Before disconnecting users, send them a message. If you disconnect when they are in the middle of a download, for example, they will lose data.

FIGURE 3-21

The Server applet, for managing your shares and keeping track of current system usage

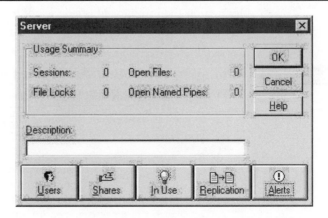

The icon for Replication is used to replicate files or directories that you have in your export directory to other computers. You use this feature if you need to have data that has to be in sync, such as a login script. You also use this to distribute files or folders—anything you put in the export directory is exported to computers that you specify. From the replication window, you select the files or folders you want to replicate, and the computers you want to replicate with. Replication is much more of an issue with Windows NT Server.

The last button that you might find helpful is the Alerts button. This is the list of computers or users you would like to receive administrative alerts when they occur on the system. Alerts can be sent if someone accesses a specific resource, or in the event of problems such as server shutdown. A few prerequisites, such as starting the Alerter and Messenger services, must be fulfilled. The Messenger service has to be installed on the receiving computer.

Sounds Icon

The Sounds icon is for assigning sounds to various system events, such as opening and closing of windows, errors, startup, shutdown, and critical stops. You can modify the default Windows sound scheme, or you can create your own custom sound assignments and save them as schemes. If the sound files provided with NT are not enough for you, there are plenty of useable sounds located on the Internet. This icon is not for installation or configuration of any devices. In the next exercise, we change a sound event.

EXERCISE 3-18

Changing the Sound Associated with a System Event

1. Click the Sounds icon located in the Control Panel.
2. In the list of events, select an event you want to change, or to which you want to add a sound association.
3. If an event has the yellow sound icon to the left of it, click that to preview the sound.
4. Use the scroll down bar to select a sound, or click the Browse button to search the directory tree for more sounds.
5. When you are satisfied with the sounds associated with the events, click the Save As button to save your custom scheme.

Mouse Icon

With the mouse icon, you adjust the parameters of your mouse, including programming the buttons, adjusting speed, and changing drivers. If you have a type of mouse other than the default two-button mouse, you can configure the special features as well. For example, the Microsoft Intellimouse® has a wheel between the two buttons that can be customized. You can adjust the speed of the wheel, the direction of the wheel, and whether to allow the wheel to be used as another mouse button. There are seven tabs in my Mouse icon for configuring the device.

Buttons Tab

The Buttons tab can be used for configuring the primary and secondary buttons on the mouse. (They are referred to as primary and secondary for the sake of left-handed mouse users. Right-click is a secondary mouse click for right-handed users, but a primary mouse click for left-handed users. Primary/secondary terms can avoid confusion.) If you have a three-button mouse, this tab is where you program the third button. Most three-button mouse users program the third button to be a double-click.

The double-click speed area of the Buttons tab adjusts the rate to suit your needs. Some users double-click very fast, while others take more time in between clicks. Use the test to select the rate comfortable to you.

Pointers Tab

The Pointers tab is most often used to configure the mouse pointer with animated cursors. The Microsoft Plus! Pack for Windows 95 introduced desktop themes that used different cursors, in addition to desktop wallpaper and custom icons. NT provides some additional cursors and pointers, and you also can get plenty of animated and custom cursors on the Internet. In the next exercise, we select a new pointer scheme from the available library supplied by NT.

EXERCISE 3-19

Selecting a New Pointer Scheme

1. From the Start menu, select Control Panel.

2. Select the Mouse icon

3. Select the Pointers tab.

4. Select the drop-down menu box for Schemes and select a scheme you wish to use. If there are no schemes present here, you did not install them. You need to go to the Add/Remove Programs icon and install the mouse pointers which are located under Accessories.

5. If you choose not to use the whole scheme, you can double-click the pointer that you wish to change, or select the Browse button and a browse window will appear. Here is where you can select additional individual pointers, rather than using a new scheme. If you cannot decide which pointers to use, and would just like to keep the original default scheme, select the Use Default button, or select None from the scheme pull-down box.

Motion Tab

The Motion tab includes the Pointer Speed and Snap To default options. The pointer speed adjusts the speed of your mouse pointer, which can be thought of as the amount of distance covered by the mouse. If you adjust the slider bar to Slower, it takes more physical movement by the user to move the mouse from one side of the screen to the other. Faster, on the other hand, can enable the mouse to cross the entire screen with just an inch or two of movement on the mouse pad.

The Snap To default enables the mouse to jump to the default button in any dialog box—usually OK or Apply. This can save a user time navigating through various windows, but also can be annoying. The mouse jumps all over the screen as each dialog box is opened, making it difficult to keep track of the mouse cursor.

General Tab

The General tab is where you install a new driver for the mouse, as the next exercise demonstrates.

EXERCISE 3-20

Changing the Mouse Driver

This exercise covers the changing of a mouse driver. The driver has to be changed when a new mouse is added to the system. You should practice accessing this icon and changing the mouse driver without the use of a mouse. If the changing of the mouse driver is not successful, you have to return to this window to change the driver again, this time without the use of the mouse. You might be surprised how lost you are without the mouse.

1. Open the Mouse icon from the Control Panel.

2. Select the General tab.

3. The Select Device window will appear. If the mouse driver you would like to install does not appear, select Show All Devices.

4. You see a screen with available manufacturers and models for which NT provides driver support. Select the driver for the mouse you are installing.

5. If the driver for the mouse you are installing is not present, click the Have Disk button. Insert the disk supplied by the manufacturer into the drive, or select the Browse button to select an alternate source, such as a network path.

6. You have to reboot your computer for the changes to take effect.

Most mice are either serial mice, or PS/2 mice. PS/2 mice are becoming more popular because they do not take a communications (serial) port, and therefore will not likely conflict with a modem, or another communications device. PS/2 mice are built into most leading brand systems purchased today.

Serial mice are attached to the computer via a serial port, so we should understand what happens with serial ports and Windows NT during system startup. When NT is booting, NTDETECT searches for devices on the serial port, such as a mouse. If it does not find a device, NT disables the port. You might not want this to happen. If the port is disabled, it doesn't appear in the Ports icon in the Control Panel. In the next exercise, we disable the serial mouse detection using the BOOT.INI file.

EXERCISE 3-21

Disabling **NTDETECT** Serial Mouse Automatic Detection

1. Find the BOOT.INI file in the root directory of your system partition, and remove the Hidden, System, and Read-only attributes. If it is hidden you have to change the View options in Explorer to Display All Files. Back up the BOOT.INI, because this file is critical.

2. Open the BOOT.INI file with any text editor.

3. Add the /NoSerialMice switch to the end of the entry in the [operating systems] for the operating system you don't want to use the automatic detection. The switch is not case sensitive.

Here is an example of a BOOT.INI with the switch added:

```
[boot loader]
timeout=5
default=multi(0)disk(0)rdisk(0)partition(1)\WINNT
[operating systems]
multi(0)disk(0)rdisk(0)partition(1)\WINNT="Windows NT
Server Version 4.00" /NoSerialMice
multi(0)disk(0)rdisk(0)partition(1)\WINNT="Windows NT
Server Version 4.00 [VGA mode]" /basevideo /sos
/NoSerialMice
```

There are a few variations on the /NoSerialMice switch that might be useful to you. The switch that we have seen in the above example disables detection on all serial ports on the system. Here are the other two variations:

```
/NoSerialMice:COMx Disables the detection of serial mice
on a COM port specified by the x.
/NoSerialMice:COMx,y,z Disables the detection of serial
mice on more than one COM port that you specify.
```

The BOOT.INI in the preceding example uses what is known as the ARC naming convention. This is used to designate the path to the installation of Windows NT. Understanding the ARC naming convention is important for troubleshooting, and for the NT Workstation exam. The very first question on *my* exam was a complex ARC naming question. Be prepared!

Keyboard Icon

The Keyboard icon is where you adjust parameters such as speed, and where you add various input locales and keyboard mappings. The keyboard is one of the devices that you can customize heavily according to your preferences. This icon also lets you change the driver for the keyboard, as we see in the next exercise.

Changing the Keyboard Driver

1. Open the Keyboard icon in the Control Panel.

2. Select the General tab.

3. Click the Change button.

4. A dialog box of Compatible Keyboard Driver will be displayed.

5. If the driver you would like to add is not present, select the Show All Devices radio button.

6. Select the driver for the keyboard model you want to add. If the driver you want to add is not present, choose the Have Disk button. This prompts you to insert the vendor-provided driver disk.

7. You might have to reboot the computer for the changes to take effect.

Speed Tab

The Speed tab is used for adjusting the keyboard's response. The first option is the Character Repeat Delay. This slider bar adjusts the time the computer waits while you are holding a key down *before* it begins to repeat the character. A mid-range setting should be fine for most users.

After this delay, but while you still hold the key down, the repeat rate takes effect. The computer begins repeating the character at a rate based on your adjustment of the slider bar. The slower the setting, the slower the characters will continue to appear. This setting is most apparent when you are using the backspace key to erase words and lines. If you set the speed too fast, you will backspace too far. If the setting is too slow, erasing a sentence or two would be time-wasting.

Input Locales Tab

The Input Locales tab is where you can set up keyboard layouts for different languages. There are about 70 input locales, including Spanish, German, English, and French. These keyboard layouts include language-specific characters not available on most users' standard keyboards. You can alternate between input locales by setting a hot key. You can see which input locale you are in by looking at the abbreviation in the taskbar. On my taskbar, there is EN for English, and ES for Spanish. I admit to having never used this feature until a co-worker was writing a letter in Spanish, and wanted to know where the upside-down question mark (¿) could be found. I had to switch input locales to enable the keyboard to remap in the desired language. Since there was no visible key on the keyboard for the ¿ key, I had to press every key in the new input locale until I typed the key that this character was mapped to, in this case the + key.

General Tab

The General tab lets you change the keyboard driver, just as it did with the mouse. You won't be in this area often. It is nice to know, however, that NT Workstation supports the extended 101/102-key enhanced keyboards, with the Start Menu key added.

FROM THE CLASSROOM

Applets Are Good For You

There are two important points that we encourage students to remember when they're using the control panel to configure NT. First, all of the applets in the control panel get information from, and put changes directly into, the Registry. This means that you don't have to use the Registry editing tool to discover settings or change information. Editing the Registry directly can be very hazardous. Even though we stress this many times during a class, we invariably find several students using the editing tools instead of the applets in the control panel.

The second point is that some of the changes you make "stay with the computer" and some "stay with the user." To avoid confusion and frustration, remember which settings are machine-level, and which are user-level. For example, with the Mouse applet, you can set pointer speed and double-click sensitivity—changes that stay with the user and are stored in the user profile. But mouse type and driver settings are computer-specific, and are the same for every user.

Consider the Display applet as another example. Desktop settings, such as color schemes and wallpaper settings, are configurable on a per-user basis. However, the resolution is a computer setting. We find that when we get support calls from former students, about 25% of them have questions relating to settings controlled by the Display applet.

When preparing for your NT certification test, you might want to review the tabs in the Display applet with an eye toward which settings are user-specific and which are computer-based.

—*By Shane Clawson, MCT, MCSE*

CERTIFICATION OBJECTIVE 3.03

Windows NT Registry

While you are making adjustments through the various areas of the Control Panel, a central repository called the Registry is keeping track. The Registry contains your system's hardware and software configuration. Previous versions of Windows NT used the Registry to store information, as does Windows 95. Before that, hardware and software settings were maintained in .INI files. Windows had its own major .INI files such as SYSTEM.INI and WIN.INI. The Registry is far more efficient than the older text-based .INI files. Sure, there are ASCII values in the Registry, but it also can support binary entries. The Registry is hierarchical, as Figure 3-22 illustrates. There are subkeys found under keys, which was not possible with the flat, non-hierarchical .INI files. What's more, the Registry is a consolidation of configuration information, whereas .INI files could be scattered all over the disk.

Great as the Registry is, it is much easier and safer to make adjustments to your system using the various applets in the Control Panel than it is to modify them directly in the Registry. You will see in a moment just how cryptic the Registry can be. Users of Windows 95 and previous versions of Windows NT have a grasp of the role the Registry plays in configuring hardware and software, but a new user could be somewhat overwhelmed. It took me months to grow confident enough to maneuver in the Registry and make changes. Of course, I never modified system settings that I was not familiar with. (Well, almost never.) After spending some time in the Registry, you will find yourself memorizing the paths to commonly configured values.

You also can use the Registry to view and modify a remote user's Registry settings. This is a handy feature if you don't want to get out of your chair, or you are the only Registry expert around. It's also a dangerous feature, because I can access your computer's Registry and modify a few settings and you won't be able to start your system. Of course, you could do the same to me unless I don't enable the Server service on my computer. When you are using REGEDT32 to view the Registry of a remote computer, you only see the HKEY_LOCAL_MACHINE and HKEY_USERS keys. This is for safety reasons. Those two keys will be more than enough for modifying. If you need to modify any other keys that are not supported in remote Registry accessing, you have to go directly to the machine and modify the Registry locally, or call the other user and have him make the adjustments for you.

Always use caution when you are editing the Registry. It is so dangerous that Microsoft issues a warning before each mention of the various parameters that are adjustable in the Registry. Please note that once you have made a change in the Registry, it is final. However, if you remember the original value you can always reenter it. To reduce the amount of accidental modifications to the Registry, you can open it in read-only mode. This is the safer method if you are just curious and won't be making any adjustments while you are there. I know I keep saying that the Registry can be disastrous, but it's nothing a LastKnownGood can't fix. You learn more about the LastKnownGood later in the chapter. Along with the LastKnownGood, there is an option to back up the Registry from NT backup. This should be done prior to modifying Registry contents to ensure that you are fully capable of returning to your original values, in case a modification cripples the system. Unfortunately, the NT backup only can save the Registry to tape, not to another directory or a floppy disk, which hampers efforts for a smooth restore, should something go wrong. Backing up to floppy disk would be out of the question anyway, as most Registries soon grow larger than the capacity of a floppy.

In Figure 3-22 you can see two of the three components of a value entry. For example, Ignore All Caps is the name, and the value is 0x00000001 (1). We cannot see the data type (REG_DWORD).

FIGURE 3-22

FIGURE 3-22

The Windows NT Registry is a hierarchical record of all the configurations on a system

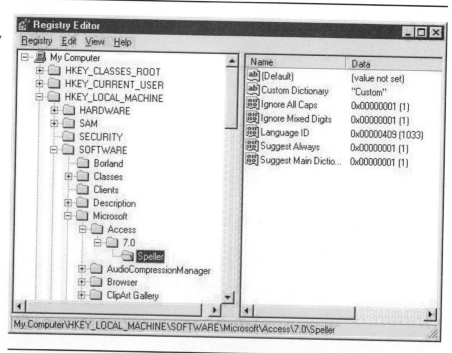

Table 3-2 gives a quick reference for each of the five main keys found in the Registry.

TABLE 3-2

Registry Folders

Key Name	Description
HKEY_LOCAL_MACHINE	Contains information about the hardware and operating system. The most common key for making modifications.
HKEY_CLASSES_ROOT	Contains file associations and Object Linking and Embedding information (OLE).
HKEY_CURRENT_CONFIG	Contains configuration data for the current hardware profile.
HKEY_CURRENT_USER	Contains the user profile for the user that is currently logged on.
HKEY_USERS	Contains all loaded user profiles, including the current user.

exam
ⓦatch

The exam doesn't ask complex Registry questions. Prepare for a question or two on what type of information is stored under a major Registry key.

EXERCISE 3-23

Creating a Start Menu Selection for the Registry Editor

If you use the Registry editor a lot, it would be beneficial to make a selection for the editor on your Start menu. This next exercise does just that. Also, note that any program can be substituted in the following exercise if you want to place a selection on the Start menu. We will discuss two ways to do this.

1. Open the Start menu, and select Settings.

2. Select Taskbar.

3. Select the tab for Start Menu Programs.

4. Click the Add button.

5. Click the Browse button to find the Registry Editor.

6. Select the Winnt directory.

7. REGEDIT will be in this directory. However, if you would like to make a Start Menu selection for REGEDT32 instead, change to the System32 directory.

8. Select Open after you have made your choice. The command line should now show the path to the Registry Editor.

9. Click Next.

10. At this point you choose which folder to place the shortcut in. We're placing it in the Start Menu folder.

11. Click Next.

12. Change the name of the shortcut if you desire, or accept the default.

13. The shortcut now is placed in the Start menu. Click Start to verify.

The other way to place a shortcut on the Start menu is as follows:

1. Open up Explorer by right-clicking the Start menu and selecting Explore.

2. Open the Winnt folder and find the icon for REGEDIT, or you can open the Winnt\System32 folder and find the icon for REGEDT32.

3. When you see the icon for the Registry Editor, right-click and drag the icon to the Start menu. Drop the icon on the Start menu.

4. The program now is a shortcut on the Start menu.

EXERCISE 3-24

Find Occurrences of a Word in the Registry

You can search for keys and values rather than manually navigating the Registry by opening keys. Remember that REGEDIT lets you search for values as well as keys, and REGEDT32 lets you search for keys. The next exercise illustrates the point of searching for keys and values in the Registry using REGEDIT.

1. Open the Start menu and click Run.

2. Type REGEDIT in the run box and click OK.

3. Click Edit, then select Find. Or you can accomplish the same thing by using CTRL-F.

4. In the space provided, enter the word **Canada**.

5. After searching the Registry, REGEDIT comes up with the first few occurrences. Some of the occurrences found are on the right side of the screen. These are the values. Some occurrences are on the left pane of the screen. These are keys that contain the word. REGEDT32 would not be able to find the occurrences in the right pane of the screen.

HKEY_LOCAL_MACHINE

The main key in the Registry is HKEY_LOCAL_MACHINE. Figure 3-23 shows the hierarchy of the main key. Here is a summary of the five keys found under this area.

The HKEY_LOCAL_MACHINE\Hardware key contains information about the components installed in the system and their associated configuration settings. This is an important key to know about when you are configuring and adjusting the Registry contents. It contains mostly binary information, so you're not likely to tamper with the settings. This key is important to your system because it contains information about the hardware components that were collected during startup. Each time the system stops, the settings under this key are lost. They are computed when the system restarts.

The HKEY_LOCAL_MACHINE\SAM key is for the security accounts of users and groups. SAM stands for the Security Account Manager. This is another area where you should not attempt to adjust the settings directly. As with the Hardware key mentioned above, it is in binary format, which is a deterrent to curious users. These security settings can be adjusted from User Manager, which is much easier to configure, and less destructive.

The HKEY_LOCAL_MACHINE\Security key houses the security for the computer, such as group memberships, user rights, and password settings. There is also a subkey under the Security key that maps to the SAM key, so settings in one key automatically appear in the other. Not only is the information here in binary format, it is grayed out to avoid tampering. That is how important this Registry subkey is to system security. The settings in this key can be adjusted from the User Manager administrative tool.

The HKEY_LOCAL_MACHINE\System key works with the Hardware key to maintain startup information, but unlike the Hardware key, which computes its settings at startup, the settings under the System key are stored for future use. This key has a few subkeys that are very important to proper system startup:

- The ControlSet000-ControlSet003 subkeys contain information used to start the machine correctly. There is more than one set for the purpose of fault tolerance. A backup copy is made of the ControlSet.

- The Hardware Profiles subkey holds the profile information for the different hardware profiles you created in the System icon of the Control Panel. We learned about hardware profiles earlier in the chapter.

- The Select key is crucial to maintaining the correct control set. The first value in the Select key is Current. This is the control set that is currently being used by the system. The Current value of 0x1 corresponds to the ControlSet001 in the left frame. The second value is Default. This value indicates which control set the system uses during boot when you have not manually overridden the value yourself. It is possible to override the default by entering a value manually that corresponds with a ControlSet here, or by invoking the LastKnownGood. My default is 0x1, which corresponds to

ControlSet001 in the left frame. The Failed value indicates which
ControlSet was replaced if you invoked the LastKnownGood. It
does not correspond to any ControlSets on the left frame. Finally, the
LastKnownGood value is a good copy of a control set that worked. In this
case, the LastKnownGood corresponds to ControlSet003 in my system.

If you are still interested in learning more about the Registry, there are
several books that show all of the available modifications to the Registry. If you
are a programmer, there are books for Registry programming, showing how to
make your applications create keys and values, or even register themselves.
There are a few neat things you can do with the Registry that have not made
their way to the Control Panel or any other front-end configuration utilities.
Here are a few that I have found useful for personal and business reasons:

■ Don't display the last username that logged into NT. If someone knows
your username, he is halfway to cracking your account. (The password
is the hard part, though!)

■ Log in as the Administrator automatically, without using the
CTRL-ALT-DEL. This is especially good for home users who get tired of
logging in to NT all the time.

FIGURE 3-23

HKEY_LOCAL_MACHINE,
the main key of the
Registry, and its subkeys

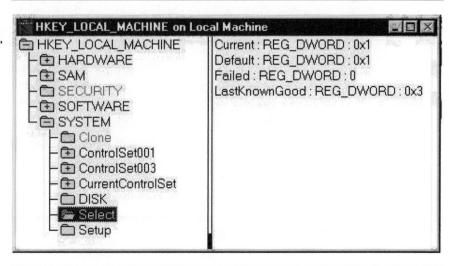

- Modify where NT looks for the source installation files. If you install from a CD-ROM, you can tell it later to look on the network when it needs another file from the CD-ROM, rather than finding the NT Workstation CD-ROM.

- Add custom messages before a person logs on. This can give a warning such as: "Use of this system in an unauthorized manner will not be tolerated."

REGEDIT vs. REGEDT32

The difference between the two Registry editing tools is minimal in terms of modifying keys and values. They differ in some important features, though. REGEDIT can search for specific values in the Registry, whereas REGEDT32 cannot. REGEDT32 can search only for keys. Only REGEDIT has secondary mouse-click support. You can right-click a key or value to bring up a context-sensitive dialog box. If you click a key, you can expand and collapse the keys. You can search, delete, and rename keys this way. You also have the option called Copy Key Name, which copies the key to the clipboard, and lets you paste it to another area. When you right-click a value, you can modify it, delete it, or rename it. If you don't click a value on the right pane of the screen and right-click any empty area instead, you have the option of creating a new value. These are some handy features for the Registry expert.

REGEDT32 has the advantage of being capable of supporting the security provided with the Registry that REGEDIT cannot. REGEDIT is the version of the Registry editor for Windows 95, which does not support security information as Windows NT does. With REGEDT32 you actually can assign permissions to Registry keys, just as you would for any folder or file in Explorer. You also can audit Registry keys, just as you would audit any other attempt to access resources, either as successful attempts or unsuccessful attempts. There are many events you can audit. However, I don't think this feature will prove all that useful. (But if Junior ever makes a successful attempt to enumerate the HKEY_CLASSES_ROOT\Esconfig.Binding.1\CLSID subkey, he's busted!)

The biggest visual difference between the two editing tools is the way the keys are positioned in the window. See in Figure 3-24 how in REGEDIT the keys are all contained within one window. They appear as subdirectories under

FIGURE 3-24

The REGEDIT utility
displays all the keys in
one window

the My Computer icon. REGEDIT must be familiar to those users who have
migrated from Windows 95. If you used REGEDIT in Windows 95, the
REGEDIT provided with Windows NT presents no problem.

In REGEDT32, shown in Figure 3-25, the keys appear as separate windows
of information, or *hives*. This is the older style and is not as easy to use. Notice

FIGURE 3-25

The REGEDT32 utility
displays the keys in
separate windows

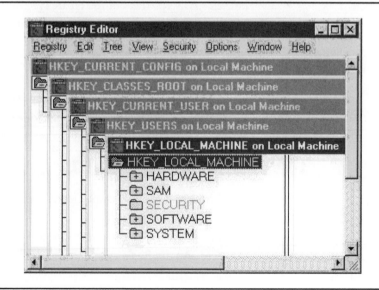

the Security pull-down menu. This is where you configure the permissions on the various keys.

Whichever Registry editing tool you use, you should become very familiar with the Registry. Being able to modify Registry parameters can set you apart from other Administrators. If you can customize environments, and tune, monitor, and troubleshoot Windows NT problems via the Registry, you will be highly regarded. This is a wonderful feature that will be around for a long time, so you might as well begin mastering it now. But remember, you won't usually make your modifications through the Registry! Windows NT provides many alternatives to Registry editing to make your life easier. Study them well and use them.

CERTIFICATION SUMMARY

In this chapter, we have done a thorough review of the many facets of configuring Windows NT Workstation 4.0. Configuring can be done at two levels, system settings and user settings, and in two places, the Control Panel and the Registry. The Control Panel is the better place from which to configure your system, because it is safe and easy to make modifications there.

The Registry keeps track of the entire system's configuration and displays all settings in hierarchical form. It provides an overview of the entire system. You should get to know your way around the Registry, but its cryptic elements, such as expressing a configuration as a numerical value, make it a dangerous place for adjusting configurations.

Always keep a hardcopy record of your system configuration. This saves future troubleshooters or administrators a lot of time, effort, and guesswork.

TWO-MINUTE DRILL

- ❏ The Control Panel is the "front end" to the Registry, where all NT configuration occurs.
- ❏ NT uses environment variables for information not stored in .INI files and the Registry.

❑ System settings affect every user in the system, whereas user settings only affect a specific user. The applets in the Control Panel can configure user or system settings or both. System setting will require administrative rights to configure.

❑ UPS is a device connected through the serial port that keeps power running to a system in the event of an emergency, such as a blackout. UPS can keep a computer running for several minutes while you shut it down correctly.

❑ A *user profile* stores user preferences such as screen savers, last documents used, and environmental settings such as program groups and network connections. A *roaming profile* is a user profile that is kept in one location so that any changes you make to the profile will be used on any computer that you log into.

❑ The recommended initial paging file size should be the size of your RAM plus 11 – 12MB, and can be split among different drives for increased performance. *Virtual memory* is the use of swapping pages of memory to the hard disk when you are out of RAM. The paging file can be used to simulate RAM when you run out.

❑ Services can be configured to start as automatic, manual, or disabled, and can also be stopped, started, and paused.

❑ Tape devices are one of the few hardware devices that NT will try to detect.

❑ The SCSI Adapters icon is for adding and removing SCSI devices and adapters as well as for IDE devices.

❑ The Registry is a collection of information about the system hardware, software, system settings, and user settings.

❑ NT provides two files, REGEDT32.EXE and REGEDIT.EXE, to edit items not controlled through the NT user interface.

❑ REGEDIT.EXE can search for keys, values, and data. REGEDT32.EXE can only search for keys, and is the only editor that allows users to change security options.

❑ The main Registry keys are:

❑ HKEY_CLASSES_ROOT

❑ HKEY_CURRENT_USER

- ❑ HKEY_LOCAL_MACHINE
- ❑ HKEY_USERS
- ❑ HKEY_CURRENT_CONFIG
- ❑ The HKEY_LOCAL_MACHINE key contains the most useful information about the local system. The five subkeys found under HKEY_LOCAL_MACHINE are:
- ❑ Hardware
- ❑ SAM
- ❑ Security
- ❑ Software
- ❑ System

SELF TEST

The following questions will help you measure your understanding of the material presented in this chapter. Read all the choices carefully, as there may be more than one correct answer. Choose all correct answers for each question.

1. You want to change the size of the paging file. Where do you go to do this?

   A. The Virtual memory button in the Performance tab of System Properties.

   B. The Performance button of the Virtual Memory tab in System Properties.

   C. The Change button on the Performance tab in System Properties.

   D. The Set button on the Virtual Memory tab in System Properties.

2. What utility lets me search the Registry for the value of "AutoAdminLogon"?

   A. REGEDT32.

   B. REGEDT.

   C. REGEDIT.

   D. You cannot search for values in the Registry.

3. Which file does the Startup/Shutdown tab modify in System Properties?

   A. BOOTUP.INI

   B. BOOT.INI

   C. BOOT.CFG

   D. START.INI

4. What is the recommended paging file size for a computer with 32MB of RAM?

   A. 40MB

   B. 42MB

   C. 44MB

   D. 48MB

5. Where would you place a shortcut so that it appears on all users' desktops?

   A. Winnt\All users\Desktop

   B. Winnt\Profiles\All users\Desktop

   C. Winnt\Profiles\Desktop\All users

   D. Winnt\All users\Profiles\Desktop

6. The paging file is actually a file called _____, and is located in the root directory of the drive you specified in the Virtual Memory dialog box.

7. Which tab of the System Properties dialog box shows how much RAM is installed in a computer?

   A. General

   B. Performance

   C. Memory

   D. Environment

8. (True/False) 17 is a higher priority thread than 23.

9. On the main Services screen, which button do you click to configure a service to start up automatically on bootup?

A. Disabled

B. Manual

C. Startup

D. Automatic

10. The _____ tab of the SCSI adapters dialog box is where you add and remove drivers for the devices.

11. Which is the only valid Registry key?

A. HKEY_CLASS_ROOT

B. HKEY_CLASSES_USER

C. HKEY_CLASSES_ROOT

D. HKEY_CLASS_USER

12. (True/False) The Advanced option of the Ports icon in the Control Panel lets you adjust the baud rate, parity, and flow control.

13. Which option is not available from the UPS Configuration dialog box?

A. Remote UPS Shutdown.

B. Power failure signal.

C. Send Administrative Alert.

D. Execute Command File.

E. Low battery signal at least two minutes before shutdown.

14. Which is not a subkey of HKEY_LOCAL_MACHINE?

A. Software

B. Classes

C. SAM

D. Hardware

15. Which menu would you select to find a key or value in REGEDIT?

A. Tools

B. File

C. Find

D. Edit

16. Which subkey of HKEY_LOCAL_MACHINE holds the CurrentControlSet key?

A. Hardware

B. SAM

C. System

D. Software

17. (True/False) You click the Install/Uninstall tab to remove components of Windows NT.

18. Location, calling cards, and area code are examples of _____ settings.

19. The _____ adapter can be used if you want to configure network settings but do not have an adapter in your system.

20. Where is the SCSI Investigator found on the Windows NT Workstation CD-ROM?

A. TOOLS\SCSI

B. SUPPORT\TOOLS\SCSI

C. SCSITOOL

D. SUPPORT\SCSITOOL

21. From which Control Panel icon do you configure a MIDI adapter?

A. Devices

B. Multimedia

C. Sounds

D. Adapters

22. The entry in the BOOT.INI file to disable serial mouse detection on COM1 is

    _____ .

23. _____ communication uses stop and start bits appended to each byte of information.

24. The _____ tab is where you change the display driver.

25. Which is *not* an available button on the Server Service main dialog box?

    A. Sessions

    B. Alerts

    C. In Use

D. Users

26. What is *not* an option in the Advanced Ports dialog box?

    A. Base I/O

    B. COM port

    C. Flow Control

    D. FIFO enabled

27. UPS stands for _____ .

28. Which portion of the HKEY_LOCAL_MACHINE key is grayed out to avoid tampering?

    A. The SAM key.

    B. The Special key.

    C. The Security key.

    D. None is grayed out.

MICROSOFT CERTIFIED SYSTEMS ENGINEER

4

Managing Users and Groups

CERTIFICATION OBJECTIVES

W indows NT was designed from the start to be used in a business network environment. In such an environment, more than one person may use the same computer. Therefore, a method of logging onto network services needs to be provided, by which users are given an "account" to access the network. Windows NT provides this capability by implementing user accounts and passwords. As an administrator, one of your primary duties will be to manage these user accounts.

A Windows NT-based computer requires all users to have a user account. A user account is required in order to gain local or network access. User accounts are defined by the combination of a unique username and password. In order to gain access, the user must enter the username and then the password after pressing CTRL-ALT-DEL.

In addition to a username and password, Windows NT user accounts typically include other account information, and are subject to system-wide account policies.

Each user account can have personal settings according to the security level or personal preferences of the user. Users can be assigned security permissions to give them access that is appropriate to them. Also, individual users can determine their desktop settings according to their own preferences.

Assigning privileges to each individual user account can be too time-consuming, especially in an environment where there are many user accounts. For this reason, user accounts can be assigned to groups. Groups have network privileges assigned to them as a unit, rather than assigning privileges individually. Since some users have higher levels of privileges on the computer, Windows NT provides a set of default user groups with pre-defined security settings.

CERTIFICATION OBJECTIVE 4.01

Default User Accounts

When Windows NT is installed, two default accounts are created: Administrator and Guest. These two accounts are very useful to you if used correctly. Initially, the account you will use the most is, of course, the Administrator account. The Administrator account allows you to set up the workstation. The Guest account, if used correctly, only allows temporary users to gain access to the workstation.

Administrator

The Administrator account is the account used to manage the workstation. This account has very powerful privileges that give it access to the entire computer. The administrator can: manage security policies; create, modify, or delete user accounts and groups; modify operating system software; create and connect to shared directories; install and connect to printers; format or partition a hard disk; back up and restore files; debug the system; take ownership of files and other objects; and install or update device drivers.

The Administrator account should be used only for administrative tasks. This follows the principle of making sure that users use the lowest level of privileges necessary to do their job. The person with access to the Administrator account should have a secondary account for everyday use. The Administrator account cannot be deleted, but it can be renamed. The Administrator account created when installing Windows NT Workstation is used only to administer the local machine. You cannot use the Administrator account on a workstation to access or administer a domain.

Password-guessing programs written by hackers attempt to gain access to this account, since it is the only account that cannot be locked out due to failed logon attempts. For this reason, you should rename this account after you install Windows NT.

FROM THE CLASSROOM

Passwords: You Can't Be Too Careful

To gain access to an NT machine, you *must* have a user ID and password. There are no tricks or "back doors" that you can use to gain access to an NT machine. Pay attention! NT is not like some other operating systems (Win95, for example) that let you in without a valid account.

FROM THE CLASSROOM

What's more, passwords in NT are case sensitive. This can take some getting used to.

In the classroom, we stress this to the students and we ask them to use a standard password so that they do not get themselves into trouble by "locking" themselves out of the computer. Of course, telling a techie type not to do something because it can cause real trouble is interpreted by some to mean, "Let's find out just how much trouble it can be."

This password issue comes up early because, during installation, you must supply a password for the account administrator. If you get it wrong at that point, after the installation you will have no way to gain access to the computer

to fix the problem. In the classroom, we often tell the students to use a blank password as the initial password for the administrator's account. (Of course, using a blank password is *not* recommended in real-world circumstances.) You probably know where this story is going. We can always count on a couple of students exploring for themselves how much trouble it can be if they use complex passwords. Sure enough, they forget the password and lock themselves out. The only fix is to re-install NT, which we generally have the students do on the Saturday morning make-up session—the one where the instructor sleeps late.

—By Shane Clawson, MCT, MCSE

Guest

The Guest account is used for limited access for remote users or users from other domains. This account is best used for temporary users to whom you do not wish to give a regular user account. Changes made to the desktop settings by a user logged on as Guest are not saved when that user logs off. When Windows NT is installed, this account is disabled by default. The Guest account is a member of the Guests built-in local group.

The Guest account is set up with a blank password. If you decide to enable it, be sure to change the password.

CERTIFICATION OBJECTIVE 4.02

Default Group Accounts

Six local groups come built in to Windows NT, and are common to all NT Workstation machines and to NT Server machines not installed as domain controllers. On an NT Domain Controller, there are three additional built-in groups.

Local Groups

Local groups affect resources only on the workstation. They can have user accounts as members, or, if the computer is a part of a domain, they may also contain global groups. Local groups can be assigned rights and permissions only for resources on the computer containing the directory database in which they are defined. Local groups can be created on any Windows NT computer. Figure 4-1 shows a local group with one user account as a member.

FIGURE 4-1

Local groups can be created on any Windows NT computer

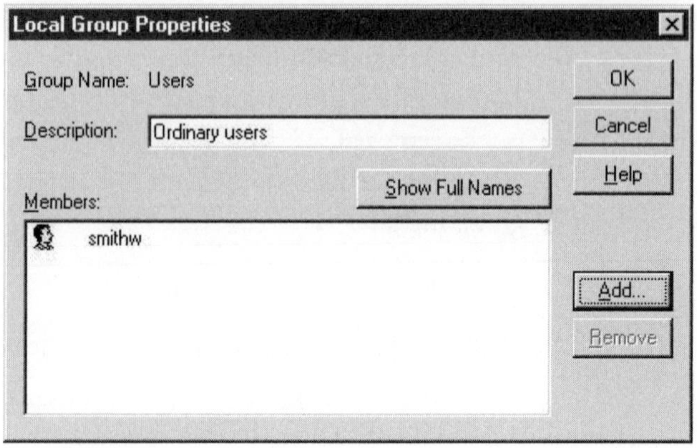

Default Local Groups

Windows NT Workstation comes with several built-in local groups for convenience in adding new users to the workstation. Each group has a default set of rights and capabilities, which makes it easy to categorize user accounts. The administrator may modify these rights and capabilities, or create custom groups after NT has been installed.

These groups are:

- Administrators
- Power Users
- Users
- Guests
- Backup Operators
- Replicator

Administrators

Administrators hold full rights and privileges over all files and other resources on the workstation. The default Administrator account created when you install NT is a member of this group. Also, if the workstation is part of a domain, then any domain administrator is part of this group. The Domain Admins global group is a part of this group in a domain environment, but it can be removed.

Operations that can be performed by members of the Administrators group include:

- Partition or format a hard disk
- Display, initialize, and control the security data
- Perform volume backups and restores
- Access system memory locations for debugging
- Take ownership of files
- Unlock a locked workstation
- Assign user rights

Power Users

Power Users are given the ability to share directories or printers. In addition, they can add Program Manager groups, change the system clock, and create or delete users and groups.

The Power Users group is useful if users are managing their own workstations in a Workgroup environment. This level of access allows them to manage their own workstations, while preventing them from accidentally changing system-critical information.

Users

This is the general classification given to most users on the workstation who are not administrators. Members of the Users group can run applications, print documents on local or shared printers, and manage their own user profiles.

All newly created accounts are automatically added to the Users group. In a domain environment, the Domain Users global group is a member of the Users local group, but it can be removed.

Guests

The Guests group provides low-level access to the workstation. The Guest account is a member of this group. In a network environment, any user may log on to the workstation as a member of the Guests group. Remember that by default, the Guest account is disabled access to system resources through the Guests group must be assigned specifically by the administrator. In a domain environment, the Domain Guests global group is a member of the Guests local group, but it can be removed.

Backup Operators

Backup Operators can use the BACKUP and RESTORE commands to backup and restore all the files on NT Workstation. Any user can back up and restore files to which he has rights, but members of Backup Operators are given full rights to any file on the workstation, as long as they are using the BACKUP and RESTORE commands. This also means that they can bypass read and write protection of files.

Replicator

Replicator is a special group used by the Replicator service. The Replicator service can automatically update files from servers to workstations in a network.

Special Access Types

There is a second set of five groups used by the Windows NT system, which are automatically assigned based on how the user is accessing the system. The administrator cannot assign anyone to these groups, and they do not show up in the User Manager.

The five special groups are:

- **Interactive**   Users that are directly logged onto a workstation.

- **Network**   Users that are connected to the computer from another computer in the network.

- **Everyone**   All users, including Interactive and Network.

- **Creator Owner**   A user who created or became the owner of a file, folder, or print job.

- **System**   Used internally by the operating system.

If you are logged onto your workstation, you are in the Interactive group. If you are connected to another workstation, you are a member of the Network group on that computer. Anyone connected to, or logged onto, any workstation is a member of the Everyone group. If you create or take ownership of a resource, you are a member of the Creator Owner group for that resource.

Global Groups

Global groups are created on domain controllers and are used to assign local permissions to domain users. To do this, global groups can become members of local groups on other Windows NT computers in the domain. In this way, domain users can be given access to local computers in a domain without assigning each domain user separately.

Naming Conventions

An important part of an administrator's job is to come up with a naming convention for naming users, groups, and resources, such as printers. The naming convention should be consistent, and easy to learn and understand. If the naming convention is hard to understand, the users won't use it!

A good naming convention for user accounts is to use the last name of the individual, followed by the first initial of the first name. For instance, the username for Joe Schmoe would be schmoej. If another person has the same first initial—Jane Schmoe—we use her middle initial or the second letter of the first name—in this case schmoeja. This naming convention is commonly used on the Internet for e-mail account names.

Keep naming conventions simple, and make them easy to understand. For instance, if we were mapping to a printer with the network name HP4SI-422, we could quickly determine that this is a Hewlett-Packard Laserjet 4SI located in room 422. If you make the convention simple enough that anyone can figure out what the name of a new user, group, or resource should be without having to ask, it should work quite well.

Group-Based Security

By placing users into groups, the system administrator can escape the tedious job of assigning permissions to individual users. Groups can be assigned rights as a unit, rather than assigning rights to each individual account. You may create your own groups or use the built-in groups that come with Windows. It is not recommended that you modify the default rights of the built-in groups, although you could do so.

To manage users effectively, don't bother trying to assign each one permissions individually. Instead, use the built-in groups to put your users in the appropriate categories. If the built-in groups don't work, you can create your own groups with their own individual permissions. If you decide to do this, it's best to group by department. For instance, sales personnel would be part of the Sales local group, while technicians would be part of the Techies local group. Above all, keep it simple enough that someone else can figure out your system by just looking at it.

In a domain environment, global groups are used to assign local permissions to domain user accounts. User accounts from the domain master account database are added to a global group that is also defined on that database. The local administrator of the workstation can then add the global group to a local group that has access to resources on that workstation. The important rule to remember here is that permissions are assigned to local groups; global groups go into local groups; and domain users go into global groups.

User Manager

User Manager, shown in Figure 4-2, is the administrative tool used for the management of all users and groups on the workstation. This is also the tool used to manage user profiles.

Creating User Accounts

Creating user accounts in Windows NT Workstation is easy. You can use User Manager to create user accounts in one of two ways: creating new accounts, or copying existing accounts.

When you create a user account, you can enter information specific to that account, assign the account to multiple groups, and set the profile information for that user. See Figure 4-3 for an illustration of the New User window. See Table 4-1 and Table 4-2 for an explanation of the fields and check boxes in this window. Remember that each user account name must be unique.

Each user account or group account created is assigned a security ID (SID) by Windows NT. Each SID is unique to that account. The SID allows certain permissions to be given to each user, since the SID is part of an access token that is given to the account whenever the user logs on. This access token is compared to the access control list of an object to determine if the user can access that object. If the user account or group is deleted, its SID is lost, as are its permissions.

FIGURE 4-2

User Manager is the
administrative tool used
for the management of all
users and groups on the
workstation

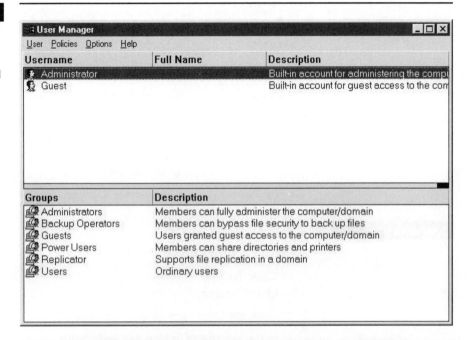

FIGURE 4-3

Creating user accounts at
the New User window

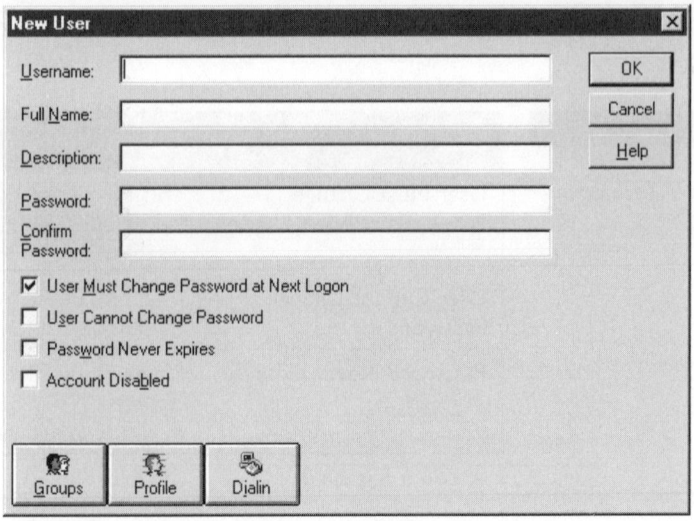

TABLE 4-1	Box Name	Description
New User Field Descriptions	Username	A unique name of up to 20 characters. Not case sensitive. A username cannot include any of the following characters: " \ / [ ] | = ; : , + * ? < >.
	Full Name	The real name of the user.
	Description	A brief description of the account or the user.
	Password	Passwords are case sensitive and cannot be longer than 14 characters. In this window passwords always appear as asterisks (*).
	Confirm Password	Re-enter the password in this field to confirm it.

EXERCISE 4-1

Creating a New User Account

1. Click the Start button and select Programs | Administrative Tools | User Manager.

2. Click the User menu and select New User.

3. In the Username field, enter **jeffersont**

4. In the Full Name field, enter **Thomas Jefferson**.

5. In the Description field, enter **Former President**.

TABLE 4-2	Box	Description
New User Check Boxes	User Must Change Password at Next Logon	This forces the user to change their password the next time they try to log on. This option is disabled once the user changes his password.
	User Cannot Change Password	Keeps the user from changing the password. Useful for accounts shared by several people.
	Password Never Expires	Keeps the password from ever needing to be changed. If this box is checked, any password expirations are ignored.
	Account Disabled	Disables the account so that nobody can log on with it.

6. Leave the Password field blank, and uncheck User Must Change Password at Next Logon.

7. Click OK.

There! You have created a new user account called jeffersont.

Group Memberships

You can add a new user account to any group. Once a user is assigned to a group, that user is given the rights and permissions inherent to membership in that group. Refer to Figure 4-4 as you do the exercise for assigning user accounts to groups.

Assigning User Accounts to Groups

1. Open User Manager.

2. Select the jeffersont account that we created in the preceding exercise.

3. Open the User menu and select Properties.

4. Click Groups.

Assigning group memberships

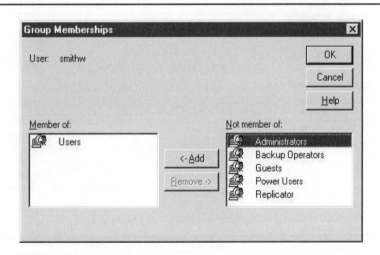

5. From the Not a Member Of list, select Administrators.

6. Click Add.

7. Click OK.

8. Click OK again.

9. Select the Administrators local group.

10. Note the jeffersont account is now a member of the Administrators local group.

Adding and Removing Users from Groups

Users can be added to groups in two ways. One way involves selecting the specific user, and adding the user to groups by selecting the Groups button in the New User dialog box, and then adding groups to the Member Of field.

With the other method, you select an individual group and add users to it, using the Add Users and Groups dialog box.

User Environment Profile

The User Environment Profile (the window shown in Figure 4-5) allows you to control the system environment according to which user is logged on. As an

FIGURE 4-5

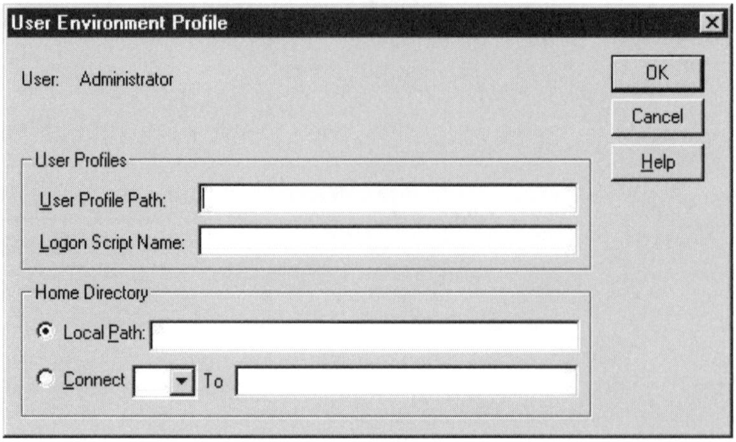

The User Environment Profile window allows the administrator to control the system environment

administrator, you can control the location of the user profile, run a logon script individual to that user, or specify the location of a home directory for the user.

User Profile Path

The user profile is the set of stored characteristics that set the default desktop configuration for each individual user account. The system looks for the user's profile in the path specified in the User Profile Path box. User profiles can be stored on the local computer or they can be located on a server. There are five basic types of user profiles:

- **System Default**   Sets the configuration of the display when no users are logged on. This information is kept in the file DEFAULT at the path \WINNT\SYSTEM32\CONFIG.

- **User Default**   Sets the default configuration for newly created users logging in for the first time. This information is kept in the file USERDEF at the location \WINNT\SYSTEM32\CONFIG.

- **Local User**   Stores the desktop configuration for a user when logged on to a particular computer. Each logged-on user has his own local profile on the computer (except for Guests). This information is kept in a file named after the user.

- **Roaming**   Used in a domain environment, roaming user profiles are created by a domain administrator and stored on a server. This profile can be assigned to one or more users and applies to them at whatever Windows NT-based computer they log on, if they log on using a domain account as opposed to a local account.

- **Mandatory**   Also used in a domain environment, mandatory user profiles are identical to roaming user profiles except that they cannot be changed by the user. Any changes made to a mandatory user profile by a user are lost when that user logs off. Instead of having the extension .DAT like other profiles, mandatory profiles use the extension .MAN.

Logon Script Name

Logon scripts are files that run every time the user logs on to the network. They allow you to assign a set of network connections to a user account each time that user logs on. Logon scripts are useful for logging on from a non-Windows NT operating system (such as DOS), that uses logon scripts to define network connections. Most of the time, logon scripts are not used on individual workstations not connected to a network.

A logon script is usually implemented as a DOS batch file with the extension .BAT. However, executable files with the extension .EXE or .CMD can be used as well.

When a logon script is run, the authenticating computer looks for the script in the NETLOGON directory of the authenticating computer. Usually this directory is found in the \WINNT\SYSTEM32\REPL\IMPORT\SCRIPTS directory. Windows NT domain controllers use directory replication to copy logon scripts from one domain controller to another.

Home Directory

Home directories provide a way for users to store their individual data in a special directory. The home directory can be a directory on the local computer in a workgroup environment, or it can be located on a server computer in a domain environment. You should make sure that a user's home directory has permissions set so that only the appropriate user has access to the files in that directory. Windows NT makes the home directory the default save location for programs that do not specify one in their Save dialog box. When an MS-DOS command prompt is launched, NT defaults to the home directory.

When you create a home directory for a user, use the variable %USERNAME% in the directory path. By doing this, Windows NT substitutes the user's name for the %USERNAME% variable, so you only have to enter the variable once, rather than type the name for each user.

Granting Dial-in Permission

Granting dial-in permission to a user account allows that user to access the workstation using the Remote Access Service (RAS). If you do not grant dial-in permission to the user, he won't be able to connect to the computer using RAS, even if he already has an account on the computer.

One way to implement security for remote connections is to implement the Call Back feature. When Call Back is enabled, if a user attempts to log on remotely, the computer hangs up and calls the appropriate number before that user is logged on.

The number called depends on which option has been selected in Call Back. In Set By Caller, the user calling in to the computer enters a number to be called back when he first connects. The computer calls the user at that number. This can be useful in situations where a long-distance phone call is being made, and you don't want the call to be billed to a remote user's home. Or, you can preset the number called back from the Dial-in Information dialog box (shown in Figure 4-6). This is the most secure way of implementing this feature, since the computer only calls the preset number before the user can log on.

Editing User Accounts

Once a user account has been created, you can come back and change it anytime by using User Manager. User accounts can be copied, deleted or renamed in User Manager.

FIGURE 4-6

At the Dial-in Information window, set the number the computer should call back when a user logs on

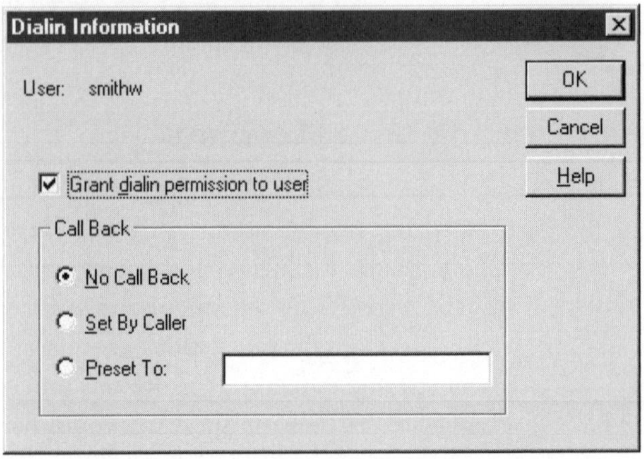

Copying an Existing User Account

Copying a user account can be useful if you need to create a large number of user accounts with the same rights. For instance, let's say that your company hires 50 new people in the Sales department. Instead of creating each account and assigning the rights to it one by one, you can create one generic Sales account and copy it whenever you want to add a new user with the same rights as Sales. This generic account is called a *template*. When you copy a user account, it is given a new security ID (SID) by Windows NT. The permissions for the old account are copied to the new one.

EXERCISE 4-3

Copying a User Account

1. In User Manager, select the jeffersont account.
2. Open the User menu and select Copy.
3. In the Username field, enter **nixonr**.
4. In the Full Name field, enter **Richard Nixon**.
5. Note that the Description field remains the same.
6. Click the Group button. Note that the group settings for the jeffersont account have been transferred to the nixonr account. Click OK.
7. Click the Profile button. The profile settings for the jeffersont account have now been transferred to the nixonr account. Click OK.
8. Click OK again. We have copied the jeffersont account to a new account called nixonr.

Deleting an Existing User Account

If a user account is no longer needed, you can delete it easily. Be careful; once you delete a user account, it's gone. There's no way to bring it back once you have deleted it. This is because once the account is deleted, the security ID (SID) is lost. SIDs are unique and, once erased, are not re-created. Because the SID identifies the permissions given to an account, when you erase an account you lose any individual permissions it may have. The permissions cannot be re-created by creating another account with the same name.

If you wish to prevent a user from logging on, but don't want to delete the user's account, you can disable the account. This prevents a logon, but all information and rights in the account are saved. Once it is enabled, the user can log back on as if nothing happened. This can be useful if a user takes a leave of absence or a vacation.

Disabling a User Account

1. In User Manager, double-click the nixonr account.
2. Check the Account Disabled field.
3. Click OK. The nixonr account has been disabled.
4. Exit User Manager and log off.
5. When Windows NT restarts, attempt to log on as nixonr.
6. Note that the operating system does not allow you to log on using the nixonr account.

Enabling a Disabled User Account

1. Double-click the nixonr account.
2. Uncheck the Account Disabled field.
3. Click OK. The nixonr account has been enabled.
4. Exit User Manager and log off.
5. When Windows NT restarts, attempt to log on as nixonr. This time, you are allowed access to the computer.

Deleting a User Account

1. In User Manager, select the nixonr account.
2. In the User menu, select Delete. (Or press DELETE on the keyboard.)
3. Click OK in the Warning box.
4. Click Yes to confirm. The nixonr account has been deleted.
5. Log off and attempt to log on as nixonr.

Renaming User Accounts

Renaming a user account allows changing the name on the account without losing any of the rights or information assigned to it. This can be used in a situation where a person leaves a company, and someone else is hired to fill the job. Renaming an account retains its SID, so no individual permissions are lost.

For instance, let's say that Fred quits your company, but he has a special set of user rights that give him access to several special directories on the computer. Your company hires Mary to fill Fred's old position. The best way to implement the change would be to disable Fred's account when he leaves, and when Mary starts, enable the account and rename it for Mary. Enter a new password for Mary, and select the User Must Change Password at Next Logon option.

exam
⚠atch

Nearly every student who has taken the Windows NT Workstation test has reported that they were given a question about the renaming scenario just given. You will receive at least two questions concerning when it's appropriate to copy, delete, disable, or rename an account.

EXERCISE 4-7

Renaming a User Account

1. In User Manager, select the jeffersont account.
2. Open the User menu and select Rename.
3. In the Change To field, enter **washingtong.**
4. Click OK. The user jeffersont has been named to washingtong.
5. Exit User Manager and log off.
6. When NT restarts, attempt to log on as jeffersont.
7. Now, log on as washingtong.

Changing Account Properties

Once a user account is created, anytime that you wish to go back and edit the properties of the account, you can do so in User Manager.

EXERCISE 4-8 **Changing a User's Environment**

1. From User Manager, highlight the washingtong account.

2. From the User menu, click Properties. (Or you can simply double-click the user account in User Manager.)

3. Click the Groups button.

4. In the Member Of box, highlight Administrators.

5. Click Remove.

6. Click OK.

7. Click OK again. We have removed the washingtong account from the Administrators group.

Creating Local Groups

In most cases, you should try to use the built-in groups for managing your users, but if these groups are not convenient, you can create your own, using the window shown in Figure 4-7.

FIGURE 4-7

Creating a new
Local group

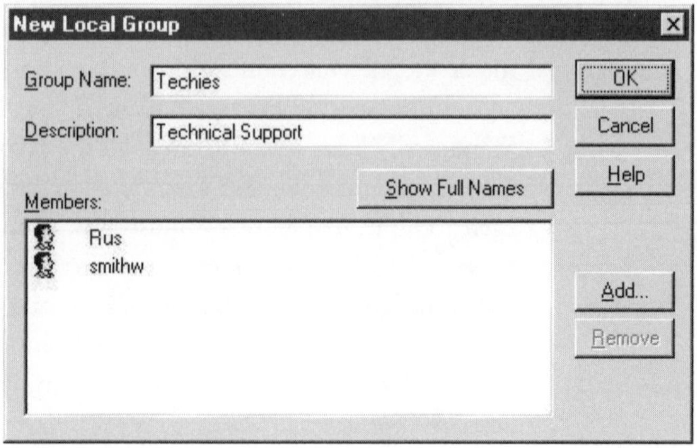

EXERCISE 4-9

Creating a New Local Group

1. In User Manager, open the User menu and select New Group.
2. In the Group Name field, type **Techies**.
3. In the Description field, type **Technical Support**.
4. Click the Add button. The Add Users and Groups menu appears.
5. Highlight the washingtong account, and click Add. Note that the washingtong account now appears in the bottom window.
6. Click OK.
7. Note that the washingtong account now appears as a member of the group Techies. Click OK to create the group.

CERTIFICATION OBJECTIVE 4.04

Account Policies

The administrator of a Windows NT computer can control the security policies for accounts on that computer. These policies affect every account that logs onto your computer in areas such as password usage, user rights, and event auditing. These policies can be enacted through the User Manager's Policies menu and affect accounts only on that computer. In a domain environment, account policies are managed through User Manager for Domains (found in Windows NT Server), and affect all the accounts in the domain.

The account policy for a workstation controls general password usage for each account. As Figure 4-8 illustrates, administrators can determine when a password expires, or lock out a user for not being able to provide the correct password after a set number of tries, among other policies. See Table 4-3 for a description of the policies, and their default settings. Remember that you can never lock out the Administrator account. Only administrators can change account policies.

FIGURE 4-8

Account Policies that
the administrator can
determine

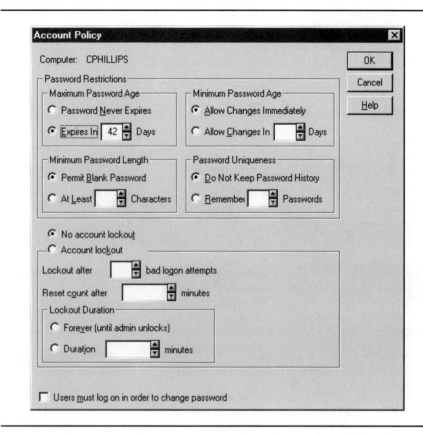

EXERCISE 4-10

Change Default Account Policy

1. From User Manager, open the Policies menu.

2. Select Account.

3. Here you can select the right to be assigned. In this example, we'll
   change the minimum password length. Click the At Least option in
   the Minimum Password Length box.

CERTIFICATION OBJECTIVE 4.05

User Rights

Administrators can assign rights that control which activities a user or group can perform on the workstation. Rights are assigned at the User Rights Policy window, shown in Figure 4-9. Rights apply to the entire computer, unlike permissions, which are assigned to specific objects like printers or directories. Table 4-4 describes the various user rights. You should not change user rights unless you know exactly what the results of your changes will be.

EXERCISE 4-11

Grant a User Right to a Group

1. In User Manager, open the Policies menu.
2. Click User Rights.
3. Select Change the System Time.

FIGURE 4-9

User rights apply to the entire computer, unlike permissions, which are assigned to specific objects

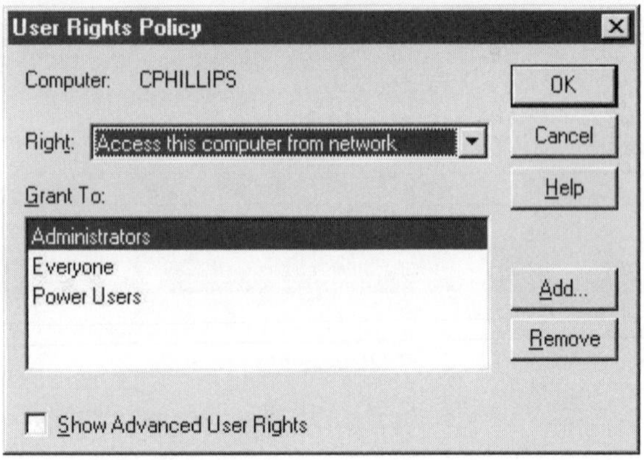

TABLE 4-4   User Rights

User Right	Description	Default Groups
Access this computer from network	Allows a user to connect to the computer over a network.	Administrators, Everyone, Power Users
Back up files and directories	Allows a user to make backups of files or directories. This right supercedes any permissions set for files or directories.	Administrators, Backup Operators
Change the system time	Allows a user to set the time on the computer's internal clock.	Administrators, Power Users
Force shutdown from a remote system	Allows a user to shut the system down remotely over the network.	Administrators, Power Users
Load and unload device drivers	Allows a user to change device drivers.	Administrators
Log on locally	Allows users to log on at the workstation.	Administrators, Backup Operators, Server Operators, Print Operators, Account Operators
Manage and audit security log	Allows a user to manage the security policy.	Administrators
Restore files and directories	Allows a user to restore files or directories from a backup.	Administrators, Backup Operators
Shut down the system	Allows users to shut down the workstation at the computer.	Administrators, Backup Operators, Everyone, Power Users, Users
Take ownership of files or other objects	Allows a user to take authority of files, directories, or other objects.	Administrators

4. Click the Add button.

5. In the top window, select the Techies group, then click Add.

6. Note that the Techies local group now appears in the bottom window. Click OK to assign this right to the Techies group.

7. Now log off and log back on as washingtong.

8. Attempt to change the system time by clicking Start | Settings | Control Panel | Date/Time.

9. When finished, log back on as administrator.

Remove a User Right from a Group

1. In the User Rights box, select Change the System Time.

2. Select the Techies group in the Grant to window.

3. Click the Remove button.

4. Log off and log back on as washingtong. Attempt to change the system time again.

5. When finished, log back on as administrator.

Advanced User Rights

Advanced User Rights are some sophisticated rights that can be assigned. You can view these rights in User Manager easily, as shown in Figure 4-10. Generally these rights are associated with software development, so you won't need to use this much in administration.

View Advanced User Rights

1. Open User Manager.

2. Open the Policies menu and select User Rights.

3. Check the Show Advanced User Rights check box.

4. Now view the Right drop-down box. Note that there are several additional rights now available.

Audit Policy

Auditing allows you to keep track of system events relating to user activity on a system. These audited events can capture the following information:

■ The name of the event or action.

■ The name of the user who performed the action.

■ The date and time of the action.

FIGURE 4-10

Advanced user rights

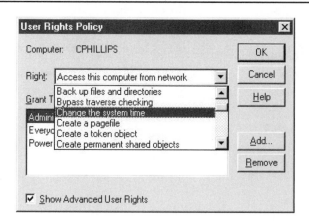

Auditing is useful for many purposes, such as tracking the occurrence of invalid logon attempts. Multiple invalid logon attempts could indicate an attempt to hack into the system. You can also use auditing to generate a report whenever a user attempts to access a resource for which that user does not have access permission. Even changes to users and groups can be audited providing an "audit trail" of all such activity.

The success or failure of an attempted action can be audited and recorded. This information can be written to the Windows NT Event Log and saved to disk. You can save audit information on the successful use of printers or other shared resources, and plan for future capacity using the information you saved. Table 4-5 describes the kinds of activities that can be audited, and explains what failure and success mean.

The ability to set up auditing is a user right called Manage Auditing and Security Log, which by default is granted only to the Administrators group. Members of the Administrators group can view the Security Log information. On Windows NT Server, the Administrators and Server Operators groups can view this information.

Be careful when you implement an audit policy. Auditing common events like file access and object access can slow your computer down. This is especially true on a server, where multiple users may be accessing the same files or objects. Audit only those events that you consider important.

TABLE 4-5   Auditing Activities with NT

Activity Audited	Event Logged if Success	Event Logged if Failure
Logon and Logoff	User logged on or off the workstation, either locally or remotely.	User attempted to log on but failed, either locally or remotely.
File and Object Access	User accessed a directory, file, printer, or other object that is set for auditing.	User attempted but failed to access a directory, file, printer, or other object set for auditing.
Use of User Rights	User succeeded in use of a user right other than logon or logoff.	User failed in use of a user right other than logon or logoff.
User and Group Management	User created, modified, or deleted a user or group account, or modified a password.	User attempted, but failed to create, modify, or delete a user or group account or modify a password.
Security Policy Changes	User made changes in User Rights or Audit Policies.	User failed in an attempt to change User Rights or Audit Policies.
Restart, Shutdown, and System	User restarted or shut down the system, or a system security event occurred.	User failed to restart or shut down the system, or a system security event occurred.
Process Tracking	User started or stopped a program or other system process.	User failed to start or stop a program or other system process.

EXERCISE 4-14

Enabling Auditing

1. Start User Manager.
2. Open the Policies menu and select Audit.
3. Select Audit These Events.
4. Find User and Group Management. Check the Success box.
5. Click OK.

Security Log

You can use the Event Viewer to display and manage the Security log. The Security log shows events that are related to security, as specified in the Audit

Policy. The Security log does not record any information until you tell it to through the Audit Policy in User Manager.

Viewing and Clearing the Security Log

1. Log onto your workstation using the Administrator account.

2. Start User Manager.

3. Copy the administrative account, giving the new account any name you like.

4. Close User Manager.

5. Log off and log on again as Administrator.

6. Click the Start Button. Select Programs | Administrative Tools | Event Viewer.

7. Open the Log menu and select Security.

8. Find the event where the Administrator account was copied, and double-click it. You can examine the entry and see details of what happened. Then close the Event Detail window.

9. Open the Log menu and select Clear All Events.

10. When asked to save the log before clearing, choose No.

11. When asked to confirm, click Yes. The Security log has been cleared.

CERTIFICATION SUMMARY

To log on to Windows NT, each user must have a user account. All usernames must be unique. Passwords do not have to be unique, but cannot be longer than 14 characters and are case sensitive. User accounts can be added into groups, which simplifies their management. Policies applied to groups apply to all the user accounts in that group as a unit.

Windows NT comes with two accounts already created: Administrator and Guest. The Administrator account is used to manage user accounts, policies, and resources. The Administrator account cannot be locked out or disabled. The Guest account provides low-level access to the computer for users that do not have a user account of their own. The Guest account is disabled by default.

User Manager is the administrative tool used to manage user accounts, groups, and policies. You can copy, rename, or delete user accounts with User Manager.

Account Policies are set from User Manager and allow you to change how passwords are used. You can also set the account lockout policy there. Enabling account lockouts can help prevent your system from being hacked into.

User Rights allow you to control which operations a user or group performs. Each right enables the user to perform specific operations on the computer.

TWO-MINUTE DRILL

- ❑ When Windows NT is installed, two default accounts are created: Administrator and Guest.
- ❑ The administrator can manage security policies; create, modify, or delete user accounts and groups; modify operating system software; create and connect to shared directories; install and connect to printers; format or partition a hard disk; back up and restore files; debug the system; take ownership of files and other objects; and install or update device drivers.
- ❑ The Guest account is used for limited access for remote users or users from other domains.
- ❑ Local groups affect resources only on the workstation.
- ❑ Windows NT Workstation comes with several built-in local groups for convenience in adding new users to the workstation.
- ❑ There is a second set of five groups used by the Windows NT system, which are automatically assigned based on how the user is accessing the system.
- ❑ Global groups are created on domain controllers and are used to assign local permissions to domain users.
- ❑ An important part of an administrator's job is to come up with a naming convention for naming users, groups, and resources, such as printers.

❑ Groups can be assigned rights as a unit, rather than assigning rights to each individual account.

❑ User Manager is the administrative tool used for the management of all users and groups on the workstation.

❑ Once a user is assigned to a group, that user is given the rights and permissions inherent to membership in that group.

❑ As an administrator, you can control the location of the user profile, run a logon script individual to that user, or specify the location of a home directory for the user.

❑ Granting dial-in permission to a user account allows that user to access the workstation using the Remote Access Service (RAS).

❑ Once a user account has been created, you can come back and change it anytime by using User Manager.

❑ Nearly every student who has taken the Windows NT Workstation test has reported that they were given a question about renaming user accounts. You will receive at least two questions concerning when it's appropriate to copy, delete, disable, or rename an account.

❑ Account policies affect every account that logs onto your computer in areas such as password usage, user rights, and event auditing.

❑ Administrators can assign rights that control which activities a user or group can perform on the workstation.

❑ Auditing allows you to keep track of system events relating to user activity on a system.

SELF TEST

The following questions will help you measure your understanding of the material presented in this chapter. Read all the choices carefully, as there may be more than one correct answer. Choose all correct answers for each question.

1. (True/False) The Administrator account can be deleted.

2. The _____ default account must be enabled before it can be used.

3. To assign permissions to a large number of users, the user accounts should be placed into _____.

4. Which groups do you need to be a member of to share a directory on your computer? Choose two.
   A. Power Users
   B. Users
   C. Backup Operators
   D. Administrators
   E. Guests

5. Which user accounts are created by default when Windows NT is installed?
   A. Administrator and Guest
   B. Administrator and User
   C. User and Power User
   D. User and Guest

6. The _____ administrative tool is used to manage all user and group accounts.

7. You want your users to be able to share their own printers, but you don't want to grant them full access to the computer. Which built-in group should you make your users members of?
   A. Users
   B. Power Users
   C. Guests
   D. Backup Operators

8. Bob is retiring from your company. Linda, a new employee, is taking over Bob's position. You want Linda's user account to have the same rights and permissions as Bob's user account. How do you do this with the least amount of administrative effort, while maintaining security?
   A. Delete Bob's account when he leaves. Create a new account for Linda and reassign all rights and permissions.
   B. Copy Bob's account to Linda's account. Then erase Bob's old account.
   C. Disable Bob's account when he leaves. When Linda starts, rename the account to Linda's username.
   D. Lock out Bob's account when he leaves. When Linda starts, rename the account to Linda's username.

9. If a user creates a file on the computer, then that user is a member of the _____ special group for that file.

10. (True/False) Users that access the computer over the network are members of the Interactive special group.

11. Members of which built-in group can take ownership of a file or folder?

    A. Users

    B. Power Users

    C. Administrators

    D. Backup Operators

12. When you copy a user account, what information is *not* transferred to the new account?

    A. Description

    B. Profile settings

    C. User Cannot Change Password

    D. Full Name

13. (True/False) If an account is accidentally deleted, it can be restored by creating a new account with the same name and description.

14. Which Administrative tool can be used to view the security log?

    A. User Manager

    B. Event Viewer

    C. Devices

    D. Security Manager

15. You believe that someone may be trying to get unauthorized access to your computer. How can you verify this?

    A. Force all users to change their password the next time they log on.

    B. Enable auditing of failed logon attempts.

    C. Enable auditing of file access.

    D. Disable all accounts except the Administrator account.

MICROSOFT CERTIFIED SYSTEMS ENGINEER

5

Windows NT File System Support

One of the ways Windows NT Workstation maintains compatibility is with file system support. Windows NT provides support for the File Allocation Table (FAT) and introduces the New Technology File System (NTFS). The FAT file system is a widely used, well-supported file system utilized by most Microsoft operating systems. To overcome prior operating system limitations, NT now supports the NTFS file system for long filenames, compression, security, and increased efficiency. This chapter will cover the features of both file systems, as well as disk management features such as volume and stripe sets for improvements in performance and fault tolerance. These disk management features are implemented through the new Disk Administrator, a graphical-based utility for managing your disks and partitions.

CERTIFICATION OBJECTIVE 5.01

File Allocation Table (FAT)

The File Allocation Table is a widely supported file system introduced with the first version of MS-DOS over fifteen years ago, and continued through Microsoft's most popular operating systems such as DOS, Windows 3.x, and Windows 95. Even OS/2 can read the FAT file system format. The file system gets its name from the method used to store data on the disk. Comparable to the index of a book, the FAT file system is used to point to the areas on the disk where data is stored. This file system was great for its time but is beginning to show its age, especially with today's large capacity hard disks and extended file attributes (discussed later in the chapter). FAT is by no means dead, however. We can make a strong case for the use of FAT partitions in Windows NT Workstation. Another point to remember about the FAT file system is that it is required for system partitions of RISC processor architectures. The FAT file system can be as small as two megabytes to support the RISC boot files, and the rest can be NTFS. If you are faced with a question on the exam about Alpha or MIPS and file systems, you now know these require FAT. Regardless of the FAT file system's limitations, in some circumstances it is appropriate to use the FAT file system in Windows NT Workstation, and therefore you should understand it.

Alpha or MIPS require FAT [handwritten annotation]

With the Windows 95 OEM Service Release 2 (OSR2), Microsoft updated the FAT file system. It's now referred to as FAT32. There are some improvements with FAT32 that are worth mentioning, including support for larger hard disks and more efficient use of space. Cluster sizes are smaller with FAT32 than with the FAT16 file system. Unfortunately, FAT32 partitions are not visible from MS-DOS, or even from the original version of Windows 95. FAT32 is still not compatible with the NTFS file system, and therefore NTFS partitions are not visible from Windows 95 OSR2.

FAT Naming Conventions Under DOS

The FAT naming convention uses the 8.3 scheme: an eight-letter filename, with a three-letter file extension. This limitation is a nuisance that has lasted for many years. Filenames such as SETUP.EXE are clear enough, but combinations of acronyms and abbreviations, made to create unique and meaningful filenames, quickly become indecipherable. Of course, the eight-letter maximum filename made sense under DOS, which requires text-based user input (unless you are using a DOS shell). The eight-character maximum would facilitate minimal typing to execute programs and change directories. Can you imagine the labor involved in typing filenames and spotting errors if there were no maximum? But today the graphical user interface (GUI) rules the operating systems, so it's only natural that restrictions inherited from DOS and FAT are being challenged. Since you will still be using DOS and FAT file systems, you must learn the concepts associated with the two, especially the naming conventions. There are a few rules regarding the FAT naming conventions:

- Filenames consist of one to eight characters with an optional extension of one to three characters.

- The period is used to separate the filename from the extension, and only one period can be used.

- The name cannot contain any spaces, nor can it contain any of these characters: / \ ^ ? * " [ ] | : = , ;

- System command names are reserved, such as COM1, LPT1, PRN, NUL, and CON.

■ Filenames are not case sensitive. Lowercase letters are transformed into uppercase automatically.

FAT Naming Conventions Under Windows NT

A new version of FAT, called Virtual File Allocation Table (VFAT), was created with Windows NT and maintains compatibility with FAT. VFAT enables the use of long filenames, while maintaining the 8.3 naming convention for older applications viewing the same file. It does this by writing two files on the disk: one for the FAT compatible 8.3 convention, and one that is the actual long filename. The only time this dual naming becomes a concern is when you have many long filenames for directories in your root directory. You are limited to 512 directory entries. So, if for some strange reason you have 200 or more directories in your root directory, you may be concerned. For most of us, this is not a problem.

The VFAT can be thought of as "middle ground" between the FAT file system and the NT file system (NTFS). It gives users with FAT partitions the enhancements in long filename support without the complete transition to NTFS. That's about the only NTFS related enhancement that you get, though—no security attributes, nor the capability to compress files. What is nice about VFAT is that you can change to directories with a wildcard character. For example, if I was in my root directory of C and I wanted to change to the Norton Utilities NT directory, I would enter this at the command prompt:

```
C:\cd nort*
```

This command would take me to the directory without having to type the whole directory path.

VFAT introduced a few modifications to the restrictions of the FAT naming conventions that you must be aware of:

■ The name can now be up to 255 characters.

■ The names now preserve case.

■ The names can also contain spaces and more than one period. The last period still separates the filename from the extension.

| EXERCISE 5-1 | **Creating a VFAT Filename and Viewing Its FAT Alias** |

1. Open up Explorer, and select the root directory of your C drive.

2. On the right of the screen, right-click the mouse and select New | Text Document.

3. Accept the default of New Text Document.txt.

4. Open a command prompt by selecting Start | Run, and typing **cmd** in the space.

5. Ensure that you are in the root of C:\ by typing **C:** at the prompt and pressing ENTER.

6. Type **dir /x /p** and scroll down until you see the New Text Document.txt that you just created.

7. Notice the FAT alias (for FAT support) to the left of the VFAT long filename entry.

CERTIFICATION OBJECTIVE 5.02

Long Filenames

Long filenames created in NT will be read by older operating systems as the 8.3 counterpart on the FAT partition. Truncated 8.3 filenames are cryptic at best. You need to know how NT creates an 8.3 version of a filename.

For example, an 8.3 version of the filename "April Report from Human Resources" would be APRILR~1. Notice that the filename consists of the first six characters (ignoring spaces between words) followed by a tilde and a number. The number after the tilde is used to distinguish among files that have the same first six characters. So a second file, "April Report from Finance," would be APRILR~2. If you had an "April Report" from every department in a large company, imagine the time wasted on a FAT file system trying to distinguish APRILR~5 from APRILR~9.

If "April Report from Human Resources" had an extension of .TXT, the 8.3 FAT alias would be APRILR~1.TXT.

Let's clarify a difference between Windows 95 and Windows NT VFAT concerning filenames. Windows 95 increments the number after the tilde for each file it finds with the identical first six characters. NT increments only through the fourth repetition and then starts using a hexadecimal number after the first two letters. In the next example you will see what NT did to my name:

CAMERO~1	cameron brandon1
CAMERO~2	cameron brandon2
CAMERO~3	cameron brandon3
CAMERO~4	cameron brandon4
CAEC68~1	cameron brandon5
CAFC68~1	cameron brandon6

Long filenames are difficult to work with if you dual-boot to an operating system such as DOS, which will not recognize the long name. Keep in mind that you can't view the NTFS partition from other operating systems that don't recognize NTFS. This makes for very taxing deciphering of long filenames from another operating system. Windows 95 will show the long filename, but DOS will not. Fortunately, if you are using NT you probably won't use DOS applications much, so you won't spend much time at the command prompt.

Remember these rules concerning the creation of FAT aliases for long filenames:

- NTFS removes all spaces from the long filename when it is creating the FAT alias.

- NT replaces all illegal characters with the underscore character (_) when it creates the FAT alias.

- Illegal characters include: ? " / \ < > * | :

- NT truncates the file extension to three characters or less.

exam
Ⓦatch

Very likely, you will be asked to choose the 8.3 version of a given long filename.

New Technology File System (NTFS)

NTFS is Microsoft's robust file system exclusive to the Windows NT operating system. This file system is much improved over its predecessor, FAT. NTFS was introduced in 1992 with the Windows NT Advanced Server, and developed to address the need for long filename support, larger capacity drive support, and extended security attributes. Keep in mind that the FAT file system is more compatible with other operating systems such as Windows 3.1, DOS, Windows 95, and OS/2 (in particular, Windows 95 cannot see NTFS partitions). If you format with FAT, you will not be able to use the features that NTFS supports. Although NT supports both FAT and NTFS, the file system of choice for the Windows NT operating system is NTFS.

It would be helpful to leave one of the partitions on your computer formatted with the FAT file system so you can observe the features and limitations provided by this file system. This is a great learning tool, and you can always convert the partition to NTFS later.

exam
Ⓦatch

Don't be surprised to see a question concerning which file system to use: FAT or NTFS. You should know the differences between the two, and when it is appropriate to choose one over the other.

Be sure you are aware of all the ramifications of choosing a file system before you start installing. For the home user this is not a major concern, but in large companies it is very common to have a standards guideline in place that you follow whenever new systems are being built and configured. If you are responsible for developing these standards guidelines, it is very important that you be aware of the differences, and make the appropriate decision as to which file system to implement. Like it or not, corporate standards are not very flexible.

Naming Conventions With NTFS

As noted earlier in the VFAT file system section, NT makes use of the VFAT file system to maintain compatibility with FAT filename conventions while allowing the use of long filenames. VFAT and NTFS naming conventions are one and the same. But be aware that NTFS is the file system that uses VFAT to maintain compatibility. In other words, you won't ever format your drive with the VFAT file system.

Features of NTFS

Although you can have both FAT and NTFS formatted partitions on the same computer, there are many features of the NTFS file system that would make it the preferred choice for your NT workstation. NTFS is most suitable in companies needing to take advantage of NTFS attribute security, or using powerful modern computers with high-capacity hard disks installed. The maximum for the FAT file system is 4GB. Exceeding this 4GB limit was unheard of just a few years ago. The NTFS architecture is designed to use numbers up to 2^{64} bytes (that is, 16 exabytes, or 18,446,744,073,709,551,616 bytes). The NTFS file system's practical limit is 2 terabytes (TB). NTFS is the culmination of several enhancements to the FAT file system and the High-Performance File System (HPFS), but can introduce a few disadvantages. Regardless of these disadvantages, as the following sections demonstrate, NTFS is an exceptional choice for your primary file system.

Fault Tolerance

hot- fix ≡ sector sparing

marks back sector as unusable & moves data

One of the fault tolerant features of NTFS is the *hot-fix* feature, often called *sector sparing*. Hot-fix moves information found in a bad sector to a different sector, and marks the original sector as unusable. The fix is completely transparent to the user. This feature cannot guarantee your data will not be damaged in the process, but at least subsequent attempts to write data to the bad sector will be avoided.

Security

One feature of the NTFS file system that makes it very secure is the invisibility of NTFS partitions from non-NTFS operating systems. This may be a nuisance to some home users who dual-boot, only to find the files they need are on the NTFS partition when they are using Windows 95. That is another reason to choose carefully regarding your file system. If you must be compatible with other operating systems, NTFS may not be for you.

With NTFS it's difficult (you need a third-party utility) to boot from a floppy disk and access the NTFS partition. This makes for a very secure environment where physical tampering of the machine is not tolerated. A would-be hacker could not reboot the computer and boot to a floppy disk to view your partition, as was the case with FAT partitions. Unfortunately, neither can you if something should go wrong. I faced this dilemma when our Exchange server went down on my first day of work at a new job. The hard disk appeared to have crashed, but it would still boot up to a certain point before the blue screen of death would appear. We needed to recover the Exchange private and public stores located on the drive. Had it been a FAT partition, we could have booted up with a floppy and then accessed the partition and retrieved our information. Since it was an NTFS partition, we couldn't circumvent the security so easily. Microsoft even recommends a 500MB FAT partition for this very reason.

In some organizations security is too important to include a FAT partition on your system. If you are ever in a situation where you need to access a failed partition, you can use a minimal install of NT in another directory to boot the system. This alleviates the need to use the less secure FAT file system as the primary partition. Please note that RISC-based systems require at least a 2MB FAT primary partition.

Advanced NTFS security allows an administrator to restrict access to folder level and even down to the file level by assigning permissions to users or groups. FAT partitions allow an administrator to grant permissions only to the folder level—not down to the file level. This is a major reason why the NTFS file system should be chosen in a business setting, or any setting where extra security is needed. This subject should be fully understood and will be discussed in later chapters. Learning NTFS security is important not only for the NT Workstation exam, but also for other exams such as those for NT Server, Exchange, Internet Information Server, and SQL Server. If you learn the concepts now, you will be in good shape for any other exams that you take.

File Recovery

When you delete a file from NT it is gone (unless it is still in the recycle bin). This unfortunate NTFS feature pretty much guarantees a tech support phone call whenever a user accidentally deletes a file. I've even heard of a user who bought three NT utilities software packages in a valiant attempt to recover a multimedia file he had been working on for weeks. Of course, an irrevocable delete feature has its value. For example, a top-secret file can be deleted after it is read and under the current inability to recover lost files it can never be resurrected and viewed by unauthorized users. (With a FAT file system, you could drop to the DOS prompt and issue the UNDELETE command.)

NTFS also uses the *lazy-write* feature—a transaction log that keeps track of whether writes to the disk have been completed. In the event the system crashes during a disk write and the write becomes incomplete, NT rolls back the transaction that was taking place during the crash. After a successful transaction, NT updates the log, confirming the transaction's completion. In the FAT file system, a power outage or an improper shutting down of the system could result in corrupt or damaged files. I once was running a disk utility on Windows 95 and I accidentally pulled the power cord. The system did not even boot completely the next time I started it. If this happens in Windows NT, CHKDSK /F will automatically be invoked upon boot up. This utility reads the transaction logs and checks to see if any writes are outstanding, or if any incomplete write needs to be rolled back.

NTFS is referred to as the "recoverable file system," because of the feature known as the Master File Table (MFT). The MFT contains information about the files and folders, comparable to FAT. MFT is critical, so it is mirrored. Pointers to both the original and the mirror of the MFT are stored in the boot sector of the disk. This provides recovery if the original MFT becomes corrupt or lost.

File and Partition Sizes

In order to understand the improvements that NTFS offers, it is important to understand the differences between FAT and NTFS when it comes to file and partition sizes. This aspect of NTFS excited users like me when we upgraded to Windows NT, and it's probably the biggest improvement the NTFS file system has made, next to the addition of extended security attributes.

The FAT file system was designed for small hard disks and for simple file and directory structures. This is because a drive formatted with the FAT file system uses clusters to store information. The larger the partition size, the larger the cluster size.

Partition size	Cluster size
0MB – 32MB	512 bytes
33MB – 64MB	1K
65MB – 128MB	2K
129MB – 255MB	4K
256MB – 511MB	8K
512MB – 1023MB	16K

You can see how the cluster size increases exponentially as the partition size gets larger. For users with large hard disks, it was necessary to format drives into smaller partitions to avoid the excessive overhead due to large cluster sizes. This is why the FAT file system is not recommended for today's high capacity hard disks. I can still remember formatting drives into 510MB partitions to retain the 8K cluster size.

In the next example, you can see how NTFS cluster size alleviates the problem of excessive file system overhead.

Partition size	Cluster size
512MB or less	512 bytes
513MB – 1024MB (1GB)	1K
1025MB – 2048MB (2GB)	2K

Partition size	Cluster size
2049MB – 4096MB (4GB)	4K
4097MB – 8192MB (8GB)	8K

Compare the FAT cluster size to the NTFS cluster size on the 512 – 1023MB partition. You can see that NTFS saves a substantial amount of space.

File Compression

One of the most popular features of the NTFS file system is its capability to compress single files or directories, without the need to compress the whole drive. In older DOS-based programs like DoubleSpace, Stacker, and DriveSpace, you had to format the whole drive. A device driver for the compression program would make one large file consisting of everything on the drive you had compressed. I once saw an 800MB file! Not to mention how much conventional memory the driver took up, giving you fits if you needed to load several device drivers. You did get a better compression ratio this way, but it was a hassle. The new NT compression is a welcome alternative to these compression programs. This individual basis of compression comes in handy when you need extra space or when certain files will not be accessed over a period of time. You probably will not even notice as the files are uncompressed when you open them, and then compressed again when you close them. The Properties window (see Figure 5-1) shows your file attribute options. Compressed files and directories also can be displayed in different colors. This is handy when you are viewing directories through Explorer, and can immediately tell if the file or folder is compressed or not.

You have the option to compress the folder, and also to compress the subfolders of a folder. When you select the Compressed check box, if there are folders underneath this selected folder, a prompt appears, asking if you would like to compress the subfolders. To compress the entire contents of a drive, just right-click an NTFS drive and select the Compress button. If you enjoy working at the command line, you can also compress files and directories with the command line compression utility called COMPACT.EXE. The syntax is:

```
COMPACT name_of_file_or_directory /C
```

FIGURE 5-1

The Properties dialog box showing the Compressed attribute set and the compressed file size

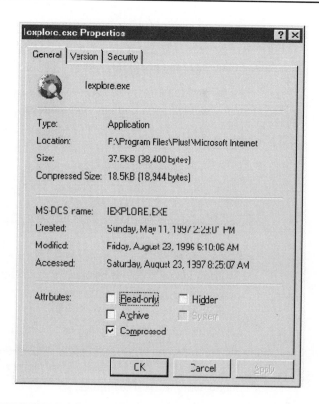

The /C switch is to compress, and the /U switch is to uncompress. As with any command-line utility or command, there are many switches that can alter the performance of the command. Incidentally, the COMPACT command with no switches displays compression statistics on the files and folders.

One of the aspects of file compression dealt with thoroughly on the exam is the matter of what results from moving and copying files on NTFS compressed partitions. The following rules appear simple enough, but in a testing environment Microsoft can fool you with complex scenarios and extraneous information.

■ On an NTFS partition, when you *move* a file or folder that is compressed to another area on the same partition, it retains its state.

The file or folder does not inherit the compression attribute of the target folder into which it was moved.

■ When a file or folder is *copied* to another area on the same partition, it inherits the compression attributes of the target folder.

■ When you are moving or copying a file or folder to another NTFS partition, the file or folder always inherits the compression attribute of the target folder. This rule also applies when you move or copy to another NTFS formatted drive, either local or network. Similarly, when you move or copy a file or folder from a FAT partition to NTFS, it always inherits the compression attribute of the target folder. Remember that, since FAT does not support compression, any file or folder that is moved or copied to a FAT volume is uncompressed automatically.

I don't want to complicate these rules by belaboring them. The key to answering questions that involve these rules is to ignore all the extra information that is given to fool you. Disregard Judy's directory name, or the read-only attribute that Mike set, or the no access permission that Garth has. *Where* is the file or folder going? Are you *moving* it or *copying* it? The bottom line is: The file or folder will either retain or inherit its compression attribute. Know when each rule applies.

POSIX Support

Portable Operating System Interface (POSIX) is an open system standard for application portability among different computer platforms, most of them UNIX based. In order to be POSIX compliant, an application must fulfill certain requirements, such as having case-sensitive filenames. For example, with POSIX applications, filenames such as Microsoft, microsoft, and MICROSOFT are all treated as separate files. POSIX applications also use *hard links,* which can be compared to Windows NT shortcuts, in which many entries can point to the same file. There are a few characters that cannot be included in an NTFS filename under POSIX compliance: / \ < > ? " * | :

Another POSIX feature is additional time stamps, which show when the file was last accessed or modified. POSIX applications are run in what is known as an "environment subsystem." The subsystem is loaded automatically when a

POSIX-compliant application is started. The POSIX subsystem interacts with the NT Executive Services, because applications are not allowed to access the hardware directly. The NT Executive Services intercept the request and make calls to the NT Win32 services for processing.

Performance

There is no clear winner between FAT and NTFS when it comes to performance. However, NTFS provides a file allocation feature that will allow it potentially to increase read/write times. When NT needs to write a file to the disk, it first searches for a contiguous area of free space in which to write the entire file. If there is no area of contiguous space large enough, then it has to fragment the file. This increases read/write times. A badly fragmented disk slows over time. The FAT file system, on the other hand, writes to the first cluster it can find—a recipe for disaster as far as fragmentation is concerned.

Usually I'm not too concerned with fragmentation on the NTFS file systems because of the file allocation feature mentioned previously. Drives that are fairly large should not have a problem for quite some time. When drives become full, fragmentation occurs. Recently I was working on a PC whose owner reported that it had been slow lately. Granted, it was a Pentium 75, but there were only a few megs of hard disk space left. When I viewed the fragmentation report from Norton Utilities Speed Disk, I saw there were over 9000 file fragments. It took over an hour to defrag the 540MB hard disk.

Another difference in performance between FAT and NTFS is in file and folder access. The two file systems have different ways of looking up information. As we noted earlier, FAT is comparable to the index in a book, in that it points to the physical areas on the disk where data is stored. When you use a book index, of course, you can go directly from the index to the page you wish to view. Unfortunately, the FAT system has to "walk the tree" to access the file. In book terms, the FAT index would be the equivalent of finding the right chapter, going there, and only then finding the right section. This might not sound like much of an issue, but if you have a folder nested deep within other folders, it could mean a drop in performance while the FAT index searches for the starting cluster for each directory.

Windows NT uses the Master File Table (MFT), which is similar to the File Allocation Table. Small files and folders can be contained entirely within the

MFT so the computer does not have to search as much as it does with FAT. If we continue our book analogy, the MFT would contain some if not all of the information within the index, and any other information that could not be contained in the MFT would have a single pointer to the remaining content.

CERTIFICATION OBJECTIVE 5.04

Converting to NTFS

Conversion to NTFS is easy. Just make sure this is what you want to do, because the conversion is one-way. You cannot return to your original file system. There are three ways to convert your partitions to NTFS.

The first way is the easiest: Make the conversion when installing NT Workstation, at the screen shown in Figure 5-2. This is also a quick way to format a partition when reinstalling NT, or when installing over another operating system.

FIGURE 5-2

The simplest way to convert to NTFS is when installing Windows NT

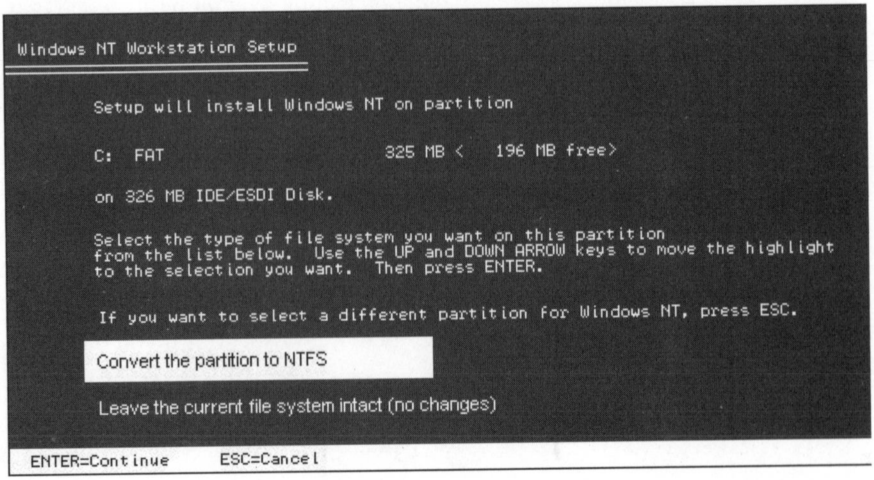

```
Windows NT Workstation Setup

    Setup will install Windows NT on partition

    C:  FAT                   325 MB <   196 MB free>

    on 326 MB IDE/ESDI Disk.

    Select the type of file system you want on this partition
    from the list below.  Use the UP and DOWN ARROW keys to move the highlight
    to the selection you want.  Then press ENTER.

    If you want to select a different partition for Windows NT, press ESC.

   ┌─────────────────────────────────┐
   │ Convert the partition to NTFS   │
   └─────────────────────────────────┘
     Leave the current file system intact (no changes)


  ENTER=Continue     ESC=Cancel
```

The second way to convert your FAT and HPFS file systems to NTFS is through the use of the command line utility CONVERT.EXE. Here are the appropriate options for the CONVERT.EXE command:

```
CONVERT e: /fs:ntfs
```

The e: in the example is the partition you wish to format. The /fs: is short for file system, and ntfs is the file system that you are going to convert the partition to, in this case NTFS.

The third way to make the conversion is to go through Disk Administrator. Select a partition that is FAT, choose Tools, and then Format. Change the file system to NTFS in the drop down box and then choose Start to convert the partition.

EXERCISE 5-2

Converting a FAT Volume to NTFS

1. Make sure you have a volume formatted as FAT that you would like to convert to NTFS.

2. From the Start menu, select Run, and type **cmd**.

3. From the command prompt, type the convert command, and enter the drive designation for the drive you wish to **convert**, followed by **/fs:ntfs**.

4. If NT cannot convert the drive at this time, you will receive a message asking whether you would like the conversion to be scheduled for the next time the system restarts.

Converting time is in proportion to the size of the drive you are converting.

Compact Disk File System (CDFS)

The Compact Disk File System is, obviously, the file system for compact disks. It provides file and directory management just as FAT and NTFS do, but for the read-only compact disk medium. Since CD-ROM is read-only, the file system supports only reads, copies, and opens of files and directories.

High-Performance File System (HPFS)

HPFS support was removed with Windows NT 4. It was supported under Windows NT 3.51, and is available only if you are upgrading from NT 3.51. I

FROM THE CLASSROOM

Save Your Data, Save Your Sanity

There are two tips I can offer to relieve stress in your life.

One tip is to select the best file system, based on your needs. NT supports three file systems. Only two are applicable to hard disks. (The third is CDFS, for the CD-ROM.) Of the two file systems for hard disks, NTFS is the file system of choice, especially for data storage. Use FAT only when you must dual-boot a machine. In most cases, a dual-boot system is neither desirable nor necessary.

We have a client who deployed over 13,000 NT Workstations in his organization. The original configuration was dual-boot to either DOS or NT. Of course, the file system was FAT, to support the dual-boot to DOS.

In this organization, many users refused to delete old mail. One user proudly told us that he had saved every piece of e-mail he had ever sent or received...since 1989! (I suppose this was in case he forgot who won the '92 presidential elections.) Users were storing mail on their local hard disks, because they had consumed too much disk resource on the servers. The client sought our advice when the local hard disks were beginning to run out of space. He found the prospect of upgrading to larger drives economically unpalatable.

Now, you should know that the client suppressed the fact that he was set up as dual-boot. We recommended that he compress the folders storing e-mail, since old e-mail rarely is accessed. (We asked the gentleman who had kept all his e-mail since '89 how often he'd had to review the mail for business purposes. He said he couldn't recall *ever* needing to do so.)

We subsequently received two more support calls. In the first call, the client couldn't understand how to compress the folder, because the compression check box wasn't available. That was an easy one. Compression is available only on NTFS partitions, which he didn't have. The client thanked us, assured us he knew how to make an NTFS partition, and hung up.

I bet you can guess what the second call was. How come he could no longer boot the computers to DOS?

By the way, that second thing you might try to relieve stress...fill out your federal tax return using Roman numerals.

—By Shane Clawson, MCT, MCSE

once was working on a computer where FDISK reported an HPFS partition. I asked the owners if they used OS/2 and they said no. I was puzzled until I found out that DOS FDISK reports any partitions that it does not recognize, including NTFS, as HPFS.

Networks as File Systems

We have learned so far that NT uses local file systems such as FAT, NTFS, and CDFS for managing data. When you are connecting to another computer on the network, you are using a remote file system, but the file system is local to that computer. When you are servicing a request from another computer, you are using your local file system to service their remote request. In order for this to work, the local computer (the one that is doing the requesting) must redirect requests to the remote computer. This is done through the redirector, which is also a file system driver in NT. In NetWare terminology, the redirector is known as the "requester." Do not be confused if you see a reference to the requester, just know that it is Novell's equivalent to the redirector. You will read more about the redirector in the networking chapters later in the book.

Here is a quick Q & A scenario to help you review the suitability of FAT vs. NTFS in different circumstances:

QUESTIONS AND ANSWERS

I am installing NT and I have HPFS…	Convert it before you upgrade. NT 4 does not like HPFS.
I do not require the capability to assign permissions or use compression…	Use FAT. Dead giveaway.
My hard disk is 120MB…	Use FAT. NTFS is not as efficient for a drive that size.
My hard disk is 1.2GB…	Use NTFS. FAT is not very effective on a large drive.
I have a RISC processor…	Then use FAT on your system partition. The remainder can be NTFS. FAT is required for the bootup files on the system partition.

Volume Sets

Volume sets let you maximize the available space on up to 32 drives by combining leftover space on each drive into one large volume with one single drive letter. Volume sets are transparent to the user, which is a good thing. NT just continues on to the next volume member when more space is required. You can have 20 partitions, each with 5MB of data, for a total of 100MB of space. What else could you do with 5MB partitions if it weren't for volume sets? What is important to remember about volume sets is that they are not fault tolerant. That is a bad thing. Imagine if the disk drive with one of your 5MB partitions were to crash. You would lose the entire volume set. If you lose one small area of the volume set, then you lose the whole volume set. Also note that other operating systems will not be able to view the data on the volume set, and volume sets do not increase performance. To summarize, here are the advantages and disadvantages of volume sets:

The advantages of volume sets:

- Free space on the drives can be combined into a single drive letter. This includes multiple spaces on one drive, as well as multiple spaces on multiple drives.

- Free space from different types of hard disks can be included (SCSI, IDE).

The disadvantages of volume sets:

- If one member of the volume set fails, the entire set is inaccessible.

- The system and boot partitions cannot be included in the volume set.

- Non-NT operating systems will not be able to see the volume set.

For the next exercise, you must have two small partitions that you would like to combine into one volume set. You may want to reserve some free space in order to complete the exercise after this one (on extending the volume set).

Creating a Volume Set

1. Highlight an area of free space. Hold down the CONTROL key and select the other areas of free space that you are going to add to your volume set.

2. From the Partition menu, select Create Volume Set.

3. Enter the size for the volume set, or accept the default maximum space. At this time the volume set is unformatted, and each member of the set is in yellow (if you have not changed the color scheme).

4. Click one member of the set, and notice that this highlights every member of the set automatically.

5. From the Partition menu, select Commit Changes Now. Notice the recommendation to update your emergency repair disk, because changes have now been made to your configuration information.

6. If the members of the set are still highlighted, select Format from the Tools menu.

7. Format the set with the file system of your choice.

The volume set is now complete. You can assign the volume set a different drive letter at this time if you wish. If you reserved some free space, we can begin to extend the volume set. One of the advantages of the volume set is that any amount of free space on any of your drives can be consolidated into the volume set for the most efficient use of space, and the set can easily be extended.

Extending a Volume Set

1. Highlight the newly created volume set.

2. Click an area of free space that you would like to include in the volume set. The area you are adding to the volume set cannot already be formatted, or have an unknown file system.

3. Select Extend Volume Set from the Partition menu.

4. Enter the total size for the volume, or accept the default maximum volume size.

The volume set is now extended. You can commit changes at this time.

Stripe Sets

A stripe set divides data into blocks (64K) and spreads them across an array of hard disks. Just like the volume set, the stripe set takes on one drive letter, and is transparent to the user.

The stripe set does not have to be created from partitions that are the same size. Nor do the physical disks in a stripe set have to be the same size, but there must be unpartitioned areas available on each disk that you want to include in the volume.

The stripe set uses the smallest partition size included in the set as the common partition sizing. For example, if three disks with 200MB of space on each were dedicated to the stripe set, those three disks would equal a 600MB stripe set. If you added a 150MB region, the stripe set would *remain* 600MB. Here is how it works:

> You are creating a stripe set with four members: three at 200MB, and one at 150MB.

> Because you can only create a stripe as wide as the smallest member, the stripe size in this case would be 150MB. Therefore the total size of the stripe set would be: 150MB + 150MB + 150MB + 150MB = 600MB.

Stripe sets improve read times because the data is being read off separate drives simultaneously. This makes them a good choice when you feel that the biggest bottleneck in your system may be the throughput from your hard disk. When you create a stripe set (RAID level 0), you are not fault tolerant. If one disk fails, you lose all the data in the stripe set. You can create a stripe set on a minimum of two hard disks, and a maximum of 32 drives.

Before we go any further, let's review the advantages and disadvantages of disk striping.

The advantages of disk striping:

- Improved performance for read/write access on your hard disks.
- Requires only a minimum of two hard disks.

■ Striping provides the best performance of all disk management options.

The disadvantages of disk striping:

■ If one disk fails, you lose the whole set.

■ You cannot use the system and boot partitions in the stripe set.

■ In order to expand a stripe set, you have to back up the data, delete the stripe set and create the new, larger stripe set from Disk Administrator, and then restore from tape.

You need equal regions of free space on each disk to make the stripe. This may be difficult to muster if you already have been using your drives. For this reason, a stripe set is something that you should plan ahead, and not a feature to implement on a whim.

EXERCISE 5-5

Creating a Stripe Set

In this exercise we will be creating a stripe set. You must have free space on two separate drives in order to complete this exercise.

1. Highlight one of the areas of free space you would like to combine into the stripe set.

2. While holding down the CONTROL key, click the other areas of free space you wish to add.

3. Choose Create Stripe Set from the Partition menu.

4. Enter the amount of space you would like to allocate to the stripe set, or just accept the default maximum amount. If you retained the default coloring scheme, your stripe members should now be green.

5. From the Partition menu, select Commit Changes Now. This step is necessary in order to format the stripe set in the next step.

6. You can now select Format from the Tools menu to format the stripe set with the file system of your choice. You can also change the drive letter assignment if you wish.

I have heard conflicting reports of performance gains by implementing the stripe set from various users. One colleague of mine performed an experiment in a lab in which he used two older PIO MODE 2 hard disks, and created a stripe set with them. (If you are unfamiliar with PIO MODE 2 drives, they are very slow.) When he benchmarked the stripe set against a modern hard disk, the stripe set barely beat the new drive. I also have heard people say that striping produced results that hardly were noticeable. Perform your own tests to see which you prefer. Next time I format my hard disks I am going to implement a stripe set.

With Windows NT Server you have the choice of creating a stripe set with or without parity. The biggest difference between the two is fault tolerance. A stripe set with parity is able to endure a crash of a single disk within the stripe. The failed drive can be replaced and then re-created by the information that is already contained in the stripe. However, NT Workstation only allows disk striping without parity. Another feature that NT Workstation does not support is the disk mirroring feature. You will encounter this in NT Server also.

There are a few tips regarding the use of volume and stripe sets that should be addressed for the exam. Just like the rules for moving and copying compressed files, the volume and stripe set rules are fairly simple, but Microsoft will go out of its way to confuse you with too many details. If you keep the simple rules in your head, you should do fine. Here is a quick reference for possible scenario questions, and the appropriate answers:

QUESTIONS AND ANSWERS

I want greater disk performance...	Do not use a volume set. Use a stripe set.
I want to increase my capacity later...	Do not use a stripe set. Use a volume set. It can be extended, whereas a stripe set cannot.
I want to use free space from several areas...	Do not use a stripe set. Use a volume set. It can combine multiple areas of free space, including space within partitions on the same drives.
I have the same amount of space on two separate disks...	Use a stripe set.
I want to include the system and boot partitions...	You cannot include the system or boot partitions in stripe or volume sets.

Disk Administrator

Disk Administrator is the graphical tool for managing disk drives. With Disk Administrator you can create partitions, volume sets, and stripe sets, format drives with both FAT and NTFS file systems, and even assign drive letters manually. It's a much better alternative to DOS's FDISK. Disk Administrator uses a graphical representation of the drives (see Figure 5-3) and color coding to make it easy to see volume and stripe sets, as well as the separate partitions for each physical and logical disk in the system. The Disk Configuration view is what you see most often, but the other option is the Volumes view. The Volumes view gives you important information such as percent and amount of free space on each drive, and total capacity. Disk Administrator's ability to create and access a partition without having to reboot the machine is a great improvement over FDISK. Incidentally, you should be an administrator to use Disk Administrator. An inexperienced end user could get into trouble with this utility!

When you start Disk Administrator for the first time, or if you have changed your configuration, you are prompted to write a signature to the disk. This is a non-destructive signature for NT to determine whether a change has occurred since the last time Disk Administrator was started.

Creating NT Partitions

You will spend most of your time in Disk Administrator creating and formatting partitions. If you are not familiar with primary and extended partitions, and logical drives, let's go over them now.

When you start Disk Administrator, you probably will see a few partitions already. If you notice in Figure 5-4, there are two primary partitions, indicated by a dark color. Usually, a primary partition is used by the operating system. There can be a maximum of four primary partitions, but if you create an extended partition (which we will discuss next), you can use only three primary partitions. This may seem like a limitation, and in some instances it is,

FIGURE 5-3

The Disk Administrator window shows partitions for each physical and logical disk in a system

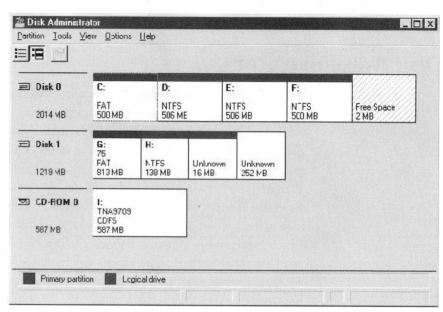

but the use of extended partitions overcomes it. An active partition is important because that is the partition the operating system uses to boot up on. It also allows you to boot to different operating systems. Most likely it is the first primary partition on the drive (C:). In RISC-based computers, this primary partition must be FAT. You can partition your entire disk as a primary, but if you would like more partitions later, you will have to destroy all the data on the drive in order to do it. I recommend that you always create an extended partition.

Extended partitions were a bit confusing for me at first. I remember needing to call a friend and have him walk me through FDISK whenever I created one. Extended partitions contain logical drives. An extended partition is not a partition that you can format like a primary partition, nor does the extended partition get a drive letter assigned. It just holds the logical drives.

Logical drives are contained within the extended partition. If you have lots of partitions, you probably are using an extended partition with many logical drives. In Disk Administrator, the logical drives are indicated by a lighter color than the primary partitions.

When you want to create a partition in Disk Administrator, you create it from free space on a drive. When you install a second hard disk in your computer, for example, you need to create a partition before the space can be used. (With stripe and volume sets, as we discussed earlier, you do not need to do this—they require that free space, not partitions, be added to the sets.) In Figure 5-4, there are nearly 4GB of free space in which you can make a partition, or several partitions.

When you partition this free space, you might create two logical drives that encompass the entire 4GB extended partition. Or you might just create another primary that spans the whole 4GB. In the next exercise we will create a

---

FIGURE 5-4

Disk Administrator
shows how much free
space is available for
creating partitions

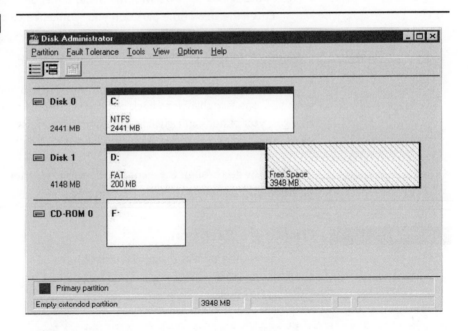

partition in Disk Administrator. In order to create a partition, you must have free space on your hard disk that is not currently allocated.

Creating a Partition

1. Open up Disk Administrator from the Administrative Tools program group.

2. Verify that you have free space to create a partition, or delete a partition that is not in use in order to free up some space. (Please make sure important data is not on the partition before you delete it!)

3. Highlight the portion of free space where you would like to create the new partition.

4. From the Partition menu, select Create.

5. If you get a dialog box regarding MS-DOS compatibility with the new partition, confirm your intentions by selecting Yes.

6. A dialog box appears with the minimum and maximum partition sizes. Enter the size of the partition you would like to create.

7. If you get another dialog box regarding MS-DOS compatibility, then confirm your intentions by selecting Yes again.

These changes do not take effect until the changes are committed, which gives you one last chance to back out if you are unsure. To commit the changes, you either can right-click the partition and select Commit Changes Now, or select the Partition menu and choose Commit Changes Now.

Let's now go through the steps of deleting a partition. You can use the partition you just created in the next exercise.

Deleting a Partition

1. Select the partition you just created.

2. From the Partition menu, select Delete, or right-click the partition and select Delete.

It's that simple. The partition now contains free space. Remember that you cannot format system and boot partitions.

Drive Letter Assignments

While *I* was working through the preceding exercises, a couple of things occurred with regard to drive letter assignments that you should be aware of. Let me begin by sharing what happened on my machine during the exercise, as illustrated in Figure 5-5. I have one drive in my computer that is divided into two partitions with the drive designators C and D. I added another drive—the 4GB drive for which I was creating the partition. When I finished creating the partition, I expected to see it take the drive designator E. I was surprised when it took drive letter N.

I realized I had about 15 network drives mapped, so I took the next available drive, which in this case was N. Needless to say, I disconnected the network drive mappings, and assigned a new drive letter. It's important to know how to assign drive letters manually.

FIGURE 5-5

When a partition is created, a dialog box offers options for assigning a drive letter to that partition

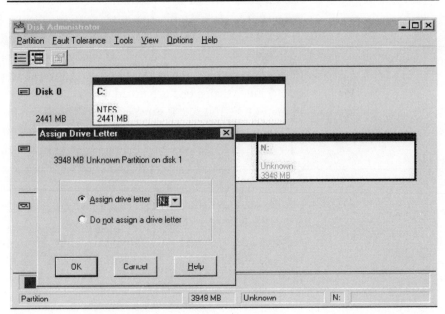

Assigning a Drive Letter

1. Highlight the partition in which you want to change the drive letter.

2. From the Tools menu, select Assign Drive Letter. You also can right-click the partition, and select Assign Drive Letter.

3. Choose the drive letter you wish to assign to the partition.

Notice that you also can choose not to assign a drive letter to the partition. This option comes in handy when you need to partition the drive, but are not sure which drive letter you would like the partition to take. It also allows you to hide the drive from any network users. Unfortunately, you can't use the drive yourself until you un-hide it by giving it a drive letter.

After my run-through of the exercise, when I restarted Disk Administrator, my CD-ROM was taking drive letter E, which is the drive designator I had wanted for the new hard disk partition. I had to select the CD-ROM (E:), and choose Do Not Assign A Drive Letter in order to free up drive letter E. After I had assigned E to the new partition, I went back to the CD-ROM and assigned it letter F. Applications that expect to see the CD-ROM at its original drive letter of E will not be able to find it, and will return an error message.

I experienced another example of what can go wrong, if you are careless, during adjustments to partitions in Disk Administrator: Once when I created a partition, a dialog box prompted me to change the reference to the drive in my BOOT.INI file. I disregarded it. When I restarted the computer the next day, I selected "Windows NT Workstation 4.0" from the menu. I noticed later that CHKDSK was busy fixing numerous problems. Had I lost my drive? When the computer finished booting, it was at the NT Server login screen. I rebooted, thinking I had selected the wrong menu item the first time, but the same thing happened again. Finally, I remembered the dialog box about the BOOT.INI modification. The references to the partitions had changed and they were pointing to the wrong partitions. While the problem was easy to fix, it was a scary situation. Take care and become familiar with the assignment procedures.

Formatting Volumes

After you have created your partition, you must format it. You can format the new partition with the FAT file system or the NTFS file system. See the preceding sections if you still have questions regarding which file system to use. Once again, be careful which partitions you are selecting to format, because all data on the partition will be erased, even if you choose to cancel while the formatting is taking place. Remember that drives formatted with NTFS will not be visible to other operating systems.

Format partitions by right-clicking them from Explorer or the My Computer icon. This brings up the dialog box in Figure 5-6. You have the choice of the normal format, or the quick format. The quick format bypasses the physical check on the disk's surface for errors. I do not recommend using the quick format the first time you format the drive.

The next exercise covers formatting the partition that we created in the earlier exercises. If you deleted the partition in the last step, now is a good time to practice creating partitions and create it again. In order to start formatting, we need to verify that you performed the steps correctly. You should see the partition with a drive letter now, and it should say Unformatted. Right-click the partition. The option to format should not be grayed out. If it is, you didn't commit the changes when you created the partition, so select Commit Changes Now.

<table>
<tr><td>EXERCISE 5-9</td></tr>
</table>

Formatting a Volume

1. Start by right-clicking the partition you wish to format, and selecting Format.

2. The formatting dialog box appears as shown in Figure 5-6. Choose FAT or NTFS for the file system.

3. Accept the default allocation size.

4. Enter a label if you wish, or just leave it blank.

5. Select the Quick Format option if you wish.

6. Click Start to begin formatting.

Just so you know, I have Novell NetWare on one of my partitions, which Disk Administrator reports as unknown. I can't really do anything with it other than delete it from Disk Administrator, which is what I am tempted to do. (I hope that does not offend any NetWare lovers out there.)

Recovering Disk Configuration Information

Even if you are extra careful while configuring partitions in Disk Administrator, you can easily make a quick decision that you will regret. Fortunately, Disk Administrator can save and restore disk configurations. When you are satisfied with a certain configuration, you can save it to floppy disk where it can be used in the event of an emergency. An emergency that would require you to restore the disk configuration would be a hard disk drive failure, where you would need to reinstall NT. After NT has been installed on the new drive, you can restore your disk configuration to the state it was in before the disk failure. This can save time while you get your computer back into its original state. Please note that this does not save data that was on the disk before the failure. Back up your data. Failure to do so is unprofessional and potentially costly.

To save the configuration information, select the Partition menu, choose Configuration, and select Save. This prompts you to insert a floppy disk on which to save the configuration. Remember that any changes you make should be updated using RDISK.EXE. You should have a recovery disk for every computer, and you cannot use the same recovery disk for every computer in your company.

To restore the information from a saved configuration, select the Partition menu, then choose Configuration, and select Restore.

Later chapters cover recovery techniques that use the emergency repair disk you just created. Microsoft always has extensive troubleshooting questions and scenarios in its exams.

Third-Party Disk Utilities

There are a number of third-party disk utilities that augment the performance of Windows NT Workstation. A thorough analysis of the available products is beyond the scope of this book. One important fact relating to the use of third-party products is that they must be compatible with NT, and more specifically, the NTFS file system. The rule is not to use third-party products that are unaware of long filenames. For example, a 16-bit program, such as an older version of Norton Utilities, will destroy them. Security attributes that you assigned to the file or folder will be lost as well. Use only 32-bit utilities that are designed to run on Windows NT. I know NT looks like Windows 95, and some products are compatible with both operating systems, but generally the file system utilities, such as DEFRAG, will not work with NTFS.

NT did not ship with a disk defragmenting utility. Fortunately, there are a few great third-party products for NT that provide a graphical way to defragment your hard disks. The most notable are Norton Utilities Speed Disk, and DiskKeeper by Executive Software. Both products support FAT and NTFS file systems, scheduling, and consolidation of free space. It would be wise to invest in one of the following disk defragmenting tools before your file system gets out of control. It is easier to control fragmentation before it begins. We all can attest to the fact that a system slows down over time. This is due mostly to fragmentation.

Norton Utilities Speed Disk

Norton Utilities have been around for a long time and have a loyal following. It was no surprise that Norton Utilities for NT included the highest-quality tools for optimizing and monitoring NT, including Speed Disk, the graphical disk defragmenting utility. Although NT tries its best to keep an NTFS volume from becoming fragmented, over time the fragmentation will increase. Speed Disk analyzes your drive and returns a percentage of fragmentation. It then recommends the necessary actions to eliminate fragmentation. Since the defragmentation process takes several minutes to complete, or even longer if you are performing the thorough option, it is nice to be able to schedule Speed Disk to execute at times you specify. I prefer Speed Disk to do a standard defragmentation a few times a week, and a thorough defragmentation every couple of weeks, depending on the environment and usage of the computer.

Executive Software's DiskKeeper

DiskKeeper from Executive Software is another of the leading disk defragmentation utilities. DiskKeeper has most of the features Speed Disk has, and can accomplish the same tasks as well. One of the features I like about DiskKeeper is the quick and easy way I can view the fragmention report on my drives with the Analyze button. This enables me to view file fragments on a percentage basis, and DiskKeeper suggests appropriate actions to take to correct problems. The detailed fragmentation report has everything you need to know about the status of fragments in your file system, including pagefile fragments, number of fragmented files, percent of disk fragmented, and even a list of the most fragmented files. The fact that DiskKeeper can run in the background using idle resources enables you to work on the system while the defragmentation is taking place. This is a welcome feature for those of us who don't have the time to just stare at the screen for 20 minutes. Another feature that is helpful is the capability to exclude files and directories from the exclusion lists. Unfortunately, DiskKeeper does not tell you what it is doing at each phase of the defragmentation process. Still, I recommend you download the DiskKeeper Lite demo and try it for yourself.

CERTIFICATION SUMMARY

Windows NT supports two files systems: FAT and NTFS. The FAT file system is provided to maintain compatibility with older operating systems, such as MS-DOS, Windows 3.x, and Windows 95. FAT partitions use the 8.3 naming scheme, and do not support long filenames, whereas NT provides long filename support with a new version of FAT called the VFAT. These long filenames are truncated when copied to a FAT partition.

While the FAT file system can be used in some situations, the NTFS file system is the system of choice for Windows NT. Some of the new features provided with NT cannot be implemented without use of the NTFS file system. This new file system, introduced with NT, supports larger hard disks, compression, extended security attributes, file-level security, fault tolerance, and long filenames.

With Windows NT you have several disk management options for increasing performance and usability. You can create stripe sets, which spread data across several hard disks so that the data can be read from multiple drives at once for greater disk throughput. You also can create volume sets that consolidate free space from any partition or disk and create one large logical drive. None of these options is fault tolerant.

Disk management is performed through the use of the Windows NT Disk Administrator. This graphical utility allows you to create and manage partitions, stripe sets, and volume sets. You also can format partitions with FAT or NTFS—even convert a FAT partition to NTFS. Disk Administrator is useful for viewing disk configuration information, such as disk capacity, free space, percent of disk free, and format.

 # TWO-MINUTE DRILL

❑ File Allocation Table (FAT) is the file system used in older operating systems such as DOS, Windows 3.x, and Windows 95.

❑ FAT naming conventions use the 8.3 syntax—eight letters for the filename, and three letters for the extension.

❏ The VFAT system enables you to use long filenames, and is completely compatible with FAT.

❏ NTFS creates FAT-compatible 8.3 names by using the first six letters of the long filename followed by a tilde and a number.

❏ NTFS supports long filenames, compression, and security attributes.

❏ NTFS partitions cannot be accessed from non-NT operating systems.

❏ You can create primary or extended partitions. Primary partitions can be active. Extended partitions contain logical drives.

❏ The lazy-write feature is a transaction log that keeps track of whether writes to the disk have been completed or not.

❏ FAT is best for volumes of less than 400MB, and NTFS for anything over 400MB.

❏ On an NTFS partition, when you move a file or folder that is compressed to another area on the same partition, it retains its state.

❏ When a file or folder is copied to another area on the same partition, it inherits the permissions of the target folder.

❏ When you are moving or copying a file or folder to another NTFS partition, it always inherits the compression attribute of the target folder.

❏ POSIX is an open system standard for application portability among different computer platforms.

❏ You can convert a drive from FAT to NTFS during installation of NT, or with the CONVERT.EXE program, or through Disk Administrator.

❏ An HPFS partition must be converted prior to NT installation.

❏ Volume sets let you combine free space on several partitions into one large volume with one single drive letter.

❏ Stripe sets spread data across an array of disks to improve read/write performance.

❏ Stripe sets and volume sets are not fault tolerant, and cannot encompass system and boot partitions.

❏ Disk Administrator is the graphical tool for creating partitions, volume sets, and stripe sets, and formatting drives.

❏ An emergency repair disk can be made through Disk Administrator, or the RDISK utility that allows you to recover disk configuration information in the event of an emergency.

SELF TEST

The following questions will help you measure your understanding of the material presented in this chapter. Read all the choices carefully, as there may be more than one correct answer. Choose all correct answers for each question.

1. Which of the following is an acceptable FAT filename?

    A. pay|day.txt

    B. Thursday memo.doc

    C. airplane.gif

    D. *newfile.txt

2. What will be the FAT alias for this long filename:
Notes from March meeting concerning X.400.txt

    A. notesfr~1.400

    B. notesf~1.txt

    C. notesfr~1.txt

    D. notes f~1.txt

3. What will be the FAT alias for this long directory name:
Current.proposal.34

    A. current.pro

    B. current~1.34

    C. curren~1.pro

    D. curren~1.34

4. What will be the outcome if I move a file called FINANCE.TXT, which is *not*

compressed, to a compressed folder on a different partition on my only hard disk?

    A. The file is compressed because I moved, rather than copied it to the new partition.

    B. The file is not compressed because it retains its compression attribute.

    C. The file is compressed because of the compression attribute of the target folder.

    D. The file is not compressed because it was not moved or copied to a different hard disk.

5. What will be the outcome if I move the file C:\job duties\Friday.txt, which is compressed, to the C:\monthly duties\ directory, on the same computer, which is not compressed?

    A. The file will not be compressed because the target folder is not compressed.

    B. The file will be compressed because it will retain its compression attribute.

    C. The file will not be compressed because it was moved, not copied.

    D. The file will be compressed because it was moved, not copied.

6. I have a Pentium 133 with 64MB of RAM and a 2GB hard disk that is partitioned into several 200MB partitions. I need to choose a file system that supports long filenames and has the capability to track file updates

by viewing their timestamps. Which file system should I use?

A. FAT, because NTFS does not use timestamps.

B. NTFS, because FAT does not support long filenames and timestamps.

C. FAT, because the partition sizes are small.

D. HPFS, because FAT or NTFS cannot fulfill these requirements.

7. I am using a 486/33 with 16MB of RAM and a 540MB hard disk. The hard disk is divided into two equal partitions. I need to restrict access to a certain directory on the computer from other users who may log on. Which file system should I use?

A. FAT, because the partitions are too small for NTFS.

B. NTFS, because only NTFS allows security attributes to be set.

C. FAT, because NTFS cannot be used on a 486/33.

D. HPFS, because NTFS cannot be installed on a partition that small.

8. I am upgrading an NT 3.51 computer that has the HPFS file system installed. What is the best way to convert the file system to FAT?

A. Use HPFS2NT.EXE to convert the partition to NT before the upgrade.

B. Use CONVERT.EXE to change the partition to NT before the upgrade.

C. Install NT normally, then convert the partition to NTFS using Disk Administrator.

D. None of the above.

9. What is the only way to convert a partition from NTFS to FAT?

A. There is no way to convert NTFS to FAT.

B. You have to use Disk Administrator.

C. You have to use CONVERT.EXE.

D. It must be converted during setup.

10. Fill in the blank.
NT uses the _____ feature that uses a transaction log to keep track of whether writes to the disk have been completed or not.

11. What is the most effective usage of space?

A. Stripe set.

B. Mirrored drive.

C. Volume set.

D. None of the above. They all require overhead.

12. (True/False) If you lose one of the members of a volume set, you only lose the data that was contained on that drive.

13. What is the total size of a stripe set created from the following free regions of space: 200MB, 450MB, 150MB, 235MB, and 180MB?

A. 1215MB

B. 850MB

C. 650MB

D. 750MB

14. I want the fastest performance from my configuration, but I do not require fault tolerance. What should I use?

    A. Stripe set with parity

    B. Volume set

    C. Stripe set

    D. None of the above. They are all fault tolerant.

15. (True/False) When you try to format a section of free space, you are prompted to create a partition before you format.

16. (True/False). A drive can have as many as four extended partitions.

17. Fill in the blank.
    The utility used to compress files and directories from the command line is

    _____.

18. What menu option would you choose in Disk Administrator to format a volume?

    A. Partition

    B. Options

    C. Format

    D. Tools

19. What would be the result if I issued this command to convert my FAT J: drive to NTFS?
    J:\>CONVERT J: /fs:ntfs

    A. It would work fine.

    B. It would not work. The syntax is incorrect.

    C. It would ask if you would like to schedule conversion for the next time the system restarts.

    D. It would ask for the allocation unit size since I did not specify it.

20. (True/False) MFT stands for Master Format Table.

MICROSOFT CERTIFIED SYSTEMS ENGINEER

6

Understanding Windows NT 4.0 Security

CERTIFICATION OBJECTIVES

Security is a key element of a networked operating system, especially one that is put onto the Internet. If a business relies on a networked computer, maintaining the right level of security for that network is vital. Unfortunately, many supervisors consider security to mean that anyone who breaks into their company's system will be caught. That isn't good enough. Once a break-in happens, the damage is done. In this chapter, I give you the information you need to take a proactive, not reactive, approach to network security. I know it's always possible to break into a networked system, but if you take reasonable steps to stop intruders, you increase your safety margin.

Security is a balancing act. There are drawbacks to implementing too much security as well as too little. A company's need for a secure system must be weighed against its goal of meeting a mission. If you apply so much security that the client company can't do its job, you've failed at applying the proper security. You need to know what level of security is required to safeguard the system, and at what level the mission suffers. This chapter explains NT security and how to implement it. How much security you implement depends on your company's policies and your ability to sell the need for security.

CERTIFICATION OBJECTIVE 6.01

Windows NT 4.0 Security Model

The NT security model is made up of four main components: logon processes, Local Security Authority (LSA), Security Account Manager (SAM), and the Security Reference Monitor. Figure 6-1 is a graphical representation of the security model. I'll give a brief explanation of each component. Later we'll examine their functions in more depth.

■ The logon process is the method by which the user gets initial access to the system. There are two kinds of logon processes: interactive logons at the computer console, and remote network logons.

■ The Local Security Authority is the heart of the security subsystem. It creates security access tokens, authenticates users, and manages the local security policy.

FIGURE 6-1   The NT security model, showing the main components

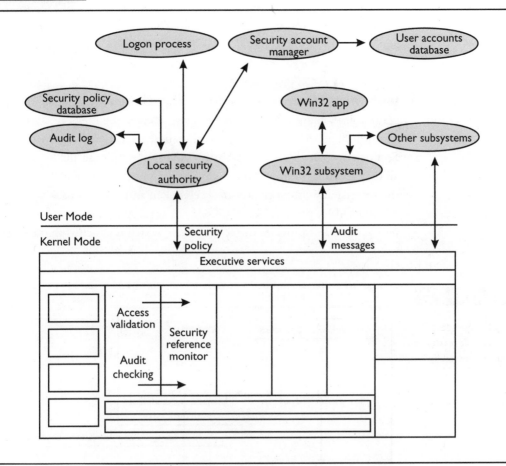

- The SAM database maintains all user, group, and workstation accounts in a secure database. The Local Security Authority validates user logons against the SAM database.

- The Security Reference Monitor verifies that the user has permissions to access the requested object, then performs that action. It also provides audit messages when needed.

Security for NT Workstation starts at logon. The user presses CTRL-ALT-DEL to activate the WINLOGON process. See Figure 6-2 for an illustration of WINLOGON's function. The user is prompted for a username and password. WINLOGON passes this information to the security subsystem. At the heart of the security subsystem is the Local Security Authority. The LSA generates access tokens, manages the local security policy, and provides interactive user authentication services. The LSA also controls audit policy, and logs the audit messages generated by the Security Reference Monitor. The security subsystem verifies usernames and passwords against the Security Account Manager database. SAM is like a hive in the Registry, where all user account information is stored. If the information passes verification, the security subsystem creates an access token and passes it back to the WINLOGON process. WINLOGON calls the Win32 subsystem to create a new process and provides the access token, which is attached to the newly

---

FIGURE 6-2

WINLOGON process passes logon information to the security subsystem

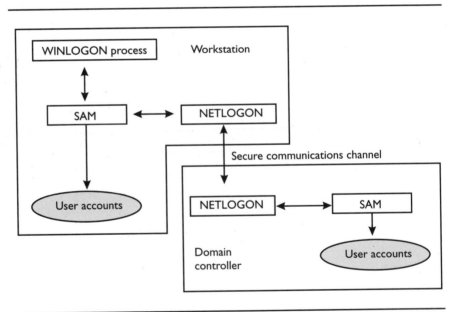

created process. The access token then functions as the user's ID card, so the username and password are no longer needed.

Logon Authentication

logon types

-local
- remote
- domain
- pass-through

NT supports four logon types: local, remote, domain, and pass-through authentication.

In a local logon, you log onto a computer at that computer's console by selecting your computer name in the Logon To dialog box.

A remote logon occurs when someone accesses your computer via the network. Your workstation receives an encrypted username and password from the requesting computer via the NETLOGON service. From that point, your workstation's security subsystem processes the request as if it were a local logon, with the NETLOGON service replacing the WINLOGON process.

To log onto a domain, you must choose which domain you wish to log onto when you enter your username and password. If your workstation is a member of that domain, it logs on using the domain logon method; otherwise, it uses pass-through authentication. Domain logon starts when you submit username, password, and domain name to the WINLOGON process. WINLOGON identifies your request as going to the network, and passes it to the NETLOGON service. The NETLOGON service establishes a secure communications channel with the domain controller. The NETLOGON service on the domain controller then passes the request to the domain controller's security subsystem, where the username and password are verified against the domain's SAM database. If the username and password are correct, the domain controller creates an access token and informs your workstation of a successful match.

Pass-through authentication occurs when you log onto a *trusted domain*— a domain in which your workstation doesn't have an account. Before the WINLOGON process even begins, NT Workstation creates a secure communications channel with the domain controller of which it is a member. When you log onto a trusted domain, your request is passed to the domain controller where your secure communications channel exists. The domain controller then processes the logon to the trusted domain for you. Your member domain controller notifies your workstation of a successful logon.

Windows NT Logon Security Features

As I've stated, NT security starts at logon. NT uses *mandatory logon* to force everyone to log on before it grants access to the system. It also protects the system by implementing Restricted User Mode, which restricts permissions to the current user.

Mandatory Logon

You need to press CTRL-ALT-DEL to activate the WINLOGON process. This prevents trojan horse viruses from being installed on your system. When you press CTRL-ALT-DEL, NT stops all programs and activates the WINLOGON dialog box. The WINLOGON dialog box then passes your logon information to the security subsystem. Mandatory logon allows NT to perform auditing and setting resource quotas, and allows you to customize your settings and desktop.

Restricted User Mode

NT doesn't allow users or programs to access the hardware directly. This means that a program must ask the operating system to open the file. The operating system verifies that the program is allowed to read the file. If the program has the proper permissions, NT opens the file for the program. If the program doesn't have the proper permissions, access is denied to the program and the user.

Windows NT Objects

To really understand NT security, you need to understand the concept of objects. In NT, just about everything is an object. A file is an object and so is a window. NT controls access to objects. A program asks the NT operating system to perform specific tasks to objects. For example, when you open a text file in Notepad called HELP.TXT, Notepad makes a request to NT to open the object HELP.TXT. NT then verifies your access permissions, and if you have the proper permissions it opens HELP.TXT. Programs are not allowed to access the hardware directly. This is why many MS-DOS programs won't work on NT.

Type

The most common type of object is a file object, but just about everything you can think of is an object; named pipes and processes are also objects. The type of object you are setting permissions for determines the type of permissions that may be set. For example, you can read, write, and delete a file. With a printer, you can manage documents, purge documents, and view the printer queue.

There are two classes of objects: container objects and noncontainer objects. A container object can contain other objects; a noncontainer object doesn't contain other objects. A container object can inherit permissions from its parent container. I'll explain this in more detail later in this chapter.

Attributes

Any object that can be secured has a security descriptor. The security descriptor describes the security attributes for the object. The security descriptor is made up of four parts.

- Owner security ID identifies the owner of the object, which allows that person to change the permissions for the object.

- Group security ID is used only by the POSIX subsystem.

- Discretionary Access Control List (ACL) identifies the groups and users who are allowed and denied access. Owners control the discretionary ACL.

- System ACL controls the auditing of messages that the system creates. The security administrators set system ACLs.

Access Control

Now that you have logged onto the system, how does NT identify you and your permissions level? NT uniquely identifies every user and group on the system. This is necessary for granting permissions to individual users or groups. It also allows you to get very granular with access permissions. To accomplish this, NT uses security IDs and group IDs.

Security ID (SID)

A SID is used to uniquely identify each NT Workstation and Server on a network. NT creates a new SID for each user added to the system. The SID is never changed and can never be re-created. Because a SID can never be re-created, you need to be very careful when deleting user accounts. In fact, it is common practice to disable accounts for a period of time before you delete them. This saves you time later if you really didn't need to delete the account. For example: Betty, a receptionist in marketing, gets mad one day and tells her boss that she quits. Her boss notifies you, the system administrator, that her account must be deleted immediately, since her account has access to sensitive information. You follow your customer's order and delete her account. The next day, Betty's replacement, Robert, comes in and needs access to all the same information that Betty had access to. So you create a new account for him, and try to assign him to the same groups and rights that Betty had—this could be a considerable task. What should you have done instead of deleting Betty's account? You should have disabled the account. This would prevent Betty from logging in and doing unsavory things to her boss's sensitive files. When her replacement came in, you simply could have renamed the account, changed the password, and then enabled the account. This would give Robert the same access that Betty had, and it would have kept your system secure by preventing Betty from logging on.

Group ID

NT uses a unique group ID to distinguish each group on your system. The group ID is then placed on the access token created for the user at logon. NT places the ID of each group that the user belongs to on the token. The user keeps that token and its access permissions until he logs off. If the administrator changes the groups the user belongs to while he is still logged on, the changes don't become effective until he logs off and logs back on. This is very important to remember when you are removing users from a group because they no longer need to have access to that group's files. Simply removing them from the group doesn't guarantee that they won't access the files shared to that group.

e x a m
ⓦ a t c h

This can be tricky if you see it on the test. The key to assigning and removing a user to a group is that the user must be logged off before the change can take effect. If the user isn't logged on when the change is made, the change takes effect the next time he logs on. If the user is logged on when the change is made, he must log off and log back on to apply the changes.

CERTIFICATION OBJECTIVE 6.02

Access Tokens and Processes

NT uses *subjects* to ensure that a program that a user executes has no more access to objects than the user does. Whatever rights and permissions a user has, so do the programs that the user executes. If a user can delete a file, so can the program. A subject is a combination of the user's access token and the program that is running on the user's behalf. Whenever a program is running, it is running in the *security context* of the user. The security context controls what access the user has to the object. Since NT follows the client/server model, there are two types of subjects:

- Simple subject: A user logs on the process is assigned a security context.
- Server subject: A process that runs as a protected server, which has other subjects, called clients. When clients request a process, the server subject takes on the security context of the client.

In order for a server process to access objects that it doesn't have permissions to, it uses a technique called *impersonation*. If the client process has proper access permissions, the server process impersonates the client process in order to access the object.

ACLs and ACEs

As I stated earlier in the chapter, ACL stands for Access Control List. An ACL is comprised of Access Control Entries (ACE). The ACE specifies auditing and access permissions for a given object, for a specific user or group of users.

There are three types of ACEs: AccessAllowed, AccessDenied, and SystemAudit. AccessAllowed and AccessDenied are discretionary ACEs, which grant and deny access to a user or group of users. SystemAudit is a system security ACE, which logs security events to the event viewer.

Every ACE must have an access mask. An access mask tells the ACE which attributes are available for a particular object type. The ACE can then grant permissions based on that mask. For example, a file can set Read, Write, Execute, Delete, Take ownership, and Change permissions, because an access mask defines these attributes. See Figure 6-3 for an illustration of the access mask's role in access validation.

FIGURE 6-3

The access validation process. ACEs specify access permissions for an object

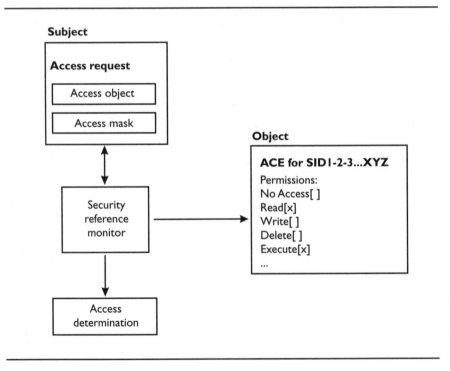

When an ACL is evaluated, every ACE is processed and evaluated in the following order:

1. AccessDenied ACEs are processed before AccessAllowed ACEs. The security ID in the user's security token is evaluated against the security ID in the ACE. If no match occurs, the ACE is not processed.

2. If access is denied, the security subsystem checks to see if the original desired access mask contains *either* a ReadControl or a WRITE_DAC. If it does, the system also checks to see if the user is the owner. *If both evaluate to true,* access is allowed.

3. For an AccessDenied ACE, the ACE access mask and the desired access mask are compared. If there are any accesses in both masks, processing stops, and access is denied. Otherwise, the next ACE is processed.

4. For an AccessAllowed ACE, the ACE access mask and the desired access mask are compared. If all accesses in the desired access mask are matched by the ACE, processing stops, and access is granted. Otherwise, the next ACE is processed.

5. If the contents of the desired access mask are not completely matched when the end of the ACL is reached, access is denied.

To better explain, here are two examples of the validation process. For the first example, refer to Figure 6-4 as we go through the steps of the process.

Example One: A user, MikeS, wants to delete a file called J:\JESSE \HELP.TXT. Figure 6-4 shows the groups MikeS belongs to, and the discretionary ACL applied to the file.

NT reads the discretionary ACL and evaluates it in the following way:

1. NT reads MikeS's desired access mask of Delete for the file HELP.TXT.

2. NT reads the AccessDenied ACE to Sales. AccessDenied, by default, is placed at the front of the discretionary ACL. Once an AccessDenied is processed, further processing of the ACL halts.

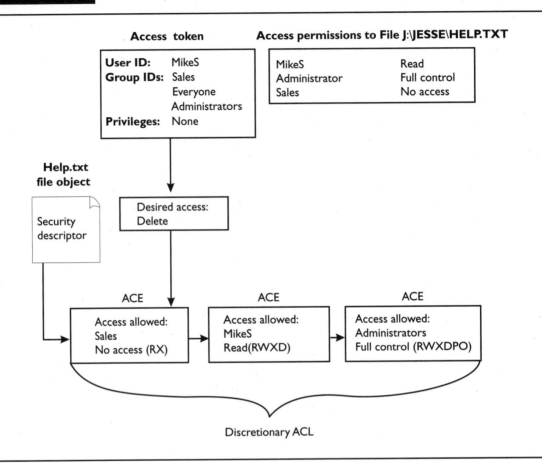

FIGURE 6-4 Delete request denied because of the AccessDenied ACE for Sales

In Figure 6-5 user MikeS is granted access to delete the file HELP.TXT. NT reads the discretionary ACL and evaluates it in the following way:

1. NT reads MikeS's desired access mask to delete the file HELP.TXT.

2. NT processes the request by first looking at MikeS ACE. No match is found.

3. NT then processes the group Sales and matches the Delete request. Further processing of the ACL halts, since the proper access is matched.

FIGURE 6-5   Delete request allowed because of Delete permission in the Sales ACE

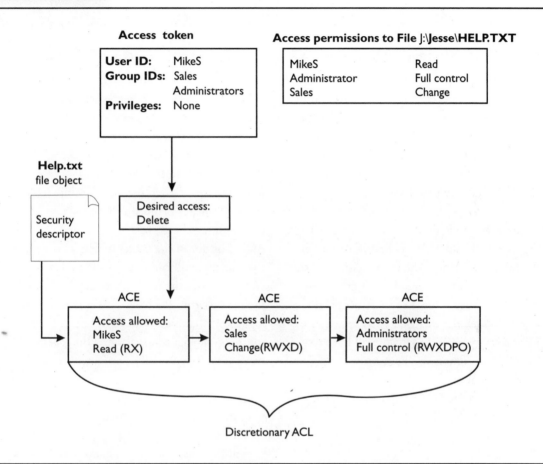

Since NT stops processing the ACL as soon as the desired access mask is matched, it is important that the No Access ACE is always processed first.

exam
Watch

Permissions are cumulative, except for No Access. You don't have to belong to a group that has all the proper permissions. If your account has Read access and you belong to a group with Write access, you will be granted Read and Write access.

FROM THE CLASSROOM

How Much Money Do You Get When You Cache the Access Token?

We see the problem of out-of-date access tokens frequently. In fact, we create this situation in one of our classroom labs to expose the students to the symptoms and the fix. Consider the following scenario: You get a call from a user who needs to access a folder on the server. You check the security permissions on the folder and grant the user permission to the folder. You tell the user that he is all set. Several minutes later, the user calls back and says he still cannot access the folder. You check the permissions and they seem okay, but the user still can't get access. Now you do what some support people do, right? You tell the user that you are not sure what is going on and that you will have to get back to him tomorrow. Tomorrow comes, and you call the user to see if anything has changed (as if you expected elves to fix the problem during the night). The user reports that everything is fine and he can access the folder. What happened?

Here is what happened. When the user logged on, the security processes created an object called an access token. The access token is cached in memory. This makes referencing the token much faster. Among other things, the access token contains portions of the Access Control List (ACL) which is how NTFS permissions are recorded, indicating who has what permissions to an object. When a user attempts to access an object, such as a folder, the security system checks the access token to verify that the user has appropriate authority to access the object. In our scenario, the user had no permissions to the folder, so his access token indicated that. When the NT administrator changed the permissions to give the user access to the folder, the permissions got updated in the ACL, but not in the access token. The result is that the user still can't access the folder.

So why was the user able to access the folder the next morning? The answer is that the user logged off that night and went home. In the morning, he logged on again. This generated a new access token, which contained updated information, and the user was able to access the folder. The quick fix for the administrator is to have the user log off and then log on again.

This scenario is fairly benign, because the user did not have access, so damage could not be done to the data. Consider a situation in which a user has Delete permission to an object. You don't want him to have it, so you change the permissions on the object. Will the user still be able to delete the object? Hint: Was the user logged on at the time you made the change?

—*By Shane Clawson, MCT, MCSE*

File and Directory Security

The type of file system you choose determines what level of security you can use on NT. FAT doesn't allow folder or file permissions, but NTFS does. Don't get file and directory security confused with share-level security. Share-level security can be applied to any file system, because it is secured via the network. File and directory security via NTFS secures the files from the actual user, whether it is from the network or from the console. This will be explained in further detail when I discuss share-level security. If you're concerned about security, NTFS is the file system to use. (Except if you have a RISC processor. RISC systems require the system partition be formatted with FAT. However, other partitions may be formatted with NTFS. For RISC systems you can secure the system partition with Disk Administrator to allow only administrators access to the system partition.)

With NTFS, the owner can set the following permissions for file level permissions.

- **No Access**   The user cannot access the file at all. This takes precedence over all other permissions. If a user is assigned to a group with Read Access, and a group with No Access, the user will not be able to read the file because No Access always takes precedence.

- **Read**   Allows the user to read or execute the file. No modifications may be made to the file.

- **Change**   Allows the user to read, write, execute, or delete the file.

- **Full Control**   Allows the user to read, write, execute, delete, change permissions, and take ownership of the file.

- **Special Access**   Allows the owner to choose individual access permissions, read, write, execute, delete, change permissions, and take ownership of the file.

File level permissions are summarized more simply in the following table.

Access Level	Permissions
No Access	None
Read	RX
Change	RWXD
Full Control	RWXDPO
Special Access	Custom
Permissions Key: (R)ead, (W)rite, e(X)ecute, (D)elete, change (P)ermissions, take (O)wnership	

The owner can also set folder-level permissions. The following permissions are available:

- **No Access**   Completely restricts the user from accessing the folder and its files. No Access takes precedence over all other permissions set for the user.

- **List**   Allows the user to view the files and folders list within the directory, but the user cannot access the files and folders.

- **Read**   Allows the user to read files within the folder, but doesn't allow the user to save changes.

- **Add**   The user can't list or read the files in the folder, but can write new files to that folder.

- **Add & Read**   Allows the user to list, read, and write new files within the folder. The user can read, but not save changes to existing files.

- **Change**   Allows the user to list, read, write new files, modify, and delete existing files within the folder. The user can also change attributes and delete the folder.

- **Full Control**   Allows the user to list, read, change, and delete the folder and the files within the folder. The user also can take ownership and change permissions of the folder and its files.

- **Special Directory Access**   Allows the owner to set custom access to the directory.

- **Special File Access**   Allows the owner to set custom access on the files within the folder.

Folder-level permissions are summarized more simply in the following table.

Access Level	Folder Access Permissions	File Access Permissions
No Access	None	None
List	RX	N/A
Read	RX	RX
Add	WX	N/A
Add & Read	RWX	RX
Change	RWXD	RWXD
Full Control	RWXDPO	RWXDPO
Special Directory Access	Custom	
Special File Access	Custom	Custom
Permissions Key: (R)ead, (W)rite, e(X)ecute, (D)elete, change (P)ermissions, take (O)wnership		

exam
ⓦatch

There is one more permission type called File Delete Child. File Delete Child is a POSIX function that allows a user with full control of a folder to delete a top-level file within that folder, even though the user doesn't have permissions to delete that file. Let's say you have full control of a folder called Sales Reports. Within that folder there is a file called MARY.XLS in which you have No Access permissions assigned. Since you have full control of the Sales Reports folder, you can delete the file MARY.XLS, even though you don't have access to that file.

Viewing and Changing Permissions

You can set permissions using the GUI interface or the command shell. The GUI is generally easier to learn and remember, but the command shell can be quicker when changing permissions on several files and folders at once. With the GUI, you can view and change permissions using Explorer, Desktop, or even the Open/Save dialog box.

EXERCISE 6-1

Changing Access Permissions for a Directory

In this exercise you learn how to change permissions on a directory. You will remove the Everyone group from the directory and give your user account full control. Before you begin, you must have an NTFS-formatted volume on your system. If you don't have an NTFS volume you must run the command:

```
CONVERT drive: /FS:NTFS
```

Where drive is the letter of the drive you wish to convert to NTFS.

1. Once you have an NTFS volume (Figure 6-6), right-click a directory in that volume and choose Properties.

FIGURE 6-6

NTFS volume

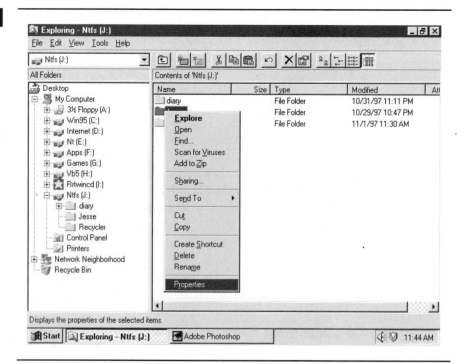

2. Next select the Security tab and then click the Permissions button (Figure 6-7).

3. Now click the Remove button to remove the group Everyone from having access to this directory. Warning: Make sure the directory isn't part of the NT system directory. Then click the Add button (see Figure 6-8). If there is more than one group in the list, ensure that the special group Everone is selected, then click the Remove button.

4. Next click the Show Users button. Select your username and click the Add button. On the Type of Access drop-down menu, choose Full Control. Finally, click OK. Select your computer name from the List Names From drop-down box (see Figure 6-9).

5. At the Directory Permissions screen (see Figure 6-10), you have the option to Replace Permissions on Subdirectories and to Replace Permissions on Existing Files. For this exercise, just choose the default.

FIGURE 6-7

The Security tab
in Properties

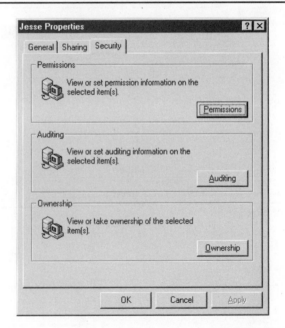

FIGURE 6-8

Directory Permissions

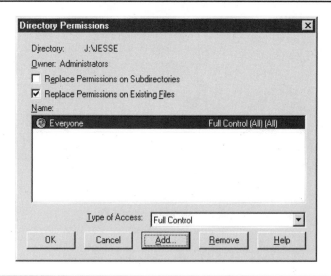

FIGURE 6-9

Adding a user

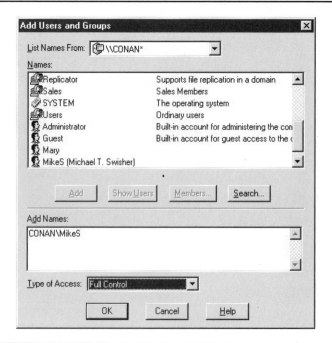

FIGURE 6-10

You have the option to
replace permissions

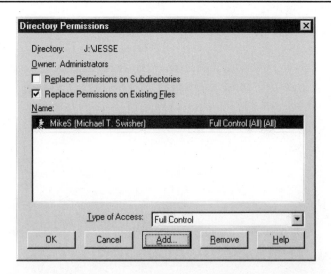

Command Prompt

You also can use the command prompt to change permissions on directories
(see Figure 6-11). The NT command shell has a built-in command called
CACLS.EXE. The following are the available switches:

```
CACLS filename [/T] [/E] [/C] [/G user:perm] [/R user [...]]
               [/P user:perm [...]] [/D user [...]]
    filename     Displays ACLs.
    /T           Changes ACLs of specified files in the
                 current directory and all subdirectories.
    /E           Edit ACL instead of replacing it.
    /C           Continue on access denied errors.
    /G user:perm Grant specified user access rights.
                 Perm can be: R   Read
                              C   Change (write)
                              F   Full control
    /R user      Revoke specified user's access rights (only
                 valid with /E).
    /P user:perm Replace specified user's access rights.
                 Perm can be: N   None
                              R   Read
```

```
                                   C  Change (write)
                                   F  Full control
             /D user        Deny specified user access.
```

CACLS: Displays or modifies access control lists (ACLs) of files
or directories.

```
Usage: cacls filename [/t] [/e] [/c] [/g user|group:perm]
[/r user|group [...]]
                              [/p user|group:perm [...]] [/d
                              user|group [...]]
Parameters: filename Displays ACLs of specified directory,
file or files.
 /t Changes ACLs of specified files in the current directory
and all subdirectories.
/e Edit ACL instead of replacing it.
   /c Continue changing ACLs, ignoring errors.
   /g user|group:perm Grant specified user or group access
   permissions.
     perm can be:
     r Read
     c Change (write)
     f Full control
/r user Revoke specified user's or group's access
permissions.
/p user|group:perm Replace specified user's or group's
access permissions.
 perm can be:
 n None
 r Read
 c Change (write)
 f Full control
/d user|group Deny specified user access.
```

You can specify more than one file, user, or group in a command. Wildcard
characters in file and directory names are supported.

Group names containing a space need to be contained in double quotes, for
example "group name".

Using CACLS to Change Permissions

Now let's change back the permissions on the folder you changed in
Exercise 6-1. You will need to remove your username and put the
Everyone group, with full control, on the desired folder.

FIGURE 6-11

You can change
permissions at the
command prompt

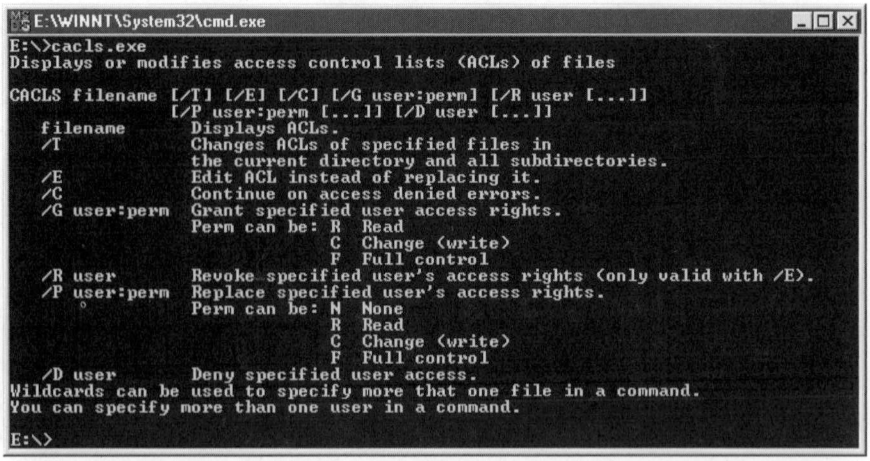

```
E:\WINNT\System32\cmd.exe                                         _ □ ×
E:\>cacls.exe
Displays or modifies access control lists (ACLs) of files

CACLS filename [/T] [/E] [/C] [/G user:perm] [/R user [...]]
                  [/P user:perm [...]] [/D user [...]]
     filename      Displays ACLs.
     /T            Changes ACLs of specified files in
                   the current directory and all subdirectories.
     /E            Edit ACL instead of replacing it.
     /C            Continue on access denied errors.
     /G user:perm  Grant specified user access rights.
                   Perm can be: R  Read
                                C  Change (write)
                                F  Full control
     /R user       Revoke specified user's access rights (only valid with /E).
     /P user:perm  Replace specified user's access rights.
                   Perm can be: N  None
                                R  Read
                                C  Change (write)
                                F  Full control
     /D user       Deny specified user access.
Wildcards can be used to specify more that one file in a command.
You can specify more than one user in a command.

E:\>
```

EXERCISE 6-2

Using CACLS to Change Access Permissions

This is a two-step process. Step 1 changes the permissions on the folder. In order to change the permissions on every file in that directory, you must use wildcard characters. That is step 2.

```
1. C:\>CACLS J:\JESSE /E /R MikeS /G Everyone:F

2. C:\>CACLS J:\JESSE\*.* /E /R MikeS /G Everyone:F
```

If you used the /T switch, it would replace the permissions on the files, but it would also replace permissions on all files and subfolders under that directory.

Transaction Logging

NTFS uses transaction logging for recoverability. NTFS uses a master file table (MFT) to find files on its volume. The first record in the MFT describes the MFT, and the second record is a mirror of the MFT. If the first record is corrupt, the second record is used. The boot sector knows the locations of the MFT and the MFT mirror file. An exact copy of the boot sector is stored at the logical center of the disk. The third record in the MFT is the log file. The log file records all file transaction information. This is the key to recoverability.

When a user changes a file, the log file service records all undo and redo information as a transaction in the log file. Undo information is used to roll back a transaction in case of an error, or if NTFS is unsure a successful transaction occurred, or if a transaction isn't completed. The redo information is used to repeat a transaction. If your system crashes, NTFS performs three data passes. The first pass is an analysis pass that checks for errors, and determines the cluster number of the error by using the log file. The second pass is a redo pass. NTFS completes transactions from the last checkpoint operation. The final pass is the undo pass. The undo pass rolls back any incomplete transactions.

The log file service maintains two objects, the restart area, and the infinite log file. The restart area is the place where the client's last checkpoint operation occurred. Two copies of the restart area are maintained for redundancy. The infinite log file is a circular logging file. When new records are added, they are appended to the end of the log file. When the log file is full, the log file service waits for transactions to be completed, so free space will be available for new entries.

Ownership

Each NTFS file and folder has one user account designated as its owner. The owner of a resource is the only account that has the right to access the resource, modify its properties, and secure it from outside access.

The file's owner can give an administrator no access to a file, but an administrator can always take ownership of the file. Once the administrator is the owner, he has full control of that file. Normally, a user is the owner of a resource, except when that user is an administrator. When a user with administrator privileges owns a file, the group Administrators is the owner of that resource. Ownership can only be taken; it can never be forced on someone. This helps protect people from malicious administrators.

Who is the owner of a file or folder? The owner is the person who created it, and he is responsible for securing those files and folders. It isn't only the administrator's job to ensure security of files and folders. This type of access control is called *discretionary access.*

Taking Ownership of a File

1. Log onto your system as a user without administrator rights.
2. Create a new file called TEST.TXT on an NTFS volume.
3. Log off.
4. Log on as an administrator.
5. Right-click the file called TEST.TXT and choose Properties.
6. Choose the Security tab.
7. Click the Ownership button.
8. Click the Take Ownership button.

e x a m
ⓦa t c h

Many people think an administrator can do anything. That isn't true, especially when it comes to resource ownership. Remember that once you take ownership, you can't give it back to the previous owner. For the previous owner to become the owner, he must follow the steps of the preceding exercise, and he must have permissions to take ownership.

Permissions When Copying and Moving Files

You must be careful when copying and moving files on NTFS partitions. Depending on the type of operation, the permissions change. When you copy a file or folder, the new copy inherits the permissions of its parent folder. As previously mentioned, container objects can inherit permissions from their parent container. These are known as *inherited permissions.* For example, when you copy a file from a directory with full control to a directory with Read permissions, the copied file has Read permissions only. This applies to the creation of new files and folders as well. However, when *moving* files and folders, it isn't quite that simple. When you move a file or folder on one partition to a different partition, the file or folder inherits the parent folder's permissions. Here's the twist: If you move a file or folder within the same partition, it keeps its previous security permissions.

The reason a file moved between partitions doesn't retain its permissions is that NTFS copies the file to the new partition, then deletes the old file. When NTFS moves a file within the same partition, it simply changes the MFT. Thus, the permissions of the file don't change.

exam
ⓦatch

This may not seem confusing at first, but when you are taking the test you might get the MOVE and COPY commands mixed up. Don't just read what I wrote. Test it out. Create two NTFS partitions on your system and try out the different possibilities.

CERTIFICATION OBJECTIVE 6.04

Share-Level Security

Share-level security gives other users access to resources on your computer via the network. Any file system that is available on NT can use share-level security. You can share folders many different ways, but using Explorer or My Computer is probably the easiest. In order to share a folder on a Windows NT Workstation computer, you must be a member of the Administrators or Power Users group. This is one right that can't be modified. You can't grant any other groups the ability to share folders, nor can you take away the power users' ability to share folders. Also, you must have permissions to list the directory contents in order to share it. This applies only to NTFS-formatted partitions.

Permissions for Shared Directories

Permissions for shared directories are much like NTFS file permissions, but not as granular. You can't set special permissions on shares, as you can in NTFS. The four types of share permissions are No Access, Read, Change, and Full Control.

- **No Access** The user is allowed to connect to the share, but no files or folders are listed. The user receives the message: You do not have permissions to access this directory.

- **Read** Allows the user to read or execute files or folders in that shared folder.

- **Change** Allows the user to read, write, execute, or delete files and folders in that shared directory.

- **Full Control** Allows the user to read, write, execute, delete, change permissions, and take ownership of the files and folders in that share. Change permissions and take ownership of the file only apply to shares on NTFS partitions.

Folder share-level permissions are summarized more simply in the following table.

Access Level	Permissions
No Access	None
Read	RX
Change	RWXD
Full Control	RWXDPO
Permissions Key: (R)ead, (W)rite, e(X)ecute, (D)elete, change (P)ermissions, take (O)wnership	

EXERCISE 6-4

Sharing a Directory for the First Time from the Desktop

Let's share a directory, giving your user account Read access. Use the same directory you used for changing permissions. Assign your user account Read access via a network share.

1. Right-click the folder and choose Properties. The window shown in Figure 6-12 appears.

FIGURE 6-12

The Sharing tab
in Properties

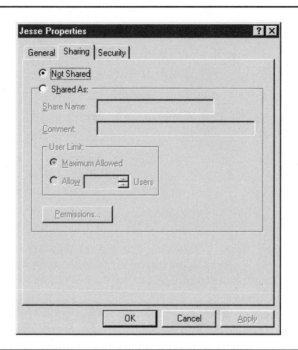

2. Choose the Shared As option button. The name of the folder defaults
   to the share name. Change the User Limit to 1, as in Figure 6-13.
   (On NT Workstation, the maximum is 10. You should change it to 1,
   because your account is the only one that will be given access, so there
   is never any need for more than one connection. This helps improve
   security by thwarting hackers trying to get into that directory while
   you are logged on. You will also be alerted of a problem if you try
   to connect to the share, and you can't because someone else is
   connected.) Then Click the Permissions button.

3. Remove the Everyone group (see Figure 6-14). Then Press the
   Add button.

4. Click the Show Users button and select your name from the list (see
   Figure 6-15). Click the Add button. Make sure the Type of Access is set
   to Read. Then press OK.

5. Your screen should look similar to Figure 6-16. Press OK.

Choosing the Shared
As option

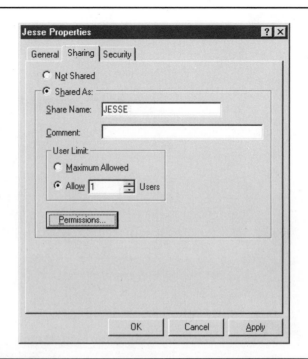

Command Prompt

You also can share a directory via the command prompt. To do so, you must use the NET SHARE command.

```
NET SHARE sharename
        sharename=drive:path [/USERS:number | /UNLIMITED]
                              [/REMARK:"text"]
        sharename [/USERS:number | /UNLIMITED]
                  [/REMARK:"text"]
        {sharename | devicename | drive:path} /DELETE
```

The proper command for sharing the same directory is

```
E:\>net share jesse=J:\jesse /USERS:1
```

This shares the directory for one user, but it puts it at the default Everyone group with full control.

FIGURE 6-14

Remove the
Everyone group

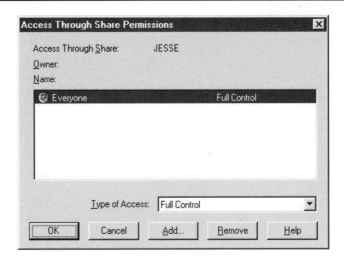

FIGURE 6-15

Giving a user account
Read access

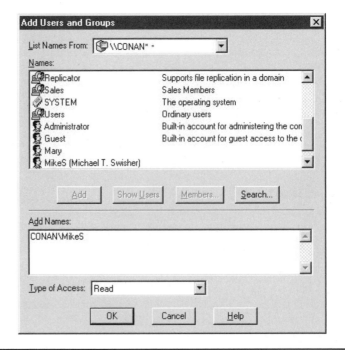

FIGURE 6-16

User MikeS now has
Read access

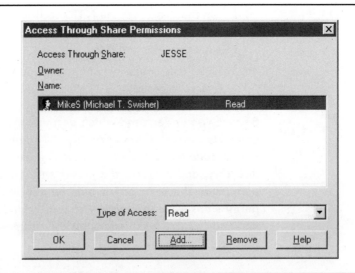

To delete a share via the command prompt type:

```
E:\>net share jesse /Delete
```

Assigning Permissions to Shared Directories

If you share a directory on an NTFS partition you can get more granular with
your permissions. You're still stuck with the four types of share permissions,
but you can change permissions on the files and folders for added security.

Assigning Directory Permissions

For this exercise, assume that you need to share a program on your
NTFS-formatted hard disk, which surveys your customers. Let's say that
everyone with access to your computer via the network is your customer. In
order to conduct your survey, you need to give all the users Read, Write, and
Execute permissions. How can you do this without allowing users to delete
the files in that directory?

1. Create a directory on your NTFS-formatted hard disk. Let's call
it Survey.

2. On the folder, set the NTFS security permissions for Add and Read. Be sure that you check the boxes to change the permissions on all subdirectories and files.

3. Share that directory, with change permissions, with the Everyone group.

e x a m
ⓦ a t c h

Be sure you understand which permissions are applied when a user connects through a network share. The most restrictive permissions always take precedence. If a user is granted Full Control on an NTFS directory, and accesses the files in that directory through a Read permission share, he only would be allowed to read the files. If the permissions were reversed—the user granted Read permissions on NTFS and Full Control permissions on the share—he still would only be able to read the files.

There are several ways to connect to a shared resource. You can map a drive using Explorer or the NET USE command. You also can access shared folders via Network Neighborhood or the Start | Run button.

EXERCISE 6-6

Connecting to a Shared Resource

For this exercise, we'll connect to a shared resource by mapping a drive via Explorer. You'll need two computers networked together, both running NT Workstation.

1. Share a folder as described in the preceding exercise, with the share name Survey.

2. On the client computer, start Explorer (if the toolbar isn't showing go to View | Toolbar).

3. Click the Map Network Drive icon.

4. Choose the drive letter you wish to assign.

5. In the path block type **\\computername\survey**.

6. Click OK.

If you are wondering what \\computername\sharename is, it's a universal naming convention (UNC). It has become an accepted standard, since Microsoft created it and they own most of the operating system software. You don't have to map a network drive to connect to a network share. In step 5 of the previous exercise, you simply typed the name of the computer you want to connect to (computername), and name of the directory share (survey).

Using Uniform Naming Conventions

Instead of mapping a drive, try connecting to a resource using only a UNC. Click your Start button and choose the Run command. Enter *computername* **survey** at the command line. A window appears with the directory share at the root level.

FROM THE CLASSROOM

Security Insecurities: Understanding how Share Security Relates to NTFS Security

One of the trickiest issues for students and new NT administrators is how share-level permissions relate to the permissions set on an NTFS partition. It's a common misperception that a user's effective permission takes precedence over either the share permissions or the NTFS permissions.

We frequently receive calls from clients relating a scenario like this: "One of our users is trying to modify a file and NT won't let him. I have reset the permissions on the file and folder numerous times, including giving the user Full Control permission. Nothing seems to work. What do I need to do?" We even know of situations where NT administrators have

re-installed NT in an attempt to fix the problem!

To help you visualize what is happening, think of a share point on your server as a doorway into the server. (You can set share security permissions in the same manner as setting permissions on other objects.) Now imagine a guard at the doorway, holding a set of keys. When a user accesses a share point, imagine the user standing at the doorway and handing the guard their "invitation," which contains the permissions set for that user. Let's say the user has Read permission at the share. The guard hands the user a Read key, and the user enters the doorway.

FROM THE CLASSROOM

The user then approaches an object (a file) and the NTFS permissions on the file are Read, Write and Delete. Each of these permissions is represented by a "lock." If the user wants to modify the file, he needs the Write key (Write permission) for the file. But, because the user came to the file through the doorway (the share) with only a Read key, he cannot modify the file. Even if the user himself has Write permission, he didn't come through the doorway with a Write key. No matter what permissions are set at the file or folder level, this user can't Write or modify the file.

Another common mistake is setting the share-level permissions to be too restrictive. It's better to set the broadest permission practical at the share level, and then restrict access at the folder and file level.

The reason that this issue is so confusing is that most of us don't think of checking the share permissions after the share is created. We tend to concentrate on the NTFS permissions, when the problem is with the share permissions. Remember, this is only an issue when access is remote. If access is local, the user never accesses the share and therefore, share permissions never apply.

—By Shane Clawson, MCT, MCSE

CERTIFICATION OBJECTIVE 6.05

Auditing Policy, Account Lock Out, and Registry Keys

There are a few more aspects to security that we should discuss. Viruses are a security risk, so I'll explain what you can do to help protect against infection. I'll also talk about auditing, and the effects it has on your system. Then I'll explain how to lock accounts out if the user fails to enter the correct password. Finally, I'll show you how to edit the WINLOGON Registry key to make your system more secure. Be very careful when editing the Registry. If you make a mistake your system might become unstable, and you'll need to rebuild your entire computer.

Audit Policy and Virus Protection

After learning about directory and file security, you now have your system file permissions secured as required, but there is one major step missing. You need to audit who is accessing your sensitive files. NTFS allows you to audit your files and directories. Auditing allows you to trace which users accessed files on your system. This is a good way to ensure that your permissions are properly set up on your system. Before you can audit events in NT, you must turn Auditing on. To activate Auditing, you must be a member of the Administrators group.

Auditing isn't a substitution for virus protection, but it can assist you in identifying a virus. If you are auditing write processes to a drive, and you notice an unusual amount of writes to it, you should check to see if it could be a virus. You'll still need a good virus protection program, but new viruses are being developed every day, and auditing can be a useful tool for identifying them.

You should take care when planning your audit policy. How much you should audit depends on your security requirements. If you have no security requirements at all, you don't need to audit. But if you have very sensitive files requiring great security, you should audit every applicable event. Be careful when auditing, because it slows your system down and it causes your hard drive to fill up with audit logs.

Figure 6-17 is the screen you'll see when you enable Auditing. Start User Manager, then on the menu bar choose Policies | Audit. Choose the Audit These Events option button. Then choose what types of functions you wish to audit. See Table 6-1 for audit event details.

In the next exercise, you'll see how to turn auditing on and how to check if someone takes ownership of the file.

EXERCISE 6-8

Auditing Attempts to Take Ownership

In this exercise we are going to audit for anyone taking ownership on the J:\JESSE\HELP.TXT file.

1. In User Manager turn on auditing for Successful Use of User Rights.

2. Access the Security tab of the file J:\JESSE\HELP.TXT (or any file you wish to audit on an NTFS partition) by going to the file's property sheet.

3. Click the Auditing button.

From the Audit Policy
window, choose which
functions you wish to audit

Audit Policy   ☒

Computer: CONAN   OK

○ Do Not Audit

◉ Audit These Events: Cancel

                                Success   Failure   Help

Logon and Logoff   ☐   ☐
File and Object Access   ☐   ☐
Use of User Rights   ☐   ☐
User and Group Management   ☐   ☐
Security Policy Changes   ☐   ☐
Restart, Shutdown, and System   ☐   ☐
Process Tracking   ☐   ☐

TABLE 6-1

Audit Event
Success/Failure

Event	Definition
Logon and Logoff	Logs all logons and logoffs, both local and remote.
File and Object Access	Logs successful actions to file, folder, and printer objects. Must be on NTFS to audit file and folder objects.
Use of User Rights	Use of anything requiring user rights.
User and Group Management	Any user accounts or groups created, changed, or deleted. Any user accounts that are renamed, disabled, or enabled. Any passwords set or changed.
Security Policy Changes	Any changes to user rights or audit policies.
Restart, Shutdown, and System	Logs all shutdowns and restarts of the local system.
Process Tracking	Tracks program activation, handle duplication, indirect object access, and process exit.

4. Set the properties to match the screenshot in Figure 6-18.

5. Now log on with a different username (make sure the user has the right to Take Ownership).

6. Repeat steps 1 and 2.

7. Click the Ownership button.

8. Click the Take Ownership button (see Figure 6-19).

9. Now run Event View and look at Security Log.

10. In Figure 6-20, look at Event ID: 578.

FIGURE 6-18

Setting the File
Auditing properties

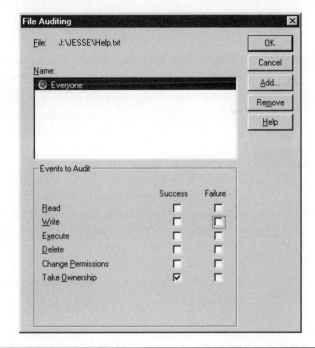

FIGURE 6-19

Choosing Take Ownership

Account Lockout

You can set NT to lock out an account after a certain number of bad logon attempts. Three bad logon attempts is a good limit to use. This prevents hackers from breaking into your account with a program that uses wordlists and brute-strength password crackers. You can set the account to be locked out forever—an administrator would have to unlock it—or you can have it automatically reset after a certain period of time.

EXERCISE 6-9

Changing Account Lockout Settings and Viewing Their Effect

To set the account lockout feature start User Manager. On the menu bar choose Policies | Account. You will see the screen in Figure 6-21.

Check the Account Lockout option button in the middle of the window. The Lockout After option sets the limit of bad attempts. The Reset Count After option sets the amount of time that must pass before the counter resets to zero. Simply put, if you log on with a bad password, NT remembers for 30 minutes (if that's the time you set) that you entered a bad password. Lockout

FIGURE 6-20

The Event Detail screen
shows the Event ID

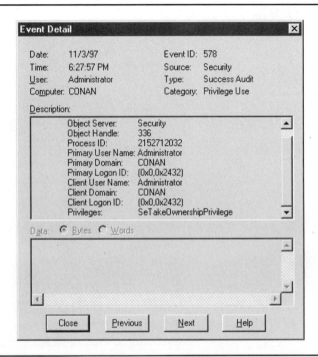

Duration can be forever, or for a certain amount of time. Lockout Duration
goes into effect after the limit of bad attempts has been reached.

Disabling the Default Username

Another security measure is not to display the username of the last logged-on
user. You need two things to break into an account: a username and a password.
Security is improved when an intruder has to guess at both. Exercise 6-10 teaches
you how to disable the default username. Before editing the Registry, make sure
you run RDISK to back up your current system configuration.

FIGURE 6-21

Changing account
lockout settings

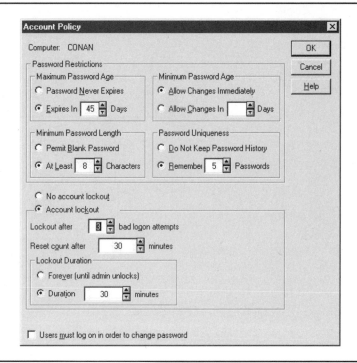

Disabling the Default Username

1. Click Start | Run.

2. Type **regedt32** and press ENTER.

3. Select the Registry key HKEY_LOCAL_MACHINE\SOFTWARE\
   Microsoft\Windows NT\CurrentVersion\WINLOGON

4. On the menu bar choose Edit | Add Value.

5. In the Value box enter DontDisplayLastUserName.

6. In the string box enter 1.

Adding a Security Warning Message

You can have NT give a security notice before logging on to your system. This
will be important if you ever want to prosecute a hacker. The government

once lost a case against a computer hacker, because the logon screen said Welcome. Exercise 6-11 explains how to enter a security notice.

EXERCISE 6-11

Changing the WINLOGON Security Notice

1. Click Start | Run.

2. Type **regedt32** and press ENTER.

3. Select the Registry key `HKEY_LOCAL_MACHINE\SOFTWARE` `\Microsoft\Windows NT\CurrentVersion\WINLOGON`

4. Double-click the value LegalNoticeCaption.

5. In the string box type a caption you want to appear in your title bar. For example: Warning this is a Private System.

6. Double-click the value LegalNoticeText.

7. In the string box type in a legal notification like, "This is a private system owned and operated by Swisher Enterprises. By logging on you consent to monitoring. Any illegal activity may and will be reported to law enforcement officials. If you don't have official business on this system, you are violating the law."

Disabling the Shutdown Button

By default, NT Workstation allows users to press CTRL-ALT-DEL and shut down the system. You can disable this by editing a Registry key. You may be thinking, Why would I ever want to disable the shutdown button? Well, what if you had a computer in a public place—say, out on the sales floor? Anyone could just press CTRL-ALT-DEL and click Shutdown. By disabling this feature you can help protect your system against unauthorized shutdowns.

EXERCISE 6-12

Disabling the WINLOGON Shutdown Button

1. Click Start | Run.

2. Type **regedt32** and press ENTER.

3. Select the Registry key `HKEY_LOCAL_MACHINE\SOFTWARE` `\Microsoft\Windows NT\CurrentVersion\WINLOGON`

4. Double-click the value ShutdownWithoutLogon.

5. In the string box enter **0**.

Automating Logons

You can automate logons by editing the Registry. I don't recommend this, because then anyone could get into your computer. But in case you need to do this, here are the steps required.

Automating Logons by Editing the Registry

1. Click Start | Run.

2. Type **regedt32** and press ENTER.

3. Select the Registry key HKEY_LOCAL_MACHINE\SOFTWARE \Microsoft\Windows NT\CurrentVersion\WINLOGON

4. On the menu bar choose Edit | Add Value.

5. In the Value box enter AutoAdminLogon.

6. In the string box enter 1.

7. On the menu bar choose Edit | Add Value

8. In the Value box enter DefaultPassword.

9. In the string box enter the password of the default user.

10. Double-click the value DefaultUserName.

11. In the string box enter the default username.

CERTIFICATION SUMMARY

In this chapter we discussed the NT security model and its four components. I explained how logons occur, and the role that the Local Security Authority plays in the logon process. You learned about the four logon types: local, remote, domain, and pass-through. We discussed ACLs and ACEs, and how they interact with access tokens.

File and directory security is an important topic that you will continuously apply as you use NT. This is how you protect shared resources on the network. There are various levels of permissions for files and directories, but you need an NTFS-formatted partition to use them. Another type of security is shared security. Shared security can be applied to any type of file system. Sometimes you need to combine shared security with NTFS file and directory security to get the right level of permissions assigned.

Finally, we discussed auditing, and making your system more secure by editing the WINLOGON Registry key. Take what you've learned in this chapter with you after you pass the exam. As the Internet grows and more companies put their networks on the Internet, those systems become more vulnerable to attack. We must apply security to our systems before we are attacked; otherwise it is too late.

TWO-MINUTE DRILL

- ❑ The NT security model is made up of four main components: logon processes, Local Security Authority, Security Account Manager (SAM), and the Security Reference Monitor.

- ❑ There are four types of logons that NT supports: local, remote, domain, and pass-through authentication.

- ❑ NT uses *mandatory logon* to force everyone to log on before they can access the system. It also protects the system by implementing Restricted User mode.

- ❑ NT uniquely identifies every user and group on the system. To accomplish this, it uses security IDs and group IDs.

- ❑ Whatever rights and permissions a user has, so do the programs that the user executes.

- ❑ The type of file system you choose determines what level of security you can use on NT. FAT does not allow folder or file permissions. NTFS allows permissions on folders and individual files.

- ❑ File Delete Child is a POSIX function that allows a user who has full control of a folder to delete a top-level file within that folder, even though the user doesn't have permissions to delete that file.

- ❑ A file's owner can give an administrator no access to a file. However, an administrator can always take ownership of the file.

❑ When you copy a file or folder, the new copy inherits the permissions of its parent folder.

❑ Any file system that is available on NT can use share-level security.

❑ Be sure to understand which permissions are applied when a user connects through a network share. The most restrictive permissions always take precedence.

❑ Auditing allows you to trace which users accessed files on your system. This is a good way to ensure that your permissions are properly set up on your system.

❑ You can set NT to lock out an account after a certain number of bad logon attempts.

SELF TEST

The following questions will help you measure your understanding of the material presented in this chapter. Read all the choices carefully, as there may be more than one correct answer. Choose all correct answers for each question.

1. The _____ creates security access tokens, authenticates users, and manages the local security policy.

   A. Local Security Authority

   B. SAM

   C. ACL

   D. ACE

2. What maintains the database of all user, group, and workstation accounts?

   A. Local Security Authority

   B. SAM

   C. ACL

   D. HKEY_LOCAL_MACHINE

3. NT supports which of the following logons? (Choose all that apply)

   A. local

   B. pass-through authentication

   C. remote

   D. domain

4. Why must you press CTRL-ALT-DEL to log on to NT?

   A. To reboot the system to refresh the memory

   B. To reboot the system to clear the security logs

   C. To prevent trojan horse viruses

   D. To erase the last username from the logon dialog box

5. Which of the following is an object? (Choose all that apply)

   A. file

   B. window

   C. process

   D. keyboard

6. A _____ is used to uniquely identify each user account.

   A. SID

   B. GUID

   C. Group ID

   D. ACL

7. If you delete a user account, how can you get it back?

   A. You can't undelete an account. You must create a new account.

   B. Choose undelete from the file menu.

   C. Run the command ACCOUNT /UNDELETE.

   D. Use the recycle bin.

8. A program always runs in the _____ of the user.

   A. subject

   B. security context

C. real mode

D. protected mode

9. User JesseS belongs to the local group Marketing. The permissions on the file DICTIONARY.DOC are as follows: JesseS has Change (RWXD) permission and the Marketing group has No Access permissions. When user JesseS tries to read the file, what access will he be granted?

A. Change

B. Read

C. Read and Execute

D. No Access

10. Which ACE does NT process first?

A. AccessAllowed

B. ReadControl

C. WriteDenied

D. AccessDenied

11. User MaryS is assigned to the local group Sales. Mary has Read permissions for all files on your system. The group Sales has special permissions of Write on all the files in the folder called Reports. If Mary requests Read and Write permissions at the same time, what will happen?

A. Access will be denied, since she doesn't have enough access in any individual group.

B. Access can't be resolved.

C. Access will be granted.

D. Access will be granted, but an administrator must approve it first.

12. If you want to limit the people who can access your system when they log on locally, how must your hard disk partition be formatted?

A. NTFS

B. FAT

C. HPFS

D. CDFS

13. Why is there a special utility to secure the boot partition of RISC computers?

A. RISC computers can't be physically secured, so the partition requires extra protection.

B. RISC computers are more secure than Intel-based computers, because they can access more security subsystems.

C. RISC systems must boot on a FAT partition.

D. Microsoft just hasn't compiled the utility to other systems yet.

14. What command allows the user to change file permissions from a command shell?

A. NET PERMISSIONS

B. SET FILE

C. CACLS

D. ACE

15. If you want to audit access to files stored on your NTFS-formatted hard disk, what must you do first?

A. Turn Auditing on in User Manager.

B. Turn Auditing on for the folder by using Explorer.

C. Do nothing. NT automatically audits all file access once NTFS is installed.

D. Use the program Security Manager to enable Auditing.

16. What does transaction logging provide for NTFS?

    A. Auditing of file access

    B. Remote access to your system

    C. Network connections made to your computer

    D. Recoverability

17. Who is the owner of a new file on a FAT partition?

    A. Administrator

    B. System

    C. Whoever created the file

    D. FAT doesn't support Owners

18. Who is the owner of a new file on an NTFS partition?

    A. Administrator

    B. System

    C. Whoever created the file

    D. FAT doesn't support Owners

19. (True/False) Only administrators can give someone ownership of a file.

20. When moving a folder from drive C: to drive D:, what permissions will the folder have? (Both drives are formatted with NTFS.)

    A. The folder will keep its original permissions.

B. The folder will inherit the permissions of drive D:.

C. NTFS will reset the folder to Everyone Full Control.

D. NTFS doesn't support permissions between drives.

21. Which file systems support share-level security?

    A. FAT

    B. NTFS

    C. CDFS

    D. All of the above

22. Which one is NOT a type of share permission on an NTFS partition?

    A. Read

    B. No Access

    C. Full Control

    D. Special Access

    E. None of the above

23. How can you share a folder on the network to allow everyone to read, write, and execute files, but not delete any files?

    A. You can't.
       Give everyone group Change share permissions.
       Give everyone group Read, Write, and Execute share permissions.
       Give everyone group Change share permissions and Read, Write, Execute Special File permissions on NTFS.

24. Which of the following are negative results from auditing all file object accesses on your system? (Choose all that apply)

    A. Slows your computer's processor down

    B. Creates more disk access

    C. Fills your security log up too fast

    D. None of the above

25. What must be turned on to allow you to audit writes to your NTFS directories?

    A. Logon and Logoff

    B. File and Object Access

    C. Use of User Rights

    D. Process Tracking

26. User RyanB is given share-level access of Full Control to share SalesRPT. However, the NTFS permissions are set to Read for the group Sales. RyanB is a member of the group Sales. When he connects to the share SalesRPT, what type of access will he have?

    A. Full Control

    B. Read

    C. No Access

    D. None of the above

MICROSOFT CERTIFIED SYSTEMS ENGINEER

7

Understanding Windows NT Networking

N T is known for its networking capabilities. It has built-in networking capabilities that allow it to operate in a heterogeneous network environment. *Heterogeneous* means a mixed network operating environment involving different operating systems like NT, UNIX, and Novell. NT uses a layered networking model, which makes it easier to write network applications and hardware drivers. The NDIS layer allows multiple protocols to bind to a single network adapter. NT has grown in popularity because of its ability to connect to so many different systems. It comes with a Microsoft redirector and a Microsoft-developed Novell redirector, allowing it to connect to NT, LAN Manager, LAN Server, NetWare, and any SMB-compliant network operating system. NT also supports many open system architectures like UNIX and Open VMS.

CERTIFICATION OBJECTIVE 7.01

Built-In Networking

NT is an operating system (OS) and a networked operating system (NOS). Years ago, the OS and the NOS were two separate software components. Your computer's OS was probably MS-DOS and your NOS was probably Novell. NT bridges the gap between the OS and the NOS by providing built-in networking.

Windows NT Network Components

NT uses several components to provide a robust NOS, capable of operating in a heterogeneous network. Redirectors are used to access other computers on the network, and server services provide other computers on the network access to your workstation. NT supports several protocols out-of-the-box, and has room to support more. NT uses an interprocess communication (IPC) to communicate with other computers. NT supports six different IPC mechanisms that we'll discuss later.

NT Networking Model

The NT networking model is made up of layers, which loosely correspond to the seven layers of the OSI networking model. Figure 7-1 shows the NT networking model and how it corresponds to the OSI model.

Each layer can talk only with the layers directly above and below it. The MAC sublayer is where the network interface card (NIC) driver resides, and this is where the model begins. The driver is responsible for linking the NIC to the network. The NDIS interface layer is the next layer. The *NDIS interface* layer is a special layer that allows hardware vendors to write NIC drivers that access the NDIS layer, regardless of which transport protocols are used. NDIS allows multiple NICs to bind to multiple protocols without requiring a separate protocol stack for each card. The third layer, transport protocols,

FIGURE 7-1

The NT networking model corresponds to the OSI networking model.

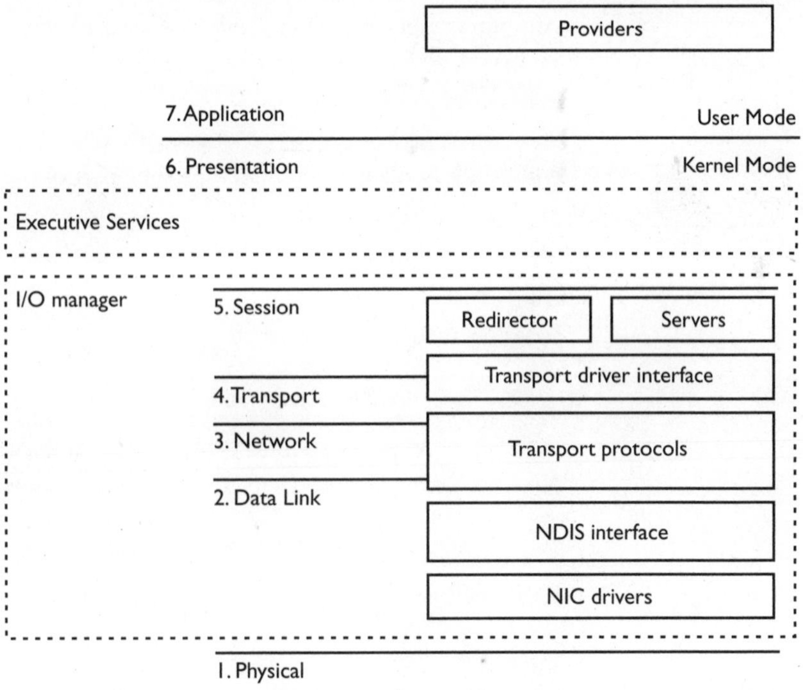

defines how data should be presented to the next receiving layer, and packages that data accordingly. The fourth layer serves a similar purpose as the NDIS layer. The *transport driver interface (TDI)* allows redirectors to be written without concern for the transport protocol being used. The fifth layer provides for the redirector. The redirector redirects local requests for shared network resources to the appropriate network share.

exam
ⓦatch

Be sure to understand that the TDI layer and the NDIS layer allow transport protocols to communicate with applications and networks seamlessly.

Servers and Redirectors

In order to access other computers and shared resources on the network, you must have a way to get out to the network. NT uses redirectors to give client computers access to server services. Now that you're on the network, it only makes sense that there must be some shared resource that you need to access. The server service enables other computers to connect to shared resources on your system. The redirector lets you out, and the server lets others in to your computer. Actually the redirector is one part of the workstation service.

Workstation

All user mode requests pass through the workstation service. The workstation service is made up of two parts:

- User mode interface, which resides in the SERVICES.EXE
- The redirector (RDR.SYS), which is a file system driver that interacts with the lower-level NIC drivers by means of the TDI

Figure 7-2 depicts the workstation service receiving a request and passing it to the redirector.

WINDOWS NT REDIRECTOR   As previously mentioned, the redirector is implemented as a file system driver. Implementing the redirector as a file system has many advantages.

FIGURE 7-2

The Workstation service receives a request and passes it to the redirector

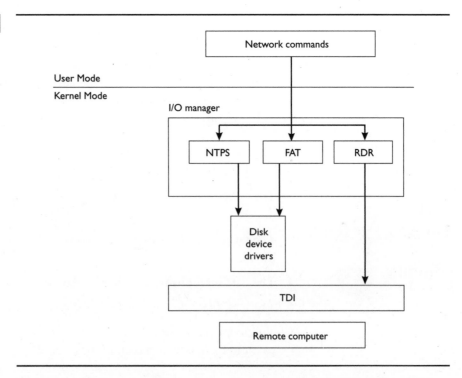

FIGURE 7-2

The Workstation service receives a request and passes it to the redirector

- It runs in Kernel mode, allowing it to call other drivers and Kernel mode components.

- It can load and unload dynamically.

- It can coexist with other redirectors.

- It allows applications to access files on a local and remote computer by calling a single API. The NT I/O Manager doesn't distinguish between accessing files locally or remotely.

PROVIDERS AND THE PROVIDER-INTERFACE LAYER   Each additional type of network must have a provider installed (Banyan Vines or NetWare). The *provider* allows NT to communicate with the network. NT Workstation comes with a provider, Client Services for NetWare. This allows NT Workstation to access resources on a Novell NetWare server.

Server

The server service allows remote computers to connect to NT Workstation. The redirector sends client computers to your workstation, where the server service provides them with requested resources. The following steps, illustrated in Figure 7-3, occur when the server service receives a request from a client workstation to read a file:

1. The low-level network drivers receive the request and pass it to the server driver.

2. The server passes a read file request to the proper local file system driver.

3. The local file system driver calls a lower-level disk driver to access the file.

4. The data is sent back to the local file system driver.

5. The local file system driver sends the data back to the server.

6. The server passes the data back down to the low-level network drivers so it can be transmitted back to the client workstation.

FIGURE 7-3

The server service receives a request from a client workstation

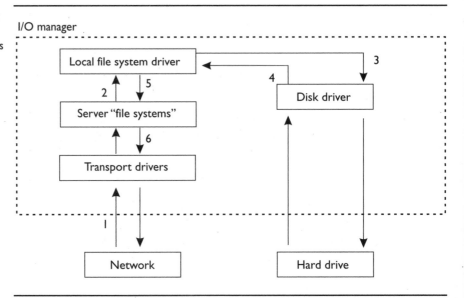

FROM THE CLASSROOM

NT Workstation on the Network *or* How to Turn Your Network Upside Down Without Really Trying

A big surprise to many of our students is that, when you install NT Workstation, it automatically installs and starts the server service. This can be a nasty surprise when you are installing Workstation back in your organization.

We were doing some wide area network design at a client's site, and it came to the client's attention that we also had a great deal of expertise in NT and NT networks. The client had recently installed 3,800 computers, all with NT Workstation. The client had set up several domains, and had the NT Workstations in various workgroups. Some of the workgroups contained only a single NT Workstation, several others contained a couple of workstations, while a number of workgroups contained 75 or 80 computers. This design is pretty funny. Well, it's funny to a serious NT person, anyway!

There are many problematic issues with the layout of this network. One of the more significant issues is the deployment of NT Workstation with the default installation that installs and starts the server service. With the server service running, NT Workstation is a server on the network. This means that each of the Workstations is sending browser registration traffic and browser announcements.

Our client did not understand the disadvantage to having the server service enabled. To illustrate the point, we asked what he would think if he had a network of 3,800 NetWare servers. He replied that the network would be unmanageable. I think he got the point.

—By Shane Clawson, MCT, MCSE

Multiple UNC Provider (MUP)

The MUP handles I/O requests containing UNCs. When an application makes an I/O call using a UNC, the MUP selects the appropriate redirector to handle the request. When a request is received containing a UNC, the MUP checks with each redirector to find out which one should process the request. The redirector with the highest-registered response is used to establish the connection. The connection remains as long as there is activity over the connection. If there is no activity for 15 minutes the MUP renegotiates to find an appropriate redirector. Figure 7-4 depicts where the MUP is logically located.

Multiprovider Router (MPR)

Applications that don't use UNC names in their I/O requests use a different method to select a redirector. MPR receives WNet commands (part of the Win32 network APIs), chooses the proper redirector, and passes the command to the selected redirector. Since different vendors use different interfaces for communicating with their redirector, there is a series of provider DLLs between MPR and the redirectors. Figure 7-5 illustrates the MPR's function.

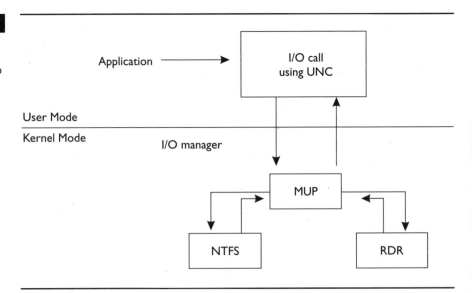

FIGURE 7-4

The MUP selects the appropriate redirector to handle a request

MPR passes WNet
commands to the
selected redirector

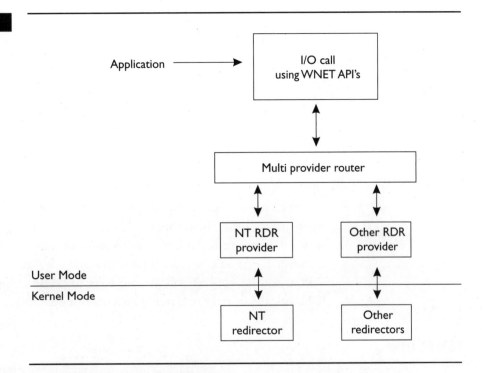

CERTIFICATION OBJECTIVE 7.02

Protocols

Protocols are languages used by computers. In order for two computers to talk
to each other they must speak the same language (use the same protocol). Why
doesn't everyone just accept a standard protocol? That's just like asking why
everyone doesn't speak the same language. Could the world tell everyone in

America that they are going to have to learn French because that's the new world standard? The same is true with computer companies developing networked computer systems. Novell developed IPX/SPX, and it's partial to its own creation. Microsoft used to be tied to NetBEUI, but now has adopted TCP/IP as its standard protocol. TCP/IP is a pseudo-standard. The Internet uses TCP/IP and, since the Internet is growing at an exponential pace, TCP/IP is growing just as fast.

NetBEUI

NetBEUI is a fast, small, and non-routable protocol. It's used mainly for backward compatibility to Microsoft's LAN Manager and IBM's LAN Server network operating systems. It's easy to install because no configuration is required. You should use NetBEUI if you have a few computers networked, with no routing between subnets. Since NetBEUI isn't routable, it can't be used with the Internet, which is why it has lost popularity.

NWLink

NWLink is Microsoft's implementation of Novell's IPX/SPX protocol. Since Novell owns the copyright on IPX/SPX, Microsoft had to reverse engineer the protocol. NWLink is a fast and routable protocol that doesn't require configuration. It's used primarily to communicate with Novell servers. NWLink by itself won't access a Novell server; it needs a redirector to access the Novell server.

TCP/IP

Transmission control protocol/Internet protocol (TCP/IP) is the default protocol for Windows NT. The Internet uses TCP/IP; therefore, TCP/IP is considered a global standard. TCP/IP is a bigger protocol than NetBEUI and NWLink, and it requires configuration. Although TCP/IP requires configuration, you can use DHCP to configure your workstation. NT Server can be used as a DHCP server to provide the TCP/IP configuration. TCP/IP is the default protocol installed when you enable networking in NT.

DLC

Data Link Control (DLC) is not a computer-to-computer protocol. It's used as a gateway protocol. SNA server uses DLC to communicate with IBM mainframes. DLC is also used for printing to network printing devices equipped with the DLC protocol. Computers communicate with the gateway server using NetBEUI, NWLink, or TCP/IP. Then the server uses DLC to communicate with the requested device.

AFP

AppleTalk Filing Protocol (AFP) ships with NT as a development tool for developers who write Macintosh applications under NT. AFP is used on NT Server to support Services for Macintosh, but it's also possible to use NT Workstation to develop AFP applications.

exam
ⓦatch

Know which protocols are routable (NWLink and TCP/IP) and which ones aren't (NetBEUI and DLC). Also know when you should use each protocol in a given situation. For example, you need to communicate with the Internet. Which protocol should you use?

Interprocess Communication (IPC)

Interprocess communications (IPC) is the process of exchanging data or instructions between two computers. IPCs support two-way communications between computers. NT supplies six methods of IPC: NetBIOS, Windows Sockets, named pipes, mailslots, NetDDE, and remote procedure calls (RPC).

NetBIOS

The Network Basic Input/Output System (NetBIOS) is a session-level interface used by applications to communicate with NetBIOS-compliant transport protocols. NetBIOS has been around since the early 1980s. Since NetBIOS has been around so long, it is now used mainly for backwards compatibility to older systems.

The NetBIOS interface is responsible for establishing logical network names, beginning sessions between two computers, and supporting reliable data transfer between computers that have an established session. The logical network name is used to uniquely identify each computer on the network. The name is made up of 1 – 15 characters. One of the drawbacks to NetBIOS naming is that it is a flat namespace. You'll need to be careful when planning a naming convention for your network. If you use last names for computer names, you'll quickly run into problems, especially if you manage a large network, or if your network grows beyond your planned size. After a session is established, computers can communicate in the form of NetBIOS requests or in the form of Server Message Block (SMB). NetBIOS can be implemented over TCP/IP, NWLink, or NetBEUI. A NetBIOS client-server application can communicate over various protocols: NetBEUI protocol (NBF), NWLink NetBIOS (NWNBLink), and NetBIOS over TCP/IP (NetBT).

Winsock

Windows Sockets (Winsock) is the windows implementation of the UC Berkeley Sockets API. Microsoft TCP/IP, NWLink, and AFP use this interface. A socket provides an endpoint to a connection. Two sockets make a complete path. The two sockets work as a bi-directional pipe for incoming and outgoing data between two computers.

Named Pipes

Named pipes provide connection-oriented communications. This means they guarantee delivery of the data. Named pipes help client-server applications by providing a secure channel between two processes for exchanging data. Named pipes also provide for *impersonation*. This allows the server to process the client request in the security context of the client. Using impersonation ensures that the client's process doesn't exceed his level of permissions.

Mailslots

Mailslots provide connectionless communications. This means they do not guarantee delivery of data. Mailslots are generally used for broadcast messages. The browser service uses mailslots to advertise your arrival on the network.

RPC

Remote procedure calls (RPC) are the most flexible and robust of the IPC mechanisms. RPC uses other IPC mechanisms to establish communications between two computers. RPC can ride over named pipes, NetBIOS, or winsocks to communicate with other computers. An RPC can be established on the same computer as a client call to a server. It does this by using the local procedure call (LPC) to transfer information between processes and subsystems.

NetDDE

Network dynamic data exchange (NetDDE) allows two applications to communicate, with a link always maintained. The link must always be maintained so that when the server registers a change, all other clients receive the message of the change. MS Hearts and Chat are two examples of NetDDE.

The NetDDE IPC by default is not started. Whenever you start a NetDDE-enabled application, the NetDDE IPC automatically starts. NetDDE depends on a hidden share called NDDE$. This share maps to a DDE process, not a folder. The share is created whenever a NetDDE-enabled application is started. NetDDE provides information-sharing capabilities by opening two one-way pipes between applications.

CERTIFICATION OBJECTIVE 7.03

Network Settings

In this section I'll take you through opening the Control Panel, adding a service, removing and reinstalling a service, installing a transport protocol, and changing the domain that your workstation participates in.

EXERCISE 7-1

Opening the Network Control Panel

1. Right-click Network Neighborhood.
2. Select properties.

Or

1. Click Start | Settings | Control Panel.
2. Double-click the Network icon.

In Exercise 7-2 we'll add Simple TCP/IP Services to your NT Workstation.

Adding a Service

1. Open Network Control Panel.
2. Select the Services tab. You see the screen in Figure 7-6.
3. Click the Add button. You see the screen in Figure 7-7.
4. Select Simple TCP/IP Services and click OK.

FIGURE 7-6

The Network properties
Services tab

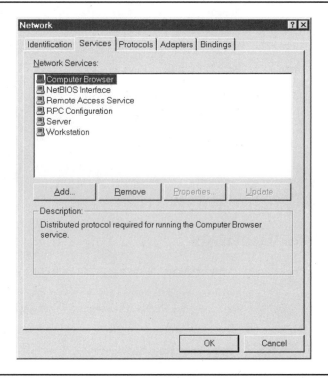

FIGURE 7-7

Adding a network service

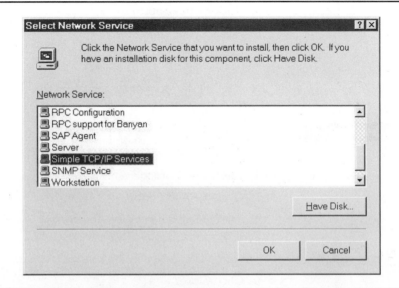

5. You are prompted for the location of your NT Workstation CD. Insert your CD and type in the appropriate path. Click Continue.

6. Click Close.

7. Restart your computer.

The next exercise teaches you how to remove a service, and then reinstall that same service. This is a necessary procedure when you think a service has a corrupted DLL file and you wish to fix it. Remember that, after installing new services or components to NT, you need to reinstall your latest NT service pack. The key to this exercise is step 5. After removing a service, you must restart your computer before adding that service back.

EXERCISE 7-3

Removing/Reinstalling a Removed Component

1. Open Network Control Panel.

2. Select the Services tab.

3. Select Simple TCP/IP Services.

4. Click Remove button.

5. Restart your computer.

6. Follow the steps in Exercise 7-2.

Exercise 7-4 shows you how to add NetBEUI as a protocol to your system.

EXERCISE 7-4
Installing a Transport Protocol

1. Open Network Control Panel.

2. Select the Protocols tab.

3. Click the Add button.

4. Select NetBEUI Protocol and click OK.

5. You are prompted for the location of your NT Workstation CD. Insert your CD and type in the appropriate path. Click Continue.

6. Click Close.

7. Restart your computer.

The next exercise teaches you how to remove your computer from a workgroup and add it to a domain. For this exercise you'll need an NT server on your network configured as a domain controller. You'll also need to have administrative rights to the domain.

EXERCISE 7-5
Changing the Domain or Workgroup

1. Open Network Control Panel.

2. On the Identification tab, shown in Figure 7-8, click the Change button.

3. You now see the screen in Figure 7-9. Select the Domain option button.

4. Enter the domain name of an NT Domain to which you have administrator rights.

5. Check-mark the Create a Computer Account in the Domain check box. (See Figure 7-10.)

FIGURE 7-8

The Identification tab in
Network Properties

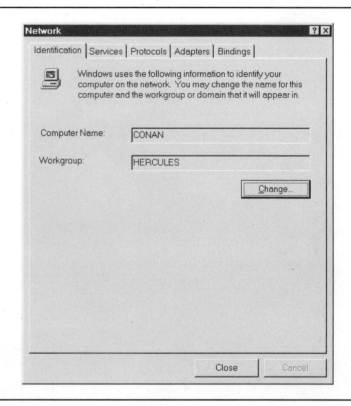

6. Enter your administrative username and password in the appropriate box.

7. Click OK.

Binding Options

The Bindings tab in Network Control Panel allows you to set the order in which protocols, adapters, and services are processed. Binding is the linking of network components on different levels to enable communication between

FIGURE 7-9

Changing the Workgroup
to a Domain

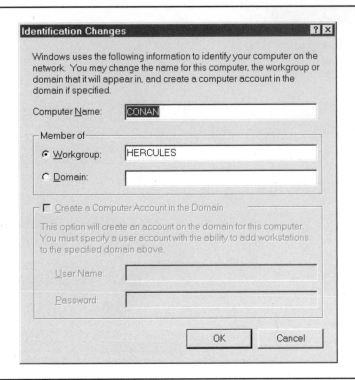

those components. A network component can be bound to one or more
network components above or below it. The services that each component
provides can be shared by all the components bound to it. The higher an
object is in the order, the faster it's accessed. You also can disable an adapter, a
protocol, or a service at the Bindings tab. Figure 7-11 shows the Network
Control Panel bindings tab.

You can view all services, all protocols, or all adapters by using the drop-
down menu Show Bindings For. By clicking the + signs, you can expand the
branches. Figure 7-12 shows all adapter bindings expanded out for adapter [3].

FIGURE 7-10

Adding a computer account
on the domain

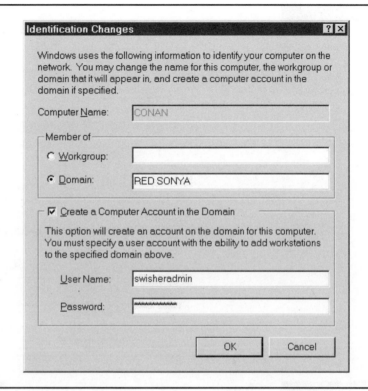

In Exercise 7-6 you go through the steps of changing the priority of the transport protocol. For this exercise you'll need at least two protocols installed on your workstation. This exercise assumes that you have TCP/IP and NetBEUI installed, and that NetBEUI is higher in the binding order before we start the exercise. Since all of our servers have TCP/IP as their default protocol, we want to make TCP/IP higher in the binding order.

FIGURE 7-11

At the Bindings tab you can set the order in which protocols, adapters, and services are processed

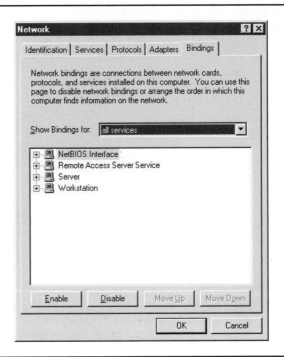

EXERCISE 7-6

Changing the Priority of Transport Protocols

1. Open Network Control Panel.

2. Select the Bindings tab.

3. Show Bindings for: All services.

4. Expand each branch by clicking the + symbol, as shown in Figure 7-13.

FIGURE 7-12

Bindings tab showing all
adapters expanded out
for adapter [3]

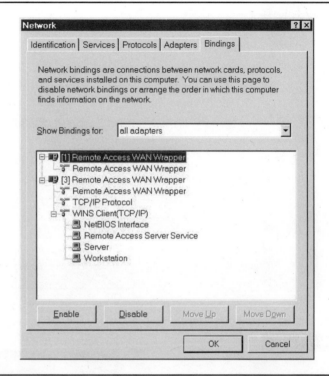

5. Every place you see NetBEUI Protocol, select it, then press the Move
   Down button.

6. Your screen should now look something like Figure 7-14.

7. Click OK.

FIGURE 7-13

NetBEUI is higher in the
binding order

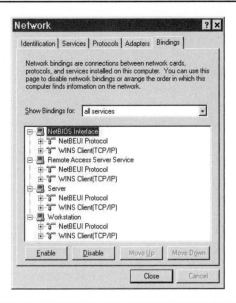

FIGURE 7-14

TCP/IP is higher in the
binding order

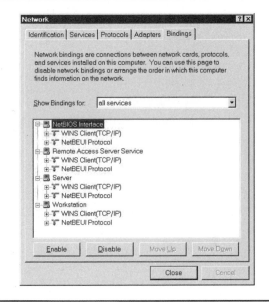

CERTIFICATION OBJECTIVE 7.04

Managing Shared Directories

Once a share is created, the best way to manage the share is through the Server applet in Control Panel. Using the Server applet you can monitor the following:

- Total number of active sessions
- Total number of open files currently accessed via the network
- Total number of file locks placed by remote users against the open files
- Total number of open named pipes between your workstation and remote clients

The Server applet allows you to enter a description of your computer that shows up in server manager. You can do more than just look at the open connections; you also can manage the connections using the control buttons located at the bottom of the Server applet.

There are five buttons on the Server applet, but we'll discuss only the first three: Users, Shares, and In Use.

The Users button opens the User Sessions dialog box. The User Sessions dialog box allows you to view a list of all the network users connected to the computer, and list all the resources opened by a selected user. Optionally, you can disconnect one or all of the users connected to the computer.

The Shares button opens the Shared Resources dialog box. Use this dialog box to view a list of the shared resources available on the computer and, for a selected resource, a list of connected users. Optionally, you can disconnect one or all of the users connected to the computer.

The In Use button the opens the Open Resources dialog box. Use this dialog box to view a list of the computer's open shared resources. You also can close one open resource, or all open resources.

Default Shares

NT creates hidden shares for administrative purposes. Two hidden administrative shares are the C$ and the Admin$. Only administrators can access both these shares. Backup Operators can access the C$. This is necessary so that they can back up all files on hard disks. The $ symbol at the end of a share makes it hidden. When users browse your computer for shared resources, shares that end with $ won't be seen. Users can still connect to hidden shares, but they must know the name of the share and have the proper permissions. You can map a drive or use a UNC to connect to a hidden share.

You can stop these shares, but they will be re-created the next time the computer restarts. However, you can use the Windows NT system policy editor to edit the Registry to always have these shares removed.

Admin$

This administrative share shares the root system root directory, regardless of which folder it was created in. This allows administrators easy access to the operating system folder on any NT computer.

C$

The C$ is created to allow administrators to the computers drive C: root directory. Administrators can quickly map a drive to a user's C$ to access files and folders. If the system has more than one partition, a similar share is created for each partition (D$, E$, and so on). CD-ROMs and floppy drives don't automatically create hidden administrative shares.

Browsing the Network

The Computer Browser is a service that allows your computer to be seen on the network. The Computer Browser service maintains a list of available servers on the network and provides that list to the clients when requested. A server is any computer that provides server services, so Windows 95 and Windows 3.11 are also considered servers if they have file and print sharing services enabled. Every workgroup on every subnet has a master browser.

Domains also have a master browser for each subnet and the primary domain controller maintains the domain-wide list.

Browsing takes place on every installed transport protocol. If you are running NWLink and TCP/IP, your browser searches for servers on the NWLink and TCP/IP. If you limit your protocols, you can increase your network performance. By limiting the number of protocols you limit broadcasts on the network. Your computer system responds faster when accessing the network, because it doesn't have to timeout on several different protocols when trying to make a connection.

There are certain situations where a master browser is needed: a client can't find its master browser, client detects that a master browser has disappeared, or a windows NT Server starts on the network. Every time a master browser is needed on a segment, an election is held. You should configure a system on each subnet to be the preferred master browser in order to reduce network traffic caused by elections. You can even turn off servers from announcing themselves to the network. To turn off announcements type this command:

```
NET CONFIG SERVER /HIDDEN:YES
```

Election Process

The browser election tries to find the most robust computer to be the master browser. A computer initiates an election by sending an election datagram out to the network. When a browser receives an election datagram, it examines the election criteria set on that datagram. If the browser has better election criteria, it sends out its own election datagram. This continues until no more election datagrams are broadcast. When a browser can't send an election datagram because it doesn't have better criteria, it attempts to find the new browse master. See Chapter 11 for more on browsing.

CERTIFICATION SUMMARY

NT has networking built in. It ships with two redirectors that allow the computer to access the network. NT provides support for five protocols:

NetBEUI, NWLink, TCP/IP, DLC, and AFP. TCP/IP is the default protocol when you install NT's networking components. TCP/IP and NWLink are routable protocols. NetBEUI is a small, fast, and efficient protocol for small networks; however, it is not routable.

NT uses IPCs to communicate between computers. RPCs are the most robust and mature of the IPC mechanisms. Other IPCs supported by NT are: NetBIOS, Winsock, named pipes, mailslots, and NetDDE.

You use the Server applet in Control Panel to manage your shared folders. In order to share folders, you can use Explorer or Server Manager. Once a folder is shared you should use the Server applet, which is also found in Server Manager.

Finally, you can improve the performance of your workstation and network by assigning a preferred master browser. Whenever a browser election occurs, network traffic is generated. By having a preferred master browser, you can help reduce the amount of traffic.

✓ TWO-MINUTE DRILL

❑ NT bridges the gap between the OS and the NOS by providing built-in networking.

❑ The NT networking model is made up of layers, which loosely correspond to the seven layers of the OSI networking model.

❑ Be sure to understand that the TDI layer and the NDIS layer allow transport protocols to communicate with applications and networks seamlessly.

❑ NT uses redirectors to give client computers access to server services.

❑ Protocols are languages used by computers.

  ❑ NetBEUI is a fast, small, and non-routable protocol.

  ❑ NWLink is Microsoft's implementation of Novell's IPX/SPX protocol.

  ❑ TCP/IP is the default protocol for Windows NT.

❑ Data Link Control (DLC) is a gateway protocol.

❑ Know which protocols are routable (NWLink and TCP/IP) and which ones aren't (NetBEUI and DLC). Also know when you should use each protocol in a given situation.

❑ IPCs support two-way communications between computers. NT supplies six methods of IPC: NetBIOS, Windows Sockets, named pipes, mailslots, NetDDE, and remote procedure calls (RPC).

❑ Once a share is created, the best way to manage the share is through the Server applet in Control Panel.

❑ NT creates hidden shares for administrative purposes. Two hidden administrative shares are the C$ and the Admin$.

❑ The Computer Browser service maintains a list of available servers on the network and provides that list to the clients, when requested.

SELF TEST

The following questions will help you measure your understanding of the material presented in this chapter. Read all the choices carefully, as there may be more than one correct answer. Choose all correct answers for each question.

1. Which of the following are advantages to implementing the redirector as a file system driver? (Choose all that apply.)

    A. It runs in Kernel mode

    B. It can load dynamically

    C. It can unload dynamically

    D. It can coexist with other redirectors

2. Which layer of the OSI model does the NDIS layer of the Microsoft Networking model operate?

    A. Session

    B. Transport

    C. Network

    D. Data Link

3. Which layer is between the TDI and the NDIS layers?

    A. Transport protocols

    B. Transport

    C. MAC

    D. Redirector

4. What does the TDI layer provide?

    A. It allows the redirector to communicate with a standard interface regardless of the transport protocols being used

    B. It allows hardware vendors to write NIC drivers without regard to the transport protocol

    C. It provides a way to send data to the network without involving the application

    D. It provides networking services for remote computers

5. What is the importance of the NDIS interface layer?

    A. It allows the redirector to communicate with a standard interface regardless of the transport protocols being used

    B. Transport protocols can't be used without the NDIS layer

    C. It allows multiple NIC drivers to be loaded against the redirector

    D. Hardware vendors can write NIC drivers to access the NDIS layer without regard to the transport protocols being used

6. What does the multiple UNC provider (MUP) do?

    A. It converts mapped drives to a UNC

    B. It sends I/O requests with UNC names to the appropriate redirector

    C. It receives WNet commands, chooses the proper redirector, and passes the command to the selected redirector

    D. It allows users to have more than one UNC-connected resource open at a time

7. Which protocol(s) could you use if you had two separate physical subnets connected by a router? (Choose all that apply.)

    A. NetBEUI

    B. NWLink

    C. TCP/IP

    D. DLC

8. Which protocol would you choose if you had a LAN with only 5 workstations and 1 server connected on a single physical subnet?

    A. NetBEUI

    B. NWLink

    C. TCP/IP

    D. DLC

9. Which protocol is used mainly as a gateway protocol?

    A. NetBEUI

    B. NWLink

    C. TCP/IP

    D. DLC

10. You want to connect two remote sites with a router, but don't want to waste time configuring a protocol. Which protocol should you choose?

    A. NetBEUI

    B. NWLink

    C. TCP/IP

    D. DLC

11. You want to create a share on your workstation, but don't want it to be visible when users browse the network. How can you do this?

    A. Since it is a hidden share it is considered an administrative share; therefore, an administrator must do this

    B. Type NET CONFIG SERVER / HIDDEN:YES

    C. Create a share with $ at the end of the share name

    D. Create a virtual share using the Server applet in Control Panel

12. Which type of IPC is used when your computer broadcasts that it is joining a workgroup?

    A. Mailslots

    B. RPC

    C. Named pipes

    D. NetBIOS

13. Your workstation has NetBEUI, NWLink, and TCP/IP installed on it. You notice that every time you browse the network, your computer takes a long time to display the available computer's list. Your friend doesn't experience any noticeable delay when browsing the network. What should you do to fix the problem? (Choose all that apply.)

    A. Remove all unnecessary protocols

    B. Remove NetBEUI

C. Adjust the binding order to put the most-used protocol higher in the binding order

D. Set a protocol standard using only one protocol, install that protocol on all machines, and remove all other protocols

14. You have several folders shared on the network from your workstation. How can you check to see which folders have connections to them?

   A. Use the Server applet in Control Panel and select the Users button

   B. Enable auditing of all shared folders

   C. Use network monitor to identify all user connections

   D. Use the Server applet in Control Panel and select the Alerts button. Set an alert to tell you whenever people access your shares

15. Which service allows your computer to be seen on the network?

   A. Messenger

   B. Server

   C. Workstation

   D. Computer Browser

16. You are developing a NetBIOS-compliant naming standard for your organization. You plan to use the following format: *CityName-Bldg#-Rm#-FirstName.* The cities where your network is installed are Dallas, Los Angeles, New York, and Orlando. Building numbers are all four digits and room numbers are all three digits. No one's first name is over ten characters in length. Will this work?

   A. Yes

   B. No

8

Installing and Configuring TCP/IP

With the tremendous growth of the Internet and networking, we have become dependent on communication among computers around the world. Communicating with many different types of computers and architectures is quite a difficult task. We need a language that everyone can agree on in order to communicate effectively. This language is the Transmission control protocol/Internet protocol (TCP/IP). This protocol has become a standard because of its proven reliability and durability. After nearly two decades in existence, this protocol has become the most used protocol for communication today. A number of components combine to make this protocol so powerful. In this chapter, you gain an understanding of what is involved in the architecture of this protocol. You become familiar with the installation and configuration of the Microsoft implementation of TCP/IP. This chapter includes an overview of its features, such as dynamically configuring client workstations and resolving names in a Windows-based computer network. We close the chapter with a discussion of the new web and file transfer servers that take advantage of the TCP/IP protocol. The web server included with Windows NT Workstation is the Microsoft Peer Web Service, which enables you to publish your own web site.

Although we have devoted a whole chapter to the TCP/IP protocol and the web server, we still don't cover these topics in exhaustive detail. There are entire books devoted to these subjects. We give you enough information to understand any TCP/IP or Peer Web Server concept that you might see on a Windows NT Workstation exam. What's more, this knowledge provides a basis for study towards future Microsoft exams, such as Internetworking TCP/IP on Windows NT 4, and Implementing and Supporting Microsoft Internet Information Server.

CERTIFICATION OBJECTIVE 8.01

Features of Microsoft TCP/IP

Transmission control protocol/Internet protocol is the protocol of choice for connecting diverse workstations such as Windows NT, UNIX, Macintosh, and even mainframe computers. It is the protocol of the Internet, which is a testament to the popularity of this protocol. TCP/IP was developed in 1969 by the Department of Defense for the ARPANET project. This project was to design a fault-tolerant network that could withstand partial destruction in the event of war. In such a fast-moving industry as computers, it's amazing that something developed so long ago is still useful today. Internet TCP/IP applications such as e-mail and file transfer played a large part in the growth of the protocol's popularity. The Internet will continue to evolve, but TCP/IP remains the glue that holds it together. TCP/IP is not just for the Internet. It is a very capable protocol for any organization. Although it is not the fastest or easiest protocol to configure, it has many advantages that would make it a wise choice for your company's primary network protocol.

Microsoft has its own implementation of TCP/IP that is supported with nearly every Microsoft operating system, including DOS, Windows 3.*x*, Windows 95 and Windows NT. In most cases, support is built directly into the operating system. The Microsoft implementation still includes standard TCP/IP components such as FTP, SNMP, Telnet, and a wide range of TCP/IP commands. On top of these, the Microsoft TCP/IP is enhanced for Windows networks with additional features such as DHCP and WINS. These subjects are discussed later in the chapter.

CERTIFICATION OBJECTIVE 8.02

TCP/IP Architecture

The TCP/IP protocol maps to a popular networking model called the open systems interconnect (OSI) model. The OSI model is used to standardize protocols so that systems of different types can still communicate. As you can see from Figure 8-1, TCP/IP does not map to the OSI model exactly. Perhaps this is because the OSI model was introduced in the late seventies, nearly a decade after TCP/IP.

Each layer of both models has a distinct function that it provides to the layer directly above or below it.

FIGURE 8-1

TCP/IP maps to the
OSI model

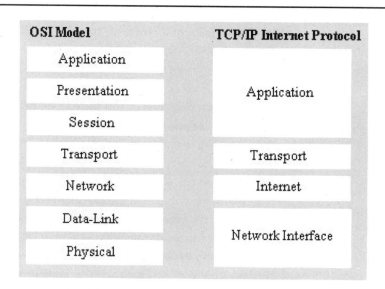

Network Interface Layer

The network interface layer is the lowest layer of the TCP/IP architecture.
It is responsible for putting frames onto the network medium. There is
another layer that separates the network interface layer from the network
device, and that is called the network device interface specification (NDIS)
interface. This is not a portion of the TCP/IP protocol suite, but a standard
for communicating between the device and the protocol. NDIS allows
an NDIS-compliant protocol, such as TCP/IP, to communicate with any
NDIS-compliant device.

Internet Layer

The Internet layer of the TCP/IP architecture is concerned with the source
and destination addresses of the computers. The Internet layer must use the
components listed below to acquire the correct address—either the physical
hardware address or a logical address such as an IP address or host name. The
components and functions of the Internet layer are described in Table 8-1.

Transport Layer

The transport layer provides communication between the hosts, and data delivery
for the layer above it. This sounds like the Internet layer, but the transport layer

TABLE 8-1

Internet Layer

Component	Function
Internet Protocol (IP)	This protocol is the core of the TCP/IP suite. IP packets are delivered on a connectionless delivery system. This means that packets are not guaranteed to arrive in the correct order, if they arrive at all.
Internet Control Message Protocol (ICMP)	A maintenance protocol used between two systems to share status and error information. The PING command uses this protocol.
Address Resolution Protocol (ARP)	Used to distinguish the hardware address of the destination computer from the Internet address.
Reverse Address Resolution Protocol (RARP)	Used when a computer must determine an Internet address while it already has a physical hardware address. Microsoft uses Dynamic Host Configuration Protocol (DHCP) instead of RARP for this purpose.
Dynamic Host Configuration Protocol (DHCP)	Allows a computer to obtain an IP address and other information from the DHCP server upon booting. Much easier than manually configuring workstations TCP/IP information.

provides frame sequencing, error detection, and acknowledgments. Which of the two available components of the transport layer is used depends on the nature of the application being used. If an application requires speed rather than guaranteed delivery, the user datagram protocol is used. If data must arrive intact, the transmission control protocol is used. The components and functions of the transport layer are described in Table 8-2.

Application Layer

The application layer contains the connection utilities and applications. This is the layer that the user and applications interact with. As we indicated before, applications in this layer determines how the lower layers should perform their jobs. Does this application require connection-oriented (TCP), or connectionless (IP) services? The applications that are run in this layer require the services of the lower layers to function. For example, the PING command makes use of the Internet layer's ICMP protocol. The components and functions of the application layer are described in Table 8-3.

TABLE 8-2

Transport Layer

Component	Function
User Datagram Protocol (UDP)	A protocol that does not guarantee the data will arrive in order, if it arrives at all. Just like IP, it is faster because it does not have to wait to receive acknowledgements from the destination computer.
Transmission Control Protocol (TCP)	A connection-oriented protocol that ensures the data will arrive in the correct order. A connection is set between the two communicating devices to send and receive data. If this data is out of order, TCP reorders the information. If the expected information was not received, it is requested again.

TABLE 8-3

Application Layer

Component	Function
Ping	A utility for verifying connectivity between two TCP/IP machines. Sends Internet control message protocol (ICMP) echo request and echo reply packets to the destination. The destination responds, proving there is connectivity. If it doesn't respond (times out) you can start your troubleshooting process. This is a very helpful utility.
Telnet	Used for terminal emulation for character-based communicating.
File Transfer Protocol (FTP)	Used to transfer files between two computers. The computer you are receiving from must have an FTP server. An FTP client and server is provided with NT Workstation, which can also allow you to upload information as well.
Trivial File Transfer Protocol (TFTP)	Similar to the file transfer protocol, but does not require user authentication.
Simple Mail Transfer Protocol (SMTP)	Used to send and receive mail over the Internet.
Domain Name Service (DNS)	Translates host names into IP addresses. (An example of a host name would be microsoft.com.) DNS Servers are used to store the host names/IP address information and are queried by the clients.
Simple Network Management Protocol (SNMP)	Used for managing SNMP-compliant network devices such as hubs and routers. A managing computer is used to get data from other computers on the network such as configuration data, error messages, protocol information, and usage statistics.

Installing and Configuring TCP/IP

Although the TCP/IP protocol is by far the most popular protocol available, it is one of the most difficult to configure. There are a number of configuration settings that must be correct before you can begin communicating. From the server end you can implement some of the newer technologies associated with Microsoft's TCP/IP to ease the burden of configuring workstations. These require plenty of time and expertise to configure, though.

Most of the installation and configuration of the TCP/IP protocol is done through the Network applet in the Control Panel. Figure 8-2 shows the

---

Installing and configuring
TCP/IP from the
Protocols tab

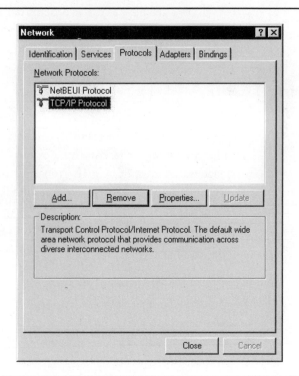

Protocols tab. (It's interesting to note that, in Network Properties, Microsoft defines the T in TCP/IP as *transport*, rather than transmission. I checked many different sources to verify the correct definition for the acronym. The vast majority use transmission. The transmission control protocol is a component of the transport layer, so they are not too far off.)

As you can see, we have already installed TCP/IP, because it is in our list of network protocols. If you do not see it in your list of network protocols, you have to install it. The next exercise covers installing the TCP/IP protocol.

EXERCISE 8-1

Installing and Configuring TCP/IP

1. Open the Control Panel, and select the Network applet.

2. Click the Protocols tab.

3. Click the Add button.

4. Select the TCP/IP Protocol and click OK.

5. We are now at the Protocols tab, and TCP/IP should be visible. You can remain in this area, because we are going to configure the TCP/IP protocol next.

Configuring TCP/IP

Once you have installed the TCP/IP protocol you still might have to revisit the Network applet frequently for adjustments. Even if you do not make any adjustments, you will visit this area to view the settings for the protocol. You reach the Microsoft TCP/IP Properties dialog box, shown in Figure 8-3, by selecting the TCP/IP protocol from the list of installed protocols and selecting Properties.

In addition to the Network Control Panel applet for viewing TCP/IP information, there are many console-based utilities. You can use these utilities to get current statistics on the state of connections, the route table, addresses, name resolution, and much more. An important console command that you should be familiar with is IPCONFIG. Issuing this command without any parameters gives you the big three TCP/IP settings: IP address, subnet mask, and default gateway. This is a convenient way to determine your current IP address when you are being assigned one through DHCP. For more detailed

FIGURE 8-3

Find the settings of a protocol at the Properties dialog box

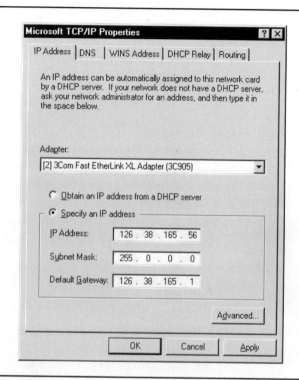

information, you can type IPCONFIG /ALL. Here is a sample of the output provided by the IPCONFIG /ALL command:

```
Windows NT IP Configuration
    Host Name . . . . . . . . . : hal-wcbrandon.mydomain.com
    DNS Servers . . . . . . . . :
    Node Type . . . . . . . . . : Hybrid
    NetBIOS Scope ID. . . . . . :
    IP Routing Enabled. . . . . : No
    WINS Proxy Enabled. . . . . : No
    NetBIOS Resolution Uses DNS : No
Ethernet adapter E190x2:
    Description . . . . . . . . : 3Com 3C90x Ethernet Adapter
    Physical Address. . . . . . : 00-60-97-42-50-63
    DHCP Enabled. . . . . . . . : Yes
    IP Address. . . . . . . . . : 198.114.201.109
    Subnet Mask . . . . . . . . : 255.255.255.0
```

```
Default Gateway . . . . . . : 198.114.201.1
DHCP Server . . . . . . . . : 198.114.201.23
Primary WINS Server . . . . : 198.114.201.23
Secondary WINS Server . . . : 198.114.201.38
Lease Obtained. . . . . . . : Wednesday, December 03,
                              1997 10:23:00 AM
Lease Expires . . . . . . . : Saturday, December 06, 1997
                              10:23:00 AM
```

Get to know this powerful command. It is a great one to have in your tool belt as a TCP/IP administrator. It is very helpful when you need to troubleshoot a system that you are not familiar with. Rather than ask the end user, you can just type the command and see for yourself. Everything you need to know about the current TCP/IP configuration can be found here. Before we get too far, let us lay the foundation of configuring the TCP/IP protocol.

IP Address

The IP address uniquely identifies a computer on the network. It is 32 bits long, with four octets separated by periods, such as 198.24.147.48. Each octet has eight bits, which equals one byte. What is so special about the IP address is the fact that it not only uniquely represents the host, but also represents the network that the host is on. You will see in the next section how this is done.

It is very important to ensure that no two hosts are using the same IP address on your network. If there is a host on the network with the same IP address, the second machine may not even initialize on the network, or may just receive intermittent errors while communicating. The latter of the two is a little more difficult to detect. Duplicate addresses on the network can be avoided by creating a list of IP addresses and updating it every time you manually assign an address. This list is also convenient if you need to look up the address for a specific machine.

Subnet Mask

The subnet mask is used to hide part of the IP address in order to distinguish the network from the host on the network. You may already have seen a few subnet masks, such as 255.255.255.0. With the subnet mask of 255.255.255.0, you can see how network can be distinguished from host.

255 = 11111111 in binary digits. Therefore the subnet mask of 255.255.255.0 would equal:

11111111.11111111.11111111.00000000

When you apply the subnet mask to the IP address, you are separating the network from the host based on the subnet mask you are using. The one binary digit is used to distinguish the network from the host. Here is an example of how the one binary digit covers, or masks, a portion of an IP address.

First, let's pick an IP address of 165.29.45.114. We will convert this IP address to binary to show you more clearly how the mask works. This IP address expressed in binary representation is shown here:

10100101.00011101.00101101.01110010   = IP address

11111111.11111111.11111111.000000000   = subnet mask

Wherever there are ones in the subnet mask, they are used to designate the network, so from this example we can draw the following conclusion: The IP address is on the 165.29.45 network, and the unique host is 114.

This means that we can use the same first three octets of the IP address for everyone on the network. The last octet, based on this subnet mask, is the unique address that we must change for each host on the network. We have a total of 254 unique host addresses on this network: 1 – 254. If we need more than that, we have to use another range for the IP address, or change the subnet mask. Custom subnet masking is a little beyond the scope of this book, but will be covered in great detail as you study for the Internetworking TCP/IP on Windows NT exam.

Default Gateway

The default gateway is used when you have an address that is not on a network you belong to. You need to send this information to another network, because it is not destined for your network. This default gateway is extremely important for this reason. One important detail concerning the default gateway is that it must be on your network. For example, if you are on the network of 214.84.153, the default gateway must have this same network address of 214.84.153. This address also can be thought of as the router address of the machine that connects you or your LAN to the outside world, or just connects you to another subnet.

I recently had to track down a problem when my boss changed the IP address of a printer to another subnet and could not communicate with the printer anymore. The printer would not reply to the PING command (a TCP/IP command to verify connectivity by pinging the IP address to see if you receive a response). He showed me how he had changed the IP address, and sure enough, he had not changed the default gateway to the new subnet. We changed the default gateway and the printer responded to the PING command.

Advanced

The Advanced Options tab for the TCP/IP protocol enables you to configure separate TCP/IP settings for multiple network adapters in your system. These multiple network adapters let your computer join separate TCP/IP networks, and possibly route packets between them. Since each network adapter takes part on a different network, you need to configure the TCP/IP settings for each network. As we said before, the IP address must reflect the network you are on. This involves configuring the subnet mask and default gateway, specific to each network.

You can also specify that you want to enable point-to-point tunneling protocol (PPTP) filtering. This is a new technology that allows remote users to access the network over the Internet. It provides a secure channel, even though you are transmitting information over the very populated Internet. It is called the tunneling protocol because it can be thought of as a tunnel that your data goes through to remain safe from prying eyes. Your data enters the tunnel at your workstation and surfaces at the server with PPTP enabled.

The button to enable security on the Advanced tab of TCP/IP settings allows you to specify which port or protocol you would like to allow for each network card. Disallowing access based on specific ports or protocols makes your network more secure against intruders gaining access.

Now would be a good time to use the PING command. This command is most commonly used to test for connectivity with remote systems, but also can be used to see if you have installed and configured TCP/IP correctly on your system. Here is the syntax to verify TCP/IP has been installed correctly:

```
PING 127.0.0.1
```

This IP address is reserved for internal loopback testing. You know you have set up TCP/IP correctly when you see the following screen:

```
C:\PING 127.0.0.1
Pinging 127.0.0.1 with 32 bytes of data:
Reply from 127.0.0.1: bytes=32 time<10ms TTL=128
Reply from 127.0.0.1: bytes=32 time<10ms TTL=128
Reply from 127.0.0.1: bytes=32 time<10ms TTL=128
Reply from 127.0.0.1: bytes=32 time<10ms TTL=128
```

If you did not receive this response, verify your installation. After you have installed and configured TCP/IP correctly, you can use this command to verify that the WINS, DNS, and default gateway settings are correct. Let me show you how, as we continue the troubleshooting steps using the PING utility.

After we have verified that we have TCP/IP set up correctly on our machine, we continue testing in this order:

1. Ping the near side of the router. Since a router has two addresses to connect networks, you should ping the side of the router that is closest to you. If you receive a response, then you can communicate on your network.

2. Ping the far side of the router. This is the address of the other side of the router from your network. This means that your packets are passing through the router.

3. Ping a computer on the far side of the router. This not only means that you can pass packets through the router and on to the other network, but that you can communicate with a specific host on the other network.

This is an effective troubleshooting technique to use to identify where the problem is on a TCP/IP-based network. I have spent many hours reconfiguring Internet settings because of connection problems, only to figure out that they were not my fault. I now have a list of certain computers to ping in order to find which link in the chain is broken.

FROM THE CLASSROOM

TCP/IP, or Life Can Be One Ping After Another

TCP/IP protocol can be a lot of fun. There are, however, a number of parameters that must be configured correctly in order for your computer to be able to communicate on the network. The mistake most frequently made, when manually configuring the IP address, is inputting the wrong IP address or the wrong subnet mask. In a class of ten students, we can count on three of the students getting the entries wrong.

The most common problem is keyboarding in the wrong IP address. This is especially true when you have subnetting in place. For example, consider the following IP address and subnet mask:

171.131.19.20 IP

255.255.255.0 Subnet Mask

If you make a transposition error and enter 171.131.20.19, and the correct subnet mask, you can't communicate with other computers on your segment, because you have the wrong net ID. This is an easy mistake to make and a hard one to find. I have observed students

staring at the IP address for many minutes without seeing the transposition error. Even seasoned instructors may struggle to find the error.

The second most common error is a typographical error made when entering the subnet mask. Look closely at the following subnet masks:

255.255.255.0

255.255.225.0

Do you see the mistake? Look closely at the third octet in both addresses. I have stood behind students while they entered the addresses, and watched them make the typo. It is especially likely to happen if they are using the numeric pad and typing quickly. Like the transposition error, this error can be hard to find, because the numbers look so similar.

Of course, you can eliminate this entire hassle if you use DHCP servers to hand out IP addresses.

—*By Shane clawson, MCT, MCSE*

Configuring for DNS

It's a safe bet that all of you have been on the Internet, or have seen ads on television for company web sites. When you type in the uniform resource locator (URL), such as www.pepsi.com, you are transported to the site. You don't have to know the 32-bit IP address. This is made possible by the use of the domain name service (DNS). DNS performs name resolution of host names to IP addresses. If there were no way around the Internet other than the IP address, there would be about a hundred people on the Internet right now, rather than millions. There are many servers out on the Internet dedicated to the sole purpose of resolving these host names. As you probably have noticed, there are different URL classifications, such as org, mil, and edu. These classifications are an attempt to organize the Internet. The com designation of commercial sites has greatly outnumbered the other designations. When DNS finds the designation of com, it searches through the lower branches of its hierarchy first—the reverse of the order in which URLs with other designations are resolved. Configure for DNS at the tab shown in Figure 8-4.

FIGURE 8-4

Configure for DNS at the DNS tab in Properties

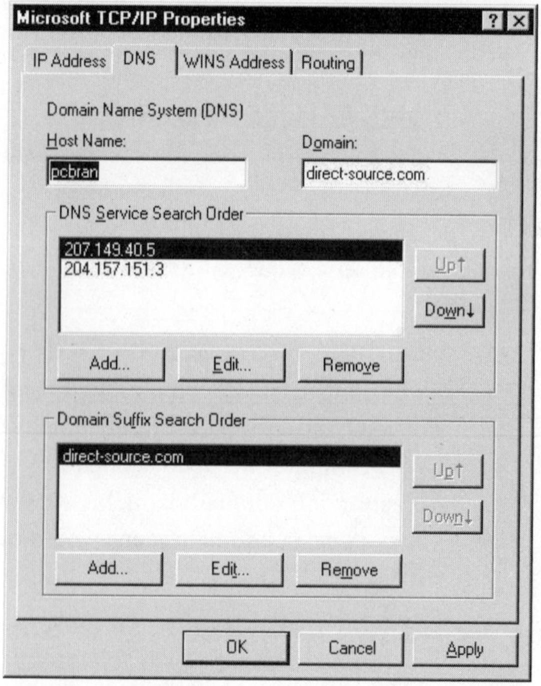

Host Name

The host name is the name you are using for your computer, and must adhere to a few rules. It can contain the letters A – Z, 0 – 9, and a hyphen. The host name is case-sensitive due to the fact the Internet is populated with many UNIX machines, which are case-sensitive. No other characters are permitted in the host name. If the name of your computer is used as the host name, which it is by default, and contains illegal characters, they are mapped to a hyphen.

Domain Name

The domain name can be a bit confusing. Earlier in the book you learned about the NT domain structure, which is a logical grouping of computers. The domain name that is used here is a bit different, and should not be confused with the NT domain name. A DNS domain is a collection of TCP/IP hosts, either physical or logical. An organization usually has one domain name, such as Microsoft.com. Under the Microsoft.com domain, you can have subdivisions, such as sales.microsoft.com, or training.microsoft.com.

DNS Service Search Order

The DNS service search order is where you specify a DNS Server to resolve host names. If you are like most people who access the Internet, you are given this DNS Server address from your Internet provider. You can have three DNS servers queried until one is found to be available.

Domain Suffix Search Order

The domain suffix search order is used to append the domain name to the end of your host name. You would enter the name of your organization here. If your computer was named engineering1, and the suffix search order (your organization's domain name) is computerking.com, then the combination of host name and domain name would be engineering1.computerking.com.

Configuring Windows Internet Name Service (WINS)

On a Windows TCP/IP network there are many names that correspond to the various machines on the network, such as the workstations, servers, and printers. These types of names are called NetBIOS names. These names also make it easier to communicate with other computers on the Windows network. I say Windows network because these NetBIOS names are not used by non-Microsoft computers such as UNIX machines. Like DNS, these NetBIOS names require translation in order to be used. Then Windows Internet Name Service (WINS) is responsible for mapping these NetBIOS names to IP addresses. There is a WINS server on the network responsible for translating these NetBIOS names. This is where WINS clients have their names registered. If they were not registered in the WINS database, they would have to broadcast their name registration across the network, which could cause unnecessary traffic. When a client would like to communicate with another NetBIOS computer, it just queries the WINS server with the NetBIOS name, and the WINS server sends back the IP address that is associated with that NetBIOS name. Here is an example of the result I got when I typed the command to view NetBIOS statistics:

```
C:\nbtstat -r
NetBIOS Names Resolution and Registration Statistics
Resolved By Broadcast        =  2
Resolved By Name Server      =  196
Registered By Broadcast      =  0
Registered By Name Server    =  31
```

If you were to type the command on your home computer you would probably not see anything. If you get a chance, type the command at work just to see how many names were resolved and registered by the name server and by broadcasting.

WINS is a dynamic replacement for the LMHOSTS file. This file was a static text file that computers would use to map NetBIOS names to IP addresses. If a computer was added to the network, this file would have to be manually adjusted on the workstations to reflect the name and IP address of the computer. Manually adjusting several LMHOSTS files on the network was a very daunting task. Now with WINS, a workstation can query the server with a name that it would like resolved to an address. The workstation no longer has to manually update the LMHOSTS file, even though it may provide fault tolerance to maintain the LMHOSTS files in a smaller network in case the WINS server fails. See Figure 8-5 to configure WINS.

FIGURE 8-5

Configure WINS at the
WINS Address tab in
Properties

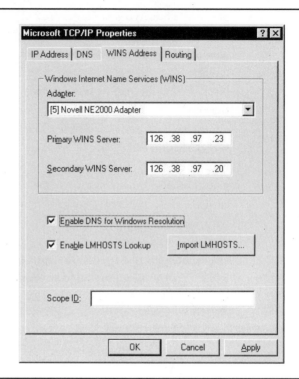

Adapter

Choose the adapter you would like to configure the WINS information for.
You can have different WINS configurations for each adapter located in
the system. This is required if you are connected to two different Windows
networks that have separate WINS servers. You can directly query the WINS
server for each network.

Primary WINS Server

The primary WINS server is the server you designate to be first on your list of
WINS servers to query. Most networks have, at most, two WINS servers to
service client translation requests. It is a very good idea to add a second WINS
server for fault tolerance.

Secondary WINS Server

The secondary WINS server can be used if the primary WINS server becomes unavailable. The secondary WINS server is used only as a backup to the primary, but contains the same information as the primary. If there were not a secondary WINS server on the network and the primary WINS server became unavailable, the clients would have to resort to broadcasting translation and registration requests over the network. This can quickly lead to traffic congestion. They can also use the static LMHOSTS file if it has been maintained.

Enable DNS for WINS Resolution

You can use the DNS Server that you configured in the DNS Configuration dialog box to resolve NetBIOS names. If WINS was not successful at resolving the name, the system then tries the DNS Server to see if it can resolve the name.

Enable LMHOSTS Lookup

As we said earlier, the LMHOSTS file is a static text file that was used to map NetBIOS names to IP addresses. You can still use LMHOSTS if you have implemented WINS. If you have selected Enable LMHOSTS Lookup, when a name is not resolved dynamically the LMHOSTS file is parsed for the computer name. You should keep this enabled as a backup name service to the WINS server should it go down.

Import LMHOSTS

The Import LMHOSTS file is where you specify the LMHOSTS file that you want to use. This can be helpful if you need to import an LMHOSTS file from another computer that has already been configured.

Scope ID

You can use the NetBIOS scope ID to isolate NetBIOS traffic to a specific set of computers. Only computers that have the matching scope ID can communicate. This can be effective if you want a group of computers to communicate separately from the rest of the network. You also can have several computers on the network with the name SERVER as long as they are using different scope IDs. An example of this would be SERVER.ENG, SERVER.SALES, and SERVER.SUPPORT. ENG, SALES, and SUPPORT would be the scope IDs. I once changed the scope ID on one of the computers here at work, and something interesting happened. After I made the change, I was prompted to restart the computer. When the computer rebooted and I tried to log in, a domain controller could not be found. The domain controllers on the network were not configured with the same scope ID, so they were not available to validate me. Oh well. It seemed like a good idea—isolate my computer from other users. Unfortunately, it isolated me from everything else, including the resources I needed to access!

With the beta release of the upcoming Windows NT Server 5, the documentation says that WINS will no longer be needed. It appears as if DNS is going to replace WINS for name resolution purposes. This was shocking news, because there are so many NetBIOS names out there on Windows networks that use WINS for resolution.

Routing

Your Windows NT computer can participate as a router between two networks. For this to be possible, you need to have more than one network card installed on your system. This makes your computer *multi-homed.* Your computer can now route information by using route tables that you create with the ROUTE command. This is known as *static* routing. Dynamic routing relieves the burden of manually configuring the route information, but can increase traffic in large networks while it dynamically builds route information. Unfortunately, only Windows NT Server can take part in dynamic routing.

Each network adapter card in the computer has a different address. This will be a valid address on the network that the network card is connecting to. When routing is enabled, the computer determines whether the address is on the same network, or must be routed to another network. If the address is destined for a remote network, the packet is sent to the default gateway, which is the address of the card that is on the remote network.

The Enable IP Forwarding check box on the Routing tab of TCP/IP Properties, shown in Figure 8-6, is where you set up your workstation to route packets to different networks. This is a lower-cost alternative to an expensive dedicated router. This is effective if you have two smaller networks that communicate occasionally, but do not require a dedicated router. Keep in mind if you are routing using Windows NT Workstation, that you have to manually configure the routing tables for the network as we discussed earlier. Routing in this way should not be a replacement for routers in your organization, especially large networks. Hardware routers are very efficient, and especially designed for this purpose.

Another reason why routing is adequate for smaller networks is that Windows NT does not support the more robust routing protocols like Open Shortest Path First (OSPF), and External Gateway Protocol (EGP). Routers

FIGURE 8-6

The Routing tab is a lower-cost alternative to an expensive dedicated router

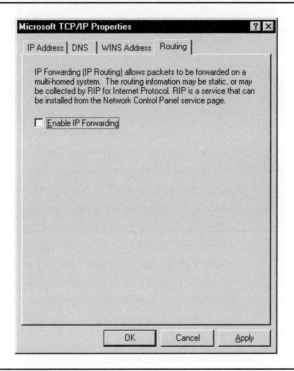

use these protocols to share route table information, in which Windows NT cannot take part.

Configuring for DHCP

As we have witnessed so far, the TCP/IP protocol is a very complicated protocol to install and configure. There are many settings, such as the IP address, subnet mask, and default gateway that must be exactly correct. A strong knowledge of these settings is imperative to supporting a TCP/IP-based network. However, to relieve some of the burden, Microsoft has created the Dynamic Host Configuration Protocol (DHCP). This will help you automatically configure a workstation's many settings. Configuring the DHCP server is not in the realm of this discussion, but an understanding of how this can affect your workstation configuration is.

exam
ⓦatch

You may be asked what is required to automatically configure client workstations. I hope that's an easy question after reading this section!

If you look back to Figure 8-3 you see the option to Obtain an IP address from a DHCP server. By clicking this radio button, you gray out the options for IP address, subnet mask, and default gateway. This is all you need to do on the workstation end to enable DHCP. Of course there is a little more to it, such as having a properly configured network card and TCP/IP installed.

As you know, you can manually assign an IP address to a computer, or you can have one assigned at random from a pool of IP addresses on the DHCP server. Deciding whether to manually assign an IP address is very important. There is a reason why you should manually assign an address to the important machines on your network. If you have a server such as a WINS or DNS Server that clients need to have access to, this would make it a great candidate for a static address. If the server were to receive its IP address through the DHCP server at random, the clients could not have a reliable way to contact the server. The workstations should have the server's IP address hard-coded in their configurations.

Here is a quick Q & A scenario to help you review the configuration of the TCP/IP protocol:

QUESTIONS AND ANSWERS

I need to configure TCP/IP in a routed environment...	You will need to configure the default gateway.
I need to configure TCP/IP in a non-routed environment...	You do not need the default gateway. The default gateway is for sending information that is not on your network.
I would like to automatically configure...	Use Dynamic Host Configuration Protocol (DHCP).
I require dynamic resolution...	Use either WINS or DNS depending on scenario. These are dynamic alternatives to static files like HOSTS and LMHOSTS. DNS is to HOSTS as WINS is to LMHOSTS.

CERTIFICATION OBJECTIVE 8.04

Peer Web Services

The Peer Web Services included with Windows NT Workstation is a scaled-down version of the Internet Information Server (IIS) that allows you to publish web pages on your company's intranet. With Peer Web Services you also can create the content for your Internet Information Server without the need to run Windows NT Server on your desktop. It may be a little limited compared to the IIS counterpart, but it should be sufficient when used as your internal company web server, and not as an Internet web server.

You can see in Figure 8-7 the WWW and FTP Services installed on the hal-wh2fctl6 computer. You have the option of selecting Properties, and connecting to a different server. You also can see the buttons to start, stop and pause the services for the computer. This screen will become familiar to you as

FIGURE 8-7

Two Internet services are
installed on this computer

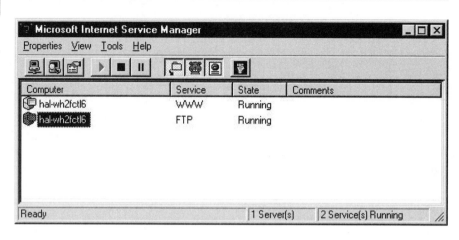

you work with Peer Web Services, because you have to stop and start the
service in order for changes that you make to take effect.

PWS Installation

Installing the Microsoft Peer Web Services is done a little differently than most
application installations. Rather than accessing a directory on the Windows
NT CD-ROM for a setup program, you use the Network applet in the
Control Panel. This makes sense because you are installing a service. This
exercise covers the installation of the Peer Web Server.

EXERCISE 8-2

Installing Peer Web Services

1. Click the Network icon in the Control Panel.

2. Click the Services tab.

3. Select Add.

4. Under Network Service, highlight Microsoft Peer Web Server and
   select OK.

5. Provide the path to the installation files located on the Windows NT
   Workstation CD-ROM.

6. Click OK on the Microsoft Peer Web Services installation screen.

7. Choose the options you would like to install. I am choosing everything with the exception of the Gopher service. Choose a destination directory or accept the default.

8. Choose a destination publishing directory or accept the default.

9. The Peer Web Services should now be installing. You may be prompted to install open database connectivity (ODBC) drivers. If so, just accept the default.

10. At this point the installation is complete and we should now be back at the Services tab, with the Microsoft Peer Web Server installed.

11. Click Close. You should not be prompted to restart your computer. You can now go straight to the Internet Service Manager to view what we just installed.

Publishing an HTML Document Using Peer Web Services

1. Find an HTML document on your hard disk for this exercise. The easiest way is to use the Find feature on the Start menu. You can search all of your local hard disks with the *.HTML, or *.HTM option. Chances are you will find a few documents rather quickly.

2. Copy one of the files you found in the last step to the Inetpub\wwwroot directory.

3. Start your web browser. If it is Explorer, click the icon on the desktop.

4. Enter the URL address for your computer, followed by the name of the file you just copied to the wwwroot directory. For example, if your computer is named Cassie, type: **http://cassie/ document_name.html**. If you do not know the computer name, start the Internet Service Manager and the first screen will show you the name of your web server. Press ENTER when you have entered the correct URL address.

5. The web page can now be viewed by others.

By far the most complicated step in the preceding exercise is step 4. Just to make sure we are comfortable with the process, here is another example of a

URL address. I have a computer called Pandora, and the HTML document I want to publish is called support.html. This is the correct URL address:

http://pandora/support.html

It's not that this step is so difficult; it's just the fact that most of us are unfamiliar with web servers, and how to access the files that we just published. It gets more difficult when you have several virtual directories to confuse you. We will discuss virtual directories later in the chapter. However, if you create links from your web pages, you don't have to remember these paths, and life will be much easier for you and your users.

Configuring WWW

Once you have installed the WWW Service, you need to configure it to your situation. You have many options concerning security, access rights, publishing directories and logging. It takes time to find the right blend for your organization. Once you have made these settings they do not have to be adjusted very often, with the exception of your published directories. This probably takes the longest to configure because you usually have to make many directories, and place the correct information in them. For example, you could make directories for different areas of your web site, such as Sales, Support, and Training. You place the corresponding web pages in each directory to be published. Just hope that you aren't the one who has to create all those web pages and link them to other pages.

Before we get too deep into the web server, let's continue with an exercise involving the web, your browser, and—most important—your MCSE and Windows NT! For this exercise you need access to the Internet and a web browser.

EXERCISE 8-4

Access the World Wide Web Using Internet Explorer and Search for Windows NT Information

1. Open up your web browser.

2. In the address field, type **www.lycos.com**. You do not have to specify http:// on the most recent browsers. You can also substitute lycos.com with your favorite search engine.

3. In the search area, type **MCSE**.

4. You will no doubt see many references to MCSE. If you search long enough, you can find some sites that will help you as you continue on towards your MCSE.

5. After you have finished reviewing your hits, type **"Windows NT"** in the search box, and be sure to include the quotation marks. These quotation marks search for the two words next to each other. This avoids hits like *stained glass windows*.

6. When you are finished, close the browser.

There is also an HTML-based Internet Service Manager, as shown in Figure 8-8. It is not possible to stop and start services with the web-based administration tool. If it is more convenient for you to configure the services remotely from a web browser, you will enjoy the web-based Internet Service

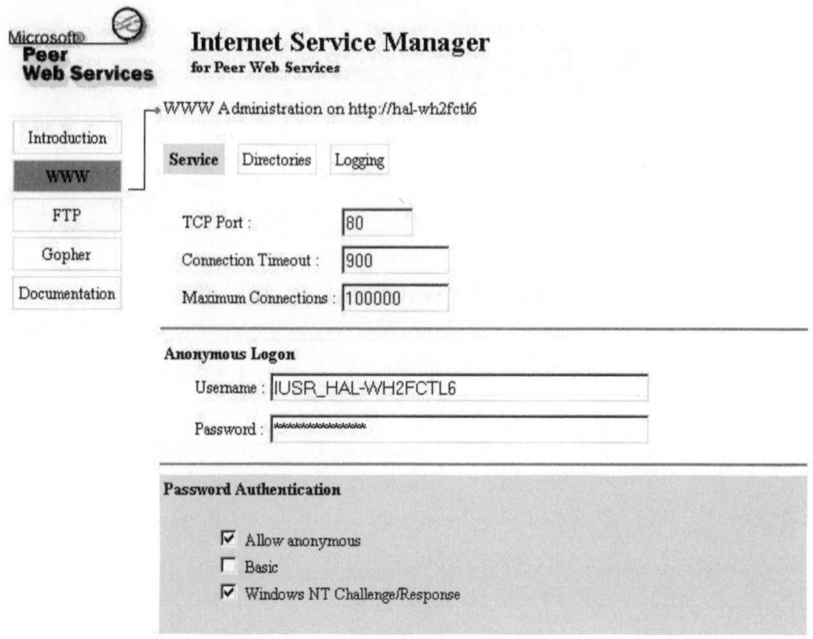

FIGURE 8-8

The HTML-based Internet Service Manager

Manager. You may have been around computers for years, but the concept of publishing web pages on your workstation is still quite new.

There is a whole exam devoted to the Internet Information Server, which covers topics, such as virtual directories, anonymous logons, and publishing of documents, that are involved in Peer Web Services. However, you must understand the components in the Workstation Peer Web Services, which is essentially a limited version of the Internet Information Server. If you continue on your MCSE track and decide to take the Internet Information Server exam, you will already have a good understanding of these concepts. At the rate that the Internet and intranets are taking off, it would be a great idea to study for that exam. Web servers are going to be here for a long time.

Here are some differences between the Peer Web Services and the Internet Information Server:

PWS	IIS
Web publishing for the corporate intranet	Web publishing for the Internet, or high-traffic corporate intranets
No virtual servers	Virtual servers
No IP address access control	Can limit access based on IP addresses
No ODBC connectivity	ODBC connectivity
Cannot limit network bandwidth	Can limit network bandwidth
40-bit SSL support	40-bit and 128-bit SSL support

WWW Service Properties

As I have described, there are two ways to configure the WWW service. For the remainder of the chapter I will be discussing the Internet Service Manager that is *not* web-based.

To access the WWW Service Properties, double-click the server that you would like to administer. Notice that your server is listed more than once if you have multiple services installed, such as WWW, FTP, and Gopher. There are a few things that are important on the Service tab. The first three settings should be sufficient when they are left at the default. Click the Help button if you are curious about these settings. The port setting is set by default at port 80.

The anonymous logon setting is created upon installation of Peer Web Services. It is created by appending the IUSR_ to the beginning of the computer name that the Peer Web Services are being installed on. An important point to remember about this logon account is that it must be the same in the Windows NT User Manager as in the Service Properties. This is a difficult problem to troubleshoot if only one of the account's password changes. To remedy this, you may want to configure this user account so that the password never expires, and the user cannot change the password. If these passwords do not match, no one can access the server, not even the Administrator.

The password authentication settings are used when anonymous access is not allowed from the clients. The two authentication methods are Basic (Clear Text) and Windows NT Challenge/Response. Windows NT Challenge/Response is the more secure of the two, because it encrypts usernames and passwords. If you are not concerned with security or encryption, you can choose Basic (Clear Text). If you enable Allow Anonymous, you do not need to worry about usernames and passwords being transmitted over the network. This is actually much safer. It sounds funny when you think that anonymous logons can be safer than encrypted usernames and passwords but it is true. If you do not require usernames and passwords, which is what anonymous logon is for, there is no chance that a hacker can capture your username and password as they travel across the network. Keep that in mind because it can be a tricky exam question! With these three options, at least one must be selected.

WWW Directories

The WWW Directories tab is where you configure the directories to be used for the WWW Service. In an earlier exercise you placed an HTML file in the wwwroot directory to be published. This wwwroot directory is called the home directory. There is only one home directory, but there can be many virtual directories. These virtual directories appear as if they are in the directory structure of the home directory, but they do not have to be. For example, the iisadmin virtual directory is actually C:\WINNT\System32\inetsrv\iisadmin. It appears to the web browser as if it is under the inetpub directory like the wwwroot was. These virtual directories can also be located on remote computers. Just specify the path that is going to be used to access the remote system. The alias is how the directory appears to the browser. We saw how the iisadmin alias is used for the physical directory path of C:\WINNT\System32\ inetsrv\iisadmin. A common usage for these directories is to not only separate site content, but to have some directories as secured. These directories can be password protected. The site can have content that is viewable by the public, but access to certain private areas can be limited to those users with a valid password.

You have the option of specifying whether the users have read or execute access. Read access is just as it sounds. If you do not check the box for read access, users cannot view or download any of the files in that specific directory. Execute access is for applications that are run on the server. The client must have execute access to the directory-run applications that are located in this directory. It is common to have the execute box checked and the read box unchecked. This allows users to run the applications or scripts, but doesn't allow them to view the information or script content.

You also have the option for Default Document. This is a handy feature that's used if a user does not specify a filename. For example, if you type www.pepsi.com without specifying a file, the default document appears. This is most likely the main site. Because of this feature, users don't have to remember long URLs to access a site.

WWW Logging

You have several options when it comes to logging information on your web browser. Logging enables you to see who is using your server, and how they are using it. The first option is to decide whether you would like to enable logging or not. The easier choice is not to enable logging, but you still need to know about the different logging options. If you do enable logging, you have to choose whether to log to a file or to a database. It is easier to log to a file on your hard disk than to log to a SQL/ODBC database. If you do choose to log to a file, you have to decide where to store the log file, whether to automatically open a new log, and when to open that new log. If you choose the database, you first need to have access to a database. Then you have to specify the Data Source Name (DSN), the table you would like to log to, and the username and password to access the database.

Configuring FTP

In addition to the WWW Services, you can have a File Transfer Protocol (FTP) Service for your users to download and upload information. Of course it's not as pretty as the web, but it is simple and efficient. It can be much easier for you to set up a site without the hassle of creating dozens of fancy HTML documents.

FTP Server Service Properties

You can see from Figure 8-9 that configuring the FTP Service looks very similar to configuring the WWW Service. The Service tab is very close to the WWW Service tab except for the Anonymous Username and Password.

Of course the TCP Port is different too. If you enable Allow Anonymous Connections, you have to provide a username and password for the anonymous connection. This is provided by default by the installation program. The installation program also creates the user of the same name in the Windows NT User Manager. How nice of them! If you do not choose Allow Anonymous Connections, the option for username and password are grayed out, because the users will provide their own username and password. You also have the option of allowing only anonymous connections to your server. We discussed the advantages of this earlier. We don't want hackers to capture our usernames and passwords, especially if we possess the magic orb: administrative access. Another nice feature of the FTP Service tab that was not available on the WWW Service tab is the Current Sessions button. Just click here to see the users that are currently connected to your server.

FTP Messages

The FTP Messages tab is unique to the FTP Service, and is not available for the WWW Service. This is where you set a custom greeting for users when they access your FTP server. It can sometimes be difficult when you log on to someone's FTP server and there is no message there to greet you. This message can give them a quick introduction to your FTP site. You can inform them of new developments, or where to access certain information. You also can specify an exit message for when they log off your server. If too many connections are reached on your FTP server, you can specify a message to the users who are unable to access your server. This can be the usual message: "Sorry, we have reached our maximum limit of users. Please try again later."

FTP Directories

The FTP Directories tab is similar to the tab for the WWW Service properties. Here is where you specify the directories that you will make accessible to your users. These can be virtual directories, either local or remote. The ftproot is provided by default as your home directory. The other option is the Directory Listing style. This can be UNIX or MS-DOS. If you specify MS-DOS, UNIX users may not be able to see the files on your FTP server. If you are publishing on the Internet, you should choose the UNIX directory listing because of the popularity of UNIX machines on the Internet. If you are just providing the

FTP Service for your company intranet, then go ahead and select the MS-DOS directory listing format.

The Directories tab is where you can create a drop box for users to upload their information. You have to be using an NTFS partition for this to work. For the folder you would like to be the drop box, give users only the write-only permission. This is done by using Windows NT Explorer and clicking the Security tab and selecting Permissions. This creates an area that everyone has access to, but cannot be viewed—quite convenient for suggestions and comments on your intranet.

FTP Logging

The FTP Logging tab is identical to the Logging tab for the WWW Service. Review the WWW Logging tab section for specific settings. Once again, it is important to enable FTP logging if you would like to know who is accessing your resources and how they are accessing them. If you do not have logging enabled you may not be able to detect intruders until it is too late. You can spot failed attempts to access resources.

CERTIFICATION SUMMARY

TCP/IP is a reliable and robust set of protocols for communicating with diverse systems such as UNIX, Windows NT, and Macintosh. With a standard protocol, these different systems can effectively communicate and share information regardless of architecture. The TCP/IP is designed as a suite of protocols that can be used in varying situations, depending on the needs of the application. The layers of the TCP/IP architecture use these protocols to provide a distinct function for the layers above and below. From top to bottom these layers are the Application, Transport, Internet, and Network Interface.

To use TCP/IP on your machine, you must configure a subnet mask, a unique IP address, and possibly a default gateway. These can be assigned to the user automatically by the Dynamic Host Configuration Protocol (DHCP). You also may need to configure your workstation to use a WINS server, which resolves NetBIOS names to IP addresses, or a DNS Server, which maps host names to IP addresses. These services replaced text-based files like HOSTS and LMHOSTS for name resolution.

With TCP/IP and Windows NT 4 you also can install your own Peer Web Server for publishing web pages on your intranet. This allows you to run a World Wide Web server, a Gopher server, or a File Transfer Protocol server. These services are managed with the Internet Service Manager, which can be the web-based version or just the standard Internet Service Manager. You can administer these services on local or remote computers. You have the ability to restrict access to directories, create private directories, allow anonymous users, require passwords, and log events.

TWO-MINUTE DRILL

- ❑ Transmission Control Protocol/Internet Protocol is the protocol of choice for connecting diverse workstations such as Windows NT, UNIX, Macintosh, and even mainframe computers. It is the protocol of the Internet.

- ❑ The open systems interconnect (OSI) model is used to standardize protocols so that systems of different types can still communicate if they share the same protocol.

- ❑ Most of the installation and configuration of the TCP/IP protocol is done through the Network applet in the Control Panel.

- ❑ DNS performs name resolution of host names to IP addresses.

- ❑ The Windows Internet Name Service (WINS) is responsible for mapping the NetBIOS names to IP addresses.

- ❑ Your Windows NT computer can participate as a router between two networks.

- ❑ The Dynamic Host Configuration Protocol (DHCP) helps you automatically configure the workstation's IP address, subnet mask, and default gateway, in addition to many other settings.

- ❑ On the exam you may be asked what is required to automatically configure client workstations.

- ❑ The Peer Web Services included with Windows NT Workstation is a scaled-down version of the Internet Information Server (IIS) that allows you to publish web pages on your company's intranet.

❑ You have many options concerning security, access rights, publishing directories and logging when configuring your WWW Service.

❑ You can also have a File Transfer Protocol (FTP) Service for your users to download and upload information.

SELF TEST

The following questions will help you measure your understanding of the material presented in this chapter. Read all the choices carefully, as there may be more than one correct answer. Choose all correct answers for each question.

1. Which is not a layer of the TCP/IP architecture?

   A. Internet

   B. Transport

   C. Network

   D. Application

2. The _____ layer of the TCP/IP model provides frame sequencing and error detection.

3. Which is the connection-oriented protocol that ensures data will arrive in the correct order?

   A. IP

   B. UPD

   C. ICMP

   D. TCP

4. Which is a valid IP address?

   A. 114.213.2

   B. 111.111.111.111

   C. 2.86.258.104

   D. 124.0.76.205

5. What would be a correct default gateway for your computer if your IP address is 106.23.86.211?

   A. 255.255.255.0

   B. 255.255.0.0

   C. 106.23.86.211

   D. 106.23.86.143

6. Which is not an option under the Advanced TCP/IP Properties tab?

   A. Disallowing specific protocol access.

   B. Enabling IP Forwarding.

   C. Enabling the PPTP protocol.

   D. Disallowing specific port access.

7. What do you need access to if you are to resolve a name of mcsehopeful.com?

   A. A DHCP Server.

   B. A properly configured LMHOSTS file.

   C. A WINS Server.

   D. A DNS Server.

8. You are network administrator of a small network. Even though you have a WINS server on the network for name resolution, you still maintain the HOSTS files for each workstation. What would happen if you could not communicate with the WINS server?

   A. You would have to load the HOSTS file and restart the computer in order to communicate.

   B. Your HOSTS file would automatically continue to resolve names.

C. You would have to use the ROUTE /ADD command to load the HOSTS file into memory.

D. You could not resolve any more NetBIOS names.

9. What does DHCP stand for?

10. (True/False) A default gateway must always be present before you can communicate.

11. Which is not a tab on the WWW Service Properties dialog box?

A. Authentication

B. Directories

C. Logging

D. Service

12. Which tab in the Internet Service Manager do you use to specify what access a user has?

A. The Service tab

B. The Logging tab

C. The Directories tab

D. You cannot configure access through the Internet Service Manager

13. (True/False) Windows NT Challenge/Response is the most effective way to eliminate stolen passwords.

14. Which tab of the FTP Service would you specify a UNIX or MS-DOS listing?

A. Logging

B. Service

C. Directories

D. The directory listing button of the Directories tab

15. You are administrator of a branch office for the Guitars Galore corporation. You've been having communication problems with headquarters, and now there's a support representative from the corporate headquarters on the phone. He tells you to issue the IPCONFIG /ALL command. You do so, and tell him the current settings. He tells you he knows what the problem is. Based on this TCP/IP configuration, which line is incorrect?
Ethernet adapter El90x2:

A. Description . . . : 3Com 3C90x Ethernet Adapter

B. Physical Address . . . : 00-60-97-42-50-63

C. DHCP Enabled . . .: Yes

D. IP Address . . .: 107.214.21.109

E. Subnet Mask . . .: 255.0.0.0

F. Default Gateway . . .: 134.27.119.1

G. DHCP Server . . .: 107.214.21.23

H. Primary WINS Server . . .: 107.214.21.23

I. Secondary WINS Server . . .: 134.27.119.138

J. Lease Obtained . . .: Wednesday, December 03, 1997 10:23:00 AM

K. Lease Expires . . .: Saturday, December 06, 1997 10:23:00 AM

16. (True/False) The LMHOSTS file is used to map host names to IP addresses.

17. (True/False) Windows NT Workstation supports Routing Information Protocol (RIP) for dynamic routing updates.

9

Connecting to NetWare Servers

Windows NT Workstation 4.0 includes Client Services for NetWare (CSNW), a network service that is exactly what its name implies—a client that enables Windows NT to utilize services on Novell NetWare servers. With CSNW, a Windows NT 4.0 computer can connect to NetWare 2.*x*, 3.*x*, and 4.*x* servers to share files, use printer queues, and run utilities to manage NetWare servers. NetWare servers comprise an impressive percentage of business and educational Local Area Network (LAN) servers and a Microsoft Certified Systems Engineer can reasonably expect to make use of CSNW at some time during his or her technical career.

Overview

Microsoft provides NetWare connectivity components for both Windows NT Workstation and Windows NT Server. These components enable Windows NT Workstation computers to connect to NetWare servers, to use files and print queues. Windows NT Server, on the other hand, can perform additional, more sophisticated operations with its NetWare tools.

Windows NT Workstations and NetWare

With the CSNW service, Windows NT Workstations can easily browse NetWare servers in the same way Windows NT computers can be browsed in the Network Neighborhood. Windows NT's multi-provider router (MPR) makes NetWare servers appear no different from Windows NT computers to network browsers. Users can map network drives and connect to network print queues on NetWare servers the same way they connect to files and printers on Windows NT servers.

NetWare management utilities such as SYSCON can also be run on Windows NT computers, enabling administrators to add users, create print queues, and perform other NetWare tasks from a Windows NT machine. The functionality of CSNW enables Windows NT Workstation 4.0 to perform as an ideal client in a NetWare server environment.

Windows NT Servers and NetWare

Windows NT Server 4.0 includes some additional NetWare connectivity features not available with Windows NT Workstation. See Figure 9-1 for a diagram of connectivity options. Another Microsoft product, Microsoft Services for NetWare, can be purchased for Windows NT Server. These tools are provided to facilitate mixed server environments and migration projects.

Gateway Service for NetWare (GSNW)

The Gateway Service for NetWare is installed as a network service on a Windows NT Server 4.0 computer, which then attaches to NetWare servers. Files, print queues, and some NetWare utilities on NetWare servers are then available to the Windows NT Server's clients, even though they are not running a NetWare-compatible protocol or client.

The translation of protocols that is necessary for the NetWare Gateway Service to operate exacts a significant toll on the performance of activity between the client and the NetWare server. It is not recommended that the Gateway Service be utilized as a permanent solution for this reason. However, Windows NT Server running NetWare Gateway Services can be an invaluable tool in a mixed or migrating environment.

Now that you are familiar with GSNW, here are some possible scenarios where GSNW or CSNW might be used and what strategy would work best.

QUESTIONS AND ANSWERS

We are migrating from a NetWare server to a Windows NT Server...	Since your Windows NT Workstations already have CSNW installed, all you need to do is uninstall CSNW on the workstations when the server migration is complete.
We need permanent access to a NetWare server, but we need it NOW!	Install GSNW on a Windows NT Server. As time permits, install CSNW on each Windows NT Workstation.
We need temporary access to a NetWare server for a large number of users...	Install GSNW on a Windows NT Server for the short time needed.
We need temporary access to a NetWare server for a few users...	Install CSNW on each Windows NT Workstation that needs to access the NetWare server.
We need to copy files from a NetWare server to a Windows NT Server...	Install CSNW on a Windows NT Workstation to connect to both servers.

A chapter discussing the NetWare Gateway Service in depth is included in the Windows NT Server book in this series.

exam
ⓦatch

Although GSNW is not a part of Windows NT Workstation, the certification exam for NT Workstation can contain general questions regarding how GSNW works and how NT Workstation users can benefit from it. While it is not necessary to have in-depth knowledge about GSNW, it is important to understand the information presented in this chapter regarding GSNW.

Migration Tool for NetWare

Microsoft anticipated the need to facilitate NetWare to NT migrations and provided the Migration Tool for NetWare to ease the pains of conversion. The Migration Tool copies files, directories, users, and groups from NetWare servers to Windows NT domain controllers. File rights and logon scripts are also included in the list of objects that the Migration Tool can copy. It is also possible to designate which files and user accounts you want to be migrated.

File and Print Services for NetWare

FPNW allows NetWare clients to access Mi Server

File and Print Services for NetWare (FPNW) is one of two pieces that comprise Microsoft Services for NetWare (see Figure 9-1). NetWare clients can access files, printers, and applications on Windows NT Server computers that are using FPNW. This enables network administrators to make use of a Windows NT Server in a NetWare environment without installing or configuring any client software.

Directory Service Manager for NetWare

Windows NT can integrate NetWare user and group information with Directory Service Manager for NetWare (DSMN), the second component of Microsoft Services for NetWare. DSMN can also merge user accounts from multiple NetWare servers into one account database that can then be sent back to the NetWare servers. This enables administrators faced with managing binderies on multiple NetWare servers to achieve single NetWare and Windows NT authentications on their networks.

FIGURE 9-1

NetWare client
connectivity options

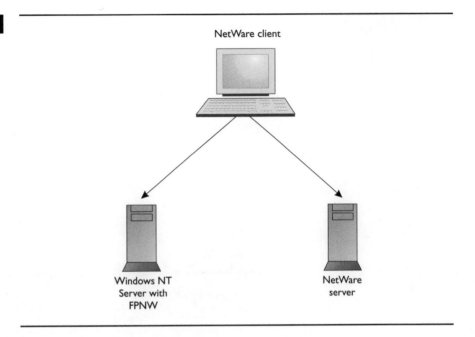

NetWare client

Windows NT
Server with
FPNW

NetWare
server

CERTIFICATION OBJECTIVE 9.01

Components for NetWare Connectivity

Two network components are required to enable Windows NT 4.0 to
function as a client to Novell NetWare servers. See Figure 9-2. NWLink
provides a protocol that is compatible with Novell's IPX/SPX transport, while
CSNW provides the NetWare Core Protocol (NCP) redirector. When these
two modules are added to a Windows NT computer, it then has the ability to
make use of NetWare file and print services.

NWLink

Windows NT computers using NWLink can communicate with NetWare
servers and with other Windows NT machines that also use NWLink.

FIGURE 9-2

Windows NT Workstation
with NWLink and CSNW
connectivity

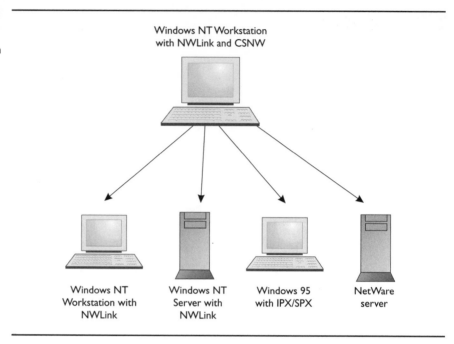

NWLink is a relatively fast and efficient protocol and should always be considered as an option when determining what protocol is best for a given network. Since IPX/SPX is routable, NWLink can also be used to communicate across WANs.

If the Windows NT client's only needs are to access NetWare servers and to share files and printers with other Windows NT computers, this may be accomplished with NWLink by itself—no need for TCP/IP or NetBEUI. Using only one protocol always improves the performance of networked clients and results in less network traffic. However, the explosive growth of the Internet is quickly reducing the number of networks that rely on just one protocol other than TCP/IP. Installing NWLink as the only protocol can be an effective method of restraining user access to the Internet. See Figure 9-3.

CSNW is completely dependent on NWLink. If it is not already present, NWLink is installed automatically when CSNW is installed. Attempts to remove NWLink without first removing CSNW will be unsuccessful.

FIGURE 9-3

Windows NT Workstation
with NWLink connectivity

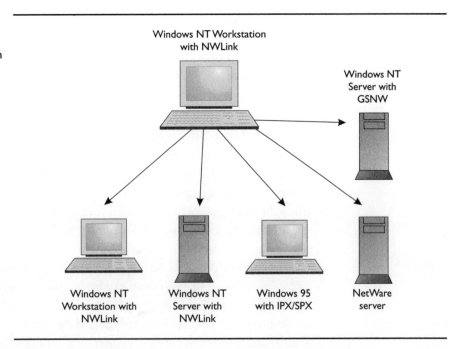

Windows NT Workstation
with NWLink

Windows NT
Server with
GSNW

Windows NT
Workstation with
NWLink

Windows NT
Server with
NWLink

Windows 95
with IPX/SPX

NetWare
server

Client Services for NetWare

NCP = NetWare Core
Protocol
file sharing language
of NetWare Server

Windows NT makes use of its built-in Server Message Block (SMB) protocol
for communicating among computers that use Microsoft-based networking
software. Microsoft LAN Manager, Digital PathWorks, Windows 95, and
Windows for Workgroups are examples of operating systems that use an SMB
redirector. In order to speak the file-sharing language of a NetWare server,
NetWare Core Protocol, Windows NT computers must install a network
service that enables it to use NCP.

Microsoft realized that NetWare connectivity would be a necessary
component for the success of Windows NT Workstation, and included this
functionality as an installable part of the operating system in CSNW. The
CSNW service acts as an interpreter between the Windows NT computer and
NetWare servers. When communicating with a NetWare machine, the CSNW

service running on the Windows NT Workstation intercepts communications being sent to the NetWare server, formats the communication according to NCP, and then passes the data to NWLink for delivery. Likewise, CSNW grabs any inbound data from a NetWare server and gives it to the Windows NT operating system in a language it knows.

File and Print Services

Windows NT users can take advantage of NetWare's legendary file and print services with CSNW enabled. Network drives can be mapped to NetWare servers, and print queues residing on NetWare servers can be utilized, with either the Windows NT command line or Explorer.

NetWare has gained wide industry recognition for having some of the most robust file and print services available on the PC platform. Since Windows NT Workstation is a powerful desktop operating system, combining NetWare servers with Windows NT clients can be an effective network strategy.

Windows NT clients can also use long filenames on NetWare servers that are running the OS/2 name space NLM. If the server does not have the OS/2 name space enabled, Windows NT users are limited to legacy 8.3 filenames.

Support for NetWare Utilities

CSNW provides support for almost all NetWare command line utilities. No real functionality is lost, since native Windows NT commands can be substituted for the few NetWare commands that do not work. The inoperative commands and their Windows NT equivalents are covered in detail later in this chapter.

Supports Burst Mode

The CSNW service on Windows NT also supports Burst Mode data transfers with NetWare servers. This feature significantly enhances performance for file transfers between NetWare servers and Windows NT clients. Large Internet Protocol (LIP) is also supported by CSNW. LIP enables computers to determine and use the largest possible packet size across routed connections, significantly improving performance in WAN environments.

Bindery Support

Users can accomplish a bindery authentication to any NetWare 3.*x* server, or to NetWare 4.*x* servers that have bindery emulation enabled. Windows NT passes the current username and password to the server for authentication. If the authentication request is denied, the user is prompted for a username and password to complete the logon.

Bindery-style logons require a user to attach or log onto a server before gaining access to services on the server. Accordingly, user accounts must be created and maintained on each server. This is quite cumbersome in an environment where users commonly need access to multiple servers. The server you want to log onto at startup can be specified in the CSNW dialog (see Exercise 9-4).

NDS Support

With version 4.0 of NetWare, Novell released NetWare Directory Services (NDS) to bring global authentication and browsing capabilities to its network operating system. NDS is a distributed database, containing information about network resources including servers, printers, users, groups, and security access lists for each network object. NDS is structured in a tree hierarchy and gives administrators and users the ability to browse and manage network objects within the tree. Users can be granted or denied different levels of access to objects within a given tree.

Windows NT 4.0 computers with CSNW installed can authenticate to NDS trees and take advantage of NDS for browsing and managing NetWare networks. The NDS tree and context for authentication can be specified in the CSNW dialog box.

A user can change his or her NDS password in Windows NT by pressing CTRL-ALT-DEL, clicking the Change Password button, and selecting NetWare or Compatible Network in the Domain field. The NetWare SETPASS command can be used to change passwords on NetWare 3.*x* servers or 4.*x* services running bindery emulation.

exam
ⓦatch

The Windows NT Help file for CSNW and NWLink, NWDOC.HLP, contains an abundance of valuable information. Click on the Overview button in the Client Service for NetWare dialog box to bring up this Help file. Taking the time to read through its contents before taking the Windows NT Workstation exam will be an excellent review of the material covered in this chapter.

CERTIFICATION OBJECTIVE 9.02

Installing and Configuring NWLink

NWLink is installed from the Protocols tab in the Network Properties dialog box (see Figure 9-4). NWLink is very easy to install and requires no configuration at the time of installation. NWLink NetBIOS also appears as an installed protocol when NWLink is installed on a computer.

NWLink NetBIOS enables Windows NT computers to use Novell NetBIOS to communicate with Novell servers and other Windows NT machines using NWLink. The NWLink NetBIOS item cannot be removed separately from NWLink, or configured in any way. Microsoft's NWLink NetBIOS includes some features not available in Novell's IPX/SPX NetBIOS. Consequently, these features are not used when a Windows NT machine communicates with a NetWare server.

EXERCISE 9-1

Installing NWLink

1. Go to the Network Properties dialog box by right-clicking Network Neighborhood and selecting Properties, or by double-clicking the Network icon in the Control Panel.

2. Select the Protocols tab and click the Add button.

3. Select NWLink IPX/SPX Compatible Transport and click OK.

4. Enter the path to the Windows NT Workstation 4.0 source files, if necessary, and click OK.

FIGURE 9-4

NWLink NetBIOS is an integral component of NWLink

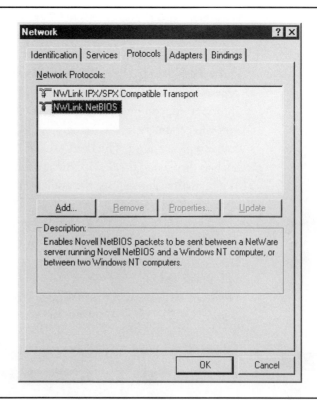

Configuring the Ethernet Frame Type and IPX Network Number

NetWare has a number of different frame types that can be used with Ethernet, and while Windows NT can automatically detect which one is in use, it may be necessary at times to force a certain frame type to be used. The following four frame types can be selected in addition to Auto Detect:

- Ethernet 802.2
- Ethernet 802.3
- Ethernet II
- Ethernet SNAP

When Auto Detect is selected, Windows NT listens for each frame type in the order previously listed. If none of these is detected, Windows NT uses the Ethernet 802.2 frame type by default.

In the NWLink IPX/SPX Properties dialog box, you can't see which frame type was detected and used when Auto Detect is selected. To see this information, you must use the IPXROUTE CONFIG command, which tells you what frame type(s) is being used, and to which network adapters each frame type is bound. The IPXROUTE command has other functions as well, such as displaying the Service Advertising Protocol (SAP) table and viewing IPX statistics. You can see the available options by entering IPXROUTE /? at the command line.

The frame type and network number can be changed from the NWLink IPX/SPX Properties dialog box. However, if you need to use multiple frame types, you must use a Registry editing tool to accomplish this with Windows NT Workstation. Configuring Windows NT Server to use multiple frame types can be done with the NWLink IPX/SPX Properties dialog box, shown in Figure 9-5. Do not attempt to configure the IPX frame type by changing the

FIGURE 9-5

NWLink IPX/SPX Properties

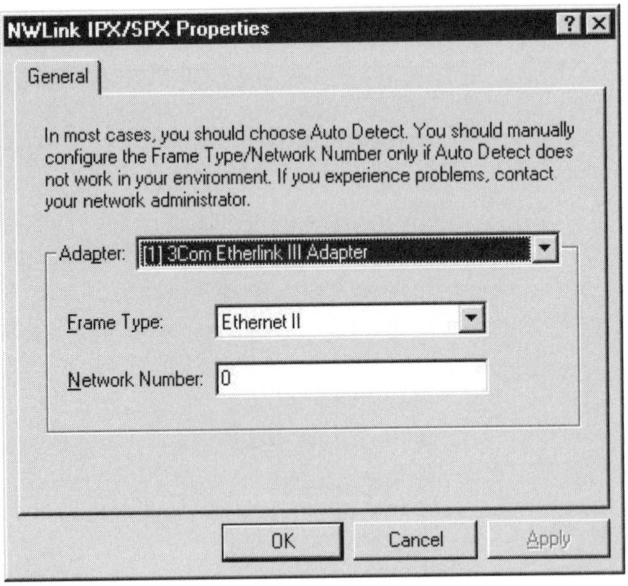

Registry unless it is absolutely necessary—your computer can crash if this Registry key is incorrectly altered. Information regarding this Registry key and its values can be obtained in the Windows NT Registry Entries Help file, in the Windows NT Workstation 4.0 Resource Kit, Microsoft TechNet, or other third-party books with Registry entry documentation.

It is possible to use more than one frame type at once, and doing so is a rather common practice. However, just as the use of multiple protocols diminishes network performance, using two or more frame types also causes network performance degradation.

The IPX network number is used to identify the physical network segment attached to the computer so that IPX traffic can be routed. Each physical network segment in an IPX environment must have one or more unique network numbers. Windows NT Workstation automatically detects the IPX network number in use on the attached segment if the frame type is set to Auto Detect, or 0 (zero) is entered as the network number.

EXERCISE 9-2

Changing the Ethernet Frame Type and IPX Network Number

1. Select the Protocols tab in the Network Properties dialog box.

2. Select NWLink IPX/SPX Compatible Transport and click the Properties button.

3. In the Frame Type field, pull down the drop-down list and select the frame type you wish to use.

4. In the Network Number field, enter the network number you wish to use, or enter the number zero, for Windows NT to automatically detect the network number. If the Frame Type is set to Auto Detect, the Network Number field will be grayed out.

Listed next are some scenarios to help in determining the best way to configure the frame type to be used by Windows NT on your network.

QUESTIONS AND ANSWERS

I only want to use one frame type although several are in use on the network...	Select the frame type you wish to use in the NWLink IPX/SPX Properties dialog box.
I need to use multiple frame types...	Use a Registry editing tool to add the frame types you need.
There is only one frame type in use on my network...	Select Auto Detect in the NWLink IPX/SPX Properties dialog box.
I used Auto Detect and I need to know which frame type it detected...	Use IPXROUTE CONFIG from the Windows NT command line.

CERTIFICATION OBJECTIVE 9.03

Installing and Configuring Client Services for NetWare (CSNW)

CSNW is installed from the Services tab in the Network Properties dialog box. It does not require any configuration at the time of installation, but will prompt each user, the first time he or she logs on, for the preferred server or preferred tree and context.

You will notice that once CSNW is installed, selecting the Client Service for NetWare item on the Network Services tab causes the Configure button to become disabled. Instead, a CSNW icon is added to the Control Panel, as illustrated in Figure 9-6. Double-clicking this icon brings up the CSNW configuration dialog box.

FIGURE 9-6

The CSNW icon in the
Control Panel

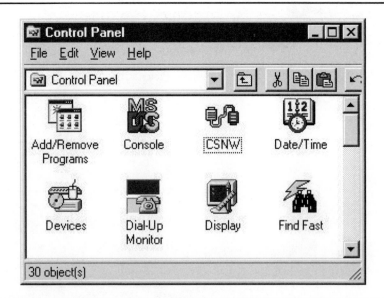

EXERCISE 9-3

Installing Client Services for NetWare

1. Select the Services tab in the Network Properties dialog box.
2. Click the Add button and select Client Service for NetWare in the Select Network Service dialog box.
3. Click OK and enter the path to the Windows NT Workstation 4.0 source files, if necessary, and click OK to finish.
4. Restart the computer for the new network changes to take effect.

EXERCISE 9-4

Configuring the Preferred Logon

1. After you have installed CSNW, the Select NetWare Logon dialog box, Figure 9-7, appears when you log onto the computer. This dialog can also be invoked after the first logon by double-clicking the CSNW icon that is added to the Control Panel. The Overview button on this dialog box brings up the CSNW Help file, which contains lots of good information.

FIGURE 9-7

The Select NetWare Logon
dialog box

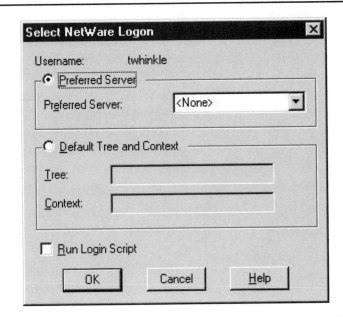

2. If you want to use a bindery logon to a specific server, select the Preferred Server radio button, and choose in the Select Preferred Server field the server to which you wish to log on at startup.

3. If you are logging into an NDS tree, select the Default Tree and Context radio button and complete the Default Tree and Context fields accordingly.

4. Check the Run Login Script check box if you want the NetWare logon script to execute at the time of authentication.

Search Order

After NWLink and CSNW are installed, Windows NT has two redirectors enabled, the Microsoft Network and the NetWare Network. By default, the NetWare Network is placed first in the network access order for both network and print providers. This order can easily be changed via the Network Access Order dialog box, which is reached by clicking the Network Access Order button that is added to the Network Services tab after CSNW is installed. See Figure 9-8.

FIGURE 9-8

Network Access Order

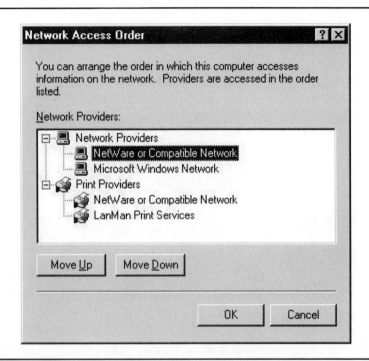

For best performance, the network that you use most should be at the top of the access order. For instance, if the file server you access most is a NetWare server, but your network printing is done through a Windows NT Server, NetWare or Compatible Network should be at the top of the Network Providers list, and LanMan Print Services should be the first Print Provider.

Changing the Redirector Search Order

1. Select the Services tab on the Network dialog box and click the Network Access Order button.

2. Select the network provider that you want to be first in the access order and click the Move Up button until it is at the top of the list.

3. Select the print provider that you want to be first in the access order and click the Move Up button until it is at the top of the list.

Connecting to NetWare Services

Once NWLink and CSNW are installed and configured, you can connect to NetWare resources with Windows NT Explorer or from the command line. This gives both users and administrators the same flexibility they have connecting to Windows NT Servers. Users can browse their way to resources, and administrators can use the command line to attach resources in logon scripts and batch files.

Connecting to NetWare Services with Explorer

Mapping network drives and browsing files on a NetWare server with Windows NT Explorer are practically the same as mapping drives and browsing files on a Windows NT Server. The most significant difference is that NetWare servers appear under the NetWare Compatible Network in the Network Neighborhood, while Windows NT Servers appear under the Microsoft Windows Network.

EXERCISE 9-6

Connecting to a NetWare Directory

1. Double-click the Network Neighborhood. If the server you wish to connect to is present, go to step 4.

2. Double-click Entire Network, and then double-click NetWare or Compatible Network. If the server you are connecting to is present, go to step 4.

3. Double-click the NDS tree that contains the server you are connecting to. Continue browsing through the organizational units until you see the server.

4. Double-click the server and then right-click a folder and select Map Network Drive to connect a network drive to the folder, or just double-click the folder to browse its contents.

FROM THE CLASSROOM

When Is Connecting to NetWare Not Like Connecting to NetWare?

With NT Workstation, Microsoft offers a reasonable NetWare client for attaching to NetWare file and print servers. This client supports both bindery and NDS modes, which makes it suitable for almost any environment.

Installing the client is easy and straightforward—just click a few places and you're done. The installation setup is even smart enough to know that you need to have the NWLink protocol installed to connect to the NetWare server. It installs the NWLink protocol while you are installing Client Services for NetWare (CSNW), if the protocol is not present. What could be easier?

We get calls from clients saying that after installing CSNW, they can attach to some of the NetWare servers and not others. What is the problem? The most frequent problem is the frame type that NT is using.

Novell servers come in general categories: 3.*x* operating systems and 4.*x* operating systems. Generally speaking, the NetWare 3.*x* servers use a frame type designated as 802.3, and the 4.*x* servers use a frame type designated as 802.2. As

a side note, 802.2 is an IEEE standard known as Logical Link Control (LLC). You might be familiar with the Microsoft implementation, Data Link Control (DLC). The 802.2 protocol is also known as Source Routing.

When you install CSNW, by default NT attempts to auto-detect which type of frame type is being used. This is really cool, because you don't have to know what the frame type is. Unfortunately, it only auto-configures for one frame type or the other. And, if it detects both frame types (802.3 and 802.2) on the network, it has a bias to auto-configure to support the 802.2 frame type.

One of our clients was a NetWare 3.*x* shop, migrating from NetWare 3.*x* to both NetWare 4.*x* and NT. The client had both frame types on the wire. NT auto-detected the 802.2 frame and configured to support that frame type. Thus the client could not attach to their 3.*x* NetWare servers.

The solution is to configure CSNW for both frame types manually.

—*By Shane Clawson, MCT, MCSE*

Connecting to NetWare print queues is just like connecting to shared printers on Windows NT computers. Three print queue configuration options are available in the CSNW dialog box, which is started with the CSNW icon in the Control Panel. If you want to eject a page at the end of each print job, check the Add Form Feed option; choose Notify When Printed to receive notification that your document has been printed; and select Print Banner for a banner page to be printed before each print job.

Connecting to a NetWare Printer Queue

1. Double-click the Network Neighborhood. If the server you want to connect to is present, go to step 4.

2. Double-click Entire Network, and then double-click NetWare or Compatible Network. If the server you are connecting to is present, go to step 4.

3. Double-click the NDS tree that contains the server you are connecting to. Continue browsing through the organizational units until you see the server.

4. Double-click the server. The contents of the server contain printer icons for each available print queue on the server.

5. Double-click the print queue that you wish to use. Continue setting up the printer by specifying make and model to install the appropriate drivers, and by naming the printer.

Connecting to NetWare Services with the Command Line

How you map network drives and connect to print queues on NetWare servers with the command line varies, depending on whether the server is using bindery services or NDS. Listed next are examples of how to use command line utilities to make drive and printer connections with either bindery or NDS servers.

exam
ⓦatch

Hands-on experience is always one of the best ways to improve the amount of information that you retain. MCSE candidates that have not been exposed to NetWare environments are encouraged to visit a site that is using Windows NT Workstation with NetWare, or to set up a NetWare server in a lab. A good idea would be to work with other MCSE candidates to pool resources and set up a NetWare server that you can take turns using at home.

QUESTIONS AND ANSWERS

I want to use the command line to map a drive to a NetWare server using bindery services…	NET USE G: \SERVER\VOLUME\DIRECTORY
I want to use the command line to map a drive to a NetWare server using NDS…	NET USE G: \\TREE\VOLUME.ORGUNIT.ORGUNIT
I want to use the command line to connect to a NetWare print queue using bindery services…	NET USE LPT1 \\SERVER\PRINTQUEUE
I want to use the command line to connect to a NetWare print queue using NDS…	NET USE LPT1 \\TREE\PRINTQUEUE.ORGUNIT.ORGUNIT

NetWare Specific Applications

Most NetWare-aware applications operate correctly running on Windows NT Workstation, although they might require extra steps for setup and configuration. They typically require the NetWare dynamic link libraries (.DLL files) that are included with the NetWare client for Windows. To fulfill this requirement, install the NetWare client for Windows onto a Windows NT Workstation computer, copy the .DLL files from the NetWare client directory to the Windows NT system32 directory, and then delete the NetWare client directory. The NWDOC.HLP file contains documentation for a few common MS-DOS and Windows NetWare-aware applications, including Btrieve and Lotus Notes.

As Windows NT Workstation becomes more common as a network client, software developers are recognizing the need to provide Windows NT-compatible software and documentation. Before attempting to make an application work on Windows NT, consult the software documentation and any technical support from the software vendor. It is likely that step-by-step instructions are available to solve the problems you are encountering. Checking for a newer version of the software is always a good idea, too. Many software companies require any new software they release to be compatible with Windows NT. Much of the PC software released prior to 1995 was not developed for, or tested on, the Windows NT platform. The latest version of any software is more likely to be compatible with Windows NT than earlier versions.

NetWare Utilities

NetWare provides command line utilities for connecting to NetWare resources and managing NetWare servers. Novell designed these utilities for computers using DOS (or OS/2) and the NetWare clients that Novell provides for those platforms. Since Windows NT does a good job of emulating DOS, most of the utilities operate as expected on Windows NT computers.

Supported Utilities

Almost all of the file and server management utilities provided with NetWare function with no problems with Windows NT. See Table 9-1 for a list of these utilities. Only two utilities, SESSION and VOLINFO, have specific problems when used. When executed from a Windows NT Workstation computer, the SESSION command does not support search mapping, and always maps as root. The VOLINFO command runs very slowly if the update interval is set to five.

TABLE 9-1		
CHKVOL	COLORPAL	DSPACE
FLAG	FLAGDIR	FCONSOLE
FILER	GRANT	HELP
LISTDIR	MAP	NCOPY
NDIR	PCONSOLE	PSC
PSTAT	RCONSOLE	REMOVE
REVOKE	RIGHTS	SECURITY
SEND	SESSION	SETPASS
SETTTS	SLIST	SYSCON
TLIST	USERLIST	VOLINFO
WHOAMI		

NetWare Utilities Supported on Windows NT

Some NetWare utilities don't function properly unless a network drive is mapped to the NetWare SYS/PUBLIC directory. If you plan to use NetWare utilities, it's a good idea to use a logon script to map a drive accordingly.

A Windows NT Help file states that the NetWare RCONSOLE command has some known problems running on Windows NT Workstation. However, the RCONSOLE command functions normally with Windows NT, and you should have no problems with it.

Unsupported Utilities

Four NetWare commands are not supported on Windows NT. Everything that is accomplished with these NetWare commands, however, can be done in Windows Explorer, or from the command line with the NET command. Table 9-2 presents the four inoperative NetWare commands and the equivalent Windows NT command. The specific syntax to use can be found by using the /? switch after the command (for example, NET LOGON /?).

CERTIFICATION SUMMARY

Windows NT Workstation includes two installable network components, CSNW and NWLink, that enable it to function as a NetWare client. CSNW is the client redirector and NWLink is the IPX/SPX-compatible network transport protocol. CSNW requires NWLink to be present for it to function, even if the NetWare server is using a network transport protocol other than IPX/SPX.

CSNW provides access to NetWare file and print services through the Network Neighborhood and Windows NT Explorer, almost exactly like Windows NT Servers are accessed. Additionally, NET USE commands can be

TABLE 9-2	NetWare Command	Windows NT Command
NetWare Utilities Not Supported on Windows NT	Login	net use device: \\server\path /user:username
	Logout	net use device: /delete
	Attach	net use device: \\server\path
	Capture	net use lpt1: \\server\queue

used to make connections to NetWare directories and print queues from the Windows NT command line. Most users will not be able to tell whether the file and print services are on a Windows NT or NetWare server. NetWare management utilities can also be run on a Windows NT Workstation with CSNW.

NWLink can automatically detect the frame type in use on the network, or it can be manually configured. Likewise, the IPX/SPX network number will be detected and set up without user intervention, but can be changed if necessary.

The Gateway Service for NetWare and the Migration Tool are available on Windows NT Server to complement CSNW on Windows NT Workstation. Microsoft Services for NetWare, which includes File and Print Services for NetWare and Directory Service Manager for NetWare, can be purchased as an add-on to Windows NT Server.

TWO-MINUTE DRILL

- ❑ Any NetWare Loadable Module that crashes can crash the entire server.

- ❑ Client Services for NetWare (CSNW) provides access to NetWare file and print services through the Network Neighborhood and Windows NT Explorer.

- ❑ Migration Tool for NetWare copies files, directories, users, and groups from NetWare servers to Windows NT domain controllers.

- ❑ NetWare clients can access files, printers, and applications on Windows NT Server computers that are using File and Print services for NetWare (FPNW).

- ❑ Windows NT can integrate NetWare user and group information with Directory Service Manager for NetWare (DSMN).

- ❑ Two network components are required to enable Windows NT 4.0 to function as a client to Novell NetWare servers: NWLink and CSNW.

- ❑ Using only one protocol improves the performance of networked clients and results in less network traffic.

❑ Windows NT makes use of its built-in Server Message Block (SMB) protocol for communicating among computers that use Microsoft-based networking software.

❑ Users can accomplish a bindery authentication to any NetWare 3.x server or to NetWare 4.x servers that have bindery emulation enabled.

❑ NDS is a distributed database containing information about network resources including servers, printers, users, groups, and security access lists for each network object.

❑ Windows NT 4.0 computers with CSNW installed can authenticate to NetWare Directory Services (NDS) trees and take advantage of NDS for browsing and managing NetWare networks.

❑ The following four frame types can be selected in addition to Auto Detect: Ethernet 802.2, Ethernet 802.3, Ethernet II, and Ethernet SNAP.

❑ CSNW does not require any configuration at the time of installation, but will prompt each user, the first time he or she logs on, for the preferred server or preferred tree and context.

❑ For best performance, the network that you use most should be at the top of the access order.

❑ Mapping network drives and browsing files on a NetWare server with Windows NT Explorer are virtually the same as mapping drives and browsing files on a Windows NT Server.

❑ Connecting to NetWare print queues is just like connecting to shared printers on Windows NT computers.

❑ The way you map network drives and connect to print queues on NetWare servers with the command line varies, depending on whether the server is using bindery services or NDS.

❑ MCSE candidates that have not been exposed to NetWare environments are encouraged to visit a site that is using Windows NT Workstation with NetWare, or to set up a NetWare server in a lab.

❏ Most NetWare-aware applications typically require the NetWare dynamic link libraries (.DLL files) that are included with the NetWare client for Windows.

❏ NetWare provides command line utilities for connecting to NetWare resources and managing NetWare servers.

❏ When executed from a Windows NT Workstation computer, the SESSION command does not support search mapping and always maps as root. The VOLINFO command runs very slowly if the update interval is set to five.

SELF TEST

The following questions will help you measure your understanding of the material presented in this chapter. Read all the choices carefully, as there may be more than one correct answer. Choose all correct answers for each question.

1. (True/False) Installing CSNW and NWLink is a difficult, time-consuming process that will require significant training for support personnel.

2. The _____ protocol and the _____ network service are the two components necessary for Windows NT to connect to NetWare servers for file and print services.

3. (True/False) Windows NT Workstation users will not be able to use long filenames when saving files to NetWare servers.

4. Which Windows NT command displays information regarding the IPX frame type in use?

    A. IPXCFG

    B. NET CONFIG

    C. IPXROUTE CONFIG

    D. NET IPXCFG

5. (True/False) CSNW is a useful component of Windows NT Workstation and a Windows NT certified professional can reasonably expect to work with it during his or her career.

6. What frame type does Windows NT use if it cannot detect the frame type in use on the network?

    A. Ethernet 802.2

    B. Ethernet 802.3

    C. Ethernet SNAP

    D. Ethernet II

7. NetWare uses the _____ protocol for network file sharing and the _____ protocol for network transport.

8. (True/False) Changing the Ethernet frame type by editing the Registry is a good idea.

9. (True/False) With Novell's NDS, it is necessary to log onto each server you wish to use.

10. When installing CSNW, when is the first opportunity to configure the preferred server or NDS tree?

    A. The first time you restart and log onto the workstation

    B. Immediately after installing CSNW, before rebooting

    C. During the installation process

    D. Never, because no configuration is necessary

11. (True/False) NWLink cannot be removed from the Windows NT client, even if the NetWare server to which it is connecting is using TCP/IP.

12. By default, what network and print providers does Windows NT access first after CSNW is installed?

    A. LanMan for print, NetWare for network

    B. LanMan for print, Microsoft Windows for network

    C. NetWare for print, Microsoft Windows for network

    D. NetWare for print, NetWare for network

13. (True/False) CSNW will allow Windows NT users to log onto NetWare 4.*x* servers only if the servers are running bindery emulation.

14. (True/False) NetWare servers are accessible through a Windows NT Server running GSNW only to Windows 3.*x* and Windows 95 clients. Windows NT Workstation users *must* have CSNW and NWLink installed on their computers to access NetWare servers.

15. When considering protocols and frame types to use, which guideline listed next results in the best network performance?

    A. Use as many protocols and frame types as possible

    B. Use at least one frame type for each protocol in use

    C. Use only one protocol and one frame type

    D. The number of protocols and frame types in use does not affect network performance

16. (True/False) Windows NT Workstation users will find that using files and printers on NetWare servers is very similar to using files and printers on Windows NT Servers.

10

Remote Access Service and Dial-Up Networking

CERTIFICATION OBJECTIVES

A s we discuss the Windows NT Remote Access Service (RAS), we'll focus on several key objectives that are important to remember. For the purposes of passing the test, it is very important to remember that RAS is a particularly strong part of the Microsoft Windows NT platform, so you need to know more than just how to set up a dial-out client. Microsoft wants you to know the infrequently used capabilities of RAS, such as point-to-point tunneling protocol, as well as the more common features, such as dial-up networking. The following section headings will guide you through the rest of the chapter. Again, review the more obtuse topics such as TAPI and RAS Security carefully, because they will be on the exam.

CERTIFICATION OBJECTIVE 10.01

Overview of RAS

The prospect of accessing network resources remotely has spawned a huge demand for remote dial-up solutions. Windows NT 4.0 Workstation ships with all the software necessary to configure the workstation as either a dial-up Internet client, or a one-connection RAS. The fundamentals of RAS all revolve around Internet connectivity standards. So as we go along, you'll not only learn about NT, but you'll also become more familiar with many of the underlying principles that govern the Internet. Our tour will include some hands-on installation work, and in-depth looks at the protocols that manage RAS connections. Please remember to draw on all you know about Network Interface Cards and local area network (LAN) protocols for a conceptual understanding of how RAS works. When we're through, you'll regard the wide area network (WAN) interfaces that RAS uses, such as modems, ISDN terminal adapters, and X.25 Packet Assembled Dissemblers, much as you would a Token-Ring or Ethernet adapters.

Features of RAS

RAS has a rich set of features that we'll review here. The important issues associated with RAS connections are link stability, bandwidth, authentication security, data security, and network fault recovery. The RAS features of

Windows NT deal with all of these problems nicely by incorporating the features directly into the operating system, rather than making them add-on products.

Point-To-Point Protocol Multi-link Protocol (PPP-MP)

If you've ever been bottlenecked by a slow WAN link, you're going to appreciate the functionality included in Windows NT 4.0 Workstation. PPP multi-link protocol is an Internet standard whereby multiple WAN media, such as modems, ISDN, or X.25, can be *bundled* into one logical pipe that has the aggregate bandwidth of the WAN interfaces. For example, if you took two 28.8Kbps modems and bundled them, the resulting logical pipe would have a bandwidth of 56Kbps. You can bundle as many modems as you want, or you can bundle different WAN interfaces. The RAS server must have just as many WAN interfaces available as the dial-up client does, and they must be bound together as well.

Point-to-Point Tunneling Protocol (PPTP)

The costs associated with maintaining a WAN backbone through leased lines can be very high. Depending on the type of line, the cost could range from $350 a month to get across town, to $10,000 a month for a coast-to-coast circuit. PPTP securely transfers encapsulated TCP/IP, NetBEUI, or IPX traffic across public networks, such as the Internet, allowing users to avoid expensive dial-up or leased line tariffs. By using the Internet you can remove many of the carrier costs, as well as the hassles that go with maintaining an extensive WAN.

Restartable File Copy (RFC)

Transient problems with phone circuits can cause a line drop on modem dial-up connections. Too often, this happens right in the middle of an important file download. Rather than starting over, the Windows NT 4.0 RFC feature automatically picks up where it left off before the line was cut off.

Auto Dial and Logon Dial

In order to log on to the domain, NT workstations must validate on a domain controller. On a LAN, the NIC provides access to the domain controller, but there's no way to authenticate for a stand-alone workstation. Windows NT Workstation 4.0 includes an option to log on to a domain using dial-up networking. Domain security is validated through the domain controller by dialing up a RAS server and pushing the logon information over the dial-up networking link. RAS also has an auto dial feature that keeps track of network resources and automatically connects to the remote resource. Auto dial maintains a list of all the RAS phonebook entries, and which network resources are accessed by the corresponding entry in the RAS phonebook.

Pay attention to the features Microsoft mentions in their marketing pushes and white papers. Many times it's tempting to skip the details on less important material, but make sure you only do that with data you know Microsoft doesn't care about. The functionality mentioned here may seem nominal compared to the larger topic at hand, but Microsoft purposely brings them into the exam to make their point.

Client/Server API Enhancements

NT 4.0 includes additional APIs that allow developers to further control RAS connections from the application. Operations such as managing connections, dialing phonebook entries, and checking the status of current connections are managed through the RAS API.

Idle Disconnect

After a connection has been idle for a period of time that the administrator specifies, the RAS server automatically terminates the link. The RAS server monitors packets traversing the WAN link, and if there is none for a specified amount of time, the line is dropped.

Windows 95 Look and Feel.

Dial-up networking and RAS maintain configuration and control parameters consistent with the Windows 95 interface. Hardware and software settings are very similar to that of Windows 95. If you know how to set up dial-up networking (DUN) in Windows 95, you only have to make a few adjustments for NT. We'll talk about the specifics of configuring DUN later in the chapter.

Supported Connections

Pay attention to the features Microsoft mentions in their marketing pushes and white papers. In this section, we'll discuss the details of each type of connection, how it works, and what its limitations are. WAN media is particularly interesting because the development of each transmission type usually spans decades. We'll pay particular attention to the advantages and disadvantages of each respective transmission type, and the public network infrastructure behind it.

Phone Lines

Phone lines are by far the most common way of connecting into a RAS server, owing to the overwhelming availability of phone lines compared to other media. Unfortunately, voice lines are analog, which means the signal a computer sends has to be converted from digital to analog. The modulator/ demodulator, also known as the modem, modulates a computer's digital signal to analog, for transmission over the phone lines. Once the signal arrives at the downstream modem, it's demodulated back to a digital signal that the receiving computer can understand. This process is controlled by a modem protocol, commonly V.34 28.8Kbps, which regulates the speed at which the modem operates. Windows NT 4.0 Workstation comes with a hardware compatibility list of the modems that have been tested to work with RAS.

Figure 10-1 is an outline of an NT 4.0 RAS session with modems. Through normal dial-up lines, the client is linked to the server—in this case, a NT 4.0 RAS server that has two interfaces. On the right is the modem interface; on the left is the LAN interface.

Modems have a couple of disadvantages. First, they are very slow compared to LAN or leased line transmission speeds. An Ethernet LAN moves at 10,000,000 bits per second, whereas a typical V.34 modem moves at 28,800 bits per second. Although RAS makes a modem act like a network card from a functionality standpoint, it's painfully slow when compared to a LAN.

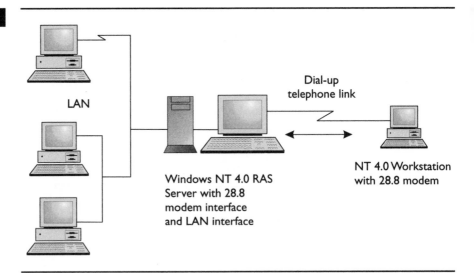

FIGURE 10-1

A RAS session with
modems. The server has
two interfaces

ISDN

Integrated Services Digital Network (ISDN) has become a popular way of
accessing remote resources as prices for ISDN lines and terminal adapters have
come down. Local telephone companies install ISDN on local premises, and
usually tariff structures are similar to regular phone lines, but more expensive.
ISDN is a digital medium, but that doesn't mean you can hook your PC
directly to it. You must install an ISDN terminal adapter, more often called an
ISDN modem (although this is a misnomer), which converts a computer's
signal to the signal that ISDN uses over its lines. ISDN is available worldwide,
although some places are still waiting for it. Traveling users find it less than
convenient, because the configuration is a bit tricky compared to modems, and
the lines aren't as readily available.

ISDN is delivered in two forms: primary rate interface (PRI), and basic rate
interface (BRI). BRI comes with two digitized channels: a B (for bearer)
channel, with a throughput of 64Kbps; and a D (for data) channel, with a
throughput of 16Kbps, that's used for channel signaling. BRI is sometimes
called 2B+D. Typically, it's used as a small office link to the Internet or in a
residential setting.

PRI is 23 B channels operating at 64Kbps, and one D channel operating at 64Kbps. This is more widely used by service providers that have multiple dial-up ISDN lines going into the RAS server.

ISDN lines are fast, and disaffected modem users, tired of slow response times, have been quick to utilize the newfound speed. The B channels are typically bound together as one logical pipe through PPP-MP, which we'll discuss later. This generates in 128,00 bits per second throughput, which, from an end-user perspective, means significantly increased response times.

X.25

X.25 is a protocol that runs on a worldwide network of packet-forwarding nodes that deliver X.25 packets to their designated X.121 addresses. X.25 connections are 56Kbps (64Kbps in Europe) and work either X.25 SMART cards or packet-assembled dissemblers (PADs). X.25 connections are just like normal dial-up connections, except the phonebook entry is the X.25 PAD type and the X.121 server address. X.25 is a parent protocol to frame relay implementations, and it carries the packet-switched network architecture (PSN) that X.25 implemented. X.25 bandwidth is purchased through companies like Sprintnet. X.25 connections come in either dial-up or permanent access connections. Dial-up connections work off of per-minute tariffs, and permanent access is billed like a leased line connection. X.25 is typically used in areas where ISDN is not available.

RS-232C Null Modem Cable

Null modem cables, or LapLink cables, can be used to connect the RAS server serial port directly to the serial port of the client machine. There are no modems involved in this configuration and the cable goes point-to-point. This is typically used in the absence of any network attachment.

PPTP

Point-to-point tunneling protocol is covered in the next section, "Supported Protocols".

Supported Protocols

If we're going to hook up a machine in Denver with a server in San Francisco, we need a set of rules that define how the data packets are going to work on our RAS links. This is the job of connection protocols—to manage and negotiate RAS links to support our upper layer protocols, such as IPX/SPX, TCP/IP, and NetBEUI.

At first glance connection protocols are mind-boggling, but we're going to simplify things by working off of what you already know. LAN and RAS connections have two common components, interfaces and media, that are easily understood and that can help us understand the big picture. Figure 10-2 is an illustration of the role of these components in a RAS connection.

An interface is a device that has one connection to a machine, such as a computer, and another connection to a transmission medium, such as an Ethernet. The interface could be Token-Ring, Arcnet, T1, or any number of media interfaces. The important thing is that an interface has one foot in the device it's attached to and one foot in the medium. The second common

FIGURE 10-2

A RAS dial-up connection

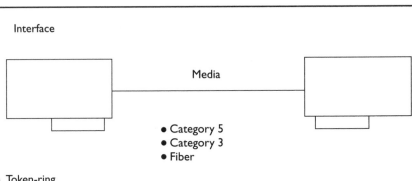

Interface

Media

- Category 5
- Category 3
- Fiber

- Token-ring
- Ethernet
- V.35
- ISDN
- X.25
- Modem

component of LAN and RAS is the media. The transmission medium could be ISDN, a telephone line, or any one of the many different types of media available. The important thing is that there is a common set of rules, or a language, which defines how data flows over the medium.

Don't allow the different types of interfaces and media that we discuss in this section confuse you. Instead, focus on the rules that govern how they are controlled.

NT 4.0 supports several different link protocols, which we'll go over here. Please keep the conceptual model in mind, as it will prove useful in understanding all of these protocols. We'll compare the advantages and disadvantages of each protocol and explain why PPP is the best-of-breed industry protocol.

Point-to-Point Protocol (PPP)

PPP is a language that allows two interfaces, with no intermediary devices, to define the rules for transmitting higher-level protocols, such as TCP/IP and IPX, over different media. See Figure 10-3 for an illustration of how PPP works. PPP was developed in the early 1990s by the Internet Engineering Task Force (IETF) to provide a standardized way to encapsulate IP datagrams across the broad spectrum of hardware vendors. PPP plays an important part in network infrastructure development, as it's the de facto standard for point-to-point communications. PPP is derivative of the High Level Data Link Control (HDLC) protocol, as are numerous other link control protocols such as SDLC, ISDN, and X.25.

That's enough background. Let's talk about what's in the name point-to-point protocol. The protocol is called point-to-point because it enables links between two points with no devices in between. It provides a number of different services to aid the upper-layer protocols, such as TCP/IP, in datagram transmission. Link Control Protocol (LCP) manages the link and negotiates the frame size of the PPP packets. PPP also provides facilities for authenticating remote links with anything from clear text passwords to encrypted passwords. Finally, the network control protocol (NCP) negotiates which upper-layer protocols, such IPX, are carried across the link.

In Figure 10-3 we can see PPP architecture of RAS. PPP owes much of its popularity to its capability to operate multiple protocols over links. NT 4.0

FIGURE 10-3   A schematic diagram of PPP

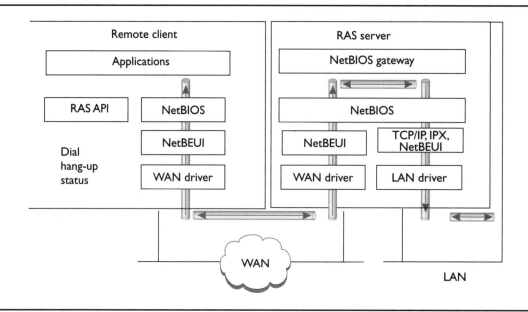

supports all 3 major network protocols over PPP links: NetBEUI, TCP/IP, and IPX/SPX. Looking at the remote client on the left side of the figure, we can see how the NetBIOS sockets, TCP/IP and IPX/SPX all are directed into the WAN driver. Applications written to these protocol specifications work over PPP. Error checking is also included within the PPP packets, as is the ability to dynamically allocate TCP/IP addresses through Dynamic Host Control Protocol (DHCP).

NT 4.0 Workstation can operate as a single-connection RAS server or, through DUN, it can access other NT RAS servers, as well as third-party PPP compliant servers.

Point-to-Point Tunneling Protocol

PPTP is an exciting extension to PPP. If you recall, PPP provides facilities for remote link validation within the packet structure. PPTP extends this by allowing multiple protocols, such as NetBEUI and IPX, to be encapsulated

within IP datagrams and transmitted over public backbones such as the
Internet. (See Figure 10-4.) Additionally, the packets are encrypted with RSA
public key technology such that the datagrams are encrypted, but none of the
validation information, such as username and password, is transmitted across
the public network.

Let's go over an example of why I said PPTP was exciting. Imagine a
telecommuter in Toledo needs to access a network resource, a UNIX host, in
San Francisco. With PPP, his only option would be to use dial-up long
distance lines to access the RAS server. Long distance is expensive, so if the
user needed to work on the UNIX host all day, the long distance tariffs would
be very high. Another option would be to put the UNIX host on the Internet,
but then anyone with a packet sniffer could find his username and password
and hack the system. PPTP is a variation on the solutions we just mentioned.
First the client system dials up a local PPP server, such as is typically provided
by an Internet Service Provider (ISP). (Note connection 1 on our Figure 10-4.)
After the client validates with the ISP, he uses DUN to connect through the
Internet to a RAS PPTP server, also located on the Internet. Connection 2
(PPTP) works on top of connection 1 (PPP) to securely transmit packets over

FIGURE 10-4	A Layout of PPTP layers

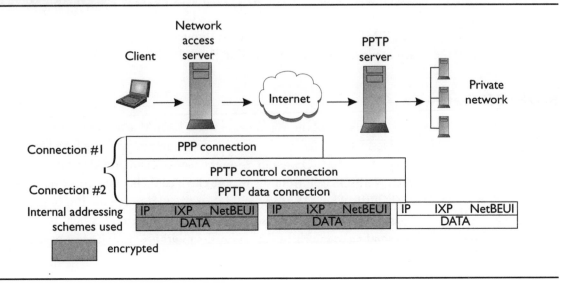

the Internet. PPTP uses Microsoft Challenge Authentication Handshake Protocol (MS-CHAP), RSA RC4, and DES technologies to encrypt the IP datagrams. The result is that the RAS server with PPTP authentication allows clients to use the Internet as a secure IP, IPX, or NetBEUI backbone. This embodies the concept of a virtual private network (VPN) that's becoming increasingly popular to lower the cost of WAN connections.

There are huge economic benefits to avoiding the long distance costs associated with PPP dial-up links that are left up for extended periods of time. In the preceding example, even if our user wanted to remain online eight hours a day, every day of the week, our only cost would be that of the account with the ISP.

PPP Multi-link Protocol (PPP-MP)

RAS connections can be very slow, especially over slower links such as 33.6 modems. PPP-MP provides a way of bundling multiple PPP links into one logical link with the aggregate bandwidth of the individual PPP links. For example, a PPP-MP NT workstation with two modems can be programmed to dial-up a PPP-MP-enabled NT RAS server with two modem lines bound together with PPP-MP. If each modem were 28.8Kbps, the aggregate bandwidth of the logical channel would be 56Kbps. The same can be accomplished with different WAN interfaces. For example, a modem could be bound in with an ISDN or an X.25 interface.

PPP-MP can significantly increase throughput, especially for applications such as file sharing, which can grind to a halt with a single WAN interface.

NetBIOS Gateway

Previous versions of the Windows NT and LAN Manager operating systems used NetBEUI loaded on the client to communicate with the RAS Server. This enabled NetBIOS resources on the network and provided a gateway by which NetBIOS calls from the remote client could be translated over to IPX and TCP/IP. The RAS server could then go out through the LAN interface to access the IPX or TCP/IP resource, and reverse the process when the resource is responding to the client. This provides multi-protocol support to some extent. The only difficulty is that the remote client is unable to run any applications that need IPX or TCP/IP loaded to function.

Serial Line Internet Protocol (SLIP)

SLIP is an older protocol used to carry TCP/IP over low-speed serial lines. SLIP dates back to 1984 and has been eclipsed by PPP in recent years, but it's still used frequently by many older dial-up clients. NT 4.0 supports SLIP both for DUN and RAS. PPP enjoys a number of advantages over SLIP: SLIP doesn't support multiple protocols; it can use only one protocol at a time. SLIP doesn't work with DHCP or bootup servers, so IP numbers have to be statically assigned to the client. SLIP requires operator intervention while it's negotiating the correct IP address, and doesn't support any kind of packet error checks as PPP does. For the most part SLIP is used only to connect to some older UNIX systems, so it's included in the dial-up networking (DUN) package.

Now that you've seen all of the connection protocols, let's look at some sample scenarios where they would be appropriate.

QUESTIONS AND ANSWERS

I'm working from home and the office is a long-distance call for me...	Use PPTP for connectivity. By utilizing the Internet as your WAN backbone, you can avoid long-distance charges.
I work off of a legacy UNIX server which doesn't support PPP...	SLIP is the right one for you. SLIP predates PPP and has a lot of support in UNIX environments.
I work from home but I need more bandwidth...	Use PPP-MP. Creating a logical pipe with multiple RAS ports increases your speed.
I use NetBIOS applications that access non-NetBIOS hosts...	Use the NetBIOS gateway. Clients can access TCP/IP or IPX hosts through the RAS server, which does a protocol conversion to allow access to NetBIOS clients.
I'm a traveling user and I need access back to the office...	Use PPP because it's simple. PPP does all the necessary negotiation and allows multiple protocols.

Enabling Remote Access Service Compression

You can approach link compression from two levels. The first is at the modem/hardware level. Modem link control standards incorporate modem hardware compression that is done by the modems themselves. The second level is the software compression that's available in the DUN client, which compresses the data at the software level. Ultimately the compression ratio is dependent on the compressibility of the data being transferred. Text files, for example, typically can get a 4:1 ratio, while bitmaps and other graphics files can't be compressed at all. Because compression at the modem hardware level involves the frequent use of interrupts, and most hardware can not handle the higher port speeds, it's recommended that software compression be used. Additionally, we'll also make sure that modem error control is enabled to further optimize our connection profile.

1. Open the Dial-Up Networking icon and select the phonebook entry you're interested in modifying.

2. Select the More button and specify Edit Entry and Modem Properties.

3. At the Edit Phonebook Entry screen pictured in Figure 10-5, select the Configure button.

4. At the Modem Configuration screen, shown in Figure 10-6, deselect the Enable Modem Compression option and make sure Enable

FIGURE 10-5

The Dial-Up Networking phonebook editor

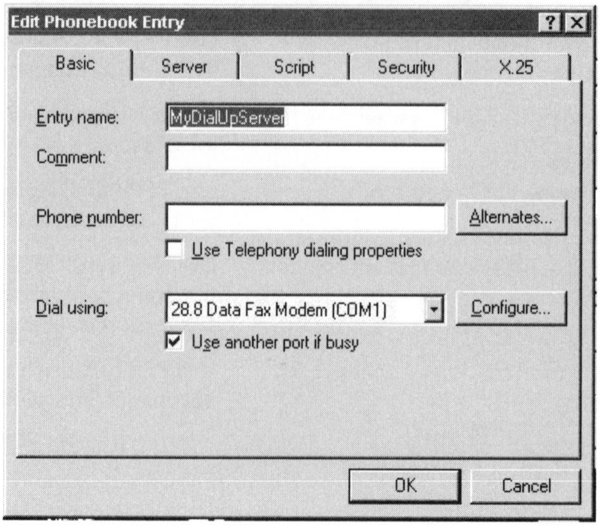

FIGURE 10-6

The Modem Configuration
settings dialog box

Hardware Flow Control and Enable Modem Error Control are
selected, then select OK.

5. To enable software compression, go back to the Edit Phonebook Entry
   screen and select the Server tab, shown in Figure 10-7. Make sure
   Enable Software Compression is selected.

FIGURE 10-7

Editing DUN Phonebook
entries

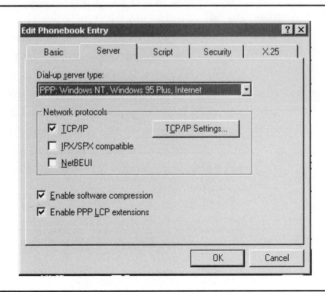

CERTIFICATION OBJECTIVE 10.04

Telephone API

Increasingly, the worlds of voice and data networks are beginning to converge. Computers and telephones exist on most corporate desktops, but there are no standardized ways of pushing and pulling information from applications to the phone system. TAPI was first introduced in 1993 and is the result of work among 40 different companies. The role of TAPI is to provide an abstraction between the application and hardware layers, which provides developers with device and network independence. TAPI enables applications to use Windows NT 4.0 on PSTN, ISDN, PBX, or IP based networks, shielding the programmer from any need to code custom interfaces. Computer-telephony integration (CTI) has typically suffered from proprietary solutions that necessitated redundant and expensive development. A good example of a telephony-enabled application would be a personal information manager (PIM) that allows automatic dial-out by clicking a name in the user's address book. This example relates specifically to the PC acting as an edge device and routing calls outbound. Windows NT 4.0 Workstation TAPI 2.0, which ships with NT, also deals with calls coming inbound from the PBX. For example, in the case of automatic call distribution (ACD), inbound calls can be routed to groups or individuals based on an identification number that the caller supplies. The key here is that any information existing on the machine—fax screens, area codes, location information, or any other kind of application data—can be passed up to the PBX for processing. In this way, rules can be developed to automate how calls are managed from the call switching level. The TAPI interface speeds application development by simplifying what programmers have to know about individual phone switches, and reducing everything to a common set of APIs that work across a broad spectrum of manufacturers.

exam
w a t c h

TAPI is the groundwork for Microsoft's development of computer telephony integration (CTI). Much of this information may seem to relate more to programmers, but Microsoft wants to get the word out, so look carefully at this information. The best way to understand the API is to spend some time browsing the settings in Control Panel under Telephony and Modems. The settings here relate directly back to the RAS and DUN parameters. Again, the key is to focus on what you know Microsoft cares about, because it will be on the exam.

Comprehensive Solution

TAPI 2.0 has a large set of features that allow developers to control telephony functionality without undue involvement in the details. It comes built in with all the APIs needed for most general-purpose applications, and it's very extensible with support for writing additional capabilities for telephone-centric applications. TAPI 2.0 supports Unicode for global support, and many application development environments provide ActiveX controls to make development even faster. TAPI 2.0 provides four levels of service for telephony-enabled applications:

- Assisted Telephony
- Basic Telephony Services
- Supplementary Telephony Services
- Extended Telephony Services

Assisted Telephony

Assisted telephony is designed for non-telephonic applications. It allows programs that don't typically get involved with placing phone calls, such as a word processor, to nest phone numbers within them and initiate phone calls. Assisted telephony very simply allows your application to make a telephone call and doesn't go beyond that.

Basic Telephony Services

For anything beyond the very simple, basic telephony is the next step in functionality. Basic telephony provides all the services of plain old telephone services (POTS). Any service provider, such as a Telco or PBX vendor, is required to offer this kind of capability, which includes: Address translation, making calls, call states and events, answering calls, dropping calls, call handle manipulation, and assisted telephony server.

Supplementary Telephony Services

Anything beyond basic usually means the application will be backed up against a PBX, so there are some additional capabilities that TAPI 2.0 can provide. The supplementary telephony services constitute the bulk of what the TAPI specification offers. This is a rich set of functions that allow easy access to telephony applications with a large spread of needs. Most of these are capabilities you have at work, but not in your home. The functions include: hold, transfer, conference, forward, park, pickup, completion, accept, redirect, reject, secure from interruptions, generating digits and tones, digit and tone monitoring, media mode monitoring, media stream routing and control, user-user info, change call parameters, and phone terminal control.

Extended Telephony Services

This service provides a well-defined device extension mechanism so vendors can write device-specific functions into TAPI. It's completely up to the vendor to write these additions to TAPI, as they are basically a standardized way of writing custom applications.

Native 32-bit and Application Portability

Windows NT 4.0 is a fully 32-bit operating system, as is TAPI 2.0. TAPI 2.0 runs under Windows NT 4.0 Workstation in a preemptive multitasking and multithreading threading environment that is capable of running under several processors and system configurations. Since Windows is a portable operating system it can be migrated to whichever CPU offers the best price/performance ratio, and can run in an SMP configuration, should additional processors be needed. All this can be done without the application being re-written, which means development investment protection. Any applications that currently run under Windows 95 and TAPI 1.4 will run on Windows NT 4.0 Workstation.

Device Sharing

Device sharing is particularly useful in the small home office where there is usually only one phone line, but there are multiple phone-enabled devices such as phones, fax machines, or modems. Device sharing prevents inbound calls from going to anything but the specified device. For example, with distinctive rings you can enable three phone numbers over one phone line. The first number produces one ring, the second two rings, and the third three rings. If a call comes in with two rings, device sharing allows you to program the TAPI 2.0 drivers to direct the call to a port that has been designated as the second number. This allows you to have voice, fax, and modem on one phone line. Inbound calls would be directed to the correct port seamlessly.

CERTIFICATION OBJECTIVE 10.05

Installing RAS

Under Windows NT 4.0 Workstation, RAS is installed as a service, and the installation varies a great deal depending on which protocols, WAN interfaces, and software options are selected. We're going to install all three step by step in the following exercises. For the purposes of this discussion, I'll use a modem because it's the most common interface, but these examples could apply to ISDN and X.25 as well.

The RAS services for NT 4.0 Server and Workstation are basically identical except that the server version can support 256 connections while the workstation version can handle only one.

Our first step will be to install the WAN interface.

Modem Installation

1. Logon to the NT workstation and go to the Settings option under the Start menu and select the Control Panel option.

2. Under the control panel select the Modems option and you will come to the Modem Properties screen pictured in Figure 10-8.

3. To add a new modem, select the Add button.

4. At the Install New Modem screen, select the Next button to begin querying the system for your modem. If you have an external modem, make sure that it's turned on, plugged into the serial port, and that the phone line is hooked up. If you have an internal modem, ensure that your port and IRQ settings don't conflict with any other previously configured device. You can check these settings with the Windows NT Diagnostics by looking under the Resource tab and checking which IRQs are already being used and making sure your internal modem doesn't conflict with them.

FIGURE 10-8

Add a new modem at the
Modem Properties window

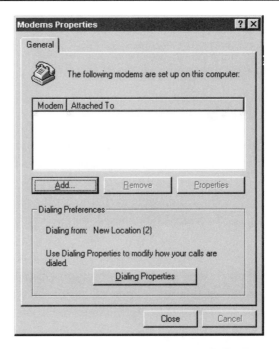

5. NT will begin to scout the COM ports to see if any modems respond to its queries. In our example, the modem is a 28.8K external modem that's attached to a serial port on COM1. If your modem is on COM port 2, 3 or 4 you'll see it go step by step through the COM ports until it arrives at the one with your modem on it. At that time it should find your modem and begin querying it. It's attempting to find the correct settings from the modem so it can plug it into the configuration. Be patient as you wait for it to complete. (If you prefer to select a modem from the list manually, you could select Don't Detect My Modem. I Will Select It From a List.)

6. When the process is finished, you see a window like the one shown in Figure 10-9, showing the name of the modem and the COM port on which it was found. In this case, it found my 28.8 modem on a serial port off of COM1.

7. The modem description is a little vague. I'd like to see if I could get a more specific description. Select the Change button to bring up the

---

NT scouts the COM ports to find your modem

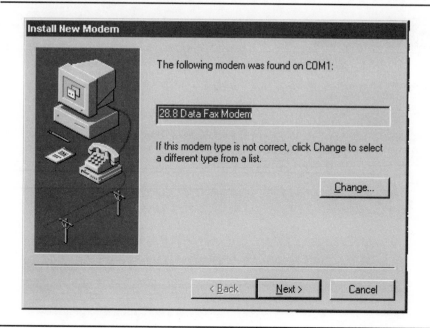

---

window in Figure 10-10. You'll receive a list of models from which you can choose. In my case I have a Hayes Acura 28.8 V.34 + FAX modem. Select the appropriate modem and press OK.

8. Going back to the previous screen (Figure 10-9), select Next and wait while NT installs your modem. After it's finished, it prompts you to select Finish to finalize the install.

Most modem installs only differ from the one in this exercise in cases where you have to select from the modem manually. As newer hardware is released after NT Workstation 4.0, you'll have to specify the correct modem. Most of the time the default installs work well, but as you experience problems reinstalling with the same specification, it's a good idea to start troubleshooting.

Once the modem is installed you can modify the settings from the Modem Properties screen at any time. By selecting the modem and clicking the Properties button, you can gain access to all the modem-specific connection information such as port speed, modem initialization strings, hardware control, and other advanced features.

FIGURE 10-10

Finding a full description of a modem

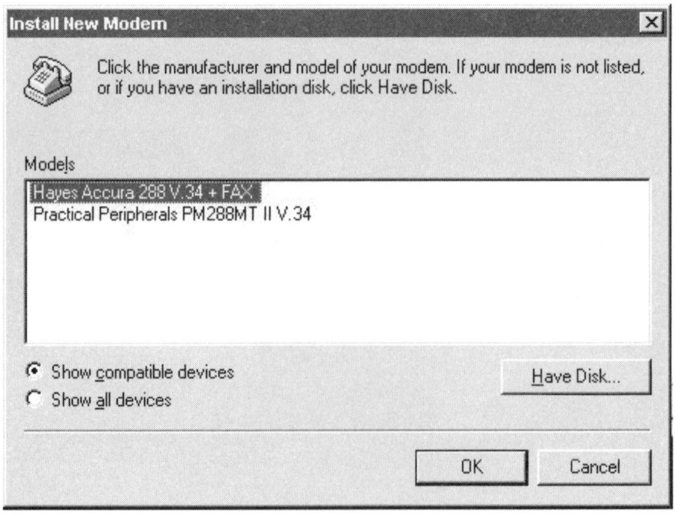

Under the Dialing Properties option on the Modem Properties screen, you'll find a number of TAPI 2.0 settings referring to the location being dialed from. If you ever need to change your default area code, calling card, or dial sequence to get an outside line, this is the place to go.

Note that you must have a RAS interface installed and recognized by NT before we can set up RAS. During the RAS install, if you haven't installed a RAS interface you will be prompted to do so. It's advisable to finish it beforehand.

Installing the Remote Access Client on NT 4.0 Workstation

The initial NT RAS install is pretty straightforward, but there are a lot of subtle differences to the software configuration that I'll point out here. Keep in mind that RAS doesn't care what connection medium it's working off of, only that it's configured properly. As we bind the WAN wrapper to the LAN protocols, take a look at the Bindings tab on the Network icon. This can give you a good conceptual understanding of how the NDIS wrapper treats LAN and WAN interfaces similarly.

1. Log on to the NT workstation and go to the Settings option under the Start menu and select the Control Panel option.

2. Select and double-click the Network icon to access the Network Configuration screen.

3. Select the Services tab, shown in Figure 10-11, to begin installing the new RAS service.

4. Select the Add button to access the NT RAS software from the installation CD-ROM. Note that you'll need access to the Windows NT 4.0 Workstation CD-ROM to complete the installation, or access to the files from another source such as a network or local drive. After you select Add you'll see Figure 10-12, showing a number of different services that NT offers. Select the RAS service.

5. Click the Have Disk button and NT prompts for the appropriate processor-specific installation directory. In this case it specifies the d:\i386\ directory from which Windows NT 4.0 was installed. After inserting the NT 4.0 CD-ROM, the setup begins copying files off of the CD-ROM.

FIGURE 10-11

At the Services tab, begin installing a new RAS service

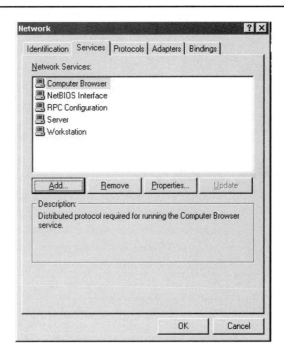

FIGURE 10-12

Select a service at the Network Service screen

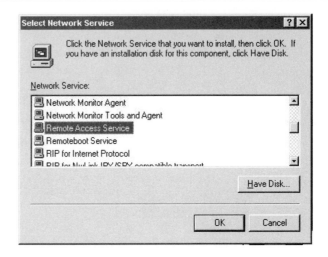

6. During the installation it needs to confirm the RAS ports so you'll see the Add RAS device screen, shown in Figure 10-13, appear with the modem you've already specified listed. Select OK to confirm the RAS port. If at this point you haven't set up any RAS interfaces, you can do so.

7. To install a modem and run through the Modem installation that we performed in Exercise 10-2, select the Install Modem button. This is the option for either ISDN or analog modems. If you need to install a PAD or Smart card select Install X.25 Pad. The PAD installation requires some specific information from your X.25 network provider, so be sure to have that ready.

8. After you select OK the Remote Access Setup screen, shown in Figure 10-14, appears. This screen has a number of important options that we'll take a careful look at. The first is the Add button on the bottom right. If you want to add more ports this button allows you to do so. If you have a device that isn't configured for RAS, but it could be, this button adds it into the configuration. If you don't have any additional RAS ports, this button takes you to the Add RAS device screen. The remove button does the obvious; it removes RAS devices from the list of RAS-enabled devices. Please note that it doesn't remove the device from the modem configuration in NT.

9. Pressing the Configure button brings up the dialog box in Figure 10-15, where you can specify whether the port will be used for the purpose of dial-in, dial-out, or both. This is an important security feature. For our purposes I'll select to enable both.

FIGURE 10-13

Add a RAS device at
this screen

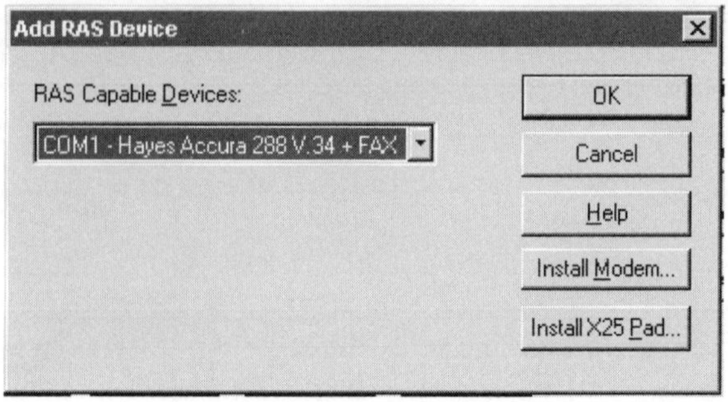

FIGURE 10-14

Add more ports at
the Remote Access
Setup window

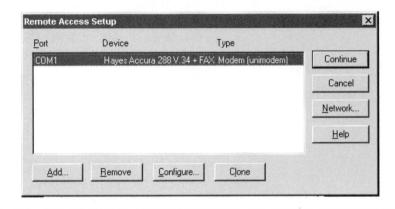

10. We'll deal with the Network button in a later section, so we're only
    left with Continue, which does precisely that.

11. When you press Continue you might receive some screens requesting
    LAN protocol information. Just cancel through those for now.

12. The Remote Access Service is now configured and you should find
    yourself back at the first Network Configuration box. This time under
    the Services menu you'll see the Remote Access Service loaded. Click
    Close and NT prompts you to reboot. Select Yes and allow Windows
    NT to reboot.

This completes the RAS installation. We'll configure the network settings in
the next section.

FIGURE 10-15

Specify dial-out or dial-in
at the Configure Port
Usage window

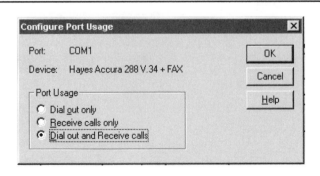

Configuring Network Settings

Now that RAS is installed let's configure the network settings for our RAS port. RAS interfaces, just like LAN interfaces, must have at least one protocol bound to them to speak to anyone on the network. Any protocol that you intend to bind to a RAS port must already be attached to the LAN port on the computer before network configuration can take place. For the next exercise I've already loaded NetBEUI, TCP/IP, and IPX/SPX on the NT workstation so that we can configure all the protocols. As you'll notice in Figure 10-16, there are two sides to the configuration: the dial-out protocols, and the dial-in RAS server protocols. We'll talk about the dial-out protocols and how they affect the dial-up networking client, as well as briefly look at the RAS dial-in protocol configuration settings. Suffice it to say that the server settings control which protocols are available for clients dialing up the NT 4.0 Workstation.

Configuring Network Protocols for Dial-Out

Since we have NetBEUI, IPX/SPX, and TCP/IP bound to the LAN interface, we can configure all of these protocols for dial-out. If you tried to select a protocol that hadn't been loaded, NT would give you an error message instructing you to load the protocol.

1. Go to the Network Neighborhood icon and right-click it. From the list select Properties to modify the network settings.

2. At the Network Settings screen select the Services tab to modify the Remote Access Service. Double-click the Remote Access Service to modify its properties.

3. Select the Network button and the screen in Figure 10-16 comes up. There are three places where the dial-out protocols have to be configured. The first is the one I already mentioned—configuring the protocols to work on the LAN adapter. The second is here underneath the dial-out protocol settings. To enable the protocols, select the box next to it. Underneath the Server Settings options are the Protocol options for clients dialing in to the RAS server. Selecting the Configure

FIGURE 10-16

Configure dial-out
protocols at Network
Configuration

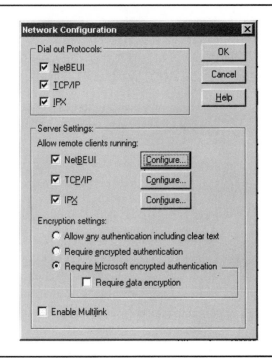

button next to each protocol allows you to configure the protocol
settings for dial-in clients. The setting they all have in common is the
option to allow RAS clients access to just the RAS server or the
network behind the RAS server. TCP/IP and IPX/SPX have some
specific information relating to the protocol configuration. On the
bottom of the dialog box are the choices for dial-in user authentication,
and the option to enable PPP-MP support for dial-in clients. If your RAS
server has multiple RAS interfaces they can be bound together into one
logical unit. Note that this doesn't cover dial-out PPP-MP connections.

4. The third place dial-out protocols are configured is in the dial-up
   networking (DUN) client configuration. Open the My Computer icon
   and double-click the Dial-Up Networking icon to access the dial-up
   networking phonebook. We're going to modify the protocol settings
   for a specific entry. Each phonebook entry must have the appropriate
   protocols configured for the server it's dialing.

5. We're going to configure a brand new server session, so press the New button and in the New Phonebook Entry page select the Server tab. You now see the screen in Figure 10-17.

6. The networking protocols section is our final stop. Each phonebook entry has its own set of protocols and dial-up server type specific to its connection. To enable NetBEUI and IPX/SPX select the box next to the Protocol. Configuring TCP/IP has a little more to it. First select the protocol and then press the Configure button to examine some more of TCP/IP settings.

7. The TCP/IP Settings screen, pictured in Figure 10-18, gives a little more control over TCP/IP's parameters. The first option specifies whether the IP address will be assigned from the server, or if there is a static IP mapping assigned on the workstation. To conserve IP numbers network managers typically use DHCP or bootup servers to pass out IP addresses. Here we'll specify to obtain it from the server. There are two kinds of Name Servers that MS TCP/IP needs to have for TCP/IP and NetBIOS over TCP/IP to work: the primary and secondary Domain Name Servers (DNS). DNS resolves TCP/IP numbers to host names by maintaining a list of host names with a record attached of their IP

FIGURE 10-17

Configure a new server session at New Phonebook Entry

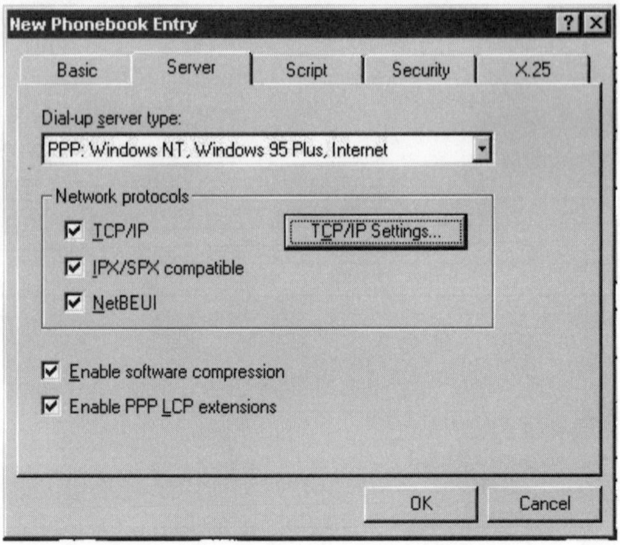

number. Primary and secondary WINS servers are used to resolve
NetBIOS names to IP numbers. The server can either specify the DNS
and WINS entries or their IP numbers can be manually entered here.
The IP header compression specifies that the PPP datagrams utilize
Van-Jacobson algorithms to compress the headers. Some older dial-up
clients might not support this. The default gateway option means that
the RAS client TCP/IP uses the default gateway number of the server
that it's dialing. This is usually the best choice, as most RAS servers are
able to move packets off their subnet.

TAPI 2.0 Location and Modem Specifications

The previously mentioned TAPI 2.0 specification contains all the modem and
location properties related to using dial-up networking. Back when we were
installing the modem the Modem Properties screen was actually a subset of the
TAPI 2.0 drivers under the telephony driver settings. The telephony drivers

Configure TCP/IP
PPP settings

also contain local dial-out information such as the current area code, number to get an outside line, calling card information, and other location-specific information. This is handy because the locations generated here can be accessed through the DUN phonebook entries. The phonebook gives you the ability not only to thumb through your dial-up servers, but also to change your location from where you're calling. Dialing-out of PBXs and to foreign countries requires a dizzying array of access codes that creates a real challenge every time you need to make a call. The Locations features allow you to plug the codes in once and forget about them. In order to access the screen in Figure 10-19, go to Telephony Drivers in the Control Panel.

Telephony Drivers

Under the Telephony options you'll also find the Telephony Drivers tab. If you have a modem you have two default drivers installed: the Unimodem

FIGURE 10-19

The Dialing Properties dialog box

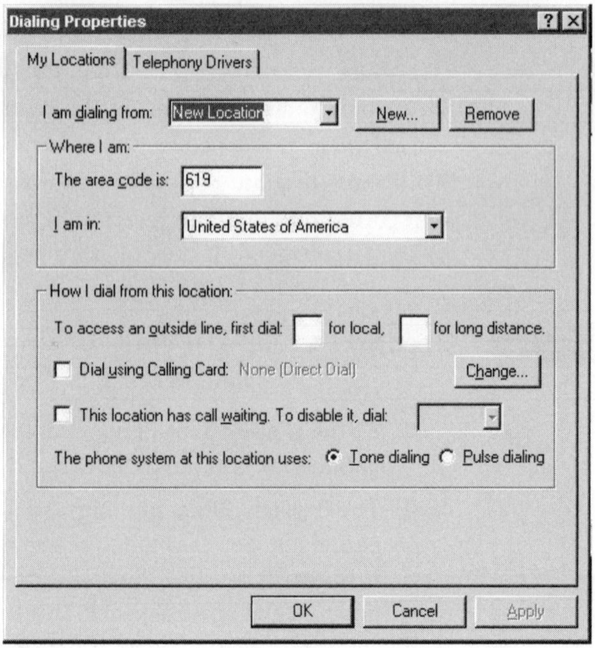

Service Provider driver, and the TAPI Kernel-Mode Service Provider. The Unimodem driver is the Modem Properties we configured previously, and the TAPI Kernel-Mode Service Provider is the TAPI 2.0 specification we've talked about.

CERTIFICATION OBJECTIVE 10.07

Dial-Up Networking (DUN)

Now that you've installed RAS protocols, connections, WAN interfaces, and TAPI information, it's time to put it all together with DUN. First, let's draw a distinction between RAS and DUN. They're very much related except that RAS concerns itself more with dial-in clients and DUN deals with dialing-out. Of course, as we've discussed, many of the settings in RAS have a bearing on how DUN works, but by and large they're separate operations. For example, RAS enables PPP-MP, but it does so for only dial-in clients. To enable PPP-MP going outbound you have to insert the parameters within DUN. Everything we've done up to this point allows you to understand all of the DUN configuration settings. As we generate the DUN parameters, ask yourself what corresponding server settings would be appropriate to match the DUN configuration. For example, if we setup DUN to use a static IP number, what corresponding settings would be appropriate for the RAS server? These exercises draw on all the information you've learned up to now.

EXERCISE 10-5

Creating a Dial-Up Networking Connection

1. Double-click the My Computer icon and open Dial-Up Networking.

2. At the Dial-Up Networking screen click the New button to create a phonebook entry. You now see the screen in Figure 10-20.

3. The first tab, Basic, provides the TAPI 2.0 information such as the phone number to dial and the modem configuration. Both of these parameters are available under the previously mentioned Telephony driver in the control panel. The entry name and comment provide a reference. This is the information you'll be looking at as you thumb

The Basic tab on New
Phonebook Entry

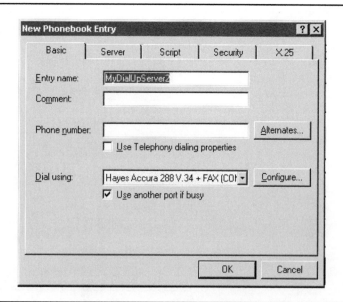

through the address book for destination servers. To use the TAPI
settings for which you have not yet designated a location, select Use
Telephony Dialing Properties and you can specify individual settings.
The modem configuration button contains the basic TAPI configuration
parameters available in the Control Panel.

4. The Server tab, shown in Figure 10-21, contains the destination server
    type, network protocol settings, and additional network settings. There
    are three dial-up server types: PPP, SLIP, and the Windows NT 3.1 and
    Windows for Workgroups server. All of these relate back to the
    supported link protocols. PPP is valid for the PPP, PPTP, and PPP-MP
    connection types. SLIP is valid for Serial Line Internet Protocol
    connection types, and Windows NT 3.1 refers to the NetBIOS gateway
    protocol using NetBEUI. The enable PPP LCP extensions parameter is
    valid only under PPP and refers to the new PPP features under LCP:
    Time Remaining, identification packets, and the callback feature. We've
    already talked about Network protocols and enabling software
    compression so I won't take that any further here.

5. Now that your basic configuration is set up, you're ready to dial. Press
    the OK button and you'll be taken back to the main Dial-Up

The Server tab on New
Phonebook Entry

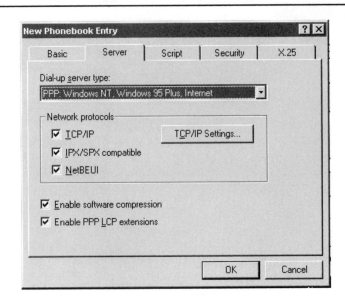

Networking screen. Notice that your configuration name appears on
the top part of the screen, the phone number comes up on the
preview, and that your location data is selected. Verify all the entries
and press OK.

6. At the DUN dialog box, shown in Figure 10-22, enter the logon data. If
   you're logging on to an NT domain, the Domain field is required. If
   you'd like to save the password, select the Save Password option.

7. At this point DUN goes out and connects to the specified server.

exam
ⓦatch

*The exam draws heavily upon the DUN configuration parameters, so
spend some time dissecting the installation. Work forwards from the RAS
port installation to the phonebook entry configuration, paying strict
attention to how the different settings interact with each other. If you
have any questions about an option, select it and press the F1 key to
receive some context sensitive help.*

FIGURE 10-22

Connecting to a
dial-up server

EXERCISE 10-6

Testing a RAS Connection

The easiest way to test a RAS connection is to look at the upper layer
protocols to see if they're making it across the line. Here we'll use the tools
that TCP/IP gives us to see if we can see other servers across the connection.

1. After you've connected to the dial-up server, check your TCP/IP
   number with the ipconfig command at a command prompt. Then find
   the IP number of the server you're connecting to.

2. At the command prompt ping localhost.

3. At the command prompt ping the IP number of your PC.

4. If both pings return, ping the host name of the RAS server. See
   Figure 10-23 if you have any questions about the ping utility.

5. The first two pings confirmed that the IP stack locally was fine. If you
   can't ping across the RAS link, or your RAS interface isn't being
   assigned an IP number through DHCP, there is probably some fault
   with the connection.

Using the PING utility to
test a RAS connection

```
C:\WINNT40\System32\cmd.exe                              _ □ X

C:\>ping dialupserver

Pinging dialupserver [207.158.5.104] with 32 bytes of data:

Reply from 207.158.5.104: bytes=32 time<10ms TTL=128
Reply from 207.158.5.104: bytes=32 time<10ms TTL=128
Reply from 207.158.5.104: bytes=32 time<10ms TTL=128
Reply from 207.158.5.104: bytes=32 time=10ms TTL=128

C:\>
```

Checking the Status of a RAS Connection

NT comes equipped with a dial-up monitor. In this exercise we'll check
the status of our dial-up connection by viewing the information in the
dial-up monitor.

1. If you're currently online you can view the DUN monitor by
   double-clicking the icon on the Windows 95 taskbar directly to the
   left of the time. If not, the monitor can be accessed through the
   Control Panel.

2. Go to the Control Panel and open the dial-up Monitor. Figure 10-24
   opens up with a variety of connection statistics that we'll discuss. The
   Device field provides a way of moving from one RAS device to the next.
   The Condition tells you whether or not the device is currently active.
   Line bps and Duration give you a summary of your session statistics.
   This is useful for troubleshooting applications that don't seem to be
   sending data across the link. Starting at Device Statistics, the columns are
   divided. On the left are the statistics for inbound traffic, and on
   the right the statistics are for outbound traffic. Device Statistics helps you
   determine whether data is going predominantly upstream or
   downstream. Connection Statistics treats everything from the standpoint
   of packets going across the network. It gives the number of frames sent
   and what the compression ratio was. Device Errors deals with the
   modem errors that are detected during transmission either due to line
   quality problems or modem issues. The Summary tab is useful for looking
   at information when there are multiple devices attached to the

FIGURE 10-24

Use the DUN Monitor
to check the status of a
dial-up connection

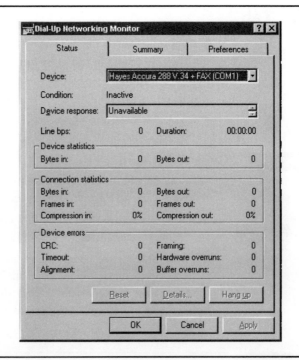

workstation. The Preferences tab deals with the Dial-up Networking
Monitor program defaults for displaying information.

EXERCISE 10-8

Disconnecting RAS Sessions

The DUN Monitor provides a couple of facilities for dropping a RAS session.
I'll show you how to use them here.

1. Open up DUN Monitor from the taskbar while your session is
   connected.

2. In the Device option box, make sure the connection you want to
   terminate is specified.

3. Press the Hang Up button and your session will be terminated.

4. You also can go to the Summary tab and under Active Lines select the
   modem you wish to terminate.

5. At the bottom press the Hang Up button.

The Script Tab

At this point we've talked about the two main DUN phonebook entries. Let's look at the role of one of the most important remaining sections, the Script tab. There are still many SLIP servers, and SLIP needs either manual logons or a script to insert the validation request from the server.

EXERCISE 10-9

Creating a Connection Script

Here is example of how to create a connection script.

1. On the DUN Edit Phonebook Entry screen, select the Script tab, shown in Figure 10-25. For PPP connections the default after dialing is None, meaning that no script runs.

2. If the SLIP server needs a terminal window for validation, select the Pop Up terminal window option. There are some SLIP systems that use this method of validation rather than requiring a script on the PC.

FIGURE 10-25

Use the Script tab with a SLIP server

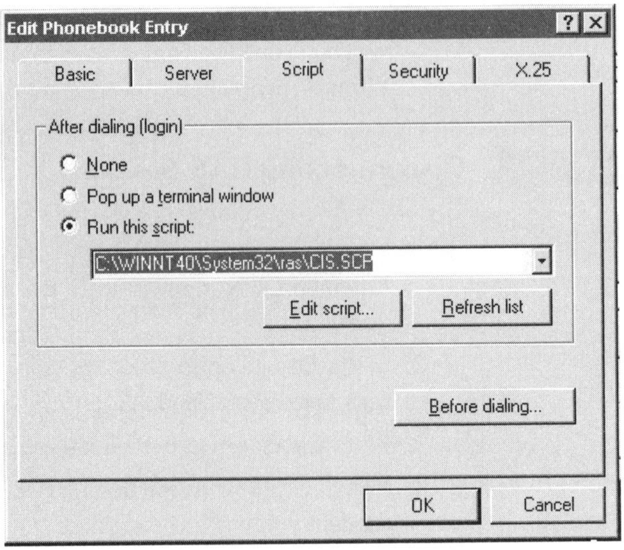

3. For our exercise, we'll use a generic script already loaded on the machine. Select the Run This Script option and press the DOWN-ARROW key on the right of the drop-down menu box.

4. We are now presented with a list of scripts that are already created for specific service providers. Select C:\WINNT40\System32\ras\ CIS.SCP to select the CompuServe CIS manager logon script.

5. From here we can edit the script by selecting the Edit Script button. Each script has some parameters laid out in the script text to customize it for the individual user.

Enabling Command Logging

Since each SLIP server must have a custom script we need to look at the commands contained within the script to adjust our specifications. This exercise deals with a very generic SLIP server, but the principles can be applied to servers requiring more sophisticated logon procedures.

1. Follow the steps from Exercise 10-9, but choose Generic Login under the script name.

2. Read the instructions within the generic login text. What I'll do here is provide a brief synopsis of what information needs to be looked at.

3. SLIP is typically used in a UNIX host environment. The UNIX prompt for logon is:
   ```
   login:
   ```
   Respond with your logon name and password. The goal of the script is to detect your login and password, and push that data to the server automatically. The first command should be:
   ```
   command=
   ```
   This tells the server you have nothing to submit before it asks you to logon. The next line should contain:
   ```
   OK=<match>"ogin:"
   LOOP=<ignore>
   ```
   This loops the system until it detects the login: prompt. The next line,
   ```
   COMMAND=<username><cr>
   ```
   pushes your login name on to the host.
   ```
   OK=<match>"assword:"
   LOOP=<ignore>
   COMMAND=<password><cr>
   ```

Follow this same sequence with your password. Every server has a different logon process, so further customization might be necessary if, for example, the server asks for data other than your username and password.

The Security Tab

The final tab we're concerned with is the Security tab. If you recall the RAS server security options, there was a list of the types of validations that the NT RAS server would accept. This is essentially the same thing in the dial-up networking client. The first option for clear text passes the username and password unencrypted to the RAS server. This lacks security because a network sniffer could decode the packets and find your password. The second option uses password authentication protection (PAP) to encode your username and password before sending them to the server. This has a pretty broad support base so it's useful for dialing up non-Windows NT RAS servers. The third option is useful only with Windows NT RAS servers, as it uses MS-CHAP. MS-CHAP utilizes RSA RC4 and DES encryption technologies for even more security. Selecting only the first option encrypts the logon data, but selecting the sub-option Require Data Encryption protects all your data with this robust form of encryption. The last option allows RAS to connect with the CTRL-ALT-DEL logon information after the password information has changed on the local machine.

Windows NT 4.0 Workstation also comes with an auto dial feature, whereby NT automatically dials the appropriate connection for a network resource once it's been accessed from the PC. For example, if you dial-up a remote system and telnet onto a UNIX host, the next time you issue the command to telnet to that host the connection is automatically created. This is handy for users with multiple RAS hosts. It might be difficult to remember which one has the appropriate server. All the user has to do is access the host and the auto dial feature creates the connection.

RAS PPP Connection Sequence

When your modem initially connects to the RAS server there are a number of settings that are automatically negotiated from the server to the workstation.

Having just seen the SLIP scripting scenario you'll really appreciate how PPP automates all the configuration necessary to maintain the WAN link.

The first step is to negotiate the Link Control Protocols. LCP manages the frame size and link management between the two connecting points. PPP encapsulates data within PPP datagrams. This shields the different hardware manufacturers from incompatibilities over RAS links. The second step is to negotiate the authentication protocols. As we just discussed, NT Workstation and RAS server can both mandate that the other party uses a certain level of authentication on the link. This can range from clear text logon validation to using RSA encryption on the data. The last step is to negotiate the Network Control Protocols. NCP manages a dialogue between the client and server to find out which network protocols, IP, IPX, or NetBEUI, will be supported over the link. PPP sessions remain active until one of the following happens.

- The client hangs up.
- The server drops the line due to an idle time out.
- The administrator on the server end hangs up the line.
- There is a fatal link error.

FROM THE CLASSROOM

Troubleshooting Remote Access

Experience has shown us that one of the most problematic areas of RAS setup is with the security settings and the point-to-point protocol. The symptoms of this kind of problem are manifested when the user attempts to dial in. The dial-in appears to be normal when the modem connects, but then the connection terminates, with no error code or other indication of a problem. There can be several causes for this. You can help isolate this problem by enabling the PPP.LOG file, through an entry in the Registry. This log details the activities of the link-level protocol bind. It might provide clues as to where the problem lies. One feature that can cause problems is something modern modems do, called fallback and fall ahead. After modems connect, they sample the line conditions and

FROM THE CLASSROOM

error rates. If they detect excessive error rates, they renegotiate the link speed, usually to a slower speed, in an effort to increase throughput by not spending so much time re-transmitting data. The modems might attempt to increase the speed, as well. This is normally a good feature. However, it can cause problems. If you are experiencing unexplained disconnects, try disabling the Auto Reliable mode of your modem.

A related problem occurs after the modems connect, and during the authentication process: The system attempts to verify your account, and then hangs up without any further indications of a problem. To help isolate this problem, set the security settings to authenticate any logon, including clear text. Dial in and see if you can establish a connection and have your account verified. Increase the encryption until authentication fails, and then use the PPP.LOG to help determine the source of the problem.

Different sets of problems occur when configuring RAS and modem options. Many modems today are set, by default, to enable compression and error checking between modems. RAS provides for error checking built into the software. It is more efficient if you disable error checking on the modem. Software compression is a different story. RAS also provides for data compression, as do most modems. It probably would be faster if you let the modems do the compression. One last setting you should check is the setting for flow control. Flow control tells the modem and/or the software when to stop sending data because of saturation. It's in your best interest to set hardware flow control rather than software flow control. Hardware flow control reacts to saturation conditions much faster than software flow control.

—By Shane Clawson, MCT, MCSE

CERTIFICATION OBJECTIVE 10.08

RAS Security

RAS incorporates a number of stalwart security features that make it pretty tough to crack. If the RAS server and client are set up properly to take advantage of NT's encryption, they make it difficult to find out what data is being sent. In this next exercise we'll configure Internet Explorer to run with RAS, taking full advantage of the security features.

EXERCISE 10-11

Running Internet Explorer with Remote Access Service

Microsoft Internet Explorer can be configured, using the auto dial feature, to establish a dial-up connection automatically when a URL is accessed on the browser. For example, if you have your start page on the Internet when you start Internet Explorer it automatically prompts you to dial your ISP. Before we begin, make sure that the following services are started: RAS, Remote Access Auto Dial Manger, and Remote Access Connection Manager. Also make sure the phonebook entry for your ISP is selected.

1. Open DUN and connect to your ISP.
2. Load up Internet Explorer and connect to the home page you had in mind.
3. On View Menu select Options and click the Navigation tab.
4. In the Page box click Start Page and select Use Current.
5. Click OK.

The next time you start Internet Explorer, and you're not connected to your ISP, the auto dial feature will make the call for you.

Support for Full Encryption

Windows NT 4.0 supports a number of different encryption algorithms to support logon validation and data transmission. At the DUN Security tab there were several methods available for logon validation and data transmission. Now we're going to take an in-depth look into the protocols that NT uses to control security.

Logon Security

Login validation to a remote NT domain follows the same security model that logging onto the domain from a LAN entails. RAS clients submit their username and password to the domain controller (DC), which checks its user database, the SAM, for rights. The DC then returns a token that authenticates the user for that session. To maintain compatibility with other dial-up servers and clients, NT has the capability to do this same authentication over RAS links with clear text. This isn't advisable, because anyone with a sniffer could look at the packets coming from the client to the server and decode your login information. For this reason NT Workstation includes several strong encryption options to secure your login information and data. The Security tab on the DUN phonebook entry screen has several encryption options available. The first option, Accept Any Authentication Option Including Clear Text, permits the password authentication protocol (PAP), which uses clear text to transfer logon information. This isn't recommended. It also permits all of the other authentication protocols including MD5-CHAP, MS-CHAP, and SPAP. CHAP comes in two versions: MD5 and Microsoft's implementation. CHAP uses a challenge response mechanism with one-way encryption to pass responses to the server. Microsoft's CHAP protocol always uses DES, the government standard encryption, when communicating with other RAS servers. The MD5-CHAP standard, from RSA Inc., is available to access other third-party servers that use the Message Digest 5 algorithm, but Microsoft never uses MD5-CHAP when talking to other Windows machines. The Shiva Password Authentication Protocol (SPAP) is used when communicating with Shiva LAN Rover server or when a Shiva client accesses a Windows NT RAS server. The Accept Any Authentication Option Including Clear Text option uses MS-CHAP to negotiate down from the strongest form of encryption (CHAP) to the mid-grade solution (SPAP) and finally to PAP.

The second option, Accept Only Encrypted Authentication, uses any of the previously mentioned protocols accept PAP. This works well in situations where there are non-Windows-based remote clients, but you don't want the security risk of using PAP.

The last option, Accept Only Microsoft Encrypted Authentication, forces the RAS server to use only MS-CHAP when validating logons. Please note that up to this point the only thing that we've encrypted is the logon information to the server. Any data sent after that goes unencrypted unless you specify Require Data Encryption. When encryption is mandated, Microsoft uses RSA, Inc.'s RC-4 algorithm to secure the packets. In North America 128-bit RC-4 encryption is permitted, but due to strong export laws that regard encryption algorithms as munitions, only the 40-bit implementation is permitted for export. This is particularly important in cases where your data may be going over public networks such as the Internet or a phone switch.

Auditing

The Remote Access manager and DUN monitor are the best ways to view events in real time, but sometimes you may have to look at a problem over time to spot the trends you're looking for. RAS by default enables auditing of any attempts to access to RAS. They are viewed in the Event Viewer. Events are generated by either success or failure conditions. An example of a successful condition is a normal logon by a user, disconnection by a user, or a normal callback procedure. A failure audit would be generated by activity such as a failed authentication, inactivity timeout, a duplicate NetBIOS name, or too many errors on the RAS link. All these are pushed into the Event Viewer, so it should be checked periodically to ensure there isn't anything unusual occurring. Check to make sure the HKEY_LOCAL_MACHINE\SYSTEM\ControlSet001\Services\RemoteAccess\Parameters\EnableAudit key is set to 1 to ensure the events are recorded.

Third-Party Security Features

RAS provides support for third-party security hosts that validate user logons before they are passed to the RAS server. Typically the host resides in between the dial-up client and the RAS server. Usually this additional security takes the form of some type of hardware key on the client side that must send a code to the host before the client is allowed access to the RAS server. One such implementation uses a pocket calculator-like device to receive access codes every minute using RF technology. When the user presses the security host, he must type in the current access code from the hand-held device to validate. At that point the host passes the user on to the RAS server for further authentication. The extra validation also could take the form of another username and password screen before you're allowed onto the RAS server.

However it's done, RAS provides an open architecture that's capable of handling secondary security.

Callback

Taking a page from the low-cost long distance providers, the callback feature allows clients to dial-up and authenticate on the RAS server. RAS then drops the line and calls the user back at a specified phone number. This saves the client from the line tariff associated with the call, and it ensures that authenticating users can only dial-up from a specific location. This discourages most hackers, because even if they obtain a user's logon information, they would also have to answer the callback at the pre-assigned phone number. The callback feature is set under the Remote Access Administrator of the RAS server. There are three options available to administrators: Preset To, Set By Caller, and No Callback, which is the default. Preset To and Set By Caller force the RAS server to dial back once the user authenticates. Preset To offers the true callback security. In the RAS Administrator, you specify Preset To for the user and specify a callback number. This has to be a number that can be dialed directly, not one that's accessed through a switchboard. Set By Caller really isn't a security feature, but it does allow the user to avoid connect charges. After the client authenticates, the RAS server prompts for the callback number for this session and the user types it in. This is ideal for roving users who want to avoid excessive long distance tariffs charged by foreign telephone monopolies. Default RAS comes configured as No Callback, which doesn't require a dial back after authentication.

CERTIFICATION SUMMARY

Windows NT 4.0 Workstation ships with TAPI 2.0, which includes APIs that allow developers to telephony enable their applications without getting mired in the details of managing RAS links. The TAPI specification is fully 32-bit, and ensures that applications can be moved across multiple processor architectures. RAS offers a rich suite of Internet-based protocols, including PPP-MP, PPP, PPTP, and TCP/IP, and continues to support the legacy connection protocols SLIP and NetBIOS gateway. There are a number of new features, including Restartable File Copy, idle disconnect, auto dial, and logon dial, that make operating and administering low-speed WAN links much easier. Windows NT 4.0 Workstation also maintains the look and feel of Windows 95, which makes operation considerably easier.

RAS treats all the supported RAS connection types—telephone, ISDN, X.25, PPTP, and RS-232C—as fully configurable WAN ports. RAS supports multi-protocols, including NetBEUI, IPX, and TCP/IP, over PPP, and can take on the role of either a dial-up networking client or a one-connection RAS server. The RAS service provides facilities for easily maintaining RAS ports and their related protocols. The dial-up networking phonebook can easily be configured to handle a variety of situations, such as multiple servers, locations, and network protocols. The phonebook entries also contain parameters for multiple connection protocols, multiple logon validation protocols, and scripted connection handling. The Windows NT 4.0 Workstation security model has modular security options with logon validation ranging from PAP to fully encrypted authentication and data links, utilizing MS-CHAP and RSA RC-4 technologies. Third-party authentication devices, RAS auditing, and callback features are also included in the security model.

TWO-MINUTE DRILL

- ❑ The chief issues associated with RAS connections are link stability, bandwidth, authentication security, data security, and network fault recovery.

- ❑ Connection protocols manage and negotiate RAS links to support upper-layer protocols such as IPX/SPX, TCP/IP, and NetBEUI.

- ❑ PPP is a language that allows two interfaces, with no intermediary devices, to define the rules for transmitting higher-level protocols, such as TCP/IP and IPX, over different media.

- ❑ PPTP is an exciting extension to PPP. PPTP extends remote link validation within the packet structure by allowing multiple protocols, such as NetBEUI and IPX, to be encapsulated within IP datagrams and transmitted over public backbones such as the Internet.

❑ PPP-MP provides a way of bundling multiple PPP links into one logical link with the aggregate bandwidth of the individual PPP links.

❑ NT 4.0 supports SLIP both for DUN and RAS.

❑ The role of TAPI is to provide an abstraction between the application and hardware layer, which provides developers with device and network independence.

❑ TAPI 2.0 provides four levels of service for telephony-enabled applications:

❑ Assisted Telephony

❑ Basic Telephony Services

❑ Supplemental Telephony Services

❑ Extended Telephony Services

❑ RAS is installed as a service and the installation varies a great deal depending on which protocols, WAN interfaces, and software options
are selected.

❑ RAS interfaces, like LAN interfaces, must have at least one protocol bound to them to speak to anyone on the network.

❑ RAS and DUN are very much related, except that RAS concerns itself more with dial-in clients and DUN deals with dialing-out.

❑ If the RAS server and client are set up properly to take advantage of NT's encryption, it's difficult to find out what data is being sent.

❑ RAS by default enables auditing of any access to RAS.

SELF TEST

The following questions will help you measure your understanding of the material presented in this chapter. Read all the choices carefully, as there may be more than one correct answer. Choose all correct answers for each question.

1. Which network protocols can Windows NT 4.0 PPP carry?

   A. MS DLC

   B. NetBEUI

   C. IPX/SPX

   D. DECnet

   E. TCP/IP

2. How many simultaneous dial-in clients can Windows NT 4.0 Workstation handle?

   A. 2

   B. 1

   C. 256

   D. 12

3. Your remote users are complaining that their applications run slowly over their RAS connections at home. What feature of Windows NT 4.0 RAS would allow you to increase the users' throughput?

   A. TAPI 2.0

   B. Dial-Up user callback

   C. PPTP

   D. PPP-MP

4. You want to make sure that the throughput for dial-up users is maximized, by enabling compression. What represents the fastest configuration for achieving this goal?

   A. Enable software compression and hardware compression with software flow control.

   B. Enable software compression and disable hardware compression with hardware flow control.

   C. Enable hardware compression and disable software compression with hardware flow control.

   D. Disable software and hardware compression.

5. (True/False) Before network protocols can be loaded on RAS interfaces, they must first be bound to the LAN adapter, in order for the NT 4.0 Workstation to operate as a RAS server.

6. Which of these pairs of RAS interfaces could be used in a PPP-MP configuration to increase your bandwidth?

   A. a 28.8 modem and 14.4 modem

   B. a 28.8 modem and X.25 PAD

   C. an ISDN and 28.8 modem

   D. a 28.8 modem and 28.8 modem

   E. all of the above

7. Dial-Out network protocols are configured from the:

   A. Remote Access Administrator

   B. DUN phonebook editor

C. Remote Access Setup screen accessed through the Network Services tab

D. Telephony options in the Control Panel

8. TAPI 2.0 has programming facilities to:

A. perform transaction processing schedules across multiple applications

B. enable basic telephony functionality within Win32 applications

C. interact with PBX and gateway servers

D. provide LAN services

9. (True/False) NetBEUI can be used to provide connectivity from TCP/IP and IPX-based hosts to NetBEUI-based clients that dial-up to a RAS server configured as a NetBIOS gateway.

10. The My Locations section of the dialing properties can keep track of which location-specific information?

A. local dialect

B. calling card information

C. dial-out parameters

D. network protocols

11. Which of the following methods would you use to test a dial-up connection?

A. try to see the dial-up server with the PING utility

B. check the PPP log file

C. check the device log file

D. check the event viewer

E. all of the above

12. You need to dial-up a UNIX host, and accessing the host with PPP isn't working.

What other connection protocol might work?

A. PPTP

B. TCP/IP

C. NetBEUI

D. SLIP

13. You want to program your RAS connection to dial-up your ISP after you load your browser. Which NT RAS feature enables you to do this?

A. Log-On Dial

B. Point-to-Point Tunneling Protocol

C. Auto Dial

D. TAPI 2.0

14. While downloading a file from your NT network, the modem line unexpectedly drops. You dial-up back to the server and file copy resumes once you connect. Which feature enabled this?

A. Restartable File Copy

B. NetBIOS Gateway

C. Remote Procedure Calls

D. PPP-MP

15. You want to make sure that your communications are secure over the RAS link you're using. What constitutes the most secure connection type available over RAS?

A. MS-CHAP with data encryption

B. PAP

C. SPAP

D. CHAP

11

Workgroups and Domains

I n this chapter, we explore workgroup and domain environments in more detail than we covered in Chapter 1. A common mistake when taking the Windows NT Workstation certification exam is to assume you don't need to know much about domains, figuring that they'll be covered in the Windows NT Server exams. But workgroup and domain environments figure prominently in networking and security for Windows NT, as well. To pass the Workstation exam, you must have a good understanding of domains.

Related to workgroups and domains is *browsing,* a process computers use to find each other on the network. The whole purpose of workgroups lies in their capability to browse together, and that feature is no less important in the domain environment.

CERTIFICATION OBJECTIVE 11.01

Windows NT Workgroups

Every Windows NT Workstation computer must belong to either a *workgroup* or a *domain.* If you're not joining a domain, you must belong to a workgroup. A workgroup simply consists of a set of one or more computers that specify a particular workgroup name in their network identification configuration. The first computer to specify a workgroup name "creates" that workgroup.

In practical terms, workgroups do very little for you. In fact, every Windows NT Workstation computer in your organization could belong to a different workgroup, and your security setup would be the same as if they were all in the same workgroup! Where workgroups *do* make a difference is in *network browsing,* or finding other computers on the network. Computers participating in a workgroup (or a domain) delegate the responsibility of keeping track of the names of other computers on the network to a few systems, reducing the load on systems that don't need to browse. We cover browsing in detail in the last section of this chapter.

Workgroups are typically used in small offices, where there are only a few computers and which need only peer-to-peer networking. Someone must be responsible for setting up user accounts and security on each workstation. If a user must change a password, for example, the change must be made on each workstation. You can see why this arrangement is impractical for larger networks.

Windows NT Domains

A Windows NT Domain is like a workgroup that shares a common account database, and provides other features we'll discuss shortly. Basically, a domain is an area of authority. For Windows NT 4.0, the domain is in the Windows networking (NetBIOS) namespace.

Where Windows NT really shines is in the domain environment. Domains are more formal than workgroups, and require planning. For example, a Windows NT Server computer must be installed as a Primary Domain Controller to create a domain. Domains are typically larger than workgroups, and offer a much wider range of services.

exam
🅦atch

Now that the Internet is so popular, you may be familiar with another usage of the word domain. An Internet domain like "microsoft.com" is in the Internet domain namespace, and lets you know that systems within it, like "www.microsoft.com" are within that domain. The Internet meaning and the Windows NT meaning are entirely different. For Windows NT 4.0 usage, you can ignore the Internet meaning. The usage will blur once Windows NT 5.0 is released with its NDS-based active directory, but we'll have a new book for that.

Single User Logon

The same username and password may be used on any system participating in a particular domain. While a user can be restricted to as many as eight workstations, by default he may log on anywhere in the domain. This is in stark contrast to the username and password required for each workstation under the workgroup model.

The administrator has the option of setting up a *roaming profile* for each user, which gives the user the same desktop environment on any workstation he logs on to. In practical terms, a roaming profile is only useful if the computers are similarly configured. What good is a user's desktop shortcut to Microsoft Outlook on a computer that doesn't have it installed, or has it installed in a different location? The "master copy" of a roaming profile is stored on a server. Each workstation the user logs on to has the profile copied down to it. The profiles for the user are synchronized at every login and logout. Since a profile contains a user's personal folder as well as temporary Internet files, it can become quite large.

Another option for user accounts in a domain is a *home directory,* which can give the user an accessible place to store files from anywhere in the domain. Some applications use the home directory as the default location to open or save files. The home directory is usually bound to a directory under a share on a server. If you wish to use this feature, you'll probably also be in the market for a third-party software package to provide disk quotas, since neither Windows NT Workstation nor Server provide any disk quota management.

A user in one domain also can be authenticated to another domain by establishing *trust relationships.* When one domain trusts another, the users and groups of the trusted domain become available to the trusting domain. If both domains in question trust each other, they have a two-way trust relationship. We'll go further into trust relationships in the Domain Models section.

A user logging on to their usual workstation can still log on if all the domain controllers are down. Cached information from their last successful logon is used to authenticate them. Of course, logon scripts, roaming profiles, and any file and printer shares or other services on those servers would be unavailable.

Centralized Administration

All account information is kept on the domain controllers. There is only one place to maintain accounts for all the users in the domain. This is what allows a few administrators to manage a large number of user accounts and workstations. Any additions or modifications are made only once.

Centralized administration doesn't mean you have to be sitting at a domain controller to perform administration tasks, however. Any system that has domain administration tools such as Server Manager or User Manager for Domains installed can view or modify (assuming the appropriate user rights) the same domain information. These client-based network administration tools for Windows NT Workstation and Windows 95 are found on the Windows NT Server CD.

Centralized Security

By joining a domain, a computer can view and use domain user accounts and global groups, just as if they were in its own local account database. Any computer within a domain can use the domain user accounts and global groups to provide or restrict access to systems and resources. For example, a Windows NT Workstation computer in a domain can allow access to a shared printer on that workstation to members of a global group, called Sales, defined in the domain. This frees users from having to add local accounts and passwords, or from having to keep track of which users are in the Sales group at a given time.

Centralized Control of Resources

A domain administrator can control resources on any system within the domain. The Domain Administrators global group is added automatically to the local Administrators group on all Windows NT systems that join the domain. It provides administrative access to the computers within the domain. Centralized security also provides centralized access control to the domain resources.

Products such as Microsoft Systems Management Server extend the ability of an administrator to manage and troubleshoot the systems and resources within the domain.

Joining a Workgroup

As I mentioned in the workgroup discussion, all that's required to create or join a workgroup is to mention its name in your network configuration. Just about every site where the setup of computers isn't centralized has several computers that are members of the workgroup called Workgroup, because that's the default in the dialog box at setup time. Most people either don't know what a workgroup is, or can't think of a better name. At my site, browsing Workgroup currently shows 58 systems! If this were a real workgroup, so many systems would make it unmanageable.

EXERCISE 11-1

Configuring Your Workstation to Join a Workgroup

1. Select Start | Settings | Control Panel.
2. Double-click the Network icon. The Network window appears.
3. Select the Identification tab. Here you can see your computer name and current workgroup or domain. Click the Change button.
4. From this window, seen in Figure 11-1, you may change your computer name and workgroup or domain. Click the Workgroup option, and then the dialog box to its right.
5. Type in the name of a workgroup you'd like to create or join. For this example, I've chosen CH11EX1.
6. Click OK. You'll have to reboot before the change will take effect.

Joining a Domain

In order for a Windows NT Workstation to join a domain, a special account for that computer must first be created in the domain. While other Windows

FIGURE 11-1

Joining a workgroup

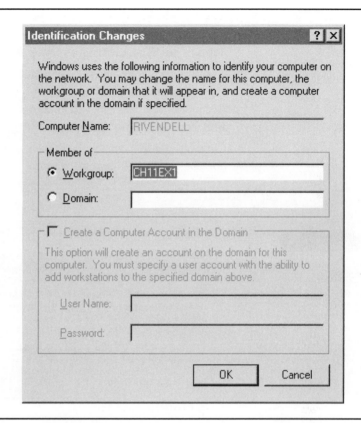

systems, like Windows 95, may participate at some level in a domain, they can't be full members, and no computer account need be created for them in the domain. We often still refer to non-Windows NT systems as domain members, even though their role is more cooperation than integration, and they can't take advantage of all the domain features.

EXERCISE 11-2

Configuring Your Workstation to Join a Domain

This is similar to Exercise 11-1, except now we need a domain to join.

1. Repeat steps 1-3 in Exercise 11-1. You see the window in Figure 11-2.

2. Click Domain and then the dialog box to its right.

3. Now type in the name of a domain that you're allowed to join. For this example, I've chosen EX2DOMAIN. If you're not allowed to join a domain, just type anything, and let it fail, or don't click OK later.

4. If your workstation hasn't been added to the domain with Server Manager, you'll need to check the box labeled Create a Computer Account in the Domain, and enter a domain administrator's username and password in the appropriate dialog boxes.

5. Click OK if you have a valid domain. You'll be welcomed to the domain, then you'll have to reboot.

FIGURE 11-2

Joining a domain

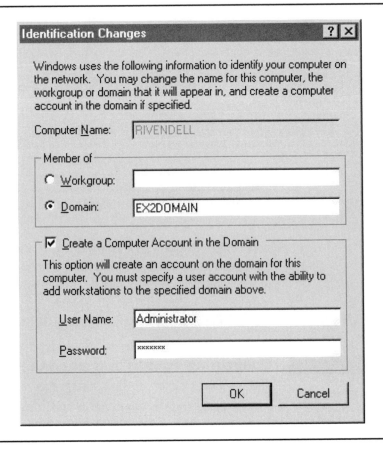

Creating a Domain User Account from the Primary Domain Controller

1. Logon to the Primary Domain Controller for your domain using an account with administrator rights.
2. Select Start | Programs | Administrative Tools | User Manager for Domains. The User Manager window appears.
3. Select User, New User. The New User window, shown in Figure 11-3, appears.
4. Fill out the fields. You may leave the Description or Full Name fields blank. I usually fill in the name field for a person, and the description field for a service account.
5. If you want to set the Groups, Profile, Hours, Logon To, Account, or Dialin options, click those buttons. When you're finished with them, you'll be back at the New User window.

FIGURE 11-3

Naming a new
user account

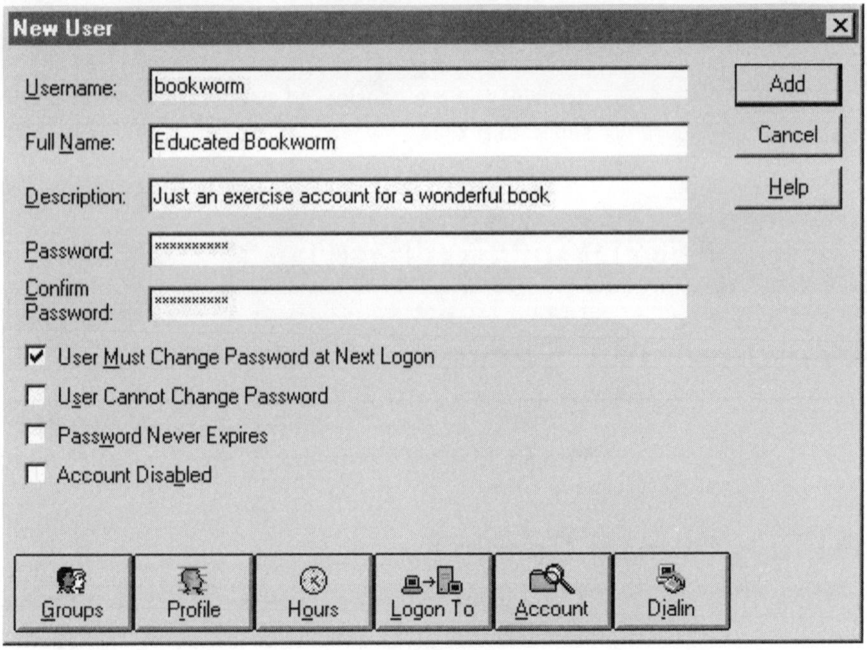

6. Click the Add button to add the account. Once it's added, click the Cancel button, and exit User Manager for Domains.

Domain Logon

If you've successfully completed Exercises 11-2 and 11-3, you're ready to log in to the domain from the workstation.

1. Bring up the logon window that you used in Exercise 11-2.

2. Enter the username and password from Exercise 11-3.

3. In the Domain window, click the down arrowhead on the right of the dialog box.

4. You should see both the workstation name and the domain name as available options. Select the domain name.

5. Click OK. You'll be asked to change your password, unless you cleared the checkbox for User Must Change Password at Next Logon during Exercise 11-3.

You're now logged on to the workstation as a domain user. If you didn't set up an existing profile when you created the account, you'll get a new default profile. Even if you have the same username on the workstation and in the domain, you are considered a separate user on the workstation, and it keeps a separate profile.

CERTIFICATION OBJECTIVE 11.05

Windows NT Servers

Windows NT Server computers may have any one of three roles in a domain: Primary Domain Controller, Backup Domain Controller, and Member Server.

Primary Domain Controller

The Primary Domain Controller (PDC) must be installed in order to create a domain. The PDC is the heart (or brain, if you prefer) of a domain. All account creation and maintenance is performed on the PDC, though the User Manager for Domains may be run on another system. Logon scripts are typically created and maintained on the PDC as well. In smaller domains, it might also serve most of the resources in the domain, and it could be the only Windows NT Server system present.

Backup Domain Controller

One or more Windows NT Servers may be installed as Backup Domain Controllers (BDC) after a domain has been created. The entire account database is basically mirrored on each BDC, and the PDC keeps the information updated within five minutes by default. If your PDC becomes unavailable, you may promote a BDC to be the PDC, which allows you to make account changes while your primary server is down. A BDC isn't automatically selected and promoted to a PDC when it becomes unavailable. This is in contrast to a PDC's role as Master Browser where a new Master Browser is selected, which is discussed later.

In addition to keeping another copy of critical account information, each BDC acts as another logon server. This means that the account database on a BDC may authenticate user logons in the domain, as well as serve any logon scripts. Adding a BDC is useful in spreading the logon load among more domain controllers. In order to keep the PDC and BDC logon scripts synchronized, the servers usually have the replication service installed. Typically, a shared export directory keeps the updated logon scripts and files, which are then replicated, on a regular basis, to the import directories of all the domain controllers. Remember that the user accounts database is automatically kept synchronized as part of Windows NT domain handling; only the logon script directory tree requires replication setup.

Member Server

A Member Server is any Windows NT Server computer in a domain that is not acting as a domain controller. Its participation in the domain is almost identical to a system running Windows NT Workstation. Member Servers are typically used as resource-intensive servers, running applications such as Microsoft SQL Server.

If a stand-alone server is being set up, it's best to make it part of a workgroup, instead of yielding to the temptation to create a domain with it. That's a common mistake, and makes the process of moving the server later to a specific domain much more painful. While a workgroup server may join a domain at any time and become a member server, a PDC or BDC requires a re-install of Windows NT Server to join another domain. You may also move a member server from one domain to another, if the need arises.

CERTIFICATION OBJECTIVE 11.06

Domain Models

As the number of users and computers in a single domain grows, it may become too complex to be handled as a single domain. Also, you may wish to distribute into smaller groups, tasks which it was once advantageous to centralize: administration, security, or control of resources. The four domain models—single domain, complete trust, master domain, and multiple-master domain—represent various stages of growth and decentralization.

In the Single User Logon section, we briefly described trust relationships. Understanding three of the models requires an understanding of trust relationships. Basically, in a trust relationship one domain trusts the authentication done by another domain. For example, if a domain called Nashville trusts a domain called Memphis, then a Memphis user could log on to a workstation in the Nashville domain using his Memphis domain authentication. Unless Memphis trusts Nashville as well, the reverse (a Nashville user logging on to a computer in the Memphis domain) is not true.

In representing trust relationships, we typically use arrows. The arrowheads point to the domain being trusted; a two-headed arrow represents a two-way trust relationship. If you always remember that a domain only knows about users in its own account database, and those in the domains to which it points, trust relationships won't give you any trouble. Using our Nashville trusting Memphis example, the arrow would point from Nashville to Memphis, like so:

Nashville → Memphis

Single Domain

The single domain model is the one we've been describing so far: it has a PDC and zero or more BDCs, along with whatever workstations it contains. It is the basis for the other models. It is the most centralized domain model.

Complete Trust

When two or more domains want to start sharing their accounts and resources with each other, you set up two-way trust relationships with each of them. Figure 11-4 illustrates complete trust relationships among four domains. These relationships are set up when, for example, departments of a company have been using separate domains, and they decide they need to share resources with each other. They keep control of their own accounts and resources, but make them available, as they wish, with other domains. This can quickly become unwieldy with more than a handful of domains. Complete Trust is the most decentralized domain model.

Master Domain

The master domain model is most popular in large organizations that wish to keep centralized account maintenance, but utilize distributed resources. Figure 11-5 illustrates such a relationship, with Memphis as the master domain. The master domain contains all of the user accounts for the entire organization. Resource domains are created which trust the master domain, and offer file, print, or application services to the master domain users. The PDC in the master domain acts as the central account administration point for the entire organization. There are usually several BDCs in the master domain for an organization of considerable size, although the resource domains may be small or large.

Multiple Master Domain

If an organization using the master domain model becomes so large that it must break up the users into more than one domain, it may use a multiple

FIGURE 11-4

A complete trust
relationship among four
domains

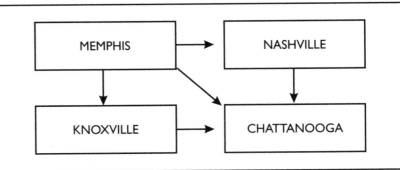

master domain model. Another good candidate for multiple master domains is
a geographically diverse organization with slow network links between
sites—the occasional user from one site can authenticate from his own site
when visiting. In Figure 11-6, Memphis and Nashville are both master
domains; Knoxville and Chattanooga are resource domains. In the multiple
master domain model, the master domains establish two-way trust
relationships with each other, while the resource domains have one-way trusts
with each of the master domains. Now there are multiple account maintenance
points, and tasks such as group membership assignments must be duplicated
manually on all master domains to keep them consistent.

exam
ᗯatch

*While the Workstation exam doesn't emphasize domain models, a basic
understanding of them adds to your understanding of domains.*

FIGURE 11-5

Nashville, Knoxville,
and Chattanooga
trust Memphis

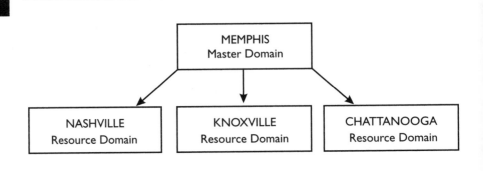

FIGURE 11-6

Memphis and Nashville are
both master domains

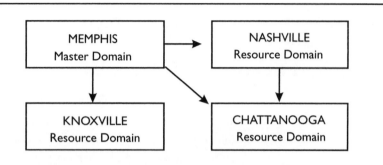

Let's take a moment for a quick question and answer session on workgroups
and domains.

QUESTIONS AND ANSWERS

My home office business uses three Windows NT Workstation computers…	Use a common workgroup.
I'm setting up a SQL Server on a new Windows NT Server in an existing domain…	Install the Windows NT Server as a member server, then install SQL Server on it.
I commonly work on two different domains. How do I set up my Windows NT Workstation for both?	If at all possible, a trust relationship should be set up. If one domain trusts another, set up your workstation in the trusted domain. If you have two-way trust, add it to the domain you use most. A computer can't be a member of multiple domains.
I'm in a domain, but would like to share the printer attached to my workstation with others…	Set up a share with permissions for a local group, to which you've added the domain users or global groups you want to allow to print there.
I want to log on to the domain but still have administrative access to my Windows NT Workstation…	Log on to your workstation as an administrator and add your domain account to the local Administrators group.
I don't want my Windows NT Workstation to be in a workgroup or domain…	You have to be in one or the other. You may choose a workgroup not in use.
I have trouble with users keeping their Windows 95 and domain passwords synchronized…	If feasible, migrate to Windows NT Workstation. Then you'll only need one password.

Browsing Microsoft Networks

No one would bother to install a network if they didn't need to communicate with other systems. In order to communicate with other systems, you first have to be able to locate them. A network browser keeps a list of domains, workgroups, computers, and other shared resources it sees on the network. This list is often called the browse list. When you explore the Network Neighborhood, a browser provides the information you see.

It's important to make a distinction at this point between a computer such as a Windows 95 or Windows NT Workstation running a server service, and a system running Windows NT Server. Any system capable of sharing resources like printers or file shares is running a server service, and is part of the browse list. When discussing browsing, we always use the term *server* to mean server service, and not a Windows NT Server, unless it is specifically mentioned.

Browsing the Network

If you've done much work with computers on networks, you've probably browsed the network many times, without knowing all the work that goes on behind the scenes. This exercise is just a quick tour of the neighborhood, for those of you who aren't familiar with the territory.

1. Double-click Network Neighborhood on the desktop. The Network Neighborhood window appears. You see an icon for the Entire Network, and your computer listed below it, perhaps with other computers in your workgroup or domain.

2. Double-click Entire Network. Which window you see depends on whether you have both Microsoft Windows Network and NetWare, or Compatible Network protocols running on your computer. If you have both, double-click Microsoft Windows Network.

3. You should be looking at little three-computer pyramid icons next to all the workgroups and domains available on your network. Find your domain or workgroup, and double-click it.

4. You should have a screen remarkably similar to the one you brought up in step 1. If you're in a domain, you should be able to double-click your domain controller and see some shares there.

5. Close out the window(s) for your workgroup or domain, and explore some others. There's a good chance you won't have access to the shares those systems have. If you're able to get to something you think you shouldn't, contact your network administrator. He or she may need to have a security discussion with someone.

FROM THE CLASSROOM

Browsing the Network: a Technique Whose Time Had Come and Gone

One of the most important issues at many of our client's sites is the issue of browsing for network resources. Browsing might well be a technique that's no longer needed. Using Network Neighborhood as a method of finding resources is inefficient, causes unnecessary network traffic, and wastes the user's time.

We were commissioned by a client to do a study of how its employees used the network, and how they got to network resources. Our job was to observe and document what was being done by whom, and why. Our findings proved to be quite interesting.

In this organization, login scripts provided users with map drives and printers to network resources. All the users' computers were running Windows 95. The client had a mix of NT and NetWare servers.

We began by collecting some network statistics, and isolating browser traffic to see how much browser traffic was on the network. It was significant. We assigned our techs to user communities, where they were to observe how

the employees connected to network resources. The analysis showed that users opened Network Neighborhood an average of six times each day. Some users browsed the network to save or open files, even though they already had a drive mapped to the resource. When we asked the employees why they did that, most replied that they had forgotten they had a drive mapped to the resource. Others opened up Network Neighborhood and browsed several servers without any apparent reason. When asked, they replied that they were curious what servers were available. All of these activities generate network traffic without any benefits.

This study led us to conclude that, on balance, users do not need to browse for network resources to be productive. Browsing several dozen servers in an attempt to find a particular resource is of questionable practical value, and seldom should be done. The study showed that users already were attached to network resources 99.7% of the time. We surveyed over 200 users who browsed the

FROM THE CLASSROOM

network over 1300 times. On only four of these occasions did users connect to a resource they did not already have. In those four cases, a printer had failed and the users wanted to connect to another one, rather than wait for the first printer to be fixed. Ironically, when the users called the help desk to find another printer, the help desk could not direct them to

an available printer, and instead had them browse until they found one.

The moral of the story is: Map the network drives and printers and then disable Network Neighborhood. Remember that users can always access network resources using the uniform naming convention (UNC).

—*By Shane Clawson, MCT, MCSE*

Browser Roles

A computer on the network can have one of many browser roles. The role it plays can change as nodes come and go. Although it's easier to imagine one role per computer, a single computer may in fact have multiple roles, if it is using multiple network protocols. A system may be a Potential Browser with TCP/IP, and a Backup Browser with IPX, for example. The roles are really only meaningful within a particular protocol, so we'll discuss each role as if we are running only one protocol.

Master Browser

The Master Browser keeps the browse list for all the systems in its workgroup or domain. The browse list for which it's responsible includes all the server resources inside its workgroup or domain, and a list of the other workgroups and domains about which it has information. In a domain, the PDC is always the Master Browser. If you have a TCP/IP network with routers, there is a Master Browser for each subnetwork, in each domain that spans subnetworks. Workgroups are not permitted to span subnetworks.

Backup Browser

The Backup Browser is to the Master Browser much like the BDC is to the PDC. It receives the updated browse list from the Master Browser, and can distribute it on request to other systems in the workgroup or domain. It updates the list every 15 minutes from the Master Browser. The number of Backup Browsers you have depends on the number of systems in the workgroup or domain.

Potential Browser

Any system that is capable of browsing, but isn't currently browsing, is a potential browser. Computers running Windows NT 3.1 or higher, Windows for Workgroups 3.11, or Windows 9x can be browsers. In a later section, we'll cover what determines which computers actually are elected to the position.

Domain Master Browser

I mentioned already that, in a domain that spans subnetworks, there is a Master Browser for each subnetwork. The Domain Master Browser is responsible for keeping track of all the Master Browsers, and keeps a master list of domain resources for them. The PDC is always the Domain Master Browser for a domain.

Preferred Master Browser

A system can be designated as a Preferred Master Browser. This gives the system preference over similarly configured systems to become a Master Browser.

Non-Browser

A system that could browse can be designated as a Non-Browser. This designation totally eliminates it from being selected as a Master or Backup Browser.

Configuring Browsers

You can influence some of the factors used to determine browsing status for a computer. We've already mentioned Preferred Master Browser and Non-Browser. Now let's discuss how to configure a Windows NT Workstation as one of these roles.

Preferred Master Browser

There is a Registry setting IsDomainMaster, which is false by default. If you wish to give preference to a computer to become the Master Browser, you can change this value to true. It gives the computer a slightly higher vote over others of its class in browser elections. The Preferred Master setting isn't sufficient for a Windows NT Server to be elected over the PDC. See Exercise 11-6 for Registry details.

Changing the Workstation's Preferred Master Browser Status

Both this exercise and Exercise 11-7 require making modifications to your computer's Registry. There's no user interface for these options, other than the Registry editor. You should exercise extreme caution when editing your Registry, as mistakes can be fatal to your system, and Microsoft won't lift a finger to help if you were playing with the Registry. Now that you've been warned, let's go edit the Registry!

1. Select Start | Run and type **regedt32** in the dialog box, and click OK.
2. If you were just going to browse around, now would be a good place to select Options, and check Read Only Mode. Since we're actually going to make changes, make sure it's not checked.
3. Inside Registry Editor, open the window titled HKEY_LOCAL_MACHINE.
4. Double-click SYSTEM in the left panel. This should show you more folders under SYSTEM in the left panel. You can ignore anything in the right panel until we get where we're going.
5. Double-click CurrentControlSet, then Services, then Browser, and finally click Parameters. You should end up with something similar to the window in Figure 11-7.

FIGURE 11-7

Changing parameters with
the Registry Editor

6. In the right panel, you should see IsDomainMaster. Double-click it to change the value.

7. Type **TRUE** to replace FALSE in the String Editor window, and click OK.

8. The value showing in the right panel should now show TRUE.

9. If you plan to do Exercise 11-7, stop here to keep from having to navigate back. Otherwise, select Registry and Exit.

Registry entries are typically listed with their full path, just as if they were actual folders. We just edited

HKEY_LOCAL_MACHINE\SYSTEM\CurrentControlSet\Services\Browser\
Parameters\IsDomainMaster

and changed it's value.

Non-Browser

There is another Registry setting "MaintainServerList" which is "Auto" by default on Windows NT Workstations, and "Yes" by default on Windows NT Servers. If you change the value to "No", the computer will never be a browser. See Exercise 11-7 for Registry details.

Automatic

The automatic setting lets the Master Browser tell the system whether or not it needs to become a Backup Browser. The Master Browser determines the number of Backup Browsers the system needs, based on the size of the workgroup or domain. If there aren't enough existing browsers, one of the systems with the automatic setting is told to become a Backup Browser.

Configuring the Workstation's Browser Status

1. Read the caution in Exercise 11-6 again, and perform steps 1-5 if you don't have the Registry editor window left from Exercise 11-6.

2. Note what value MaintainServerList has. You may wish to reset your Registry back to this value later.

3. Double-click MaintainServerList. You can set the value to Yes, No, or Auto, which have already been explained. Click OK after you've typed in the value you want.

4. Select Registry and Exit.

The Browsing Process

Browsing is somewhat more organized than the name might imply. "Designated listener" would probably be a more descriptive term than Master Browser, but it's called browsing, for better or worse. The basic elements of the browsing process are:

- **Announcing**   Each computer acting as a server sends an announcement of the services it has available. The Master Browser maintains a list of these announcements, and makes them available to the Backup Browsers.

- **Browse List Copy Pass**   Each Backup Browser retrieves an updated list every 15 minutes.

- **Call Master Browser** (Initial List Request)   The first time a system wishes to browse the network, it sends a request to the Master Browser for a list of Backup Browsers. It selects and stores three of the names. It then continues with step 4.

- **Call Backup Browser** (Server List Request)   The actual request for a list of network resources is sent to a Backup Browser. One of the three stored in step 3 is selected at random.

- **Contact Resource Server**   Once the resource server has been identified, it can be contacted about the resource in question.

- **Access Resource**   Finally, the server contacted provides access to the resource it announced in step 1.

Browser Elections

Browser elections are often viewed as things of great mystery. Heads nod knowingly when you speak of browsing trouble and browser elections. Actually, understanding which browser wins an election is not that complicated. But the cause of an election can be difficult to determine, if you're having network connectivity problems.

A browser election occurs when a system sends out an *election datagram.* This is a packet that includes that system's election criteria. All browsers receive the datagram. A system whose own criteria beat the criteria it receives sends out its own datagram, and enters an *election in progress* state. It's similar to a bid process at an auction, but you can only bid a predetermined amount. If the bidding has already passed what you can "afford", you keep silent and listen to see who wins. In order to speed up the election process, each bid is made after a delay, with likely winners having a shorter delay. This usually means that systems unlikely to win the election remain silent during the process.

A system should send out an election datagram when any one of the following happens:

- It can't locate the Master Browser (the most common trouble).

- It's set as a Preferred Master Browser and comes online.

- It's a domain controller (PDC or BDC) and comes online.

Operating System

The major determining factor of who wins a browser election is the operating system. Windows NT Server beats Windows NT Workstation, which beats Windows 95 or Windows for Workgroups.

Since Windows NT makes a much better browser than other Windows systems, you can improve the browsing in a workgroup with other Windows operating systems by adding a couple of Windows NT Workstations to the mix. They'll automatically end up as the browsers for the workgroup.

Operating System Version

Later versions of operating systems get preference over earlier versions. There are certain other "version bonuses" which are given. Here they are in order of importance:

1. Being the Primary Domain Controller (PDC) (huge bonus)

2. Running a WINS server (fairly large bonus)

3. Preferred Master Browser

4. Currently the Master Browser

5. MaintainServerList is Yes instead of Auto

6. Currently a Backup Browser

The bonuses are cumulative, so a system running a WINS server, Preferred Master Browser set, and MaintainServerList set to Auto beats out a system running a WINS server, without Preferred Master Browser set, and MaintainServerList set to Yes.

Browser Longevity

If all the previous criteria match, the system that has been browsing the longest wins. This is more likely to be the tiebreaker in a workgroup, with all systems having the same operating system and default settings.

Computer Name

In the unlikely event that the browsers also have been running the same length of time, the final tiebreaker is the node name. The node that comes first alphabetically wins. At this point, one system would have no advantage over the other, so an arbitrary choice based on node name is as good as any other method.

Browser Communications

We've seen how the browsing process and browser elections work. There are just a few more items worth mentioning before we can conclude our discussion on browsing.

Routine Communications

In the section on the browsing process, we briefly described routine browser communications. The announcements happen every 1-12 minutes. (The new announcements happen in intervals of 1, 2, 4, 8, and 12 minutes. Once 12 minutes is reached, it remains the interval between subsequent announcements.) The Master Browser listens to these announcements, and maintains a list.

If you can see Microsoft Networking workgroups and domains, but are having trouble browsing IPX servers, the trouble is often with the frame type on the Master Browser. This is a problem especially when you select the default auto-detection of frame types, and someone adds a system using a preferred frame type over the one you were using. For example: If you're using Ethernet II on your servers as the frame type, and someone adds a node using 802.2-type frames, communications and browsing will be disrupted the next time networking is started on a system and it's elected a Master Browser (because of the preference order in auto-detection).

If you want to tell which systems are your Master and Backup Browsers, there's a diagnostic utility in the Windows NT Server Resource Kit called Browser Monitor (BROWMON.EXE). It shows the Master Browser for each protocol, and double-clicking a Master Browser shows all Backup Browsers, as well as the list of systems and domains they are maintaining in their lists.

Abnormal Shutdowns

If a server makes no announcement for three consecutive announcement intervals, the Master Browser removes the system from the list. If the system that crashes *is* the Master Browser, we've already seen that the first system that notices it's gone will force a new election.

Backup Browsers

Backup Browsers get an updated list from the Master Browser every 15 minutes. This interval is long enough to ensure that a complete announcement cycle has passed and been processed. Since it's the Backup Browsers that serve the lists to clients, there is some lag time after a system actually disappears, before it disappears from a client's browse list. The maximum length of time to be removed from the Master Browser list is: 36 minutes (3 times 12 minutes), plus up to 15 minutes for the Backup Browser to get the updated list, for a total of 51 minutes.

The number of Backup Browsers depends on the size of the workgroup or domain. With one computer, there's just a Master Browser and no backups. With 2-31 computers, there is one Backup Browser. For each additional 32 computers in the workgroup or domain, another Backup Browser is added. If you're dealing with subnetworks, the rules apply for each subnetwork.

CERTIFICATION SUMMARY

Workgroups and domains are important Windows NT concepts to master. Workgroups do little more than determine the systems that participate in browsing together. Windows NT Workstations and Servers may participate in workgroups, as can Windows 95 and Windows for Workgroups 3.11. The only time a Windows NT Server can't enter and leave workgroups or domains is when it's a domain controller.

Domains are the cornerstone of Windows NT networking, and offer much more than just browsing groups. Single-user logon and centralized administration, security, and control of resources are a domain's main features. A Windows NT Server may be a primary domain controller (PDC), a backup domain controller (BDC), or a member server. You must have a PDC to start a new domain.

Browsing allows computers on a network to find each other. A Master Browser listens to all the server announcements, and maintains a list. This list is periodically retrieved by Backup Browsers, which in turn serve the information to Non-Browsers whenever requested. The primary determining factor of who is elected Master Browser is the operating system type. Other factors include the operating system version, certain Registry settings, other roles of the computer, and current browsing status.

In order to pass the certification exam, you should have a through knowledge of workgroups and domains, and understand the role of browsing and the fundamentals of how it works.

TWO-MINUTE DRILL

- ❑ Every Windows NT Workstation computer must belong to either a *workgroup* or a *domain*.
- ❑ A Windows NT Domain is like a workgroup that shares a common account database, and provides other features.
- ❑ An Internet domain like "microsoft.com" is in the Internet domain namespace, and lets you know that systems within it, like "www.microsoft.com" are within that domain.
- ❑ The administrator has the option of setting up a *roaming profile* for each user, which gives the user the same desktop environment on any workstation he logs on to.
- ❑ All account information is kept on the domain controllers.
- ❑ Any computer within a domain can use the domain user accounts and global groups to provide or restrict access to systems and resources.
- ❑ In order for a Windows NT Workstation to join a domain, a special account for that computer must first be created in the domain.
- ❑ Windows NT Server computers may have any one of three roles in a domain: Primary Domain Controller, Backup Domain Controller, and Member Server.
- ❑ All account creation and maintenance is performed on the Primary Domain Controller.
- ❑ The entire account database is basically mirrored on each Backup Domain Controller.
- ❑ If your PDC becomes unavailable, you may promote a BDC to be the PDC, which allows you to make account changes while your primary server is down.

❑ Member Servers are typically used as resource-intensive servers, running applications such as Microsoft SQL Server.

❑ The four domain models—single domain, complete trust, master domain, and multiple-master domain—represent various stages of growth
and decentralization.

❑ While the Workstation exam doesn't emphasize domain models, a basic understanding of them adds to your understanding of domains.

❑ A network browser keeps a list of domains, workgroups, computers, and other shared resources it sees on the network.

SELF TEST

The following questions will help you measure your understanding of the material presented in this chapter. Read all the choices carefully, as there may be more than one correct answer. Choose all correct answers for each question.

1. Sally, Bob, and Ed are engineers using computers running Windows NT Workstation. They occasionally like to share files with each other, and the files are too big to fit on a floppy, but they don't want just anyone to be able to access the files. What is the best solution to their problem?

   A. Buy another computer, install Windows NT Server, and have them all join the domain. Then, set up a shared directory on the new server for the files.

   B. Buy them all larger removable drives, and let them swap them around the office.

   C. Use a software compression program to pack the files on floppies.

   D. Set up accounts for all three of them on each workstation, and set up shares for the files with these accounts.

   E. Tell them to use whatever workstation has the files they need.

2. A workgroup consists of a Windows NT Server, a Windows NT Workstation, a Windows 95 system, and a Windows for Workgroups system. The Windows NT Workstation has MaintainServerList set to Yes and Preferred Master Browser set. Each of the others has default browser settings, and all are using the same network protocol. Which of the following is true:

   A. The Windows NT Server will be the Master Browser, and the Windows NT Workstation will be the Backup Browser.

   B. The Windows NT Workstation will be the Master Browser, and the Windows NT Server will be the Backup Browser.

   C. The Windows for Workgroups system will be the Master Browser, and the other systems will be Backup Browsers.

   D. Each system will browse for itself, because they're running different operating systems.

   E. None of the above, because you can't have a Windows NT Server in a workgroup.

3. A system shows up in the Network Neighborhood, but the user is unable to connect to its resources as he has in the past. Which of the following are good hypotheses to troubleshoot the problem:

   A. The user just thought he was able to connect to the resources in the past. Ignore him.

   B. The system is actually down, but hasn't been down long enough to be removed from the browse list as yet.

   C. It must be a problem with user security access to the resource.

D. The target system is in the same workgroup, and the user has changed his password recently.

E. The target system is in the same domain, and the user has changed his password recently.

4. A user has just changed his password while logged into the domain on one workstation. He logs out and immediately goes to another workstation in the domain and can't get logged in. Which of the following might be true:

A. CAPS LOCK might be in a different state.

B. He's trying his old password, thinking he hasn't changed it on this workstation yet.

C. The current workstation happened to authenticate from the Backup Domain Controller, and it hasn't been updated yet.

D. He's not allowed to log on at that workstation.

E. This workstation was down when the password change was made.

5. Ted, Jill, and Janet are users on Windows NT Workstations belonging to a domain. They always log on to the domain at their workstations. They have administrator access to their workstations, but aren't domain administrators. They'd like to share files on their workstations with each other using group access, with the ability to make changes themselves (without a domain administrator). Which option is the best:

A. Each one should set up workstation accounts for the others, just as they would in a workgroup, and add them to a local group.

B. Each one should create a local group on their workstation, and add the domain usernames of all of them to the group.

C. One of them should create a global group on their workstation, letting the others use it.

D. One of them should create a global group on a member server, letting the others use it.

E. What they want to do can't be done without the aid of a domain administrator.

6. Which of the following give a computer preference in browser elections?

A. Being a Backup Domain Controller.

B. Being a Primary Domain Controller.

C. Running Windows Internet Naming Service.

D. Currently the Master Browser.

E. MaintainServerList is Auto.

7. Which of the following are true statements about workgroup and domain membership?

A. A workstation can be a member of both a workgroup and a domain.

B. A user logging on to a domain has only one username and password to remember.

C. A system running Windows NT Server may be a member of a workgroup.

D. A system running Windows NT Server is required for domain creation

E. If you give a workstation a workgroup name that matches an existing domain, it will browse with that domain without being a domain member.

8. David is a domain administrator running Windows NT Workstation at his desk. Which of the following are true statements:

A. David can log on to the domain and have administrator access to his workstation.

B. David can log on to the domain and have administrator access to the domain.

C. David must have a roaming profile to log on to another workstation.

D. David enjoys the power he wields over other users, who are subject to his every whim.

E. David is always the Master Browser.

9. Jane wants her Windows NT Workstation to join the domain. She has selected Domain and typed in the correct name in the Identification Changes window. What can she do:

A. If she's a domain administrator, she can check the box Create a Computer Account in the Domain and enter her username and password and click OK to join.

B. Even if she's not an administrator, she could do as in answer A, as long as she's the current logged on user.

C. She can contact a domain administrator to add her node name in Server Manager before clicking OK to join.

D. She can have a domain administrator come to her workstation and enter his own username and password as in answer A.

E. Since Windows NT Workstations must select their workgroup or domain at installation, she can't join the domain without reinstalling.

10. Twenty-five users running Windows NT Workstations in a workgroup wish to share resources. What's their best solution?

A. Set up accounts for everyone on each workstation.

B. Invest in a Windows NT Server and add it to the workgroup. Place all the resources on the server.

C. Invest in a Windows NT Server and create a domain, adding all the workstations to the domain. Any resources may be moved to the server if desired.

D. Same as answer A, but publish and maintain a list of usernames and passwords, so that each user can keep his own workstation's account information for all users synchronized with the rest.

E. Invest in a Windows NT Server and create a domain. Have each workstation join its own individual workgroup, so that no two are in the same group.

11. The Marketing domain spans multiple subnetworks on a routed network. The PDC server becomes unavailable due to hardware problems, but you have a couple of BDCs. After a while, users report problems seeing other nodes on the network. What happened, and how do you fix the problem?

    A. Since the PDC must be the Master Browser for the domain, there is none now, and other nodes are unreachable. Wait for a BDC to automatically be promoted to PDC.

    B. Since the PDC was the domain Master Browser, each subnetwork's Master Browser only sees computers on its subnetwork. Promote a BDC to PDC, so that it will become a new domain Master Browser.

    C. Since a domain requires a PDC to run, quickly promote your workstation to be a new PDC for the domain. Disappearing nodes are the least of your problems!

    D. The problem is temporary, and will go away once a browser election is held and a new domain Master Browser is elected.

    E. Since the PDC was both domain Master Browser and Master Browser for its subnetwork, browsing can't continue in the domain until you replace the server with another.

12. Ned and Lonnie work different shifts at the rock quarry. They use the same Windows NT Workstation, which is a member of a domain. Which of the following could be true for Ned to log on to the workstation:

    A. Ned has a local account on the workstation.

    B. Ned has a domain account in the workstation's domain.

    C. Ned has a domain account in a domain trusted by the workstation's domain.

    D. Ned has a domain account in a domain that trusts the workstation's domain.

    E. Ned has a local account on a workstation that this workstation trusts.

13. Ned's shift has been changed, and he now works with Lonnie. There are now two Windows NT Workstations that either may log on to, with identical software setups. What's the best way to preserve their desktops for both computers?

    A. Have an administrator copy their last used profile over to the other workstation every day.

    B. Use the same mandatory profile for everyone, so the desktop is consistent everywhere without tracking changes.

    C. Set up roaming profiles for Ned and Lonnie.

    D. Assign each his own workstation, and tell them to log on only to the one to which they're assigned.

    E. Tell them if they can't agree on a desktop, they're going back to busting rock!

14. Earnest has an account in each of the two domains, Seeming and Being. Earnest is a domain administrator in Being, but just a normal user in Seeming. Domain Seeming trusts Being, and also has added Being\Domain Admins to the local Administrator's group on the PDC for Seeming. If Earnest wants to log on to the PDC for Seeming to administer it, what must he do?

    A. He can't do anything; he's just a user in the Seeming domain.

    B. He can log on to the Seeming PDC using his Seeming account, then switch to an administrative user.

    C. He can log on to the Being PDC using his Being account and set his environment to the Seeming PDC.

    D. He can log on to the Seeming PDC using his Being account.

    E. He can log on to the Being PDC using his Seeming account.

15. You're looking at the Network Neighborhood for your domain. You see systems listed for which you know you haven't set up a computer account in the domain, and they don't appear in Server Manager. Which of the following could explain the situation?

    A. The systems aren't Windows NT Workstations or Servers, and have been configured to participate in the domain.

    B. The systems used your domain name as their workgroup name.

    C. Someone added the Windows NT Workstations or Servers by checking Create a Computer Account in the Domain instead of using Server Manager.

    D. The Master Browser for your domain is on the same subnetwork as the Master Browser for their domain.

    E. Your domain didn't have any potential browsers after your PDC crashed, so the other systems were added to make browsing possible.

MICROSOFT CERTIFIED SYSTEMS ENGINEER

12

Printing

CERTIFICATION OBJECTIVES

T his chapter covers printing using NT Workstation. First, we'll discuss terminology. NT uses a slightly different definition for printers and print queues than you are probably used to. We'll take a look at the NT print model and how it uses print drivers and print processors. Then we will discuss how to create, share, and connect to printers. After creating a printer, I'll explain in depth the configuration options, including editing the Registry to change some settings. Finally, we'll look into troubleshooting print problems.

CERTIFICATION OBJECTIVE 12.01

Overview of Printing

Microsoft defines printing terms a little differently than you probably have in the past. To begin a discussion about printing using NT, you must first understand some key definitions.

Printing Devices

Printing devices are what we commonly refer to as printers. It's the actual hardware that prints the document. Why did they change printer to printing device? Because they use the term printer to mean the software that manages the printing devices.

Printing Software

Printing software is considered the printer. A printer is software that manages a specific printing device (or devices, in case of printer pooling). The printer determines how the print job gets to the printing device. Does it go directly to parallel port, serial port, or via the network? One printer can manage multiple printing devices or just one. NetWare refers to this as the print queue, but Microsoft considers the print queue to be the actual documents waiting to be sent to the printing device via the printer.

Windows NT Print Model

Here is how the printing process works under NT:

1. The user at an NT Workstation prints a document. The Windows application calls the graphics device interface (GDI). GDI calls the print driver for the appropriate printing device. Using the print device information from the print driver, and the document information from the application, the GDI renders the print job in the appropriate language.

2. The print job is sent to the spooler. The client side of the spooler makes a Remote Procedure Call (RPC) to the server side spooler, which makes a direct application programming interface (API) call to the router. The router passes the print job to the local print provider, which then spools it.

3. The print job is modified, if necessary, to print properly. The local print provider polls the print processors. Once the print processor recognizes the job's data type, it receives the print job and modifies it, if necessary, according to its data type.

4. Control of the print job passes to the separator page processor. If enabled, it adds a page to the front of the print job.

5. The job is despooled to the print monitor. If the printing device is not bidirectional, the job goes directly to the port monitor, which transmits the print job to the printing device. If the printing device is bidirectional, the monitor is a language monitor, which handles bidirectional communications with the printer and then passes the job to the port monitor.

6. The print device receives the print job, translates it to a bitmap, then prints it.

Figure 12-1 depicts the NT print model graphically.

Graphics Device Interface

The GDI controls the display of graphics on the monitor and printers. It provides a set of standard functions that let applications communicate with

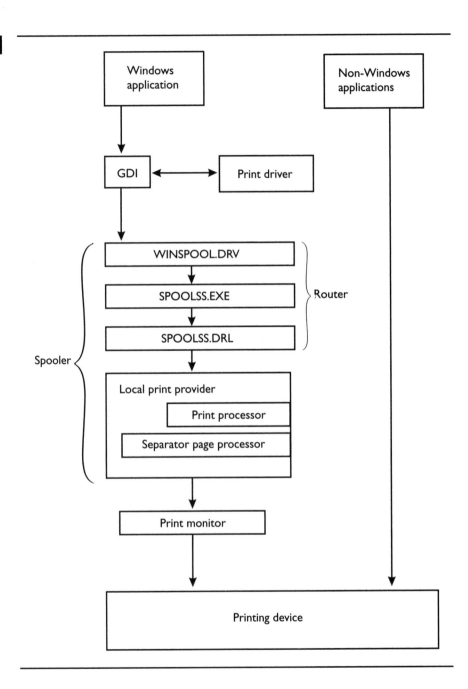

A graph of the printing process in NT

graphics devices, without knowing anything about the devices. The GDI enables application code to be independent of the hardware devices and their drivers. Hardware vendors only have to write a minidriver to interact between the GDI and their hardware. The application sends commands to the GDI and the GDI sends commands to the hardware via the minidriver.

Print Driver

Print drivers are the software that allows an application to communicate with printing devices. Print drivers are composed of three files, which act together as a printing unit.

- **Printer graphics driver**   The printer graphics driver is always called by the GDI and provides the rendering portion of the printer driver.

- **Printer interface driver**   The printer interface driver provides the user interface for configuration management of the print driver.

- **Characterization data file**   The characterization data file contains all the printing device-specific information, such as page protection, graphics resolution, memory, paper size and orientation, and printing on both sides of the paper. The printer interface and the printer graphics driver use this file whenever they need printing device-specific information.

Print drivers usually are not binary-compatible. This means that each different type of operating system and hardware platform that prints to a printing device has to have a print driver compiled for it. You can't use a Windows 95 print driver on a Windows NT machine, nor can you use a Windows NT 3.51 print driver on a Windows NT 4.0 machine. However, because the core components of NT Workstation and NT Servers are identical, these two operating systems can use the same print drivers, but they have to have the same hardware platform. (In other words, Intel print drivers can't be used for an Alpha.)

Windows NT provides three generic print drivers to support the three basic types of print devices. The three basic types of print devices are raster, PostScript, and plotter. The three generic print drivers are as follows:

- **Universal print driver** (unidriver)   Also known as the raster driver because it provides raster graphics printing. The unidriver carries out requests on most types of printers. Each hardware vendor writes a printing device minidriver that operates with the unidriver to communicate with its print devices.

- **PostScript print driver**   Uses Adobe version 4.2-compatible PostScript printer description (PPD) files. The PPD files are the only printer driver files that are binary-compatible across operating systems.

- **HP-GL/2 plotter driver**   Supports several different plotters that use the HP-GL/2 language. It doesn't support the HP-GL language.

Print Router

The print router routes the print job from the spooler to the appropriate print processor.

Print Spooler

The print spooler is a service that actually manages the print process. It's responsible for the following:

- Tracking what print jobs are going to which printing device
- Tracking which ports are connected to which printing device
- Routing print jobs to the proper port
- Managing pooled printers
- Prioritizing print jobs

The spool file folder is located at the %systemroot%\system32\spool\ printers folder. To stop and start the spooler service, you can use the Control Panel Service application, or use the NET START SPOOLER or NET STOP SPOOLER command.

Print Processor

The print processor completes the rendering process. *Rendering* is the process of translating print data into a form that a printing device can read. Since each type of client creates print jobs differently, different print server services are required to receive and prepare the jobs. The print processor performs different tasks, depending on the data type. The default data type is Enhanced Metafile for PCL printers and RAW for PostScript printers. Exercise 12-1 explains how to change the default data type.

EXERCISE 12-1

Change the Default Data Type for a Printer

1. Click Start | Settings | Printers.
2. Right-click the printer for which you want to change the default data type.
3. Click Properties.
4. Click the General tab.
5. Click the Print Processor button.
6. In the Default Datatype list box, choose the data type.
7. Click OK.

Windows NT provides two print processors: Windows print processor and Macintosh print processor. Printing device vendors can develop a custom print processor, if needed.

Windows Print Processor

WINPRINT.DLL performs the print processor functions. It supports five data types:

1. EMF: Print jobs received from NT clients are Enhanced Metafiles (EMF). In contrast to RAW printer data being generated by the printer driver, EMF information is generated by the GDI before spooling.

After the EMF is created, control returns to the user. The EMF is interpreted in the background on a 32-bit printing subsystem spooler thread and sent to the print driver. Two advantages of EMF are: It returns control of the application to the user more quickly than printer calls can be directly interpreted by the print driver; and EMF files can be printed on any printing device.

2. RAW: Raw files are fully rendered print data, which require no processing from the print processor. Encapsulated PostScript (EPS) is an example of a raw data type, because it doesn't need print processor interpretation. EPS files are sent directly to the spooler for routing to the graphics engine.

3. RAW (FF Auto): This type tells the spooler to append a form feed character to the end of each job if it isn't already present. This is used to print the last page on a PCL printing device, if the application doesn't send a form feed.

4. RAW (FF Appended): Like RAW (FF Auto) this data type appends a form feed character to the end of the job. The difference is, it always adds a form feed character even if one is already present.

5. TEXT: Raw text with minimal formatting. The print job is in ANSI text. It uses the printing device's factory defaults for printing the document. This is used for printing devices that can't accept simple text jobs, like PostScript printers.

Macintosh Print Processor

This print processor (SFMPSPRT) is installed when Services for Macintosh is installed. It supports the PSCRIPT1 data type. It indicates that the print job is level 1 PostScript code, but the printing device isn't a PostScript printer. The images are converted into monochrome raster graphics for printing to the printing device.

Print Monitors

Print monitors control access to the printing device, monitor the status of the device, and communicate with the spooler, which relays this information via the user interface. They control the data going to a printer port by opening, closing, configuring, writing, reading, and releasing the port.

NT has the following print monitors built in:

- Local Port: LPT1, LPT2, Com1, Com2, and so on.
- Digital Network Port: Supports both TCP/IP and DECnet protocols for digital network printing devices. DECnet protocol doesn't ship with NT.
- Lexmark DLC Port: Supports Lexmark DLC printing devices.
- Lexmark TCP/IP Port: Supports Lexmark TCP/IP printing devices.
- LPR Port: Supports printing to UNIX LPD printing devices.
- Hewlett-Packard Network Interface: Supports printing to HP Jet Direct enabled printers.
- Macintosh Printer Port: Supports printing to AppleTalk printers.
- PJL Language Monitor.

Print Jobs

Print jobs are source code consisting of both data and commands for print processing. All print jobs are classified into data types. The data type tells the spooler what modifications need to be made to the print job so it can print correctly on the printing device.

CERTIFICATION OBJECTIVE 12.02

Installing Printers

You can create printers two ways in NT. You can use the Add Printer Wizard or you can use Point and Print. To manage printing, you use the Printers folder. The Add Printer Wizard is located inside the Printers folder. There are three ways to access the Printers folder:

- Click Start | Settings | Printers
- In Control Panel, double-click the Printers Folder shortcut
- In My Computer, double-click Printers Folder

Creating a Local Printer

A local printer can be connected directly to a port on your computer or a printing device directly connected on the network. Don't confuse a printing device directly connected to the network with a shared network printer. The reason a printing device connected directly to the network may be a local printer is because your spooler can send jobs directly to the printing device. If the printing device is connected directly to the network, but you first send the print job to a different computer, it is then considered a shared network printer. Exercise 12-2 teaches you how to create a local printer.

EXERCISE 12-2

Creating a Local Printer

1. Open the Printers folder.
2. Double-click the Add Printer Wizard.
3. Choose the My Computer option button. Click Next.
4. Click the check box for the port your printer is connected to (probably LPT1). Click Next.
5. Choose the printer driver by selecting the manufacturer on the left side pane, then select the correct model. If your model doesn't show up on the list, you'll need to click the Have Disk button and supply the path to the driver. Click Next.
6. Give your printer a name (up to 32 characters) and choose whether or not you want it to be the default printer. Click Next.
7. You can now share your printer, but for now make sure Not Shared is chosen. Click Next.
8. Choose Yes to print a test page. Click Next.
9. Click Finish. Make sure your NT Workstation CD is in your CD-ROM drive.

Sharing a Printer

Sharing a printer on the network allows other users to print to a printing device connected to your computer. Users' workstations will first spool the print job to their spooler, then it will be sent to your spooler for final processing and printing.

Before you can share a printer on the network, you first must create it locally on your computer. (See Exercise 12-2 for creating a local printer.) You can share the printer when you create it locally, or later after it's already created. Exercise 12-3 will show you how to share a printer on the network after it has already been created locally on your system.

Sharing a Printer on the Network

1. Select the Sharing tab in the Printer Properties dialog box.
2. Give it a share name (the default is the first eight characters of the printer name).
3. Choose what other operating systems will print to this printer. When you do this, NT loads the drivers for each of the selected operating systems, so when users point and print, the driver automatically is copied to their system.
4. Click OK.

Connecting to a Remote Printer

To connect to a remote printer on another NT Workstation, you only need to double-click the Printer icon to install that printer on your system (assuming the correct drivers are loaded). This is called Point and Print. Another way is to use the Add Printer Wizard. In Exercise 12-4 we'll connect to a remote printer using Point and Print. First, you need to have a printer shared on another Windows NT 4.0 Workstation or server. If it has a different hardware platform, the appropriate driver for your system must be installed on the shared printer's server. (See Exercise 12-3 to share a printer.)

EXERCISE 12-4

Connecting to a Shared Printer

1. Browse the Network Neighborhood and double-click the computer that has the printer you wish to connect to shared.

2. Double-click the printer you wish to connect.

3. NT then starts the Add Printer Wizard and installs the printer on your system.

Network Printers

A network printer is a printer that attaches directly to your network. It isn't connected to a computer's serial or parallel port. NT supports Hewlett-Packard JetDirect cards using the DLC protocol, DEC network printing devices using DECnet or TCP/IP protocols, Lexmark network printing devices with DLC or TCP/IP protocols, and any other device that supports LPD using TCP/IP. You can set printers on all your workstations to print directly to a networked printer, but it is common practice to set up a print server to print to the printers, and share that printer out using NT network shares. This improves performance on the workstations by not requiring additional protocols to be loaded on the clients.

exam
Watch

Be sure to understand that Hewlett-Packard JetDirect cards require the DLC protocol to be loaded on your system. DLC is not a routable protocol, so the print server and the printing device must be on the same side of a router.

FROM THE CLASSROOM

NT and the Art of Printing

In the following discussion, we'll talk about setting your NT Workstation to be the most effective network client to an NT print server that it can be. In other words, we are addressing printing between an NT Workstation and an NT Server acting as a print server. No other cases apply. If you are printing from NT Workstation to a NetWare or UNIX print

FROM THE CLASSROOM

server, or to a network-attached printer using an adapter (such as an HP JetDirect card) this discussion does not apply.

In the past, the conventional way to print to a print server was to "create" a printer at the client machine and assign it to a local port (such as LPT1), and then redirect the print job away from the port and to the print server. This technique involved installing the print driver to the client machine's hard disk.

When you are printing from an NT system to an NT print server, you *don't* need to create a printer and redirect the output. You simply "connect" to the print server. No print driver is copied to the client machine's hard disk. The client machine connects to the print server, and the print driver is downloaded to the client, where it is cached in memory. The driver

remains in cache for the duration of the session (as long as the user is logged on). The advantage of this system is that there is only one print driver installed at the print server—not at several hundred client machines. When you want to update the printer driver, you only have to update the driver at the print server, and not all of the clients individually. They will get the updated driver automatically.

A potential issue arises if you are using screen fonts that are rendered by the printer driver and you are not connected to the network, so that the driver is downloaded to your computer. TrueType fonts are not a problem, but printer-specific fonts might be. You should do some research to understand this before you make a decision.

—By ShaneClawson, MCT, MCSE

CERTIFICATION OBJECTIVE 12.03

Configuring Printers

The options you can configure depend on the printing device you have and the driver that manages it. Some printing devices allow printing on both sides, printing from different paper trays, different fonts, and various other options. These options are configured using the Device Settings tab. Although some options differ from driver to driver, there are several common options that can be configured on all printers. To configure the common options, use the following tabs: General, Ports, Scheduling, Sharing, and Security.

General Tab

The General tab, shown in Figure 12-2, is used for settting which driver you want to use, describing the printer, and telling network users where it's located. It also allows you to select a separator page, change the print processor, and print a test page.

Separator Page

The Separator Page, shown in Figure 12-3, is used to identify the start of a print job. It helps users identify where their print job stops, and the next one

FIGURE 12-2

The General tab on a printer properties window

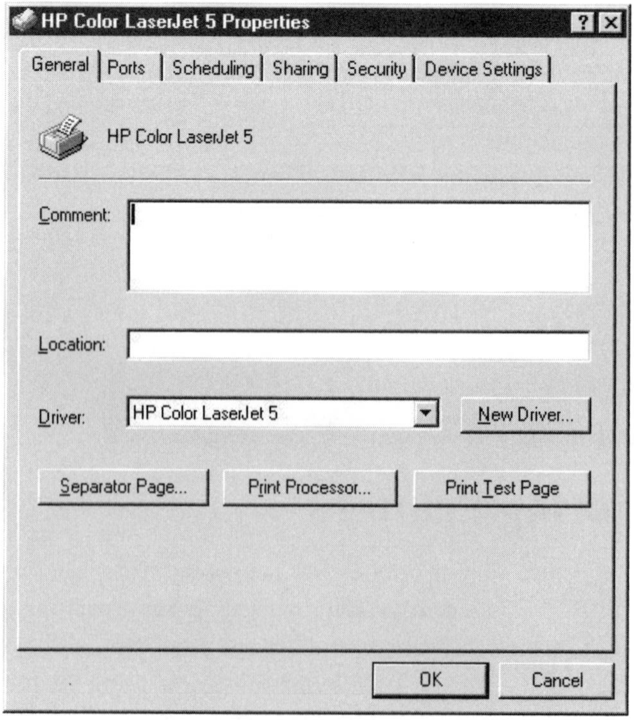

FIGURE 12-3

The Separator Page
identifies the start of a
print job

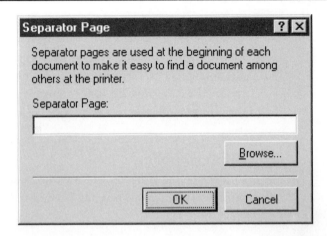

begins. A separator page also is used to switch between PostScript and PCL printing. By default, NT does not print a separator page. You must first configure a separator file. NT provides three separator files:

- **PCL.SEP**   Switches Hewlett-Packard printers to PCL mode for printers not capable of auto-switching. It also prints a separator page before each document. It's located at %systemroot%\system32.

- **PSCRIPT.SEP**   Switches Hewlett-Packard printers to PostScript mode for printers not capable of auto-switching. It's located at %systemroot%\system32.

- **SYSPRINT.SEP**   Prints a separator page for PostScript printers. It's located at %systemroot%\system32.

Print Test Page

Printing a test page prints a document to the printing device. The document lists the .DLLs the print driver uses. Windows NT asks you whether the document printed correctly. If you answer No, a step-by-step Help feature appears, to assist you in troubleshooting the problem.

Ports Tab

The Printer Properties Ports tab, shown in Figure 12-4, lets you choose a port for the printer, and allows you to add or delete ports from your system. This is also where you enable printer pooling. The Configure Port button lets you specify the Transmission Retry Timeout setting. This is the amount of time the printer is allowed not to respond, before NT sends the user notification.

Printer Pooling

Printer pooling is an efficient way to streamline the printing process. It sends print jobs to a pool of printing devices, in which only one printing device

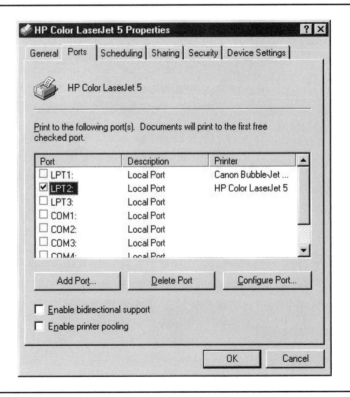

FIGURE 12-4

Choose add and delete ports at the Ports tab

actually prints the document. In order to use printer pooling, you need at least two printing devices that can use the same print driver. The printing devices should be located next to each other, since users aren't notified which printing device actually prints the document.

To create a printer pool, check the Enable Printer Pooling check box and select more than one port to print. Be sure the ports you choose have printing devices that use the same print drivers attached.

Scheduling Tab

The Scheduling tab, shown in Figure 12-5, lets you specify the times the printer is available, and allows you to set the printer's priority. This tab also provides an option to change the way the printer spools.

Priority

Your priority choice tells NT which printer gets to print to the printing device first. Printers with higher priority print before printers with a lower priority. The printer priority can be a range from 1 (the default) to 99. This does not affect the document priority. It is only useful when you have more than one printer printing to the same printing device. A good use of printer priority would be to give the most important users a printer with the highest priority. Then, for less important users, create another printer that has a lower priority. Set the proper permissions (discussed later) and the important people will be given access to the printing device first.

exam
Watch

Be sure to understand that changing the priority of a printer doesn't affect the priority of the print queue. When you use two printers, printing to the same printer device, a printer with a higher priority will print to the device, when it's available, before a printer with a lower priority. If the lower-priority printer is busy printing a document, it finishes printing the job before releasing control to a higher-priority printer.

Set a printer's priority at
the Scheduling tab

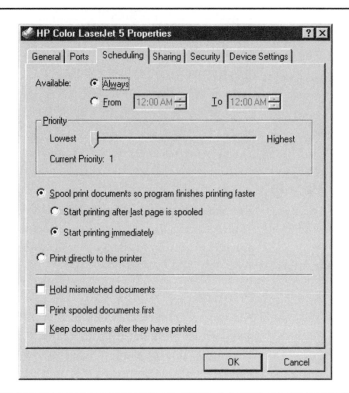

Spooling Options

You can change the spooling options to troubleshoot or speed up your print
jobs. The default is optimized for typical print jobs.

SPOOL PRINT DOCUMENTS VS. PRINT DIRECTLY TO THE
PRINTER   Spooling print documents is the default, and normally shouldn't
be changed. However, if you are troubleshooting a print problem, it might
help to print directly to the printer. If you can print directly to the printer,
except when you spool, you probably have a spooling problem. Spooling is
more efficient than printing directly to the printer, because the printer and the
computer don't have to wait for each other. When you select spooling, you can
have the print job start immediately (default) or after the last page is spooled.

Printing after the last page is spooled might seem like a better choice than starting immediately, but if a user is sending a big print job, it may take a long time before the printer starts printing. It is more efficient to start printing immediately.

HOLD MISMATCHED DOCUMENTS   If a print job is sent to the printer that doesn't match the printing device's configuration, it can cause the printer to hang with an error. To prevent this, choose the Hold Mismatched Documents check box. NT will examine the configuration of the print job and the printing device to make sure that they are in sync before sending the print job to the printing device.

PRINT SPOOLED DOCUMENTS FIRST   By default, NT prints documents on a first-come, first-served basis. By checking the Print Spooled Documents First box, you can have NT print documents that are completely spooled while another document is still spooling, even when the spooling document arrived first.

KEEP DOCUMENTS AFTER THEY HAVE PRINTED   This keeps the document in the printer's queue window, even after the print job is finished printing. This allows all users access to see what print jobs have printed.

Sharing Tab

The Sharing tab, shown in Figure 12-6, is used to share your printer on a network.

Security Tab

The Security tab, shown in Figure 12-7, is where you set permissions for users who print to your printer. It also allows you to enable auditing (if you have auditing turned on in User Manager), and it allows you to take ownership of the printer if you have the proper permissions to do so.

FIGURE 12-6

Use the Sharing tab to
share your printer on a
network

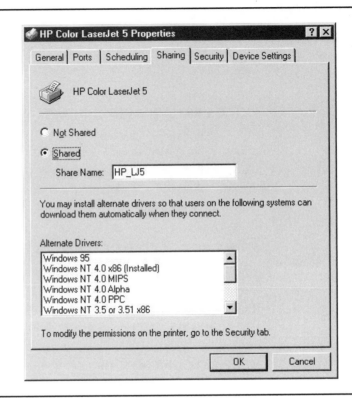

Permissions

Printers are objects that have access control lists. To set permissions, a user
must be an administrator, owner, power user, or a user who has Full Control
permissions assigned. At the Printer Permissions window, shown in Figure
12-8, you can assign four types of permissions to printer objects.

- **No Access**   The user isn't able to access the printer at all. This takes
  precedence over all other permissions. If a user is assigned to a group
  that is allowed Print Access, and a group with No Access, the user
  cannot print, because No Access always takes precedence.

- **Print**   Allows users to print, and to control the setting and print status
  of their own print jobs.

Set permissions, enable
auditing, and take
ownership at the
mSecurity tab

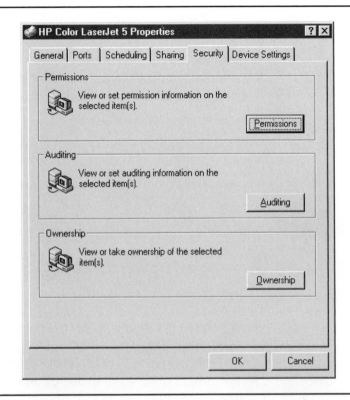

Assigning printer
permissions

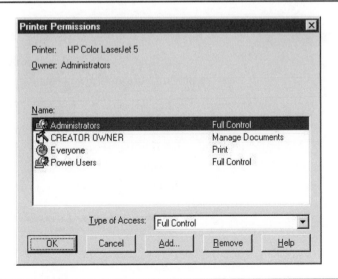

■ **Manage Documents**   Allows the user to print, and to control the settings and print status for all print jobs.

■ **Full Control**   Allows the user to print, and to control the settings and print status for all print jobs, including the printer itself. Users with full control can share, stop sharing, change permissions, take ownership, and delete the printer.

The default permissions for printers, both local and shared, are as follows:

Administrators	Full Control
Creator Owner	Manage Documents
Everyone	Print
Power Users	Full Control

Auditing

Click the Auditing button to audit print events. Figure 12-9 shows the Printer Auditing screen. Just add the users or groups you want to audit, and select which events you want to audit. Audit events show up in the Event Viewer Security log. Before you can audit, you must turn auditing on using User Manager.

Ownership

To take ownership of a printer, just click the Ownership button, then click the Take Ownership button. Once you take ownership, you can't give it back.

Device Settings Tab

The Device Settings tab offers various options, depending on which print driver you are using. Figure 12-10 shows the Device Settings tab for an HP LaserJet 5, and Figure 12-11 shows the Device Settings tab for a Canon BJC-4100.

FIGURE 12-9

At the Printer Auditing
screen add users, groups,
and events to be audited

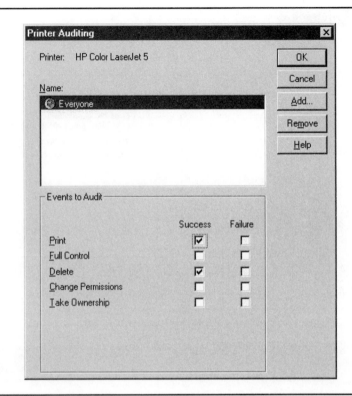

CERTIFICATION OBJECTIVE 12.04

Managing Print Jobs

By default, the creator owner of a print job can manage his own print job.
Figure 12-12 depicts what the screen looks like when you manage a print
queue. Exercise 12-5 will teach you how to manage a print queue.

FIGURE 12-10

Device Settings tab for HP
LaserJet 5

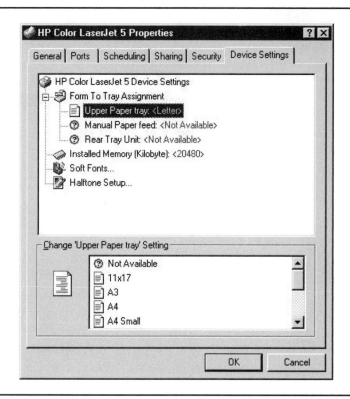

EXERCISE 12-5

Managing Print Jobs

1. Double-click the printer you'll print to in the Printers folder.

2. Choose Printer | Pause Printing on the menu bar. (This is done so the print jobs will remain in the queue for this exercise.)

3. Open a text document on your hard drive using Notepad.

4. Print the document four times.

5. Double-click the Printer icon on the lower-right corner of your task manager to bring up the print queue.

6. Click the second document in the list.

7. On the file menu choose Document | Pause.

8. Resume the print job by choosing Document | Resume.

9. To remove the print job click Document | Cancel.

FIGURE 12-11

Device Settings tab for
BJC-4100

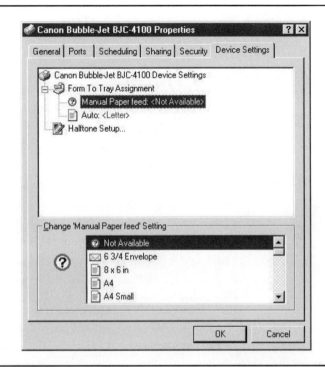

10. To pause all print jobs in the queue select Printer | Pause Printing. (This is the same thing we did in step 2.)

11. Now repeat step 8 on all jobs in the queue to end this exercise.

FIGURE 12-12

Managing a queue of
print jobs

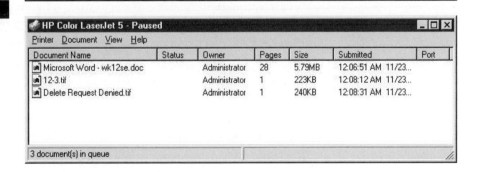

Troubleshooting Printers

If you've worked with computers and networks for any length of time, you know how troublesome printers can be. NT handles printing better than most operating systems, but there can still be problems.

A common problem is when the printer spool file located at the %systemroot%\system32\printers folder runs out of disk space. To prevent this, make sure the drive the spooler is on has plenty of available space. You should also defragment your hard disk. NT doesn't provide a defrag utility, so you'll need to purchase a third-party program. You can move the default spooler location by editing the Registry. Use extreme caution when editing the Registry. Add the value called DefaultSpoolDirectory with type REG_SZ with the new path to the following key:

HKEY_LOCAL_MACHINE\System\CurrentControlset\Control \Print\Printers

You also can change the spool directory for a specific printer by adding the value called DefaultSpoolDirectory with type REG_SZ with the new path to the following key:

HKEY_LOCAL_MACHINE\System\CurrentControlset\Control\Print \Printers\<printer>

Where <printer> is the name of the printer you want to change.

After making these changes, you have to stop and restart the spooler service.

If your system crashes while it has a print job in its spool, it tries to complete the print job after the computer restarts. Sometimes when a system crashes the spooled file becomes corrupt and remains in the spool directory. When this happens you'll need to stop the spooler service, go to the spooling directory, and delete the files that won't print. To determine which files are old, check the time date stamp on the files.

If you have NT Workstation acting as a print server and it appears to be running slowly, you can increase the priority of the spooler service. By default,

NT Workstation assigns a priority of 7 to the spooler service. To change the priority for the spooler service, you'll have to edit the Registry. Add a value called PriorityClass with type REG_DWORD with the value of the priority you want to the following Registry key:

HKEY_LOCAL_MACHINE\System\CurrentControlset\Control\Print

You also can use the Printer Troubleshooting Wizard. To start the Troubleshooting Wizard, print a test page and answer No to the question Did the Test Page Print Correctly?

CERTIFICATION SUMMARY

In this chapter you learned that NT refers to printers as the software that manages the process of sending print jobs to the printing device. You learned how the spooler service manages the process of printing. You also learned about print monitors, print drivers, print processors, print routers and print jobs.

I took you through the steps of creating a local printer and connecting to a remote printer. I explained the difference between a network printer that attaches directly to the network, and a shared network printer that prints via a share on an NT Workstation.

We configured printers to use a separator page, changed the default data type, and shared a printer on the network. We also looked at how to apply permissions security and audit printing.

Finally, I explained some troubleshooting techniques you can use to identify print problems, like changing the default spooling folder.

 # TWO-MINUTE DRILL

- ❑ Printing software is considered the printer. A printer is software that manages a specific printing device (or devices, in case of printer pooling).
- ❑ The printer determines how the print job gets to the printing device.

❑ The graphics device interface controls the display of graphics on the monitor and printers.

❑ Print drivers are the software that allows an application to communicate with printing devices.

❑ The print router routes the print job from the spooler to the appropriate print processor.

❑ The print spooler is the service that actually manages the print process.

❑ Rendering is the process of translating print data into a form that a printing device can read.

❑ Print monitors control access to the printing device, monitor the status of the device, and communicate with the spooler, which relays this information via the user interface.

❑ Print jobs are source code, consisting of both data and commands for print processing.

❑ There are two ways to create printers in NT. You can use the Add Printer Wizard or you can use Point and Print.

❑ Don't confuse a printing device directly connected to the network, with a shared network printer.

❑ Before you can share a printer on the network, you first must create it locally on your computer.

❑ A network printer is a printer that attaches directly to your network. It isn't connected to a computer's serial or parallel port.

❑ Hewlett-Packard JetDirect cards require the DLC protocol to be loaded on your system. DLC is not a routable protocol. Therefore, the print server and the printing device must be on the same side of a router.

❑ How you configure print options depends on the printing device you have and the driver that manages it. Options are configured using the Device Settings tab.

❑ Printer pooling is an efficient way to streamline the printing process. It sends print jobs to a pool of printing devices, in which only one printing device actually prints the document.

❑ Changing the priority of a printer doesn't affect the priority of the print queue.

❑ You can change the spooling options to troubleshoot or speed up your print jobs.

❑ Printers are objects that have Access Control Lists. To set permissions, a user must be an administrator, owner, power user, or a user who has Full Control permissions assigned.

❑ To take ownership of a printer, click the Ownership button, then click the Take Ownership button. Once you take ownership, you can't give it back.

❑ A common printing problem occurs when the printer spool file, located at the %systemroot%\system32\printers folder, runs out of disk space.

❑ You should defrag your hard disk to prevent problems.

❑ Use extreme caution when editing the Registry.

SELF TEST

The following questions will help you measure your understanding of the material presented in this chapter. Read all the choices carefully, as there may be more than one correct answer. Choose all correct answers for each question.

1. What are two advantages of the EMF data type?

   A. It requires less bandwidth to print over the network.

   B. It returns control of the application to the user more quickly.

   C. EMF files can be printed on any printer.

   D. EMF files are in PSCRIPT1 format.

2. What are the two types of print processors shipped with NT?

   A. Windows Print Processor (WINPRINT.DLL)

   B. PostScript Print Processor (PSCRIPT1.DLL)

   C. Macintosh Print Processor (SFMPSPRT)

   D. UNIX Print Processor (LPD)

3. If you want to add an HP JetDirect networked printer to your computer, what two things must you do?

   A. Install DLC protocol on your computer.

   B. Configure the DLC protocol address on the printer.

   C. Print a test page to get the MAC address of the JetDirect Card.

   D. Install AppleTalk on your computer.

4. You shared an HP LaserJet 5 on your system for everyone in your department to use. When users try to connect to the printer using Windows 95, they get the following error: "The server on which the printer resides does not have a suitable driver installed. Click OK if you wish to select a driver to use on your local machine." What should you do to prevent users from receiving this error message?

   A. Share the printer on an NT Server, because Workstation can't provide the correct drivers.

   B. Give them the proper access permissions.

   C. Install an appropriate Windows 95 print driver on your workstation.

   D. Change the default data type to RAW.

5. (True/False) A local printer must have a port on your system.

6. You want to set up a printer pool using two printers. Neither printing device can use a common driver. How can you enable both printing devices to be in a printer pool?

   A. You can set up a printer for each printing device, then add a third printer to manage the two independent printers.

B. Install DLC protocol to bridge the printing drivers.

C. Add both printing devices to the Ports Property page and check Enable Printer Pooling.

D. You can't, because they have to share a common driver.

7. Your boss needs to print to his secretary's printer, but he doesn't want to wait for his print job behind anybody else's print job. How can you share the printer, giving your boss a higher priority?

A. Share the printer and give him full control of the printer.

B. Set the printer to print directly to the printer.

C. Create two printers. On one printer give your boss permissions to print, and set the priority to 99. On the second printer give everyone else permissions to print and set the priority to 1.

D. Create one printer, but share it out twice. On one share give your boss permissions to print, and on the other share give everyone permissions to print.

8. User JamieS sent a print job to an NT Workstation acting as a print server. When she went to the printer to pick up her print job, she noticed a 200-page report was printing out. She didn't want to wait for her print job, so she printed her document on a different printer. JamieS is environmentally conscious, so she doesn't want to waste paper printing the first print job. How can she delete her first print job? (Choose the best answer)

A. Double-click the Printer icon and select her print job, then press the Delete button.

B. She should tell the administrator to delete the print job for her.

C. There is nothing she can do.

D. She should turn off the printer as soon as the 200-page report finishes printing.

9. To what group must a user be added before he can manage other people's print jobs? (Choose all that apply)

A. Administrators

B. Creator Owner

C. Power Users

D. Users

10. Drive C: has 10MB of available disk space on it. Drive D: has 300MB of disk space available. Windows NT is installed on Drive C:, which is almost out of space. Sometimes when you print, your computer locks up and you have to restart your system. What should you do to prevent this problem in the future?

A. Use Disk Administrator to combine the two drives as one logical drive.

B. Use Explorer and move your WINNT directory to the D: drive.

C. Move the printer spooler to the D: drive.

D. Move the print monitor to the D: drive.

13

Configuring
Applications

T his chapter provides you with a background on the Windows NT architecture for supporting applications—more specifically, the subsystem architecture that allows you to run many different types of applications from DOS and 16-bit Windows programs, even OS/2 and POSIX applications. You will learn how these subsystems communicate with each other, and with the Windows NT operating system. You also will learn how applications can be configured under these various subsystems. Supporting applications is an important portion of the exam. For this reason, we will cover the ways you can start applications to increase their performance as well as their stability and how applications affect each other and the system.

CERTIFICATION OBJECTIVE 13.01

Subsystem Architecture

Windows NT uses modular components for the subsystem architecture that enable compatibility for applications. These subsystems provide the application programming interfaces (APIs) that are specific to the operating system they are mimicking. This specificity is the reason there are several environment subsystems, such as OS/2, POSIX, and the Virtual DOS Machine. The subsystems are run in User Mode and are 32-bit, preemptively multitasked with other applications on the system.

Looking at Figure 13-1, you can see just how important the primary Win32 subsystem is to the rest of the environment subsystems. These other subsystems call upon the Win32 subsystem with requests for translation. You will learn more about the Win32 subsystem later in the chapter.

Figure 13-1 also shows how each subsystem not only communicates with the Win32 subsystem for translation, but with the Windows NT Executive Services. The subsystems are communicating with each other by passing messages through the *Local Procedure Call Facility,* which we will discuss later. I mention this message-passing facility to show you that subsystems do communicate by requesting and providing services to each other, invisible to you. The subsystems also call on the system services, because that is the only way they can gain access to the NT Executive.

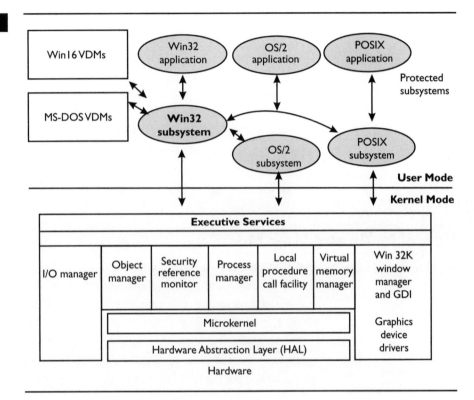

FIGURE 13-1

The Subsystem Architecture, with the Executive Services components

Subsystems

Environment subsystems enable Windows NT to remain compatible with existing software. Windows NT provides support for various subsystems and Virtual DOS Machines.

- MS-DOS VDM
- Win16 VDM
- OS/2 subsystem
- POSIX subsystem
- Win32 subsystem

All of these subsystems are protected from each other to prevent errant applications from affecting other applications running in a different subsystem. They too are run in User Mode, so as not to affect the performance of the critical system components, such as the Executive Services.

Another subsystem, called the Client Server Runtime Subsystem (CSRSS), provides console, shutdown, and error handling functions to the other environment subsystems. This subsystem is not covered in this chapter, because it does not provide a subsystem for applications to run. There are also integral subsystems, such as the security subsystem, which are very important, but not for the purpose of running applications.

Kernel Mode and User Mode

The difference between Kernel Mode and User Mode concerns whether or not direct access to the hardware is given. Kernel Mode, otherwise known as Privileged Mode, has this capability. Only a select few components are run in Kernel Mode. This is to provide stability by limiting the amount of components that are allowed to access the hardware. If every component or application were allowed to directly access the hardware, chances are the system would continually crash as these components or applications made incorrect or improper function calls.

User Mode is the mode in which the majority of Windows NT code, environment subsystems, and all of the applications are run. This is also known as Nonprivileged Mode, because it is not privileged to access the hardware directly. It must have its calls to the hardware intercepted and translated by the NT Executive Services before processing. There is a concern that some applications will need to access the hardware directly, but unfortunately, they cannot be run on Windows NT. Since Windows NT has restricted access in this way, it has become a very stable operating system. Unless you have applications that are unsupported due to this restriction, you will be very pleased with the stability that NT provides.

Kernel Mode Components

The Kernel Mode is comprised of several components that work together to maintain the system. As mentioned before, this mode has full access to the system hardware. Only a select few components run in this mode.

Windows NT Executive Services

The Windows NT Executive Services, combined with the NT Kernel, are at the top of the Kernel Mode component hierarchy. The Executive Services have separate components that perform the various operating system functions. The following components each have a responsibility to carry out a specific function when called upon.

OBJECT MANAGER   The Object Manager is responsible for the creation and use of objects. This includes naming, managing, and security for objects. Objects are everywhere in Windows NT, and have a type, various attributes, and a set of operations. They can be physical devices such as a COM port, or they can be abstract, such as a thread. Other parts of the operating system and programs access these objects by the name of the object. The Object Manager gets a request, and uses an *object handler* to provide a pointer to locate the actual object and the information about the object. The Object Manager also cleans up objects that have been orphaned. These orphaned objects might consume system resources if not properly terminated.

PROCESS MANAGER   The Process Manager is responsible for process and thread objects, including deleting, creating, and managing these objects. A process is a program, or a part of a program, that has an address space, contains objects, and spawns threads that need to be processed. A process object, which is overseen by the Process Manager, watches over the threads that it produces, including their priorities and the amount of time they spend in execution. The Kernel itself is responsible for scheduling these threads to be processed.

VIRTUAL MEMORY MANAGER   The Virtual Memory Manager (VMM) is responsible for the use of virtual memory and the paging file in the system. The VMM keeps track of all mapping between the physical and virtual memory. It is responsible for swapping the pages in and out of memory as needed. This can be a demanding task, because you can have up to 4GB of virtual memory, thanks to the 32-bit flat memory model. Half of the virtual memory is reserved for the operating system storage, and the other half is for applications.

LOCAL PROCEDURE CALL FACILITY   The Local Procedure Call Facility is responsible for passing information between processes. Applications make calls to the environment subsystem for service. This relationship is based on a client/server model. This is not the client/server model you are familiar with, such as an NT Server sharing files to workstations on the network. The client/server relationship in this respect is within one computer. The applications or processes (clients) requiring service make calls to the environment subsystem (server). This is a local procedure call, and this is how the Local Procedure Call Facility got its name. If you are familiar with the Remote Procedure Call (RPC), you can see that the Local Procedure Call (LPC) works the same way, only it is local to the machine.

SECURITY REFERENCE MONITOR   The Security Reference Monitor is responsible for access to the resources in the system. It has to provide validation for users, access to objects, and generating audit messages. This is also a very demanding task, because Windows NT has a great deal of security, even down to the file level. The Security Reference Monitor works with the logon process and security subsystem to make up the entire security model for the system. The Security Reference Model uses the logon process to verify that a user has access to the system. After the user has been granted permission to access the system, there is still constant access validation to verify that the user has access to the object. Successful and failed attempts to access resources also have to be audited by the Security Reference Monitor.

I/O MANAGER   The I/O Manager is responsible for all input and output for the operating system. Since input and output usually are handled by hardware devices, the I/O Manager has to spend a great deal of time communicating with the device drivers. These drivers, as we will see later in the section, are for communicating with the various devices in the system. The I/O Manager communicates with the drivers so it does not have to be aware of how the device functions. It only calls upon the driver to perform the functions. In addition to communicating with the device drivers, the I/O Manager communicates with the file systems and the Cache Manager, which are subcomponents. The I/O Manager must route information to the file system drivers to be able to access the drivers for the devices. It also communicates with the redirector to access files stored on a network file system, just as it does with the local file system. The Cache Manager is responsible for managing the cache for the entire system, and is controlled by the I/O Manager.

GRAPHICS DEVICE INTERFACE AND WINDOWS MANAGEMENT (USER)   The Graphics Device Interface (GDI) is the graphics engine. It is responsible for communication between applications and the graphics devices. Applications call on the GDI for graphic output, and in turn the GDI calls upon the graphics device driver. This is another example of the Kernel Mode components using a driver to communicate with the hardware in the system. Kernel Mode components can communicate to any driver in the same way. Developers can make use of this powerful GDI to make their work easier, adding only hardware-specific code to their drivers and letting the GDI do most of the work.

The Window Manager (USER) is the component that creates the screen interface for the user. When applications call on USER functions, the call is communicated to the GDI, which in turn communicates with the device drivers to perform the function. An interesting fact about the Window Manager is that it draws 16-bit application windows using the Win32 GDI functions. This explains why my old applications appeared different when I first ran them on the new operating system. The dialog boxes were drawn differently, and the placement of the buttons had changed.

Both the Graphics Device Interface and the Window Manager ran in User Mode in the Win32 subsystem in previous releases of NT, but now have been moved into the Windows NT Executive, which runs in Kernel Mode. This will speed up calls to the graphics devices by reducing the amount of costly translation calls from User Mode to Kernel Mode. For example, Microsoft's PowerPoint, a graphically intensive multimedia application, resulted in a 15-20% increase in performance compared to Windows NT 3.51.

DEVICE DRIVERS   Device drivers are used to communicate with the various hardware components in the system. These drivers are just small programs that are called upon when the system needs to communicate with the device. The Executive Services are designed so that the Kernel Mode components communicate with every device the same way. The device driver is what performs the specific features of the device. Although some device drivers can be used to communicate with many different devices, it is more common to see a device driver for each device, including drivers for each brand and model of the device. Finding compatible drivers to work with Windows NT is a concern. The number of device drivers for NT is limited, and you cannot use other operating system drivers.

Microkernel

The Microkernel, or Kernel, is the core of the Windows NT operating system. Before we get too specific, we should say that the Kernel is responsible for all actions that take place on the system. This means that the Kernel is extremely busy and very important, because most system functions have to pass through it. The Kernel uses modular components to help with the various system operations. These components all work together, and are known as the Executive Services, which we have been discussing. The Kernel is not only a member of the Executive Services, but also is the head of the Executive Services. It is responsible for scheduling and managing threads, and handling exceptions and interrupts. Interrupts are natural, common occurrences in the system, but exceptions occur when a process has performed an operation that is not permitted, such as writing to a portion of memory already in use, or dividing by zero.

Hardware Abstraction Layer

The Hardware Abstraction Layer (HAL) is the layer between the operating system and the hardware located in the computer. The HAL is what makes NT able to be ported to other architectures. A new HAL is required for different architectures, and you even require a new HAL for a multiprocessor system. For this reason, there are two Hardware Abstraction Layers provided for each processor architecture: one for a single processor configuration, and one for a multiprocessor configuration. The goal is to write the new HAL to allow for different architectures, and to compile the rest of the operating system code.

CERTIFICATION OBJECTIVE 13.02

Configuring Applications

In order to get some applications to run in Windows NT, you may have to do some configuring of the application or environment. Most applications run just fine, but you still may want to maximize their performance, or increase their stability. In subsequent exercises, you will see how to do this using the various types of applications and subsystems. You also will see how applications can be adjusted on a per-application basis, and how the environment can be adjusted so that subsequent applications use the same settings. Refer to Figure 13-2 for an overview of the applications and memory spaces.

FIGURE 13-2

Applications and their associated architectures

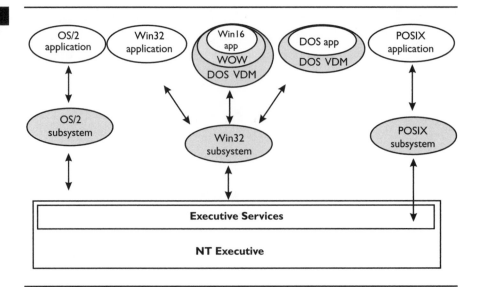

FROM THE CLASSROOM

Zen and the Art of Performance Monitoring

The most prevalent mistake, made by users and students alike, when attempting performance monitoring, is not getting *baseline data*. Baseline data must be collected when you first set up NT, and before you load any applications or connect the computer to the network. Think of baseline data as the performance characteristics of your computer before you ask it to do any work—how your machine performs without a load. Without this baseline, it is literally impossible to discern the health of your computer, or how well it is performing under given conditions, or load.

We get calls from clients all the time with questions like: "My computer seems slow, what can we do about this?" You can imagine what our first question to them is: "What evidence do you have to support this conclusion?" We invariably get back the response: "It just *feels* slower."

Believe me when I tell you that there are two people in your life who really like to cater to your feelings: your psychiatrist, and your time-and-expenses consultant. And neither works cheap! The good news for you is that, as a consulting engineer, I actually can quantify for you the variables that comprise your feelings

FROM THE CLASSROOM

about your computer. Once we quantify these variables, we can measure them across time. Thus, we can measure the relative performance of your computer.

It is the *relative* performance of your computer that is the important issue. Relative to what, you ask? Relative to how it was performing before you made changes, or added hardware or software. Relative to the performance you measured when you first got the computer. Relative to the baseline data.

First, you establish what performance criteria are important to you. Then you run the test, using Performance Monitor, to establish the baseline data. Each time you make a change, such as a configuration change, or adding hardware or software, you again run the performance measurement test that you ran to create your baseline. This process tells you exactly what performance impact the changes you made have created.

There is one more important fact about baseline data. All computer systems have different performance characteristics, even if you buy them from the same manufacturer at the same time. The individual components in the system perform differently. Therefore, it is important that you establish a baseline on each individual computer. Yes, I know what you're thinking. We hear it all the time from our clients and students when we make this suggestion. "Who has time to do all of this? And exactly what drugs are you taking?"

Experience has shown us that a little work up front saves a lot of work later. Deep down in your hearts, you all know the truth of that statement. On the other hand, as time-and-expenses consultants, we really appreciate the attitude that you are too busy to do all this preparatory work. That's what keeps us in business! Thank you.

—By Shane Clawson, MCT, MCSE

Win32 Applications

The Win32 subsystem is the primary subsystem for Windows NT. This is where most of your applications designed for Windows 95 and NT are run. These Win32 applications give you the most performance and stability, because they are designed to run on Windows NT, a Win32 operating system. You don't spend as much time trying to get these applications to run as you would with DOS or Win16 applications. If you are using 16-bit versions of programs, you will see better results after upgrading these programs to the 32-bit version.

Win32 is what provides the user interface, as well as control for the input devices such as the mouse and keyboard. When an application is running from another subsystem, it must have its calls directed through the Win32 subsystem for translation. You will learn more about this technique, called *thunking*, later in the section. For now just understand how important this subsystem is. It doesn't even appear that other subsystems are running, because you see the Win32 subsystem user interface the whole time you are running NT. If it is not the familiar Windows interface, then it is the character-based window, called a *console*.

This subsystem uses a separate memory space and message queue for each application. This provides stability if one of the applications were to crash. The other Win32 applications would remain unaffected. As a matter of fact, any other applications running are not affected if a Win32 application crashes or hangs.

Although it appears as if the DOS and Win16 Virtual DOS Machines (VDMs) are separate, they actually are a part of the Win32 subsystem. It's easier to understand how these VDMs work when they are isolated from the Win32 subsystem for discussion.

EXERCISE 13-1

Viewing the Processes in NT as You Run a Win32 Program

1. Make sure you are logged on as Administrator of the system.

2. Press CTRL-ALT-DEL to bring up the NT Security dialog box.

3. Click the Task Manager button.

4. Click the Processes tab.

5. Start the NT calculator by typing **CALC** in the Run dialog box. (Start Menu | Run.)

6. Notice that CALC.EXE now appears on the processes list. No other components are needed to run this application.

7. Close the calculator.

8. Exit the Windows NT Task Manager.

Multithreading

Windows NT Win32 applications can be multithreaded for increased performance. These 32-bit applications are designed to have more than one thread for the process. These multiple threads can be executed on any processor in the system. Threads in general are a good idea for performance. If processes were not broken down into smaller threads, one large file could take a long time to execute, and cause the other processes to wait their turn. Smaller threads can be executed in such a rapid manner that they appear to let many applications run at one time. Of course, on a single processor system these threads cannot be run at the exact same time. However, with a multiprocessor system you receive this benefit of multithreading between the processors on the system. Now you can have threads executing at the same time. These threads can be from the same process, or different processes.

Memory Space

The default for Win32 applications is to use a separate memory space. This separate memory space prevents an application from affecting other applications and the operating system if it becomes unstable. You won't see an option to run these applications in their own memory space, because they are already run in their own space by default.

Message Queues

Just as with the memory space, Win32 applications use separate message queues. When we say separate, we mean separate from every other running Win32 application, as well as separate from the 16-bit applications. These Win32-based applications provide better recovery if an application crashes or hangs. In other words, the application can still receive events from its own message queue. If the message queue were one large queue for all applications, one application could stop another from receiving its messages. You will see later in the chapter how Win16 applications use the message queue by default. You can compare and contrast the use of message queues between the two, and how applications are affected.

Base System Priorities

Processes have base system priorities, and the threads that are spawned from the processes inherit the priority of the process. However, these priorities can be altered. Priorities are assigned to threads and processes so the highest priority processes or threads, most likely system processes, are processed first. Executing threads based on priority is one method that preemptive multitasking uses to multitask applications. The other method is to use a time slice, known as a *time quantum*, that executes a thread until the time slice has expired for that thread. The next thread in line will then be processed.

You can start applications at different priority levels from the command line. This is useful if you know beforehand that you would like this application to be more responsive to requests, or less responsive. If you do not alter the priority of an application, it runs at the default priority level of 7. This is on a priority level of 0 - 31, with 31 being the highest priority. When an application is in the foreground, it receives a priority boost to level 9. Here are the different levels you can start an application in:

/LOW, which begins the application at the priority level of 4. This is considered the IDLE priority class.

/HIGH, which begins the application at the priority level of 13. This is considered the HIGH priority class.

/REALTIME, which begins the application at the priority level of 24. This is considered the REALTIME priority class.

Of course, if you do not specify a priority level when starting the application, it receives the default priority class of 7, which is considered the NORMAL priority class. Assigning a new priority class should be done with caution, because a high priority such as REALTIME can put a tremendous strain on your system. REALTIME applications do have the advantage of not being paged to disk, and that can be very useful. You can try these priority levels on your own computer, but try not to mess with them too much in a business environment unless you know what you are doing.

In addition to adjusting priority levels from the command prompt, you can adjust priority levels for the applications using the Windows NT Task Manager. The applications are running processes that can be adjusted. One application may have more than one process, but in most cases you can tell which process correlates with the program you would like to alter. For example, I have Microsoft Word open, and the process that appears for Word is WinWord. I can right-click WinWord and choose Set Priority to adjust the priority level. You have the same priority level options here as you did from the command prompt. WinWord is currently running at the default of Normal. It is a little off the subject, but you can also start applications as minimized or maximized from the command prompt. Here is the syntax for starting the applications either minimized or maximized:

START /MIN application_name

START /MAX application_name

exam
ⓦatch

You probably will be asked on the test to choose the correct command line for starting an application, based on the situation. This will include the priority levels, separate memory space, and whether it will be minimized or maximized. Know your syntax! You can type START /? |MORE at the command prompt for an overview.

FROM THE CLASSROOM

Using NT and Applications, or What's It Like to Pop Corn Without a Lid?

There are really three different categories of programs in NT. Let's talk about POSIX programs, 32-bit programs, and the old stuff (DOS and 16-bit Windows programs). We are not going to talk about OS/2 programs, because the out-of-the-box NT runs only 16-bit character-based OS/2 applications. That is assuming you actually had an OS/2 application that you wanted to run!

On to the big three, and let's start with the easy one. In every class I teach, I ask the students to raise their hands if they have, or are running, any POSIX applications. In a class full of students, it is not unusual that no one raises a hand. Not because they are too shy—the NT class mix these days always includes a contingent of UNIX people who have come to see what NT is all about. Undaunted by the no-show of hands, I ask, "OK, who knows what

FROM THE CLASSROOM

POSIX *is*?" In a room full of UNIX Admin types, this question brings some interesting responses, such as, "It's another variant of UNIX" or, "It's the follow-up effort to LINUX." In the rare case where somebody actually knows what POSIX is, I ask if he is running any POSIX-compliant applications. I get to interact with 120 different clients a year, and I have yet to find anyone who is running a POSIX application (or who will admit to it, anyway). The key thing to remember about the POSIX subsystem is that it is not running unless you start a POSIX application. I guess even Bill G. figured this wouldn't be a big seller.

By now I suspect that everyone is aware that there are 32-bit Windows application programs. There are two points to focus on relative to 32-bit programs. First, not all 32-bit programs run on Windows NT. We've had a number of students tell us that they bought a 32-bit

program, only to find it wouldn't run on Windows NT. Be sure to check before you break the shrink-wrapping. Just like the sign in the china shop, "You break it, you buy it!" The second point is that you really want your 32-bit program to have an uninstall program, and you want this program to remove any Registry entries that the installation program put there.

The final NT program category is DOS programs. When you make the decision to put NT on the desktop, you really are leaving the world of DOS behind. This troubles many of our clients. We are amazed at how traumatized some of them feel at having to replace their DOS programs. In some cases, we've had clients spend more money on our consulting services than it would cost to replace their DOS programs with the good stuff. We try to encourage them to leave the past behind.

—By Shane Clawson, MCT, MCSE

DOS Applications

Windows NT can run MS-DOS applications as well as, or even better than DOS can. This is amazing when you consider that Windows NT does not have any DOS code at all. These DOS applications are run in a Win32 application called the NTVDM, or NT Virtual DOS Machine. Each VDM has its own address space, and can be preemptively multitasked with other applications on the system. This is where you see the performance increase. You also can have multiple VDMs running on the same system. The DOS application running in the VDM is fooled into thinking it has full access to the system resources, just as it did when it was run in its native operating system. Windows NT even uses Virtual Device Drivers (VDDs) to trick applications that require sole use of a device. This might not work every time an application requires direct access to the hardware. Unfortunately, Windows NT does not allow direct access to the hardware for applications, so these applications probably will not run on NT. No amount of configuring changes the fact that the application requires direct access to the hardware.

EXERCISE 13-2

Viewing the Processes in NT as You Run a DOS Program

1. Make sure that you are logged on as Administrator of the system.
2. Press CTRL-ALT-DEL to invoke the NT Security dialog box.
3. Click Task Manager.
4. Click the Processes tab.
5. Use the Start Menu | Programs | Command Prompt to open a command prompt, which is CMD.EXE.
6. Notice in Task Manager that CMD.EXE appears as an only process.
7. Type **QBASIC** in the Command Prompt window. Now look in Task Manager and see the NTVDM process that has been created for the QBASIC program. This is because QBASIC is a DOS program that requires the NTVDM to function.
8. In the QBASIC window, press ESC to clear the dialog box. You can now exit the Command Prompt window by pressing ALT, then F for file, and then X for Exit.
9. Type **exit** to close our Command Prompt window.
10. You can see the CMD.EXE and NTVDM no longer appear in Task Manager.
11. You can now close Task Manager.

VDM Components

These are the key components to the Virtual DOS Machine:

- NTIO.SYS, the equivalent of the IO.SYS file
- NTDOS.SYS, the equivalent of the MSDOS.SYS file

- NTVDM.EXE, VDM component
- NTVDM.DLL, VDM component
- REDIR.EXE, the redirector for the VDM

Virtual Device Drivers

As we indicated earlier, Virtual Device Drivers (VDDs) are used to trick an application into believing it is communicating with a device. Windows NT has provided these VDDs for the mouse, keyboard, printer, COM ports, and for network support. These VDDs are loaded in every VDM, with settings based on the Registry entries. The following Registry key is for VDD information:

HKEY_LOCAL_MACHINE\System\CurrentControlSet\Control\
VirtualDeviceDrivers

Configuring DOS Applications

Just as you did in Windows 95 and Windows 3.*x*, you can configure the Program Information File (PIF) for a DOS application, only this time it is the Properties dialog box for the application. There is no longer a PIF editor for this purpose. The Properties dialog box configures the environment for the DOS application when it is running in Windows. In other words, you are configuring the VDM. The PIF for the application is automatically created in the same directory as the executable for the application. If there is no PIF associated for the application, then the _DEFAULT.PIF will be used. The default values for the VDM may be sufficient to run the application, but if the application still refuses to run, we can make adjustments to the program properties.

Some DOS programs allow you to right-click them and configure a number of environment settings for the application. You need to make a shortcut to others before you can modify the environment settings. For example, you can use the CMD.EXE in the %SystemRoot%\System32 directory. This program is available for each installation of Windows NT Workstation, so we will use it. If you right-click CMD.EXE, you see only a few tabs, most likely General, Version, and Security. We need to make a shortcut to the CMD.EXE program before we can adjust any of the properties. The quickest way to create a shortcut is to right-click CMD.EXE, and select Create Shortcut. You should now be on the shortcut, so go ahead and right-click the shortcut that we just made. You should now see more tabs that can be used to adjust the environment for the DOS program. Here are a few things you can adjust that are useful:

- On the Shortcut tab, shown in Figure 13-3, you can place the cursor in the Shortcut Key area and press a key to make this the hot key that opens this application. I use function keys for this. This also works for other applications, such as Explorer. You can make a shortcut to the Windows NT Explorer and give it a hot key so that whenever you press the hot key, Explorer comes up. This is convenient for commonly used programs.

- If you would like the dialog box to be opened full screen rather than windowed, use the Full Screen display option under the Options tab.

- Also on the Options tab, you can click the QuickEdit mode check box to allow the use of the mouse in the DOS environment.

- The Font tab lets you change the size of the font for the environment.

- The Colors tab lets you change the color of the characters and background for your environment.

Of course, there are many more settings available to configure a custom DOS environment for the application. These settings can be adjusted on a per-application basis, or you can configure your shortcut to the Command prompt so that every time you click it, the environment receives your custom settings. This can be done by finding the shortcut to the Command Prompt under your profile. I am logged on as Administrator of this machine, so I would look under Winnt\Profiles\Administrator\Start Menu\Programs. You should now see the shortcut. Right-click this shortcut and make the necessary changes to the environment that you wish. These changes will be available every time you click this shortcut.

FIGURE 13-3

Configuring DOS
applications at the Shortcut
tab in Properties

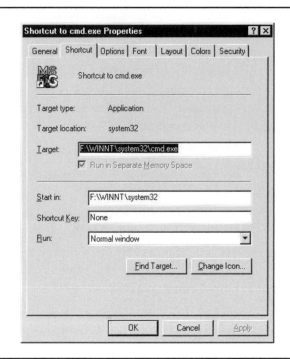

There are some DOS applications that let you configure even more than
what we just saw in the previous example. For these applications you would
just right-click the icon for the program. For example, I have used the
BACKUP.EXE in the %SystemRoot%\System32 directory. When you
right-click this application you see a few tabs that were different from the
CMD.EXE properties. (Once again, I used BACKUP.EXE as an example,
because everyone should have this in a Windows NT installation. I tried
clicking on the BACKUP.EXE after I configured the environment, but this is
not a type of DOS application that is meant to be clicked from Windows. You
can adjust the properties of your favorite DOS-based applications rather than
for these applications that I have shown you.)

Returning back to the properties for BACKUP.EXE, we see four new tabs:
Program, Memory, Screen, and Misc. Program has most of the same settings
that the Shortcut tab does for the CMD.EXE shortcut that we saw in Figure
13-3. Here is a summary of the available features of each of the tabs.

■ The Memory tab is where you configure how much initial memory to give to the application. If you do not give the application enough memory, it doesn't run. If you give it too much memory, you leave less memory available for other applications. You can adjust the amount of conventional, expanded, or extended memory to give this application. If you would like a more detailed description of the various settings, click the ? at the top right of the dialog box, and then click any topic that you would like to know more about. A dialog box appears with more information on that topic.

■ The Screen tab is where you can adjust settings for Usage, Window, and Performance. The most useful feature here is the ability to start the program in a window or full screen. Once again, use the Help feature for more information on these settings.

■ The Misc tab has many different settings to change, including foreground and background response, as well as Windows shortcut keys. Use the Help feature to find more information for these settings.

There are also two configuration files that can be adjusted for environment variables, called CONFIG.NT and AUTOEXEC.NT. They reside in the %SystemRoot%\System32 directory of your computer (see Figure 13-4), and work just the way you would expect from the equivalent DOS files. When the VDM is loaded, it processes these two files. Here is where you can place commands and environmental settings that you would like to be loaded with every VDM.

Adjust two configuration files at the Windows NT PIF Settings dialog box

Windows NT PIF Settings   [?] [X]

Custom MS-DOS Initialization Files

Autoexec Filename: `%SystemRoot%\SYSTEM32\AUTOEXEC.NT`   [OK]

Config Filename: `%SystemRoot%\SYSTEM32\CONFIG.NT`   [Cancel]

☐ Compatible Timer Hardware Emulation

You can reach this Windows NT PIF settings dialog box by the Programs tab when you right-click a DOS application. Click the button called Windows NT.

When you have configured your DOS applications, there is something that you should be aware of. First, the NTVDM is not loaded until you start your first DOS application. Every other DOS application that you start after the first DOS application uses the VDM that was created by the first application. If subsequently you were to start an application that had custom environment settings that you specified, your changes would not be in effect. This is because it was not the first VDM loaded, and it's inheriting the settings of the first VDM. You would have to start the custom application first to take advantage of the settings that you specified.

There is a chance that your DOS applications won't run for another reason. Some DOS applications check to see if you are running the correct version of DOS. You can find out what version of DOS you are running yourself by typing VER at the command prompt. If you type VER while in Windows NT 4, you receive the answer: Windows NT Version 4.0. But the VDM reports DOS version 5.0 to the application that is checking. This could cause the application not to run, if it requires a higher version of DOS than 5.0. This can be remedied easily with the program included with DOS, SETVER. This lets you trick the application into thinking it is running in the correct version of DOS. It reports the version of DOS that you specify to the application.

Win16 Applications

There is a huge need for Windows NT to remain compatible with the large amount of 16-bit programs still in existence. The last statistic that I heard concerning operating systems was that Windows 3.*x* still retains the market share for desktop operating systems. This might seem strange to the more advanced user like ourselves who demand performance, reliability, and stability, and continue to upgrade to the latest and greatest operating systems. •However, many businesses still have these 16-bit applications. They rely on these applications for important facets of their company, including accounting, record keeping, and payroll. You'd better have a compelling reason to migrate or upgrade these applications if they are being used for these critical purposes.

I cannot believe some of the applications we still use at our company are compatible with Windows NT. If these applications were not compatible with NT, there would be a gigantic concern over migrating to NT. There is still a concern if you find an application that can be replaced with a newer version, or a product from another vendor that performs the same function. You have to migrate the data, or even worse, re-create the data. This is why application support is so important to the design of Windows NT. It is important to understand how these Win16 applications are run in Windows NT. You may find yourself having to configure these applications, or troubleshoot a faulty application. If you know how these Win16 applications are run by default, you are halfway to understanding how they can be configured if the default is not acceptable.

16-bit Windows applications run in a Virtual DOS Machine with another layer for the Win16 functionality. These applications by default are run in a single VDM, with a single thread for processing. This VDM can be preemptively multitasked with the other applications in the system. However, the 16-bit applications within the VDM are cooperatively multitasked with each other. This is very important to remember, not only for the exam, but also for troubleshooting purposes. Preemptively multitasking the single VDM with other applications can increase the performance of the Win16 applications. This also protects other applications that are running on the system from being affected if another VDM becomes unstable. Cooperatively multitasking the Win16 applications by default still leaves them prone to simultaneously crashing or hanging, just as they did in their native 16-bit environment. We will see later in this section how using a separate memory space for these Win16 applications can help performance.

Since Win16 applications require DOS to function, the same rules apply in terms of access to the hardware. If this Win16 application needs to have direct access to the hardware, it doesn't function. To illustrate the fact that these Win16 applications require DOS (or what we now use as the NTVDM) to function, watch the results of the following exercise.

Viewing the Processes in NT as You Run Win16 Programs

1. Make sure you are logged on to the system as Administrator.
2. Press CTRL-ALT-DEL to bring up the NT Security dialog box.

3. Click the Task Manager button.

4. Click the Processes tab.

5. Find a 16-bit application on your system and start the application.

6. If you have Task Manager open while you are starting the 16-bit application, you will see it load the NTVDM.EXE, then the WOWEXEC.EXE, then the application itself.

7. Start another instance of the 16-bit application, or if it does not let you, start another 16-bit application while you are running the first one.

8. Notice how the second 16-bit application runs in the same NTVDM as the first. You can continue to open more 16-bit applications and they will continue to appear under the same NTVDM.

9. Exit all of the applications that you have just started, and notice the NTVDM and WOWEXEC still remain.

10. Exit the Windows NT Task Manager.

WOW Components

When 16-bit applications are being run they need to communicate with the primary Win32 subsystem. As noted earlier, the Win32 subsystem is responsible for translating requests from the applications in the various other subsystems. These 16-bit subsystems use a process known as *thunking* to translate between the 16-bit and 32-bit requests. WOW, which stands for Win16-on-Win32, is this translation layer. There are several components in addition to the VDM involved for the WOW.

- **WOWEXEC.EXE** The program for the Windows 3.x emulation.

- **KRNL386.EXE** The modified version of the Windows 3.x kernel used for translating kernel operations.

- **USER.EXE** A modified version of the Windows 3.x file of the same name used for translating user operations.

- **GDI.EXE** Is also a modified version of the Windows 3.x file of the same name used for translating graphics functions.

Remember that the Win32 detects the Win16 executable and loads the NTVDM. Once the NTVDM is started, the WOW environment is loaded.

You witnessed this in the preceding exercise. Subsequent Win16 applications are run using this same NTVDM and WOW environment that was just created.

Separate Memory

Running 16-bit programs in separate memory spaces can be effective if you are using older 16-bit applications that are not very stable. The faulty 16-bit application can be isolated and run separately from the other applications in its own memory space. If the application were to crash or hang in this separate memory space, it would not affect the other applications running. This does require more memory, so not every Win16 application should be run in a separate memory space. These unstable 16-bit applications are ideal candidates for separate memory space. Be warned that some Win16 applications expect to share a memory space with other applications, and if you are running applications in a separate memory space they cannot communicate.

As you can see from Figure 13-5, you can check the box to indicate that you would like the 16-bit application to start in a separate memory space.

There is another way to configure Win16 applications to run in a separate memory space. It is through use of the command line. This method is useful if you would like to run this application in separate memory for one instance only. Here is the syntax for the command:

START /SEPARATE application_name

FIGURE 13-5

Choose to start an application in a separate memory space

If you were to not include the SEPARATE parameter, the 16-bit application would start in the default environment, which is in the same memory space as the other 16-bit applications.

Configuring Win16 Applications

Rather than constantly starting an application in a separate memory space, you can configure the Win16 application to start in a separate memory space every time you execute the program. This is demonstrated in the next exercise.

EXERCISE 13-4

Creating a Shortcut for a Win16 Application that Executes Separately

Locate a 16-bit application on your system that can be used for the next exercise. You will know it is a 16-bit application when the option to run the application in a separate memory space becomes available.

1. Find the executable for the application, and drag the application to the desktop. This creates a shortcut.
2. With the icon on the desktop, right-click it and select Properties.
3. Click the Shortcut tab.
4. Under the target path for the application, check the box to run in a Separate Memory space.
5. Click OK to save your changes.

Every time you start the program using this shortcut, it will be started in a separate memory space. You also can make a shortcut for the application not to run in the separate memory space. You then will have the choice of starting the application the way you choose.

There is another way to find out if you are using a 16-bit or 32-bit application. The next exercise shows you how.

EXERCISE 13-5

Determining if an Application is 16-bit or 32-bit

1. Press CTRL-ALT-DEL to open the Security dialog box.
2. Click Task List
3. The Windows NT Task Manager now appears. Click the Processes tab.

4. In the Options pull down menu, make sure that Show 16-bit Tasks is checked.

5. If there are any 16-bit applications currently running on the system, they are indented under the NTVDM.EXE, and also have the WOWEXEC.EXE running. If this were the last 16-bit application running on the system, and you were to close the program, the default NTVDM and WOWEXEC still remains open.

We have now seen the most important ways to configure DOS and 16-bit Windows applications. Before we continue, we should go over some possible exam scenarios. I was surprised to see about ten questions on my exam covering these very topics.

QUESTIONS AND ANSWERS

You have a 16-bit application suite and one application is faulty…	Run the faulty application in a separate memory space so it cannot affect the other applications running. Be aware that running every 16-bit application in a separate memory space is an option, too.
One 32-bit application crashes…	Don't worry. It will not affect the other applications running on the system.
Three 16-bit applications are running in the default space, and one crashes…	Once the faulty application that has frozen the message queue has been terminated, the other applications should be able to continue processing. You must know the defaults that these applications are run in. All three shouldn't crash, just the faulty application. Once the faulty application that has frozen the queue is terminated, the other two applications should be able to continue processing.
You want to start a program minimized and in a separate memory space…	Remember the syntax for starting applications from the command prompt. You know the command is START, and you know the switch for separate is /SEPARATE, and you know the switch for minimized is /MIN. Look for the answer with these choices, and of course, in the correct order. Here is the proper syntax for the command: START /MIN /MAX /SEPARATE application_name
You would like to start a program with a higher priority level…	Start the application using the HIGH priority class. This too is done from the command prompt. Know the syntax and the correct order. Once again, here is the proper syntax for the command with priority levels: START /LOW /NORMAL /REALTIME /HIGH application_name

QUESTIONS AND ANSWERS

How are 32-bit applications run in relation to...	They are preemptively multitasked with other applications in the system.
How are DOS applications run in relation to...	They also are preemptively multitasked with other applications in the system, including other DOS applications.
How are 16-bit applications run in relation to...	They are cooperatively multitasked within their own VDM and preemptively multitasked with other applications in the system.

Message Queues

Message queues were very important for older 16-bit applications that were cooperatively multitasked with each other. They shared the same message queue. An application would be written to check the message queue for other applications that request processing. If there were other programs waiting for processing, this application had to yield control of the processor and allow the other applications to execute. If the application refused to check the message queue, it could "hog" the CPU, and other applications that required processing would stop responding. This was a common frustration with 16-bit operating environments, such as Windows 3.x.

Now that I have told how bad a single message queue can be, let me continue by saying that NT still uses this single message queue for compatibility. This only causes concern if the application fails because it interferes with the other 16-bit applications in the same VDM. It does not, however, interfere with the rest of the system and other applications that are run outside of that VDM.

Threads

In the Win16 environment, we learned that these applications are run in a VDM. This VDM is a single-threaded process. This means that the program does not spawn many threads like a Win32 program can. This is no great concern; you just are not able to take advantage of NT's multithreading ability. Threads that are running in User Mode cannot read or write outside their own memory space. This is the protection offered for applications that are running in a separate memory space.

OS/2 Applications

OS/2 application support in Windows NT is not as strong as it is for DOS and Windows applications. This is due in large part to the scarcity of OS/2 applications and the limited popularity of the operating system itself. In fact, RISC-based systems do not even support OS/2 applications, unless they are bound applications, which we will see later. An interesting note is that the primary subsystem for Windows NT, which is currently the Win32 subsystem, was originally designed to be the OS/2 subsystem. It appeared that OS/2 was going to be the dominant desktop operating system, until Windows 3.*x* gained in popularity.

OS/2 Version 1.*x*

OS/2 Version 1.*x* applications are supported in Windows NT. Anything above this version of OS/2 is not supported under NT. The applications that are supported are character-based, rather than GUI-based. For this reason it is very uncommon that you will be running an OS/2 application on Windows NT. Since native OS/2 applications are difficult to find, the older character-based applications are even more difficult to find. You do have the opportunity of forcing the OS/2 applications to use the VDM if they are bound applications. We will learn about bound applications and forcing the DOS VDM later in this section.

OS/2 Components

There are several components of the OS/2 subsystem used to provide support for OS/2 applications:

- **OS2SS.EXE**   The main component of the subsystem. This loads only when an OS/2 application is run.
- **OS2.EXE**   Passes the call for the OS/2 application to the OS/2 application launcher, OS2SRV.EXE.

- **OS2SRV.EXE** The application launcher that starts the application for the subsystem.

- **NETAPI.DLL** Contains the Application Programming Interfaces (APIs) to communicate between the OS/2 applications and the subsystem.

Bound Applications

Bound applications refer to applications that are designed to run under either OS/2 or MS-DOS. If you run one of these applications, it will run in the OS/2 subsystem if it is available. For RISC-based computers this is the only way to run OS/2 applications. However, you can edit the Registry to disable the application from using the OS/2 subsystem and using the VDM instead. In addition to disabling the OS/2 subsystem, you also can delete it.

Using the VDM to run OS/2 applications rather than the OS/2 subsystem is accomplished through the use of the FORCEDOS command. The command has this syntax:

FORCEDOS application_name

If you use graphical-based OS/2 programs that are also bound, you most likely have to use this command to run them in the NTVDM, because you may not have the Presentation Manager add-on subsystem for these types of applications. In fact, many bound applications will perform better when run under a VDM than the OS/2 subsystem.

OS/2 Configuration

You can configure OS/2 applications through the Registry, or through the use of an OS/2 text editor. The Registry entries that are used to configure the OS/2 subsystem mostly involve the path to the executable file used to start the subsystem. The OS/2 applications also use a CONFIG.SYS file, just as older DOS and Windows applications did, to configure startup information. You need an OS/2 text editor to make these adjustments to the CONFIG.SYS file. In Windows NT, the calls to the CONFIG.SYS file are intercepted, and redirected to the OS/2 entries in the Registry. This is to avoid having the CONFIG.SYS altered if you also boot to MS-DOS, or to an operating system that uses the CONFIG.SYS, such as Windows 3.*x* or Windows 95. Here is the appropriate Registry key for the OS/2 entries:

HKEY_LOCAL_MACHINE\Software\Microsoft\OS/2 Subsystem for

NT\Config.sys

The information found in this key is also under this key:

HKEY_LOCAL_MACHINE\System\CurrentControlSet\Control\Session

Mananger\Subsystems\Os2\Config.sys

POSIX Applications

POSIX stands for Portable Operating System Interface based on UNIX. The name alone gives you an idea of what POSIX applications are. The POSIX applications are mainly for the UNIX environment, but Windows NT has provided that the POSIX subsystem remain compatible with these applications. There are several standards for POSIX compatibility, and NT is POSIX.1 compliant. The POSIX application must adhere to the rules for compatibility, which include support for hard links, traverse checking, additional time stamps, and case sensitivity. POSIX applications also must be run from the command prompt, due to their non-graphical nature. Refer to Chapter 5 for additional details about the POSIX compatibility.

POSIX Components

The components that make up the POSIX subsystem are as follows:

- **PSXSS.EXE** Is the POSIX subsystem server. This file is not loaded until a POSIX application is started. This file remains in memory until it is paged out, or the computer is restarted.

- **POSIX.EXE** Is the session manager that communicates between the subsystem server and the NT Executive Services. Just like PSXSS.EXE, it is not loaded until a POSIX application is started. However, unlike the PSXSS.EXE, which never has more than one instance running, a copy of POSIX.EXE opens for each POSIX application that is running.

■ **PSXDLL.DLL** Is the dynamic link library that contains all of the functions required. This file handles the communication between the application and the subsystem.

The exam may ask what types of applications are supported in Windows NT. This should be an easy question after what we have covered in this chapter.

CERTIFICATION SUMMARY

The environment subsystems are what enable Windows NT to provide such diverse application support. These subsystems run in User Mode and, in most cases, are not even loaded into memory until they are needed. They are 32-bit, protected, and preemptively multitasked. While they run in User Mode, they must make calls to System Services to access the system hardware. Access to these devices is available only to Kernel Mode components, such as the Kernel, NT Executive, and the Hardware Abstraction Layer. The Kernel is the core of the operating system and is a member of the NT Executive. The NT Executive is comprised of several components that are responsible for their own functions:

■ Object Manager
■ Process Manager
■ I/O Manager
■ Local Procedure Call Facility
■ Security Reference Monitor
■ Virtual Memory Manager
■ Graphics Device Interface and Windows Management (USER)

Win32 applications are run in the primary subsystem, the Win32 subsystem. This subsystem also is responsible for fulfilling requests by the other subsystems that are running. The Win32 subsystem runs the 32-bit applications in their own memory space, message queue, and address space.

DOS applications are run in the Virtual DOS Machine, which is a 32-bit, preemptively multitasked, separate memory space. They do not have access to the system hardware, but are fooled into believing so by the use of Virtual Device Drivers. Just like Win32 applications, these DOS applications do not crash the system or other applications that are currently running, if they become unstable.

Win16 applications require the use of the NTVDM, but also require another layer of functionality called the WOW environment. This environment must translate the calls between the Win16 APIs and the Win32 APIs. This process is known as *thunking*. Win16 applications are cooperatively multitasked within the same VDM, but preemptively multitasked with other applications on the system. They share the same message queue and memory space by default. They can run in a separate memory space, which can be configured a number of ways.

OS/2 and POSIX applications are 32-bit, preemptively multitasked, protected environment subsystems, also. They both make use of character-based applications and pass messages to the primary Win32 subsystem. OS/2 bound applications differ in that they can be forced into using the VDM, rather than the OS/2 subsystem.

TWO-MINUTE DRILL

- ❑ Windows NT uses modular components for the subsystem architecture that enable compatibility for applications.
- ❑ Environment Subsystems enable Windows NT to remain compatible with existing software.
- ❑ Kernel Mode, otherwise known as Privileged Mode, has the capability to access hardware directly.
- ❑ User Mode is the mode in which the majority of Windows NT code, environment subsystems, and all of the applications are run.

❑ The Windows NT Executive Services, combined with the NT Kernel, are at the top of the Kernel Mode component hierarchy.

❑ The Object Manager is responsible for the creation and use of objects. This involves naming, managing, and security for objects.

❑ The Process Manager is responsible for process and thread objects. This involves deleting, creating, and managing these objects.

❑ The Virtual Memory Manager is responsible for the use of virtual memory and the paging file in the system.

❑ The Local Procedure Call Facility is responsible for passing information between processes. Applications make calls to the environment subsystem for service.

❑ The Security Reference Monitor is responsible for access to the resources in the system. It has to provide validation for users, access to objects, and generating audit messages.

❑ The I/O Manager is responsible for all input and output for the operating system. Because input and output usually are handled by hardware devices, the I/O Manager spends a great deal of time communicating with device drivers.

❑ The Graphics Device Interface is the graphics engine. It is responsible for communicating between applications and the graphics devices.

❑ The Window Manager (USER) is the component that creates the screen interface for the user.

❑ Device drivers are used to communicate with the various hardware components in the system.

❑ The Kernel, the actual core of the Windows NT operating system, is not only a member of the Executive Services, but also is the head of the Executive Services. It is responsible for scheduling and managing threads, and handling exceptions and interrupts.

❑ Windows NT Win32 applications can be multithreaded for increased performance.

❑ Know your syntax! You will probably be asked on the test to choose the correct command line for starting an application based on a given situation. This will include the priority levels, separate memory space, and whether it will be minimized or maximized.

❑ Virtual Device Drivers are used to trick an application into believing that it is communicating with a device.

❑ POSIX stands for Portable Operating System Interface based on UNIX. The POSIX applications are mainly for the UNIX environment, but Windows NT has provided the POSIX subsystem to remain compatible with these applications.

SELF TEST

The following questions will help you measure your understanding of the material presented in this chapter. Read all the choices carefully, as there may be more than one correct answer. Choose all correct answers for each question.

1. Which facility is used when environment subsystems need to communicate?

   A. Process-passing

   B. Thread-passing

   C. Message-passing

   D. Procedure-passing

2. What does CSRSS provide?

   A. Security for the subsystems

   B. Logon Authentication

   C. Translation for the subsystems

   D. Error handling for the subsystems

3. What component is responsible for keeping track of the time that threads are being processed?

   A. Thread Manager

   B. Process Manager

   C. The Kernel

   D. Object Manager

4. (True/False) The Security Reference Monitor works with the CSRSS and Object Manager subsystem to make up the entire Security model for the system.

5. Which priority class is considered IDLE?

A. Priority level 4

B. Priority level 6

C. Priority level 7

D. Priority level 9

6. Fill in the blanks.
   Both the _____ and the _____ ran in User Mode in the Win32 subsystem in previous releases of NT, but now have been moved into the Windows NT Executive, which runs in Kernel Mode.

7. Which is not a component of the Virtual DOS Machine?

   A. NTDOS.SYS

   B. NTVDM.DLL

   C. REDIR.SYS

   D. NTIO.SYS

8. (True/False) If there is no PIF associated for the application, the DEFAULT.PIF is used.

9. I have a DOS application and three Win16 applications running on the system. When I switch from the DOS application to one of the Win16 applications, they are all unresponsive. What is the best way to remedy this situation?

   A. Run each one of the Win16 applications at the priority level of HIGH, so they do not become unresponsive.

B. Run the DOS application at the priority level of LOW, so that it does not consume too many resources.

C. Run each of the Win16 applications in its own memory space, so they do not interfere with each other.

D. Increase the priority level of the NTVDM in which all of the Win16 applications are running, so they will appear more responsive.

10. Which is the proper syntax for loading an application in a separate memory space with a HIGH priority level?

A. START MSPAINT.EXE /SEP /HIGH

B. START /SEP /HIGH MSPAINT.EXE

C. START MSPAINT.EXE /SEPARATE /HIGH

D. START /SEPARATE /HIGH MSPAINT.EXE

11. Which of the following are ways you can start a Win16 application in a separate memory space?

A. From a batch file that uses the /SEPARATE option.

B. From Task Manager by File, then New Task, and then checking the box for Separate Memory.

C. From the command prompt.

D. From the Run dialog box.

E. Creating a shortcut that has the separate memory check box marked.

12. Which is not a component of the OS/2 Subsystem?

A. NETAPI.DLL

B. OS2SS.EXE

C. OS2LIB.DLL

D. OS2.EXE

13. (True/False) The OS/2 Subsystem cannot run OS/2 2.x applications.

14. Which is not a Kernel Mode component?

A. Cache Manager

B. Security Subsystem

C. I/O Manager

D. Local Procedure Call Facility

15. Fill in the blank.
If you do not alter the priority of an application, it will run at the default priority level of _____.

14

Performance Tuning

O ne might ask, why is it important that you keep your car tuned? One might also ask, why is it necessary to tune your Windows NT system? Just as it's important that your vehicle be tuned to allow for maximum efficiency, it's important to optimize your Windows NT system, in order to maximize its capability.

Windows NT has several methods available, by which to maximize its potential. Prior to optimizing your Windows NT system, you must be able to recognize where bottlenecks may exist. In the first section of this chapter we examine what a bottleneck is, and methods for detecting and eliminating them. Next we look at self-tuning mechanisms, by which Windows NT can optimize itself.

No discussion of optimizing Windows NT would be complete without mention of the Performance Monitor application, which we discuss in the second section of this chapter. The Performance Monitor is a valuable tool in assisting you with diagnosing bottlenecks within your system.

CERTIFICATION OBJECTIVE 14.01

Performance Tuning

Performance-tuning Windows NT 4.0 is the art of taking your existing configuration and maximizing its performance to achieve the optimal outcome. It is a systematic approach that starts by finding the process that is hindering your system the most, and resolving it. However, tuning your system does not stop there; it is an ongoing process.

In this section we exam what a bottleneck is, ways to detect bottlenecks, and ways they can be eliminated. After our discussion on bottlenecks, we move on to ways in which Windows NT assists you in helping your machine run smoothly.

Bottlenecks

Imagine you are drinking your favorite soda from a bottle. As you look at the bottle you see that the bottom of your soda bottle is wider than the neck. If you turn the bottle upside down the flow is restricted, due to the narrowness of the neck. The term bottleneck within the computer industry indicates a component within your system, whose limitations impede the system as a whole from operating at its maximum potential. Another way to look at this is that a bottleneck is the resource that consumes the most time while a task is executing. One indication that you have a bottleneck is a high rate of use on one resource, while other resources have a relatively low usage rate.

Detecting Bottlenecks

All computer systems have bottlenecks that impede their performance capabilities. You may never notice a bottleneck within your system, depending on how you use your system. If you routinely use it to balance your checkbook, it may perform fast enough for you that you do not see a noticeable bottleneck. On the other hand, if you use it for designing a 3D CAD drawing of the room you're adding to your house, and it slows down immensely while rendering, then you definitely will notice that you have a bottleneck.

However, just knowing your system is slow does not help you in identifying what resource may be causing the problem. Is it the memory, the hard disk drive, the processor, or possibly an application, or Windows NT service? If you constantly have to fetch data from your paging file, is the hard disk causing the problem, or a lack of memory in your system? If your system slows to a crawl, is it due to processor-intensive calculations or an application that is stealing processor time?

To determine what is the bottleneck in your system, you must evaluate a set of metrics based upon the number of requests for service, the arrival time of the requests, and the amount of time requested. Usually, the resource with the lowest maximum throughput capability becomes the bottleneck if it is in high demand. It is important to realize that a resource doesn't have to be at 100% utilization for a bottleneck to occur. Later in this chapter, when we begin using the Performance Monitor, we will discuss different levels of utilization that typically indicate a bottleneck.

The Task Manager is a useful tool for short-term monitoring of your system and can be extremely valuable in detecting an application or Windows NT service that has become a CPU or memory bottleneck. Using the Task Manager, you can see which applications and processes, and the number of threads that are running in your system. While an application is listed under the Application tab, it is also listed in the Processes tab, along with other processes such as Windows NT services and drivers. A single process can have one thread or many threads running at the same time. A thread is what allows a process to run different portions of its program concurrently (and possibly on different processors, which we will look at in detail, later in the chapter). Figure 14-1 displays the Task Manager Processes tab. A process is running that is consuming more memory than it should, thereby slowing the system. Can you identify it?

If you said that LEAKYAPP.EXE looks like it is using more memory than it should, you are correct! This is just one way that the Task Manager can help you determine bottlenecks within your system.

FIGURE 14-1

Use Task Manager for short-term monitoring of your system

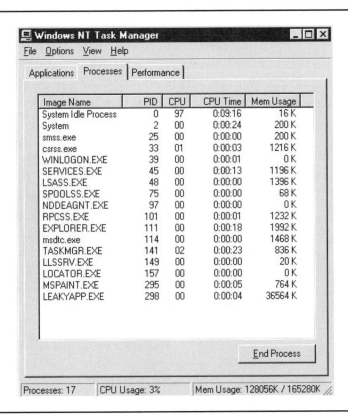

Now it is your turn to start up the Task Manager and take a look at what is happening within your system. Exercise 14-1 leads you through the steps of starting up a few applications and looking at all three tabs on the Task Manager. These three tabs help you detect application and Windows NT services bottlenecks within your system.

EXERCISE 14-1

Viewing Applications, Processes, and Threads

1. Use your right mouse button and click once on your taskbar.
2. Select Task Manager from the menu.
3. Click the Start button and select Programs | Accessories | Notepad.
4. Click the Start button and select Programs | Accessories | Clock.
5. Select the Applications tab on the Task Manager. You should see the two applications that you just started, and to the right of the applications' names, you should see "running". If one of the programs had stopped responding, you would see "not responding" instead.
6. Select the Processes tab on the Task Manager. This displays all the processes currently running within your system. The majority of processes listed are Windows NT services or drivers, with the exception of the two applications that you started. The Processes tab is very useful in helping you to determine CPU usage and memory being consumed by each process.
7. Select the Performance tab on the Task Manager. This screen shows you the total amount of threads that are currently running in your system.
8. Close the Task Manager.

Eliminating Bottlenecks

Once you have determined that you have a bottleneck, you are halfway to solving your problem and speeding up your system. The steps you take in eliminating the bottleneck vary, depending on what type of bottleneck you have. In some situations you might need to terminate an application. In Figure 14-1 simply highlighting LEAKYAPP.EXE and clicking the End Process button can solve the bottleneck. In other situations you may need to add more memory, a faster hard disk, or more processors.

Once you have eliminated the most significant bottleneck in your system, try to find the next bottleneck and eliminate it. Performance Tuning is a constant cycle of improvement and there is always a bottleneck to overcome, unless your system is so fast that you do not perceive a bottleneck.

Self-Tuning Mechanisms

Windows NT ships with several mechanisms in place to assist with optimizing your system performance automatically, including:

- Methods to avoid fragmentation of physical memory
- Utilizing multiple pagefiles
- Multiprocessing capability
- Thread and process prioritization
- Caching disk requests

Methods to Avoid Fragmentation of Physical Memory

Windows NT utilizes two types of memory, *physical memory*, which is the actual RAM, and *virtual memory*, which is hard disk space acting as though it is additional RAM. Virtual memory is used when the amount of physical memory is not enough to run the current applications, processes, and threads. Data is transferred transparently between physical memory and virtual memory under the control of the *virtual memory manager* (VMM). The VMM swaps unused data from RAM to the hard disk, and swaps in data from the hard disk to RAM so that it can be accessed faster.

The size of the smallest portion of memory that can be managed is 4KB (kilobyte). This 4KB section of memory is called a *page*. Both physical memory and virtual memory (the file stored on the hard drive is called PAGEFILE.SYS) are treated equally with regard to the size of the pages. This allows the virtual memory manager to manipulate data that is being moved back and forth between physical memory and virtual memory, without having to worry about different page sizes. Any available space in physical memory or virtual memory can be used for the transferred page without the need to worry about a large amount of fragmentation.

Fragmentation occurs when there is unused space within contiguous pages. If there is sufficient fragmentation, you have areas of memory that cannot be used by other applications, leading to wasted memory. Other operating systems do not use 4KB pages, but use much larger pages—up to 64KB in size. Let's do a comparison of storing data within a Windows NT 4KB page and another operating system that has a 64KB page size. If there were 3KB of information stored within a 64KB page, 61KB of that memory is wasted. If that same 3KB of data were stored within a Windows NT page, there would only be 1KB of unused memory. Another example would be if we have a thread executing that needed 26KB of memory. On Windows NT it uses 7 pages ($7 \times 4KB = 28KB$), with only 2KB being unused. On the operating system that uses 64KB pages, 38KB of memory is wasted. Keep in mind that this example is for only one thread. Remember when you performed Exercise 14-1 and saw the number of threads running in your system? Now imagine the amount of memory that would be wasted if Windows NT did not use 4KB pages. By optimizing the size of the pages in this manner Windows NT leaves more physical memory available for use by your application, without having to do as much swapping to virtual memory. It is important to have as much physical memory in your system as possible, to reduce the page swapping that the virtual memory manager has to perform.

Utilizing Multiple Pagefiles

It is not always possible to add more memory to your system to reduce page swapping, but the virtual memory manager within Windows NT can recognize more than one pagefile. When you first launched the Windows NT setup program, it created a file called PAGEFILE.SYS on the physical drive on which the operating system was being installed. The default size of PAGEFILE.SYS is the amount of physical RAM plus 12MB (megabyte).

It is possible to have more than one pagefile if you have multiple logical or physical drives. Windows NT supports a maximum of 16 pagefiles per system. There can be one pagefile per logical disk, but for maximum efficiency you should create additional pagefiles—one per physical disk. The reason you want to place the additional pagefiles on separate physical drives is that you will see significantly increased levels of input/output (I/O) if your hard disk controller is capable of reading and writing to multiple hard disks at the same time. If you place additional pagefiles on logical drives, you may notice a slowdown in your system as the drive head has to move between the multiple pagefiles that exist on the physical drive hosting the logical drives. Exercise 14-2 shows you how to split your paging file among multiple hard disks. Keep in mind that to perform this exercise you must have more than one physical drive in your system.

Splitting the Paging File Among Multiple Disks

1. Right-click the My Computer icon.
2. Select Properties from the menu.
3. Select the Performance tab.
4. Click the Change button located in the Virtual Memory section.
5. Select the Primary Volume on the first drive.
6. Set the Initial Size to 8MB.
7. Set the Maximum Size to 16MB.
8. Click the Set button. You see that the settings you just made are now reflected in the Drive window.
9. Select the Primary Volume on the second drive.
10. Set the Initial Size to 8MB.
11. Set the Maximum Size to 16MB.
12. Click the Set button.
13. Click the OK button.
14. Click the Close button.
15. Answer Yes for your system to be restarted. The changes you have made will then take effect.

Figure 14-2 shows multiple pagefiles in use on a Windows NT system. Notice that the minimum pagefile size that Windows NT allows is 2MB.

Multiprocessing Capabilities

Windows NT can increase the performance of your system by taking advantage of more than one processor in a system. In a single-processor

FIGURE 14-2

Virtual Memory handles
multiple pagefile settings

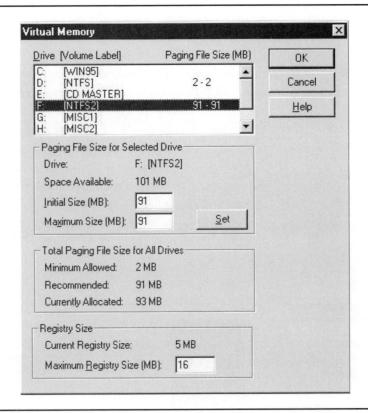

system, only one thread can be executed at a time. In a multiprocessor system, each processor can handle a thread, thereby improving performance.

Not all multiprocessing systems are created equal. A multiprocessing system falls into one of two different categories: asymmetric or symmetric. An *asymmetric multiprocessing* (ASMP) system assigns specific threads to a specific processor, which could lead to wasted processor time, if one processor is waiting on a thread that is not being executed. An example of asymmetric multiprocessing would be if the operating system was running on one processor, and applications were running on the other processor(s). When an application is not running, that processor sits idle. Figure 14-3 shows an asymmetrical multiprocessing system with four processors. As you can see,

Processor 1 is being used for the operating system, and Processor 3 for an application. Processors 2 and 4 are not being utilized and thus are wasted.

By contrast, a *symmetric multiprocessing* (SMP) system uses any available processor, as needed. Windows NT supports symmetric multiprocessing, which allows it to distribute application needs and system load evenly across all the available processors. Figure 14-4 shows a symmetrical multiprocessing system with four processors. Each processor is sharing in the load of the operating system and the application.

Multiprocessing systems do not double the performance capability of two-processor systems, as you might think they would. Overhead for resource sharing and scheduling must be factored in. It is generally accepted that two processors give you roughly 150% of the performance of one processor, but this depends on how your system is used.

FIGURE 14-3

In Asymmetric Multiprocessing, memory can be wasted

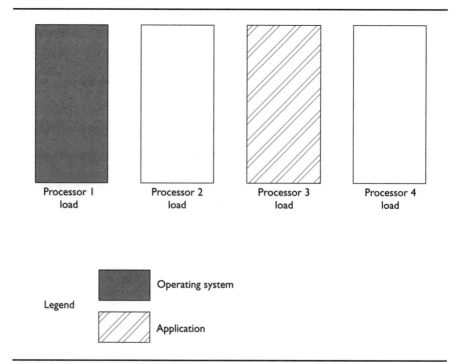

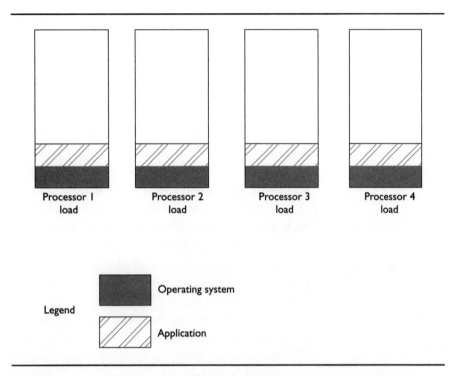

FIGURE 14-4

In Symmetric
Multiprocessing, the load is
distributed

Windows NT Workstation supports two processors out of the box. If you
need support for more than two processors, contact your computer
manufacturer to acquire the appropriate support files.

exam
ⓦatch

*Many people taking the exam get confused by the number of processors
that are supported by Windows NT Workstation and Windows NT
Server. Be sure to recognize the differences in supported quantities
of processors between the two different operating systems as they
are shipped.*

Thread and Process Prioritization

As we discussed earlier in this chapter, a process can be made up of multiple
threads that are executed at the same time in a *multiprocessing* system.
However, if you look at a *preemptive multitasking* operating system, it only
appears that the threads are being processed at the same time. In reality, the

threads are processed based upon their priority. Since Windows NT is a preemptive multitasking operating system, there must be a way to manipulate the priorities of the processes and threads. Windows NT always schedules the highest-priority thread to run, even if it has to interrupt a lower-priority thread. In this way, it keeps the processor running the highest-priority task.

The priorities within Windows NT are handled in a hierarchical manner, and have a number range of 0 to 31, with 31 being the highest priority. The priorities fall into one of the four base priority classes. Table 14-1 illustrates the four classes and the priority numbers associated with them. Each process starts with a base priority of 7, which is within the normal base priority. The threads of a process inherit the base priority of the process. Windows NT can raise or lower this number by two priority levels, which allows the system to prioritize itself as it is running.

If there are multiple threads running at the same priority, they share the processor(s) by taking equal turns until the threads have finished. Periodically, all threads receive a priority boost from Windows NT. This helps to prevent the lower-priority threads from locking onto a shared resource that may be needed by a higher-priority thread.

Dynamic applications use priority levels 0-15, while real-time applications operate with the priority levels from 16-31. A dynamic application would be a user application or operating system component that is not critical to the performance of the system and may be written to the pagefile. A real-time application would be a mouse driver that is critical to system performance and therefore cannot be written to the pagefile. Real-time applications access the processor quite frequently in order to respond to a real-time event, such as a user moving the mouse cursor across the monitor screen.

TABLE 14-1	Base Priority	Number Range
	Low	0-6
Base Priorities for Processes and Threads	Normal	7-10
	High	11-15
	Real-time	16-31

It is important to note that, in order to start a process with a priority higher than 23, you must be an administrator. This is because a process running at this high a priority really slows the entire system down and makes even moving the mouse cursor a slow procedure.

As already discussed, Windows NT can automatically change the priorities on processes. For example, if you bring an application to the foreground, the operating system automatically raises the priority level of the processes that the application is running, to make sure that it responds to your requests quickly.

It is possible to change the responsiveness of the foreground application by adjusting the Application Performance Boost slider. Figure 14-5 shows the Performance tab from System Properties, where the Application Performance Boost slider is located. As indicated by the hash marks under the slider, there are three possible settings for boosting the foreground application. The Maximum setting increases the foreground application by two priorities. If you have an application that started with a priority of seven, and move the slider to the Maximum position, it raises the priority level to nine as long as the application is in the foreground. The middle setting increases foreground application priority by one priority level. With the slider set to the None position, the foreground and background applications run with the same priority level. Exercise 14-3 shows how to change foreground application priority levels.

EXERCISE 14-3

Changing the Foreground Application Responsiveness

1. Right-click the My Computer icon.
2. Select Properties from the menu.
3. Select the Performance tab.
4. Move the slider from Maximum to None.
5. Click the OK button.
6. Answer Yes for your system to be restarted. The changes you have made will then take effect.

Be sure to set the Application Performance Boost slider back to Maximum after you have completed experimenting with the None setting.

FIGURE 14-5

At the Performance tab
from System Properties,
you can boost an
application's priority

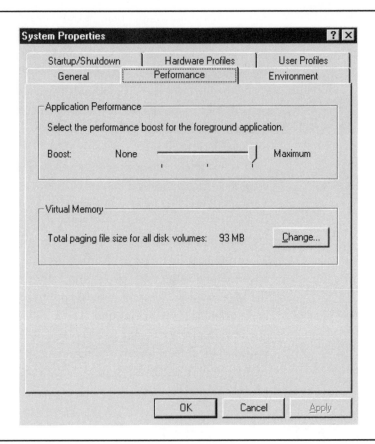

If you have several applications running and you want them all to operate at
a high-priority level regardless of which application may be in the foreground,
you can adjust the behavior of Windows NT by manually changing the
applications while they are running or before they are started.

To manually change the priority of an application that is already running,
use the Task Manager. Priority levels changed with the Task Manager remain
in effect as long as the process is running. Figure 14-6 shows an example
of changing the priority for TCPSVCS.EXE. Exercise 14-4 shows you how
to use the Task Manager to change the priority of an application that is
already running.

Changing the priority
of a process using
Task Manager

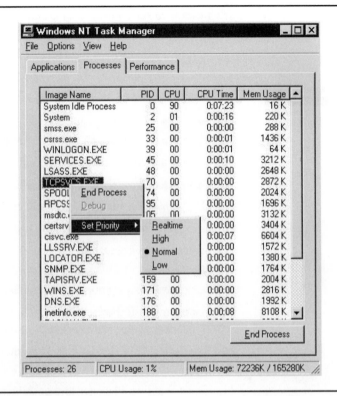

EXERCISE 14-4

Changing the Priority of a Running Process

1. Click the Start button and select Programs | Accessories | Notepad.

2. Use your right mouse button and click once on the taskbar.

3. Select Task Manager from the menu.

4. Select the Processes tab.

5. Locate NOTEPAD.EXE and click it with your right mouse button.

6. Select Set Priority from the menu. Normal is the priority at which this process is currently running.

7. Select High from the menu.

8. Notepad is now running at the High priority.

If you want to start a process at a higher priority, start it from a command prompt, using one of the switches listed in Table 2. Exercise 14-5 shows you how to start a process with a priority other than normal.

EXERCISE 14-5

Starting Processes with Other Than Normal Priority

1. Click the Start button and choose Programs | Command Prompt.
2. Type **start /low clock**. Your clock starts at a low priority level.
3. Type **start /high clock**. A second clock starts at a high priority.
4. Type **start /realtime clock**. A third clock starts at a higher priority.
5. Use your right mouse button and click once on the taskbar.
6. Choose Task Manager from the menu.
7. Select the Processes tab and see that three different clock processes are running.
8. Select the View menu and choose Select Columns.
9. Place a mark in the Base Priority box. This shows you the priorities for all processes that are currently running.
10. Check each CLOCK.EXE and see that each is running at the priority that you started it with from the command prompt.
11. Close the Task Manager and each instance of the clock.
12. Close the Command Prompt.

Caching Disk Requests

Windows NT improves the performance of your system by utilizing disk caching, which the disk cache manager controls. The disk cache manager reduces the amount of I/O traffic to your hard drive. It does this by storing

TABLE 14-2

Command Line Switch Settings to Change Process Starting Priority

Switch	Priority Level
/LOW	4
/NORMAL	7
/HIGH	13
/REALTIME	24

frequently-used data in physical memory, rather than having to read it each time from your hard disk. Reducing the amount of I/O increases your system performance.

The caching system is dynamic, so the size of the cache file changes as necessary, based upon the amount of memory that the operating system requires. If you start a new process, Windows NT changes the cached memory that is available, to ensure a balance between the memory used for caching and the virtual memory pagefile. This maximizes the physical memory that is present.

It is not possible to configure manually the size used by the cache, since the size is determined by all the applications running on the system. The best way to optimize the size of the disk cache is to have as much physical memory as possible in the system. This allows Windows NT sufficient resources to manage itself optimally.

In most situations the tuning that Windows NT performs on itself is sufficient to have an optimally configured system. However, in those cases where self-tuning does not solve your problems, you need to turn to other methods of optimization such as the Performance Monitor.

FROM THE CLASSROOM

The Dangers of Dual-Boot Machines

Many clients, especially if they are new to NT, want to configure their computers with both NT and the operating system they have in place. This scenario is common enough that we create a dual-boot operating system in the classroom so the students have some experience in the environment. We find that most clients dual-boot between NT and DOS (or DOS/WIN). Over the past several years, the upgrade choice has been between Windows NT and Windows 95. As NT's popularity has grown, and the next release of Windows 95 (called Windows 98) is around the corner, we see more upgrades to NT from Windows 95. Users prefer to upgrade to NT, rather than upgrade from Windows 95 to Windows 98, and then be faced with an upgrade to NT later.

FROM THE CLASSROOM

The first point to remember, when setting up a dual-boot machine, is to have DOS (or Windows 95) installed first, and then install NT. If you try it the other way around, you won't be able to start NT after you make the hard disk a DOS-bootable drive. When you install NT, the installation process makes an image of the DOS boot sector and stores it in a file called BOOTSEC.DOS. Don't delete this file. When you start your computer, you are presented with the Boot Loader Menu. When you select DOS from the menu, NTLDR needs the information in BOOTSEC.DOS in order to start DOS.

The second point to remember concerns the C: drive. We feel that it is most effective to have each operating system on its own separate partition. Experience has shown that this is an easier way to manage the system. Whether you create separate partitions or not, you must pay close attention to the file system for the C: drive. On a dual-boot machine, the file system must be FAT. After working with NT for a while, you will become comfortable with the NTFS file system and the features and benefits that it has to offer. And there is the really neat little command-line utility to convert your FAT partitions to NTFS partitions without destroying the data. Just run the utility, wait a few seconds, reboot the machine (in some cases you don't have to reboot the machine) and you're done. What could be easier? Maybe it's too easy. If you get carried away and convert the C: drive (which is a FAT partition so that DOS will boot) to NTFS, you can't dual-boot to DOS again. And there's no way to convert from NTFS to FAT, so you're stuck. Don't underestimate the possibility that this could happen to you. In the classroom, we stress this point before the students do the conversion exercise. Yet, in a class of 10 students, we can count on at least one mistakenly converting the C: partition instead of the D: partition. If this can happen in the relatively controlled environment of the classroom, imagine what can happen in the chaos of the real world.

—By Shane Clawson, MCT, MCSE

CERTIFICATION OBJECTIVE 14.02

Performance Monitor

The Performance Monitor is a tool included with Windows NT 4.0 that tracks the performance of system components and applications. By tracking different components of your system, it can help you to see what is degrading the performance. The Performance Monitor can serve a variety of purposes.

- Identify bottlenecks
- Identify trends over a period of time
- Monitor real-time system performance
- Monitor system performance history
- Determine the capacity the system can handle
- Monitor system configuration changes

The Performance Monitor is used to establish a *baseline* of your system. A baseline is a snapshot of your system under normal operating conditions, and a yardstick to measure future abnormalities. When you start Performance Monitor, as with any application, you use a portion of processor time to run the program. If you turn on the switch that allows disk monitoring, that minimally affects I/O for the local hard disk(s). This should, in essence, have no effect on the results of the measurements you are taking. Figure 14-7 shows the Performance Monitor after it has first been started. Exercise 14-6 shows you how to start the Performance Monitor on your system. It is best to make sure that your hard disk has finished all logon processing prior to starting the Performance Monitor. This ensures that your results do not include any of the logon processing.

FIGURE 14-7

Performance Monitor is used to establish a baseline of your system

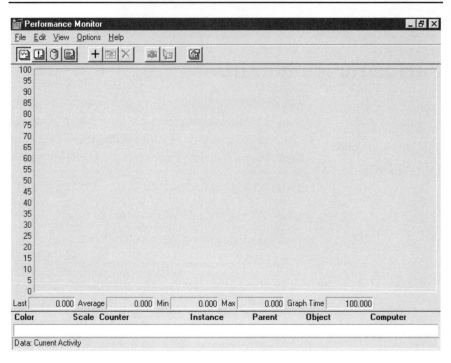

EXERCISE 14-6

Starting the Performance Monitor

1. Click the Start button.

2. Select Programs.

3. Select Administrative Tools.

4. Select Performance Monitor.

5. Leave the Performance Monitor running to complete the rest of the exercises in this section of the chapter.

Performance Monitor utilizes three different types of items to view the system. They are objects, counters, and instances.

■ *Objects* are system components, such as Memory, Processor, or Disk. See Table 14-3 for other Objects.

■ *Counters* are specific features of the Object that you have chosen. For example, the %Processor Time is a counter for the Processor object. Objects can be made up of many different counters.

■ An *instance* is a single occurrence of a counter activity. An example would be if your system has two processors and you start the %Processor Time counter for each processor.

Measurements are always occurring throughout the processes running on your Windows NT system. The Performance Monitor is the tool that displays this measurement based upon which objects you choose.

Counters are incremented each time an object performs its functions. For example, each time the processor services a request from an I/O device, the interrupts/sec counter would be incremented.

Many of the counters are used by Windows NT so that it may monitor itself and perform self-tuning. Table 14-3 lists several of the objects that can be measured with

TABLE 14-3	**Object Name**	**Description**
Description of Objects Measured by Performance Monitor	Browser	Monitors browser activity for the domain or workgroup to include elections and announcements
	Cache	Monitors the disk cache usage
	LogicalDisk	Monitors hard disk partitions
	Memory	Monitors memory usage and performance
	Paging File	Monitors the usage of pagefiles
	PhysicalDisk	Monitors a hard disk that contains one or more partitions. This object can be used to monitor the whole drive instead of individually monitoring partitions
	Process	Monitors all processes that are running on the system
	Processor	Monitors each processor in the system
	System	Monitors counters that affect all hardware and software in the system
	Thread	Monitors all threads running in the system

Performance Monitor. This list is not exhaustive, and your applications may be written to let the system monitor their performance via objects.

Creating a Performance Monitor Chart

A Performance Monitor chart measures the objects that you add and reflects the current activity. If you save the chart under a filename, it performs constant logging, which you can view whenever you want to see an update of the measurement.

Figure 14-8 shows the Add to Chart dialog box. As you can see, you can vary the color, scale, width, and style of each counter that you add to the chart. When Performance Monitor is started, it uses a default scale. However, if you are viewing more than a single counter, you may want to utilize a different scale than the default on each counter, in order to analyze the data appropriately.

Analyzing a Performance Monitor Chart

A chart like that shown in Figure 14-8 shows the activity of every object, counter, and instance that is being monitored. The scale on the left of the

FIGURE 14-8

Creating a chart with Performance Monitor

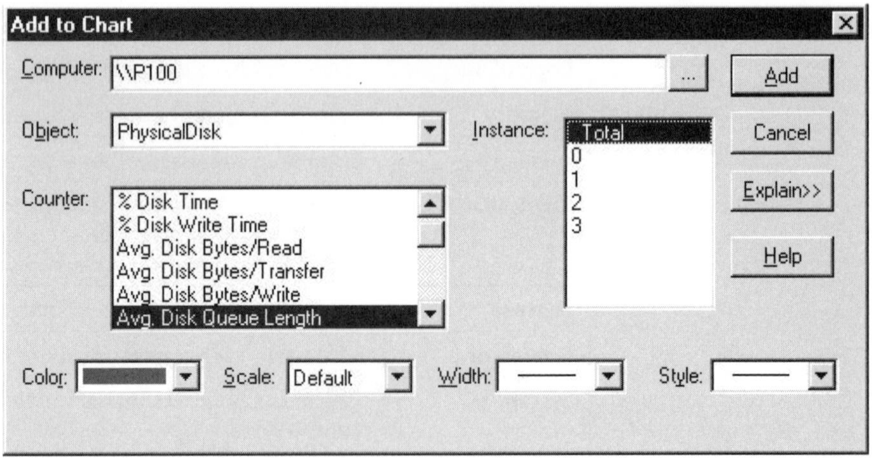

chart always starts at zero and is displayed by default. The scale can be changed if your activity goes above one hundred. The default time interval is set to one second for each counter. Table 14-4 describes the other values displayed by the Performance Monitor.

When you use the Performance Monitor, it is important to monitor actions that can cause bottlenecks in your system. In the following sections we will use Performance Monitor to examine processor performance, disk drive performance, and memory performance. As you will notice in the following discussions, things are not always as they appear at first. The item that you suspect to be causing your bottleneck might, in reality, be disguising the real bottleneck.

Processor Performance

Normally, within your computer the processor is the fastest component, and tends to waste a lot of time waiting on other processes. The processor in modern systems is usually not the bottleneck in a system, unless you are using applications that are very graphical or math-intensive. However, you might want to measure the performance of your processor to ensure that a bottleneck is not present, especially if you are using a earlier processor than one from the Pentium family.

TABLE 14-4	Value	Purpose
Performance Monitor Value Bar Descriptions	Last	Displays the counters value during the last poll
	Average	A running average of the counter during the charts history
	Minimum	The minimum value of the counter during the charts history
	Maximum	The maximum value of the counter during the charts history
	Graph Time	The total amount of time it takes for a complete chart to be created across the screen

When monitoring processor performance there are three important counters to observe.

- Processor:%Processor Time
- Processor:Interrupts/sec
- System:Processor Queue Length

Processor:%Processor Time

The Processor:%Processor Time counter is an indicator of how busy the processor in your system is. There is no need to be alarmed if your processor has spikes of 100%, as this is expected in some situations, such as starting up an application. However, a bottleneck can occur if your processor is so busy that it does not respond to service requests for time. If you are experiencing a consistent processor load of 80% or more, then you have a processor bottleneck. Exercise 14-7 will lead you through the steps necessary to add the counter to the Performance Monitor.

EXERCISE 14-7

Adding Processor:%Processor Time to the Performance Monitor

1. Select the Edit menu and choose Add to Chart.
2. Select Processor from the Object drop-down list.
3. Select %Processor Time from the Counter scroll-down list.
4. Click the Add button.
5. Click the Done button to close the Add to Chart window.

Let your system sit idle for a few seconds and then open up any application, such as Notepad. What happens to your Performance Monitor chart? You should see quite a bit of %Processor Time measurement being recorded as the application is opening.

Processor:Interrupts/sec

The Interrupts/sec counter measures the rate of service requests from I/O devices. If you see a significant increase in the value of this counter, without an

tem activity, then a hardware problem exists, in which a
orking properly. This counter should not normally be
r, an occasional spike above 2000 is acceptable. Exercise
to add this counter to your system.

or:Interrupts/sec to the
onitor

t menu and choose Add to Chart.

sor from the Object drop-down list.

pts/sec in the Counter scroll-down list.

button.

e button to close the Add to Chart window.

or Queue Length

r Queue Length counter is an important indicator of
as it watches the number of threads that are asking for
thread requires a certain amount of processor cycles. If
ssor cycles exceeds what the processor can supply, a long
lops and degrades system performance. You should never
ssor queue that is greater than two. If you have a queue
o, there are too many threads waiting for the processor,
become a bottleneck. Exercise 14-9 shows you how to
r queue length.

EXERCISE 14-9   **Adding System:Processor Queue Length to the Performance Monitor**

1. Select the Edit menu and choose Add to Chart.
2. Select System in the Object drop-down list.
3. Select Processor Queue Length in the Counter scroll-down list.
4. Click the Add button.
5. Click the Done button to close the Add to Chart window.

Processor Performance Troubleshooting

Once you have determined that the processor in your system is causing the bottleneck, do not automatically go out and buy a new processor. There are some things you can check within your system to see if they are causing the processor to be a bottleneck.

■ Check to see if the processor only becomes a bottleneck when a certain application is running. If so, find a new application to replace it (if feasible). Screensavers, especially OpenGL screensavers, are very processor-intensive.

■ Check that your level 2 cache (L2 cache) has been enabled in your Built In Operating System (BIOS). If your L2 cache has not been enabled, it puts a strain on your processor.

■ Check that you have a sufficient size of L2 cache. At a minimum, you should have 256KB of L2 cache. If you have recently added physical memory to your system, you might want to increase the size of your L2 cache (if your mainboard allows it). After you add physical memory to a system, the L2 cache must map the larger physical memory, which can result in a lower cache hit ratio, and more work for the processor having to retrieve data from other I/O devices.

■ Check to see if you are using low-bit network or disk adapter circuit cards. An 8-bit card uses more processor time than a 16-bit card, and a 16-bit card uses more processor time than a 32-bit card. Using a 32-bit card provides the most efficiency for your system, since it transfers the most bits of data on each transfer from the card to memory.

If after checking the preceding items, you still have a processor bottleneck, you might have no other choice but to replace the processor in your system. If your mainboard supports multiprocessing, add another processor.

Figure 14-9 shows a processor bottleneck that has been caused by a screensaver. The %Processor Time counter is the white line. As you can see, the screensaver has kept the processor in use 100% of the time, which prevents other tasks from operating efficiently.

Processor utilization
at 100%, caused
by a screensaver

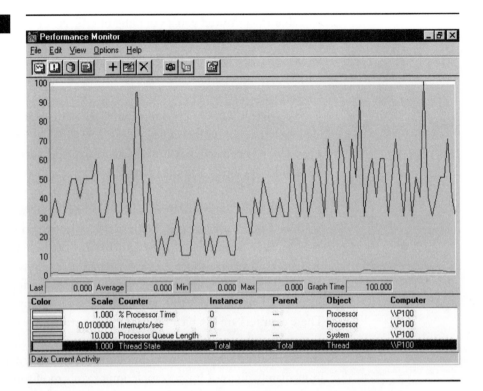

Disk Drive Performance

Disk drives contribute significantly to creating a bottleneck in your system.
The hard disk in your system participates in everything from booting your
system and loading applications, to storing and retrieving data from your hard
disk and pagefile. With your hard disk involved in all these processes, you can
see that the speed of your drive can impact the performance of your system.

The first sign that you might have a disk drive bottleneck could be the
amount of time that the disk drive indicator stays illuminated. This should be
verified by using the Performance Monitor. If the Performance Monitor shows
sustained rates of disk activity above 85%, a disk drive bottleneck is present.
Keep in mind that the disk drive might not be the root cause of the bottleneck,
so you need to investigate further to make a final determination.

Table 14-3 showed you a sampling of Objects that can be monitored with Performance Monitor. If you recall there were two Objects that were related to disk drive performance, *LogicalDisk* and *PhysicalDisk*. The LogicalDisk Object measures performance at a much higher level than the PhysicalDisk Object does.

The LogicalDisk Object can measure the performance of a partition of a hard disk that has been assigned a drive letter such as C: or D:. Initially, this is a good way to detect a disk drive bottleneck before moving on to use the PhysicalDisk Object. Another good use of LogicalDisk is to monitor which partition may be busy due to a particular application.

The PhysicalDisk Object measures real transfers to and from actual hard disks, and not just partitions. You use this object when you want to isolate differences in performance between drives in your system, or if you want very detailed information about the performance of a specific drive.

To monitor either LogicalDisk or PhysicalDisk performance, you must enable the Disk Drive Performance Counters by running the Diskperf utility. These counters are disabled by default, as they degrade overall system performance by interrupting the processor during I/O. The counters should only be enabled when you want to monitor disk performance, and should be immediately disabled upon completion of your monitoring. When you enable the counters, Diskperf installs the Disk Drive Performance Statistics Driver that actually collects the data for Performance Monitor, and also a high-precision timer that times each disk drive transfer. The driver and timer have been measured to take 1% – 2% of overhead on Intel-based processor systems.

In order to run the Diskperf utility, you must belong to the Administrator's local group. Exercise 14-10 shows you how to enable the Disk Drive Performance Counters.

EXERCISE 14-10

Enabling the Disk Drive Performance Counters

1. Click the Start button.
2. Select Programs.
3. Select Command Prompt.
4. Type **diskperf –y**

5. Press the RETURN key. A message states: "Disk Performance counters on this system are now set to start at boot. This change will take effect after the system is restarted."

6. Restart your system.

exam
ⓦatch

You must use diskperf –ye if you want to monitor a physical drive in a stripe disk set. Using diskperf –ye installs the Disk Drive Performance Statistics Driver low in the disk driver stack, so that it can see individual physical disks before they are logically combined.

When monitoring disk drive performance, there are four important counters to observe.

■ Memory:Pages/sec

■ %Disk Time (Applies to both LogicalDisk and PhysicalDisk Objects)

■ Disk Bytes/sec (Applies to both LogicalDisk and PhysicalDisk Objects)

■ Average Disk Bytes/transfer

■ Current Disk Queue Length (Applies to both LogicalDisk and PhysicalDisk Objects)

Memory:Pages/sec

The Memory:Pages/sec counter watches pages that are swapped and written to your disk drive. Remember that the virtual memory of your system is kept in a file named PAGEFILE.SYS that is located on your disk drive. If you monitor this counter and the %Disk Time counter, you will see how much the PAGEFILE.SYS affects the overall performance of your system. Exercise 14-11 shows you how to add the Memory:Pages/sec counter to Performance Monitor. This counter can be used to indicate that there is not enough physical memory in your system.

EXERCISE 14-11

Adding Memory:Pages/sec to the Performance Monitor

1. Select the File menu and choose New Chart. This clears the counters from the previous exercises.

2. Select the Edit menu and choose Add to Chart.

3. Select Memory from the Object drop-down list.

4. Select Pages/sec in the Counter scroll-down list.

5. Click the Add button.

6. Click the Done button to close the Add to Chart window.

%Disk Time

The %Disk Time counter shows how much time the processor is spending servicing disk requests. It can be a broad indicator of whether your disk drive is a bottleneck. If you use this counter in addition to the Processor:%Processor Time counter used earlier in this chapter, you can see whether disk requests are using up your processor time. Exercise 14-12 shows you how to measure the amount of time that is being used servicing disk requests. For this exercise we will stay at the high level and use the LogicalDisk Counter.

EXERCISE 14-12

Adding LogicalDisk:%Disk Time to the Performance Monitor

1. Select the Edit menu and choose Add to Chart.

2. Select LogicalDisk from the Object drop-down list.

3. Select %Disk Time in the Counter scroll-down list.

4. Click the Add button.

5. Click the Done button to close the Add to Chart window.

Disk Bytes/sec

The Disk Bytes/sec counter shows you how fast your disk drives are transferring bytes of data. This is the primary measure of disk throughput. Exercise 14-13 shows you how to add this counter to Performance Monitor.

EXERCISE 14-13

Adding LogicalDisk:Disk Bytes/sec to the Performance Monitor

1. Select the Edit menu and choose Add to Chart.

2. Select LogicalDisk from the drop-down list.

3. Select Disk Bytes/sec in the Counter scroll-down list.

4. Click the Add button.
5. Click the Done Button to close the Add to Chart window.

If you have more than one disk drive, copy a few large files from one disk drive to another disk drive, while you monitor the Disk Bytes/sec counter to see the speed at which your drives are performing.

Average Disk Bytes/transfer

The Average Disk Bytes/transfer counter measures throughput of your disk drive. The larger the transfer size, the more efficient your disk drive performs and the faster your system executes. Exercise 14-14 shows you how to monitor the Average Disk Bytes/transfer counter.

EXERCISE 14-14

Adding LogicalDisk:Average Disk Bytes/Transfer to the Performance Monitor

1. Select the Edit menu and choose Add to Chart.
2. Select LogicalDisk from the drop-down list.
3. Select Average Disk Bytes/transfer in the Counter scroll-down list.
4. Click the Add button.
5. Click the Done button to close the Add to Chart window.

Current Disk Queue Length

The Current Disk Queue Length counter shows how much data is waiting to be transferred to the disk drive. It measures requests, not time. It includes the request being serviced and those waiting. A disk queue of more than two can indicate that the disk drive is a bottleneck. Exercise 14-15 shows how to add this counter to Performance Monitor.

EXERCISE 14-15

Adding LogicalDisk:Current Disk Queue Length to the Performance Monitor

1. Select the Edit menu and choose Add to Chart.
2. Select LogicalDisk from the drop-down list.
3. Select Current Disk Queue Length in the Counter scroll-down list.

4. Click the Add button.

5. Click the Done button to close the Add to Chart window.

Now that you have completed measuring different counters using the Disk Drive Performance Counters, it is time for you to disable them so they do not degrade system performance when they're not in use. Exercise 14-16 shows you how to disable the counters.

Disabling the Disk Performance Counters

1. Click the Start button.

2. Select Programs.

3. Select Command Prompt.

4. Type **diskperf –n**

5. Press the RETURN key. A message will state: "Disk Performance counters on this system are now set to never start. This change will take effect after the system is restarted."

6. Restart your system.

Disk Drive Performance Troubleshooting

Once you have determined that the disk drive in your system is causing the bottleneck, do not immediately go out and buy another disk drive. There are some things you can check within your system to see if they could be causing the disk drive to be a bottleneck.

■ Check to see that you have plenty of physical memory in your system. By having as much physical memory in your system as possible you increase the size of your disk cache and reduce the size of your pagefile. By reducing the need to go back to your disk drive for data, or to swap pages into or out of the pagefile, you increase the performance of your system immensely.

■ Check your disk drive controller card. If you have a card that transfers in 8-bit or 16-bit increments, you would see a drastic improvement by switching to a 32-bit controller card. If possible, make sure that the 32-bit controller card is a bus-mastering direct memory access (DMA) controller, rather than a controller that uses programmed I/O. Programmed I/O uses the processor to setup disk drive transfers. A bus-mastering DMA controller uses the disk drive controller to manage the I/O bus, and the DMA controller to manage the DMA operation. It leaves the processor free for other uses.

If you have determined that you do indeed need another disk drive, and you are going to add it to your existing disk drive configuration, place the drives on separate I/O buses to ensure maximum performance potential. There are also some things you can do to improve disk drive performance when you have more than one disk drive in your system.

- Check to see if you have enough disks drives to use a disk drive stripe set. Using a stripe set can increase the speed of a logical disk by splitting it across 2 – 32 physical disk drives. Disk drives operate simultaneously, and you can see a speed increase from a stripe set up to the maximum speed of the bus. Stripe sets are created using the Disk Administrator that is covered in Chapter 5.

- You also might want to use a Redundant Array of Inexpensive Disks (RAID) controller card along with multiple disk drives. A RAID controller card contains its own processor and cache memory that speed up the transfers to and from the controller card. This also translates into improved system performance, as there is no load placed on the system processor or system memory when utilizing a RAID controller. RAID controllers are expensive and usually only installed in a system that is being utilized as a server.

exam
Watch

Windows NT Workstation can create Volume and Stripe sets with the Disk Administrator. Windows NT Server is also capable of creating certain levels of RAID from the Disk Administrator. Some people taking the exam get confused on the differences in Disk Administrator between the two operating systems.

Figure 14-10 shows an example of a situation in which a faster disk drive is needed. The white line displays the %Disk Time at a sustained rate of 100%. The black line is the Current Disk Queue Length that has had a maximum of 5 items in the queue, and the average has been about 2.5 items.

FIGURE 14-10

Disk drive performance is
at 100%; a faster disk drive
is needed

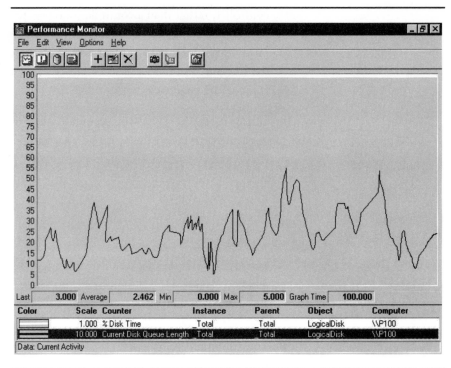

Memory Performance

Memory can contribute significantly to creating a bottleneck in your system
and is normally the most common source of bottleneck. Windows NT uses a
virtual memory system that consists of a combination of physical memory, a
virtual memory pagefile that is located on a disk drive, and hard disks where
applications and data can exist. Data is stored on the disk drive until needed
and then moved into physical memory. Data that is no longer actively being
used can be written back to the disk drive. However, if a system does not have
enough physical memory, data has to be moved into and out of your disk drive
more frequently, which can be a very slow process. Data pages that have
recently been referenced by a process are stored in physical memory in a
working set. If the process needs data that is not in the working set, it creates a
page fault, and the memory manager adds new pages to the working set.

The first step you should take in investigating a suspected memory problem is to measure the amount of paging that is occurring. There are three important counters you should use when you investigate a memory bottleneck. They indicate how often a process has to look outside of its working set to find data it needs. The three counters are:

- Memory:Page Faults/sec
- Memory:Pages Input/sec
- Memory:Page Reads/sec

Memory:Page Faults/sec

The Memory:Page Faults/sec counter measures the number of times that data is not found in a process's working set. This includes both *hard page faults*, in which additional disk drive I/O is required, and *soft page faults*, in which the pages are located elsewhere in memory. If you continuously experience a lack of data being found in the process's working set, the amount of memory in your system is probably too limited. The best indicator of a memory bottleneck is a continuous, high rate of hard page faults. Exercise 14-17 shows you how to add this counter to Performance Monitor.

EXERCISE 14-17

Adding Memory:Page Faults/sec to the Performance Monitor

1. Select the File menu and choose New Chart. This clears the counters from the previous exercises.
2. Select the Edit menu and choose Add to Chart.
3. Select Memory from the Object drop-down list.
4. Select Page Faults/sec from the Counter scroll-down list.
5. Click the Add button.
6. Click the Done button to close the Add to Chart window.

Memory:Pages Input/sec

The Memory:Pages Input/sec counter is used to see how many pages are retrieved from the disk drive to satisfy page faults. This counter can be used in conjunction with Memory:Page Faults/sec to see how many faults are being satisfied by reading from your disk drive, and how many might be coming from elsewhere, such as other locations in memory. Exercise 14-18 shows you how to add this counter to Performance Monitor.

EXERCISE 14-18

Adding Memory:Pages Inputs/sec to the Performance Monitor

1. Select the Edit menu and choose Add to Chart.
2. Select Memory from the Object drop-down list.
3. Select Pages Input/sec from the Counter scroll-down list.
4. Click the Add button.
5. Click the Done button to close the Add to Chart window.

Memory:Page Reads/sec

This counter reflects how often the system is reading from your disk drive due to page faults. If you sustain more than five pages per second, you have a shortage of physical memory. Exercise 14-19 shows you how to add this counter to the Performance Monitor.

EXERCISE 14-19

Adding Memory:Page Reads/sec to the Performance Monitor

1. Select the Edit menu and choose Add to Chart.
2. Select Memory from the Object drop-down list.
3. Select Page Reads/sec from the Counter scroll-down list.
4. Click the Add button.
5. Click the Done button to close the Add to Chart window.

Memory Performance Troubleshooting

Once you have determined that the memory in your system is causing the bottleneck, you might want to rush out and get more physical memory. It might not be necessary to add more physical memory, even though it never hurts to have as much physical memory as your system can handle. There are some things you can check within your system to see if they could be causing the memory to be a bottleneck.

■ Check the size of your L2 cache if you have recently added physical memory to your system. The L2 cache has to map the larger memory space that occurs after physical memory has been added to a system.

■ Check to see if you have any drivers or protocols running that are not in use. They use space in all memory pools even if they are idle.

■ Check to see if any of your applications have memory leaks by monitoring their use.

■ Check to see if you have additional space on your disk drive that you can use to expand the size of your pagefile. Normally, the bigger your pagefile is, the better. This is especially true if you have recently added memory to the system. PAGEFILE.SYS might need to expand to map the additional memory. If the PAGEFILE.SYS cannot expand, it could appear as a memory bottleneck.

Figure 14-11 shows an example of the three memory counters that we discussed in this section. The white line is the Page Faults/sec, which is the total page fault rate during this measurement, and it averages 81 per second. Page faults do cause an interruption to the processor, but to significantly slow the system down takes a hard page fault. The black line is Pages Input/sec that measures the hard page faults by counting the number of pages that have to be taken from disk drive to satisfy the fault. The area between the white and black lines shows the amount of soft page faults during this measurement. Remember that a soft page fault is a page that was found elsewhere in physical memory, such as cache memory. The dark gray line is the Page Reads/sec, which is the number of times the disk drive had to be read to satisfy a page fault.

CERTIFICATION SUMMARY

To optimize your Windows NT system, it is important to take all the steps available to improve performance capability. Windows NT assists you in this

Three memory
measurements from
Performance Monitor

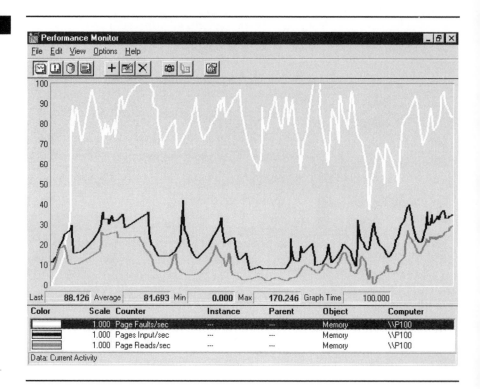

endeavor by providing counters for every object that the operating system can measure. Windows NT can use the counters for automatic self-tuning, and they also can be used manually with Performance Monitor.

Some of the self-tuning that Windows NT performs automatically is in the areas of: thread and process prioritization, caching disk requests, multiprocessing capability, utilizing multiple pagefiles, and avoiding fragmentation of physical memory.

The Performance Monitor tool that is shipped with Windows NT allows you to be very granular, when investigating the performance of your system, by measuring different objects and counters. The Performance Monitor displays in real time what is occurring within your system and helps you to isolate a bottleneck rapidly.

A bottleneck is something within your system that is prohibiting the system from operating at peak efficiency. The three main areas to concentrate on in looking for a bottleneck are Processor Performance, Disk Drive Performance, and Memory Performance.

Performance-tuning a Windows NT system is an ongoing process that starts with finding and resolving the most significant bottleneck. After resolving the most significant bottleneck, find the next most significant one, and keep doing this until you resolve all possible bottlenecks. After you resolve all possible bottlenecks, your system will achieve the greatest performance possible.

TWO-MINUTE DRILL

❑ Tuning your system is an ongoing process.

❑ To determine a bottleneck in your system, you must evaluate a set of metrics based upon the number of requests for service, the arrival time of the requests, and the amount of time requested.

❑ The Task Manager is a useful tool for short-term monitoring of your system, and can be extremely valuable in detecting an application or Windows NT service that has become a CPU or memory bottleneck.

❑ Windows NT ships with several mechanisms in place to assist with optimizing your system performance automatically.

❑ Methods to avoid fragmentation of physical memory

  ❑ Utilizing multiple pagefiles

  ❑ Multiprocessing capability

  ❑ Thread and process prioritization

  ❑ Caching disk requests

❑ Be sure to recognize the differences, in terms of supported quantities of processors, between Windows NT Workstation and Windows NT Server as they are shipped.

❑ The Performance Monitor can be used for a variety of reasons including:

  ❑ Identify bottlenecks

  ❑ Identify trends over a period of time

  ❑ Monitor real time system performance

❏ Monitor system performance history

❏ Determine the capacity the system can handle

❏ Monitor system configuration changes

❏ When monitoring processor performance there are three important counters to observe:

❏ Processor:%Processor Time

❏ Processor:Interrupts/sec

❏ System:Processor Queue Length

❏ If Performance Monitor shows sustained rates of disk activity above 85%, a disk drive bottleneck is present. Keep in mind that the disk drive itself might not be the root cause of the bottleneck. You need to investigate further.

❏ Windows NT Workstation can create Volume and Stripe sets with the Disk Administrator. Windows NT Server is also capable of creating certain levels of RAID from the Disk Administrator.

❏ Memory can contribute significantly to creating a bottleneck in your system and is the most common bottleneck you will encounter.

SELF TEST

The following questions will help you measure your understanding of the material presented in this chapter. Read all the choices carefully, as there may be more than one correct answer. Choose all correct answers for each question.

1. Using the /HIGH switch when starting an application from the command prompt will cause it to start at what priority?

   A. 24

   B. 13

   C. 7

   D. 4

2. While using the Processor:%Processor Time counter in Performance Monitor you see it spike to 100% when starting an application, but then it drops to 43%. What do you need to do?

   A. Upgrade to a faster processor

   B. Increase the size of your pagefile

   C. Add more physical memory to your system

   D. Nothing, the system is performing within acceptable parameters

3. Windows NT divides memory into _____ pages.

   A. 2KB

   B. 4KB

   C. 8KB

   D. 16KB

4. Windows NT Workstation supports _____ processors.

   A. 1

   B. 2

   C. 3

   D. 4

5. (True/False) It is not possible to change the priority of the foreground application so that it runs at the same priority as all background applications.

6. By how many levels can Windows NT automatically adjust the priority of an application?

   A. 4

   B. 3

   C. 2

   D. 1

7. You suspect a disk drive is creating a bottleneck within your system. You use the LogicalDisk:%Disk Time counter to take measurements, but have a consistent reading of zero. What is the problem?

   A. The disk drive no longer functions properly

   B. Disk drive performance counters are enabled

   C. The wrong object:counter is being used

   D. Disk drive performance counters are disabled

8. Multiprocessing supported by Windows NT is _____ .

   A. asymmetrical

B. symmetrical

C. both asymmetrical and symmetrical

D. neither asymmetrical nor symmetrical

9. (True/False) Using two processors in your Windows NT system doubles the performance capability.

10. Where does Windows NT perform automatic self-tuning optimizations?

   A. Thread and process prioritization

   B. Asymmetrical processing

   C. Swapping among multiple pagefiles

   D. Caching disk requests

   E. All the above

11. The cache system used by Windows NT is _____ .

   A. static

   B. fixed

   C. dynamic

   D. inert

12. The Disk Drive Performance Counters are enabled using what utility?

   A. Perfdisk

   B. Diskenable

   C. Diskperf

   D. Enabledisk

13. (True/False) The Task Manager cannot be used to change the priority of a thread.

14. Using Performance Monitor, you have determined that you have a disk drive bottleneck. What action(s) could alleviate this problem?

   A. Create a RAID 5 set using Disk Administrator

   B. Add more physical memory to the system

   C. Use an 8-bit disk drive controller card

   D. Buy a new processor

   E. All the above

15. Using Performance Monitor, you have determined that you are encountering a memory bottleneck. What action(s) will eliminate it?

   A. Increase the size of pagefile.sys

   B. Add a new high-speed controller card

   C. Unload any drivers that aren't in use

   D. Decrease the size of the L2 cache

   E. All of the above

16. (True/False) Hard page faults are more detrimental to system performance than soft page faults.

17. (True/False) Once you have manually performance-tuned your system, you never have to do it again.

18. (True/False) Disk Drive Performance Counters should only be enabled when monitoring disk drive performance.

19. How would you change the priority of an application that is already running?

   A. Use Performance Monitor

   B. The Performance tab from System Properties

   C. Use the /REALTIME switch

   D. Task Manager

MCSE
MICROSOFT CERTIFIED SYSTEMS ENGINEER

15

Booting, Troubleshooting, and Service Packs

CERTIFICATION OBJECTIVES

Wouldn't life be wonderful if we could install an operating system and never have to worry about it failing to work correctly? In all my years of dealing with a variety of operating systems, I have never encountered one that didn't need coaxing at some point in time. Windows NT is no different, so it's very important that you be intimately familiar with the boot process for different processor-based configurations. In this chapter, we discuss the boot process for Windows NT on Intel-based and RISC-based machines. We also discuss systems that have been set to multiboot between two or more operating systems.

Next, we look at troubleshooting your hardware and software to include having a Windows NT boot disk and emergency repair disk for your system. Not all problems you encounter are boot-specific, and you may need other utilities to help with your troubleshooting. We examine the Event Viewer, and we learn what Windows NT Diagnostics, also known as WinMSD, can offer you in determining faults within your system.

No operating system is bug free, but when Microsoft makes significant fixes to bugs in Windows NT, it issues a Service Pack. In one section of the chapter, we discuss installing Service Packs.

No chapter on troubleshooting Windows NT would be complete without a discussion on the "Blue Screen of Death."

In the last section of the chapter, we look at a variety of resources available to you, to help keep your Windows NT system operating smoothly.

Boot Process for Intel-Based and RISC-Based Machines

The boot process for Intel-based and RISC-based machines is essentially the same. You turn on your machine, the screen flickers a little, a bunch of words scroll across the screen, and eventually a menu appears, prompting you to select what flavor of Windows you want. But what is going on behind the scenes? What does all that chugging, churning, and chattering really mean? The answers to these questions and more will be exposed over the next several pages. You are probably familiar with the way in which a normal PC boots. It does a Power On Self Test (POST), reads the Master Boot Record (MBR), loads the operating system, sets the environment, and then brings everything up. You can refer to Figure 15-1 for more information on this process.

FIGURE 15-1

As a PC boots, it checks
the hardware configuration
prior to initializing the
operating system

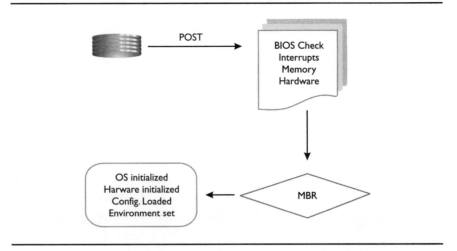

Windows NT boots up in a similar fashion; it does a POST, reads the
MBR, and loads it into memory. However, when NT is installed, it changes
the boot sector to load NTLDR, which takes over at that point. The changes
take place after the MBR is read. See at Figure 15-2 to visualize this process.

FIGURE 15-2

Windows NT boots in a
similar fashion to other
operating systems, until
the MBR is read

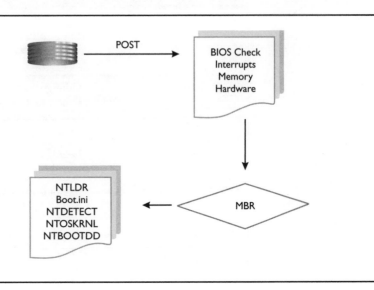

At this point you might be tempted to ask why we are having this involved discussion about boot sequences. Well, in addition to being on the MCSE test, this information is important for understanding the boot process from a troubleshooting standpoint. Users often are not sophisticated enough to give you an informed description of what is going on when they're having a computer problem. Quite often, the problem is simply stated as, "the stupid thing is broken." Eliciting a better description of the event, from the user standpoint, can tell you where in the boot process to begin looking for what has caused the problem.

Table 15-1 lists the files that are required to boot up Windows NT 4 Workstation on an Intel-based machine.

How do the files in Table 15-1 work together? First, NTLDR reads the BOOT.INI and builds a menu of operating system choices. If you choose to start Windows NT rather than another operating system, it starts NTDETECT.COM. NTDETECT.COM scans over the hardware in your system and tells NTLDR what it has found. Then NTLDR loads NTOSKRNL.EXE for further processing. We will see what additional processing occurs when we discuss Windows NT load phases.

TABLE 15-1		
	Windows NT Files	**Description**
Files for Intel-based Machines	NTLDR	Loads the operating system for Windows NT. It can also load other operating systems (such as Windows 95) if the machine is configured to dual-boot.
	BOOT.INI	Configures the start-up menu that launches NT. Points to the location of the boot partition for NT, and to the location of other operating systems on the machine.
	BOOTSECT.DOS	Is only used if starting an operating system other than NT (such as DOS or Windows 95).
	NTDETECT.COM	Examines the hardware on an Intel machine to build a list that is passed to the NTLDR.
	NTOSKRNL.EXE	This is the NT kernel.
	NTBOOTDD.SYS	Only used if the machine has SCSI hard disks (and the SCSI adapter has the bios disabled).

The BOOT.INI file also points out an important concept: the boot partition and the system partition do not have to be the same thing. The boot partition is where the Windows NT system files are stored. The system partition is simply where you boot from. (The names might have lead you to think it would be the other way around.) On Intel-based computers, the system partition must be on the first physical hard disk. The boot partition can be the same as the system partition, or it can be on a different partition on the same hard disk, or it can be on a different hard disk.

Table 15-2 lists the files needed to boot Windows NT 4 Workstation on a RISC-based machine. Notice the differences between the two different processor platforms.

exam
ⓦatch

It is important to note that on RISC-based machines the system partition has to be on a FAT partition.

Table 15-3 displays the differences between the two processor platforms' pre-boot sequences.

Now that we have discussed the files needed to boot Windows NT, let's look at the process NT uses to load so it can run successfully.

Windows NT Load Phases

As Windows NT begins to load the system files, it does so in a predetermined fashion. It moves from a character mode into a graphical mode—this transition is crucial—and as this takes place, it engages many different facilities.

As Windows NT loads, it goes through four distinct phases. These phases are the Kernel load phase, the Kernel initialization phase, the Services load

TABLE 15-2	Windows NT Files	Description
Files for RISC-based Machines	OSLOADER.EXE	Loads the operating system on a RISC machine. Basically the same as NTLDR on an Intel machine.
	NTOSKRNL.EXE	The NT kernel.
	NTBOOTDD.SYS	Only used if the machine has SCSI hard disks (and the SCSI adapter has the bios disabled).

TABLE 15-3	Intel-based Pre-boot Sequence	RISC-based Pre-boot Sequence
Comparison of Boot Sequences	POST routines are run.	ROM firmware reads boot precedence table.
	MBR is read into memory.	Firmware reads first physical sector of boot drive (MBR) into memory.
	Active partition is located, and boot sector is read into memory.	Firmware examines BIOS Parameter Block (BPR) to determine support for file system.
	NTLDR is loaded.	OSLOADER.EXE is loaded.

phase, and finally the Windows subsystem start phase. The process is complete when a user successfully logs on. Let's look at each of these phases.

Kernel Load

The Kernel load phase begins when NTOSKRNL.EXE is loaded into memory. At this point you see the message, "NTDETECT is checking hardware". Then the hardware abstraction layer (HAL) is called into play. The function of HAL is to hide differences in hardware from the operating system. In this manner, HAL virtualizes the hardware specifics from Windows NT (which in turn enhances portability). This comes at a cost, however, both in performance and in the range of applications that NT can run. This is becoming much less of an issue. Basically, any program that relies upon direct hardware calls does not run under Windows NT. The programs affected by this are primarily games.

After HAL is constructed, the Registry is consulted to determine which drivers are to be loaded, and in what order. So where in this vast database is the information found? If you look at Figure 15-3, you see the Service Group order key.

The last step of the Kernel load phase occurs when the screen turns black and dots progress across the top of the screen. It is at this stage that the drivers in the Service Group Order subkey are loaded into memory. If you had selected the /SOS option in your BOOT.INI, you actually would see the names of the drivers being loaded. This is a valuable troubleshooting technique, and will be visited later.

FIGURE 15-3

The Service Group Order subkey controls the order in which Windows NT loads the drivers

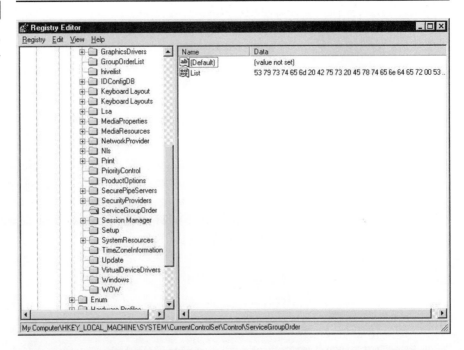

Kernel Initialization

It is now time to begin initialization of the Kernel. This occurs when the screen turns blue. Each driver loaded during the Kernel load phase is initialized. As this occurs, dots parade across the screen. If the progression appears to hang, a driver either is taking a long time to load, or is having trouble loading. You can get a rough idea of what caused the hang by counting the dots which preceded it. How Windows NT treats a failed service is governed by the settings found in HKEY_LOCAL_MACHINE\SYSTEM\CurrentControlSet\Services\ servicename\ErrorControl. There are four levels of settings:

- **Ignore: 0x0**   If a service has this error control code, and Windows NT has trouble loading or initializing the service, it is ignored and the boot sequence proceeds. You aren't even given an error message.

- **Normal: 0x1**   When this level is set, the error is ignored, and boot progresses in a normal fashion, but this time you are given an error message.

- ■ **Severe: 0x2**   When a severe level is set, and you are not booting using the LastKnownGood configuration, the boot process fails and restarts using the LastKnownGood configuration. If you are already booting using the LastKnownGood, the error is ignored and the boot process continues. LastKnownGood configuration will be discussed in depth later in the chapter.

- ■ **Critical: 0x3**   If a critical service fails and you are not booting using the LastKnownGood configuration, the boot process fails and restarts using the LastKnownGood configuration. However, if you already are using the LastKnownGood configuration, and you receive the critical error control code, then the boot fails and an error message is generated. Refer to Figure 15-4 to see how these error control codes are displayed in the Registry.

FIGURE 15-4

During Kernel initialization, the error control level assigned to each service determines how Windows NT handles exceptions

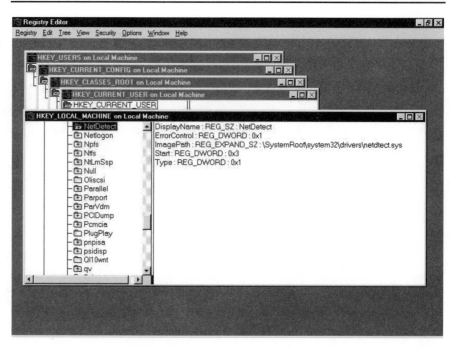

Services Load

We are now ready to begin the Services load phase. At this point, Windows NT reads the contents of the following key: HKEY_LOCAL_MACHINE\ SYSTEM\CurrentControlSet\Control\Session Manager\BootExecute. The default entry for this particular key is shown in Figure 15-5. The autocheck autochk * is roughly equivalent to the old DOS utility CHKDSK. You can customize this key to tell NT to fix any problems found on the disk automatically, if you change the autochk * to autochk /p *. It then checks each partition on your system for errors. If you change it to autochk /p \DosDevices\c:, it checks drive C: for errors.

The Session Manager subkey of the Registry contains global variables used by the Session Manager. These items are stored in the following Registry path: HKEY_LOCAL_MACHINE\SYSTEM\CurrentControlSet\Control\Session Manager. In order to explore these settings, we have to use the Registry editor to view them. The Registry contains critical configuration information,

FIGURE 15-5

The Session Manager subkey details global variables that are loaded during the Services load phase

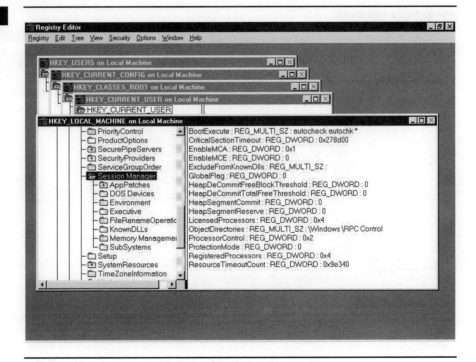

without which Windows NT is severely lobotomized. It is with the utmost respect and caution that we examine this database. Prior to working with the Registry, make sure that you have a good backup (just in case). Remember that some settings are changed dynamically, and therefore enacted without warning or prompting. It is for this reason that I prefer REGEDT32 set to Read Only mode. It can prevent transient fingers from inadvertently making real-time changes to your workstation. This is illustrated in Figure 15-6.

EXERCISE 15-1

Viewing the Session Manager Registry Settings

1. Select Start | Run and type **REGEDT32** in the run box.
2. Select Options | Read Only Mode.
3. Select the HKEY_LOCAL_MACHINE pane from the cascaded windows.
4. Select the System key.
5. Select the CurrentControlSet subkey.

FIGURE 15-6

When exploring in the Registry, the Read Only mode of REGEDT32 is a handy feature

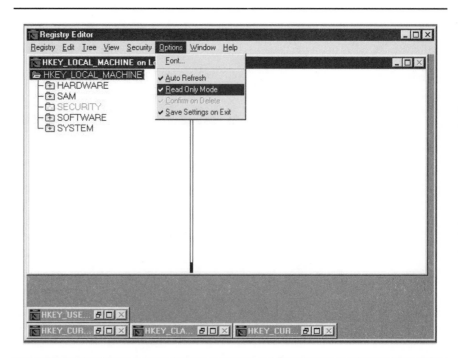

6. Select the Control subkey.

7. Scroll down until you see the SessionManager subkey.

8. Choose File | Exit when you're finished examining the details of the key.

Windows Subsystem Start

When the Windows Subsystem starts, it starts WINLOGON.EXE, which starts the Local Security Authority (LSA). The LSA is the main element of the Windows NT security system, and is responsible for showing the CTRL-ALT-DEL logon dialog box.

The next thing that happens is that the Service Controller executes and takes a final look through the Registry, checking for services that are marked to load automatically.

The process is complete after a successful logon has been accomplished. After a successful logon has occurred, the Windows NT Kernel copies the Clone Control Set to LastKnownGood. The system does not consider the boot to be successful unless the Clone Control Set has been copied to LastKnownGood. Later in the chapter we discuss how LastKnownGood can be utilized for your benefit.

Now that we have seen what happens while Windows NT is starting, let's take a closer look at the BOOT.INI file it uses during startup.

BOOT.INI

The BOOT.INI file is a critical .INI file created by Windows NT when it is first installed. This file is where you can configure the many ways your system behaves when Windows NT is booted. If this file becomes damaged or corrupted, Windows NT simply doesn't load.

There are two sections that make up the content of the BOOT.INI. As seen below, the first is the boot loader section and the second is the operating systems section. No matter how many operating systems are installed, you must still have a BOOT.INI file.

```
[boot loader]
timeout=30
default=multi(0)disk(0)rdisk(0)partition(7)\WINNTWS
```

```
[operating systems]
multi(0)disk(0)rdisk(0)partition(7)\WINNTWS="Windows NT
    Workstation Version 4.00"
multi(0)disk(0)rdisk(0)partition(7)\WINNTWS="Windows NT
    Workstation Version 4.00 [VGA mode]" /basevideo /sos
multi(0)disk(0)rdisk(0)partition(6)\WINNT="Windows NT Server
    Version 4.00"
multi(0)disk(0)rdisk(0)partition(6)\WINNT="Windows NT Server
    Version 4.00 [VGA mode]" /basevideo /sos
    C:\="Windows 95"
```

exam
ⓌＡｔｃｈ

The importance of the BOOT.INI cannot be stressed enough. Know what will happen if the BOOT.INI file is damaged, missing, or otherwise errant. You must also know how to edit it, and be very familiar with reading it.

EXERCISE 15-2

Edit the BOOT.INI File

1. Select Start | Programs | Windows NT Explorer and go to the root of your C: drive.

2. Make sure all files are displayed so that you can see the BOOT.INI file (which is a system, read-only file).

3. Once you find the BOOT.INI file, right-click it, choose Properties, and uncheck the Read-only box.

4. Click the OK button and then open BOOT.INI with Notepad.

5. Change the Timeout setting from 30 seconds to 15 seconds.

6. Make sure that when you save changes created with Notepad, you select the All Files Type, or else you will end up with BOOT.INI.TEXT and it will not work!

7. Right-click BOOT.INI, choose Properties, and check the Read-only box.

Boot Loader

The boot loader section contains two basic entries: timeout, and the default operating system. The timeout is simply a countdown timer to give you a chance to make a selection other than the default. When timeout reaches 0, the default operating system is loaded. If you want your system to start up more quickly, you can either make a selection or change the timeout setting. However, if the timeout setting is changed to 0, you won't have a chance to make any selection.

If you are dual-booting your system, you can make changes here to
select the default operating system by pointing the default setting to the one
preferred. Rather than directly editing the BOOT.INI to make changes to the
boot loader section, it is preferable to utilize the Startup/Shutdown tab under
System Properties. As seen in Figure 15-7, the graphical tools provided are easy
to use—much easier than trying to edit the Advanced RISC Computing
(ARC) naming path to the default OS.

Operating Systems

The operating systems section of the BOOT.INI file is perhaps the most
ominous looking portion of this important file. Although it is poorly
understood even by many professionals, you need to learn this section, as
it might be on your exam. So what is the operating systems section of the
BOOT.INI? Its function is to tell you what operating systems are installed on

FIGURE 15-7

Use the System Properties
tab under Startup/
Shutdown to edit the
boot loader section of
the BOOT.INI file

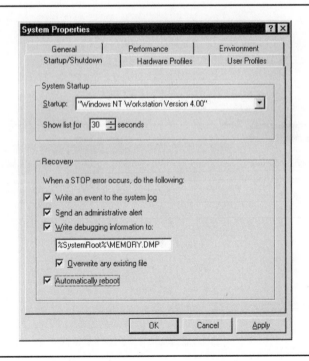

the machine, and to tell Windows NT where to find them. Even if you are not dual-booting your machine, the BOOT.INI file still has this section.

ARC Naming Convention

The ARC naming convention comes to us from the RISC world. It is useful in identifying partition information on multidisk/multipartition machines. For instance, look at Figure 15-8.

If we look at the BOOT.INI for this machine, we see the following:

```
[boot loader]
timeout=30
default=multi(0)disk(0)rdisk(0)partition(7)\WINNTWS
[operating systems]
multi(0)disk(0)rdisk(0)partition(7)\WINNTWS="Windows NT
    Workstation Version 4.00"
multi(0)disk(0)rdisk(0)partition(7)\WINNTWS="Windows NT
    Workstation Version 4.00 [VGA mode]" /basevideo /sos
multi(0)disk(0)rdisk(0)partition(6)\WINNT="Windows NT Server
    Version 4.00"
multi(0)disk(0)rdisk(0)partition(6)\WINNT="Windows NT Server
    Version 4.00 [VGA mode]" /basevideo /sos
C:\="Windows 95"
```

From this we can see the boot partition is on partition number 7. But what is all this other stuff? Let's look and see.

FIGURE 15-8

Disk Administrator shows a graphical representation of the disk layout of a particular machine

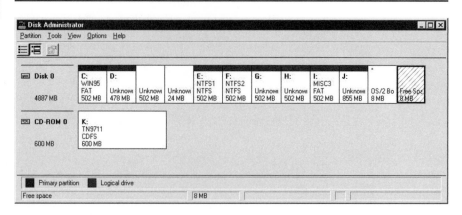

SCSI(n) or multi(n)

A SCSI controller that has its resident BIOS disabled uses the SCSI ARC name. All other controllers (IDE controllers, and SCSI controllers with BIOS enabled) are listed as multi. The numbers that follow SCSI or multi start counting with 0. In the preceding example, the multi (0) indicates that it is the first controller (either IDE or SCSI with the BIOS enabled).

exam
ⓦatch

If your BOOT.INI does not list the SCSI ARC name then NTBOOTDD.SYS will not be used.

disk(n)

Disk is only used if SCSI is listed as the first word of the ARC path. If Disk is used, the SCSI bus number is used here. It starts counting with 0. If you have multi in the first space, then Disk will always be 0.

rdisk(n)

Rdisk indicates the SCSI Logical Unit Number (LUN), when SCSI is the first word in the ARC path. It indicates the ordinal number of the disk, if the first word is multi. Remember the counting here also starts with 0.

partition(n)

This is simply the partition number on the disk. The important thing to remember is that the counting starts with 1. In Figure 15-7, even though the OS/2 Boot Manager is at the physical end of the drive, it is counted as number 1 partition, since the system boots from it, then moves up in count from the C: drive.

To put this all together now, if we have the following:

```
multi(0)disk(0)rdisk(0)partition(7)\ WINNTWS="Windows NT
Workstation Version 4.00"
```

we know it is either an IDE controller or a SCSI controller with the BIOS enabled. It is the first controller on the system. Disk (0) in this instance is ignored. Rdisk (0) means that it is the first drive on the system. Partition (7) means that Windows NT Workstation is located on the seventh partition.

Please note that if changes are made to the system, and this section of the BOOT.INI is not updated, Windows NT will not load on the next boot.

You may be wondering about the "unknown" partitions listed in Figure 15-8. The unknown partitions are valid, but unknown to Windows NT 4 Workstation, as it does not recognize OS/2, LINUX, or FAT32 partitions.

\path

The path listed in the preceding BOOT.INI is simply the path to the location of each operating system.

BOOT.INI Switches

There are several switches that can be used to customize the way Windows NT boots up. Some of these are used for troubleshooting purposes. These can be used in the BOOT.INI file.

/NOSERIALMICE=[COMx | COMx,y,z...]

This switch tells Windows NT that you do not have a serial mouse on a particular COM port, and as a result it does not poll the port for a mouse. You might want to use this if you have a serial device attached to a particular COM port. If NT detects the device, it might think it is a mouse, and as a result the device would not function properly under Windows NT. If you were to use /NOSERIALMICE without a particular COM port specified, this disables polling on all COM ports. If you say /NOSERIALMICE=COM1 then only polling on COM1 is disabled.

/BASEVIDEO

This switch causes Windows NT to load the standard VGA driver in 640 by 480 mode. This is useful if, for instance, you make a change to a video driver and then reboot, only to find you cannot read anything on the screen. In the /BASEVIDEO mode you can get the machine up, and change the settings back to something supported by your particular hardware configuration. By default Windows NT sets this option up for you. It appears on the screen as VGA mode of BOOT.INI.

/CRASHDEBUG

This switch enables the automatic recovery and restart options, and is set up when you make changes to the Recovery section of Startup/Shutdown under System in Control Panel. While you can add it to the BOOT.INI manually, the safest way to change this is through Control Panel.

/SOS

SOS mode does pretty much what it sounds like; it tells you what drivers Windows NT is loading during startup. Remember the dots that go across your screen as drivers are loaded? This switch causes NT to echo the names onto the screen. It is useful for determining which driver is hanging during startup. This entry is also added by default to the VGA mode entry in BOOT.INI.

/NODEBUG

The /NODEBUG switch tells NT that no debug information is being monitored. When this information is being used, there is a pretty significant performance hit as a result. This switch is useful to developers.

/MAXMEM:n

If you use the /MAXMEM switch, you can tell Windows NT how much memory it is allowed to use. Why would you want to limit how much memory NT uses? Normally you wouldn't, but if you suspected that you had bad memory modules, you can play with these settings until you locate the bad module.

/SCSIORDINAL:n

The /SCSIORDINAL switch is used if you have two identical SCSI controllers in the same system. You would use this switch to tell NT which one was which. The numbering on this begins with 0, so 1 would indicate the second controller.

We have edited the BOOT.INI with a text editor, so let's take a look at how to modify it using a Control Panel applet.

Editing BOOT.INI with Control Panel

1. Select Start | Settings | Control Panel.
2. Select the System applet.
3. Select the Startup/Shutdown tab.
4. Change the timeout setting from 15 seconds to 30 seconds.
5. Click the OK button.
6. The settings take effect after the next reboot.

Earlier in this section, we mentioned dual-booting different operating systems. In the next section, we discuss multiboot configurations.

CERTIFICATION OBJECTIVE 15.02

Configuring Multiboot Systems

Windows NT supports multibooting between Windows NT and additional operating systems, if your system partition contains the Windows NT boot sector.

When you install Windows NT, setup copies the first sector of the system partition (the boot sector) to a file named BOOTSECT.DOS. NT then replaces the original boot sector with its own boot sector.

When you start your computer, and the system partition contains the Windows NT boot sector, the code in the boot sector loads the Windows NT boot loader, NTLDR. The operating system menu, which is built from the BOOT.INI file, enables you to choose the operating system to be loaded.

If you select an operating system other than Windows NT from the operating system menu, NTLDR loads and starts the BOOTSECT.DOS file. This functionality results in the other operating system starting, as if NTLDR had not intervened.

If you want to dual-boot between Windows 95 and Windows NT, you should install Windows 95 first and then install Windows NT. If the Windows 95 boot sector replaces the Windows NT boot sector, it causes a problem for Windows NT accessing any NTFS volume. Why would it cause this problem? Because the Windows 95 boot sector is for FAT partitions, and does not recognize NTFS partitions.

So, now we have a fully-functioning Windows NT Workstation, in which everything will work perfectly from here on out, correct? Not on your life! As I said in the beginning of the chapter, I have never seen an operating system that doesn't need to be massaged from time to time. In the next section, we start looking at methods to help you in troubleshooting hardware and software.

CERTIFICATION OBJECTIVE 15.03

Troubleshooting Hardware/Software

Any discussion about troubleshooting hardware and software could easily fill this entire book, so we will limit ourselves to only a few topics on the matter. Let's start the section off with a look at boot failures and methods available to overcome them.

Boot Failures

Boot failures can take many different paths to lead your system to failure. It can be anything from a boot file being corrupted to a bad video driver not allowing your system to complete the boot process.

The first item to ensure is that you have a Windows NT boot floppy, in case one of the boot files for your system ever gets deleted. With a boot floppy on hand, you might be able to get your system back up quickly, and might be able to copy the missing or corrupt file back to your hard disk. You must use a special boot disk that has been formatted on a Windows NT system and modified to mimic the boot configuration of the system that won't boot. When you create the boot disk, you may need to modify the BOOT.INI file to show the ARC path to the boot partition on the bad system. Exercise 15-4 leads you through the steps of creating a Windows NT boot floppy for an Intel-based machine.

Creating a Windows NT Boot Floppy for Intel-based Machines

1. Log on as Administrator and select My Computer.
2. Right-click 3 ½ Floppy (A:) and select Format from the menu.
3. Make sure you have a blank floppy disk in the drive and click the Start button.
4. Acknowledge the warning by clicking the OK button.
5. When the format completes, click the OK button.
6. Copy the following files to the newly formatted disk: NTLDR, NTDETECT.COM, BOOT.INI, and NTBOOTDD.SYS (if your system uses NTBOOTDD.SYS).
7. Reboot your system with the boot floppy you just created. It is better to try the boot floppy now, and make sure it works properly, than to find out that it doesn't work when you need it.

While the Windows NT boot disk can save you from several boot problems, it doesn't solve them all.

Using the LastKnownGood Configuration

What happens if you load a new device driver that doesn't function correctly, and prohibits the system from booting correctly? Is all lost, and is your only option to reload Windows NT? I hope you answered with a big resounding NO! You can get around this problem by reverting to the LastKnownGood configuration. LastKnownGood is the configuration that was saved to a special control set in the Registry after the last successful logon to Windows NT. So instead of reloading the operating system, you can restart the computer without logging on, and select LastKnownGood during the boot sequence. This loads the previously known good control set, and bypasses the bad device driver. Exercise 15-5 leads you through the process of booting, using the LastKnownGood configuration.

Booting Windows NT with the LastKnownGood Configuration

1. Start Windows NT Workstation.

2. When the BOOT.INI displays the OS menu, select Windows NT Workstation.

3. A message appears, telling you to press SPACEBAR for the LastKnownGood. Press the SPACEBAR immediately, as you have only a few seconds to make this choice before it disappears.

4. Select L to choose the LastKnownGood configuration from the Hardware Profile/Configuration Recovery menu.

5. Press ENTER to confirm your choice. After the system boots, it displays a message confirming that it loaded from a previous configuration.

While the LastKnownGood configuration can save your day, like the Windows NT boot floppy it doesn't work in all situations. Another tool available for your use is the Emergency Repair Disk.

Using the Emergency Repair Disk

The Emergency Repair Disk (ERD) can be used to return a Windows NT system back to the configuration it was last in, based on the last time you updated your Emergency Repair Disk. This disk can repair missing Windows NT files, and restore the Registry to include disk configuration and security information. To create an ERD, use the Repair Disk Utility. Figure 15-9 shows the Repair Disk Utility after it has been started.

If you choose the Update Repair Info button, the Repair Disk Utility overwrites some of the files located in the %systemroot%\Repair directory. After the %systemroot%\Repair directory has been updated, the program

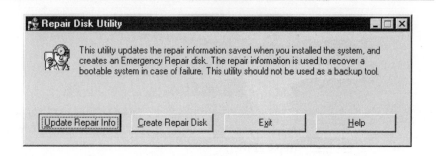

prompts you to create an Emergency Repair Disk. The disk it creates is the same as if you had chosen the Create Repair Disk option.

If you choose the Create Repair Disk button, the Repair Disk Utility formats the disk prior to creating the ERD. This occurs whether you use a prior ERD or a new disk. Exercise 15-6 shows you how to create an ERD.

EXERCISE 15-6

Creating an Emergency Repair Disk

1. Log on as Administrator.
2. Select Start | Programs | Command Prompt.
3. Type **rdisk** in the prompt window.
4. Choose the Update Repair Info button.
5. After the program updates your %systemroot%\Repair directory, it prompts you to create an ERD. Select OK after inserting a disk.
6. A message is displayed showing that configuration files are being copied.
7. Choose Exit after the files are copied to the disk.

If you look at the files on the ERD you will notice some of them end with a ._. This indicates that those files have been compressed. You can decompress those files using the expand utility that comes with Windows NT.

exam
Ⓦatch

The Security Accounts Manager (SAM) and security files are not automatically updated by rdisk. To update those files, you need to use the /S switch in conjunction with rdisk.

Now that we have an up-to-date Emergency Repair Disk, it is time to use it in the Emergency Repair Process. The Emergency Repair Process is used when your system doesn't function correctly, and using the LastKnownGood configuration doesn't solve the problem. This process requires the original installation disks from when you first installed Windows NT Workstation. You also need the ERD that you created in the preceding exercise. Please note that ERDs are computer-specific, so don't get them mixed up if you have several systems. Exercise 15-7 shows you how to complete the Emergency Repair Process.

Using the Emergency Repair Disk with the NT Setup Disks

1. Start your system using the Windows NT Setup boot disk.

2. Insert disk 2 when the system prompts you for it.

3. When the first screen appears press R to start the Emergency Repair Process.

4. Four selections are displayed on your screen. Follow the on-screen instructions to select *only* the option Inspect Registry Files.

5. Select the Continue (Perform Selected Tasks) line and press ENTER.

6. Windows NT wants to perform mass storage detection, so go ahead and let it do that.

7. Insert disk 3 when prompted, and press ENTER.

8. Press ENTER to skip the Specify Additional Mass Storage Devices step.

9. When the system prompts you, insert the ERD you created in Exercise 15-6.

10. Several choices are displayed on your screen. Select *only* the DEFAULT (Default User Profile) choice.

11. Select Continue (Perform Selected Tasks) and press ENTER.

12. The correct data is copied back to your Windows NT Workstation partition. Once the data has been copied, remove the ERD and press ENTER to restart your system.

System Recovery

Windows NT features a Recovery utility that can perform selected tasks in the event of a STOP error. You configure the recovery options within the Startup/Shutdown tab of System Properties. You should remember this tab from earlier in the chapter when we discussed changing the boot loader options of the BOOT.INI file. Figure 15-10 shows the Startup/Shutdown tab.

The Recovery options are, for the most, part self-explanatory. However, it is worth mentioning that the Automatically Reboot option allows your system to be returned to normal operation quickly after a system crash, instead of it having to be rebooted manually. The most important option in the Recovery utility, as far as troubleshooting goes, is the Write Debugging Information To utility. When this option is checked and a STOP error occurs, the entire contents of memory get dumped to the pagefile. When your system restarts,

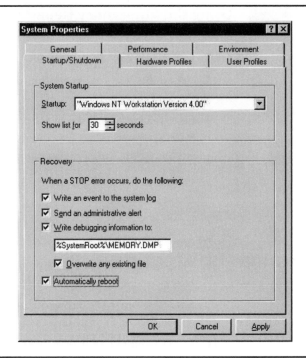

this information is copied automatically from the pagefile to the name you
specified in the Recovery option block.

Since the entire contents of your system's memory are dumped to the
pagefile, the pagefile has to be as large as the amount of physical memory
installed in your system. A system that has 64MB of physical memory needs to
have a pagefile that is at least 64MB in size. One other caveat: The pagefile has
to be located on the boot partition. Exercise 15-8 gives you a chance to
configure your system for memory dumps.

EXERCISE 15-8

Configuring for Memory Dumps

1. Select Start | Settings | Control Panel.

2. Double-click the System applet and select the Startup/Shutdown tab.

3. Under Recovery, select the Write Debugging Information To box. It is
   your choice to either accept the default path and filename, or pick one
   of your own.

4. If you want the next memory dump to overwrite any file that has the same name, select the Overwrite box. If you leave this block unchecked, Windows NT doesn't write a memory dump file if one already exists with the same name.

Task Manager

The Task Manager should look familiar to you. We examined it in Chapter 14 while discussing Performance Tuning. Let's look at one more function that it can perform with regard to troubleshooting your system. It has the capability to end a task that may be causing your system to hang. Under normal operating conditions you see the word "Running" underneath the status column, as illustrated in Figure 15-11. However, if a task is no longer responding, the words "Not responding" are in the status column. Exercise 15-9 leads you through the process of shutting down a task.

FIGURE 15-11

Applications tab of the Task Manager shows whether a task is responding

   ## Shutting Down a Task with Task Manager

1. Use your right mouse button and click once on your Taskbar.

2. Select Task Manager from the menu.

3. Click the Start button and select Programs | Accessories | Paint.

4. Click the Start button and select Programs | Accessories | Clock.

5. Click the Start button and select Programs | Accessories | Notepad.

6. Select the Applications tab on the Task Manager. You see the three applications that you just started. To the right of the applications is listed the Status of each application.

7. Let's assume that the Clock application has run rampant and is using 100 percent of the CPU, and needs to be shut down. Click Clock so that it is highlighted, and click the End Task button.

8. On a real task that is not responding, you might receive a dialog box stating that the task is not responding, and asking if you would like to wait. Click End Task.

9. Close all remaining applications that are running.

10. Close the Task Manager.

Taking Ownership of a Resource

If you share your Windows NT Workstation with other people, at some point the inevitable happens: someone loses access to a resource. Of course, this only happens if you are using the NTFS file system. Assuming you have Administrator privileges, you can easily solve the dilemma by taking ownership of the resource and sharing it to the person who needs access with full control, so he can gain ownership of the resource. In my experience, this action normally occurs when someone is fired or quits. Exercise 15-10 shows you how to gain ownership of a resource and allow someone else to take ownership of it. In the exercise, User1 is the person who quits the organization and User2 is the person who takes his place.

EXERCISE 15-10

Taking Ownership of a Resource (Troubleshooting Security Problems)

1. Log on to your system as Administrator and create two new user accounts named User1 and User2.

2. Log off the system and log back on as User1. Create a folder named user1test and set the permissions so only User1 has access to it. This folder is the one that User2 needs to access in order to retrieve valuable data.

3. Log off the system and log back on as User2. Try to access the user1test folder.

4. Log off the system and log back on as Administrator.

5. Open Windows NT Explorer and right-click the user1test folder.

6. Select Properties and choose the Security tab.

7. Select the Ownership button.

8. Select the Take Ownership button. The system prompts you with a dialog box stating that one or more of the items is a directory. Click the Yes button.

9. Select the Permissions button and give User2 full control of the user1test folder.

10. Select the OK button.

11. Select the OK button.

12. Log off the system and log back on as User2.

13. Access the user1test folder and follow steps 5-8 to gain ownership of the folder.

Not all of your problems will be boot-related, or easily identified with any of the methods described so far. You might need to use other tools to help you diagnose the problem your system is having. In the next section, we look at two tools available to you: the Event Viewer and Windows NT Diagnostics.

Event Viewer

The Event Viewer, located in the Administration submenu, allows you to examine various events that have been generated by the Windows NT system, services, and applications, or through user actions that have been audited. Figure 15-12 shows an example from the Event Viewer.

Log Files

The event viewer can display three separate logs. Depending on the type of item you need to view, it dictates which log you will open.

■ The System Log contains events that are provided by the Windows NT internal services and drivers.

■ The Security Log contains all security-related events when auditing has been enabled.

■ The Application Log contains events that have been generated by applications.

By default, each log file is a maximum of 512KB in size, and overwrites events older than seven days. These default settings are configurable by changing the Maximum Log Size and Event Log Wrapping options. The maximum size of the log can be changed in 64KB increments. The three event

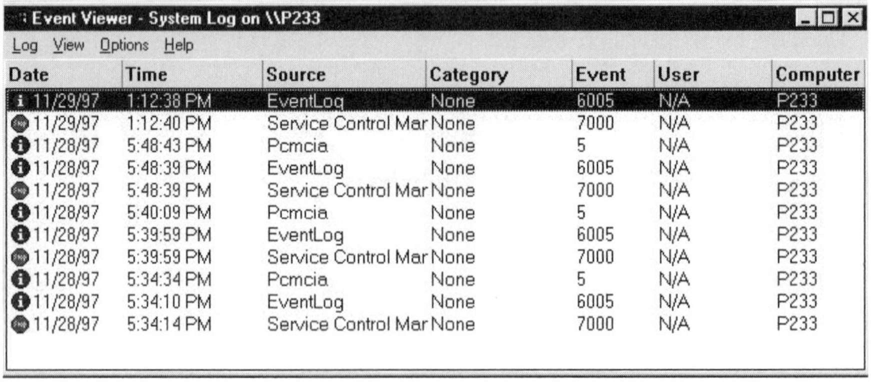

FIGURE 15-12

Event Viewer allows you to examine various events that have been generated by the Windows NT system

	Event Viewer - System Log on \\P233					_□×

Log View Options Help

Date	Time	Source	Category	Event	User	Computer
11/29/97	1:12:38 PM	EventLog	None	6005	N/A	P233
11/29/97	1:12:40 PM	Service Control Mar	None	7000	N/A	P233
11/28/97	5:48:43 PM	Pcmcia	None	5	N/A	P233
11/28/97	5:48:39 PM	EventLog	None	6005	N/A	P233
11/28/97	5:48:39 PM	Service Control Mar	None	7000	N/A	P233
11/28/97	5:40:09 PM	Pcmcia	None	5	N/A	P233
11/28/97	5:39:59 PM	EventLog	None	6005	N/A	P233
11/28/97	5:39:59 PM	Service Control Mar	None	7000	N/A	P233
11/28/97	5:34:34 PM	Pcmcia	None	5	N/A	P233
11/28/97	5:34:10 PM	EventLog	None	6005	N/A	P233
11/28/97	5:34:14 PM	Service Control Mar	None	7000	N/A	P233

log wrapping options are: overwrite events as needed, overwrite events older than (n) days, and do not overwrite events (clear log manually).

Event log files can be saved in three different formats; event log file with the .EVT extension, text file with the .TXT extension, or a comma-delimited text file with the .TXT extension. The .EVT file is a binary file that can be read only by the event viewer utility. Any ASCII editor can read both types of text files.

Log File Events

There are five types of events you might encounter in the various logs. A unique icon identifies each event type, so that you can locate rapidly the type of event you may be interested in finding. Table 15-4 describes each of the events corresponding to an icon.

Log Event Details

Events can be seen in greater detail by using the mouse to double-click the event, or by choosing Detail from the View menu while the event is highlighted. The detail dialog box displays a text description that can help in

TABLE 15-4	Icon	Event	Description
Types of Events Displayed in the Event Viewer		Error	A significant problem has occurred, such as a service that may not have started properly.
		Warning	An event has occurred that is not currently detrimental to the system but may indicate a possible future problem.
		Information	A significant event that describes a successful operation. For example, a service starting successfully may trigger this type of event.
		Audit Success	Audited security access attempt that was successful. For example, access to an audited directory.
		Audit Failure	Audited security access attempt that was not successful. An example is a failed logon attempt.

analyzing the event. Hexadecimal information may also be provided, depending on the event. If you save the log file, the text description is saved no matter what format of log file, but the hexadecimal data is saved only if you use the .EVT format. Figure 15-13 shows the Event Details for an event from the System log.

Exercise 15-11 shows you how to use the Event Viewer to see the logs on your system.

Using the Event Viewer

1. Select Start | Programs | Administrative Tools | Event Viewer.

2. Select the Log menu and choose Application. Review any entries that are in this log.

3. Select the Log menu and choose Security. Review any entries that are in this log.

FIGURE 15-13

Event Detail from the System log

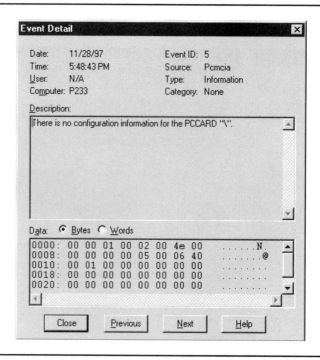

4. Select the Log menu and choose System. Review any entries that are in this log.

5. If you have entries in your System Log, highlight one of them and press ENTER. The details for that event are displayed.

6. Click the Close button to close the Event Detail window.

7. Select the Log menu and choose Exit to close the Event Viewer.

FROM THE CLASSROOM

Troubleshooting NT—Where to Begin?

NT has some wonderful tools to help you find out what is happening in your computer. Of course, tools are only valuable if you use them. If you are accustomed to the DOS/Windows environment, which offers few tools bundled with the operating system, you probably don't even look to the operating system for information about what is happening with your system. Habits can be tough to change, but you should try to change this one.

It's interesting to observe student behavior during an NT class when computer problems pop up, especially when the problems are not part of the troubleshooting labs. When this happens, more than half the students revert to old troubleshooting patterns. After the students pursue these lines fruitlessly for a while, you actually can see them becoming aware of the tools in NT and beginning to use them.

The tool to start with, when a problem occurs, is the Event Viewer. From there you can look over the three log files to see what activities have been logged. Consider the following scenario: You are having trouble connecting to a remote host and are running the TCP/IP protocol.

When we introduce this problem in class, the students start flying through their troubleshooting techniques for IP. They begin pinging away, wondering about default gateways and routers, checking subnet masks, and changing IP addresses. None of these activities involves using the Event Viewer and checking the System Log file. When they finally get around to checking the logs, they discover that the network adapter has failed.

Even though I've been working with NT a long time, I find myself doing the same type of thing—launching into some process or another, trying to get information before I remember to check the Event Viewer. Old habits die hard.

—By Shane Clawson, MCT, MCSE

CERTIFICATION OBJECTIVE 15.04

Windows NT Diagnostics (WinMSD)

Windows NT Diagnostics (also called WinMSD) has several tabs that reflect a lot of information about your Windows NT Server system. Figure 15-14 shows Windows NT Diagnostics after it has first been started.

Version

The Version tab shows the NT version number, build, and type, the CPU architecture, and multiprocessor support. The serial number and the name of the person to whom the copy of Windows NT is registered are also displayed on this tab.

FIGURE 15-14

The Windows NT Diagnostics opening window

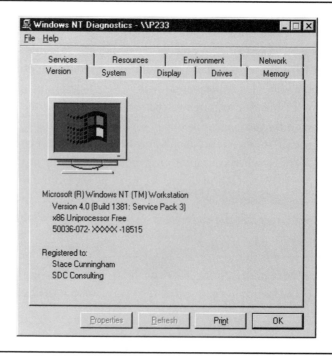

System

The System tab shows system-level information about the hardware, including the vendor ID, the Hardware Abstraction Layer (HAL) type, the BIOS date, and a description of the CPU(s).

Display

The Display tab shows the video BIOS date, the display processor, the video resolution, the quantity of video RAM, the vendor, the digital to analog (DAC) type, and the driver type and revision.

Drives

The Drives tab provides a tree display that can be sorted by drive letter or drive type for each logical disk drive. Selecting any drive brings up a Properties window that shows information such as the drive letter, the serial number, the disk space available, and how much disk space is in use. A File System tab on the Properties window gives information about the file system being used, including the maximum number of characters in a filename. The File System tab also shows whether the case will be preserved in filenames, the support of case-sensitive filenames, support for Unicode in a filename, file-based compression, and security preservation and enforcement.

Memory

The Memory tab shows in-depth details on memory utilization in your system, including the total number of processes, handles, and threads in use. This tab also displays the total amount of physical memory and the page file space available and currently in use.

Services

The Services tab displays information on all services and devices on your Windows NT Server. Highlighting a selection and selecting the Properties button brings up a Service Properties dialog box for the service or device.

Information is displayed that shows the executable file associated with the service or device, the start type, the user account with which it is associated, and any error associated with it. The service flags are also displayed, indicating whether the service runs in its own memory space, whether it is a kernel driver, and whether it can interact with the Windows NT desktop. A Dependencies tab shows you if the highlighted choice depends on another service or device. If it does depend on another service or device, it may help you in troubleshooting why a service or device failed to start.

Resources

The Resources tab displays information about hardware resources, including interrupt requests (IRQ), I/O ports, direct memory access (DMA), physical memory, and device drivers. If you select an item, it displays a dialog box indicating the associated device driver, bus, and bus type. A check box on this tab allows you to choose whether you want resources owned by the NT HAL to be displayed on the list.

Environment

The Environment tab displays all environment variables and values. It can display either values for the system or values for the local user for user-specific entries.

Network

The Network tab provides you with a great deal of information: the number of logged on users, the transport protocols in use—along with the media access control (MAC) address of each transport, the internal network settings, and the system statistics regarding server bytes sent, hung sessions, and more.

Now that you are familiar with all the tabs offered by Windows NT Diagnostics, Exercise 15-12 gives you the chance to see how your system is functioning.

Using the Windows NT Diagnostic Tools

1. Click the Start Button.
2. Select Programs.
3. Select Administration Tools.
4. Select Windows NT Diagnostics.
5. Select the Drives tab.
6. Click the + to the left of Local Hard Disks.
7. Double-click the C: drive.
8. Select the File System tab. Observe the statistics that are applicable to the drive.
9. Click the OK button.
10. Select the Services tab.
11. Highlight Workstation and click the Properties button. Observe the Service Flags that are applicable for the workstation service.
12. Select the Dependencies tab. Notice that the workstation service has group dependencies on transport driver interface (TDI).
13. Click the OK button.
14. Click the OK button to close Windows NT Diagnostics.

There are times when, no matter how much troubleshooting you do to your system, nothing fixes it. The reason could be a bug within Windows NT. In the next section we discuss how Microsoft handles this type of situation.

CERTIFICATION OBJECTIVE 15.05

Windows NT Service Packs

Microsoft periodically issues a Service Pack to fix bugs that have been detected in the Windows NT operating system. At the time of this writing, the latest service pack issued is Service Pack 3.

Obtaining Service Packs

The latest Service Pack can be ordered from Microsoft by phone or from their FTP site. The FTP address is ftp.microsoft.com/bussys/winnt/winnt-public/fixes/usa/nt40/ussp3/i386 for Intel-based machines.

Installing Service Packs

The first thing you need to do prior to installing a Service Pack is to read the README.TXT file that comes in the archive to see what bugs have been fixed, and whether there are any peculiarities that might affect the installation on your system. Installing a Service Pack is not a complex task; there are only a couple of decisions that need to be made. It is wise to err on the side of caution, as a Service Pack can render your machine inoperable. Exercise 15-13 shows you the process of installing Service Pack 3.

| EXERCISE 15-13 |

Installing a Service Pack

1. Obtain Service Pack 3 (NT4SP3_I.EXE) via FTP from ftp.microsoft.com/bussys/winnt/winnt-public/fixes/usa/nt40/ussp3/i386. Save the executable file to a folder.

2. Select Start | Programs | Windows NT Explorer and open the folder where you stored the Service Pack archive.

3. Double-click the NT4SP3_I.EXE file. The file starts extracting files to a temporary location and starts UPDATE.EXE automatically. After the files have been extracted, you are prompted with a Welcome screen that explains the procedure. It is wise to follow the instructions about updating your ERD and backing up all system and data files.

4. Click the Next button. The Software License Agreement is shown. After reading it, click the Yes button.

5. Service Pack Setup prompts you to pick the type of installation desired. Be sure the Install the Service Pack radio button is selected, and click the Next button.

6. The next screen asks you if you want to create an Uninstall directory. As always, it is wise to err on the side of caution so be sure the radio button Yes, I Want To Create an Uninstall Directory is selected, and

click the Next button. If you do not create an Uninstall directory, you can't use the Uninstall feature of the Service Pack.

7. The next screen tells you that it is ready to install the Service Pack. Click the Finish button to complete the process. The Service Pack changes only those files that were originally set up on your system.

Reapplying Service Packs

Do not delete the Service Pack archive from your system. Anytime you change hardware or software on the system you will have to reapply the Service Pack. If you reapply it, you must also choose to create a new uninstall directory.

Removing Service Packs

You may find that the Service Pack does not function correctly on your system. If this happens, you have to remove it from your system. Keep in mind that you can only uninstall the Service Pack if you originally installed the Service Pack with the Uninstall Directory option selected. Exercise 15-14 shows you how to remove a Service Pack from your system.

Removing Service Packs

1. Select Start | Programs | Windows NT Explorer and open the folder where you stored the Service Pack archive.

2. Double-click the NT4SP3_I.EXE file. The file starts extracting files to a temporary location and starts UPDATE.EXE automatically. After the files have been extracted, you are prompted with a Welcome screen that explains the procedure.

3. Click the Next button. The Software License Agreement is shown. After reading it, click the Yes button.

4. Service Pack Setup prompts you to pick the type of installation desired. Select the Uninstall a Previously Installed Service Pack radio button and click the Finish button.

5. After your system restarts, the UPDATE.EXE program replaces the files that were updated by the Service Pack with the files from the previous installation.

The "Blue Screen of Death"

"Blue Screen of Death" is just about the most frightening phrase you can say to clients when dealing with their Windows NT systems. Blue screens are actually text mode STOP messages identifying hardware and software problems that have occurred while Windows NT has been running. The reason for producing the blue screen is to alert you to the fact that an error message has been generated. The blue screen gives you information to help in troubleshooting the problem, rather than the system failing in an invisible manner. As shown in Figure 15-15, the blue screen consists of a STOP message, the text translation, the addresses of the violating call, and the drivers loaded at the time of the STOP screen.

FIGURE 15-15

A typical "Blue Screen of Death"

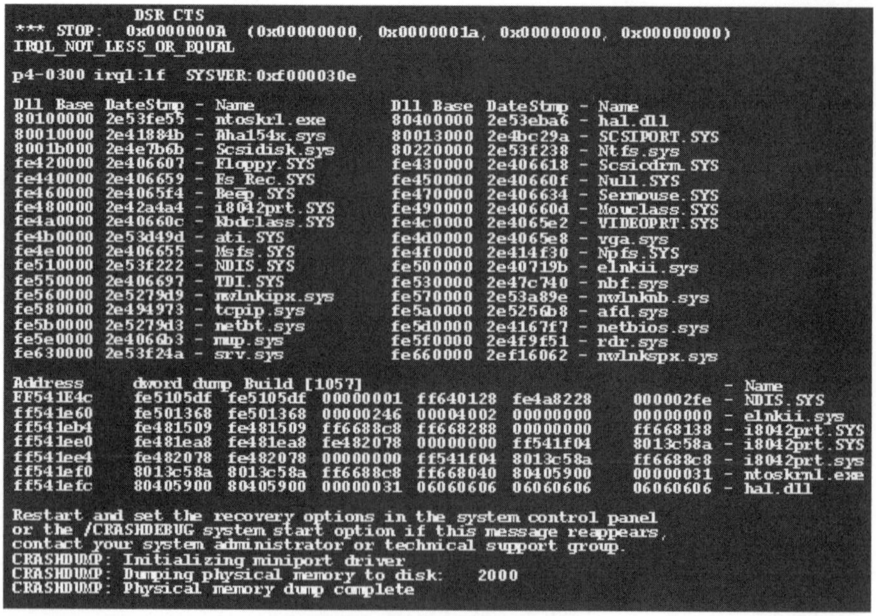

```
                DSR CTS
*** STOP:   0x0000000A   (0x00000000,  0x0000001a,  0x00000000,  0x00000000)
IRQL_NOT_LESS_OR_EQUAL

p4-0300 irql:1f   SYSVER:0xf000030e

Dll Base DateStmp - Name             Dll Base DateStmp - Name
80100000 2e53fe55 - ntoskrl.exe      80400000 2e53eba6 - hal.dll
80010000 2e41884b - Aha154x.sys      80013000 2e4bc29a - SCSIPORT.SYS
8001b000 2e4e7b6b - Scsidisk.sys     80220000 2e53f238 - Ntfs.sys
fe420000 2e406607 - Floppy.SYS       fe430000 2e406618 - Scsicdrm.SYS
fe440000 2e406659 - Fs_Rec.SYS       fe450000 2e40660f - Null.SYS
fe460000 2e4065f4 - Beep.SYS         fe470000 2e406634 - Sermouse.SYS
fe480000 2e42a4a4 - i8042prt.SYS     fe490000 2e40660d - Mouclass.SYS
fe4a0000 2e40660c - kbdclass.SYS     fe4c0000 2e4065e2 - VIDEOPRT.SYS
fe4b0000 2e53d49d - ati.SYS          fe4d0000 2e4065e8 - vga.sys
fe4e0000 2e406655 - Msfs.SYS         fe4f0000 2e414f30 - Npfs.SYS
fe510000 2e53f222 - NDIS.SYS         fe500000 2e40719b - elnkii.sys
fe550000 2e406697 - TDI.SYS          fe530000 2e47c740 - nbf.sys
fe560000 2e5279d9 - nwlnkipx.sys     fe570000 2e53a89e - nwlnknb.sys
fe580000 2e494973 - tcpip.sys        fe5a0000 2e52568 - afd.sys
fe5b0000 2e5279d3 - netbt.sys        fe5d0000 2e4167f7 - netbios.sys
fe5e0000 2e4066b3 - mup.sys          fe5f0000 2e4f9f51 - rdr.sys
fe630000 2e53f24a - srv.sys          fe660000 2ef16062 - nwlnkspx.sys

Address     dword dump Build [1057]                             - Name
FF541E4c    fe5105df fe5105df 00000001 ff640128 fe4a8228 000002fe - NDIS.SYS
ff541e60    fe501368 fe501368 00000246 00004002 00000000 00000000 - elnkii.sys
ff541eb4    fe481509 fe481509 ff6688c8 ff668288 00000000 ff668138 - i8042prt.SYS
ff541ee0    fe481ea8 fe481ea8 fe482078 00000000 ff541f04 8013c58a - i8042prt.SYS
ff541ee4    fe482078 fe482078 00000000 00000000 8013c58a ff6688c8 - i8042prt.sys
ff541ef0    8013c58a 8013c58a ff6688c8 ff668040 80405900 00000031 - ntoskrnl.exe
ff541efc    80405900 80405900 00000031 06060606 06060606 06060606 - hal.dll

Restart and set the recovery options in the system control panel
or the /CRASHDEBUG system start option if this message reappears,
contact your system administrator or technical support group.
CRASHDUMP: Initializing miniport driver
CRASHDUMP: Dumping physical memory to disk:    2000
CRASHDUMP: Physical memory dump complete
```

CERTIFICATION OBJECTIVE 15.07

Troubleshooting Resources

Having access to a variety of troubleshooting resources can make your life much easier when dealing with Windows NT. In this section, we discuss some of the resources that are available to you.

Microsoft's WWW and FTP Sites

Microsoft maintains World Wide Web (WWW) servers and FTP (File Transfer Protocol) servers that can provide you with updated drivers, current product information, and more. The web address is www.microsoft.com and the FTP address is ftp.microsoft.com. The FTP site allows anonymous logons, so feel free to explore the site.

The Knowledge Base

The Knowledge Base, developed by Microsoft product support specialists, contains support information about problems that they have solved. I cannot stress enough the value of the Knowledge Base, the first place I look when I encounter an unusual problem. It's always possible that someone else has encountered the problem, and solved it. The Knowledge Base is available in many different places. It can be accessed on Microsoft's web site, the TechNet CDs, and Resource kit CDs.

Resource Kits

The Resource Kits contain detailed information that is an in-depth, technical supplement to the documentation included with the product. Resource kits also come with a CD that is full of useful utilities. Resource kits can be obtained from your local dealer, and they also are included on the TechNet CDs.

TechNet CD-ROM

The TechNet CDs are an invaluable tool for supporting any Microsoft product. We already have discussed a couple of the items included on the TechNet CDs, when we looked at other troubleshooting resources. There are over 1.5 million pages of technical documentation available on the TechNet CDs, along with drivers, updates, and Service Packs. TechNet is available by yearly subscription and delivers new CDs to you every month as they are updated.

Help

Windows NT Help is no farther away than a few mouse clicks. Help is available in three different contexts. You can use the Contents tab in Help to find topics grouped by subject, or use the Index tab to find specific topics listed alphabetically, or use the Find tab to search for information by typing in a subject, title, specific word, or phrase. Figure 15-16 displays the Help Index tab. Exercise 15-15 gives you an opportunity to use Help to find a specific phrase.

FIGURE 15-16

The Index tab of Help displays topics alphabetically

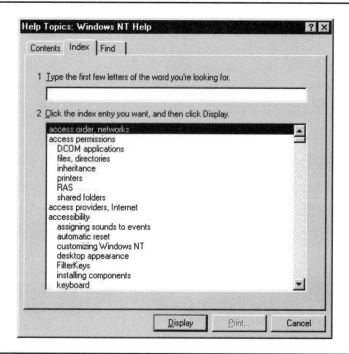

Opening Help Files

1. Select Start | Help. The Help Topics window is displayed.
2. Select the Index tab and type **netwo** in dialog box 1.
3. The words Network Adapter are highlighted in dialog box 2.
4. If you double-click on Network Adapter, you are presented with the Topics Found dialog box.
5. Double-click To Install a Network Adapter, to receive help on that topic.
6. Close Help after you have finished reading the information displayed.

CERTIFICATION SUMMARY

The boot processes for Intel- and RISC-based machines are quite similar. The main difference concerns the files used during the booting of each type of machine. Windows NT loads in four distinct phases. It is helpful during troubleshooting to realize what is supposed to happen during each phase. Windows NT depends on the BOOT.INI file to load the operating system properly. The BOOT.INI file is made up of two sections, boot loader and operating systems. The ARC naming convention is used throughout BOOT.INI. It is possible to modify the way Windows NT starts up by using a variety of switches in BOOT.INI.

Windows NT supports multibooting between multiple operating systems. This can be useful when you need to use more than one operating system on a single machine. If you are going to run Windows 95 and Windows NT on the same system, it is best to install Windows 95 first.

Troubleshooting hardware and software is never an easy process. Problems can include a variety of boot failures in which you may need to use the LastKnownGood configuration or the emergency repair disk. System recovery can assist in troubleshooting by providing a dump of your physical memory that can be further analyzed when appropriate. If an application stops responding, you can use the Task Manager to shut it down. In some situations you may need to take ownership of a resource to clear up a security problem that exists. Other tools available to help with troubleshooting Windows NT are the Event Viewer and Windows NT Diagnostics (WinMSD).

When Microsoft fixes a significant amount of bugs, it issues a Service Pack. Service Packs can be obtained from the Microsoft FTP site. Installing a Service Pack is not a complex task, but you should read the README.TXT file prior to installation.

The "Blue Screen of Death" can be intimidating, and it's something that no one dealing with Windows NT looks forward to seeing. It reflects that a serious problem has occurred and gives information to help you find out what caused the STOP error.

There are many resources available to help you troubleshoot Windows NT. Some of the resources available include Microsoft's web site, the TechNet CD subscription, and the online Help file that is included with Windows NT.

TWO-MINUTE DRILL

- ❑ Apart from the fact that it's on the MCSE test, it is helpful to understand the boot process from a troubleshooting standpoint.

- ❑ It is important to note that on RISC-based machines the system partition has to be on a FAT partition.

- ❑ As Windows NT loads, it goes through four distinct phases: the Kernel load phase, the Kernel initialization phase, the Services load phase, and finally the Windows subsystem start phase.

- ❑ The BOOT.INI file is a critical .INI file created by Windows NT when it is first installed. If this file becomes damaged or corrupted, Windows NT simply doesn't load.

- ❑ Know what happens if the BOOT.INI file is damaged, missing, or otherwise errant. You must also know how to edit it, and be very familiar with reading it.

- ❑ The ARC naming convention is useful in identifying partition information on multidisk/multipartition machines.

- ❑ Windows NT supports multibooting between Windows NT and additional operating systems, if your system partition contains the Windows NT boot sector.

- ❑ Ensure that you have a Windows NT boot floppy in case one of the boot files for your system ever gets deleted.

❏ LastKnownGood is the configuration that was saved to a special control set in the Registry after the last successful logon to Windows NT.

❏ The Emergency Repair Disk (ERD) can repair missing Windows NT files and restore the Registry to include disk configuration and security information.

❏ To create an ERD, use the Repair Disk Utility.

❏ The Security Accounts Manager (SAM) and security files are not automatically updated by rdisk. To update those files, you need to use the /S switch in conjunction with rdisk.

❏ Windows NT features a Recovery utility that can perform selected tasks in the event of a STOP error. Configure the recovery options within the Startup/Shutdown tab of System Properties.

❏ Task Manager has the capability to end a task that may be causing your system to hang.

❏ The Event Viewer, located in the Administration submenu, allows you to examine various events that have been generated by the Windows NT system, services, and applications, or through user actions that have been audited.

❏ Windows NT Diagnostics (also called WinMSD) has several tabs that reflect a lot of information about your Windows NT Server system.

❏ Microsoft periodically issues a Service Pack to fix bugs that have been detected in the Windows NT operating system.

❏ The "Blue Screens of Death" are actually text mode STOP messages identifying hardware and software problems that have occurred while Windows NT was running.

❏ Troubleshooting resources include Microsoft's WWW and FTP Sites, The Knowledge Base, Resource Kits, TechNet CD-ROM, and Windows NT Help.

SELF TEST

The following questions will help you measure your understanding of the material presented in this chapter. Read all the choices carefully, as there may be more than one correct answer. Choose all correct answers for each question.

1   Which of the following would be valid in a BOOT.INI file?

 A.   multi(0)disk(1)rdisk(0)partition(0)\
      winnt="Windows NT Version 4.0"

 B.   multi(0)disk(0)rdisk(0)partition(5)\
      winnt="Windows NT Version 4.0"

 C.   scsi(0)disk(1)rdisk(0)partition(3)
      winnt="Windows NT Version 4.0"

 D.   scsi(0)disk(2)rdisk(0)partition(4)\
      winnt"Windows NT Version 4.0

2   (True/False) The /SOS switch is used in the BOOT.INI file to enable the capture of debugging information.

3   What files are required to be on a Windows NT boot disk for a non-SCSI Intel-based machine?

 A.   NTLDR

 B.   BOOT.INI

 C.   NTBOOTDD.SYS

 D.   OSLOADER.EXE

 E.   NTDETECT.COM

4   NTDETECT.COM is used to _____ .

 A.   load the operating system services

 B.   load SCSI drivers when the SCSI BIOS has been disabled

 C.   configure the operating system menu

 D.   examine the hardware on an Intel-based machine

5   You are sent out on a trouble call and told that the system hangs ever since the user added a new video driver. What would you do?

 A.   Use the Emergency Repair Disk to replace the Registry

 B.   Boot the system with a Windows NT boot disk

 C.   Reboot the system and choose the LastKnownGood configuration

 D.   Reload Windows NT Workstation on the system

6   Your system has 32MB of physical memory and you have set the System Recovery to write debugging information to %systemroot%\memory.dmp. What else needs to be done to ensure that the debugging information will be saved?

 A.   Your pagefile has to be at least 32MB

 B.   Your pagefile has to be smaller than 32MB

 C.   Your pagefile has to be located on a partition other than where Windows NT is installed

 D.   Your pagefile has to be equal in size to your boot partition

7 What tool do you use to detect the group
dependencies for a service?

   A. Event Viewer System Log

   B. Event Viewer Application Log

   C. WinMSD Resources Tab

   D. WinMSD Services Tab

8 (True/False) The only way to change the
default timeout is to edit the BOOT.INI
file manually.

9 Which load phase can be identified by the
screen turning blue?

   A. Kernel load

   B. Kernel initialization

   C. Services load

   D. Windows subsystem start

   E. ARC load

10 Paul has been fired and his replacement,
Ann, needs to access the fourth-quarter
report located in a folder that belonged to
Paul. How can Ann access this folder?

   A. Have Ann log on to the system and take
ownership of the folder

   B. Have Paul come back to work so he can
give Ann access to the folder

   C. Have an Administrator log on to the
system and assign ownership of the
directory to Ann

   D. Have an Administrator log on and take
ownership of the folder, and give Ann
full control of the folder

11 (True/False) The Session Manager subkey
of the Registry contains local variables that
are used by the Session Manager.

12 If a service has been set in the Registry for
an error control of 0x2, it reflects a level of
_____ .

   A. Ignore

   B. Critical

   C. Normal

   D. Severe

13 To update your Emergency Repair Disk,
you would type _____ from a
Command Prompt.

   A. fdisk

   B. rdisk

   C. ERD

   D. update

   E. repair

14 (True/False) A Service Pack can easily be
removed from your system, even if you do
not have the uninstall folder.

15 What causes the "Blue Screen of Death"?

   A. a STOP message

   B. a HALT message

   C. a SEVERE message

   D. a CRITICAL message

16 (True/False) Any ASCII editor can be used
to read an Event Viewer .EVT log file.

17 The partition(n) portion of an ARC name starts counting with _____ .

   A. 0
   B. 1
   C. 2
   D. 3

18 Your system is set to dual-boot between Windows 95 and Windows NT. You receive the following message as you try to boot into Windows 95: I/O Error accessing boot sector file. What has caused this to occur?

   A. NTLDR is missing
   B. NTDETECT.COM cannot detect the Windows 95 folder
   C. The BOOT.INI file is missing
   D. BOOTSEC.DOS is missing

19 A system you have been sent out to troubleshoot will not boot. You attempt to use the LastKnownGood configuration and it does not correct the problem. What would you do next?

   A. Format the drive and reload Windows NT
   B. Use the Emergency Repair Disk for that system
   C. Use your Windows NT boot disk to replace a missing script file
   D. Use the Emergency Repair Disk for the neighboring system

20 (True/False) The SAM and security files are automatically updated when you use the Repair Disk Utility.

A

Self Test
Answers

Answers to Chapter 1 Self Test

1. What does RISC stand for?
   C. Reduced Instruction Set Computing.
   These processors only execute a small amount of instructions, but do so very fast and efficiently.

2. Windows NT is written in the
   _____ language.
   C programming language. This language is very portable across many different architectures. Other portions of NT were written in assembly language that required faster processing.

3. _____ applications use conventions such as case-sensitive naming and hard links.
   POSIX. These applications are run in the POSIX subsystem.

4. What does TCP/IP stand for?
   D. Transmission Control Protocol/Internet Protocol. This is the most popular protocol available, and the default protocol for Windows NT.

5. (True/False) DLC is the protocol used for communicating with DEC Pathworks networks.
   False. DLC is used for communicating with mainframe computers and stand-alone printers that have an HP JetDirect network card installed.

6. What is the fastest network protocol supported by NT?
   B. NetBEUI. This is a small, efficient protocol, but it is not routable.

7. I have one DOS application running, and a suite of five 16-bit applications running. One of the 16-bit applications continually crashes when I use the DOS application. What is the best way to keep this from happening?
   D. Run the faulty application in a separate memory space. This is the best way to resolve the situation. Running every 16-bit application in its own memory space might work too, but not if the applications expect to share the same address space with each other. What's more, there would be a much greater demand on memory involved in creating five separate VDMs.

8. Windows NT Workstation provides support for up to _____ processors.
   Two. NT Server can support 4 processors out of the box, and up to 32 processors through OEM.

9. (True/False) If you share a file that is on a FAT partition over the network, the file cannot be seen by non-NTFS-compatible operating systems.
   False. The file can be seen by non-NTFS-compatible computers. An NTFS partition can't be seen if you dual-boot to a non-NTFS-compatible operating system, or if you boot your computer using a floppy disk.

10. NT uses a process called _____ to translate the calls from one subsystem to another.
Thunking. This is required to pass parameters from 16-bit into 32-bit functions and vice-versa.

11. Which is not a component of the Windows NT Executive?
C. Process Scheduler. There is no such thing as a Process scheduler, although the Windows NT Kernel is responsible for creating, managing, and scheduling threads, which is code from a process.

12. (True/False) Environment subsystems are run in User Mode.
True. Almost everything in Windows NT is run in User Mode, with the exception of critical operating system components.

13. Kernel mode is also commonly referred to as _____.
Privileged mode. This is because it has the privilege of directly accessing the hardware, which is not available for User Mode components or applications.

14. _____ is the term used to describe the process of moving paging files to and from the disk as needed.
Demand Paging. This is accomplished through use of the Virtual Memory Manager and the paging file.

15. How many inbound client connections does NT Workstation support?

Unlimited. Windows NT Server allows unlimited client connections. You should reevaluate your choice of Windows NT Workstation if you are constantly reaching the maximum of ten concurrent client connections.

16. How many RAS connections does NT Workstation support? How many does NT Server support?
Workstation: One. NT Server: 256. Once again, you should reevaluate your choice of Windows NT Workstation if you would like to receive more than one concurrent RAS connection to your system.

17. I have a network of 4 computers with very inexperienced users. Which model (workgroup or domain) would be the better choice for my network, and why?
C. Domain model, because you have very inexperienced users. Although it's true that a workgroup model is suitable for networks with fewer than ten users, your inexperienced users won't know how to share resources, as the workgroup model requires.

18. What is the lowest level of the Windows NT operating system architecture?
The Hardware Abstraction Layer (HAL). This is the layer between the hardware in the computer and the Windows NT Executive services.

Answers to Chapter 2 Self Test

1. Holden wants to upgrade his workstation to Windows NT 4.0 Workstation. What choices does he have?
   A,C. Windows NT 4.0 Workstation can be upgraded only from a Windows 3.1 or previous version of Windows NT, such as NT 3.1 or Windows 3.51.

2. Phoebe's boss wants her to install Windows NT 4.0 Workstation onto some legacy hardware. What choices does she have?
   B,C. To install Windows NT 4.0 Workstation, you must meet the minimum hardware requirements: 486 /33, 12MB of RAM, 120MB of hard disk space.

3. Nuala Anne wants to verify that all of the hardware that she is going to use for Windows NT Workstation is compatible. How should she verify the hardware?
   B. Before installing Windows NT 4.0 Workstation, it is a good idea to check that the hardware you are using is on the Hardware Compatibility List. You can find the HCL on Microsoft's web site and on the latest version of the Microsoft TechNet CD-ROM.

4. To partition your hard disk you use the _____.EXE utility.
   FDISK.EXE. The FDISK.EXE utility allows you to create and delete partitions on your hard disk.

5. Ken accidentally lost his three setup floppies for installing Windows NT 4.0 Workstation. What command-line utility can he use to re-create them?
   D. The /OX switch allows you to create the three Windows NT setup floppies in case you lose the originals. The /U switch specifies an unattended installation and the /B switch specifies a floppy-less installation.

6. Dermot is doing top-secret work and wants to take advantage of Windows NT's security model. He is using a Pentium II 266, 4.3GB hard disk with 64MB of RAM. What file system should he use?
   C. Using NTFS partitions with your Windows NT 4.0 Workstation allows you to take advantage of the Windows NT 4.0 security model or file and directory permissions. The other advantages are fault tolerance and better performance for hard disks over 500MB.

7. Danielle needs to install Windows NT 4.0 from the network from an MS-DOS workstation client and does not need to create floppies. What setup utility should she use?
   C. The /B switch denotes a floppy-less installation. Since the installation will be done over the network, only the WINNT.EXE command can be used. The WINNT32.EXE command only works on previous versions of Windows NT.

8. Michael was instructed to come up with a plan to implement unattended installations

throughout his company's enterprise-wide network. He also needs to pre-install applications and set up machine-specific parameters such as computer names and IP addresses. What files does Michael need to use?

B,C,D. To automate a Windows NT 4.0 Workstation rollout, you need an UNATTEND.TXT file to script the installation, SYSDIFF.EXE to pre-install any applications with the base setup, and Unique Database Files to provide unique parameters that are specific to the machine, such as TCP/IP address and computer name.

9. Your company has just purchased four new Hewlett-Packard printers for your network. TCP/IP is already installed on your network yet you cannot connect to the printers. What protocol must be installed to talk to the HP printers?

C. The DLC protocol is mainly used for connecting to Hewlett-Packard JetDirect printers and Mainframes.

10. You accidentally edited the Registry of your computer. After you restart your computer, Windows NT will not load. What will help you restore your system?

A. If your Windows NT 4.0 Workstation fails to boot or is damaged in some way, you can use the Emergency Repair Disk to repair it. The ERD contains necessary configuration information that is used to repair the Registry and important configuration files.

11. While installing Windows NT 4.0 Workstation, you encounter errors during installation of your network card. You still want to install a network device to continue the installation. What option should you pick?

C. If your computer does not recognize your network card during installation, you should select the MS Loopback Adapter and enter any configuration information necessary to complete the installation. Once the information is entered and the installation is finished, you can change or install your original network card.

12. What command lets you change the boot loader on your hard disk from Windows NT to Microsoft DOS?

B. If you want to change your boot loader from NTFS to MS-DOS, you must "SYS" the boot partition to remove NTLDR. Once this is completed, NT relinquishes control over the hard disk.

13. Holly is upgrading a previous installation of Windows NT Workstation 3.51 to Windows NT Workstation 4.0. She already has the three Windows NT setup floppies. What version of the Windows NT setup utility can she use?

A,C,D. Since the upgrade is going to come from a previous version of Windows NT 4.0, the WINNT32.EXE command can be used. Because Holly already created the three Windows NT boot floppies there is no reason to create a new set with the /OX switch.

14. What are the benefits for using NTFS partitions on your Windows NT 4.0 Workstation?
A, C, D. The benefits for using NTFS partitions include the Windows NT security model, fault tolerance, and better performance with hard disks greater than 500MB.

Answers to Chapter 3 Self Test

1. You want to change the size of the paging file. Where do you go to do this?
C. The Change button on the Performance tab in System Properties. The Virtual Memory dialog box appears. Here is where you can adjust the size and location of the paging file.

2. What utility lets me search the Registry for the value of "AutoAdminLogon"?
C. REGEDIT. This is the only utility that allows you to search for values in the Registry.

3. Which file does the Startup/Shutdown tab modify in System Properties?
B. BOOT.INI. This is the read-only file in the root directory of your system drive.

4. What is the recommended paging file size for a computer with 32MB of RAM?

C. 44MB. The recommended size for the paging file is the amount of RAM in the system plus 12MB. Other sources have stated 11MB rather than 12MB.

5. Where would you place a shortcut so that it appears on all users' desktops?
B. Winnt\Profiles\All users\Desktop. Profiles is the main folder under Winnt that holds user information. None of the other folders exists.

6. The paging file is actually a file called _____, and is located in the root directory of the drive you specified in the Virtual Memory dialog box.
PAGEFILE.SYS. Windows NT always creates and uses a paging file.

7. Which tab of the System Properties dialog box shows how much RAM is installed in a computer?
A. General. This tab contains the registration information, operating system version, and memory installed.

8. (True/False) 17 is a higher priority thread than 23.
False. The higher the number, the higher the thread priority.

9. On the main Services screen, which button do you click to configure a service to start up automatically on bootup?
C. Startup. You must select the service and click this button to access the service startup type.

10. The _____ tab of the SCSI adapters dialog box is where you add and remove drivers for the devices.
Drivers. Use this tab to add/remove drivers, and the Devices tab to view the devices currently installed in the system.

11. Which is the only valid Registry key?
C. HKEY_CLASSES_ROOT. This is one of the main Registry keys. The rest are fictional.

12. (True/False) The Advanced option of the Ports icon in the Control Panel lets you adjust the baud rate, parity, and flow control.
False. The Advanced option lets you override the default port and IRQ values.

13. Which option is not available from the UPS Configuration dialog box?
C. Send Administrative Alert. Every other option listed can be configured from the UPS Configuration section.

14. Which is not a subkey of HKEY_LOCAL_MACHINE?
B. Classes. The five subkeys under the HKEY_LOCAL_MACHINE are Hardware, SAM, Security, Software, and System.

15. Which menu would you select to find a key or value in REGEDIT?
D. Edit. Select Edit, then Find. You can also use CTRL-F.

16. Which subkey of HKEY_LOCAL_MACHINE holds the CurrentControlSet key?

17. (True/False) You click the Install/Uninstall tab to remove components of Windows NT.
False. You would click the Windows NT Setup tab to add or remove Windows NT components.

18. Location, calling cards, and area code are examples of _____ settings.
Telephony. Telephony settings are used for dialing by TAPI-compliant devices and applications.

19. The _____ adapter can be used if you want to configure network settings but do not have an adapter in your system.
MS Loopback. You can add protocols and services, and adjust the binding order without having a network card installed.

20. Where is the SCSI Investigator found on the Windows NT Workstation CD-ROM?
D. SUPPORT\SCSITOOL. Will verify SCSI settings, but only for Adaptec and Buslogic SCSI adapters.

21. From which Control Panel icon do you configure a MIDI adapter?
B. Multimedia. This is where you install and configure multimedia adapters, as well as other audio devices. The Sounds icon is not used for adding or removing devices.

22. The entry in the BOOT.INI file to disable serial mouse detection on COM1 is _____ .

C. System. This also holds the Clone, and other ControlSets 000-003.

/NoSerialMice:COM1. This disables detection only for COM1. To disable all COM ports, use the /NoSerialMice entry with no parameters.

23. _____ communication uses stop and start bits appended to each byte of information.
    Serial, or Asynchronous. This is because only one bit can be sent at a time. Synchronous devices use a clocking signal, rather than bits appended to each character, for timing.

24. The _____ tab is where you change the display driver.
    Settings. Click the Display Type button to change the display driver.

25. Which is *not* an available button on the Server Service main dialog box?
    A. Sessions. The Server applet can view sessions on the computer, but there is no button for it.

26. What is *not* an option in the Advanced Ports dialog box?
    C. Flow Control. The Advanced Ports dialog box does not contain settings for Flow Control, start bits, stop bits, parity, or baud rate.

27. UPS stands for _____ .
    Uninterruptible Power Supply. A device that connects through the serial port of a computer and maintains power in the event of power loss.

28. Which portion of the HKEY_LOCAL_ MACHINE key is grayed out to avoid tampering?
    C. The Security key. Tampering with this key could alter important security features such as passwords, group access, and permissions.

Answers to Chapter 4 Self Test

1. (True/False) The Administrator account can be deleted.
   False. The administrator account cannot be deleted or locked out.

2. The _____ default account must be enabled before it can be used.
   Guest. The Guest account is disabled by default.

3. To assign permissions to a large number of users, the user accounts should be placed into _____.
   Groups. User accounts are placed into groups. This simplifies administration by allowing user accounts to be given permissions as a unit.

4. Which groups do you need to be a member of to share a directory on your computer? Choose two.
   A,D. The Power Users and Administrators groups can share directories.

5. Which user accounts are created by default when Windows NT is installed?

A. The administrator and guest account are the default accounts created at installation.

6. The _____ administrative tool is used to manage all user and group accounts.
   User Manager.

7. You want your users to be able to share their own printers, but you don't want to grant them full access to the computer. Which built-in group should you make your users members of?
   B. The Power Users built-in group can share printers or directories, but does not have all the powers of the Administrator group.

8. Bob is retiring from your company. Linda, a new employee, is taking over Bob's position. You want Linda's user account to have the same rights and permissions as Bob's user account. How do you do this with the least amount of administrative effort, while maintaining security?
   C. By disabling the account, security is maintained; and if the account is renamed, it retains all rights and permissions. Answer A is incorrect, since deleting Bob's account would lose all of the properties of his account. Answer B is also incorrect. In order to maintain security, unused accounts should be disabled. Answer D is incorrect, because the account cannot be locked out manually. This only occurs when the

account lockout option is enabled and logon failures are exceeded.

9. If a user creates a file on the computer, then that user is a member of the _____ special group for that file.
   Creator Owner. Anytime a user creates a file, folder, or print job, that user becomes a member of the Creator Owner special group for that file.

10. (True/False) Users that access the computer over the network are members of the Interactive special group.
    False. Users that access the computer over a network are members of the Network special group. Users that access the computer locally are members of the Interactive special group.

11. Members of which built-in group can take ownership of a file or folder?
    C. Only members of the Administrator local group can take ownership of a file or folder on the computer. Administrators can also take ownership of a print job.

12. When you copy a user account, what information is *not* transferred to the new account?
    D. The account description, group memberships, profile settings, User Cannot Change Password, and Password Never Expires fields are transferred when you copy a user account. The Username, Full Name, User Must Change Password at Next

Logon, and Account Disabled fields are not transferred.

13. (True/False) If an account is accidentally deleted, it can be restored by creating a new account with the same name and description.
False. Once an account is deleted, it's gone. You cannot restore deleted accounts.

14. Which Administrative Tool can be used to view the security log?
B. The Event Viewer administrative tool is used to view the security log.

15. You believe that someone may be trying to get unauthorized access to your computer. How can you verify this?
B. If someone was attempting to hack into the system by guessing passwords, auditing failed logon attempts shows a large number of failures.

Answers to Chapter 5 Self Test

1. Which of the following is an acceptable FAT filename?
C. The other three files contain illegal characters or spaces.

2. What will be the FAT alias for this long filename: Notes from March meeting concerning X.400.txt
B. NOTESF~1.TXT. The first six letters of the name are used. Spaces between words are removed. A subsequent file with the same first six characters would have the number 2 after the tilde.

3. What will be the FAT alias for this long directory name: Current proposal.34
D. Curren~1.34. The rules are the same for filenames concerning the first six letters and the tilde symbol. NT takes the last period it finds, and uses whatever is directly to the right of it for the extension (up to three characters).

4. What will be the outcome if I move a file called FINANCE.TXT, which is *not* compressed, to a compressed folder on a different partition on my only hard disk?
C. The file is compressed because of the compression attribute on the target folder. This falls under the rule: "When you are moving or copying a file or folder to another NTFS partition, it inherits the compression attribute of the target folder."

5. What will be the outcome if I move the file C:\job duties\Friday.txt, which is compressed, to the C:\monthly duties\ directory, on the same computer, which is not compressed?
B. It will be compressed because it retains its compression attribute. This falls under the rule: "On an NTFS partition, when you move a file or folder that is compressed to another area on the same partition, it retains its state."

6. I have a Pentium 133 with 64MB of RAM and a 2GB hard disk that is partitioned into several 200MB partitions. I need to choose

a file system that supports long filenames and has the capability to track file updates by viewing their timestamps. Which file system should I use?
C. FAT, because the partition sizes are small. FAT is the best choice for drives smaller than 500MB because it uses less system overhead than NT.

7. I am using a 486/33 with 16MB of RAM and a 540MB hard disk. The hard disk is divided into two equal partitions. I need to restrict access to a certain directory on the computer from other users who may log on. Which file system should I use?
B. NTFS, because only NTFS allows security attributes to be set. Ordinarily the small size of the drive would suggest the FAT file system. However, FAT does not support security attributes so you must select NTFS.

8. I am upgrading an NT 3.51 computer that has the HPFS file system installed. What is the best way to convert the file system to FAT?
B. Use CONVERT.EXE to change the partition to NT before the upgrade. HPFS was supported under NT 3.51, but now only FAT and NTFS are supported.

9. What is the only way to convert a partition from NTFS to FAT?
A. There is no way to convert NTFS to FAT. Yes, you could delete an NTFS partition, and reformat it as FAT, but that is not converting. Your data will be lost.

10. Fill in the blank. NT uses the _____ feature that uses a transaction log to keep track of whether writes to the disk have been completed or not.
Lazy-write. This is NT's built-in fault tolerant feature.

11. What is the most effective usage of space?
C. Volume set. This maximizes space by consolidating free space on available drives into one large logical drive.

12. (True/False) If you lose one of the members of a volume set, you only lose the data that was contained on that drive.
False. Volume sets are not fault tolerant. When you lose a member of a volume set, you lose all the data contained in the volume.

13. What is the total size of a stripe set created from the following free regions of space: 200MB, 450MB, 150MB, 235MB, and 180MB?
D. 750MB. The smallest region of space on one of the members is the size of the stripe across all drives.

14. I want the fastest performance from my configuration, but I do not require fault tolerance. What should I use?
C. Stripe set. This configuration has the fastest read times because the data is being read from a stripe by multiple hard disks simultaneously.

15. (True/False) When you try to format a section of free space, you are prompted to

create a partition before you format.
False. The option to format is grayed out when you have selected free space.

16. (True/False). A drive can have as many as four extended partitions.
False. You can have only one extended partition. You can have four primary partitions, or three primary partitions plus one extended partition.

17. Fill in the blank. The utility used to compress files and directories from the command line is _____.
COMPACT.EXE

18. What menu option would you choose in Disk Administrator to format a volume?
D. Tools. You also can assign a drive letter and view the properties of the volume you have selected.

19. What would be the result if I issued this command to convert my FAT J: drive to NTFS?
J:\>CONVERT J: /fs:ntfs
C. It would ask if I would like to schedule conversion for the next time the system restarts. The system cannot gain exclusive access to the drive because I issued the command from the drive it wanted to convert.

20. (True/False) MFT stands for Master Format Table.
False. MFT stands for Master File Table.

Answers to Chapter 6 Self Test

1. The _____ creates security access tokens, authenticates users, and manages the local security policy.
A. The LSA is the heart of the security subsystem.

2. What maintains the database of all user, group, and workstation accounts?
B. The SAM is actually a hive in the Registry that has all user account information.

3. NT supports which of the following logons? (Choose all that apply.)
A,B,C,D. All are types of NT logons.

4. Why must you press CTRL-ALT-DEL to logon to NT?
C. Pressing CTR-ALT-DEL activates the WINLOGON process and shuts down all other programs. This ensures that a password capture program won't operate on NT at logon.

5. Which of the following is an object? (Choose all that apply.)
A,B,C. Almost everything is an object in NT, if it can be managed by the operating system. The operating system does not manage a keyboard.

6. A _____ is used to uniquely identify each user account.
A. The security identifier is unique to every

user. This is how NT distinguishes among users.

7. If you delete a user account, how can you get it back?
    A. Once you remove the account, the SID is destroyed and can never be re-created.

8. A program always runs in the _____ of the user.
    B. A program is assigned the same permissions as the user. This is known as a security context.

9. User JesseS belongs to the local group Marketing. The permissions on the file DICTIONARY.DOC are as follows: JesseS has Change(RWXD) permission and the Marketing group has No Access permissions. When user JesseS tries to read the file, what access will he be granted?
    D. No Access is processed before any other ACE. Processing stops as soon as No Access is identified.

10. Which ACE does NT process first?
    D. AccessDenied must be processed first to ensure that users denied access don't get to the files.

11. User MaryS is assigned to the local group Sales. Mary has Read permissions for all files on your system. The group Sales has special permissions of Write on all the files in the folder called Reports. If Mary requests Read and Write permissions at the same time, what will happen?

C. Access permissions are cumulative. Each ACE is processed until enough permission is given.

12. If you want to limit the people who can access your system when they log on locally, how must your hard disk partition be formatted?
    A. NTFS is the only file system on NT 4.0 that allows file and folder permissions.

13. Why is there a special utility to secure the boot partition of RISC computers?
    C. Since FAT doesn't allow file permissions, the tool is required to ensure that only administrators can have access to the boot files. RISC systems can have other partitions formatted with NTFS.

14. What command allows the user to change file permissions from a command shell?
    C. The other answers aren't even commands.

15. If you want to audit access to files stored on your NTFS-formatted hard disk, what must you do first?
    A. Remember that you must turn Auditing on before you can audit anything. Although the Audit button appears on the file's properties, nothing happens until you turn it on.

16. What does transaction logging provide for NTFS?
    D. Recoverability is the purpose of transaction logging in NTFS. In other

systems it may serve more roles, but don't let that confuse you.

17. Who is the owner of a new file on a FAT partition?
    D. NTFS is the only file system on NT that has owners.

18. Who is the owner of a new file on an NTFS partition?
    C. NT uses discretionary access to control permissions to files and folders. Owners are responsible for securing the files they own. You become an owner whenever you take ownership or create a new file.

19. (True/False) Only administrators can give someone ownership of a file.
    False. Ownership can only be taken, NEVER given away.

20. When moving a folder from drive C: to drive D:, what permissions will the folder have? (Both drives are formatted with NTFS.)
    B. When you move a file between partitions, NT actually copies the file and deletes the original. Since a new copy of the file is created, it inherits the parent folder's permissions.

21. Which file systems support share-level security?
    D. Share-level security is supported by all file systems on NT. File and folder level permissions are only possible with NTFS.

22. Which one is NOT a type of share permission on an NTFS partition?
    D. This may have tricked you. There are only four share-level permissions on any type of file system (No Access, Read, Change, and Full Control). Special Access is a directory permission for an NTFS volume.

23. How can you share a folder on the network to allow everyone to read, write, and execute files, but not delete any files? File permissions on NTFS.
    D. To get more granular with sharing files, you can assign NTFS permissions to the same files to control access. You'll need to be familiar with this for the test.

24. Which of the following are negative results from auditing all file object accesses on your system? (Choose all that apply.)
    A,B,C. Auditing file access takes time away from your CPU and it causes your hard disk to log the actions.

25. What must be turned on to allow you to audit writes to your NTFS directories?
    B. It's pretty simple. You just need to know Table 6-4.

26. User RyanB is given share-level access of Full Control to share SalesRPT. However, the NTFS permissions are set to Read for the group Sales. RyanB is a member of the group Sales. When he connects to the share SalesRPT, what type of access will he have?
    B. Although he has Full Control at the

share, his file permissions only allow him to Read. Remember the most restrictive permissions always take precedence when combining share permissions with file and folder permissions.

Answers to Chapter 7 Self Test

1. Which of the following are advantages to implementing the redirector as a file system driver? (Choose all that apply.)
A,B,C,D. All four are advantages to implementing the redirector as a file system driver.

2. Which layer of the OSI model does the NDIS layer of the Microsoft Networking model operate?
D. The NDIS layer works with the NIC driver. Both are located at the Data Link layer of the OSI model.

3. Which layer is between the TDI and the NDIS layers?
A. The TDI and NDIS layers allow applications and NIC drivers to operate without regard to the transport protocol being used.

4. What does the TDI layer provide?
A. Same reason as #3.

5. What is the importance of the NDIS interface layer?
D. Same reason as #3.

6. What does the multiple UNC provider (MUP) do?
B. The MUP is a driver that accepts I/O requests and then sends the request to the appropriate redirector.

7. Which protocol(s) could you use if you had two separate physical subnets connected by a router? (Choose all that apply.)
B,C. NWLink and TCP/IP are the only routable protocols listed.

8. Which protocol would you choose if you had a LAN with only 5 workstations and 1 server connected on a single physical subnet?
A. NetBEUI is the best protocol to use, since it doesn't require configuration and it is efficient in small networks.

9. Which protocol is used mainly as a gateway protocol?
D. DLC is used as a gateway protocol to IBM mainframes using SNA server.

10. You want to connect two remote sites with a router, but don't want to waste time configuring a protocol. Which protocol should you choose?
B. NWLink is the only routable protocol that doesn't require configuration. TCP/IP can be configured automatically using DHCP.

11. You want to create a share on your workstation, but don't want it to be visible when users browse the network. How can you do this?

C. Placing a $ at the end of a share hides it from the list of available shares.

12. Which type of IPC is used when your computer broadcasts that it is joining a workgroup?
A. When you join a workgroup your computer doesn't require acknowledgment, so it sends a broadcast message using mailslots.

13. Your workstation has NetBEUI, NWLink, and TCP/IP installed on it. You notice that every time you browse the network, your computer takes a long time to display the available computer's list. Your friend doesn't experience any noticeable delay when browsing the network. What should you do to fix the problem? (Choose all that apply.)
A, D. You might have protocols installed on your computer that aren't in use on the network. If this is the case, remove them. If you are using three different protocols on the network you should try to find one protocol to use. The reason C isn't a correct answer is because the browse service uses all available protocols to browse the network. Changing the binding order won't speed up the process because all the protocols need to be used.

14. You have several folders shared on the network from your workstation. How can you check to see which folders have connections to them?

A. The Server applet is the only tool that allows you to view which folders are in use. You can access the Server applet via Control Panel or by using Server Manager.

15. Which service allows your computer to be seen on the network?
D. The Computer Browser service broadcasts your computer to the network.

16. You are developing a NetBIOS-compliant naming standard for your organization. You plan to use the following format: *CityName-Bldg#-Rm#-FirstName*. The cities where your network is installed are Dallas, Los Angeles, New York, and Orlando. Building numbers are all four digits and room numbers are all three digits. No one's first name is over ten characters in length. Will this work?
B. This naming standard will exceed the NetBIOS limit of 15-character computer names.

Answers to Chapter 8 Self Test

1. Which is not a layer of the TCP/IP architecture?
C. Network. The Network layer is a portion of the OSI model, not the TCP/IP architecture. The TCP/IP does, however, contain the Network Interface layer.

2. The _____ layer of the TCP/IP model provides frame sequencing and

error detection.
Transport. This layer contains the User
Datagram Protocol (UDP) and the
Transmission Control Protocol (TCP).

3. Which is the connection-oriented
    protocol that ensures data will arrive
    in the correct order?
    D. Transmission Control Protocol (TCP).
    This is a Transport layer protocol that
    maintains a connection between the source
    and destination computers for the duration
    of the transfer.

4. Which is a valid IP address?
    B. 111.111.111.111. It may look strange
    but it is a valid IP address. All of the other
    addresses contained an illegal number (0),
    did not have enough octets, or had a
    number that is too high (258).

5. What would be a correct default gateway
    for your computer if your IP address is
    106.23.86.211?
    D. 106.23.86.143. The default gateway
    must be on your network. The first two
    answers are subnet masks. The third answer
    is your own computer's address, which will
    not be the correct address to route to
    remote networks.

6. Which is not an option under the
    Advanced TCP/IP Properties tab?
    B. Enabling IP Forwarding. This is an
    option under the Routing tab in TCP/IP
    Properties, not the Advanced portion.

7. What do you need access to if you are to
    resolve a name of mcsehopeful.com?

D. A DNS Server. The Domain Name
Service performs name resolution of host
names to IP addresses.

8. You are network administrator of a small
    network. Even though you have a WINS
    server on the network for name resolution,
    you still maintain the HOSTS files for each
    workstation. What would happen if you
    could not communicate with the WINS
    server?
    D. You could not resolve any more
    NetBIOS names. This would most likely be
    the case because you have not maintained
    the LMHOSTS file, which would resolve
    NetBIOS names to IP addresses in the
    event the WINS server was unreachable.

9. What does DHCP stand for?
    Dynamic Host Configuration Protocol.

10. (True/False) A default gateway must always
    be present before you can communicate.
    False. The Default Gateway is used in a
    routed environment when you have packets
    destined for a remote network. If you do not
    communicate with remote networks, then
    you do not need to specify a default gateway.

11. Which is not a tab on the WWW Service
    Properties dialog box?
    A. Authentication. The authentication
    settings are adjusted from the main Service
    tab in the Internet Service Manager.

12. Which tab in the Internet Service Manager
    do you use to specify what access a user has?
    C. The Directories tab. This is where you

specify whether the users have Read or Execute access to the directories.

13. (True/False) Windows NT Challenge/Response is the most effective way to eliminate stolen passwords.
False. With Windows NT Challenge/Response, usernames and passwords are sent encrypted over the network, but this is not the most effective way. Allowing Anonymous access is the most effective, because usernames and passwords are not transmitted over the network.

14. Which tab of the FTP Service would you specify UNIX or MS-DOS listing?
C. Directories. The UNIX directory listing style is most often used on the Internet due to the abundance of UNIX machines, but you can use the MS-DOS directory listing on your own intranet if you have no UNIX machines.

15. You are administrator of a branch office for the Guitars Galore corporation. You've been having communication problems with headquarters, and now there's a support representative from the corporate headquarters on the phone. He tells you to issue the IPCONFIG /ALL command. You do so, and tell him the current settings. He tells you he knows what the problem is. Based on this TCP/IP configuration, which line is incorrect?
F. Default Gateway: 134.27.119.1. I cannot stress too strongly the importance of a correctly configured default gateway. Make sure this is on the same network as the IP address of the computer. If you received this address via the DHCP server, you have more problems. The DHCP server is assigning a default gateway that is not on the same network as the IP addresses.

16. (True/False) The LMHOSTS file is used to map host names to IP addresses.
False. The HOSTS file is used to map host names to IP addresses. LMHOSTS is used to map NetBIOS names to IP addresses.

17. (True/False) Windows NT Workstation supports Routing Information Protocol (RIP) for dynamic routing updates.
False. Windows NT Workstation does not support dynamic routing, but Windows NT Server does. NT Workstation can take advantage of static routing.

Answers to Chapter 9 Self Test

1. (True/False) Installing CSNW and NWLink is a difficult, time-consuming process that will require significant training for support personnel.
False. CSNW and NWLink are very easy to install and configure. A capable computer support professional can complete the process with little or no training, and it only takes a few minutes to install. Waiting

for the computer to reboot will probably be the most time-consuming step of the setup process.

2. The _____ protocol and the _____ network service are the two components necessary for Windows NT to connect to NetWare servers for file and print services.
NWLink, CSNW. These two components must be installed for Windows NT Workstation to function as a client to a NetWare server. With OEM software, the only other way for a Windows NT Workstation to access a Novell server is through a Windows NT Server running the Gateway Service for NetWare.

3. (True/False) Windows NT Workstation users will not be able to use long filenames when saving files to NetWare servers.
False. Windows NT Workstation users can use long filenames on NetWare servers if the OS/2 name space NLM is running. Consult the NetWare documentation if you need help installing the NLM on the server.

4. Which Windows NT command displays information regarding the IPX frame type in use?
C. The IPXROUTE command displays information and statistics about NWLink. When used with the CONFIG switch, it displays the frame type(s) in use, and to which network adapter it is bound. This command is most useful when Auto Detect is selected for the frame type and you need

to find out what frame type was detected and used.

5. (True/False) CSNW is a useful component of Windows NT Workstation and a Windows NT certified professional can reasonably expect to work with it during his or her career.
True. The number of installed NetWare servers guarantees that CSNW will be used on a significant percentage of corporate, government, and educational Windows NT Workstations. A Windows NT certified professional should be familiar with the capabilities of CSNW and comfortable with its installation and configuration.

6. What frame type does Windows NT use if it cannot detect the frame type in use on the network?
A. Ethernet 802.2 is the frame type that is used by default if Windows NT can't detect at least one frame type. This is the default frame type for NetWare 3.12 and NetWare 4.x servers, as well as 3.5 and later versions of Windows NT.

7. NetWare uses the _____ protocol for network file sharing and the _____ protocol for network transport.
NetWare Core Protocol (NCP), IPX/SPX. Microsoft Networking uses the Server Message Block (SMB) protocol for file sharing, while NetWare uses NCP. Novell's robust and routable IPX/SPX transport protocol is the foundation for NetWare communications. CSNW enables Windows

NT to communicate with NCP, and NWLink is the IPX/SPX-compatible network transport protocol.

8. (True/False) Changing the Ethernet frame type by editing the Registry is a good idea. **False.** If the Registry data that contains the frame type configuration is not valid, it can cause the computer to crash. Editing the Registry should only be done when there is no other way to implement the desired configuration. Use the NWLink IPX/SPX Properties dialog box whenever possible.

9. (True/False) With Novell's NDS, it is necessary to log on to each server you wish to use. **False.** NDS provides global logon authentication. Once a user logs on to an NDS tree, he can access any network objects within the tree that he been given permission to use. One NDS tree can contain all of the servers and printers for an entity's global network, and a user can be given access to anything on that network with just one logon.

10. When installing CSNW, when is the first opportunity to configure the preferred server or NDS tree? **A.** Windows NT automatically prompts you to enter the preferred server or preferred tree and context information when you restart and log on to the workstation, after installing CSNW. Each

user that logs on to the workstation is prompted for the same information.

11. (True/False) NWLink cannot be removed from the Windows NT client, even if the NetWare server to which it is connecting is using TCP/IP. **True.** NWLink is necessary for CSNW to function and it cannot be removed until CSNW is removed. Even if the NetWare servers on your network are using TCP/IP, you must still have NWLink installed to use CSNW.

12. By default, what network and print providers does Windows NT access first after CSNW is installed? **D.** Windows NT places NetWare at the top of the access order for both network and print providers after CSNW is installed. Adjusting this order may be necessary if you use a Windows NT Server computer as your primary file or print server.

13. (True/False) CSNW will allow Windows NT users to log on to NetWare 4.x servers only if the servers are running bindery emulation. **False.** Windows NT users can connect to NetWare 4.x servers through NDS authentication, as well as through bindery services. This gives Windows NT Workstation users the same functionality as any other NetWare NDS client.

14. (True/False) NetWare servers are accessible through a Windows NT Server running GSNW only to Windows 3.x and Windows 95 clients. Windows NT Workstation users *must* have CSNW and NWLink installed on their computers to access NetWare servers.
False. Windows NT Workstation users can access NetWare servers through a Windows NT Server using the Gateway Service for NetWare. GSNW is designed to function as a gateway for any client that can connect a Windows NT Server.

15. When considering protocols and frame types to use, which guideline listed below results in the best network performance?
C. Using only one protocol and one frame type reduces the number of broadcasts a computer must make to communicate with other network devices. Using only one protocol on a network is always the best choice, as long as it can meet the needs of the network.

16. (True/False) Windows NT Workstation users will find that using files and printers on NetWare servers is very similar to using files and printers on Windows NT servers.
True. Most users don't notice a difference between using file and print services on a NetWare server, and using the same services on a Windows NT server. Once a drive is mapped or a print queue is connected, only the most computer-savvy users can tell

whether the connections are to a NetWare server or to a Windows NT computer.

Answers to Chapter 10 Self Test

1. Which network protocols can Windows NT 4.0 PPP carry?
B,C,E. Microsoft currently supports the three major network protocols. These protocols were chosen to offer the widest range of connects. IPX accommodates Netware environments, NetBEUI provides backwards compatibility with RAS NetBIOS gateways, and TCP/IP provides connectivity to the widest range of hosts.

2. How many simultaneous dial-in clients can Windows NT 4.0 Workstation handle?
B. Windows NT 4.0 Workstation can support one dial-up client. NT 4.0 Server can support 256 connections, and Windows NT 3.51 Workstation can support two connections.

3. Your remote users are complaining that their applications run slowly over their RAS connections at home. What feature of Windows NT 4.0 RAS would allow you to increase the users' throughput?
D. PPP-MP allows you to bind multiple RAS ports together, which gives the link the aggregate bandwidth of each RAS port.

4. You want to make sure that the throughput for dial-up users is maximized, by enabling compression. What represents the fastest configuration for achieving this goal?
B. Software compression provides superior performance compared to hardware compression, because the PC has more memory and processor space. If you use the modem for compression, you're more likely to end up with buffer overruns and lost connections.

5. (True/False) Before network protocols can be loaded on RAS interfaces, they must first be bound to the LAN adapter, in order for the NT 4.0 Workstation to operate as a RAS server.
True. In order to support dial-up user access to LAN behind the RAS server, the protocols have to be loaded on each interface.

6. Which of these pairs of RAS interfaces could be used in a PPP-MP configuration to increase your bandwidth?
E. Neither the interface nor the bandwidth has to be symmetric in order to support PPP-MP.

7. Dial-Out network protocols are configured from the:
B. The Remote Access Setup screen configures the protocols for RAS. The DUN phonebook editor configures the protocols for each phonebook entry.

8. TAPI 2.0 has programming facilities to:
B,C. TAPI has a broad base of APIs that make it easy for developers to telephony-enable their applications. TAPI can be used for anything from basic dial-out functionality to interacting with phone systems.

9. (True/False) NetBEUI can be used to provide connectivity from TCP/IP and IPX-based hosts to NetBEUI-based clients that dial-up to a RAS server configured as a NetBIOS gateway.
True. The NetBIOS gateway on the RAS server provides protocol translation for NetBEUI clients. Keep in mind, however, that IPX- or TCP/IP-based applications still need their respective protocol loaded, in order to run.

10. The My Locations section of the dialing properties can keep track of which location-specific information?
B,C. The My Locations feature allows users to create customized dial-out scripts once and reuse them. DUN also provides facilities for keeping multiple server entries, which can be used interchangeably with the locations.

11. Which of the following methods would you use to test a dial-up connection?
E. Each answer represents the testing of a different layer of the RAS connection. The device log provides a hardware-level perspective on the errors. You could catch a buffer overrun or poor line quality error. The PPP log provides a look at protocol

errors and multi-protocol errors. The event log alerts you to major errors, and allows you to monitor security. The PING utility checks to see if the basic protocol will work. Mapping a drive checks the file server connection and validation.

12. You need to dial-up a UNIX host, and accessing the host with PPP isn't working. What other connection protocol might work?
    D. Many legacy UNIX servers still use the predecessor to PPP, SLIP, for their connections. SLIP doesn't support dynamic IP allocations, multiple protocols, or encryption.

13. You want to program your RAS connection to dial-up your ISP after you load your browser. Which NT RAS feature enables you to do this?
    C. The auto dial feature correlates network connections, for example a telnet session to a UNIX host, back to the DUN phonebook entry that enabled the connection. So for example, if you access your home page automatically upon opening your browser, the auto dial feature activated the RAS connection, which then enabled you to see the web server with your home page.

14. While downloading a file from your NT network, the modem line unexpectedly drops. You dial-up back to the server and file copy resumes once you connect. Which

feature enabled this?
    A. The restartable file copy feature does precisely what the question describes. This is particularly handy over modem connections where link failure is pretty common.

15. You want to make sure that your communications are secure over the RAS link you're using. What constitutes the most secure connection type available over RAS? AMS-CHAP secures the authentication procedure while logging onto the RAS server. Utilizing data encryption means that every packet sent and received is scrambled.

Answers to Chapter 11 Self Test

1. Sally, Bob, and Ed are engineers using computers running Windows NT Workstation. They occasionally like to share files with each other, and the files are too big to fit on a floppy, but they don't want just anyone to be able to access the files. What is the best solution to their problem?
   D. Setting up two extra accounts on each workstation is manageable, and allows the users to share resources however they wish. Answer A is overkill for this situation, and is expensive. The other options are cumbersome and unnecessary.

2. A workgroup consists of a Windows NT Server, a Windows NT Workstation, a

Windows 95 system, and a Windows for Workgroups system. The Windows NT Workstation has MaintainServerList set to Yes and Preferred Master Browser set. Each of the others has default browser settings, and all are using the same network protocol. Which of the following is true:
A. Since there are four systems, there will be a Master Browser and one Backup Browser. Windows NT Server wins the browser election based on operating system, which is the predominant criterion. While the Windows NT Workstation would probably have been the Backup Browser anyway, having MaintainServerList set to Yes means the Master Browser won't even have to ask one set to Auto to start browsing.

3. A system shows up in the Network Neighborhood, but the user is unable to connect to its resources as he has in the past. Which of the following are good hypotheses to troubleshoot the problem:
B,D. For B, remember that it can take up to 51 minutes for a system to be removed from the Network Neighborhood. If the system in question had been up a while, it would take at least 24 minutes to disappear from the neighborhood, assuming it went down just before its announcement, and that the Backup Browser updated its list immediately after the Master Browser removed it. For D, remembering that the passwords have to be maintained on each system in a workgroup is a clue, if the user

tells you he had recently changed his password. While security *might* be the problem, C is wrong because it could have been one of the other things mentioned. E is unlikely in a domain, though user access could still have been set up using a local user database. A is only an option after you've eliminated everything else and determined that he never had access to begin with.

4. A user has just changed his password while logged into the domain on one workstation. He logs out and immediately goes to another workstation in the domain and can't get logged in. Which of the following might be true:
A,B,C,D. The CAPS LOCK problem is so common, it's mentioned in the error window that pops up when a failed logon attempt occurs. B would be a misunderstanding on the part of the user. Since the BDC may take up to 5 minutes to get the update from the PDC, scenario C occasionally happens. The administrator could have filled out workstation names using the Logon To button in User Manager for Domains, so D is also correct. E is false because the new workstation would have played no part in the change; the information is kept on the domain controllers.

5. Ted, Jill, and Janet are users on Windows NT Workstations belonging to a domain. They always log on to the domain at their workstations. They have administrator

access to their workstations, but aren't domain administrators. They'd like to share files on their workstations with each other using group access, with the ability to make changes themselves (without a domain administrator). Which option is the best?
B. In order to use groups while not involving a domain administrator, local workstation groups must be used. Using the domain user accounts will make the access work. Option A would require the users to log on to their workstations instead of the domain, and maintain additional passwords on each workstation. Option C is impossible: global groups don't exist on Windows NT Workstation. Option D won't work because only global groups on a domain controller are available to the domain. Since B works, E is also false.

6. Which of the following give a computer preference in browser elections?
B,C,D. Being the PDC has the most effect, so B is true. Running a WINS server gives the next biggest bonus, so C is also true. Being the current Master Browser does give an advantage as well, so D is true. BDCs get no special treatment, so A is false. If MaintainServerList were Yes, it would help, but it is of no advantage when set to Auto, so E is false.

7. Which of the following are true statements about workgroup and domain membership?

B,C,D,E. Option E can be used to improve browsing for workstations that may later be joining the domain. They will show up in the Network Neighborhood just like the domain members, although they can't participate in any other domain functions.

8. David is a domain administrator running Windows NT Workstation at his desk. Which of the following are true statements?
A,B. Since David is a domain administrator, and the Domain Administrator group is added to the local Administrators group on every workstation that joins the domain, he's also a local administrator. Not only is he a domain administrator, but he may install the domain administrator tools on his workstation, and run User Manager for Domains as well as the local workstation User Manager. Roaming profiles aren't required to log on to different workstations; they just help keep the same desktop environment if they have been set up, so C is false. While D is just a humorous response, if it were true, David's career as an administrator would be very short. E is false because users aren't browsers, computers are. Since David is using a domain, the Master Browser will be the PDC if it's available.

9. Jane wants her Windows NT Workstation to join the domain. She has selected

Domain and typed in the correct name in the Identification Changes window. What can she do?

A,C,D. An administrator is required to create a computer account in the domain before the computer may join. This can be accomplished either in Server Manager or by entering any domain administrator's username and password after selecting Create a Computer Account in the Domain. B is false because she's not a domain administrator in that answer. E is also false: the only time a reinstall is required is when a Windows NT Server that was installed as the BDC or PDC for another domain wishes to join.

10. Twenty-five users running Windows NT Workstations in a workgroup wish to share resources. What's their best solution?

C. This is the only option that gives a central account database that can be used by all the workstations. Option A is basically unmanageable, while the additional suggestion in D just does away with any security you might have had. Just adding a Windows NT Server to the workgroup doesn't change the situation, so B is out. Option E is actually worse than B, because now the systems aren't even browsing together.

11. The Marketing domain spans multiple subnetworks on a routed network. The PDC server becomes unavailable due to hardware problems, but you have a couple

of BDCs. After a while, users report problems seeing other nodes on the network. What happened, and how do you fix the problem?

B. While the subnetwork the PDC was on will elect a new Master Browser, there is no domain Master Browser to tie the subnetworks together without a PDC. Therefore, promoting a BDC is the quickest way to restore network connectivity. Option A has pretty much everything wrong: the domain Master Browser is missing, not a Master Browser (one would have been elected), and promoting a BDC to the PDC is a manual process. Option C is also totally wrong: domains will still run with no PDC (though not well in the case of browsing subnetworks), NT Workstations can't be domain controllers, and systems must be installed as domain controllers before they may be promoted. Option D is false because there is no election process for a domain Master Browser; it's *always* the PDC, though a new Master Browser would have been elected for the old PDC's subnetwork. While the first half of the statement in E is true, the Master Browser is a red herring, and you should promote a BDC instead of trying to replace the hardware and restore the old server (takes too long, though you might end up doing that in addition after promoting a BDC).

12. Ned and Lonnie work different shifts at the rock quarry. They use the same Windows NT Workstation, which is a member of a domain. Which of the following could be true for Ned to log on to the workstation: **A,B,C.** The workstation can validate from its local account database, the account database of the domain of which it's a member, or another domain trusted by that domain. If you said D, you'd better review the direction of trust relationships. E is totally bogus, since a workstation (or even a server) can't enter a trust relationship; it's a domain attribute.

13. Ned's shift has been changed, and he now works with Lonnie. There are now two Windows NT Workstations that either may log on to, with identical software setups. What's the best way to preserve their desktops for both computers? **C**, though B gets honorable mention. Roaming profiles will provide them with their desktop regardless of which workstation they log on to. Option B gets honorable mention because it's probably easier to maintain in their environment, though it doesn't preserve any modifications they might make. Option A would work, but would be a lot of manual work. Option D might work depending on the situation, but begs the question of preserving the desktop across systems, so it's not the best answer. Option E won't make for very happy employees, and may not be

what you want to say to someone who can bust rock.

14. Earnest has an account in each of the two domains, Seeming and Being. Earnest is a domain administrator in Being, but just a normal user in Seeming. Domain Seeming trusts Being, and also has added Being\Domain Admins to the local Administrator's group on the PDC for Seeming. If Earnest wants to log on to the PDC for Seeming to administer it, what must he do?
D. The importance of Being\Earnest lies in Earnest as a member of Being\Domain Admins, and that group is a member of Administrators on the PDC. The Seeming\Earnest is a totally different account, and by default wouldn't even be able to log on locally to the PDC, so option B is out. There's no way to set environments as mentioned in C. E isn't possible because there's no trust relationship mentioned of Being trusting Seeming, and he wouldn't be able to log on locally by default with that account, even if the trust existed.

15. You're looking at the Network Neighborhood for your domain. You see systems listed for which you know you haven't set up a computer account in the domain, and they don't appear in Server Manager. Which of the following could explain the situation?
A,B. Only Windows NT computers need

computer accounts in the domain to participate. Any Windows system, even a Windows NT one, may give your domain name as its workgroup name and participate in browsing, but not the domain. Any computers added as in option C would also show up in Server Manager. Options D and E are total fabrications, and have no validity under any circumstances.

Answers to Chapter 12 Self Test

1. What are two advantages of the EMF data type?
   B,C. EMF files return control of the application to the user more quickly, because EMF spools to the spooler and then becomes a background process to print. EMF files also can be printed on any printer, because the print process renders the document based on the printing device selected.

2. What are the two types of print processors shipped with NT?
   A,C. These are the only two types of print processors supplied with NT. Vendors can make other print processors if needed.

3. If you want to add an HP JetDirect networked printer to your computer, what two things must you do?
   A,C. To use an HP JetDirect card, you must have DLC installed on your system. Since DLC uses MAC addresses to print,

you need to print a test page to identify the MAC address of the JetDirect Card. Also, note that DLC is not a routable protocol.

4. You shared an HP LaserJet 5 on your system for everyone in your department to use. When users try to connect to the printer using Windows 95, they get the following error: "The server on which the printer resides does not have a suitable driver installed. Click OK if you wish to select a driver to use on your local machine." What should you do to prevent users from receiving this error message?
   C. Windows 95 supports Point and Print like Windows NT does. However, you must have the proper driver installed. Print drivers are not hardware platform and operating system independent. You must have a driver compiled for each operating system and hardware platform.

5. (True/False) A local printer must have a port on your system.
   True. A local printer is just that—local. It must have a local port. A local port can be a serial port, parallel port, or a network enabled port.

6. You want to set up a printer pool using two printers. Neither printing device can use a common driver. How can you enable both printing devices to be in a printer pool?
   D. In order to set up printer pooling, all printers must use the same print driver.

7. Your boss needs to print to his secretary's printer, but he doesn't want to wait for his

print job behind anybody else's print job. How can you share the printer, giving your boss a higher priority?
C. You must create two different printers, so you can assign different priorities to the printers.

8. User JamieS sent a print job to an NT Workstation acting as a print server. When she went to the printer to pick up her print job, she noticed a 200-page report was printing out. She didn't want to wait for her print job, so she printed her document on a different printer. JamieS is environmentally conscious, so she doesn't want to waste paper printing the first print job. How can she delete her first print job? (Choose the best answer.)
A. Since she is the creator owner of the document, she can delete her own print job. If you selected B as the answer, that would work, but it isn't the best solution.

9. To what group must a user be added before he can manage other people's print jobs? (Choose all that apply.)
A,C. Administrators and Power Users can manage other users' print jobs. Creator Owner can only manage his own print job.

10. Drive C: has 10MB of available disk space on it. Drive D: has 300MB of disk space available. Windows NT is installed on Drive C:, which is almost out of space. Sometimes when you print, your computer locks up and you have to restart your

system. What should you do to prevent this problem in the future?
C. The printer spool file is probably causing the hard drive to fill up, thus causing the system to lock. Moving the printer spooler to Drive D: should alleviate the problem. Although having only 10MB of available disk space still can cause problems with other applications.

Answers to Chapter 13 Self Test

1. Which facility is used when environment subsystems need to communicate?
C. Message-passing. Messages are passed to subsystems through the Local Procedure Call Facility.

2. What does CSRSS provide?
D. Error handling for the subsystems. This is known as the Client/Server Runtime subsystem, and also provides the console, as well as shutdown.

3. What component is responsible for keeping track of the time that threads are being processed?
B. Process Manager. The Process Manager is responsible for the deleting, creating, and managing of processes and threads. The Kernel is responsible for scheduling these threads.

4. (True/False) The Security Reference Monitor works with the CSRSS and Object

Manager subsystem to make up the entire Security model for the system.
False. The Security Reference Monitor works with the Logon Process and Security Subsystem to make up the entire Security model for the system.

5. Which priority class is considered IDLE?
A. Priority level 4. This is the priority level for /LOW. Priority levels 7 and 9 are for the background and foreground levels, respectively.

6. Fill in the blanks. Both the _____ and the _____ ran in User Mode in the Win32 subsystem in previous releases of NT, but now have been moved into the Windows NT Executive, which runs in Kernel Mode.
Graphics Device Interface, Window Manager. Window Manager (USER) functions are communicated to the GDI, which then communicates to the device driver.

7. Which is not a component of the Virtual DOS Machine?
C. REDIR.SYS. The redirector component of the Virtual DOS Machine is implemented as an executable, not SYS.

8. (True/False). If there is no PIF associated for the application, the DEFAULT.PIF is used.
False. The _DEFAULT.PIF will be used if there is no PIF associated with the application.

9. I have a DOS application and three Win16 applications running on the system. When I switch from the DOS application to one of the Win16 applications, they are all unresponsive. What is the best way to remedy this situation?
C. Run each of the Win16 applications in its own memory space, so they do not interfere with each other. Although increasing the priority may fix the problem, using a separate memory space is a better idea if the Win16 applications are becoming unresponsive. If you isolate the problem to just one Win16 application, you could run just that application in its own memory space to avoid using too much memory.

10. Which is the proper syntax for loading an application in a separate memory space with a HIGH priority level?
D. START /SEPARATE /HIGH MSPAINT.EXE. The options for priority and memory space should appear *before* the application name. You also should have realized that /SEP is not correct. If you are really on your toes, you know that MSPAINT.EXE is a Win32 application that is already run in a separate memory space by default! The switch is just ignored.

11. Which of the following are ways you can start a Win16 application in a separate memory space?
A,B,C,D,E. They are all ways of running a Win16 application in separate memory. I did not cover the use of Task Manager for starting new applications. It appears as the

Run dialog box and still has the check box to run 16-bit applications in a separate memory space.

12. Which is not a component of the OS/2 Subsystem?
C. OS2LIB.DLL. OS2SRV.EXE was the other component not listed, which is the application launcher for the subsystem.

13. (True/False) The OS/2 Subsystem cannot run OS/2 2.x applications.
True. The OS/2 subsystem only supports OS/2 1.x character applications, not OS/2 2.x applications.

14. Which is not a Kernel Mode component?
B. Security Subsystem. We did not discuss this subsystem in the chapter. Using your knowledge of the Kernel Mode components and the process of elimination, you should have been able to choose this answer.

15. Fill in the blank. If you do not alter the priority of an application, it will run at the default priority level of _____.
7. This is the default priority level of an application, and also is the background priority level. By virtue of being in the foreground, an application receives a boost of 2, with a priority of 9.

Answers to Chapter 14 Self Test

1. Using the /HIGH switch when starting an application from the command prompt will

cause it to start at what priority?
B. Table 14-2 illustrates the four switch possibilities and their associated priority level.

2. While using the Processor:%Processor Time counter in Performance Monitor you see it spike to 100% when starting an application, but then it drops to 43%. What do you need to do?
D. The processor only becomes a bottleneck if it sustains a utilization rate of 80% or higher.

3. Windows NT divides memory into ____ pages.
B. Windows NT uses a 4KB page size to help avoid fragmentation of memory.

4. Windows NT Workstation supports ____ processors.
B. Windows NT supports two processors. If you need to support more processors, contact your computer system manufacturer.

5. (True/False) It is not possible to change the priority of the foreground application so that it runs at the same priority as all background applications.
False. It is possible to make the foreground application equal to background applications by moving the slider to None on the Performance tab of System Properties.

6. By how many levels can Windows NT automatically adjust the priority of an

application?
C. Windows NT can automatically raise or lower priority by a maximum of two levels.

7. You suspect a disk drive is creating a bottleneck within your system. You use the LogicalDisk:%Disk Time counter to take measurements, but have a consistent reading of zero. What is the problem?
D. You must enable the Disk Drive Performance Counters prior to using either the LogicalDisk or PhysicalDisk Objects.

8. Multiprocessing supported by Windows NT is _____ .
B. Windows NT supports symmetrical processing so that it can effectively share the load among all the processors.

9. (True/False) Using two processors in your Windows NT system doubles the performance capability.
False. Overhead for resource sharing and scheduling between two processors prohibits you from seeing double system performance.

10. Where does Windows NT perform automatic self-tuning optimizations?
A,C,D. Windows NT adjusts thread and process priority, swapping among multiple pagefiles, and caching disk requests, as part of its self-tuning optimizations.

11. The cache system used by Windows NT is _____ .
C. Windows NT uses a dynamic cache so that it can adjust itself for maximum performance.

12. The Disk Drive Performance Counters are enabled using what utility?
C. Diskperf is the utility used to enable and disable the Disk Drive Performance Counters.

13. (True/False) The Task Manager cannot be used to change the priority of a thread.
True. Task Manager can change the priority of processes, not threads.

14. Using Performance Monitor, you have determined that you have a disk drive bottleneck. What action(s) could alleviate this problem?
B. Adding more physical memory to a system can alleviate a disk drive bottleneck by minimizing the amount of paging to the disk drive if physical memory is low.

15. Using Performance Monitor, you have determined that you are encountering a memory bottleneck. What action(s) will eliminate it?
A,C. Expand the size of your pagefile, because if your pagefile is too small it can appear to be a memory bottleneck. Unloading unused drivers will free memory that the system can use.

16. (True/False) Hard page faults are more detrimental to system performance than soft page faults.
True. Hard page faults indicate that additional I/O has occurred, and soft page faults indicate the data was located elsewhere in memory.

17. (True/False) Once you have manually performance-tuned your system, you never have to do it again.
False. Performance tuning your system is an ongoing process.

18. (True/False) Disk Drive Performance Counters should only be enabled when monitoring disk drive performance.
True. The Disk Drive Performance Counters degrade overall system performance by interrupting the processor during I/O. They should only be enabled when you are going to measure disk drive performance.

19. How would you change the priority of an application that is already running?
D. The Task Manager can change the priority of an application that is running. If you stop and restart the application it goes back to the original priority.

Answers to Chapter 15 Self Test

1. Which of the following would be valid in a BOOT.INI file?
B. The only choice that fulfills ARC naming requirements is B.

2. (True/False) The /SOS switch is used in the BOOT.INI file to enable the capture of debugging information.
False. The /SOS switch is used to display the drivers that are loading as Windows NT is booting.

3. What files are required to be on a Windows NT boot disk for a non-SCSI Intel-based machine?
A,B,E. The other two files are used for SCSI systems and RISC-based machines.

4. NTDETECT.COM is used to
_____ .
D. NTDETECT.COM examines the hardware on an Intel-based machine.

5. You are sent out on a trouble call and told that the system hangs ever since the user added a new video driver. What would you do?
C. Reboot the system using the LastKnownGood configuration with the original video driver.

6. Your system has 32MB of physical memory and you have set the System Recovery to write debugging information to %systemroot%\memory.dmp. What else needs to be done to ensure that the debugging information will be saved?
A. The pagefile has to be at least the same size as physical memory so that it can dump everything from memory to the pagefile for debugging.

7. What tool do you use to detect the group dependencies for a service?
D. WinMSD Services tab shows you dependencies for services.

8. (True/False) The only way to change the default timeout is to edit the BOOT.INI file manually.

False. The timeout can be changed from the Startup/Shutdown tab of System Properties.

9. Which load phase can be identified by the screen turning blue?
B. Kernel initialization occurs when the screen turns blue.

10. Paul has been fired and his replacement, Ann, needs to access the fourth-quarter report located in a folder that belonged to Paul. How can Ann access this folder?
D. An Administrator has to take ownership of the folder, but if Ann is given full control, she can access the folder and take ownership for herself.

11. (True/False) The Session Manager subkey of the Registry contains local variables that are used by the Session Manager.
False. The variables for the Session Manager subkey are global.

12. If a service has been set in the Registry for an error control of 0x2, it reflects a level of _____ .
D. 0x2 reflects an error control of severe.

13. To update your Emergency Repair Disk, you would type _____ from a Command Prompt.
B. You would type **RDISK** from a command prompt to update your ERD.

14. (True/False) A Service Pack can easily be removed from your system, even if you do not have the uninstall folder.
False. If you did not create an uninstall folder, you cannot easily remove the Service Pack.

15. What causes the "Blue Screen of Death"?
A. A STOP message causes the "Blue Screen of Death".

16. (True/False) Any ASCII editor can be used to read an Event Viewer .EVT log file.
False. The .EVT log file is stored in a binary format.

17. The partition(n) portion of an ARC name starts counting with _____ .
B. The partition(n) starts with a count of one.

18. Your system is set to dual-boot between Windows 95 and Windows NT. You receive the following message as you try to boot into Windows 95: I/O Error accessing boot sector file. What has caused this to occur?
D. If BOOTSEC.DOS is missing, it creates that error.

19. A system you have been sent out to troubleshoot will not boot. You attempt to use the LastKnownGood configuration and it does not correct the problem. What would you do next?
B. You should use the ERD for that system to try and fix it.

20. (True/False) The SAM and security files are automatically updated when you use the Repair Disk Utility.
False. You must use the /s switch with rdisk if you want to back up the SAM and security files.

B

About the CD

CD-ROM Instructions

T his CD-ROM contains a full web site accessible to you via your web browser. Browse to or double-click **index.htm** at the root of the CD-ROM and you will find instructions for navigating the web site and for installing the various software components.

Electronic Book

An electronic version of the entire book in HTML format.

Interactive Self-Study Module

An electronic self-study test bank linked to the electronic book to help you instantly review key exam topics that may still be unclear. This module contains over 300 review questions, the same questions that appear at the end of each chapter. If you answer a multiple choice question correctly by clicking on the right answer, you will automatically link to the next question. If you answer incorrectly, you will be linked to the appropriate section in the electronic book for further study.

Sample Exams

Demos from market-leading certification tools vendors, including Self-Test Software's PEP, Transcender's CERT, VFX Technologies' Endeavor, BeachFront Quizzer's BFQuizzer, and Microhard Technologies' MCSEQuest. These exams may be installed either from the "Exams and Simulations" web page or from Windows Explorer. See the following for instructions on either type of installation.

From the Web Page

Internet Explorer users will be prompted to either "open the file" or "save it to disk." Select "open the file" and the installation program will automatically be launched, installing the software to your hard disk. Follow the vendor's instructions. The software will be installed to the hard disk. Once installed, you should run the programs via the Start Programs taskbar on your desktop.

Netscape Navigator users will be asked to "save as..." the setup file. You should save it to a folder on your hard drive, then click on it in Windows Explorer to launch the installation. Follow the vendor's instructions. The software will be installed to the hard disk. Once installed, you should run the programs via the Start Programs taskbar on your desktop.

From Windows Explorer

You can also launch the installation of any of these programs from Windows Explorer by opening the "Demo Exams" folder on the CD. Each vendor's installation program is inside the designated folder. Click on the appropriate SETUP.EXE file and then follow the vendor's instructions. The software will be installed to the hard disk. Once installed, you should run the programs via the Start Programs taskbar on your desktop.

MCSE
MICROSOFT CERTIFIED SYSTEMS ENGINEER

C

About the Web Site

Access Global Knowledge Network

A s you know by now, Global Knowledge Network is the largest independent IT training company in the world. Just by purchasing this book, you have also secured a free subscription to the Access Global web site and its many resources. You can find it at:

http://access.globalknowledge.com

To acquire an ID to use the Access Global web site, send e-mail to access@globalknowledge.com and type **Access ID Request** in the subject field. In the body of the message, include your full name, mailing address, e-mail address, and phone number. Within two business days you will receive your Access Global web site ID. The first time you visit the site and log on, you will be able to choose your own password.

What You'll Find There. . .

You will find a lot of information at the Global Knowledge site, most of which can be broken down into three categories:

Skills Gap Analysis

Global Knowledge offers several ways for you to analyze your networking skills and discover where they may be lacking. Using Global Knowledge Network's trademarked Competence Key Tool, you can do a skills gap analysis and get recommendations for where you may need to do some more studying (sorry, it just may not end with this book!).

Networking

You'll also gain valuable access to another asset: people. At the Access Global site, you'll find threaded discussions as well as live discussions. Talk to other MCSE candidates, get advice from folks who have already taken exams, and get access to instructors and MCTs.

Product Offerings

Of course, Global Knowledge also offers its products here—and you may find some valuable items for purchase: CBTs, books, courses. Browse freely and see if there's something that could help you.

Glossary

10Base-2   An Ethernet topology using thin Ethernet coaxial cable, also known as Thin Ethernet or thinnet.

10Base-5   Also called thicknet, this form of cable was once commonly used for backbones in Ethernet networks. It is now being replaced by 10Base-T.

10Base-T   An Ethernet topology that uses unshielded twisted pair cable. 10Base-T has become the most popular Ethernet cable, because many buildings are already wired for 10Base-T, it is inexpensive and easy to work with, and if the cable specifications are CAT5, it can transmit data at 100Mbps.

access permissions   Access permissions set your rights and privileges to manipulate files and directories. Depending on your permissions, you may or may not be able to copy, delete, or otherwise manipulate files and directories on the network.

Account   An account or user account provides access to the network. It contains the information allowing a person to use the network, including user name and logon specifications, password, and rights to directories and resources.

account restrictions   Restrictions on an account determine when and how a user gains access to the network.

acknowledgment (ACK)   A packet of information sent from the recipient computer to the sending computer, for the purpose of verifying that a transmission has been received and confirming that it was or was not a successful transmission. Similar to a return receipt.

active hub   A hub device used in a star topology to regenerate and redistribute data across the LAN. Unlike a passive hub, the active hub requires electricity. See also hub, and passive hub.

adapter   A network adapter card, also called a network interface card, transmits data from the workstation to the cable that connects the machine to the LAN. It provides the communication link between the computer and the network. See also Network Interface Card.

administrator account   The account used to administer the settings on an NT Server and network. This account is created during install and has unlimited access to the server. Care must be taken when logged into a server as an administrator, because administrator access rights include the ability to shut down the server or erase critical data.

alias   A name used to reference a person, or group on a computer system. Mail aliases are a common use of the alias feature. When an alias is used, the computer system still recognizes a person by a user name, but an alias can be set so that people can send mail or other information using the alias name instead of the user name.

analog   A continuous, non-digital data transmission usually associated with telephone communications.

AppleTalk   The set of network protocols used by Macintosh computers.

archiving   A process that allows you to move old files off the file server to preserve disk space for new files. If the old files are later needed, they can be unarchived and retrieved. Archived data can be saved to CD-ROM, WORM, or tape.

ArcNet (Attached Resource Computer Network)   A bus network topology that is similar to token ring, in that it uses a token to transmit data across the network. ArcNet transmits data at 2.5Mbps and can run on coaxial, twisted-pair, and fiber optic cable.

ASCII (American Standard Code for Information Interchange)
A representation of standard alphabetic and other keyboard characters in a computer-readable, binary format.

Asynchronous Transfer Mode (ATM)   A packet-switching network technology for LANs and WANs that can handle voice, video, and data transmissions simultaneously.

ATM   See Asynchronous Transfer Mode (ATM).

Attachment Unit Interface   A connector on a NIC used to connect a cable to the card. Frequently used with coaxial cable.

attributes   The characteristics of files and directories. On networks such as Windows NT, attributes are set by the administrator, and define the rights for users and groups to manipulate files. On a stand-alone system, the main user can set file attributes. Attributes affect whether a file can be opened, copied, deleted, executed, modified, or otherwise manipulated.

AUI   See Attachment Unit Interface.

back door   Used by system administrators to access the network at an administrator's level, if something happens to the network administrator's home account. This provides a means to rebuild the administrator's account, or otherwise fix the network.

back up   The process of saving files to a separate location, usually an offline storage location, such as tape.

backbone   The main cable that connects file servers, routers, and bridges to the network.

backup   Copies all of the files on a network to some form of offline storage. Backups should be performed nightly, and full copies of the backup should be stored off-site.

Backup Domain Controller (BDC)   A computer that contains a backup of a domain's security policy and domain database, maintained by the NT server. Serves as a backup to the primary domain controller. A BDC is not required but is recommended.

bad sector   A damaged or non-working area of a hard disk. If data has been saved to that area, it cannot be accessed.

bandwidth   The capacity to transmit data across a communications link. Bandwidth is usually measured in bits per second (bps).

base I/O address   The address that identifies a hardware device to the computer.

baseline   The baseline captures the activity on the network on a normal day. This can be used to compare future readings for diagnostic purposes.

BNC (British Naval Connector)   Also known as a barrel connector, the connector type used in 10Base2 (thin Ethernet) networks to connect two cable segments, creating a longer segment.

bootup   The process a computer executes when powered up is known as bootup. This includes the files that initialize the hardware, and the starting of the operating system.

bridge   A hardware device that connects two LAN segments of either the same or different topologies.

buffer space   A reserved portion of RAM that provides room for the storage of incoming and outgoing data.

bus A network topology that connects all computers to a single, shared cable. In a bus topology, if one computer fails, the network fails.

cache An area in memory that duplicates information to provide faster access.

CD-ROM A device, similar to a musical compact disc, that stores data.

client A machine used to access the network.

client/server network A network architecture, based on distributed processing, in which a client performs functions by requesting services from a server.

coaxial cable A cable used in networks, consisting of a conductive center surrounded by a layer of insulation and a non-conductive outer layer.

command line A character mode interface for computer applications that relies on commands instead of a graphical interface to process information.

compression A mathematical technique that analyzes computer files in order to compress them to a smaller size. Most backup systems, and many file servers, compress files to provide increased storage capacity.

computer virus A computer program built to sabotage or destroy a computer or network.

concentrator A device that connects workstations to the path of the file server. Concentrators typically have 8 – 12 ports into which workstations attach.

conventional memory The memory below 640K. If you have room, your LAN drivers are loaded in conventional memory.

CSU/DSU (Channel Service Unit/Data Service Unit)   A piece of hardware that sits between a network and a digital telephone line, to translate data between the two formats. CSU/DSUs are most commonly used to attach a network router to a T1 or other digital telephone line.

DAT (Digital Audio Tape)   A hardware option for tape backup. Some are 4mm while others are 8mm.

Database Management System   A software application that manages a database, including the organization, storage, security, retrieval, and integrity of data in a database.

DBMS   See Database Management System (DBMS).

differential backup   Backing up only the files that have changed since the last backup, this differs from a full backup, in that a full backup saves all files regardless of when they changed. A differential backup differs from an incremental backup, in that archive attributes are not reset.

directory path   The path to a directory on a file system, including the server, volume, and other names leading to the directory.

directory tree   The file structure, including directory and subdirectory layout below the root directory.

disk mirroring   Provides redundancy by mirroring data from one hard drive to another. If a crash or other problem occurs on the active drive, Windows NT automatically begins to use the backup drive, and notifies you of the switch.

distributed-star   A combination of a bus and star topology used by ARCnet.

DLC (Data Link Control)   A method that allows token ring-based workstations to connect to IBM mainframes and minicomputers. It has also been adopted by printer manufacturers to connect remote printers to print servers, which is how Windows NT uses DLC.

DLL   See Dynamic Link Library (DLL).

DLT (Digital Linear Tape)   A hardware solution for tape backup and storage that allows multiple tapes to be loaded into the system, providing unattended backups and easy access for keeping data in online storage.

DMA (Direct Memory Addressing)   Matches an area in memory with an area on the NIC, so that when information is written to memory, it is copied to the NIC and vice versa.

DNS   See Domain Name Service (DNS).

Domain Name Service   DNS is a hierarchical name service that translates host names to IP addresses. It is used with TCP/IP hosts.

domain   A set of workstations and servers, on a network, that are administered as a group.

driver   Coordinates the communications between hardware and the computer. For example, it is a driver that allows a LAN adapter or other card to work.

Dynamic Host Configuration Protocol (DHCP)   Designed by Microsoft to handle IP address ranges through temporary assignments of addresses, DHCP provides automatic IP address allocation to specific workstations.

Dynamic Link Library (DLL)   A module of executable code that is loaded on demand. Used in Microsoft Windows products.

edge connector   The portion of an expansion board inserted into an expansion slot when the card is seated in the computer. The number of pins, and the width and depth of the lines, differ depending on the various types of interfaces (i.e., ISA, EISA, PCI, Micro Channel).

EIDE (Enhanced IDE)   EIDE is a disk drive interface that can support up to four 8.4GB drives.

EISA (Extended Industry Standard Architecture)   A standard for the PC bus that extends the 16-bit ISA bus (AT bus) to 32 bits EISA; also provides bus mastering.

electronic mail (e-mail)   Mail messages transmitted electronically from one network user to another, or across the Internet.

emergency startup disk   Provides a bootup option for Windows NT if the server will not boot from its hard disk.

encryption   An algorithm that hides the contents of a message, or other file or communication, by deliberately scrambling the elements that compose the item. The item must then be decrypted to its original form before it can be read.

Ethernet   The most popular LAN network topology.

event logs   Log files containing the system events, including security and application events.

Explorer   The file system navigation tool for Microsoft's Windows 95 and NT 4.0 operating systems.

FAQ (Frequently Asked Questions)   Appear in specific areas of bulletin boards and web sites, and contain answers to questions about a product or service that are frequently asked. These are used in newsgroups to cover questions that have appeared often.

Fast Ethernet   Ethernet provides 100Mbps data transmission.

FAT (File Allocation Table)   Originally the layout of a DOS disk storage system. In Windows NT, a FAT is a NT Server volume that is accessible by DOS and that is using the DOS file storage system instead of NTFS.

fault tolerance   A computer system that is resistant to hardware problems and software errors is said to be fault tolerant.

FDDI (Fiber Distributed Data Interface)   A very fast and expensive fiber-based network access method. FDDI provides 100Mbps network access.

fiber-optic cable   Instead of electrical impulses, fiber-optic cables move light. This type of cable is built around conductive elements that move light, not electricity. For most fiber-optic cables, the conductive element is most likely a form of special glass fiber, rather than copper or some other conductive metal. The beauty of fiber-optic cable is that it is immune to electronic and magnetic interference, and has much more bandwidth than most electrical cable types.

file server   A network computer that runs the network operating system and services requests from the workstations.

file system   The network operating system's rules for handling and storing files.

firewall   A hardware or software solution that protects a computer system from external intrusion. Firewalls have become more instrumental on computer systems as access to the Internet has grown more popular.

full backup   A complete copy of all the data on the network. These should be run frequently, and at least one current copy should be stored off-site.

gateway   A device that connects two or more dissimilar computer systems. Gateways can be electronic or software devices, and are becoming more common as the need for cross-platform communications increases.

GB   The abbreviation for gigabyte, which is treated as equivalent to a billion bytes.

Hardware Abstraction Layer (HAL)   A translation layer between the NT kernel and I/O system, and the actual hardware.

HCL (Hardware Compatibility List)   Lists all the hardware tested by Microsoft that works with NT. Check this before purchasing hardware.

host   A server that is accessed by clients. In a TCP/IP network, any computer connected to the network is considered a host.

hot-swappable parts   Parts that can be replaced without shutting down the system.

hub   The device used in a star topology that connects the computers to the LAN. Hubs can be passive or active. See also passive hub, active hub.

incremental backup   Backs up all the files that have been changed since the last backup. The file is not replaced on the backup, it is appended to the backup medium.

interference   Noise that disturbs the electrical signals sent across network cables.

intruder   Any person trying to break in to a network.

IP (Internet Protocol)   A common protocol that sets up the mechanism for transferring data across the network. Usually seen in TCP/IP.

IPX   The native transport protocol for Novell's NetWare. It is also available in the Windows NT environment.

ISA (Industry Standard Architecture)   The bus used in most PCs since it was introduced in 1985.

Kbps   See kilobits per second.

kilobits per second (Kbps)   A data transfer speed of 1,024 bits per second.

lag   The slowing of network performance usually caused by increased demand for available bandwidth.

LAN (Local Area Network)   Consists of any two or more computers joined together to communicate within a small area, usually not larger than a single building.

LAN driver   Provides the information to allow the NIC to communicate with the network.

legacy system   An existing system that either needs updating or is no longer capable of maintaining required performance.

load   The amount of data present on the network. Also known as network traffic.

log off (or log out)   The procedure for exiting the network.

logical printers   Created by NT, logical printer capability allows you to set a single print definition that can be serviced by multiple physical printers.

log on (or log in)   The procedure for checking on to the network so that you can access files and other network information. When you have access to the network, you are said to be logged on. When you exit the network, you log out.

loopback test   A test which allows a NIC to talk to itself to see if it is working.

MB   megabyte

Mbps (megabits per second)   Used to measure throughput or communication speed. A communications rate of 1,048,576 bits per second.

media filter   Used on token ring networks to change the type of media from Type 1 (shielded twisted-pair) to Type 3 (unshielded twisted-pair) or vice versa.

mirroring   The process of duplicating data so that if one system fails, another can take its place.

modem   A device used to translate digital signals from the computer into analog signals that can travel across a telephone line.

multi-disk volume   A storage system that uses multiple hard disks connected with the OS, so that they act as a single entity with a single drive name/letter.

multistation access units (MAUs)   MAUs are the central hubs in a token ring LAN.

multithreading   The process that allows a multitasking operating system, such as Windows NT, to multitask the threads of an application.

NDIS (Network Driver Interface Specification)   A network device driver specification, NDIS provides hardware and protocol independence for network drivers. A benefit of NDIS is that it offers protocol multiplexing, which allows multiple protocol stacks to coexist in the same host.

near-line backups   These backups differ from offline backups, in that they are kept on devices connected to the network for faster restoration of files. They require more effort to restore than accessing a file from a hard disk, but less effort than restoring a file from an offline backup.

NetBEUI (NetBIOS Extended User Interface)   A transport layer driver that is the Extended User Interface to NetBIOS. It is used by Windows NT and other operating systems to deliver information across a network. NetBEUI cannot be routed.

NetBIOS (Networked Basic Input-Output System)   A networked extension to PC BIOS. NetBIOS allows I/O requests to be sent and received from a remote computer.

NetWare   Novell's network operating system.

network   Two or more computers linked together so that they can communicate.

network adapter   See network interface card.

network infrastructure   The physical equipment that hooks computers into a network. This includes the cables, hubs, routers, and software used to control a network.

Network Interface Card (NIC)   The card that allows the computer to communicate across the network. The network cable attaches to the NIC.

network map   A detailed map of information about what's on the network. Includes an inventory of machines and other hardware, a map of cable layout, and other information to document the network.

Network Operating System   An operating system that permits and facilitates the networking of computers. Windows NT is one.

NIC   See network interface card (NIC).

node   Each device on a network is an individual node. It can be a workstation, a printer, or the file server.

NOS   See Network Operating System.

NT File System (NTFS)   The file system used by Windows NT. It supports large storage media, and file system recovery, in addition to other advantages.

NTDETECT   The hardware recognition program used by Windows NT.

offline backups   Backups that are kept offline. They are removed from the operation of the server and require the medium, usually tape, to be loaded in order to restore.

off-site storage   A place in a separate location from the file server, used to store backup tapes. A complete backup should always be kept off-site.

online backups   Backups that are stored online so that they are immediately available.

overhead   The control attached to packets transmitted across a network. Overhead data includes routing and error-checking information. Overhead also refers to the bandwidth used to sustain network communications.

packet   A unit of data transmitted across a network as a whole.

packet burst   Used in IPX when a packet burst-enabled source sends multiple packets across a network without waiting for an acknowledgment for each packet. Instead, one acknowledgment is sent for the group of packets.

partition   A logical division on a physical hard disk that is treated as though it were a separate hard disk.

passive hub   A hub device used in a star topology that connects machines to the network and organizes the cables, but does not regenerate or redistribute data.

password   The key to access the network during logon.

patch   A program that edits the binary code of another program to insert new functionality, add more capability, or correct a bug in the earlier release. Patches provide software updates in between full releases of the program.

PCI (Peripheral Component Interconnect)   A PC local bus that provides high-speed data transmission between the CPU and a peripheral device.

peer to peer network   A network in which any machine can serve as the server or as a client. These networks are used to allow small groups to share files and resources, including CD-ROM drives, printers, and hard drives.

Performance Monitor   A utility that provides performance information about your network to help you locate bottlenecks, determine which resources are too taxed, and plan upgrades to the system's capacity.

permissions   Sometimes called rights, permissions regulate the ability of users to access objects such as files and directories. Depending on the permissions, a user can have full access, limited access, or no access to an object.

platform   A type of computer system (e.g., Intel x86, or UNIX).

Point-to-Point Protocol (PPP)   A communications protocol that provides dial-up access to a network. It's commonly used to connect to the Internet.

PostScript   Defined by Adobe Systems, PostScript is a page description language. A printer must be PostScript-compatible in order to print PostScript files; otherwise, reams of garbage code prints.

POTS (Plain Old Telephone Service)   The standard analog telephone system, like the one used in most houses.

PPP   See Point-to-Point Protocol.

preemptive multitasking   A method of multitasking that has the capability to prioritize the order of process execution, and preempt one process with another.

Primary Domain Controller (PDC)   The NT Server running the master copy of the WINS service for an NT domain. It contains the domain's security policy and domain database. It handles synchronization with the Backup Domain Controller.

print queue   The line that handles printing requests and supplies files to the printer in their proper order. From the British word queue meaning line.

print server   Controls network printing, and services printing requests. Print servers can be hardware devices or a software solution.

properties   Object descriptors set in the Windows NT naming system or Registry, depending on the type of object.

protocol   A set of rules of formatting and interaction, used to permit machines to communicate across a network. Networking software usually supports multiple levels of protocols. Windows NT supports several protocols, including TCP/IP and DLS.

QIC (Quarter Inch Cartridge)   A tape cartridge format common for backup tapes.

RAID (Redundant Array of Inexpensive Disks)   A disk mirroring scheme that duplicates data across several disks, creating a fault-tolerant storage system. A RAID system can maintain data integrity as long as one disk has not failed.

RAM (Random Access Memory)   Short-term storage memory, physically residing in the computer on memory chips. Since computer applications use RAM in their processing, the amount of RAM in a computer is a major determinant of how well the computer works.

RAS (Remote Access Server)   A Windows NT server configured to use the dial-up service to provide remote access.

redirector   Also called a requester, a redirector is software that accept I/O requests for remote files, and then sends the files to a network service on another computer.

Registry   The Windows NT database that stores all information about the configuration of the network.

Remote Access Server   See RAS.

Remote Access Service   The dial-up service in Windows NT that allows users to access the network remotely by telephone lines.

rights   Authorizes users to perform specific actions on a network. Similar to permissions.

ring   A network topology that connects the computers in a circular fashion. If one computer fails, the complete network fails, so this topology is rarely used.

root   The top level of a directory structure, above which no references can be made.

router   A device that connects more than one physical network, or segments of a network, using IP routing software. As packets reach the router, the router reads them and forwards them to their destination, or to another router.

RPC (Remote Procedure Call)   A request sent to a computer on the network by a program, requesting the computer to perform a task.

scaleable   The capacity to change with the network. As requirements change, a scaleable network can grow or shrink to fit the requirements.

script   Used to describe programs, usually those written in an interpreted language, as opposed to a compiled language, because the instructions are formatted similar to a script for actors.

SCSI (Small Computer System Interface)   A high-speed interface used to connect peripherals such as hard disks, scanners, and CD-ROM drives. SCSI allows up to seven devices to be lined in a single chain.

Security Accounts Manager (SAM)   The application that handles the assignment of rights and permissions to users, groups, resources, and other objects in Windows NT.

Serial Line Interface Protocol (SLIP)   A TCP/IP protocol that provides the ability to transmit IP packets over a serial link, such as a dial-up connection over a phone line.

server   The computer running the network server software that controls access to the network.

server mirroring   Duplicating a complete server to reduce the demand on the main server.

services   Options loaded on computers allowing them to help each other. Services include the capability to send and receive files or messages, talk to printers, manage remote access, and look up information.

share   A setting to make resources such as printers, CD-ROM drives, or directories available to users on the network.

shell   A program that provides communication between a server and a client, or a user and an operating system.

shielded twisted pair   A twisted pair cable that has foil wrap shielding between the conducting strands and the outer insulation.

SLIP   See Serial Line Interface Protocol.

SNA (Systems Network Architecture)   The basic protocol suite for IBM's AS/400 and mainframe computers.

SNMP (Simple Network Management Protocol)   Used to report activity on network devices, SNMP is a popular network monitoring and control protocol.

star   A network topology, in which separate cables connect from a central hub to individual devices.

stateless   The most efficient type of network communication, a protocol that needs no information about communications between sender and receiver.

subnet masking   Used in TCP/IP communications, the subnet mask allows the recipient of IP packets to distinguish the Network ID portion of the IP address from the Host ID portion of the address.

swap file   An area on a disk that allows you to temporarily save a program, or part of a program, that is running in memory.

Switched Multimegabit Data Service (SMDS)   SMDS is a 1.544Mbps data service that supports many common LAN architectures.

Synchronous Optical Network (SONET)   A fiber-optic network communications link, SONET supports rates up to 13.22Gbps.

system administrator   Manages the network. It is this person's responsibility to ensure that network functions are running smoothly—for example, that backups are complete, network traffic is running smoothly, and drive space is available when needed.

T-1   A widely-used digital transmission link that uses a point-to-point transmission technology with two-wire pairs. One pair is used to send, and one to receive. T-1, also written as T1, can transmit digital, voice, data, and video signals at 1.544Mbps.

T-3   Designed for transporting large amounts of data at high speeds, T-3, also written as T3, is a leased line that can transmit data at 45154Mbps.

T-connector   A device used in Thin Ethernet cabling to connect the cable to the NIC.

TCP/IP (Transmission Control Protocol/Internet Protocol)
An industry standard set of protocols used to connect computers within a network, as well as to external networks such as WANs and the Internet. TCP/IP is the most widely-used networking protocol and can be used to connect many different types of computers for cross-platform communication.

TechNet   The technical support CD-ROM published by Microsoft. It includes thorough information about Windows NT and other Microsoft products.

Telnet   A TCP/IP network service that allows a computer to connect to a host computer over the network and run a terminal session.

template   A template is a partially completed object, designed to help you start a task. Windows NT Server provides templates to help the new administrator configure objects and complete other tasks.

Thick Ethernet   See 10Base-5.

Thin Ethernet   See 10Base-2.

throughput   A measure of the rate at which data is transferred across a network measured in bits per second (bps).

token   An electronic marker packet, used in ArcNet and FDDI networks, that indicates which workstation is able to send data on a token ring topology.

token ring   A networking topology that is configured in a circular pattern and circulates an electronic token on the ring to pass data.

topology   The physical configuration of a network, including the types of cable used. Common topologies include bus, ring, and star.

transceiver   A device that allows you to connect a NIC for one medium (cable) to another medium. Most commonly used to translate thin or thick Ethernet to unshielded twisted pair.

Transmission Control Protocol/Internet Protocol   See TCP/IP.

trust relationship   Used on NT networks with multiple domains, trust relationships occur when users from one domain are given permission to access resources from another domain without having to log onto that domain explicitly.

twisted pair   A cable type in which conductive wires are twisted to help reduce interference. There are two types of twisted pair: shielded and unshielded.

Uninterruptible Power Supply   See UPS.

unshielded twisted pair   A twisted pair cable that does not have any shielding between the conducting strands and the outer insulation.

UPS (Uninterruptible Power Supply)   A battery backup system commonly used on file servers to protect in times of power outages.

URL (Uniform Resource Locator)   The URL provides the address to a document on the World Wide Web.

user account   An account on a network designed for a particular user. Based on user account options, a person has access to specific files and services. See account.

User Manager   What you use to create users and groups, assign passwords, and control access rights to files, directories, and printers.

User Profile Editor   What you use to set several user options.

user   Any person who accesses the network.

username   A name used by a user to log on to a computer system.

volume   A logical division of a disk on a Windows NT file server.

WAN (wide area network)   While a LAN is a network where all machines are in close proximity to each other—usually in the same building—a WAN is extended over longer distances, ranging from a few miles to across the world. TCP/IP is the primary WAN protocol and was developed to provide reliable, secure data transmissions over long distances.

Windows Internet Name Service   See WINS.

WINS (Windows Internet Name Service)   The Windows NT service that provides a map between NetBIOS computer names and IP addresses. This permits NT networks to use either computer names or IP addresses to request access to network resources.

wireless networking   A network configured to use communication techniques such as infrared, cellular, or microwave, so that cable connections are not required.

workgroup   A group of users who share files and resources on a network. Members of a workgroup usually have related job functions. For example, they may be in the same department.

workstation   The client machine used to access a network.

WORM (Write Once, Read Many)   An optical storage medium that only permits you to write to it once, but allows you to read from it many times. CD-ROM drives are basically WORM devices.

INDEX

SYMBOLS and NUMBERS

%Disk Time counter, Performance Monitor and hard disk performance, 572
10BASE-2, defined, 672
10BASE-5, defined, 672
10BASE-T, defined, 672
16-bit applications. *See* Win16
32-bit applications. *See* Win32
32-bit flat address space, memory architecture, 24
32-bit operating systems, TAPI and, 406-407

A

abnormal shutdowns, browsers and, 463
access control, security model, 251-253
Access Control Entries. *See* ACEs
Access Control Lists. *See* ACLs
access permissions
    See also permissions
    defined, 672
Access Through Share Permissions dialog box, read access, *275*
access tokens and processes, 253-258
    ACEs (Access Control Entries), 253-257
    ACLs (Access Control Lists), 253-257
    caches, 258
account lockout, 282-283
account policies, 192-194
    changing default, 193-194
    passwords and, 193-194
account restrictions, defined, 672
accounts
    default group, 175-180
    defined, 672
    SIDs (Security IDs) and. *See* SIDs
    user. *See* user accounts
ACEs (Access Control Entries), 253-257
    types of, 254
    validation process, *254*, 255-257
acknowledgment (ACK), defined, 672
ACLs (Access Control Lists), 253-257
    CACLS.EXE for changing permissions, 265-267
    discretionary, *256, 257*
Across a Cable option, Network Settings, 75
Across a Wire option, Network Settings, 75

active hubs, defined, 673
active partitions, defined, 47
activities, auditing, *199*
adapters
    See also NICs (Network Interface Cards)
    Bindings tab (Network Control Panel), 309-314
    defined, 673
    installing, 129-131
    removing, 131
    WINS (Windows Internet Name Service) and, 340
Adapters tab, Network icon (Control Panel), *129*
Add Users and Groups dialog box
    adding users, 263, *264*
    read access, *274*
Add/Remove Programs icon, 135-139
    components check boxes, *140*
    Control Panel, 135-139
    Install/Uninstall tab, 137
    installing software exercise, 138
    removing software exercise, 136
    Windows NT Setup tab, 138-139
Address Resolution Protocol (ARP), function of, *327*
addresses
    base I/O, 675
    IP. *See* IP addresses
Admin$, default shares, 316
administration, centralized, 442-443
administrative tools, User Manager, 180-192
Administrator account
    account policies, 192-195
    default local groups, 176
    default user accounts, 173
    defined, 673
    naming conventions, 179
Administrators
    Control Panel and, 100
    managing users and groups, 171-204
    operations performed by, 176
    system, 691
Advanced Options tab, configuring TCP/IP, 334-335
advanced user rights, viewing, 197
AFP (AppleTalk Filing Protocol), 303
aliases, defined, 673
analog, defined, 673
answers, Self Test, 631-664

B

C

Q

R

W

X

Custom Corporate Network Training

Train on Cutting-Edge Technology   We can bring the best in skill-based training to your facility to create a real-world, hands-on training experience. Global Knowledge Network has invested millions of dollars in network hardware and software to train our students on the same equipment they will work with on the job. Our relationships with vendors allow us to incorporate the latest equipment and platforms into your on-site labs.

Maximize Your Training Budget   Global Knowledge Network provides experienced instructors, comprehensive course materials, and all the networking equipment needed to deliver high quality training. You provide the students; we provide the knowledge.

Avoid Travel Expenses   On-site courses allow you to schedule technical training at your convenience, saving time, expense, and the opportunity cost of travel away from the workplace.

Discuss Confidential Topics   Private on-site training permits the open discussion of sensitive issues such as security, access, and network design. We can work with your existing network's proprietary files while demonstrating the latest technologies.

Customize Course Content   Global Knowledge Network can tailor your courses to include the technologies and the topics that have the greatest impact on your business. We can complement your internal training efforts or provide a total solution to your training needs.

Corporate Pass   The Corporate Pass Discount Program rewards our best network training customers with preferred pricing on public courses, discounts on multimedia training packages, and an array of career planning services.

Global Knowledge Network Training Lifecycle: Supporting the Dynamic and Specialized Training Requirements of Information Technology Professionals

- Define Profile
- Assess Skills
- Design Training
- Deliver Training
- Test Knowledge
- Update Profile
- Use New Skills

College Credit Recommendation Program   The American Council on Education's CREDIT program recommends 34 Global Knowledge Network courses for college credit. Now our network training can help you earn your college degree while you learn the technical skills needed for your job. When you attend an ACE-certified Global Knowledge Network course and pass the associated exam, you earn college credit recommendations for that course. Global Knowledge Network can establish a transcript record for you with ACE that you can use to gain credit at a college or as a written record of your professional training that you can attach to your resume.

Registration Information:

COURSE FEE: The fee covers course tuition, refreshments, and all course materials. Any parking expenses that may be incurred are not included. Payment or government training form must be received six business days prior to the course date. We will also accept Visa/MasterCard and American Express. For non-U.S. credit card users, charges will be in U.S. funds and will be converted by your credit card company. Checks drawn on Canadian banks in Canadian funds are acceptable.

COURSE SCHEDULE: Registration is at 8:00 a.m. on the first day. The program begins at 8:30 a.m. and concludes at 4:30 p.m. each day.

CANCELLATION POLICY: Cancellation and full refund will be allowed if written cancellation is received in our office at least six business days prior to the course start date. Registrants who do not attend the course or do not cancel more than six business days in advance are responsible for the full registration fee; you may transfer to a later date provided the course fee has been paid in full. Substitutions may be made at any time. If Global Knowledge Network must cancel a course for any reason, liability is limited to the registration fee only.

GLOBAL KNOWLEDGE NETWORK: Global Knowledge Network programs are developed and presented by industry professionals with "real-world" experience. Designed to help professionals meet today's interconnectivity and interoperability challenges, most of our programs feature hands-on labs that incorporate state-of-the-art communication components and equipment.

ON-SITE TEAM TRAINING: Bring Global Knowledge Network's powerful training programs to your company. At Global Knowledge Network, we will custom design courses to meet your specific network requirements. Call (919)-461-8686 for more information.

YOUR GUARANTEE: Global Knowledge Network believes its courses offer the best possible training in this field. If during the first day you are not satisfied and with to withdraw from the course, simply notify the instructor, return all course materials and receive a 100 percent refund.

US:
1 888 762 4442
Canada:
1 800 465 2226
US:
www.globalknowledge.com
Canada:
www.global-knowledge.com.ca
CALL
1 888 762 4442 US
1 800 465 2226 Canada
FAX
1 919 469 7070 US
1 613 567 3899 Canada
MAIL
Check and this form to:
US
Global Knowledge Network
114 Edinburgh South,
Suite 200
P.O. Box 1187
Cary, NC 27512
Canada
393 University Ave.,
Suite 1601
Toronto, ON M5G 1E6

REGISTRATION INFORMATION

Course title _____

Course location _____ Course date _____

Name/title _____ Company _____

Name/title _____ Company _____

Name/title _____ Company _____

Address _____ Telephone _____ Fax _____

City _____ State/Province _____ Zip/Postal Code _____

Credit card _____ Card # _____ Expiration date _____

Signature _____